African American Religious Cultures

African American Religious Cultures

VOLUME 1: A–R

Anthony B. Pinn
General Editor

Stephen C. Finley
Associate Editor

Torin Alexander
Paul Easterling
Derek S. Hicks
Margarita Simon Guillory
Assistant Editors

A B C CLIO

Santa Barbara, California • Denver, Colorado • Oxford, England

Library of Congress Cataloging-in-Publication Data

African American religious cultures / Anthony B. Pinn, general editor ; Stephen C. Finley,
    associate editor ; Torin Alexander, assistant editors . . . [et al.].
        p. cm.
    Includes bibliographical references and index.
    ISBN 978-1–57607–470–1 (hardcover : alk. paper) — ISBN 978-1–57607–512–8 (ebook)
1. Blacks—America—Religion—Encyclopedias. I. Pinn, Anthony B. II. Finley, Stephen C. III.
Alexander, Torin.
BL2500.A37   2009
200.89´9607—dc22   2009013494

13 12 11 10 9   1 2 3 4 5

This book is also available on the World Wide Web as an eBook.
Visit www.abc-clio.com for details.

ABC-CLIO, LLC
130 Cremona Drive, P.O. Box 1911
Santa Barbara, California 93116-1911

This book is printed on acid-free paper ∞

Manufactured in the United States of America

Dedicated to the Ancestors who gave birth to these traditions.

Contents

VOLUME 2

PART 2 ESSAYS 449

Acknowledgments

This encyclopedia appears almost ten years after it was first proposed. And, without the support and assistance of a good number of people, it would still be no more than a few email exchanges and computer files. I would like to take this opportunity to thank those who made this project possible. At ABC-CLIO, Steven Danver made contact with me after the project seemed to have slipped through the cracks and encouraged me to continue work on this project. Lynn Jurgensen and Kim Kennedy-White have been a delight to work with; their good humor, patience, and sharp insights have been of tremendous help. Thank you. I also appreciate the hard work done by Kathy Breit, who copyedited the manuscript.

I would also like to thank my students—Stephen C. Finley, Torin Alexander, Derek S. Hicks, Paul Easterling, and Margarita Simon Guillory—who served as editors on the project. Their careful attention to tasks assigned made it possible for me to split my time between this project and other responsibilities. I hope participation in this project proved to be a useful and informative experience for them.

The editors would like to thank the many contributors to this project for their essays; this includes authors from other ABC-CLIO encyclopedias who met the use of their materials in this current project with support and encouragement. Finally the editors thank their colleagues, families, and friends for their patience and the numerous ways in which they provided assistance.

The appendix includes three pieces for which permission was required. The editors acknowledge with gratitude permission to include the following:

Mother Divine and the Trustee Board of the Peace Mission Movement authorized the reprinting of *The Peace Mission Movement as Explained by Mrs. M. J. Divine* (Philadelphia: Imperial Press, Inc./Palace Mission, Inc., 1982), 44–46; 99–102.

Norm Allen and the Council for Secular Humanism (African Americans for Humanism) authorized the preprinting of "An African American Humanist Declaration." Published in *Free Inquiry*, Volume 10, Issue 2 (Spring 1990): 13–15.

Orbis Books granted permission to reprint "The Black Manifesto," James H. Cone and Gayraud S. Wilmore, editors. *Black Theology: A Documentary History, Vol. 1* (1993), pp. 27–36.

I would also like to acknowledge with gratitude ABC-CLIO's authorization of my use of materials from *African American Religious Experience in America*, a book I published with Greenwood Press in 2005. The licensing agreement between Greenwood Press and ABC-CLIO made possible the inclusion in this encyclopedia of many of the sidebars and material for the following entries: "Buddhism," "Roman Catholicism," "Church of the Living God," "Church of God and Saints of Christ," "Unitarian Universalist Association," "Religious Humanism," and "Lutheran Church."

Thanks to all who live these traditions, and to those who have helped us—in our modest way—share the importance and vitality of these traditions.

Introduction: The Forging of African American Religious Cultures

The Americas

The term "America" at times has been used as a reference by citizens of the United States to describe their culture and geography. This rather narrow use of the term was challenged during the first few decades of the twentieth century in light of the history of this area of the world that helped shape the United States and its borders and that also involves a plurality of countries and worldviews (Levander and Levine 2008). The use of "America" to name a particular nation was challenged, and in its place, the "Americas" became a way to describe a particular hemisphere composed of numerous countries with interrelated histories and cultures. There were in fact, as historians have demonstrated, overlapping moments of contact, conquest, and development that bind the various areas of the Western Hemisphere together and that allow for synergy on a variety of levels, including the political, economic, and cultural. For example, the interests of Spain and France in the so-called "New World" involved more than one geographic location—spreading across various islands, North America, and South America. As a result, these areas represent something of a historical and cultural whole in that they share influences and experiences (Thomas 1997; Palmié 1995; Klein and Vinson 2007).

The individual nations that currently comprise this hemisphere are formed and influenced not only from within their particular geography but also by other peoples and nations beyond their borders. They involve similarities of experience but also differences. The histories of various areas of this hemisphere converge and inform each other, but are not identical, resulting in a shared reality that extends beyond the story of any one country. This shared reality that constitutes the overlapping stories of life in the American hemisphere share a fundamental reality that also shapes this encyclopedia —the presence of people of African descent and the history of the Atlantic Slave Trade.

It would be a significant mistake to assume what we refer to as the Americas was an unclaimed area of the world simply awaiting arrival and use by European explorers and economic speculators. No, European exploration did not involve the discovery of new lands, but rather the renaming and use of thriving populations and their homes. The area of the world of concern in this encyclopedia was invented; and this involved the applying of new names, new systems of politics, social life, and so on to existing societies. There were rich and diverse cultures already present. Within this encyclopedia, culture is understood as the beliefs and practices that shape the self-understanding, thinking, and activities of a particular group and the signs, symbols, and other ways in which these beliefs and practices are expressed. Yet, as the entries in this encyclopedia will suggest, these cultures are porous, open to influence and change as they are brought in contact with other cultures.

While communities across the hemisphere do not necessarily refer to themselves as "American" in part because of the earlier and problematic use of the term, there are ways in which the word "American" serves as a marker of related developments and formations that shape the cultural worlds within this hemisphere. It is in this sense, in this way, that the term is used in the context of this encyclopedia: The term "American" is not used here to designate members of a particular nation. It is not political in that way, and it is not concerned foremost with economic and political realities. Rather, the term is used here as a way to think about overlapping religious realities.

It is not uncommon for those of African descent in the Americas to refer to themselves in a way that notes their African heritage and their particular geographic location. Afro-Brazilian and Afro-Caribbean serve as two examples. And while noting and respecting this naming, this encyclopedia seeks to present religious culture in a way that sweeps across the hemisphere, recognizing points of religious overlap and difference. This does not rule out more localized approaches to naming such as the two noted above, but it allows for a more comprehensive (yet not definitive) examination of religious cultures of the hemisphere in a way that recognizes particular nations while putting the religions of these individual nations within a larger framework. In so doing, it uses a reference that considers the full range of this geography and the African cultural influence present in the American hemisphere—"African American."

Africans in the American Hemisphere: African Americans

Martin Bernal (Bernal 1987, 1991) and Cheikh Anta Diop (Diop 1974), among other scholars, have championed research that points out the impact of Africa on world civilization. But this cultural influence was not limited to contact between Africa and Europe. Scholars such as Ivan Van Sertima have argued with great academic force that Africans made contact with the American hemisphere long before the introduction of the slave trade. In fact, for example, he argues African influence on American culture(s) is still evident in the sculptures, inscriptions, and other artifacts associated with particular areas such as Mexico (Van Sertima 1976). The pre-Columbus presence of Africans in the American hemisphere is important in that it speaks to the rich cultural heritage of Africa and it also notes the manner in which the cultural life and practices in the American hemisphere were influenced by an African worldview. Yet, the number of Africans within the American hemisphere becomes significant numerically only with the slave trade.

One of the most significant markers of the Modern Period, the age of science and exploration, is the development of the so-called "New World" (over against the Old World of Europe)—the Americas—as the major geography for the trade in enslaved Africans and the production of new wealth and new cultures. Numbering in the millions and moved to this location over the course of centuries, the enslavement of Africans from West Africa forged economic growth for Europe through the production of rum, crops, and other items in the Americas and transported elsewhere in the world. Over the course of the slave trade, more than 10 million Africans were brought to the American hemisphere to labor on plantations and to provide other forms of labor necessary to maintain the economic interests of Europe. This trade in Africans was an early example of the global market—a transnational economy—a web-like and interconnected structure that helped fuel the industrial, intellectual, and social advances marking the "Modern World" (Davis 2001).

The forced movement of Africans across the Atlantic involved the entire American hemisphere and many European nations. The system of slavery, once begun in the "New World," was a system based on the full participation of a good number of European countries. "Ironically," notes historian David Davis, "the only New World colony that barred the importation of slaves was Georgia, whose founders sought a refuge for England's deserving poor as well as a secure buffer between South Carolina's menacing black majority and the hostile Spaniards in Florida, who were accused of inciting slave rebellions and encouraging runaways by offering freedom to those who escaped into Spanish territory. By 1749, however, Georgia's trustees realized that it was impossible to exclude slaves from the colony and agreed to end their fourteen-year experiment with 'free soil' " (Davis 2001, 179).

Justification for Slavery

One might ask a question at this point: How could humans enslave other humans, and what would encourage this behavior on such a large scale? The answer most often given to this perplexing question suggests the physical difference between Africans and Europeans, along with their cultural differences, was used to justify the slave trade. Even countries initially reluctant to participate in this trade would come around due to the potential for economic gain. Religion offered a firm way of justifying this activity (Haynes 2002). With time, the Hebrew Bible was brought into the service of slavery when the story of Ham (the son of Noah) and his son Canaan—both assumed to be African—was used as justification for the enslavement of Africans:

> Noah was the first tiller of the soil. He planted a vineyard; and he drank of the wine, and became drunk, and lay uncovered in his tent. And Ham, the father of Canaan, saw the nakedness of his father, and told his two brothers outside. Then Shem and Japheth took a garment, laid it upon both their shoulders, and walked backward and covered the nakedness of their father; their faces were turned away, and they did not see their father's nakedness. When Noah awoke from his wine and knew what

his youngest son had done to him, he said, "Cursed be Canaan; a slave
of slaves shall he be to his brothers." (Genesis 9:20–25)

If Canaan is cursed to be a slave, some argued, and Africans are the offspring of
Ham (and his son Canaan), then Africans are slaves due to divine action. This was
not the only rationale offered for slavery, but its link to a sacred text gave it a certain
type of authority and appeal. Regardless of the inconsistencies and flaws of the argument, it and others like it (e.g., physical difference marked inferiority) were held tena-
ciously. And at times, religious justifications would expand to include the pretext of
introducing Africans to the Christian faith; but this evangelizing was spotty at best
and was typically a thin veil covering economic motivations.

The Practice of Slavery

There is evidence in written records of "Black" slaves present in Europe as of the
1300s. And many historians who study the Atlantic Slave Trade give special notice
to the 1444 transport of Africans to Portugal by Antam Gonçalves and his crew. This
did not mark an expanded interest in African servants in that the Portuguese were more
interested in gold than in servants. However, limited interest in Africans would change
as economic opportunity, particularly through the production of sugar, in the Americas
generated need for laborers that could not be met through European indentured servants and the forced labor of indigenous populations. Having developed some familiar-
ity with the capture and use of Africans as servants in Europe, the labor shortage was
resolved by systematic introduction of enslaved Africans—a system of forced labor
that would last some 350 years, and unmatched by earlier examples of slavery elsewhere in the world (Palmié 1995, 44).

As many scholars note, Spanish authorities allowed the movement of 50 Black
slaves to the island of Hispaniola to assist with sugar production at the start of the sixteenth century. Other islands such as Puerto Rico would also receive an influx of
enslaved Africans provided to assist with gold mining. Cuba, for example, established
late in the fifteenth century, had few slaves who worked the gold mines and a few other
economic ventures such as tobacco (Thomas 2002). It was not until the revolution in
Saint Domingue (Haiti) damaged its ability to produce large sugar exports that Cuba
was able to develop a significant reputation as a prime location for economic growth.
Whereas Saint Domingue lost much of its hold on the sugar industry, Cuba expanded
its production of sugar. Labor was necessary for this work, and the import of slaves
met this need. In fact, Cuba would become one of the largest importers of slaves in
the nineteenth century. Islands such as Barbados, Jamaica, Martinique, and others
would receive good numbers of Africans. The Portuguese moved into Brazil as of
the 1500s, but gave limited attention to its economic potential until later in that century. This is in part because it had some difficulty determining the best way to exercise
its claim to that territory over against the growing interests of Spain and France in Brazil. With time, however, Portugal would begin to develop trade in dyewood, cotton,
and sugar. The number of Africans imported to provide necessary labor would increase

and eventually accounted for almost 40 percent of the total number of Africans brought to the American hemisphere (Klein and Vinson 2007).

The North American colonies entailed a smaller market than the Caribbean and Latin America, but this did not mean a lack of slave presence in the North American territories. The British, when they finally entered the slave trade in earnest, would surpass European competitors in the number of slaves transported annually to the Americas (Segal 1995, 12–14, 22). Although there were enslaved Africans in New England representing roughly 10 percent of the population by 1775, the bulk of this forced labor was on the tobacco and rice plantations of southern colonies where slaves represented a much larger percentage of the overall population. The first 20 Africans were brought to Virginia in 1619, but with time there would be an increase in the African presence throughout the colonies and this presence would revolve around labor. The presence of enslaved Africans in New England is first noted in Boston and is dated to the 1630s. And although one might speculate that trading in slaves was a practice more likely associated with southern colonies, Puritans in New England began trips to Africa to gain slaves as early as the 1640s. Although a rather dangerous undertaking, Massachusetts merchants took the lead in New England, supplying New Englanders as well as southerners with enslaved Africans. Yet prior to the eighteenth century, the number of slaves in the Puritan colonies was fairly small, much less than 10 percent of the total population. In the northern, middle, and southern colonies, the colonial period was marked by the labor of enslaved Africans. Enslaved Africans never outnumbered Europeans in the northern colonies, and this helped shape the nature of slavery in those colonies. However, and although most farmers did not have slaves, the labor of enslaved Africans in the South on sugar, cotton, and rice plantations, for example, was vital. Over the course of time, roughly 500,000 enslaved Africans were brought to North America. This is a number that pales in comparison to the number of Africans taken to Brazil during the centuries of the slave trade. Although numerous nations participated in the Atlantic Slave Trade, the British and the Portuguese dominated the transportation of Africans (Thomas 1997).

One should not think, however, that enslaved Africans taken to one location necessarily stayed in that location. To the contrary, political challenges such as the North American Revolutionary War resulted in the movement of slaveholders and Africans from one New World location to others. With respect to North America, the Revolutionary War resulted in a movement of colonists loyal to England and their enslaved Africans relocated to Canada. According to David Brion Davis, there were slaves in British Nova Scotia as of the 1750s (Davis 2001, 179). Also, the Revolution in Saint Dominigue—the most productive revolution in the American hemisphere— resulted in slaves' and slaveholders' movement to other areas of the Caribbean and North America. In addition, it was the case that some enslaved Africans were "seasoned" or prepared for work as slaves in the Caribbean and then transported, for instance, to North American plantations. While economically rewarding, the dirty business of transporting enslaved Africans was brutal and resulted in the deaths of millions of Africans. The infamous "slaver" was one typically involved in a variety of ventures. "The typical slave trader was interested in all kinds of commerce as well as slaves: he might be a banker . . . or always also concerned in whaling, in order to make spermaceti candles. . ." (Thomas 1997, 291).

Transportation of Enslaved Africans

Many of the first enslaved Africans in the Americas were transported from Europe, but with time colonists would request shipment directly from Africa. By the mid-1500s, the number of slaves transported to the Americas was roughly 7,000 per year but this number would grow, and with time roughly 5 million Africans would be taken from western-central Africa (Klein and Vinson 2007; Thomas 2002). The trade in slaves was big business. For example, slave traders in France held more wealth than any other group of merchants. Slave trade became a complex enterprise—involving cooperation between various European nations and generating great wealth and advancement. "America became," note Herbert Klein and Ben Vinson, "the great market for an estimated 10 million African slaves in the course of the next five centuries, and it was in the New World that African slavery most flourished under European rule" (Klein and Vinson 2007, 17).

There was significant money to be made, but the initial costs were high and the risk great; and much of this risk and cost was defrayed through partnerships by which groups carried the expense and split the proceeds. The routes taken and the stops made reflected the desire to maximize profits. However, it was typically the case that the journey involved movement from Europe to Africa, where slaves were secured with payment made in the form of manufactured goods. Then the enslaved Africans were taken to the Americas and the ships loaded with produce from the Americas. The labor to carry out this route included the ship captain and a variety of others, such as officers, crew, doctor, and the person responsible for recording the various business transactions. Armed to prevent theft at sea by pirates, the ships loaded the cargo and began the arduous journey across the Atlantic (Thomas 1997, 301).

Whether purchased or stolen, enslaved Africans were brought to the coast of West Africa for transporting. This movement to the coast in and of itself was a horrific process, involving movement over hundreds of miles with limited supplies and limited rest. It was not uncommon for some Africans to die prior to reaching the coast because of fatigue and lack of proper food and water. Others would not make it to the cost with their initial group because they were sold to other slavers along the route to the coast (Segal 1995, 29). After travel to the coast, survivors were stored in far from comfortable and healthy environments. Little attention was given to arranging them in accordance with cultural groups—the Ibos here and the Madingos over there for instance. The rapid growth in the need for and movement of Africans made such distinctions inefficient economically. They were loaded onto ships once they were available. " 'When our slaves,' wrote, again Captain Thomas Phillips, 'were come to the seaside, our canoes were ready to carry them off to the longboat . . . if the sea permitted, and she convey'd them aboard ship, where the men were all put in irons, two and two shackled together, to prevent their mutiny or swimming ashore. The negroes are so willful and loth to leave their own country, that they have often leap'd out of canoes, boat and ship, into the sea, and kept underwater till they were drowned, to avoid being taken up. . ."

(Thomas 1997, 404). It was often the case that this process of movement to the ships did not take place until enslaved Africans had been branded with a hot iron to indicate to whom they had been sold and who now held them as property. This practice was replaced in time with the use of a piece of metal worn around the neck or wrist that bore the symbol of a particular slaveholder. Bodies were not simply branded or otherwise differentiated as a physical marker of ownership. Many countries, such as Portugal, also required that enslaved Africans be baptized.

Sufficiently marked and in some cases baptized, enslaved Africans began the long and terrifying journey we call the "Middle Passage"—the movement from the West coast of Africa to the American hemisphere. This journey was dreadful regardless of who captained the ship, or which nation sponsored the voyage. "It," notes Thomas, "was the sea, the vast, mysterious, terrifying 'green sea of darkness,' which gave the Atlantic slave trade its special drama" (Thomas 1997, 407). We have no recorded accounts from enslaved Africans concerning the nature of this experience—the feel of the crowded boat, smell, the terror of darkness below deck, and pain caused by the movement of the water as it generated seasickness, as well as the mental and physical trauma of the journey itself. Instead, we must rely on the accounts provided by Europeans involved in the trade who recounted various aspects of the journey. For example, a doctor on one of the ships reported that:

> The slaves that are out of irons are locked "spoonways," according to the technical phrase, and closely locked to one another . . . Those which do not get quickly into their places are compelled by the cat [whip] and, such was the situation when stowed in this manner, and when the ship had much motion at sea, that they were often miserably bruised against the deck or against each other . . . I have seen their [the slaves'] breasts heaving and observed them draw their breath, with all those laborious and anxious efforts for life which we observe in expiring animals subjected by experiment to bad air of various kinds. (Thomas 1997, 413)

Because volume translated into high profits, as many Africans as possible were loaded naked unto the ships. And to avoid revolts, adult males were bound and guarded. Women and children did not pose the same threat, so they were allowed a greater degree of movement. Yet, to avoid suicide due to the terror and uncertainty of the journey, they too had to be monitored and controlled. The conditions under the deck, where the vast majority of slaves were held, were stifling, and seasickness only added to the deplorable conditions. The small and confined space meant adults had restricted mobility and had to lie on their backs, or on some ships they sat up but without the possibility of standing upright. The desire to maximize profits also meant keeping as many of the enslaved Africans alive during the journey as possible. To accomplish this, slave ships required periods of exercise that involved "dancing" or other practices on the deck; and feedings—at times of spoiled food—took place typically a couple of times each day by force if necessary. Some supporters of the slave system argued dancing slaves were a sign of good humor and enjoyment on the part of the enslaved (Pinn 2003). However, it does not take much thought to recognize that this would be far from the case. Slaves moved around the deck not because of enjoyment but because they were forced to do so under the threat of physical punishment. The poor conditions—large numbers in confined spaces—cruel treatment, suicides, and disease resulted in fewer Africans arriving the Americas than had been loaded initially on the ships.

Selling Africans

Upon arrival to various ports spread throughout the Americas, enslaved Africans were prepared for market and sold to planters in North America, South America, and the Caribbean. The process of selling slaves held some similarities across the Americas, in each instance suggesting that enslaved Africans were treated as if indistinguishable from cattle and goods. In Brazil, the process was often as follows:

> . . .the slaves would be prepared to be sold, being shaved, fattened, and if necessary painted (to give the illusion of health) . . . Slaves would also be made to dance and sing, in order to raise their spirits, in the same way as abroad the ship which had brought them from Africa. Buyers would again patiently examine the wares, feeling the Africans' limbs and bodies much as butchers handled calves. The slaves were often asked, as they had been told to do before leaving Africa, to show their tongues and teeth, or to stretch their arms . . . Often slaves would be sold at auction by one or other of the houses which specialized in the business, the bidding being at the door of the customs house. Occasionally the merchants would seek to sell their slaves by hawking them, chained, from house to house. (Thomas 1997, 432)

Slaves that were not purchased for whatever reason were often left behind, without proper shelter or means to sustain life.

In North America the following description was offered concerning the sale of Africans:

> The slaves are put in stalls like the pens used for cattle—a man and his wife with a child on each arm. And there's a curtain, sometimes just a sheet over the front of the stall, so the bidders can't see the "stock" too soon. The over-seer's standin' just outside with a big blacksnake whip and a pepperbox pistol in his belt. Across the square a little piece, there's a big platform with steps leadin' to it. Then, they pulls up the curtain, and the bidders is crowdin' around. Them in back can't see, so the overseer drives the slaves out to the platform . . . they have white gloves there, and one of the bidders takes a pair of gloves and rubs his fingers over a man's teeth, and he says to the overseer, "You call this buck twenty years old? Why there's a cup of worms in his teeth. He's forty year old, if he's a day." (Mellon 1988, 291)

Treatment and conditions for enslaved Africans across the Americas varied depending on a variety of factors including the ratio of Africans to Europeans, the type and location of work (e.g., mining, cultivation of crops—rural or urban), and the disposition of slaveholders. Regardless of policies or laws, slaveholder disposition determined the food available to enslaved Africans as well as living conditions and the types of punishment inflicted. Nonetheless, throughout the Americas life for enslaved Africans entailed status as "non-free" and hence a hard and torturous existence. This reality starts early and is noted by, for example, the fact that they were seldom referred to by name during shipment and distribution (Segal 1995). In this way, they were deemed similar to livestock.

One should not think that enslaved Africans did nothing to challenge their condition. There are too many accounts of revolts and rebellions for that to be the case. According to historian Hugh Thomas, the first recorded rebellion in the American hemisphere took place on the island of Hispaniola (now Haiti and the Dominican Republic) in 1522, and it was followed by other attacks on the slave system elsewhere in the Americas (Thomas 1997, 104). The Maroons of Jamaica, for example, were able to maintain their independence through settlement in remote areas and strong physical resistance to British efforts. And in North America, slave rebellions were also noted and others were able to escape slavery by moving to free states or Canada. The most famous revolt is perhaps that which took place in Saint Dominque (Haiti) during which enslaved Africans on the island were able to resist the French and gain their freedom. The fear of rebellion both during transport and once in the Americas was an undeniable dimension of the slave trade throughout its history. Most enslaved Africans, however, remained confined to the system of chattel slavery.

Forging Life in the American Hemisphere

In some regions, it was not uncommon for large numbers of enslaved Africans to arrive from particular African cultural regions. For instance, during some of the sixteenth century, most of the enslaved Africans brought to Mexico and Peru were from Upper Guinea. In the seventeenth century many of the enslaved Africans in Mexico and Peru were believed brought from Angola (Klein and Vinson 2007, 136). In eighteenth century North America, the presence of enslaved Africans from the Kongo presented itself in cultural formations such as dance, the visual arts, and other practices. For example, "black American traditional burials," writes art historian Robert Farris Thompson, "reveal telling regularities, like the importance of depositing on the tomb the last-used objects of the dead, plus seashells, pipes, pierced vessels, and planted trees" (Thompson in Gundaker 1998, 38). All such elements suggest the complex movement of cultural elements across the Atlantic Slave Trade.

The African presence in the American hemisphere was not limited to enslaved Africans but also included those who were free—by escaping, purchasing their freedom, being granted their freedom, and in some cases having been born free. Together they made every effort to forge cultures that helped them survive the hardships of life in a hemisphere marked by slavery and oppression. This process involved a blending of their African cultural heritage, elements of European culture brought to the Americas, and elements of the cultural worlds of the indigenous population. These two volumes will help readers better understand the cultural worlds developed by enslaved Africans, free Africans, and their descendants in the American hemisphere.

The process of enslavement and the nature of life in the Americas—a new and foreign environment—made the full-scale maintenance of culture worlds impossible. However, cultural memories in stories, folktales, songs, quilts, elements of language, and so on were shared. This cultural information spread through newly formed communities and families particularly on large plantations and in towns where Africans from the same regions of Africa could be in contact. The remembering and passing along of this information allowed for the preservation of certain elements of African culture, which were combined with cultural influences from Europe expressed by colonists as well as cultural influences from the indigenous Americans. As one might imagine, where there were large numbers of Africans and fewer colonists—such as much of the Caribbean and Brazil—African retentions (e.g., language and customs) were more substantial and more highly visible to both Africans and Europeans.

Groupings of Africans from particular regions and other factors may have contributed to the presence of African cultural retentions in the Americas, and these retentions would have revolved heavily around materials that allowed enslaved Africans to make sense of their new surroundings and circumstances. While these elements of African culture would have covered a variety of daily activities and thought patterns, some would be more easily transferable than others. That is to say, "those beliefs relating the individual to health and well-being, interpersonal relationships, and relation of the self to the cosmos were most likely to retain their power in the New World" (Klein and Vinson 2007, 143). Drawn from a variety of sources and forged within a context of oppression, enslaved Africans developed practices and beliefs, structures and worldviews, that helped them make sense of their world, maintain some sense of self-worth and importance, and link individuals with larger communities and the larger natural environment. Regarding this, religion is a prime example of the cultural worlds developed by African Americans in every region of the Americas. "The gods of Africa," remarks historian Albert Raboteau, "were carried in the memories of enslaved Africans across the Atlantic. To be sure, they underwent a sea change. African liturgical seasons, prescribed rituals, traditional myths, and languages of worship were attenuated, replaced, and altered, or lost. Still, much remained..." (Raboteau 2002, 16).

The slave trade and system of slave labor that had so greatly impacted the American hemisphere would shift and change as colonial politics shifted, revolutions occurred, moral and ethical reflection on slavery grew, and centers of economic power changed. During the first three decades of the 1800s, various European nations would rethink and eventually end their participation in the Atlantic Slave Trade—but it would continue until close to the end of the nineteenth century. The suppression of the slave trade begun in the early nineteenth century resulted in an influx into various locations in the Americas of free Africans who had been taken from slave ships on their way to American ports. Settling in locations such as Cuba and Brazil, these free Africans and their presence would create tension that persisted until the slave system was dismantled fully: Should they live in separate communities? Should free Africans labor on plantations, and if so under what rules? Would their presence result in rebellion on the part of enslaved Africans? A complex and interconnected array of reasons—abolition, changing economic structures among them—would eventually bring the forced labor model to an end.

African American Religious Cultures

The nature and practice of religion was transformed within the crucible of the slave trade. What follows are just a few examples of religious developments provided as a way to introduce the general subject of this encyclopedia and to give readers a sense of the proper backdrop for the religious practices and beliefs discussed in the pages following this introductory essay.

Historian of religion Charles Long provides great insight when saying, from the start of the age of exploration in the fifteenth century through our current period, "the Western world, through conquest, trade, and colonialism, made contact with every part of the globe. These encounters and confrontations with other cultures raised again the issue of religion" (Long 1986, 3). Religions follow and are shaped by the changing patterns of the slave trade and the raising and lessening in importance of particular slave ports. As one might imagine, this pattern of religious development draws on the strength of numbers, the size of populations from various areas of Africa in one colonial location, as well as the types of labor and "free" time afforded them. Such factors influenced the nature of the religious beliefs and practices formed as well as the modes of their expression available in the American hemisphere during the period of slavery. Denominations expanded their reach and revised their theology and practices, and traditional African forms of religiosity were planted in a new geography. There were no neat divides between these various belief systems. To the contrary, elements were transposed and new dimensions added. Within the context of communities of enslaved and free Africans in the Americas, a rich environment of religious pluralism emerged—one that involved various combinations of Christianity and traditional African-based religious beliefs and practices. In some instances, what emerged was Christianity with an African outlook; but in other cases, there developed African-based traditions.

Slaveholders believed African-based religions, as well as unsupervised gatherings of Christianized Africans, dangerous because they could serve as inspiration for revolts and rebellions throughout the American hemisphere. Two examples are offered here. First, one of the most famous rebellions took place in Saint Domingue (Haiti). This event, marked by the efforts of key leaders such as Toussaint Louverture, is known to history as the Haitian Revolution. Occurring from 1791 to 1803, and resulting in the establishment of the independent nation of Haiti, it was the most damaging and successful slave revolt to ever take place in the Americas. Some argue that a Vodou ceremony held on August 14, 1791, sparked the revolution and gave it great energy and determination by connecting physical struggle to spiritual powers and religious authority given by the African gods. As would also be the case elsewhere in the Americas, the ability to gather in sustained ways, to live in close proximity with limited interference from Europeans, only served to enhance the growth of African-based traditions. Economic changes in the nineteenth century combined with an absence of Catholic missionary effort from the Revolution until 1860 served as a locus for religious growth: "The consolidation of the Revolution, and the land grants to former slaves it made possible, transformed Haiti into a rural nation of subsistence farmers working their small plots. This new peasantry organized itself around small villages that functioned as extended family compounds . . . they opened a new space for the preservation" of African-based religious systems such as Vodou (Olmos and Paravisini-Gebert 2003, 103). In Brazil as well, religion was often related to rebellion, in one instance resulting in the conspirators—Muslims from Nigeria—being sent back to Lagos to avoid any additional trouble (Johnson 2002, 74).

In North America, famous rebellions during the 1800s were led by professed Christians such as Nat Turner, Denmark Vesey, and Gabriel Prosser. In each case, these men and those who fought on their side believed God required them to strike a blow for their freedom, and they used biblical passages to justify this stance. Turner, a minister, saw signs and other spiritual indicators that a great mission was his. He had been set aside by God to accomplish a great mission; he need only wait for the proper sign (the eclipse of the sun). It came in 1831:

> Before midnight, with only a hatchet and a broadax, they set out for the home of the man who at the time was Nat's own master, John Travis. At the Travis house they slaughtered everyone—Travis, his wife, and five others. They took what guns and ammunition they could find, and, dressing their lines like infantrymen, they marched off to perform the bloodiest slave insurrection in American [i.e., United States] history. By Tuesday morning, August 23, at least seventy slaves had killed fifty-seven whites in a twenty-mile area of the Boykins district of Southampton County [South Carolina]. (Wilmore 1983, 70)

Turner was eventually caught and executed, but he never repented of his deeds. He continued to assert that the Christian faith and his ministry required this fight against slavery. It was clear that religion, regardless of how slaveholders might seek to use it to preserve the system of slavery, could be used by enslaved Africans to demand and secure their freedom. Whether embraced to secure their survival by helping them make sense of the world or used to push for freedom (in body or spirit) from the slave system, religion maintained its importance for enslaved Africans and free Africans in the Americas. And these various religious traditions emerged through a process of contact and exchange.

While scholars debate the proper naming of this process of blending African, European, and American elements into the formation of new religious traditions and the reshaping of the Christian faith, less argued over is the importance and strong presence of a rich mosaic of religiosity marking the American hemisphere. And although different in many ways, the African-based traditions developed in the American hemisphere do share certain elements including a rich pantheon of deities, spirits, ancestors, and other forces, spiritual power in all living things, the necessity of interaction between humans and other forces mediated through those with religious knowledge, the use of ritual practices, and the existence of sacred objects (Olmos and Paravisini-Gebert 2003, 9–11).

The Caribbean

The population of enslaved Africans in Cuba combined with mulattos and free Blacks to create a sizable Black population on the island. Growth was the consequence of work needs and a decreased fear of slave revolts. The crown, local authorities, and the church worked to guarantee stability through legal regulations (supposing humanitarian concerns such as health care, housing, and food) and, in the case of the latter entity, religious and theological structures and instruction. A great deal was taken from Africans during the process of enslavement; however, the ability of the African gods to travel, housed in memories, remained intact.

The central elements of the Catholic faith operating in Cuba involved the basic sacraments—baptism, confirmation, matrimony, extreme unction, the Eucharist, penance, and holy orders—as well as the practice of cult-like devotion to the saints. The Catholic Church found it fairly easy to control formal practices (e.g., the sacraments) because they involved traditional training and access. However, devotion to the saints did not require the same level of knowledge and laity was able to exercise great authority over the cult of the saints (Pinn 1998). Cubans did not need priests to announce what the saints desired or what they were willing to perform for those in need. Nonclergy persons were able to gather, interpret, and work with this information. And these developments took place within three primary locations—the mutual aid societies (the *cabildo*) initiated by church leaders, slave quarters, and mountain settlements—and involved a blending of religious sentiments and practices drawn from a range of regions of Africa but dominated by the Bantu from the Congo and Yoruba of West Africa, Europe, and indigenous practices. Within this context numerous African-based traditions developed, including Regla de Ocha (the religion of the *orisha*) or what we commonly refer to as Santería (Olmos and Parvaisini-Gebert 2003, 24–25).

The Church had no reason to like the attention given to African-based tradition, but there was little it could do to prevent such devotion. The best alternative was to tolerate these popular practices and hope the Africans would eventually grow tired of them. Commitment to the religious education of slaves was spotty due to issues such as economic growth and the nature of slaves: Are they humans with souls that must be saved? Are they capable of understanding the gospel of Christ? Yet there was another factor that with time became major; the African slaves brought within them a religious orientation capable of incorporating elements from the Catholic Church. Dominican representatives of the church and others worked to address the needs of African slaves very early, attempting to ensure that they were churched and churched accurately and adequately (Pinn 1998). This was much easier with slaves found within cities, but measures were also taken to bring those living on plantations outside the cities into the church through proper and consistent instruction.

A similar situation occurred elsewhere in the Americas. For example, although ultimately concerned with wealth, slaves in Saint Domingue (Haiti) did receive religious attention from Spaniards. The Catholic Church actively encouraged missionary activity, following the activity of the conquerors, on the island. However, the geography of the island, combined with a relatively limited number of religious leaders limited the complexity and depth of missionary work.

By the second decade of the sixteenth century, enslaved Africans were being imported to Saint Domingue from various areas of West Africa, but were eventually dominated by groups from current Benin (once known as Dahomey). When the French took over, troubles with religious instruction for enslaved Africans would intensify. However, this would change some in 1685 with the Code Noir that regulated life for French colonies and required baptism and religious instruction for enslaved Africans. And while this push for religious instruction included a ban on African-based religious practices, the latter were not so easily removed (Pinn 1998). As one priest notes, African practices were not abandoned by enslaved Africans, but rather were combined with the Christian teachings offered them:

> The Negroes have no scruples . . . They intermix Dagon's ark and secretly keep all the superstitions of their ancient idolatrous cult with the ceremonies of the Christian religion. All the Negroes have much devotion for the communion wafer. They eat it only when they are ill, or when they are afraid of some danger. In regard to the holy water, the little bit of water that is consecrated during the Sunday Mass, it is rare that one finds one drop of it when the ceremony has ended; they carry it in little calabashes and drink some drops when they rise (in the morning) and pretend that it will guarantee their welfare against all the witchcraft that might befall them. (Desmangles 1992, 26–27)

The Catholic Church could not wipe out Vodou (meaning "spirit" or god and referenced as Voodoo in much of the United States), the African-based tradition first named Vaudoux in the eighteenth century, in Saint Domingue. Instead, it had no choice but to make peace with it. There remained a tension, however, in that during particular periods of history practitioners had to maintain a level of secrecy. Such need to practice undercover certainly helped to promote a fusion of Catholicism and African-based tradition as the saints and certain other elements from the former were used to cover the gods and rituals present in the latter (Pinn 1998). That is to say,

> what ever the content of the religion brought by the slaves from Africa might have been . . . it was evidently influenced by several factors: the ecology of the plantation, the slave's daily schedules, their acquisition of new friends or comrades, a new language for communication, new types of housing, new diet, new patterns of social organization and political power, new kinds of work specialization . . . and a new calendar of events that included Catholic religious feasts and national holidays. (Laguerre 1980, 24)

What emerged is perhaps one of the most elaborate and complex religious traditions to emerge in the Americas (Olmos and Paravisini-Gebert 2003, 102).

Throughout the Caribbean African-based traditions would develop and evolve, and while they would experience both periods of growth and decline, they remained vital and viable sources of religious meaning. Not all religious practices, however, are community based. In addition to those noted above, rather individualized practices such as Obeah in Jamaica and other Caribbean locations emerged in the seventeenth century and helped Africans make sense of their new surroundings and circumstances. The range of religious traditions within the Caribbean is expansive. Furthermore, the European influence on African American religion was not limited to the Christian Church. In addition, practices such as Spiritualism (communication between humans and the deceased) moved from France into the Caribbean and, for example, resulted in the emergence of traditions such as Espiritismo in Puerto Rico as well as Spiritual churches in North America.

North America

Vodou (Voodoo) and other African-based religious traditions would continue an exchange with Christianity, particularly Roman Catholicism. However, with time, North America came to be associated not with Roman Catholicism (with few exceptions such as Maryland and Louisiana) but with Protestant denominations. This impacted the development of African American religion in North America in that Roman Catholicism's structure (such as the importance of Saints) allowed for connection to African gods in function; but Protestantism lacked this structure (e.g., attention to saints) and lacked the same type of elaborate rituals. Nonetheless, African-based practices did develop in North America, alongside African American Christian churches. But these practices were typically without the same level of complexity found elsewhere in the Americas where there were larger numbers of Africans with greater opportunity through societies and other community organizations to exchange information without interference from Europeans.

Baptism was not enforced in the same way in the British colonies of North America, and in fact there was strong debate over whether it was necessary or advisable to introduce enslaved Africans to the Christian faith. Some believed doing so might require their emancipation: To baptize them would be an acknowledgement that they are human, and if they are human can they be rightly held in bondage? Others argued Africans did not have the necessary intellect or soul to benefit from the Christian faith. This would differ in the areas once held by the French and the Spanish: Where Catholicism dominated, Africans were baptized, and African-based traditions such as Vodou (Voodoo) would thrive. However, in the British colonies, the seventeenth century entailed limited attention to the spiritual needs of Africans. In the northern colonies of North America, figures such as John Eliot and Cotton Mather sought to give some attention to converting enslaved Africans as did the Quakers. And in the eighteenth century, the Society for the Propagation of the Gospel in Foreign Parts would push for religious instruction to enslaved Africans in the middle and southern colonies (Pinn and Pinn 2002).

Efforts in the colonies were hampered not only by the limited number of traveling ministers but also by the weak interest on the part of many slaveholders to open their plantations to religious instruction. They feared such instruction might interfere with an ability to secure work in that Africans might begin to resent their condition. Also, they believed, as noted above, spirituality might result in rebellion. This uncertainty concerning the benefits of instruction meant spotty attention to the spiritual needs of Africans in the colonies. In so many of these cases, conversion was hampered by the requirements to learn catechisms, which was a difficult process in that enslaved Africans, by law, could not be taught to read and write. It was also clear to Africans that much of what they were being taught was meant to safeguard the system of slavery —a reality they found offensive in that it suggested God ordained their enslavement and required them to obey their masters.

The conversion of enslaved Africans was slow under these conditions, until the 1730s and the First Great Awakening. This was a period of revival in the colonies during which many colonists and Africans (free and enslaved) developed energetic relationships with God and moved into churches, particularly Baptist and Methodist churches that allowed more involvement in ministry without formal training and that had fewer strict rituals and structures. This event, combined with another Awakening in the 1800s, marked the movement of large numbers of Africans into Christian churches, both majority-White churches as well as independent churches run by Africans.

One should not think, however, that African American religion in North America was limited to various approaches to the Christian faith. To the contrary, Christian churches in North America existed alongside African-based traditions and also alongside modified forms of Islam. The latter, Islam, arrived with enslaved Africans and according to the historical record available through diaries and other written materials persisted. African-based traditions also took root in these colonies. Hoodoo, voodoo, conjure, and other modes of religious expression and practice lived alongside Christian churches—finding expression in the quiet and more secretive moments of life. That is to say, particularly in somewhat isolated areas in Georgia and South Carolina,

> the coastal plantations that absorbed the slave traffic were remote from one another. The jungle swamps of the low country and the wide expanses of water separating the coastal islands made communication difficult among the plantation laborers of this section. With the continued arrival of Africans to these isolated plantation communities native ceremonies and customs were renewed or exchanged. (Georgia Writers' Project 1972, xxii)

The movement of enslaved Africans from islands in the Caribbean to North America also served to reinforce African-based traditions by bringing to communities of enslaved Africans expertise and additional practitioners.

Latin America

Making use of what freedom of movement they could manage, and using the resources available to them, free and enslaved Africans forged religious realities in the context of Latin America that merged the African past and the American (European and indigenous) present. "Through a variety of means—ritual, communal, familial, aesthetic, etc.—Africans and their descendants," writes Rachel Harding, "created alternative spaces, alternative definitions of themselves and of the meaning of their presence in the New World" (Harding 2000, xvii).

Numerous traditions mark the religious landscape of Latin America, but it is perhaps in Brazil that the thickest collection of Africa-influenced traditions is located because of the dominance of Brazil in the slave trade. West Africans, for a good stretch of time Ewe speaking and Yoruba speaking, as well as those from West Central Africa, brought with them African religious sensibilities and worked them in light of their new environment and an array of available religious orientations (Harding 2000). This blending resulted in the development of religious traditions such as popular Catholicism and Candomblé. Concerning the latter, based on the circumstances encountered, what had been communally based practices or regional variations lost much of their force and attention as religious beliefs and practices became more standardized and revolved around a more generally held arrangement of divine figures. To some extent this new religious arrangement was made necessary by the softening boundaries separating various groups of Africans—Hausas, Angolans, and so on—and the development of communities reflecting less clearly defined cultural groupings (Johnson 2002, 67).

Although African-based religions existed in Brazil long before observers decided to make mention of them, according to many sources, the term "Candomblé" was used first in the early nineteenth century to name a new religious tradition in Brazil, specifically Salvador and Reconcavo (Harding 2000). While the exact moment when Brazilian religions such as this one began to emerge, it is safe to say that, as elsewhere in the Americas, these traditions emerged in accordance with the need of Africans to frame their world and life experiences in ways that connected them to realities larger than enslavement. The number of Africans in Brazil over against the number of Europeans made it difficult to control, and certainly prevented an ability to stop, the practice of African-based religions. Roman Catholic officials at times attempted to co-opt these practices, or assumed the availability of Catholicism would eventually supersede African religion they considered inferior practices. The Church was incorrect.

Africans might incorporate certain elements of Catholicism, such as the saints, but the continuing presence of Candomblé makes clear its persistence and importance as a distinct religious tradition. In other words, "the use of Brazilian Catholic institutions such as lay confraternities and devotions as a base for the maintenance and cultivation of African spiritual values and traditions was very common through the colonial period and into the first half of the nineteenth century in Bahia," which was the location for Candomblé. In fact, Harding continues, efforts to suppress African practices during the 1800s, around the time Brazil became independent from Portugal, also correspond to the growth in houses of the Candomblé practice called *terreiro* (Harding 2000, 50). What one notes here is the manner in which these New World religious traditions are both flexible enough to adopt new practices and beliefs but firm enough to resist efforts to dismantle them. This is the case not only with Candomblé but also with other traditions such as Batuque and Tambor de Mina that nourish spiritually some of Brazil's residents.

Learning about African American Religious Cultures

Numerous traditions developed over the course of the Atlantic Slave Trade. Overlapping in some ways and distinctive in others, these traditions frame life and the worldview of African Americans to the present. While some have waned in influence, others have grown in visibility and influence. However, regardless of the number of participants or other visible markers of importance, these various religious traditions help to define the shape and content of life in the American hemisphere. Through the religious cultures they entail, one gains a great deal of insight into the history of this hemisphere and the various groups of African Americans who inhabit it.

This encyclopedia is concerned with the religious worlds of African Americans—the wide-ranging and complex communities of people of African descent who populate the hemisphere. Why these peoples are called African American here, regardless of their particular national home, should be clear at this point, and some sense of what it has meant and what it has entailed to create religious cultures should also be somewhat clear. What remains to be given is some attention to the structure of the encyclopedia—its various components and what they are meant to offer readers.

This two-volume encyclopedia is meant to provide a glimpse into the religious worlds created by African Americans. But such a project cannot hope to capture and discuss every religious tradition present in the American hemisphere. The number of traditions is too large. What is offered in these pages is a "snap shot" of the religious heritage of the New World, and the traditions selected for inclusion are meant to signal a sense of the rich religious terrain that is the Americas. This is only a limited look into the religious worlds created over the course of centuries and under extreme circumstances. In a sense it provides a general mapping of the religious world that is the New World. Not everything is covered, but as is the case with any map, enough is presented to provide a working sense of the area being observed. This mapping of African American religious cultures is, in fact, a charting of particular traditions as a way of suggesting the complexity and diversity of religious beliefs and practices in the American hemisphere. As is the case with any encyclopedia, there are "thin" spots and areas given greater attention than others. This is the nature of such a project, and this tendency is further enhanced by the secrecy covering some traditions and the more public posture of others. No preference is given to particular religious traditions. None are considered more "important" or "better" than others. To the contrary, they are all presented as vital in that they are embraced by members of particular communities and are understood as life affirming and beneficial by adherents. With this in mind, the length of particular entries is not a marker of greater or lesser value; rather, length is simply a function of available information and overlap between some traditions.

The encyclopedia begins with religious traditions in the Americas, presented in alphabetical order. These essays, of varying lengths, are meant to provide basic information such as historical development and major beliefs/practices. While not covering every nation within the American hemisphere, an effort has been made to give some coverage to the three large geographies that typically come to mind within thinking about this hemisphere—North America, Latin America, and the Caribbean. An effort has also been made to provide some attention to biographical information on key figures. These biographical sketches outline the contributions of particularly important figures in the development of the traditions covered. In some instances, where traditions are less formally structured, little can be offered regarding key figures. However, where and when available, every effort has been made to offer a sense of "who's who" within the religions of African Americans. The biographies are sketches, not full presentations. They will not give readers a full sense of the life and accomplishments of those presented here. Some of the leaders noted will be familiar to readers—perhaps this is the case in terms of some of the Christian denominations covered. With respect to other biographical entries, readers will encounter some leaders for the first time in their educational process.

While the first section of the encyclopedia is concerned with a sense of religion in the Americas by means of attention to particular traditions, the second section of the encyclopedia provides more sustained focus on major issues and concerns. Arrangement of the essays in the second section of the encyclopedia is not meant to suggest greater importance of the United States, but rather to show sensitivity to the context of the major market for the encyclopedia. These essays tend to focus on North America because it is assumed most users of this encyclopedia are situated in North America, particularly the United States. And these documents will help such readers better contextualize major topics in religion within their national context. However, it is hoped that these essays will also be of value to readers outside the United States as well in that, while focused on a particular context, the overlapping nature of life in the Americas will allow these essays to offer information relevant to other areas of the Americas. For example, while highlighting the United States, the "Megachurch" phenomenon is certainly not limited to the United States. It is also a relevant conversation beyond the United States as the broadcasts, Web sites, and publications of U.S. ministers impact the thinking and actions of Christians on a global level. The environment and religion essay is also a topic impacting life beyond the United States. These are just a few examples of how the topical essays might offer information and insights extending beyond the particular context of the United States.

In addition to presentation of traditions and special topics, this encyclopedia also provides a chronology of major happenings as a way to help readers further contextualize the development and spread of the traditions covered. Additional context is given through the appendix in which primary materials that focus on some of the issues and concerns noted in the other entries are included. The appendix is limited in size, a necessity considering the length of the overall project, but it provides interesting detail. A second appendix provides information related to particular practices and various elements of religious ritual. This encyclopedia is a resource and is meant to provide a basic understanding that can then be supplemented by more in-depth readings. And the bibliographies offer additional readings for those interested. It is hoped that the images also found in the encyclopedia will encourage readers to think about the "look" of some of the practices covered.

Move through this encyclopedia as you see fit. Read the entries in whatever order you find suitable. But however you decide to use this work, it is hoped that it will leave you with a greater understanding of the complexity, richness, historical importance, and ongoing meaning of the religious cultures made by African Americans in the American hemisphere.

SELECTED BIBLIOGRAPHY

Bernal, Martin. *Black Athena: Afroasiatic Roots of Classical Civilization, Volume I: The Fabrication of Ancient Greece, 1785–1985* (Piscataway, NJ: Rutgers University Press, 1987).

Bernal, Martin. *Black Athena: Afroasiatic Roots of Classical Civilization, Volume II: Archaeological and Documentary Evidence* (Piscataway, NJ: Rutgers University Press, 1991).

Davis, David B. *The Problem of Slavery in Western Culture* (New York: Oxford University Press, 1988).

Davis, David B. *In the Image of God: Religion, Moral Values, and Our Heritage of Slavery* (New Haven, CT: Yale University Press, 2001).

Desmangles, Leslie G. *The Faces of the Gods: Vodou and Roman Catholicism in Haiti* (Chapel Hill: The University of North Carolina Press, 1992).

Diop, Cheikh Anta. *The African Origin of Civilization: Myth or Reality* (New York: Lawrence Hill and Col, 1974).

Duncan, Carol. *This Spot of Ground: Spiritual Baptists in Toronto* (Waterloo, Canada: Wilfrid Laurier University Press, 2008).

Gundaker, Grey, ed. *Keep Your Head to the Sky: Interpreting African American Home Ground* (Charlottesville: University Press of Virginia, 1998).

Harding, Rachel E. *A Refuge in Thunder: Candomblé and Alternative Spaces of Blackness* (Bloomington: Indiana University Press, 2000).

Haynes, Stephen R. *Noah's Curse: The Biblical Justification of American Slavery* (New York: Oxford University Press, 2002).

Johnson, Paul C. *Secrets, Gossip, and Gods: The Transformation of Brazilian Candomblé* (New York: Oxford University Press, 2002).

Klein, Herbert S., and Ben Vinson III. *African Slavery in Latin America and the Caribbean*, 2nd ed. (New York: Oxford University Press, 2007).

Laguerre, Michel S. *Voodoo Heritage* (Beverly Hills, CA: Sage Publications, 1980).

Landes, Ruth. *City of Women*, 2nd ed. (Albuquerque: University of New Mexico Press, 2006).

Levander, Caroline F., and Robert S. Levine, eds. *Hemispheric American Studies* (Piscataway, NJ: Rutgers University Press, 2008).

Long, Charles. *Significations* (Philadelphia: Fortress Press, 1986).

Mellon, James. *Bullwhip Days: The Slaves Remember* (New York: Weidenfeld & Nicolson, 1988).

Olmos, Margarite Fernández, and Lizabeth Paravisini-Gebert, *Creole Religions of the Caribbean: An Introduction from Vodou and Santería to Obeah and Espiritismo* (New York: New York University Press, 2003).

Palmié, Stephan, ed. *Slave Cultures and the Cultures of Slavery* (Knoxville: The University of Tennessee, 1995).

Pinn, Anthony. *Varieties of African American Religious Experience* (Minneapolis: Fortress Press, 1998).

Pinn, Anthony B. *Terror and Triumph: The Nature of Black Religion* (Minneapolis: Fortress Press, 2003).

Pinn, Anthony, and Anne Pinn. *Fortress Introduction to Black Church History* (Minneapolis: Fortress Press, 2002).

Postma, Johannes. *The Atlantic Slave Trade* (Westport, CT: Greenwood Press, 2003).

Raboteau, Albert. *Slave Religion: The "Invisible Institution" in the Antebellum South* (New York: Oxford University Press, 2002).

Savannah Unit, Georgia Writers' Project, Work Projects Administration. *Drums and Shadows* (Athens: University of Georgia Press, 1986 [1972]).

Segal, Ronald. *The Black Diaspora: Five Centuries of the Black Experience Outside Africa* (New York: Farrar, Straus and Giroux, 1995).

Thomas, Hugh. *Cuba*, 3rd ed. (London: Pan Books, 2002).

Thomas, Hugh. *The Slave Trade: The History of the Atlantic Slave Trade, 1440–1870* (New York: Simon & Schuster, Inc., 1997).

Van Sertima, Ivan. *They Came Before Columbus: The African Presence in Ancient America* (New York: Random House, 1976).

Wilmore, Gayraud. *Black Religion and Black Radicalism* (Maryknoll, NY: Orbis Books, 1983).

Part I

ENTRIES

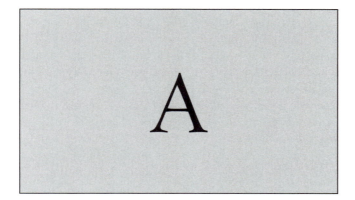

AFRICAN AMERICAN MYSTICISM

Historical Development

Experiences that engender and enable religious faith are arguably among the most important predictors and precipitants of culture in African America. However, despite the cultural capital often associated with religion, commentators who write about the black estate seldom if ever deal with the topic of mysticism. It is interesting to note, for example, how scholars have neglected the mystical flowering of the African Diaspora from Old World indigenous and ethnic permutations to New World Christian conversionary accounts. Certainly, not every experience by peoples of African descent of the sacred can or should be subsumed under the rubric of mysticism, but careful examination reveals the mystical tradition to be an integral aspect of African American religious culture and life.

"Mysticism" as a term has been too insulated and largely associated with elite discourses in the academy, church, and society for most African Americans to view it as having any importance in their own religious culture. Indeed, a cursory review of American popular and scholarly literature reveals that mysticism has been generally identified with the cultivated inwardness of groups like the Society of Friends (Quakers) and the ecstatic otherworldliness of groups like the United Society of Believers in Christ's Second Coming (Shakers). At the same time, there is a pronounced revival of interest in mystical religion among twenty-first-century religious seekers. On the whole, mainstream accounts of mysticism demonstrate a perennial preoccupation with individuality, an absence of socially formative power, and a disregard for the concern of the whole. So interpreted, about the best that can be hoped for with respect to mysticism is an intuited and parallel relationship of like-minded individuals in pursuit of a marginally common goal.

The expressions of African American mysticism recounted here offer a dramatically different departure where issues of meaning, power, and value are concerned.

There is no single substantial definition for mysticism. That being said, a working definition at least is in order: *Mysticism is a generic term for intimate discourse and practices that speak to what it means to be human in relationship to the transcendent and the mundane.* Not an uncommon experience, mysticism is translated into a diversity of religious and metaphysical positions —Christian, Muslim, African derived, humanist, and everything in between—in relation to the lived social context. Mysticism, simply considered, is a more focal and fontal experience of religion. Mysticism can constitute a life way or a moment in life. In the context of African America, mysticism places the question of black being—identity and community—at the center of its most urgent formulations (Pollard 1990, 28–42).

Mystic ancestors include known and unknown members of the "Invisible Church": Harriet Tubman, the inspirited and providentially appointed "General" and "Moses of her people"; the freedom-obsessed insurrectionists Nat Turner, Denmark Vesey, Gabriel Prosser, and David Walker; and God-intoxicated visionaries James Smith, Rebecca Cox Jackson, Julia Foote, Zilpha Elaw, and Amanda Berry Smith (Harding 1981; Dodson 1982, 276–89; Humez 1984, 129–43). There is Martin Luther King Jr. in Montgomery, Alabama, in 1956, faced with escalating threats against his family, seated at his kitchen table praying when "rationality left me . . . and almost out of nowhere I heard a voice that morning saying to me: 'Preach the Gospel, stand up for the truth, stand up for righteousness'" (Carson 2000, 114–15). Malcolm X, who was transforming into El Hajj Malik El Shabazz and was the featured speaker at the Harvard Law

---

JARENA LEE (1783–?)

Born in 1783 in the state of New Jersey, Jarena Lee began working as a "servant maid" at the age of seven and would continue as a domestic into her adult life. Prior to her conversion, knowing the depths of suffering and oppression, she had been tempted on several occasions to "destroy her life." Lee's spiritual awakening also occurred at an early age and rescued her from social and possible physical death. But Lee's mystic visions contained an ecclesial as well as social imperative, challenging male leadership prerogatives with a fierce insistence that God had called a woman to preach. Now a widowed mother of two, she committed herself to full-time ministry, fired by denominational rebuff and righteous discontent. Lee's mystic articulations are a beautifully human counterpoint to the unfathomable brutality, demonic design, and intended perpetuity of raced, gendered, social, and religious bondage she faced. Lee is one among the many of African American women visionaries, mystic insurgents who not only envisioned divine agency but established a course of action in the quest for human survival and wholeness. Lee's spiritual autobiography, first published in 1836, is the earliest known to be written by an African American woman and predates the more familiar fugitive slave narratives.

Malcolm X (1925–1965) during a press conference for Dr. Martin Luther King Jr. in 1964. (Library of Congress)

School Forum in 1964, glanced out the window when "awareness came surging up in me . . . how deeply the religion of Islam had reached down into the mud to lift me up, to save me . . . " (Malcolm X 1965, 293).

The exemplars are also twentieth- and twenty-first-century writers like Zora Neale Hurston whose novels, folklore, and research from *Tell My Horse* to *Sanctified Church* is concerned with the serious and substantive evolution of black

---

SOJOURNER TRUTH (1797–1883)

The life of Sojourner Truth is further testament to the surging power of the African American womanist mystic tradition. It is often rather conveniently forgotten that Isabella Bomefree, born into slavery in upstate New York in the late eighteenth century, had long seen visions and dreamed dreams about the role she would play in helping her people. She recounts the authenticating power of mystical religion in *The Narrative of Sojourner Truth*. The racist and patriarchal macrocosm serves as a vivid reminder that here was a woman continually confronted by her negative and anonymous status in the extant social order. Truth, having experienced the ignominy of being sold on repeated occasions, now experiences the agony of having her son sold away. She determines that she will get him back. Like other nineteenth-century African American women, Sojourner Truth, too, knew well the seeming permanence of gendered and racial proscription. Under the aegis of African American mysticism, Truth engaged in a fierce interplay between her emerging womanist sensibilities and the rupturing of social and religious conventions. She was a "true believer," freed by this most intimate of experiences to challenge prevailing social norms and expectations.

religious belief and practice from Africa throughout the Diaspora. There is W. E. B. DuBois's triumph "Of the Faith of our Fathers" and lament "Of the Passing of the First Born" in the *Souls of Black Folk*. James Baldwin's *Go Tell it on the Mountain*, Octavia Butler's *Parable of the Sower*, Alice Walker's *By the Light of My Father's Smile*, and Toni Morrison's *Beloved* are all soaring and unconventional (and by definition controversial) stories of spiritual and corporeal redemption. There are artists, dancers, painters, poets, musicians, and filmmakers like Katherine Dunham, John Coltrane, Nina Simone, Julie Dash, Maya Angelou, Tupac Shakur, Meshell Ndegeocello, Bob Marley, John Biggers, and countless more. Mysticism, that is to say, a people's most intimate experiences of faith and hope, compassion and critique, abounds in African American religion, culture, and life.

Beliefs and Practices

The African American encounter with mysticism is far-reaching in scope and extensive in time. It is a saga of mythic beginnings and the myriad of experiences of Africa's children predating antiquity and stretching forward to the transatlantic epic, to the vast millions of women, children, and men who were snatched from Africa over a period of some 400 years and their yearning to finally and at last be at home. It is an originating orientation whose roots also lie in the oft-forgotten and perhaps never to be told discomforting remembrances of African families, elders, chiefs, and clans, entire communities who grieved for the return of their relatives to the Old World. Despite their movement into the New World, the descendants of Africa never stopped

searching for ways to reunite the severed links. Differences of region aside—throughout the Americas—in lands claimed by Portuguese, Spanish, Dutch, French, and English the children of Africa everywhere found powerfully creative ways to transcend the degradation of their estate. Out of the great diversity of oppressed black humanity was forged a common bond, a unified set of experiences, the constituent universals that would lead to a proverbial recognition throughout the Diaspora: "The blood that unites us is thicker than the waters that divide us," and a positive if rather enigmatic understanding on both sides of the Atlantic—we are Africans (Gomez 2005).

This mystic revalorization or imagination of origins, and a people's concern to authenticate their utter humanity takes a seminal shift in the land that was to become the United States of America. Mystic-laden traditions from the African inheritance to Azusa Street and beyond were to leave an indelible imprint on a people having undergone the horrific terror of the Atlantic world (the triumphant "rise of the West") to call forth oppositional and independent understandings of themselves. At the middle point between the competing worldviews of the modern and postmodern world they found resident an alternative vision. The basis for this new critical stance of human renewal and possibility, of resistance and contestation, sprang from the visions, dreams, and contemplations of (in this instance) the descendants of Africa in North America. The interrelationships of these meanings and events—challenged, contradicted, and sometimes even reversed—are at the heart of an inchoate mystic experiencing endemic to African American religious and social life.

Alton B. Pollard III

SELECTED BIBLIOGRAPHY

Carson, Clayborne, ed. *The Papers of Martin Luther King, Jr.* (Berkeley: University of California Press, 2000), IV: 114–15.

Dodson, Jualynne. "Nineteenth Century A.M.E. Preaching Women." *Women in New Worlds*, ed. Hilah F. Thomas and Rosemary Skinner Keller (Nashville: Abingdon, 1982), 276–89.

Gomez, Michael. *Reversing Sail: A History of the African Diaspora* (New York: Cambridge University Press, 2005).

Harding, Vincent. *There Is a River: The Black Struggle for Freedom in America* (New York: Harcourt, 1981).

Humez, Jean M. " 'My Spirit Eye': Some Functions of Spiritual and Visionary Experience in the Lives of Five Black Women Preachers, 1810–1880." *Women and the Structure of Society*, ed. B. J. Harris and J. K. McNamara (Durham, NC: Duke University Press, 1984), 129–43.

Malcolm X. *The Autobiography of Malcolm X* (New York: Grove Press, 1965).

Pollard, Alton B., III. "Howard Thurman and the Experience of Encounter: A Phenomenological View." *The Journal of Religious Thought* 46, no. 2 (Winter-Spring 1990): 28–42.

Pollard, Alton B., III. *Mysticism and Social Change: The Social Witness of Howard Thurman* (New York: Peter Lang, 1992).

Thurman, Howard. *Jesus and the Disinherited* (Nashville: Abingdon-Cokesbury Press, 1949).

Thurman, Howard. *Deep Is the Hunger* (New York: Harper and Brothers, 1951).

Thurman, Howard. *The Creative Encounter* (New York: Harper, 1954).

Thurman, Howard. *The Inward Journey* (New York: Harper and Brothers, 1961).

Thurman, Howard. *The Search for Common Ground* (New York: Harper & Row, 1971).

AFRICAN AMERICANS AND THE LUTHERAN CHURCH

Historical Development

When Christianity in African American communities is mentioned, the typical image is of people gathered in one of the

---

HOWARD THURMAN (1899–1981)

Howard Thurman is the most expressive figure in African American mysticism. Thurman is best known for the San Francisco congregation he co-founded and co-pastored from 1944–53, the Church for the Fellowship of All Peoples (Fellowship Church), considered to be one of the first authentically inclusive models of institutional religion in the United States. A former dean of the chapel at Howard University (1932–1944), he would gain further renown at Boston University as the first African American dean at a major white university (1953–1965). Years would pass before Thurman would begin to identify his early and almost unconscious "experience of encounter" and "sense of Presence" with mysticism. Fully attuned to the collaborative forces of bigotry and how the social order was set against him and the African American community, his formidable mystic perceptions made him wary of any group or entity claiming exclusive jurisdiction over the whole of life, including church and state. In Thurman's thinking it is vital religious experience, an ontological and epistemological reordering, that provides an aperture for the worlds' disinherited to operate with freedom and integrity as individuals and communities in the social sphere.

predominantly African American denominations—living out the religious heritage of Richard Allen, Sojourner Truth, Martin Luther King Jr., and Fannie Lou Hamer, among others. But to think this way entails a limited view of African American religious life, a perspective that ignores a good percentage of African Americans and their Christian commitments.

African American Christians dominate the religious landscape of African American communities in the United States. But one should not assume that all African American Christians are affiliated with historically African American denominations. Nothing could be further from the truth. They are spread across numerous denominations, including the Lutheran Church.

From its initial beginning in Europe, the basic patterns of Lutheranism spread, eventually moving into the North American context as Europeans sailed to the colonies beginning in the 1600s. Lutheranism, like other forms of Protestantism—so named because those associated with the general movement protested against what they considered problems in the Catholic Church—spread across a great territory (Noll 2001, 12). In 1649 a group of Lutheran colonists established themselves in an area stretching from what is currently Manhattan to Albany. In spite of this movement, congregations had a difficult time recruiting clergy willing to undertake the dangerous and frustrating work of leading new congregations in the "New World." The few ministers available had to spread their services over large geographic areas, attempting to meet the basic needs of several congregations at one time—each receiving a few sermons during a year. Based on this shortage of clergy for the growing Lutheran presence, it was not until 1669 that those in New York celebrated communion.

It would take roughly a century for these small congregations to solidify into a formal network. The first *synod* (the Ministerium of Pennsylvania)—a regional grouping of congregations—was developed in 1748 when Henry Muhlenberg gathered together a group of Lutherans for the purpose of better organizing their activities and developing communication between various churches. This push toward firm organizational structure was matched in 1786 by liturgical conformity through the production of a book of service and a hymnal.

At this point in the eighteenth century, Lutherans numbered roughly 7,000 spread across 70 churches (Lagerquist 1999, 55). The number of Lutherans would grow with time, as would the mechanisms (e.g., schools, magazines, missions organizations) used to conduct their work. This growth, however, was not without controversy and splits. For example, debate over the extent to which the uniqueness of the North American context should impact the presentation and application of traditional Lutheran doctrine—should there be a liberal application of Lutheran doctrine, or should there be a more orthodox application—resulted in the formation of various synods. In 1847, as a result of this debate, the Lutheran Church Missouri Synod formed with an interest in preserving a traditional or conservative application of doctrine. Other synods formed were the General Synod and the United Synod (Noll 2001, 21).

Such difficulties and divisions were only intensified during the early twentieth century as a new wave of Lutheran immigrants reached the United States with their assumptions concerning church life in tow.

The twentieth century was marked by continued disagreement and splits over theological issues, but also efforts to merge like-minded Lutherans. In either case, the significance of Lutheranism and its appeal remained. The numbers tell the story in that two of the largest denominations in the United States are Lutheran—the Evangelical Lutheran Church in America with over 5 million members as of 2002 and the Lutheran Church Missouri Synod with roughly 2.5 million members. This membership is diverse, representing various racial and ethnic groups. Within this communion of Lutherans who work to safeguard and enhance their church are African Americans. Theirs is a history of involvement that moves through numerous difficulties, always pushing for a richer participation in Lutheranism. It is a story of religious commitment beginning during the period of slavery.

In 1669 an African was baptized into fellowship within the Lutheran Church in New York (Lagerquist 1999, 26). Starting out with a few scattered conversions and baptisms, Africans slowly gained access to Lutheran churches with a noticeable increase as a result of the revivalism and pietism that marked the 1730s and the early 1800s, in the northern colonies and southern colonies, respectively. Not all Africans became members of predominately white congregations. For example, Jehu Jones formed an African Lutheran church in New York in 1832. But much of this work took place within the context of tension over slavery—with many Lutherans seeking to aid Africans without disrupting the system of slavery. Daniel Payne, a Lutheran of African descent who eventually joined the African Methodist Episcopal Church, spoke to this contradiction and called for Lutherans to fight against slavery because of the manner in which it damages the God-human relationship. The strategies used to approach Africans certainly involved a compromise with slavery. Yet in some areas such as the Southeast there was a noteworthy increase in African membership, with estimates approaching 10,000 before 1860.

Consensus did not exist in Lutheran circles concerning the proper response to slavery, although most Lutherans in the nineteenth century were not concerned with what might be considered the political ramifications of religion. Some objected to it, while others endorsed segregation and did nothing to change the social status of Africans. There was little interest in using Lutheranism as a way of transforming the socioeconomic and political nature of American life. The segregation model fueled developments such as support for the formation of separate regional conventions. Creation of the Alpha Evangelical Synod of Freedmen resulted from such an effort, but its independence was rather limited as Black leadership was replaced by White leadership.

The relationship of African Americans to Lutheranism was troubled at times, but efforts were made sporadically to ease this tension. One such attempt involved the Lutheran Church, prior to its merger with two other Lutheran churches, in America's consultation on Minority Group Interests. African Americans and other representatives of the minority presence in the church suggested goals for improving the relationship between people of color and Lutheranism. Some of the goals were rather ambitious, such as a call for aggressive evangelization of minorities until the makeup of the church represented the population breakdown of the United States (Lagerquist 2001, 142). In such efforts the American Lutheran Church devoted resources to educational opportunities for African Americans, and in the early 1980s the Board of American Lutheran Church Women put in place a policy requiring the presence of women of color on the board as a way of ensuring the development of policies and plans that were sensitive to the needs and wants of women of color. Lutherans would approve the ordination of women, and the first woman would become a bishop in 1995.

The efforts of the American Lutheran Church, the Lutheran Church of America, and the Association of Evangelical Lutheran Church were combined to some degree through the development of the African American Lutheran Association, an organization of the Evangelical Lutheran Church in America (a 1988 merger of the American Lutheran Church, the Lutheran Church of America, and the Association of Evangelical Lutheran Churches). Conferences related to the experiences of African Americans in the Lutheran Church and financial support of mission activities, for example, are used to push Lutheranism to confront issues of race. This work includes fostering an ongoing conversation concerning the legacy of slavery and the reparations debate.

Progress has been slow with respect to an increase in black membership. As of 1999, the Evangelical Lutheran Church in America—the largest Lutheran Church in the United States with some 5 million members—reported African American membership of less than 54,000, roughly 1 percent of the total membership of the denomination.

Beliefs and Practices

While it is not completely accurate to argue that Lutherans, in spite of the name of the denomination, are committed to the teachings of Martin Luther, it is reasonable to suggest that the Book of Concord containing some of his religious thought guides the theological sensibilities of most Lutherans in the United States (Lagerquist 1999, 5–6).

Luther began to ask questions concerning the nature of the Roman Catholic faith and the activities of the Church. In keeping with the traditional academic practice of his time and location, Luther posted 95 theses for debate in Wittenberg, in 1517. Church officials considered this a challenge, and he was eventually asked to recant his views. Luther refused because to do so would be to reject

---

ADDIE BUTLER (1946–)

Addie Butler holds a doctorate from Columbia University and has held numerous posts in higher education. In addition, Butler has had great influence within the Lutheran Church. For example, she has chaired the Worship and Music Committee of the Reformation Lutheran Church in Philadelphia. On the regional level, she has served as the Vice President of the Southeastern Pennsylvania Synods of the Evangelical Lutheran Church of America. Butler has also held the post of Vice President of the Evangelical Lutheran Church in America (1997–2003). She has also served on the Board of Trustees for the Lutheran Theological Seminary in Philadelphia. Her service to the church has been recognized in a variety of ways, including the church's Service to God Medal.

Scripture and the ministry of Jesus the Christ as he understood them. Luther did not reject Catholic Church per se; rather, he rejected what he considered its troubled teachings and attitudes.

Luther developed a reformation of the Catholic Church's position on the nature of salvation. The Church's theology and actions suggested that salvation could be secured through good works, but Luther's reading of Scripture posed an alternative: Salvation is simply a gift from God, given to humans through divine Grace and accepted by faith. Humans do not merit salvation, nor can they behave consistently in a way that would earn it. Furthermore, he believed preoccupation with the monastic system and priesthood as exceptional modalities of service to God did not recognize the manner in which people could serve God in productive ways through their daily lives, within the context of their secular employment.

Luther believed that each individual was capable of developing a relationship with God and was capable of understanding Scripture with the aid of the Holy Spirit, when sermons and liturgy were made available in the language of the "common" people (Balmer and Winner 2002, 37). That is to say, there is something to be said for the notion of a calling from God to service, but Luther understood this call as a general process by which people should attempt to live righteously within all professions and all dimension of life. Hence, all believers should be active in the worship experience because all believers are equal in the sight of God, regardless of their socioeconomic circumstances. In essence he argued for what is commonly called the priesthood of all believers. In addition, Luther argued that only baptism and communion should be recognized as sacraments.

The Augsburg Confession (1530) outlined the underpinning of this new theological and liturgical position, and it provided the framework for the doctrinal commitments of Lutherans. Shaped by the Augsburg Confession, the most recent statement of faith found on the Evangelical Lutheran Church in America (the largest Lutheran communion in the United States) Web site summarizes basic dimensions of its theological heritage. It does so by highlighting the saving work of God through Jesus Christ, who "is the Word of God incarnate, through whom everything was made and through whose life, death, and resurrection God fashions a new creation." Furthermore, "the proclamation of God's message to us as both Law and Gospel is

NATHANIEL CARTER (1875–1904)

Carter was trained and ordained into the Lutheran ministry in 1896, after having arrived in Baltimore, Maryland, four years earlier. He was attracted to the missionary work being done amongst African Americans in that area of the country by the Lutheran Church. Carter's ordination made him one of the first African Americans to reach that status within the denomination. Among his responsibilities was a fund-raising tour conducted in the Midwest. The success of his efforts resulted in enough money to build, in 1897, St. Philip's Evangelical Lutheran Church. He pastured that church until his death in 1904.

the Word of God, revealing judgment and mercy through word and deed, beginning with the Word in creation, continuing in the history of Israel, and centering in all its fullness in the person and work of Jesus Christ." The nature and purpose of Jesus Christ is presented, according to Lutherans, through the canonical Scriptures, which tell the story, inspired by God, of God's work through Jesus Christ. These Scriptures provide all information necessary for salvation (http://www.elca.org/co/faith.html).

Anthony B. Pinn

SELECTED BIBLIOGRAPHY

Balmer, Randall, and Lauren Winner. *Protestantism in America* (New York: Columbia University Press, 2002).

Braaten, Carl F. *Principles of Lutheran Theology* (Minneapolis: Fortress Press, 2007).

Lagerquist, L. Anne. *The Lutherans* (Cleveland: Greenwood Press, 1999).

Lull, Timothy F., and Mark S. Hanson. *On Being Lutheran: Reflections on Church, Theology and Faith* (Minneapolis: Fortress Press, 2005).

Noll, Mark. *The Old Religion in a New World: The History of North American Christianity* (St. Louis: Eerdmans Publishing, 2001).

AFRICAN AMERICANS AND RELIGIOUS HUMANISM

Historical Development

While there remains a good deal of debate concerning the nature and meaning of "Religious Humanism," it is reasonable to claim that it is an umbrella category used to capture a full range of religious and spiritual perspectives, involving a general suspension of belief in the supernatural and focusing on human accountability and responsibility for what takes place in the world. It, like secular humanism, holds claims related to divine beings and notions of transcendence suspect. But unlike secular humanism, it finds a more general and natural or earthbound sense of religiosity useful and healthy. That is to say, religious humanism is a form of religious belief and practice, but one without notions of the divine and without appeal to transcendent realities such as heaven, hell, angels, and demons. Its commitments and perspectives are less concerned with relationship with God or gods, and more concerned with framing and celebrating proper human living through good practice, or ethics. In this respect, religious humanism as an umbrella category can, in practice, include agnosticism to aggressive atheism and every orientation in-between.

Many reduce this mode of humanism to atheism—a rejection of God; religious humanism tends to give less attention to disproving the existence of God than does secular humanism, although critiques of traditional forms of theism are not uncommon. Instead, its primary concern is with providing moral and ethical principles that promote healthy life options for humans and a proper relationship to the larger, natural environment. Religious humanism, as the phrase suggests, is a human-centered religious orientation. It is religious or religion because it, as other traditions discussed in this encyclopedia and as defined in the introduction to the encyclopedia, provides life orientation. It is religion or religious because it provides adherents with an "ultimate" life orientation, complete with thought and practices that shape and guide movement through the world. Some refer to this orientation as religious naturalism.

Attention to religion within African American communities typically revolves around discussion of theistic orientations such as black churches, Islam, and so on. And, in part, this narrow focus is premised on an assumption that people of African descent in the Americas are theists, or believers in God or gods. Although it is certainly the case that many African Americans acknowledge divine beings as part of their religious thought and practice as evidenced by the large number of African Americans who claim to pray, for example. However, not all people of African descent have held to theism. In fact, there is substantial historical and cultural evidence to suggest that many African Americans, from their early presence in the American hemisphere have rejected theism and have embraced various modes of religious humanism.

As the spirituals, a musical form established by African Americans early in their presence in North America, speak to an early belief in divine figures who impinge on human history, the blues, another early mode of musical expression created by free and enslaved Africans, point to a deep suspicion concerning the supernatural and the idea that the world is managed by a kind and loving God. The sentiment expressed in cultural forms such as the blues were also present within popular conversation and established within the minds and sensibilities of some enslaved Africans (Pinn 1998). A popular example of this disregard for the supernatural, for early examples of religious humanism, is found in the reflections of Rev. Daniel Alexander Payne, an African American minister during the nineteenth century. Chronicling the feeling of enslaved

Africans to the religious hypocrisy of those who profess Christianity yet hold slaves, he wrote the following words in 1839: " . . . they hear these masters praying in their families, and they know that oppression and slavery are inconsistent with the Christian religion; therefore they scoff at religion itself—mock their masters, and distrust both the goodness and justice of God. Yes, I have known them even to question his existence" (Pinn 1998, 161). This rejection of theism, typically in the form of Christianity, is not limited to a few voices during the period of slavery. Early African American expressive culture such as folktales and folk wisdom also speak to this nontheistic stance. From the Br'er Rabbit stories told early in African American history, in which human ingenuity and accountability are highlighted over against divine intervention, to more forceful presentations, cultural wisdom speaks to a range of religious possibilities, including the humanism of a figure such as John Junior, a chimney sweeper (Pinn 1998). In this particular story, John rails against Christianity, the dominant symbol of theism for many: "I strictly have my fun. No, I ain't tendin' been' no Christian . . . What in the world is they prayin' fo'? Tryin' to get to heaven? They is goin' to get there anyhow. There ain't no other hell but this one down here" (Brewer 1968, 268). John expresses the human-centered orientation that some African Americans embraced over against Christianity or other theistic orientations.

Examples of humanism as life orientation, as religious system, are found throughout African American culture, from the period of slavery, through Reconstruction, and into the twentieth century. And perhaps the most forceful and clearly presented presentation of humanism as religion within African American communities is found in the literature produced during what we commonly refer to as the Harlem Renaissance. While this cultural movement's dates are difficult to claim with great certainty, it is reasonable to argue that the Harlem Renaissance spread from roughly 1919 to the 1930s. More certain is the impact artists associated with this movement, such as Paul Laurence Dunbar, James Weldon Johnson, and Zora Neale Hurston, had on the cultural self-understanding of African Americans in particular and Americans in general during the early twentieth century (Pinn 1998).

These artists provided rich and thick depictions of African American life, including its religious dimensions. Of note is the manner in which standouts such as Johnson expressed as part of their work and personal orientation an undercurrent of humanism in African American communities. Johnson argues that theism works for some, and their attention to such an orientation should be respected; but he moves in another direction. As a student at Atlanta University (now Clark Atlanta University), Johnson read leading agnostic writers such as Thomas Paine, and those materials

James Weldon Johnson left his mark in so many areas of African American culture during the early part of the twentieth century that he is not easily categorized: he was a songwriter, poet, novelist, scholar, diplomat, and civil rights activist. (Library of Congress)

served to reinforce and name a nontheistic (or humanistic) orientation he had first embraced as a much younger man. In other words, "his doubts concerning religion and the church increased with each year. He could not, however, resolve the tension

---

ANTHONY B. PINN (1964–)

Anthony B. Pinn is the Agnes Cullen Arnold Professor of Humanities and Professor of Religious Studies at Rice University. Prior to Rice, Pinn taught at Macalester College (St. Paul, Minnesota). He is also the executive director of the Society for the Study of Black Religion. Pinn received the BA from Columbia University, and the MDiv from Harvard Divinity School. Pinn also completed the MA and PhD at Harvard University. His teaching interests include liberation theologies, black religious aesthetics, religion and popular culture, and African American Humanism. His work in African American Humanism has served to further clarify its presence and practice within African American communities.

solely out of his narrow experience with his family or church. It would take a few years, and a sense of life styles beyond the provincialism of Jacksonville, for Johnson to find his answer in agnosticism" (Levy 1973, 15). Such a move away from Christianity does not always involve for African Americans a move into agnosticism—for some it is a much more direct path to overt atheism, with a heightened concern for human accountability and responsibility for the quality of life for humans and the rest of the natural environment.

The changing nature of life for people of African descent in the Americas challenged long-held assumptions concerning the nature and meaning of religion. Continued racial discrimination, the Great Migration—the mass movement of African Americans in the United States from rural areas to cities in the North—and numerous other economic and political issues pushed for greater clarity but complexity with respect to what it means to be "black" and "religious." While black churches and other religious orientations presented throughout this encyclopedia continued to maintain adherents, humanism was not without its share of committed persons. Some of these adherents were rather critical of black churches and belief in God in more general terms. In particular, one sees this with African American involvement in the Communist Party during the first several decades of the twentieth century. It was not uncommon for some African American communists to push a materialist agenda, one that had little room for notions of transcendence and divine intervention—preferring instead a read of human history and proper mechanism of socioeconomic and political advancement (Pinn 1998). The optimism that marked much of life in the United States prior to World War I was broken, and in its place was a measured realism and suspicion concerning the nature of labor—the "haves and the have nots." While not all African American Communists and Socialists were opposed to theistic religion—in fact several African American Socialists were leaders of black churches—it was not uncommon for some to critique and reject theism. Take, for example, the words of Hosea Hudson (who maintained belief in God) speaking about Communist colleagues during the 1930s. "I had heard,"

ALICE WALKER (1944–)

One of the most significant writers of the twentieth century, Alice Walker received her undergraduate degree from Sarah Lawrence College. Holding a variety of jobs, she wrote her first book in 1968, which generated opportunities, including a faculty appointment at Wellesley College. Walker continued to write, producing such important books as *The Color Purple* and *In Search of Our Mothers' Gardens*. The definition of "womanism" found in the latter became a significant conceptual framework for a turn in African American Religious Studies called womanist theology and ethics. Within many of her works of fiction as well as more autobiographical writings, elements of humanism are present and are combined with a more general regard for the environment or nature as the source of meaning. Her contributions to humanism were acknowledged in 1997 when she was named "Humanist of the Year" by the American Humanist Association.

recounts Hudson, "other Party people talking. Some of them had never been members of no church, talking about there wont no such thing as God: 'Where is he at? You say it's a God, where is he at? You can't prove where he's at' " (Painter 1979, 133). This humanism (in the form of atheism) noted in the statement above is further evidenced in literature extending beyond the Harlem Renaissance and the 1930s flirtation with Communism.

Richard Wright, at one point a member of the Community Party and a writer, comes into prominence on the heels of the Harlem Renaissance during a phase of literary production at times referred to as Black Realism during the 1940s and 1950s. Wright, like many African American humanists, moves to this religious orientation in response to what is perceived as the inadequate response of Christianity to human suffering through a theodicy (doctrine related to the question "what can one say about divine justice in light of human misery?") that embraces and celebrates suffering as a sign of divine favor, deserved punishment, or necessary condition leading to great reward or gain. From Wright's perspective only a human-based, human-centered, life orientation gives African Americans the proper perspective on life that can address suffering and produce mature strategies for living. His position, based on this recognition, involves a disregard for God—not love for God, not hatred toward God, but disinterest (Pinn 1998). Wright expresses this stance when reflecting on a conversation had with a young man when Wright was a child. "It would have been impossible," Wright recounts, "for me to have told him how I felt about religion. I had not settled in my mind whether I believed in God or not; His existence or nonexistence never worried me. I reasoned that if there did exist an all-wise, all-powerful God who knew the beginning and the end ... this God would surely know that I doubted His existence ... And if there was no God at all, then why all the commotion?" (Wright 1991, 134).

Rejection of theism as evidenced in the literature of figures such as Richard Wright and in political activism such as

---

RICHARD WRIGHT (1908–1960)

One of the leading figures of Black Realism in literature, whose writing represents for many the height of the "protest novel," Richard Wright came into public view with a collection of short stories titled *Uncle Tom's Children* (1938). This book was followed by a string of texts that would secure his reputation, including *Native Son* (1940), *Black Boy* (1945), and *The Outsider* (1953). Within his early writings one finds much thought drawn from his Communist leanings developed during his time in Chicago (1927–1937). Wright grew disillusioned with the Communist Party and with the possibility of racial equality in the United States, and, after some time spent in New York City, he moved to Paris in the latter part of the 1940s. In Paris he was influenced by the existentialist thought of figures such as Jean-Paul Satre. Within Wright's fiction one finds a strong critique of traditional, Christian religion, and in its place he suggests a form of humanism.

found with African American Communists does not always involve an explicit rejection of theistic communities such as black churches. In some cases, holders of humanist sensibilities have maintained a more pragmatic relationship with Christian organizations in that these organizations: (1) hold significant sway within African American communities; and, (2) provide optimal organizing and recruitment opportunities because churches represent large numbers of African Americans. This is the case, for instance, with some political activity during the 1960s as promoted by the Student Nonviolent Coordinating Committee (SNCC). Initially aligned with the Civil Rights Movement and its Christian orientation, this organization of students committed to social transformation became somewhat disillusioned with the manner in which the Christian ethos of the movement tended to cripple more aggressive strategies (Pinn 1998). In such instances, some members of SNCC who appreciated more humanistic orientations voiced their perspective over against

Christianity. James Forman, the executive secretary of SNCC during its formative years and later member of the Black Panther Party, frames his political perspective and activism in terms of a human-centered viewpoint:

> I reject the existence of God. He is not all-powerful, all-knowing, and everywhere. He is not just or unjust because he does not exist. God is a myth; churches are institutions designed to perpetuate this myth and thereby keep people in subjugation. When a people who are poor, suffering with disease and sickness, accept the fact that God has ordained for them to be this way—then they will never do anything about their human condition. In other words, the belief in a supreme being or God weakens the will of a people to change conditions themselves. (Pinn 2001, 272–273)

Forman was not alone in recognizing the theological problems often associated with theism. However, some members of the Black Panther Party (an organization started in the 1960s in California to combat racism) appreciated this critique

---

JAMES FORMAN (1928–2005)

James Forman, after service in the military, received his undergraduate degree at Roosevelt University where he also worked out the initial framework of his humanism. While doing graduate work at Boston University, racial discrimination and the mounting civil rights activities caught his attention and resulted in him beginning work as a community activist in Tennessee. In 1961, he would become a member of the new Student Nonviolent Coordinating Committee that served as an arm of the Civil Rights Movement. He played a major role in SNCC's activities, but his militant stance on many issues meant disagreement with SNCC. Forman eventually left the organization and played a leadership role in other groups such as the Black Panther Party. As part of the Black Economic Development Conference held in Detroit (1969), he is remembered for his taking over of a worship service at Riverside Church in New York City during which he read the Black Manifesto calling for economic and political justice. Forman continued his education, receiving a PhD in 1982, and organized various journalism projects.

but also felt at times the need to maintain cordial connections to churches.

The examples of SNCC and the Black Panther Party raise an interesting question regarding African American humanism as a religious orientation in that they point out the possibility of this religious orientation within the context of a defined community. It is not simply the intellectual agenda of individuals; rather, it is also a religious commitment expressed within the context of groups. In addition to the political organizations noted above, African American humanism is also expressed up to the present in organizations such as the Unitarian Universalist Association—a non-creedal denomination (Pinn 1998). Although African Americans make up roughly only 1 percent of the denomination's 150,000 members, the leadership of the organization reflects their involvement. For example, Rev. Dr. William Sinkford, an African American, is president of the Association (see the entry on the Unitarian Universalist Association). Others who are less vocal about their humanism and are not markedly atheistic maintained membership in traditional churches, choosing to simply interpret church creeds and theology in light of their humanist sensibilities.

Beliefs and Practices

Regardless of their particular setting, and the range of perspectives within the framework of Religious Humanism, it is marked by allegiance to an assortment of guiding principles and assumptions, including the following:

1. Humanity is fully and solely accountable and responsible for the human condition and the correction of humanity's plight.

2. There is a general suspicion toward or rejection of supernatural explanations and claims, combined with an understanding of humanity as an evolving part of the natural environment as opposed to being a created being. This can involve disbelief in God(s).

3. There is an appreciation for African American cultural production and a perception of traditional forms of black religiosity as having cultural importance as opposed to any type of "cosmic" authority.

4. There is a commitment to individual and societal transformation.

5. There is a controlled optimism that recognizes both human potential and human destructive activities. (Pinn 2004)

WILLIAM R. JONES (1938–)

Recently retired from Florida State University where he was Professor of Religion and Director of African American Studies, William R. Jones also taught at Yale Divinity School. He received the BA from Howard University, the Master of Divinity degree from Harvard Divinity School, and the PhD from Brown University. Working in philosophy and theology, Jones is best known for his critique of African American theism and liberation theology found in *Is God a White Racist?* as well as his analysis of race-based discrimination. Jones has been active in the Unitarian Universalist Association and has held numerous leadership positions within the organization.

While there is some variation, these principles represent the general sense of ethics that frames religious humanism within African American communities. These five concerns entail, to some degree, what we might identify as core concerns, and it is these principles that frame anything one might label humanist practices.

Unlike many of the religious traditions found within African American communities, there is little about the core humanist principles that necessitate a central or common space for practice. That is to say, unlike black churches such as the African Methodist Episcopal Church, the stated creed does not require or even work best in the context of collective worship. In fact, the notion of worship does not fit well into the humanist vocabulary. Instead one might talk in terms of humanist celebration that range from rather mundane activities engaged in by individuals to more formal and recognizable moments of communal celebration such as a Sunday service in any number of Unitarian Universalist Churches. What the humanist aims for involves the development of a healthy relationship with self, community, and the larger environment. Such appreciation for life, in a general sense, for the humanist is sacramental. The lack of attention to transcendence and the supernatural means for the humanist "mundane" activities—like a walk through the woods, gatherings with loved ones, community service, and so on—have a celebratory or sacramental nature to them. In short, any activity that sharpens commitment to healthy life and that promotes strong and positive relationships, that connects humans to the earth and each other, can involve for the humanist a moment or practice of celebration.

Anthony B. Pinn

SELECTED BIBLIOGRAPHY

Allen, Norm, Jr., ed. *Personal Paths to Humanism* (Amherst, NY: Prometheus Books, 2003).

Brewer, J. Mason, ed. *American Negro Folklore* (Chicago: Quadrangle Books, 1968).

Forman, James. "God Is Dead: A Question of Power." *The Making of Black Revolutionaries* (Washington, DC: Open Hand Publishing, 1985). In *By These Hands: A Documentary History of African American Humanism*, ed. Anthony B. Pinn (New York: New York University Press, 2001).

MARK MORRISON-REED (1950–)

Rev. Mark Morrison-Reed has pastored numerous Unitarian churches, including Toronto Unitarian Church. He also served from 2001 to 2003 as the first African Canadian president of the Canadian Unitarian Council. Morrison-Reed's publications on the history and contributions of people of African descent to Unitarianism are groundbreaking and continues to inform conversation with the Unitarian Universalist Association and beyond. In addition to his pastoral and administrative work, Morrison-Reed has also taught at Meadville Lombard Theological School in Chicago, Illinois. He is known and highly regarded for his race relations work within Unitarian Universalist communities, helping the organization address issues that began to emerge in significant ways in the 1970s.

Jones, William R. *Is God a White Racist? A Preamble to Black Theology* (1973; Boston: Beacon Press, 1996).

Levy, Eugene. *James Weldon Johnson: Black Leader, Black Voice* (Chicago: The University of Chicago Press, 1973).

Morrison-Reed, Mark D. *Black Pioneers in a White Denomination*, 3rd ed. (Boston: Skinner House Books, 1994).

Painter, Nell Irvin. *The Narrative of Hosea Hudson: His Life as a Negro Communist in the South* (Cambridge, MA: Harvard University Press, 1979).

Pinn, Anthony B. *Varieties of African American Religious Experience* (Minneapolis: Fortress Press, 1998).

Pinn, Anthony B. *African American Humanist Principles: Living and Thinking Like the Children of Nimrod* (New York: Palgrave/Macmillan, 2004).

Pinn, Anthony B., ed. *By These Hands: A Documentary History of African American Humanism* (New York: New York University Press, 2001).

Walker, Alice. *The Color Purple* (New York: Harcourt, Brace, Jovanovich, 1982).

Walker Alice. "The Only Reason You Want to Go to Heaven Is That You Have Been Driven Out of Your Mind." *Anything We Love Can Be Saved* (New York: Random House, Inc., 1997).

Wright, Richard. *Native Son* (New York: Harper Brothers, 1940).

Wright, Richard. *Black Boy (American Hunger)* (New York: Harper Collins Publishers/The Library of America, 1991).

AFRICAN AMERICANS AND SECULAR HUMANISM

Historical Development

Humanism is a nonreligious life stance drawing upon reason, experience, and observation to formulate ethical ideas and to develop wisdom and scientific knowledge to further human advancement.

Humanism has a very long tradition. It can be traced back to ancient India, China (Confucianism and Buddhism were originally human-centered religions), and Greece. Protagoras (481–411 BCE) summed it up in his work *Of the Gods*: "Man is the measure of all things, of the reality of those which are, and of the unreality of those which are not." Or in today's terms, human thought and human action must be at the center of human existence. The welfare of the human race—rather than the supposed will of God—must be humanity's chief concern.

Confucius (551–471 BCE) believed that morality could be derived without reference to the gods. He taught that, in order to attain wisdom, human beings must strive toward kindness, righteousness, and social justice. He stressed education, but not prayer. Centuries before the birth of Christianity, he stressed the silver rule: Do not do to others what you do not want done to yourself.

In about the third century BCE, humanists founded the Carvaka and Lokayata movements in India. The Carvakas and Lokayatas stood in opposition to superstition and literal interpretations of Hindu teachings. They were atheists, rationalists, and materialists. They repudiated belief in the soul, reincarnation, immortality, and other religious beliefs in their day. They believed that priests were unnecessary and that people should focus on enjoying life in the here and now. They critiqued the Vedas and the Upanishadas, the leading religious books among the ancient Indians. Eventually, religionists successfully hindered the movements and obliterated most of their writings. The Carvakas lasted until about 1400 CE.

There have been many other humanist movements throughout the world since ancient times, including the Renaissance and the Enlightenment. Today there are humanist groups in several nations. There are thousands of humanist publications and numerous books on the history and philosophy of humanism. Humanism has been embraced as an alternative to religion and as a response to White supremacy by African Americans.

The Harlem Renaissance was essentially a Black humanist movement. In 1923, Jean Toomer wrote *Cane*, a superb collection of poems, stories, and sketches about life for Blacks in the United States. Toomer once attended a lecture by the agnostic Clarence Darrow, which caused him to abandon his belief in a universe operated in accordance with God's divine laws. In *Cane*, Toomer has a story called "Kabnis," in which the character Kabnis is highly critical of Black preachers. Layman, another character, goes further and says *all* preachers are parasitic.

Nella Larsen, the author of the novella *Quicksand*, was deeply humanistic. Helga, the main character in the novella, is forced to embrace theism, but in the end, she rebels and comes to view theism as a tool of oppression against Black people.

The poet Sterling Brown wrote "Slim in Hell," in which a Black man named Slim Greer dies and is transported to heaven. Saint Peter meets him, gives him angel wings, and instructs Slim to find out what is going on in hell. Slim is shocked to find out that hell and the Deep South look remarkably similar and gets the surprise of his life.

Langston Hughes, James Weldon Johnson, and other major writers contributed to the Harlem Renaissance. It was one of the most creative periods in African American history, and many of the works that came from that time are still widely read and appreciated today.

In 1966, Huey Newton and Bobby Seale formed the Black Panther Party. Drawing upon Marxist-Leninist ideals, they developed a theory that Newton called "revolutionary humanism." They advocated "community control of police" and led a successful breakfast program for school children. They established a completely secular ten-point program listing their demands and worked closely with poor and progressive people from varied backgrounds.

In the same year, Ron Karenga, now known as Maulana Karenga, created the Kwanzaa celebration. Karenga, a nontheist, has always been careful to note that celebration is not religious, but cultural. It is held December 26 to January 1 to promote Black pride, unity, and an appreciation for African culture and values. It is now embraced by millions of people throughout the world.

These are just a few examples of Black involvement in the promotion of humanist ideas. However, organized humanism in the United States has primarily been led by Whites.

Huey Newton (right), founder of the Black Panther Party, sits with Bobby Seale at party headquarters in San Francisco, July 1967. (Ted Streshinsky/Corbis)

In 1980, Paul Kurtz founded *Free Inquiry*, the nation's leading journal of secular humanist thought and opinion, and the Council for Democratic and Secular Humanism (CODESH) in Buffalo, New York. (In 1996, the world witnessed the fall of the former Soviet bloc, the Berlin Wall, and communism. The group then changed the name to simply the Council for Secular Humanism.)

Kurtz founded the organization and the journal in response to the Religious Right's continual assaults upon secular humanism. The Council is primarily an educational organization. Among its main concerns are the development of a secular ethics, church/state separation, the promotion of good science, and achieving the good life for human beings in the here and now.

The Council published the first issue of *Free Inquiry* in the fall of 1980. The magazine featured *A Secular Humanist Declaration* that Kurtz put together. Many famous leaders and thinkers signed it, including science fiction writer Issac Asimov, philosophers Sir A. J. Ayer and Sidney Hook, DNA co-discoverer Francis Crick, and psychologist B. F. Skinner.

The declaration called for unfettered free inquiry into all areas of human endeavor. It opposed religious intolerance and stressed the importance of self-reliance and human-centered thought and action, as opposed to supposed divine intervention. The *New York Times* featured the statement on its front page, and publications throughout the world ran stories about the declaration.

In 1983, the Council established the International Academy of Humanism. Humanist laureates include:

- Wole Soyinka, Nobel Laureate in Literature
- Léopold Sédar Senghor (1906–2001), former president of Senegal
- Taslima Nasrin, author, physician, social critic
- Salman Rushdie, author, Fellow of the Royal Society of Literature (U.K.)
- Neil deGrasse Tyson, Director, Hayden Planetarium

In 1985, Jim Christopher founded Secular Organizations for Sobriety (SOS), an alternative recovery group to groups depending upon a "higher power" to fight their addictions to alcohol, illegal drugs, tobacco, and other substances. The group has based its mission around the premise that it is unnecessary to believe in a Supreme Being to battle addiction. The program is international and has helped to save thousands of lives, from prison inmates to professionals. Though the program is nonreligious it is not *antireligious* and religious people are welcome to join. SOS also stands for "Save Our Selves." The group, a program of the Council for Secular Humanism, has published many pamphlets and books on the subject of sobriety from secular perspectives.

On August 31, 1989, Norm R. Allen Jr. became the executive director of African Americans for Humanism (AAH), a subdivision of the Council. The group's concerns include:

- The promotion of ethical values
- The defense of church/state separation
- Opposition to racism in all of its forms
- The fostering of skepticism of untested claims to knowledge
- Critiques of religion, bad science, pseudoscience, and claims of the paranormal
- Education

- The defense of democratic values
- The pursuit of happiness for individuals and society

AAH was formed in an effort to help attract more African Americans to organized humanism. Historically, there have been few non-Whites involved in organized humanism. Today, though, largely due to the efforts of AAH, the Council, and Prometheus Books headquartered near Buffalo, New York, and headed by Paul Kurtz, there are several humanist groups in Africa, Asia, and Latin America. However, there is still not much involvement among non-Whites in the West with organized humanism. AAH has had success where other efforts have failed. The organization has had news articles and essays in most of the Black newspapers throughout the United States. Representatives of the group have been featured on many of the Black radio stations throughout the United States.

In 1991, Allen edited *African-American Humanism: An Anthology*, the first book to demonstrate the extent to which humanism has substantively influenced and developed African American thought, intellectualism, and activism. In the same year, Allen became editor of the *AAH Examiner*, the international newsletter of AAH. The quarterly newsletter features essays, articles, poems, reviews, news, and other items of relevance to humanists of African descent.

In 1995, the National Center for Science Education, Inc., published several statements on science titled *Voices for Evolution*. Though very few African American organizations weigh in on the topic of evolution versus Intelligent Design or Creationism, AAH issued a statement. It read in part:

> AAH is concerned that Blacks and other minorities are woefully underrepresented in the sciences. It will become

---

JAMES FARMER, JR. (1920–1999)

James Farmer joined the advisory board of African Americans for Humanism in 1989. Farmer came to fame as one of the Civil Rights Movement's Big Four leaders (with Roy Wilkins, Whitney Young, and Martin Luther King, Jr.). In 1942, he co-founded the Committee of Racial Equality, which was later changed to the Congress of Racial Equality (CORE). In May of that year, CORE, in opposition to racial discrimination, led a successful boycott of a restaurant in Chicago. In 1961, Farmer participated in the first major Freedom Ride in the American South. The event was successful and persuaded many to embrace the cause of passive resistance. As a result, CORE became one of the most successful and influential civil rights groups in the U.S. In 1973, Farmer signed *Humanist Manifesto II*, a document that offered humanistic solutions to humanity's problems. A. Philip Randolph, another African American humanist widely regarded as the grandfather of the Civil Rights Movement, also signed the manifesto. Both men were friends of Paul Kurtz, the founder of the Council for Secular Humanism. In 1997, historians, columnists, civil rights leaders, and several members of Congress petitioned the White House to bestow the Medal of Freedom, the nation's highest civilian honor, upon Farmer. Early the following year, the NAACP gave Farmer, then 77, its Lifetime Achievement Award. Shortly thereafter, then-President Bill Clinton awarded Farmer the Medal of Freedom.

increasingly difficult to attract and retain minority students to the sciences if they are constantly bombarded with pseudoscientific misinformation and unscientific methods of investigation. For these reasons, AAH opposes the introduction of Creationism into all science curricula of the U.S. public schools.

Other groups that presented statements included People for the American Way, the American Association for the Advancement of Science, the National Academy of Sciences, the American Psychological Association, and numerous religious groups.

Another topic that most Black leaders have been reluctant to tackle is the exploitation of Black people by faith healers. Allen has written on this topic for *Free Inquiry*, and many Black newspapers throughout the United States reprinted the article. In the 1990s, psychic hotlines were big business. According to financial analysts, psychic phone networks earned about $2 billion by 1999. Black celebrities such as Dionne Warwick and Latoya Jackson promoted the phone networks, and Blacks were largely represented among those using these services.

Allen and AAH member Patrick Inniss wrote strong critiques of the hotlines for *Free Inquiry* and the *AAH Examiner*, respectively. Allen demonstrated that a belief in psychic hotlines among African Americans is part of a long history of African Americans' belief in prophecy and paranormal claims. Many Black newspapers reprinted either Allen's or Inniss's article.

In 2001, Christopher C. Bell Jr., who later joined AAH, wrote *The Belief Factor and the White Superiority Syndrome*. Bell argued that an image of a White Christ had a devastatingly negative effect upon the collective psyche of Black people. He discussed research that showed that fundamentalist religion tended to create an unscientific mind-set in its

---

REGINALD FINLEY (1974–)

Reginald Finley, aka the Infidel Guy, has been involved with African Americans for Humanism since the late 1990s. Finley likes the term "infidel" because he says that everyone is an infidel in the opinions of millions of people. (Christians are infidels to many Muslims, Muslims are infidels to many Christians, Muslims and Christians are infidels to many Jews, etc.) Finley, a former R&B singer from Atlanta, Georgia, is a former phone "psychic." He and his wife, Amber, worked in that capacity and were surprised at how easily they were able to cull information from unsuspecting callers. Sometimes the callers would volunteer information without any prodding. Most callers were impressed at the supposed paranormal powers of the phone psychics, and the work was fairly lucrative. However, after a while, Finley and his wife grew tired of the game and moved on to something new. Finley eventually started his own Web site, www.infidelguy.com. Featured on the site are such programs as "The Infidel Guy Show," in which the host interviews leading scientists and freethinkers. "The Debate Hour Show" hosts debates on the existence of God, Intelligent Design versus evolution, and other topics. "Infidel Radio" is a program that features first-rate theologians, philosophers, and scientists.

adherents. He argued that though an image of a White Christ gives Blacks a sense of inferiority, on the other hand, it gives Whites a sense of *superiority*. Bell called for a moratorium on the display of White Christ figures.

In 2003, Allen edited his second book, *The Black Humanist Experience: An Alternative to Religion*. The book included essays by African American humanists discussing their personal paths to humanism and the various ways in which humanism could benefit society. Contributors included writers from the United States, Ghana, Uganda, Nigeria, Ethiopia, and South Africa. In the introduction, the editor discusses highly successful secular primary and secondary schools in Curacao, the Netherlands Antilles, and Nigeria, respectively. In his essay on his personal path to humanism, the editor discusses the importance of AIDS prevention and stem cell research, as well as religious barriers to these areas. Further, he argues for a rational and scientific approach to the study of the natural world. African American humanists and African American religious leaders/observers differ in how far they are willing to go to critique harmful religious ideas and their sources.

For example, progressive religionists might critique sexism, patriarchy, and homophobia in the church. However, they might not be willing to thoroughly critique the biblical passages that give support to these reactionary messages. Furthermore, they are unlikely to be willing to question theism itself, which some humanists believe is a major source of human misery. Humanists seem more likely to embrace an unwavering commitment to free inquiry into all areas of human endeavor, which, indeed, is the mission statement of

the Council for Secular Humanism, than are most religionists. It is for this reason that African American humanists must continue to be involved in intellectualism and activism geared toward the liberation of African Americans.

Norm R. Allen Jr.

SELECTED BIBLIOGRAPHY

Kurtz, Paul. *Embracing the Power of Humanism* (Oxford: Rowman & Littlefield Publishers, 2000).

Kurtz, Paul. *Affirmations: Joyful and Creative Exuberance* (Amherst, NY: Prometheus Books, 2004).

Kurtz, Paul. *What Is Secular Humanism?* (Amherst, NY: Prometheus Books, 2006).

Madigan, Timothy J. *Promethean Love: Paul Kurtz and the Humanistic Perspective on Love* (New Castle, England: Cambridge Scholars Press, 2006).

AFRICAN AMERICANS IN THE EPISCOPAL CHURCH

Historical Development

When the first Africans to arrive in the parts of North America settled by English were carried to Virginia aboard a Dutch slave ship in 1619, they arrived in a colony served by the Anglican Church, a direct ancestor of today's Episcopal Church. Thus the connections, good, bad, and indifferent, between African Americans and what was to become the Episcopal Church are more longstanding than those with any other English denomination.

The definition of the Africans' relationship to the church was crucial in helping to shape slavery in its North American manifestations. At first, the

English thought that their Christian identity was a defining characteristic as opposed to the African peoples that they bought from the slave traders. Still, many English slaveholders feared that Christian conversion and baptism of their slaves might result in the slaves being granted freedom, and for good reason. One of the claims made by Elizabeth Key, a mixed-race daughter of an English planter, in her eventually successful suit for freedom filed in 1655, was that as a Christian baptized as a child in the Anglican Church in Virginia, she was entitled to her freedom and could not be held as a slave. The court record is unclear as to which of Key's claims were decisive in her being granted freedom, but in any event White Virginians—it turned out— were not willing for her case to serve even as a possible precedent for African slaves who came within the embrace of the Anglican Church. In 1667 the Virginia legislature enacted a law providing that baptism did not change the condition of a person as to whether he or she was slave or free, hoping thereby to encourage masters, who would no longer harbor doubts that they would lose slave labor, to permit Christian instruction of their slaves. Legislatures in other provinces where Anglicanism was established— New York and the Carolinas—enacted similar laws. All of these laws helped to contribute to a caste system where privilege was allotted to "whites"; religion turned out to play a subservient role in the social construction of race, as a means of determining who could be subject to enslavement.

The first widespread and systematic, yet halting, attempts to convert African Americans to Christianity under Anglican auspices came in 1703, with the establishment of the Society for the Propagation of the Gospel in Foreign Parts (SPG) as a missionary arm of the Anglican Church. While the SPG's missionary work focused on European Americans and Native Americans as well as African Americans, several of their missionary workers, including Elias Neau in New York and Francis Le Jau in South Carolina, found that much of their work would focus on the religious instruction of African American slaves. Slave masters were often suspicious, if not downright hostile, to the work of Neau and Le Jau, fearing that freedom for the slaves might be part of the missionaries' hidden agenda. The missionaries, consequently, had to emphasize the utility of their religious instruction for the slave masters as well as the slaves. Far from making slaves "proud and Undutifull," Le Jau was at pains to show that his missionary work resulted in Christian slaves "who behave themselves very well." Still, the slave revolts and rumors of revolts that occurred in both South Carolina and New York in the early eighteenth century left both master and missionary stirring with unease. Le Jau regarded it as "a singular Providence" that not one of his Christian converts had been implicated in a 1714 slave plot in South Carolina (Sernett 1999, 30, 32). Neau's work did not emerge from a 1712 Negro revolt quite so unscathed. Of the 21 African Americans executed, Neau had to emphasize that only two of the alleged revolters had been his students, and only one of those had been baptized; he also noted that the baptized slave was exonerated posthumously. The work of Le Jau and Neau was limited in other ways as well. Only oral instruction of potential converts was allowed; instruction in literacy was forbidden. Given all the limitations and opposition to their work, the number of converts gained by SPG missionaries was meager.

In the middle of the eighteenth century, several events converged to make black Christianity, and with it black Anglicanism, more feasible. Most noteworthy was the Great Awakening, an evangelical outbreak preached by George Whitefield and others along the North American Atlantic coast and into the frontier. Whitefield and the preachers of John Wesley's Methodism were part of a new dissent only loosely associated with the Anglican Church, and many of these evangelical preachers left Anglicanism for Methodism. But that was not the case with all, and the first black preacher who ended up embracing Anglicanism and being ordained as a priest did so not in the numerous states in which Anglicanism had once been an established church, but in the state of Pennsylvania, where Anglicanism had been a tolerated outsider. Absalom Jones, a 47-year-old evangelical preacher, had led a group of African Americans out of the St. George's Methodist Church in 1793 when a white deacon had contested their choice of seats during worship. In the following year, African Americans in Philadelphia opened their first church in that city. Prior to 1794, African Americans had been organized nondenominationally in the Free African Society, but the opening of a church presented an occasion to choose. The majority of the new congregation rejected the Methodists who had so recently presented an affront and chose the Protestant Episcopal Church whose Philadelphia-based bishop, William White, had been their strong supporter. Religious leadership of this new congregation was first offered to Richard Allen, later to become famous as a founder of the African Methodist Episcopal Church; but when Allen, who desired to remain Methodist, declined, the leadership of the new congregation was assumed by his close friend Absalom Jones. The new congregation adopted the name of St. Thomas African Episcopal Church and was received in the diocese of Pennsylvania in 1794. Jones received the ordination of deacon in 1795 and of priest in 1804; he was the first African American to be ordained to the Episcopal priesthood.

The establishment of other African American Episcopal congregations followed closely behind the establishment of the St. Thomas congregation. The Free African Church of St. Philip, established in 1809 but tracing its roots to Elias Neau's school more than a century earlier, adopted an Episcopalian identity in 1818 and became St. Philip's Episcopal Church. Strong leadership was provided by Peter Williams Jr., owner of a tobacco store, ordained in 1820 to the office of deacon and six years later as the second African American Episcopal priest. In 1910, it was one of the first black churches to relocate to Harlem. Black Episcopal congregations were also established in Baltimore, Providence, Detroit, and Newark prior to the Civil War.

Most African American Episcopalians in the South remained in mixed-race churches. They were generally subject to the full range of oppression and vagaries offered by American slavery; the church usually provided no recourse. A notable example is Harriet Jacobs (1813–1897), who, in the 1830s, attended the segregated services for the few but very respectable African American members at the stately St. Paul's Episcopal Church in Edenton, North Carolina, one of the first Episcopal parishes to be organized in the state in 1701. Most ministers there emphasized the Apostle Paul's teachings for slaves to obey their masters; an exception, William Cairnes, who was friendly toward slaves, lasted only one year in the post. Jacobs's master, James Norcom, who subjected her to relentless sexual persecution and other cruelties, eventually joined this church, and she affirmed that she received worse treatment from him after he had become a church member. Later, after escaping from slavery and reflecting from the safe distance of England, she admitted her "prejudice against the Episcopal Church," because of its "contemptuous" treatment of African Americans and the numerous misdeeds of slaveholding clergy and laity; consequently, the whole Episcopal service had seemed to her "a mockery and a sham" (Jacobs 1987, 278). If Jacobs's experience should be seen as at all representative of that of African Americans in the South, it would not furnish a strong foundation for retention of African Americans in the Episcopal Church after emancipation.

African Americans in the Episcopal churches of the North struggled against racial oppression and slavery, often against the wishes of the white Episcopal bishops who had supervision over their black congregations. Peter Williams of St. Philip's received an appointment to the Board of Managers of the American Anti-Slavery Society in 1833, but when New York Bishop Benjamin T. Onderdonk, a supporter of colonizationism, requested Williams's resignation from this post, Williams felt constrained to comply. When Alexander Crummell, a protégé of Williams, applied to undertake a seminary education at the General Theological School of the Episcopal Church in New York, Onderdonk vetoed his admission solely on the basis of his race. Crummell informally attended classes at Yale University, received ordination as deacon and priest in 1842 and 1844, and ended up receiving formal ministerial training at the University of Cambridge in England, graduating in 1853. Like Williams, Crummell was also active in the American and New York State Anti-Slavery Society.

Race oppression in the church and secular arenas, in both the North and the South, was severe enough in the early

THE REV. ABSALOM JONES,
Rector of St. Thomas's African Episcopal Church in the City of Philadª.

The Reverend Absalom Jones, Rector of St. Thomas African Episcopal Church in Philadelphia. Absalom Jones was the first African American to be ordained to the Episcopal priesthood when he received the ordination of deacon in 1795 and of priest in 1804. He led St. Thomas African Episcopal Church in Philadelphia. (Schomburg Center/Art Resource, New York) nineteenth century that many African American Episcopal clergy felt that their best chances to make a living and to contribute to humanity lay outside the United States. James Holly, a Catholic who converted to the Protestant Episcopal Church at age 26 in 1855, vigorously promoted African American emigration to Haiti. In 1861, Holly moved to Haiti, along with more than 100 members of his family and church. Within a year, the Protestant Episcopal Church had agreed to grant financial support for Holly's mission effort, and in 1874, Holly was consecrated in a New York Episcopal Church as a bishop; his episcopal responsibilities were in Haiti, as head of the Orthodox Apostolic Church, in communion with other Episcopal Churches. He was the first African American to be consecrated as a bishop in the Episcopal Church. Holly continued to advocate Haitian emigration until the time of his death in 1911.

A diverse cadre of leaders, white and black, were involved with the Liberian branch of the Episcopal Church. The Episcopal Church was first established in the portion of Liberia settled by African Americans from Maryland in 1836. Its two leading personalities, who often clashed, were the white American John Payne, who arrived as a missionary in 1838 and was elevated to the post of Missionary Bishop in 1851, and Alexander Crummell, the African American recent graduate of the University of Cambridge who arrived in 1853. Payne envisaged an Episcopal Church in Liberia under white American oversight and with primarily Americo-African clergy; Crummell envisioned an Episcopal Church under the control of black men, a church that would make a strong contribution to building a Liberian nation. He marveled at the way that "God, after carrying on His work of preparation in the black race in America in dark, mysterious, and distressful ways, has at length brought out a 'remnant' of them and placed them in a free Republic, to achieve high nationality, to advance civilization and to subserve the highest interests of the Cross and the Church!" (Crummell 1891, 446). Crummell's Pan-Africanism was widely known among African Americans in the United States as a result of his numerous publications and an influential visit to the United States in 1861 and 1862. A worn-out Payne resigned in 1871, and Crummell, weary of conflicts in both church and state in Liberia, returned to the United States in the same year. The Episcopal Church in the United States would subsequently consecrate two black bishops for service in Liberia, Samuel D. Ferguson in 1885 and Theophilus Momulu Gardiner (as suffragan) in 1920. Both consecrations took place in New York's Grace Episcopal Church. Ferguson, a native South Carolinian who had emigrated with his parents to Liberia at age 6 in 1848, presided over a thriving Episcopal church, with 7,688 baptisms and 3,949 confirmations during his 22 years as bishop. Gardiner was the first native-born African consecrated as an Episcopal bishop.

The Union Army's victory in the Civil War and the coming of emancipation sparked an exodus of a different sort. Many African Americans left the Episcopal churches in the South, mostly in favor of independent black Methodist and Baptist congregations, where African Americans could experience self-determination in church affairs and where there were no racial bars to advancement. One example was James Porter, an influential lay leader

---

GEORGE FREEMAN BRAGG, JR. (1863–1940)

George Freeman Bragg, Jr. (1863–1940) knew the power of the printing press from his early childhood, when he was hired as a valet by the editor of the *Petersburg Index*. His early life included service as a page in the Virginia legislature, employment as a teacher, and studies at the Theological School for Negroes, from which he was expelled for lack of humility but to which he later returned. He was ordained an Episcopal deacon two weeks prior to his 24th birthday, and within two years was ordained as priest, married, and assigned to a church in Norfolk, Virginia. He authored about 25 books. The most important of his books is *History of the Afro-American Group of the Episcopal Church* (1922). His most notable pastorate was in Baltimore, beginning in 1891. He worked closely with both Booker T. Washington and W. E. B. DuBois on such issues as opposing disfranchisement of African Americans in Maryland, but increasingly was identified more closely with DuBois and the Niagara Movement. For three and a half decades, he was general secretary of the Conference for Church Workers among Colored People within the Episcopal Church.

(chairman of the Board of Vestry, lay reader, choir director) in St. Stephen's Church in Savannah, Georgia. He was not permitted to fulfill his aspirations to become an ordained Episcopal priest, so, by 1873, he had joined the African Methodist Episcopal Church and had been ordained as an elder in that church. In South Carolina and Alabama, the decline of black membership was an overwhelming 80–90 percent. Some of the African Americans who remained in the Episcopal Church did so precisely because they were part of a small wealthy elite who had little desire to mix with African Americans of lower social ranking or of darker skin coloring. Others, of course, had nurtured profound long-term ties with the Episcopal Church and would not relinquish these under any circumstances. Thus, Alexander Crummell played an active role within the denomination after his return from his almost-two-decades-long sojourn in Liberia. In 1874, he founded an African American congregation in Washington, D.C., St. Luke's

Episcopal, and he became its first rector. Crummell's rhetoric was changed, however. He was no longer a fervent African emigrationist, and he was now much more focused on improving social conditions within the African American community.

As was fashionable among white Protestants in the immediate postwar years, the Episcopal Church founded an agency to look after the freed slaves, the Protestant Episcopal Freedmen's Mission, in 1865. If possible, the Mission wanted to keep African Americans within the Episcopal fold. (This organization later changed its name to the Commission of Home Missions to Colored People; its existence was discontinued in 1878, due to the evaporation of financial support in the North, and active opposition among southern white Episcopalians.) This mission accomplished less than some competing majority white denominations, such as the Congregationalists and the Methodist Episcopal Church. One accomplishment was the founding of St. Augustine's Normal School and

Collegiate Institute in Raleigh, North Carolina, in 1867. St. Augustine's (now a college) survives as of this writing. Two later schools founded by Episcopalians for African Americans also survive: St. Paul's Normal and Industrial School (now a college), in Lawrenceville, Virginia, in 1888, and Voorhees College in Denmark, South Carolina, in 1897 by a 23-year-old African American woman, Elizabeth Evelyn Wright. Differing emphases have been given to Booker T. Washington's industrial style of education and W. E. B. DuBois's classical style of education throughout these colleges' histories. While all of these institutions eventually added a four-year collegiate program of education, all three did so decades after their origins, between 1924 and 1944.

One significant educational institution for African Americans that does not survive today was a theological seminary founded in Petersburg, Virginia, in 1878, because the Episcopal bishops did not want African American students in their all-white seminaries. The seminary for African Americans was named in 1884 the Bishop Payne Divinity and Industrial School, after Alexander Crummell's antagonist in Liberia. (In 1910, the name was shortened to the "Bishop Payne Industrial School.") The life and demise of this chronically underfunded theological seminary, which educated many African American Episcopal clergy over the next seven decades, would mirror almost precisely the history of racial attitudes within the Protestant Episcopal Church.

Much of the debate within the Protestant Episcopal Church focused on the question as to the structural relationship of African Americans and predominantly black congregations to the denomination

as a whole. Significant factions of the denomination, especially southern white laity, resisted any relationship for African Americans to the denomination that did not give full license to white domination and control. In 1875, the predominantly black St. Mark's Church in Charleston, South Carolina, was denied full membership in their diocese, an action that precipitated the withdrawal of six African American Episcopal congregations in that state. An 1883 conference at Sewanee, Tennessee, rejected the proposal for a bishop to be appointed for black congregations, instead backing a proposal that African American congregations be segregated into a special missionary organization supervised by the white bishop of their diocese. Alexander Crummell opposed this plan, urging more black ministers in the cities where large numbers of African Americans lived, more black professors and teachers to mold those ministers, and an additional seminary for African American ministers in the Southwest. While Crummell thought it important that there be a strong black ministry, he did not explicitly take a position on appointing black bishops for work within the United States.

Crummell had some support among white ministers, and the Sewanee plan received a mixed reception at the 1883 General Conference, where it was supported by the House of Bishops but failed at gaining the endorsement of the House of Deputies. Nonetheless, many southern dioceses unilaterally implemented plans to segregate or exclude black parishioners, in effect denying power to black laity through setting up segregated colored convocations. The Virginia and South Carolina dioceses denied African Americans representation at their yearly conventions. Crummell and his supporters organized the Conference of Church Workers among Colored People (CCW) in an attempt to gain more respect for African American Episcopal clergy and laity; they followed Crummell's position on more black leadership for black congregations within the Protestant Episcopal Church, and strongly denounced any measure, like those of the Virginia and South Carolina dioceses, that denied representation to African Americans in church affairs. When the CCW presented a petition covering these points to the 1889 General Convention, the Convention did not endorse their stance, holding that there would be no interference from any national body in the southern dioceses' administration of their own affairs. One vocal critic of this sorry series of church decisions was W. E. B. DuBois, scion of several generations of Episcopalians; he had been baptized in an Episcopal church in Connecticut. In a 1907 letter, DuBois excoriated the Protestant Episcopal Church as lagging behind other churches on human rights questions. He saw Southern Episcopalians as morally bankrupt on racial issues and criticized Northern Episcopalians for their timidity in not standing up against the oppressive attitudes of their southern coreligionists.

Crummell died in 1898, and a diverse, but not always harmonious, cadre of African American Episcopal leaders emerged in the decades following his death. George Freeman Bragg, Jr., a graduate of Bishop Payne Theological Seminary, served as rector of St. James' First African Church in Baltimore for nearly a half century after 1891. He provided steady leadership for the CCW, arguing for a racial missionary district where African American Episcopalians could govern their own affairs without constant supervision from whites. He presented his argument often at General Convention meetings, but his ideas were rejected by that body. Bragg made a fine contribution as an historian, publishing his *History of the Afro-American Group of the Episcopal Church*. Anna Julia Haywood Cooper, a prominent African American educator and Episcopal lay leader, testified both to the mistreatment of African Americans and ministers and to the appeal of the "quiet, chaste dignity and decorous solemnity" of the Episcopal Church to some in the African American community (Cooper 1892, 34).

William Montgomery Brown, the white bishop of Arkansas and a strict segregationist, was one of the first Episcopal leaders to support the appointment of African American bishops, as long as those bishops did not have authority over whites. In 1905, he appointed George Alexander McGuire as archdeacon for colored work in Arkansas, a position that McGuire held for only three years, as he found it impossible to get along with Brown's racism. McGuire eventually became chaplain-general of Marcus Garvey's Universal Negro Improvement Association and left the Episcopal fold to found the African Orthodox Church. Under Brown's successor, James Winchester, the Arkansas diocese resolved to appoint an African American suffragan (assistant) bishop, and Edward Demby, who had served several African American Episcopal parishes throughout the South before accepting appointment as archdeacon for colored work in Arkansas, was consecrated to the position of suffragan bishop on September 29, 1918. Henry Delany received an identical position in North

ALEXANDER CRUMMELL (1819–1898)

Alexander Crummell was born in New York on March 3, 1819, of free African American parents. He studied at the Noyes Academy and Oneida Institute, and, with the support of Peter Williams, Jr., determined to pursue priesthood in the Episcopal Church as his vocation. The General Theological Seminary in New York barred his admission on racial grounds. At the age of 30, Crummell matriculated at the Queens' College in Cambridge. His studies were impeded by illness, poverty, and the death of one of his children, and he attempted to juggle his studies and his anti-slavery lecturing, with mixed success. In 1853, however, he earned his B.A. degree, and he embarked for Liberia where he and his family could live under black authorities. In Liberia, Crummell served as missionary, preacher, college professor, and politician. He was the author of several books, including *The Future of Africa* (1862). In 1871 Crummell returned to the United States. He served Episcopal Churches in Washington, D.C., until his retirement in 1894. In 1882, he helped to found the Conference of Church Workers among the Colored People, and in 1897, one year prior to his death, he founded the American Negro Academy.

Carolina, and he was consecrated two months after Demby. These two men were the first two African Americans consecrated as bishops by the Protestant Episcopal Church for work within the United States (and the third and fourth overall, after Holly and Ferguson). The CCW, however, did not extend full support for these new bishops, criticizing Demby and Delany for allowing themselves to be subject to manipulation by whites; Bragg believed that they had been selected because whites saw each of them as "a good and safe Negro." Bragg undoubtedly was disappointed over having been denied elevation to the office of bishop twice in the previous decade, in 1911 and 1917, despite much support from black clergy. He may indeed have been a more activist bishop than either Demby or Delany, who were relegated to the sidelines and given little to do.

The position of the Episcopal Church changed substantially in the 1940s and 1950s, as the Church swung toward a more racially inclusive and integrationist position. Several black clergy played a role in the Church's transition. Bravid Harris, a graduate of St. Augustine's and Bishop Payne Divinity School, was appointed "Executive Secretary for Negro Work" in 1943; in the same year, the Church's National Council committed the Church to oppose racial segregation in everything pertaining to the church's program. Harris remained in this position only two years. In 1945, he was consecrated Missionary Bishop to Liberia, a post he was to fill successfully for almost two decades. He was succeeded as Executive Secretary for Negro Work by Tollie Caution Sr., who was to fill a variety of leadership positions regarding the Church's work in racial justice matters until 1967. Caution was relatively conservative in his approach to racial politics, but he also found himself in a position where liberal whites in the Episcopal hierarchy often set the agenda on racial matters without consulting him. Twice his position with the denomination was abruptly altered, in 1957 with an early "retirement" and later rehiring to another position, and again in 1967 upon his dismissal with the concurrence of the presiding bishop because he ran afoul of white liberals' priorities in racial justice matters. Even those African American Episcopal clergy who disagreed with Caution's politics regarded the insensitivity that whites in the denomination had shown toward him a cause for indignation and protest.

A decision was made to close a dilapidated Bishop Payne Divinity School by its trustees in 1949. Embarrassment at its inferior condition and the refusal to sink further funds into a two-tiered system of theological education signified an early, though still tentative, denominational change of heart on segregation. In Virginia and elsewhere in the South, the bishops edged toward integrating the previously all-white Episcopal seminaries; the most profound struggle took place at the University of the South in Sewanee, where a mass resignation of theology faculty in 1951 and a public scolding by James Pike, who declined a honorary degree from Sewanee in 1953, were necessary before the Sewanee trustees would agree to admit African Americans to their School of Theology. (Segregation at the undergraduate level at Sewanee, however, would not be abandoned until 1961.) Several black Episcopalians played an important role in persuading the U.S. Supreme Court to issue its 1954 *Brown v. Board of Education* decision mandating desegregation. Lead counsel Thurgood Marshall, himself later appointed to the U.S. Supreme Court by President Lyndon Johnson in 1967, was one of the black Episcopalians whose efforts were notable in this regard. But Marshall did not have great influence with the denomination's leadership, which

continued to be quite ambivalent in regard to the southern freedom movement.

In 1951, Alger Adams, an African American priest from Yonkers, New York, criticized the Episcopal Church as "Church Jim Crow." Those last few African American congregations that had been excluded from white Southern dioceses in the aftermath of the Civil War and Reconstruction were finally restored to the membership they should have had all along. Thus, in 1954, St. Mark's Church in Charleston and other African American Episcopal congregations in Charleston were finally admitted into fellowship with the state Episcopal convention. But black priests in South Carolina in the 1950s were expected not to speak out on civil rights issues. Henry Parker, an African American deacon at St. Paul's Church in Orangeburg, South Carolina, was accused of shirking his duties and was dismissed in 1956 by his white bishop; many in the denomination were convinced that the real reason for Parker's dismissal was his membership in the NAACP. Moreover, integration was not a panacea if it meant simply that black Episcopal congregations were to be absorbed by white ones; the Episcopal Church lost 10,000 members between 1948 and 1958, a loss attributed to simply transferring members of closed black churches to neighboring white congregations, without empowerment of the black membership.

Activist Episcopal laity and clergy, however, placed continuing and relentless pressure on their denomination. A key role was played by the interracial Episcopal Society for Cultural and Racial Unity (ESCRU) founded in 1959 and active subsequently in demonstrations and nonviolent direct action against segregation and racial injustice, whether perpetuated within or outside of the Episcopalian fold.

Meanwhile, in 1962, one northern diocese, Massachusetts, decided to elevate an African American priest, John Burgess, to the office of suffragan bishop. Two other dioceses, Los Angeles and Long Island, followed suit in appointing assistant or interim African American bishops in the 1960s. Then in 1970, Burgess became the diocesan bishop in Massachusetts, and the first African American to preside over a predominantly white diocese. As of 2006, 38 black bishops (at some time during its history) have been consecrated by the Episcopal Church for service in the United States, Liberia, or countries in the Caribbean or Central America. (To place this in perspective, more than 1,000 bishops have been consecrated by the Episcopal Church since its formal organization in 1784.)

Some Episcopalians played a prominent role in the civil rights and black power movements of the 1960s. In the St. Augustine, Florida, civil rights campaign in 1964, it was widely noticed when three Episcopalian women— Esther Burgess, the African American wife of John Burgess, as well as the white wives of former bishops in Central New York state and Los Angeles—were refused service when they tried to order a meal at a segregated restaurant. Continuing civil rights activism eventually landed these three women briefly behind bars in the St. Augustine jail.

Six African American Episcopal clergy were among the 49 signers of the inaugural "black power" statement by the National Conference of Negro Churchmen in July 1966. This statement provided support for the controversial positions of Stokely Carmichael, then a leader of the Student Nonviolent Coordinating Committee, and criticized the easy assumptions that integration could be achieved merely by

absorbing African Americans into white institutions. "We understand the growing demand of Negro and white youth for a more honest kind of integration; one which increases rather than decreases the capacity of the disinherited to participate with power in all of the structures of our common life" (Sernett 1999, 558). Perhaps the most notable of the Episcopalian signers of this declaration was Nathan Wright (1923–2005), a priest and the director of urban work in the Newark, New Jersey, diocese. His book *Black Power and Urban Unrest: The Creative Possibilities*, published in 1967, was one of eighteen that he published. His emphasis on the need for black empowerment, rather than integration with whites, was one of his most significant and consistent themes. Also responding in a favorable way to the economic empowerment themes of Carmichael was the Union of Black Clergy and Laity, better known by its subsequent name, the Union of Black Episcopalians. This black caucus of Episcopalians, founded in 1968, superseded the CCW that had owed its existence to the ministries of Crummell and Bragg. One indication that African American religious music and culture was breaking through to the wider denomination could be seen in the Episcopal Church's publication of an excellent hymnbook of African American sacred music, *Lift Every Voice and Sing*, in 1981.

At the turn of the twenty-first century, the Episcopal Church turned more firmly and decisively to antiracist policies. A 1994 letter from Episcopal bishops declaring racism to be "totally inconsistent with the Gospel" has been followed by other actions, including mandatory antiracism training for Episcopal leaders beginning in 2000 and an initiative taken in 2006 by some Episcopal dioceses to

---

BARBARA C. HARRIS (1930–)

Barbara Harris was born in Philadelphia on June 12, 1930. She was active in the civil rights struggle in the 1960s, especially in the voters' rights part of the campaign. Her human rights activism naturally expanded to include activism in women's rights. She pressed successfully for women's admission to an organization that came to be known as the Union of Black Episcopalians. She experienced a strong calling to become a priest. Her theological study in the late 1970s consisted mostly of correspondence courses from Villanova University and the Metropolitan Community Center in Philadelphia. She was ordained as a deacon in 1979, and as a priest the following year. Her ministry was diverse in the forms that it took. Harris was elected suffragan bishop of the Massachusetts Diocese in 1988, the first female priest anywhere in the worldwide Anglican Communion to be elevated to the office of bishop. In the fifteen years prior to her retirement from the Massachusetts diocese in 2003, she continued to be a very vocal campaigner for gender equity and other human rights' issues. From 2003 to 2007, she was an assisting bishop in the Episcopal Diocese of Washington, D.C.

---

begin to reexamine their own past with an eye to documenting their own complicity with slavery and discrimination. African American Episcopal clergy and laity have often taken the lead in other human rights campaigns as well. They have generally supported women's rights, including the struggle for women's ordination within the Episcopal Church. In 1977, Pauli Murray became the first African American woman ordained to the Episcopal priesthood. She was a noted author and lawyer whose research had been instrumental in the finding for school integration in *Brown v. Board of Education*. In 1989, Barbara Clementine Harris, an African American Episcopal activist on women's ordination and other issues, was consecrated as the suffragan bishop of the diocese of Massachusetts, thus becoming the first female bishop consecrated throughout the worldwide Anglican communion. Harris retired in 2003. More varied has been the African American response to the consecration of V. Gene Robinson, an openly gay man, as Episcopal bishop

of New Hampshire in 2003. In the Diocese of Long Island, for example, the presiding bishop, Orris G. Walker Jr., an African American, supported Robinson's elevation to the post, but many African American priests and parishioners in his diocese were opposed to Robinson becoming a bishop.

Since 1973, the first African American priest, Absalom Jones, has been celebrated as a saint in the Episcopal Church; his life is commemorated on February 13 of each year. The 2006 General Convention took initial steps toward adding a commemoration of Thurgood Marshall to the Episcopal Church calendar. His life would be celebrated on May 17, the date in 1954 that the Supreme Court handed down its decision on *Brown v. Board of Education*.

Beliefs and Practices

In 1887, Alexander Crummell argued that the Episcopal Church could not model its ministry to African Americans after "the old plantation ministry," which too often had featured uneducated ministry with little attention to elevating the culture of African Americans. Crummell's prescriptions consequently focused on ensuring an excellent education for African American ministers; he was fully cognizant of the "tendency," evidenced among all African Americans at that time, to emphasize "racial autonomy and racial self-training." With the slow progress of racial integration within the Episcopal Church during the last half of the twentieth century, the sense of a special mission for black ministers and congregations within the Episcopal Church has been maintained, while there is also a strong recognition that the mission of black congregations is meant to benefit the whole church. The Office of Black Ministries is a place within the denomination where these varying emphases can be nurtured.

As one might expect, a contribution that black Episcopalians (from Williams, Crummell, and Bragg onwards) have made is to emphasize the social dimension of the gospel. A recent manifestation of this is the global movement of Afro-Anglicanism, which has taken on racism as a worldwide problem. In a 1985 statement, Afro-Anglicans affirmed that they are "an integral part of the one, holy, catholic and apostolic church" who maintained an "Anglican emphasis on scripture, tradition, reason, liturgy, ministry, and social witness" (Conference 1987, 85). However, they protested against the "cultural captivity" that continued to be evident in the Anglican tradition (Conference 1987, 90). A variety of affirmative measures were proposed to free the church from "the considerations of color, class, and sex [which] still mar the freedom of Christian fellowship," ranging from championing black religious icons to opposing the "increasing expenditure on armaments to the detriment of basic social and economic needs" to establishing an "effective dialogue with persons of other faiths, especially with Islam, Judaism, and the traditional religions of Africa, Asia, and the new world" (Conference 1987, 86, 88, 89).

Stephen W. Angell

SELECTED BIBLIOGRAPHY

Archives of the Episcopal Church USA. *The Church Awakens: African-Americans and the Struggle for Justice* (Austin, TX: Domestic and Foreign Missionary Society of the Protestant Episcopal Church, 2008). Online exhibit available at http://www.episcopalarchives.org/Afro-Anglican_history/exhibit/index.php (accessed February 19, 2008).

Beary, Michael J. *Black Bishop: Edward T. Demby and the Struggle for Racial Equality in the Episcopal Church* (Urbana: University of Illinois Press, 2001).

Bragg, George F., Jr. *The History of the Afro-American Group in the Episcopal Church* (Baltimore: Church Advocate Press, 1922).

Conference on Afro-Anglicanism. "The Codrington Consensus." *Journal of Religious Thought* 44, no. 1 (Summer-Fall 1987): 84–93.

Cooper, Anna Julia. *A Voice from the South* (Xenia, OH: The Aldine Printing House, 1892), 34.

Crummell, Alexander. *Africa and America: Addresses and Discourses* (Springfield, MA: Willey and Company, 1891), 446.

DuBois, W. E. B. *The Souls of Black Folk: Essays and Sketches* (Chicago: A. C. McClurg and Co., 1903).

Encyclopedia of African-American Culture and History, 2nd ed., s.v. "Episcopalians," by Lillie Johnson Edwards (Farmington Hills, MI: Gale, 2005).

Encyclopedia of African American Religions, s.v. "Episcopal Church," by Harold Dean Trulear (Farmington Hills, MI: Gale, 2005).

Hein, David, and Gardiner H. Shattuck, Jr. *The Episcopalians* (Westport, CT: Praeger, 2004).

Hewitt, John H. *Protest and Progress: New York's First Black Episcopal Church Fights Racism* (New York: Garland Publishing, 2000).

Jacobs, Harriet A. *Incidents in the Life of a Slave Girl: Written by Herself*, ed. Jean Fagan Yellin (Cambridge, MA: Harvard University Press, 1987).

Montgomery, William E. *Under Their Own Vine and Fig Tree: The African-American Church in the South, 1865–1900* (Baton Rouge: Louisiana State University Press, 1993).

Oldfield, J. R. *Civilization and Black Progress: Selected Writings of Alexander Crummell on the South* (Charlottesville: Published for the Southern Texts Society by the University Press of Virginia, 1995).

Sernett, Milton. *African American Religious History: A Documentary Witness* (Durham, NC: Duke University Press, 1999).

Shattuck, Gardiner H., Jr. *Episcopalians and Race: Civil War to Civil Rights* (Lexington: University Press of Kentucky, 2000).

Spencer, Jon Michael. *Black Hymnody: A Hymnological History of the African-American Church* (Knoxville: University of Tennessee Press, 1992).

AFRICAN AMERICANS IN THE PRESBYTERIAN CHURCH

Historical Development

Similar to other black Christian denominations, the formation of blacks in the Presbyterian denomination began with slavery and early efforts to convert southern and free northern slaves to

---

JOHN "JACK" GLOUCESTER (? –1822)

A former slave, John Gloucester founded the First African Presbyterian Church in June 1807 along with twenty-two other members. Having been the slave of Gideon Blackburn who was a white Presbyterian missionary, he was taught theology and was said to be quite gifted as a preacher and educator. Demonstrating a concern and passion for missions, he was approved by the General Assembly to conduct missionary work among his own people. He was formally received by the Philadelphia Presbytery in 1811 in which at this time his church had grew to over one hundred members. Not only was Gloucester a key leader in his own community, he also placed high value on education, and founded a school for African American youth. Later on, he managed to raise money to purchase the freedom of his wife and four children. Among other notable accomplishments of this Presbyterian pioneer, in 1847 Gloucester traveled to England and managed to raise over four-thousand dollars for the ministry of the Lombard Street Church. There, he became the first Presbyterian minister to be presented with a Black clerical gown, black or white. Gloucester died of tuberculosis in 1822.

Presbyterianism. While the first African American Presbyterian Church was formed in 1807 (by ex-slave John "Jack" Gloucester), other churches were simultaneously being formed in areas such as New York, New Jersey, Maryland, and Washington, D.C. Unlike in the North, southern Presbyterian efforts were often less successful than other denominations such as the Baptists and Methodists, given their ambivalent support of and often rocky relationship with the issue of slavery. Aside from churches, the Presbyterian Church has also been highly successful in establishing schools for blacks in southern regions, such as Lincoln University and Stillman College.

Analogous to the complex and hybrid nature of black Christianity in general, the black presence in the Presbyterian denomination tells a similar saga of struggle, continued existence, and, above all, hope. Historically, Presbyterianism in general was resettled from Great Britain to larger North America, but initially was not a denomination that was at the outset appealing to black people in both the eighteenth and nineteenth centuries, particularly due to the issue of slavery in general. Presbyterianism was introduced to the "New World" around 1630, but it would not be until the period leading up to the Revolutionary War of 1776, that one feels a pulse of the developing and sprouting relationship and encounter between blacks, mainly slaves, and white Presbyterians. It has been suggested in pamphlets such as *The Early History of the Presbyterian Church in the USA among Negroes*, written by an early black Presbyterian educator, that most blacks were introduced to Presbyterianism within the white homes of

employers. Within the context of domestic employment, many slaves were taught by their employers how to read certain passages of both the Bible and Catechisms. In 1747, organized efforts led by Presbyterian minister Rev. Samuel Davies were among the first aggressive Presbyterian conversion efforts of slaves. Many scholars believe that Rev. Davies baptized over 150 slaves. Although the Presbyterian denomination displayed and projected an ambivalent and inconsistent posture and practice regarding the issue of slavery, the attractive educational and social benefits of Presbyterianism continued to draw many blacks into the white denominational fold.

Unlike the African Methodist Episcopal Church (AMEC), no separate African American Presbyterian denominations were specifically founded in the North. There was one specific Presbyterian denomination founded in the South during the historical split of Cumberland Presbyterian Church in 1869, which culminated in the still active Second Cumberland Presbyterian Church in 1874, originally referred to as the Colored Cumberland Presbyterian Church. In the South, black families in both the Carolinas and Georgia have strong Presbyterian ties dating back to roughly six generations. In 1807, the country's first African American Presbyterian congregation was founded by a slave named "Jack," renamed by his Presbyterian missionary owner to "John Gloucester," in Philadelphia, Pennsylvania.

Having been taught theology by his owner, Gloucester was said to have a strong and fervent gift for preaching. The First African Presbyterian Church of Philadelphia was strongly supported by white Presbyterians, who were especially proud of their day school and educational ministry. During this time, Philadelphia had a small population of a little more than 50,000 overall, which included roughly 5,000 free blacks and 30 slaves. Overall, blacks were disadvantaged and impoverished, but managed to squeeze into a southeastern section of downtown Philadelphia. This historical moment was overshadowed by racial awakening and solidarity among many blacks in general in terms of the formation of social clubs, organizations, and fraternities that emphasized racial pride and self-help. During an 1807 General Assembly, Gloucester met with the white pastor of Philadelphia's Third Presbyterian Church (now called Old Pine Street) named Archibald Alexander, who thought it was time that the Reformed family of Presbyterianism made room for a church that met the needs and allowed space for the cultural and social particularity of Africans. Alexander was impressed with Gloucester's gifts and was able to persuade his owner Gideon Blackburn to transport Gloucester to Philadelphia. The following spring, Gloucester would find himself preaching in a vacant lot in South Philadelphia. Receiving their charter from Pennsylvania Supreme Court on December 12, 1809 (but not accepted as a mission congregation by Philadelphia Presbytery until October 1811), this black Presbyterian congregation began with as few as 50 members. Gloucester emphasized social welfare and education in his denomination, and when he passed away in 1822, his congregation was numbered at about 300 members. Because of financial and familial hardships of Gloucester in specific and the congregation in general, the church was outstripped by the Second African

John Gloucester founded the first African American Presbyterian Church in Philadelphia in 1807. (Schomburg Center for Research in Black Culture)

Presbyterian Church, a congregation that was composed of a faction of parishioners who split under the guidance of Gloucester's son, Jeremiah. With the erection of First African Presbyterian Church along with other churches in the North before the Civil War, high value was often placed on evangelism, education, and social reform, a distinct black Presbyterianism was blossoming.

During the antebellum period, key black Presbyterian pioneers used their intellectual and educational resources to combat racism not only in the larger society, but also within the churches themselves. Along with giants such as Gloucester, folk such as Samuel E. Cornish, editor of the first black newspaper, *Freedom's Journal*, who also founded First Colored Presbyterian

Church in New York City, zealously served the economically impoverished areas of lower Manhattan. The seeds of congregational independence were occurring in the North and in 1897 southern Presbyterians likewise encouraged black independence with the creation of the Afro-American Presbyterian Synod, attracting the participation and enthusiasm of many black members. Unfortunately, this enthusiasm soon waned given the overall racist and suspicious disposition of the white denomination. Such feelings often caused many black members to yearn for ecclesiastical separation, but many chose to remain in mostly white dominated congregations. Given the complicity of many white Presbyterian denominations toward aggressive antislavery and civil rights policies and social action, black Presbyterians were intentional about creating and organizing a caucus prior to the Civil War. Undergoing a few transitions, this caucus currently exists under the name of the National Black Presbyterian Caucus (NBPC), which currently continues to carry on the spirit and tradition of black Presbyterianism.

Against the backdrop of the political climate of the 1960s coupled with a rough and tumultuous uphill struggle with an all-white denomination for over 100 years, black Presbyterianism began to flourish. Connecting with the black consciousness of the 1960s and much influenced by the message of Dr. Martin Luther King Jr., folks such as Elder G. Hawkins, Robert P. Johnson, and other clergy-activists created the Commission on Religion and Race in 1963. Almost consistently since the Civil War, caucuses have played a formative and meaningful role among black Presbyterians. Five years later,

the Black Presbyterians United (BPU) was formed to encourage younger and more radical leaders to the forefront of the struggle with an emphasis on self-development and a commitment to racial solidarity.

There are many organizational resources in the Presbyterian Church (PCUSA) that are focused on servicing the needs and concerns of blacks in the Presbyterian Church. For example, one of the more pressing concerns of black Presbyterian congregations has been a decline in membership. This was one of the foremost concerns for the Office of Black Congregational Enhancement (BCE) developed in 1988, which drew heavily upon the scholarly work of Gayraud Wilmore (1998 edition of *Black and Presbyterian: The Heritage and the Hope*). Wilmore's work provided a seminal foundation for the BCE, and drawing from Wilmore's work, the BCE identified five historic resources important for the ministry of black Presbyterians specifically and the black community in general: a focus on freedom with an emphasis on liberation, importance of origins, more specifically keeping in mind the image of Africa as the land of those origins, keeping justice at the center of the God concept, incorporating cultural creativity in religious practice, and lastly, recognizing the blending of sacred/secular unity of everyday life. Moreover, Wilmore's work included important challenges that were incorporated into the mission and focus of the BCE, including intentional models for black leadership that were sensitive to both black consciousness and a sustained faithfulness to traditional Presbyterian polity. The incorporation of Wilmore's work enabled wide reaching additions in the area of congregational life, Christian education, outreach ministries, and evangelism, among other areas. Black Presbyterian organizations have worked earnestly to provide ongoing support to black Presbyterians in general, working hard to empower black Presbyterian congregations and continually encouraging and developing strategies and resources for congregations centered on and within black heritage. Between the years of 1991 and 1994 consultations were held within many presbyteries in which both lay leaders and black congregations had the opportunity, among other things, to express their concerns and commitments about being black and Presbyterian. Some of the concerns noted and shared included issues such as conflicts regarding the mission of particular congregations, issues regarding how to deal with the legalism of Presbyterian polity in general, concerns regarding increased attention toward the black middle class with less attention toward the black poor, lack of sustained attention toward black history, heritage, and identity, and concerns regarding various worship styles that were not meeting the needs of black members, among a host of other concerns, which included economic, criminal justice, education, and sociopolitical concerns central to the black community. In fact, in 1994 a new paper was released by the 1994 committee entitled "Is This New Wine?" which challenged black Presbyteries to strengthen their commitment regarding black identity in general and increased attention to the black poor in particular. Even more pressing, the paper made the stated challenge that, "If Black Presbyterian leaders thought that Presbyterian polity prevented them from making this commitment they should withdraw from the PCUSA and form their own denomination." The

African American advisory committee continues to play an important role in developing church growth strategies as well as serving as an important source for the NBPC. Similarly, the BCE likewise continues to develop both resources and strategies to educated Presbyterian leaders regarding the life, history, and sources specific to black life and heritage.

According to an ethnographic survey conducted by Scott C. Williamson of Louisville Presbyterian Theological Seminary, a demographic profile of blacks in the Presbyterian denomination suggested that blacks comprise roughly 2.7 percent of the PCUSA, consisting of more than 70 percent females with a median age of 57. This median age for black females in the PCUSA is slightly two years older than the median age of the whole denomination in general. Findings also suggest that black members hold long and consistent membership in the denomination, with most black members maintaining membership for 19 years, five years longer than the average length of membership for all PCUSA members. A third of black PCUSA members (36 percent) have been members of their congregation for more than 25 years. These numbers suggest that black membership is strong, durable, stable, and long-standing, with 41 percent of black members attending church nearly every week. Black members also hold varieties of positions in the PCUSA, but only a few as organist and choir director. Although blacks comprise roughly 39 percent of PCUSA church choirs, they make up only about 4 percent of employment positions of choir director or organist.

Given the ambivalent and rocky relationship between blacks and the mostly all-white denomination, the question of religious roots is an interesting one.

Findings report more than a few noteworthy insights into the familial and religious roots of blacks in the Presbyterian denomination. It is likely that most black PCUSA members come from religious households that attended church worship services quite frequently, although these familial religious roots have certainly undergone some form of grafting. About 62 percent of black members were not raised Presbyterian, with 36 percent claiming religious ties to the Baptist denomination and with 26 percent belonging to other religious groups. Approximately one-quarter (24 percent) of those raised Presbyterian by familial tradition still belong to their childhood congregations. These findings suggest that blacks in the Presbyterian denomination are not only committed members, but have likely contributed much to the denomination as a whole. Black members tend to be female, urban, and highly educated, with almost half hailing from the South, more specifically the Carolinas, with almost half being married. Occupationally, over half are employed with the remainder in retirement status and most black members tend to be middle to upper-middle class, contributing much of their financial capital to their churches along with other organizations and social causes. Most are overwhelmingly Democrats in a largely Republican denomination, in comparison to the only 25 percent white members self-identifying as Democrats. Most black members identify themselves as theologically moderate, with the remainder classifying their theological posture as directly to either the "right" or "left." Overall, black members in the PCUSA demonstrate a zeal for and participation in social and economic justice, along with an emphasis on core Christian values.

Beliefs and Practices

Historically, the PCUSA holds a strong commitment to what is referred to as Reformed Faith and is characterized as being very much confessional with strong emphasis on creeds and confessions such as the Nicene (325 C.E.) and Apostle's creeds along with others such as the Westminster Confession (1646) and the Heidelberg Catechism (1646). Most black clergy and ordained persons in the PCUSA accept these confessions and statements, making use of and emphasizing their core tenets in sermons, worship, and preaching. The theological stance of most black Presbyterians has been characterized as theologically moderate to liberal, especially regarding tenets such as the Virgin Birth and the Second Coming, although less orthodox in their position compared to other groups of color (Korean and/or Hispanics) in the PCUSA, they do express a more orthodox posture in general compared to overall membership. This theological commitment to core orthodox tenets are reflected in findings that suggest nine out of ten black Presbyterians believe that Jesus was born of a Virgin along with eight out of ten who believe in core themes such as the Second Coming of Jesus Christ, life after death, as well as the existence of Satan. Interestingly enough, although roughly 83 percent reported believing in heaven, only 65 percent believe in hell. Similar to many white members, about 25 percent of blacks expressed moderate uncertainty regarding the uniqueness of God's revelation in Jesus Christ when asked about whether or not only followers of Jesus can be saved, with over 50 percent of black respondents reporting that belief in Jesus was only one of many ways to find salvation. Black Presbyterians also express an almost equal balance between church and individual authority, supporting individual rights to arrive at religious beliefs independent of the governing authority of the church. While individual rights are emphasized, many do not believe that the final authority regarding issues of morality rest solely on individual authority; rather many opt to seek religious truth in acceptance (not refusal) of church doctrine. Compared to the majority of white PCUSA members, black Presbyterians are less likely to be theologically conservative, displaying an open disposition toward other religions. That is to say, most black Presbyterians do not display an exclusivist posture toward the subject of salvation, but almost 75 percent believe in the centrality of the Bible as the Word of God, making them more orthodox overall compared to their white counterparts, in their view of the Bible. According to the black Congregational Enhancement of the PCUSA, most black Presbyterians believe in the universal unconditional love of God, which empowers black Presbyterians to be prophetic witnesses in the world. Although there may be an expressed uncertainty regarding central theological tenets such as God's revelation in Jesus, many black Presbyterians are more than certain of their commitment and call to social justice, especially in the areas of taking care of the poor and the elderly, as well as fighting for and on behalf of social and economic justice. Many blacks in the Presbyterian denomination also hold a strong commitment to evangelism and social outreach.

Black Presbyterians also seek to reflect on the black experience in light of their developing theological commitments. In 2003, Gayraud S. Wilmore provided the NBPC with a concept, which later developed into a book project entitled *Pragmatic Spirituality: The Christian Faith Through an Africentric Lens*, that greatly impacted the incorporation of black cultural resources into theological beliefs and tenets. Drawing from Wilmore's definition of "pragmatic spirituality," which focused on the working of the Holy Spirit to provide both inward and outward transformations, four "corresponding negations" for the larger historic Presbyterian commitments were provided: no praise without performance, no peace without justice, no reconciliation without liberation, and no participation without power.

By way of current expressions and historical connection, many black Presbyterian congregations are informed by and incorporate an Afrocentric perspective into both worship and congregational life. This not only includes worship expressions but more than that it likewise is characterized by a reflection on the Christian Gospel from the context and needs of the black experience in general. Similar to other black denominations in general, Black Presbyterian congregations integrate Afrocentric rituals and traditions into their religious lives. Most black Presbyterian Churches claim to proclaim the Gospel from Afrocentric Christian spirituality, with an emphasis on liberating people in order to become disciples of Jesus. In fact, almost three-quarters of black Presbyterians belong to black churches in particular. As such, black Presbyterian churches blend cultural resources in the areas such as congregational life whereby curriculum makes use of the cultural resources and takes the specificity of black religious reality into account. Other incorporations include appropriating traditional hymnals, developing and broadening black liturgies to include elements from various countries, and even displaying images such as the Black Christ and the Black Madonna. In this sense, many black Presbyterian congregations encourage the incorporation of Africanized symbols by making them particular to their Christian orientations. For example, such symbols may include West African Adinkra symbols such as *Gye Nyame* (the supremacy of God), *Puntunfunefu Deneyemfunefu* (unity in diversity), or *Nyame Birlbi Wo Soro* ("God is in the heavens: A Symbol of Hope). Other resourceful ways in which denominations have incorporated cultural particularities can be seen in the sourcing of a wide range of sacred texts such as writings and passages from Frederick Douglass or the use of poetry from Alice Walker.

Worship within many black Presbyterian congregations is reflective of an influence from not only Pentecostalism but also the spirituality and use of Gospel songs, fervent preaching, and even liturgical and praise dance. It is likewise characterized by the utilization of black music, and elements such as dancing, banners, processionals, and even the incorporation of liturgical elements outside of the Presbyterian tradition itself. As many black Presbyterian churches seek to negotiate the balance between their commitments to Reformed theology and their own cultural particularities, such tensions are notably seen within the areas of music and praise. As Gospel songs along with contemporary praise melodies from within and outside of popular culture grow in popularity, many black Presbyterian churches are increasingly questioning the relevance and adequacy of more traditional hymns. While historically it has been argued that the preaching style of

the black Presbyterian minister reflected a stronger emphasis on sound doctrine, accurate hermeneutics, and Reformed distinctness, this is also beginning to change with the demands and expectations of Afrocentricism, which emphasizes a more lively and cultural sensitive form of worship. Many black Presbyterians seek to hold the Reformed tradition with high regard while also acknowledging and asserting the important role of black cultural life.

The NBPC affirms their commitment to a racially diverse ministry while also acknowledging the authenticity of the black witness and advocating for racial justice, with an emphasis on maximizing black participation in the life of the church in conjunction with the development of strategies that focus on celebrating black religious heritage and cultural plurality. Other caucuses such as the BCE offer many resources to assist the continued incorporation of black life into elements of faith, practice, and congregational life by providing numerous print, periodical, and online resources to offer members of the PCUSA access to strengthening the mission and life of black Presbyterian churches. Currently, they are focused on increasing ethnic membership by 20 percent, taking seriously the critical necessity of evangelism and church growth strategies.

Black Presbyterianism has a rich past and present history of educational, political, and religious activism and advancement. Earlier notable people, such as Lucy Craft Laney, a slave and the daughter of a Presbyterian minister responsible for founding a pioneering black school, along with others such as Daniel Jackson Sanders, a former slave who eventually became the first black president of Biddle University, now referred to as John C. Smith University, along with everyday people such as Albert Byron McCoy who worked tirelessly for many years as a director of Sunday school missions in North Carolina, give glimpses into the reality that black Presbyterianism is full of a rich participative dimension by blacks. Noted earlier, many black Presbyterians creatively formulated their own strategies of social protest by utilizing and appropriating the intellectual resources and skills offered to them by Presbyterianism. Such tactics can be seen within the legacy of ministers such as Samuel Cornish and Theodore S. Wright, who, along with other notable figures such as Henry Highland Garnet, J. W. C. Pennington, and Francis Grimke, labored diligently in the Presbyterian church and often combined the resources of the skilled and trained mind with their racial and political passions to assist in creating a more racially just society for all humans. Additional accomplishments of these pioneers include Cornish becoming the first black editor and founder of the First Colored Presbyterian Church of New York City, along with Wright becoming the first black graduate from a theological seminary (Princeton Seminary) in 1828, eventually taking over Cornish's congregation, which eventually became the second largest black church in New York City. Figures such as Pennington and Garnet encouraged members to take progressive and radical stances toward racial justice, and it was Wright's mentee Garnet whose 1843 address to slaves encouraged many of them to embark on armed struggle. When National Missions created a specialized board called the Division of Work with Colored Persons headed by Rev. McCoy in 1938, many blacks began to feel a sense of relief and self-determination within the white denomination. McCoy was asked to serve as secretary of this new unit, which was created to help serve its black constituency. With the social unrest of the Supreme Court's 1954 "separate but equal" decision, blacks in the Presbyterian church began to caucus again, this time creating a group called Concerned Presbyterians, in which the efforts of

SAMUEL ELI CORNISH (1795–1858)

As a black abolitionist, journalist, and Presbyterian minister, Cornish was the first editor of the black newspaper, *Freedman's Journal* (along with John Russworm) and later editor of *Colored American* in 1827. After moving to New York City in 1821 and under the mentorship of John Gloucester, Cornish was able to organize a group of black Presbyterians establishing what was officially established as the New Dempster Street Presbyterian Church while also having the privilege of founding the First Colored Presbyterian Church of New York City, officially becoming ordained in 1822. Cornish was said to be more of an educator and journalist than a minister. In 1828 he became an agent for the New York African Free Schools, often visiting parents to encourage attendance. Before dying in 1858, Cornish organized Emmanuel Church in New York City for a brief time, which he led until 1847. Cornish remains an important figure in the early abolition movement, although his later reputation became overshadowed by young more radical colleagues. Most of Cornish's legacy rests on his journalist achievements and skills.

KATIE GENEVA CANNON (1950–)

Born in 1950, Katie Geneva Cannon became the first black woman to be ordained as a Presbyterian minister. Growing up in rural North Carolina, issues of race and gender have always been central issues of exploration for Cannon. Cannon enrolled in Barbara-Scotia College, a school initially founded in 1867 for freed women slaves. Rising to the top of her class, education became central in Cannon's life. After a trip to Africa in 1971, Cannon studied at the seminary of Interdenominational Theological Canter (ITC) in Atlanta, Georgia, where she realized that ministry was much more than just a vessel for political and social action. Cannon received a PhD from Union Theological Seminary in New York in 1983. She is currently the Annie Scales Rogers Professor of Christian Ethics at Union Theological Seminary and the Presbyterian School of Christian Education (PSCE), where her work is dedicated to exploring the areas of Christian ethics, womanist theology, and women in religion and society. She lectures widely on various topics related to theology and ethics, and is the author of numerous articles and seven books, which include her notable works, *Katie's Canon: Womanism and the Soul of the Black Community* and *Black Womanist Ethics.*

clergy involved in activism, such as Hawkins, Johnson, and Bryant George, culminated in the creation of the Commission on Religion and Race in 1963.

Other major leaders include important people on local levels such as Sarah Mapps Douglass, who was the daughter of one of the founders of First African Presbyterian Church. Mapps Douglass was responsible for administering the primary department of Institute for Colored Youth, which was a Quaker-sponsored school in Philadelphia. Later on, she became the vice-chairperson for the Women's Pennsylvania Branch of the American Freedman's Aid Commission. Having taught in the Institute for Colored Youths for seven years, Mary Jane Patterson graduated from Oberlin College in 1862, giving her the distinction of being the first black woman to receive the bachelor's degree. Figures such as Hawkins, who became the first black moderator of the Presbyterian Assembly in 1964, along with others such as Katie G. Cannon, who became the first black woman to be ordained a Presbyterian minister in 1974 and Thelma Blair who became the first black woman to be elected moderator of a Presbyterian General Assembly, contributed much to the rich history of black Presbyterianism.

Monica Miller

SELECTED BIBLIOGRAPHY

Dubois, W. E. B. *The Souls of Black Folk: Essays and Sketches* (New York: The Modern Library, 1963).

Hageman, Howard. *Pulpit and Table: Some Chapters in the History of Worship in the Reformed Churches* (Richmond: John Knox Press, 1962).

Haney, Marsha Snulligan. *Evangelism Among African American Presbyterians: Making Plain the Sacred Journey* (Lanham: University Press of America, 2007).

Newberry, Edward B. "Reformed Theology and African American Presbyterian Worship." *The Bulletin of the Institute For Reformed Theology* 4, no. 1 (Winter 2004).

Newbold, Robert E. *Worship Old and New: A Biblical, Historical, and Practical Introduction* (Grand Rapids, MI: Zondervan Publishing House, 1994).

Paris, Peter. *The Spirituality of African Peoples* (Minneapolis: Fortress Press, 1995).

Periscope 4. "African American Presbyterians Living into the 21st Century." Available at http://www.pcusa.org/blackcongregations/pdf/periscope4.pdf.

Web site for the Black Congregational Enhancement of the PCUSA, which includes links to online resources: http://www.pcusa.org/blackcongregations/resources.htm.

White, William P. *The Presbyterian Church in Philadelphia. A Camera and Pen Sketch of Each Presbyterian Church and Institution in the City* (Philadelphia: Allen, Lane & Scott, 1895).

White, William P., et al. *Still Philadelphia: A Photographic History, 1890–1940* (Philadelphia: Temple University Press, 1983).

Williamson, Scott C. "African American Members of the Presbyterian Church (U.S.A.): Survey Results." Louisville Presbyterian Theological Seminary, May 1999.

Wilmore, Gayraud S. *Black & Presbyterian: The Heritage and the Hope* (Philadelphia: Geneva Press, 1983).

Wilmore, Gayraud S. "Identity & Integration: Black Presbyterians and Their Allies in the Twentieth Century." *The Diversity of Discipleship: Presbyterians and Twentieth Century Christian Witness*, ed. Milton J. Coalter, John M. Mulder, and Louis B. Weeks (Louisville, KY: Westminster John Knox Press, 1991).

AFRICAN AMERICANS IN THE ROMAN CATHOLIC CHURCH

Historical Development

African American Catholics claim the same faith and understand themselves as an important part of the Roman Catholic presence in the United States. The style of expression may differ in some cases, but there are no significant differences in liturgy between White and African American Roman Catholics. Differences are more a matter of perspective—viewing the faith from the vantage point of African American culture—than the theological or ritual content of the Church's practices. In short, the story of African American involvement in Roman Catholicism is more a story of the struggle for inclusion in the full life of the Church, rather than a story of diverse practices. In other words, as Professor Jamie Phelps remarks, it is the story of the struggle to "make it possible to be Black, Catholic, and American without being cursed and spit upon, devalued and marginalized" (Phelps 1997, 18–19).

In the context of what becomes the United States, the first Catholic of African descent was Estebam, a slave who in 1536 was brought to the territory comprising present day Florida, Texas, and Arkansas (Davis 1991, 28). It was not uncommon for Spanish and French colonists to baptize their slaves into the Catholic faith. In addition, in the eighteenth century, conflicts between the Spanish and the English in the Southeast also resulted in some slaves converting to Catholicism as they were encouraged by Spaniards to flee their English slaveholders and live free in Florida, if they converted. The strength of Catholicism in Florida fluctuated for some of the eighteenth century depending on who controlled it at any given moment. Even so, by 1791 there were roughly 100 African Catholics in Pensacola alone (Davis 1991, 31).

There was a rhetoric of conversion regarding enslaved Africans but, as was

Mother Frances Fieldien (left), superior general of the Oblate Sisters of Providence, and Sister Mildred Howard (right) standing in front of Saint Frances Orphan Asylum, Baltimore, Maryland, in 1915 with a group of orphans in their care. (Courtesy Oblate Sisters of Providence)

the case with Protestants, this did not mean that most slaves owned by Catholics received sustained religious instruction. A suspicion concerning the consequences of instruction, combined with a limited number of priests to service the needs of slaves and whites made outreach difficult. Attention to Africans was spotty at best, and the ability to practice their faith was often hindered. In spite of this dilemma, blacks joined the Roman Catholic Church.

Estimates suggest that there may have been 1,000 African Catholics in Louisiana prior to the start of the Civil War. Growth of the Church's African membership, however, was not limited to Florida and Louisiana, although they represent an early African Catholic presence. To get an accurate picture of the movement of Catholicism within early African communities in North America, one must also note the growth that took place in what would become Missouri, Kentucky, Pennsylvania, and Maryland. For example, before the end of the eighteenth century, there were roughly 3,000 African Catholics in Maryland. While the number of Africans who communed in the Roman Catholic Church grew in the Mid-Atlantic area and the South. Scholars generally agree, however, that the first African Catholic parish—Chapel of the Nativity—developed in Pittsburgh in 1844.

Such growth is impressive, and it provides a sense of the makeup of Roman Catholic community; but numbers do not suggest very much with respect to the religious life of enslaved Africans. Nonetheless, enslaved Africans and free Africans who were part of the Catholic

Church, according to historian Albert Raboteau, "were attracted to the centuries-old rituals of Catholicism. They found deep meaning in the Mass, the sacraments, and in personal devotion to the Virgin and the Saints" (Raboteau 1996, 119). Regarding this, it is likely that most African Catholics had a worship experience in keeping with the dominant social sensibilities that meant segregated worship in white churches.

Prevailing social attitudes made it difficult for Africans to undertake the sacrament of ordained church ministry, and African women were not encouraged to become women religious. In fact, it is not until roughly 1829 that African women, who had developed a school for young girls, made their profession and successfully entered religious life through the formation of the Oblate Sisters of Providence. The four women—Marie Madeleine Balas, Rosine Boegue, Almeide Ducheniea Maxis, and Elizabeth Lange—and their work were recognized and approved by Pope Gregory XVI in 1831. Some years after being approved by the pope, the Oblate Sisters of Providence expanded by opening a short-lived school for African children in Philadelphia in 1863. In addition to providing this educational opportunity, they also worked with orphans in New Orleans.

Thirteen years after the formation of the Oblate Sisters of Providence, the Sisters of the Holy Family formed in New Orleans to take care of destitute Africans. Three of the women associated with the Sisters of the Holy Family took their canonical vows in 1852. Life for these women was intense, as free as possible of "worldly" distractions: "The sisters arose at 4:30am and they retired at 8:45pm. At 5:00am there was morning prayers, after half an hour of meditation, followed by Mass . . . . The meals were in silence with reading. Individual spiritual reading in French or English preceded supper" (Davis 1991, 108). Other communities of African sisters developed over the course of time, each with a commitment to focusing life on service to God through attention to others.

The work of these women is important in itself, but it is also significant in that it points to the striving of the African Catholic population, marking its efforts to experience the full life of the Church and to bring the best of the Catholic heritage to those of African descent. This striving for participation in the life of the Church did not simply involve women religious. It also entailed the efforts of African men to enter the priesthood.

The practice of ordaining Africans was adopted in the eighteenth century in

---

GEORGE CLEMENTS (1932–)

Clements earned two degrees from St. Mary of the Lake Seminary. And after completing his education in 1957, he began work in the pastorate. During his time in Chicago, Clements was very involved in the civil rights struggle, including serving as chaplain for the local black panthers. In 1969 he was made pastor of Holy Angels Church in Chicago. Clements, in addition to civil rights activism, took a great interest in the adoption of children in need, founding the One Church-One Child, One Church-One Addict and One Church-One Inmate initiatives. In 1981, he became the first priest to adopt a child.

keeping with the vision of the Congregation for the Propagation of the Faith. Pope Gregory XV developed this organization for the purpose of organizing ministry within the various mission areas. However, for the most part its work involved Africans outside the United States. In North America, the idea of ordaining blacks met with opposition through the early twentieth century. Early efforts to bring black men into ministry date back to the late 1800s when the Congregation of the Holy Ghost received three men interested in preparing for the brotherhood (Davis 1991, 145–146). Marking the concern of a minority of the Church, such efforts met with very limited success.

The first Africans ordained priests in the United States happened to be brothers, born the slaves of Michael Morris Healy. With the encouragement of the bishop of Boston, John Fitzpatrick, James Augustine, Patrick Francis, and Alexander Sherwood were educated at Holy Cross College. James Healy not only became a priest in 1854 but also the first African American bishop (Portland, Maine). Alexander was ordained in 1858, and after receiving a doctorate in canon law he joined the faculty of a seminary in New York state. Patrick, after further study, but before receiving his doctorate in philosophy, was ordained in 1864. After holding several posts, Patrick eventually became the president (1874) of Georgetown College (now Georgetown University).

Mention must also be made of Augustus Tolton who was born a slave, but without the socially derived benefit of skin that could pass as white. He, because of his dark complexion, unlike the Healys, had the fact of his African ancestry presented during the process of his push for training and ordination. After demonstrating an interest in ordination and after struggling for enrollment in college, Tolton was ordained in Rome in 1886. The initial idea was for Tolton to train for missionary work in Africa, but this did not happen. Instead he was sent to the difficult pastorate of a small African American church in Quincy, Illinois. After a short time in Illinois, Tolton was transferred to a new African American parish in Chicago, one with limited resources. His reputation for commitment to African American Catholics spread beyond Chicago and, according to historian Cyprian Davis, "more than he realized, he was the inspiration for the remarkable movement of faith and evangelization among the African American Catholic laity in the last decade of the 19th century" (Davis 1991, 162). Tolton's ordination was followed by that of others such as Randolph Uncles. This slow increase in the number of African American priests inspired the creation of a seminary in Mississippi for the training of African Americans. African Americans were interested in the priesthood and were making efforts to secure ordination, but a nagging question persisted: What should be done with African American priests and African American Catholic laity?

The number of black Catholic parishes increased during the late nineteenth century, but the problem of racial discrimination persisted. The Roman Catholic Church of the nineteenth century was not certain what to do with its African membership. So, it was often the case that treatment varied from one diocese to another as each bishop determined what constituted the proper place for those of African descent in the

Church. There was no interest on the part of most in losing African American members to Protestant churches; yet, there was no agreement on a strategy for making fellowship in the Catholic church attractive and rewarding for African Americans. How and by whom should African Americans be evangelized? Should there be separate churches for them? Should they be included in ordained ministry?

African American Catholics did not rely on the good graces of white Catholics to promote their full inclusion in the life of the Church. Figures such as Daniel Rudd, who founded the *American Catholic Tribune*, worked to organize a national conversation concerning the state of the Church and the work of African Americans within the Catholic community. It was argued that a national conversation, beginning in 1889, spearheaded by African Americans would increase their visibility and would foster substantive changes within the Church in the United States. There was also an implicit assumption that the increased visibility of African American Catholics might have significance with respect to the general perception of African Americans, and might contribute to the push for the larger social transformation. That is to say, the presentation of African American Catholic's spiritual and moral commitments might contribute to a national shift with respect to civil engagement between the races in that it would point to the merits and capabilities of African Americans.

Through a series of congresses the objectives for the better treatment of African Americans outlined by Rudd and others were expressed. These objectives or goals were very similar to those expressed by African Americans in Protestant churches. In both cases the emphasis involved the Church as a religiously oriented clearinghouse of sorts for a synergy of spiritual, educational, economic, political, and moral growth and opportunity. In short, religious commitments well lived should foster transformation on all levels of individual and communal existence. Good Catholics should be good citizens who strive for racial equality. One can easily argue that African American Catholics sparked a self-evaluation of Roman Catholicism in the United States based on a strong commitment to religiosity sensitive to the unique U.S. cultural context and historical moment. This process involved both an affirmation of the Catholic Church's potential and also a critique of its shortcomings with respect to issues of racism both inside and outside the Church.

In response to the work of the congresses initiated by Rudd, the Church formed the Catholic Board of Negro Mission. However, the issues it was charged with addressing—such as mixed churches versus segregated congregations—were so intense that the Board accomplished little. Some church leaders, including Pope Benedict XV, made an effort to address the concerns and needs of African American Catholics. But the Church relied so heavily on the goodwill of individual bishops and congregations that little systemic progress was made. Irrespective of shortcomings, there were signs of promise, including the development of educational opportunities for African Americans interested in service to the Church.

The middle of the twentieth century marked a change in the status of African Americans in the Roman Catholic Church. This shift was part of a larger trend toward

JAMES AUGUSTINE HEALY (1830–1900)

Healy was born near Macon in Georgia. He received his early education at a Quaker school in New Jersey. He was also given an opportunity to study at Holy Cross College in Massachusetts. Holly was baptized into the Roman Catholic Church in 1844. His relationship with the Church would continue to grow and flourish, resulting in a groundbreaking development when he became the first African American priest in 1854. He was made the first African American bishop in 1875. In 1900, he was appointed Assistant to the Papal Throne, only one step below the office of a cardinal.

diversity as the descendants of immigrants gained authority and positions of privilege within the church. Neighborhoods changed. The descendants of immigrants moved out of the inner city and African Americans moved in. Former immigrants who once simply identified themselves as Catholics from a particular place in Europe, now understood themselves as white in keeping with the racial structure and hierarchy of the United States. This phenomenon was a sociological fact with religious ramifications in that churches experienced changes in membership and were forced to address issues of race. According to John T. McGreevy, "change from a Euro-American Catholic to an African-American neighborhood moved to a different rhythm . . . These developments—neighborhood changes, a growing distinction between 'black' and 'white' and a blurring of lines between Euro-American Catholic groups" occurred across the urban landscape (McGreevy 1998, 35, 36). Racial issues within the Church notwithstanding, African Americans continued to find the ritual and teachings of the Church spiritually appealing, and a key source of what they considered the most appropriate manner for connecting to God.

As the size of African American membership increased, it became difficult to continue thinking of them as an "add on," an aberration on the fabric of Catholic community. This did not mean that discrimination against African Americans ended, nor did it mean the kind of active participation in the struggle for equal rights the Church could have mustered. (For example, Catholic schools were only integrated slowly and this was typically done over strong objections.) Rather, it entailed greater space within the Church structure for African Americans to express their concerns and exercise their gifts and talents.

As the Civil Rights Movement heated up and in light of Vatican II, some, but certainly not most, African American priests and laity—figures such as Chicago's Father George Clements—fought (often against both the Church and the larger society) for a more liberationist agenda with regard to civil rights and for the development of a religious identity that was true to the growing concern with black consciousness that marked the late twentieth century. These more progressive Catholics developed various organizations such as the Black Clergy Caucus (founded by George Clements) to provide a structure for the immediate action they felt was necessary if the Church wanted to be relevant to the lives of African Americans. Some

African American priests gave this push an aesthetic dimension by using artistic representations of an African Christ and Virgin Mary, as well as by appealing to the importance of African saints (McGreevy 1998, 224–225). Such structural and aesthetic action was not without opposition.

The Church addressed issues of racism through pastoral letters coming from American bishops and also from the African American bishops (more than ten by the late twentieth century). Subtle moves were made to improve the visibility and power of African Americans in the Catholic Church, including the establishing in 1988 of Eugene Marino as the first African American archbishop in the United States, in Atlanta, Georgia. Some of the roughly 2 million African American Catholics wanted more than the addition of African Americans to a troubled system, one that still contained only a small number of African American priests—roughly one for every 5,000 African American Catholics (Raboteau 1996, 117; McGreevy 1998, 381). Churches were being closed, African American churches included, and there was little from the perspective of many to suggest a deep concern on the part of Church hierarchy. Some African Americans called for fundamental theological and ritual changes that recognized and celebrated the history and talents of African Americans. One of the more noteworthy advocates for radical change is George Stallings.

Stallings, educated in Rome and ordained in 1974, gained attention in the late 1980s because of his fiery rhetoric directed at the Roman Catholic Church for its failure to creatively address moral issues such as the celibacy of priests and its failure to develop rituals in keeping with the cultural heritage of African Americans. Stallings's services in Washington, D.C., drew thousands of African American Catholics (as well as African Americans from other religious communities) interested in the Afrocentric style of worship that greatly resembled the energetic services associated with African American Pentecostalism. Afrocentrism is a philosophy of life premised on the idea that people of African descent should view life from the perspective of Africa. That is to say, Africa and the welfare of those of African descent should be at the center of their thought and actions. According to Stallings, "I realized the church is a white racist institution controlled by a preponderantly Euro-American white male hierarchy that for a century had decided the fate of black people in the Catholic Church. . . . My blackness could no longer tolerate it!" (www.bccandidates.com/ StallingsBio.htm).

He developed a new congregation without the approval of the bishop. The first Mass at this new church, Imani Temple (The African American Catholic Congregation), took place on July 2, 1989. Following this, it declared its independence from Rome on January 31, 1990. The mission of this new organization was stated on the church program as follows:

> It is the mission of the African American Catholic Congregation to be a preeminent holistic provider of spiritual and educational development. The African-American Catholic Congregation, an autonomous and independent Catholic institution, understands that a people who do not take control of their destiny, moved by the genius of their culture, can never achieve full spiritual, economic, social, cultural, and psychological maturity. Therefore, the African-American Catholic

Congregation and its parishioners and [*sic*] committed to the movement and struggles of our days, in hope of preserving our tomorrows.

More troubling for Church hierarchy than the worship style referred to as the "Gospel Mass" was Stallings's theological position on the issue of ordination that marked a clear rejection of church authority and tradition. Rejecting restrictions on who could be ordained, Stallings ordained a former nun in 1991, and boldly stated that his church was pro-choice, supportive of the gay and lesbian lifestyle, in favor of marriage for priests interested in it, and committed to the right of couples to divorce. In taking this position Stallings knowingly disregarded canon law. He rejected the general authority of the pope and the local authority of the bishop.

It should come as no surprise that Stallings's teachings and actions resulted in the development of a religious movement that led to his excommunication from the Roman Catholic Church. But his removal from Roman Catholicism did not stop him from fulfilling his religious agenda in that he developed an independent church housed in six locations, serving as its archbishop (consecrated by Richard Bridges of another independent church). It is estimated that his organization has a total membership of over 3,000.

Stallings's activities have taken an odd twist. In recent years, and over the objections of some of his followers, Stallings has developed a relationship with Rev. Sun Myung Moon, going so far as to marry a member of Moon's Unification Church. In response to questions concerning the marriage, Stallings said: "Jesus was an Asiatic Jew with black blood flowing through his veins. Look at me, a man of African descent about to marry a woman of Asian descent. We are about to have some new Jesuses" (www.cesnur.org/2001/moon_may23.htm). This connection to the Unification Church marks a theological shift within Stallings's organization. He seems to be moving even further away from anything recognizable as Roman Catholicism. Where he and his followers will ultimately settle in terms of theology and ritual structures remains to be seen.

Beliefs and Practices

Stallings's work involves a break with many of the traditional beliefs and practices of Roman Catholicism. A major distinction between Roman Catholicism and Stallings's position as well as that of other Christian denominations revolves around the infallibility of the Pope with respect to issues related to the faith and its practice. Declared during the First Vatican Council in 1870, this perspective on the pope is significant in that it promotes a strong hierarchical structure within the Church and centralizes formal authority within one figure, whose authority stems from the Apostle Peter as the first leader of the Church. This understanding of Peter and his ministerial descendants is drawn from Jesus Christ's comments regarding Peter:

> When Jesus came into the region of Caesarea Philippi, He asked His disciples, saying, "Who do men say that I, the Son of Man, am?" And they said, "Some say John the Baptist, some Elijah, and others Jeremiah or one of the prophets." He said to them, "But who do you say that I am?" And Simon Peter answered and said, "You are the Christ, the Son of the living God." And Jesus answered and said

to him, "Blessed are you, Simon Bar-Jonah, for flesh and blood has not revealed this to you, but My Father who is in heaven. And I also say to you that you are Peter, and on this rock I will build My church, and the gates of Hades shall not prevail against it. And I will give you the keys of the kingdom of heaven, and whatever you bind on earth will be bound in heaven, and whatever you loose on earth will be loosed in heaven." (Matthew 16:13–19, King James Version)

This authority held by the pope is deeply important in that it results in the pope having the right at times to teach what Catholics are to believe regarding the faith in ways that are not open to question because they contain no errors.

The pope is not the only figure in the church permitted to teach Catholics what to believe and how to conduct themselves. Bishops can teach the principles of Catholic life, but this involves teachings that are subject to revision and change. That is to say, what bishops teach is subject to alteration; if this were not the case, their authority would in fact challenge that of the pope. In both cases —teachings open to change and teachings not subject to alteration—the fundamental source of information is the revelation from God housed in sacred Scripture and more contemporarily in the working of God's spirit in the modern world.

Much of what is taught within the Church results from councils called by the pope to discuss with the bishops important and pressing issues. The teachings generated by these councils can be declared infallible. And members of the church, to varying degrees, are familiar with the basics of the councils' work; but less well known is Canonical Law, revised in 1983, that provides a code for the general processes guiding the Roman Catholic Church. This law is not as directly theologically framed and formulated as are the workings of the various councils. Furthermore, Canonical Law is the product of the pope in consultation with a small group of canon lawyers as opposed to the gathering of the pope and bishops that defines the work of a council.

In a sense the importance and authority of the bishops and the pope speak to the Roman Catholic Church's deep appreciation for those who have committed themselves to the service of God and God's Church on the highest levels. This type of appreciation might also play into the significance of saints—individuals who displayed unusually strong devotion to God expressed through extraordinary events associated with their lives—within Roman Catholicism. For Roman Catholics, the saints are important on some level because they are able to intercede for the living and thereby help them in their effort to live a proper life. Of particular importance with respect to the saints is the Virgin Mary, the mother of Jesus.

There are similarities between Roman Catholicism and many of the other traditions outlined in this volume in that doctrine and ritual are of fundamental importance for the assurance of good spiritual health. Participation in the life of the Church requires markers, ceremonies or "rites," that denote the movement of the individual into the community of the faithful. There are three such ceremonies or sacraments in Roman Catholicism: baptism, confirmation, and communion. The first involves a symbolic "death" of the sinful person through the sprinkling of water on the child or adult. This ceremony opens the person to a relationship with God within the context of the community of believers. One of the activities made available to the person through baptism is communion. This ritual involves recognition of the crucifixion of Jesus Christ for the sins of the world. Jesus Christ died for the sins of the world on the cross, and the ritual of communion is a remembrance of this event. Communion is a part of the ritual of the churches but unlike many other Christian churches, Roman Catholics argue that the wine and bread consumed during this ceremony become the actual body and blood of Jesus Christ. This belief is referred to as transubstantiation. The final sacrament involves a public pronouncement of the person's embrace of Catholic teachings, and it takes place after the person has studied the doctrine of the Church. It is what one might consider the final phase of initiation into the Roman Catholic Church.

In addition to the previously mentioned sacraments, there are ritualized activities that are quite important to Roman Catholics. Confession is one such ritual through which the believer is given an opportunity to confess shortcomings and receive instructions for overcoming sin. Since Vatican II, the nature and frequency of confession has changed. Fewer people undertake it on a regular basis, and limited church resources (including a declining number of priests) make it difficult for priests to provide this service regularly. Furthermore, the shift follows a theological change regarding perceptions of sin through which "sin is less juridical, so that the faithful focus upon their fundamental life's direction toward God rather than evaluating every act independently" (Gillis 1999, 171). Much of the connection to God's will that some might have felt through the process of confession is undertaken by many through the process of prayer in both formal and informal spaces set apart for this activity.

Anthony B. Pinn

RICHARD ALLEN (1760–1831)

The person who spearheaded the foundation of the AME Church was Richard Allen. Allen was born a slave, in the Philadelphia household of Benjamin Chew, Pennsylvania's Attorney General and a Quaker turned Anglican. When Allen was six years old, he, his mother, and several siblings were sold to Stokely Sturgis, a struggling small farmer in Delaware. Despite the fact that Sturgis sold Allen's mother and three of his brothers and sisters in 1777, Allen remembered him as a humane man. When Methodist preachers first visited Allen's neighborhood in Delaware in 1780, Allen was a ready convert and invited the preachers, with Sturgis's permission, to hold services at his master's house. He became recognized as a leading Methodist preacher. In Philadelphia, Allen attended St. George's Methodist Church, a mixed (although segregated) congregation, and held services for African American Methodists at 5 AM every Sunday. He also took part in the activities of the Free African Society, along with Absalom Jones; the Free African Society was a self-help organization aiming to build up institutions for the African American community, such as a cemetery, a church, and schools. Allen's 15-year bishopric proved to be an important and consequential one. Allen died in 1931.

SELECTED BIBLIOGRAPHY

Davis, Cyprian. *The History of Black Catholics in the United States* (New York: Crossroads, 1991).

Gillis, Chester. *Roman Catholicism in America* (New York: Columbia University Press, 1999).

Hayes, Diana L. *Hagar's Daughters: Womanist Ways of Being in the World* (Boston: Paulist Press, 1995).

Hayes, Diana L., and Cyprian Davis, eds. *Taking Down Our Harps: Black Catholics in the United States* (Maryknoll, NY: Orbis Books, 1998).

McGreevy, John T. *Parish Boundaries: The Catholic Encounter with Race in the Twentieth-Century Urban North* (Chicago: University of Chicago Press, 1998).

Phelps, Jamie T., ed. *Black and Catholic: The Challenge and Gift of Black Folk* (Milwaukee: Marquette University Press, 1997).

Raboteau, Albert J. *A Fire in the Bones: Reflections on African-American Religious History* (Boston: Beacon Press, 1996).

AFRICAN METHODIST EPISCOPAL CHURCH

Historical Development

The African Methodist Episcopal (AME) Church is the largest of the independent African American denominations in North America. The AME Church originated as an early protest against racial discrimination among American Methodists, and simultaneously as an arena in which black culture and leadership could be lovingly and systematically nurtured.

In 1792, Richard Allen, Absalom Jones, and other African Americans were attending the services at St. George's Methodist Church in Philadelphia, but an incident during prayer where a white deacon threatened to pull Allen and his friends off their knees because they were not situated far enough back in the gallery caused the group of black men to walk out of St. George's, and this highlighted the urgency of beginning a church expressly for African Americans in Philadelphia. By 1794, many of the members of the Free African Society had built just such a church; it would be named St. Thomas' Church, and they decided that it should affiliate with the Episcopalians. When they asked Allen, the leading black minister in Philadelphia, to become their pastor, Allen declined. The black Episcopalians' second choice was Absalom Jones, who accepted the post. However, Allen strongly wished to remain a Methodist.

Instead, in that same year, Allen turned a discarded blacksmith shop into a new black Methodist congregation, which he called "Bethel." The Bethel African Methodists were still tied to the white Methodists. Bishop Francis Asbury helped Allen to dedicate his church in 1794, and, five years later, Asbury would ordain Allen as a deacon. However, attempts by white Methodist ministers to exert control over the Bethel church during the next two decades would pose severe problems for Allen. Bethel's articles of incorporation, drawn up by a white Methodist, were amended at Allen's direction in order to ensure that Bethel's black church members had control over their own church affairs. Pennsylvania courts upheld these actions over against the complaints of the white Methodist ministers, culminating in an 1816 decision by the Pennsylvania Supreme Court. The Supreme Court absolved Allen's congregation of any obligations to the white Methodists of St. George's, effectively establishing its independence.

Allen seized the moment by convening a gathering of black clergy from five states with a view to establishing a new denomination. One attendee was Peter Spencer, who, three years earlier, had established the independence of his African Union Church in Wilmington, Delaware. His presence may have signified a willingness to consider merging these two forms of independent black Methodism, but the results of Spencer's consideration must have been negative because this juncture never occurred, and Spencer took no further part in the work of the AME Church. Another attendee was a mixed-race Methodist preacher from Baltimore, named Daniel Coker (c. 1780–1846). Coker had been born into slavery in Maryland, but Coker had become a fugitive, ending up in New York City. Quakers assisted him in purchasing his freedom. He then returned to Baltimore where he preached and taught school. Unlike Allen, he was highly literate; one expert on African Methodism stated that Coker "possessed more information on all subjects than usually fell to the lot of colored men in his day" (Payne 1891, 89).

Allen's Philadelphia gathering decided to organize as an independent denomination and to elect a bishop to preside over the new denomination. The man elected to serve was Coker, perhaps because of his literacy. Coker declined the episcopacy, however, although the reasons for his action remain unclear; some authorities state that it was thought, on further reflection, better to have a bishop who was purely African (like Allen) rather than a mixed-race bishop like Coker; others state that Allen was out of town when the election occurred, and was angry when he heard of the election's outcome and was able to have it reversed. In any event, after Coker declined the office, Allen was elected and consecrated the first bishop of the AME Church, and his friend Absalom Jones assisted in his consecration.

One unanticipated challenge faced by Allen was a request from a woman, Jarena Lee (1783–1851?), to preach the gospel in the context of the AME Church. On the first occasion that Lee approached him, Allen gently dissuaded her from pursuing what she understood to be her calling. When, in 1818, some years later, she stood up on the floor of Bethel Church and renewed her request, Allen changed his mind and agreed to support her in an evangelistic ministry outside the ordained offices of deacon and elder, which structured the upper levels of the Methodist ministerial hierarchy, including most of the paid pastorates. Lee proved to be an indefatigable and effective traveling evangelist, who was remembered especially in midwestern states like Ohio, along with William Paul Quinn (1788?–1873), another traveling evangelist who would later become an AME bishop. Quinn and Lee had much to do with the spread of the AME Church through the states carved out of the Northwest Territory.

In expansion of his denomination, Allen did not only look west, he looked south also. A large group of black Methodists broke off from the Methodist Episcopal Church in Charleston, South Carolina, in 1817, and they moved to affiliate with Allen's denomination. Harassment from the authorities in South Carolina did not deter them; by 1820,

DANIEL ALEXANDER PAYNE (1811–1893)

Daniel Alexander Payne was born in Charleston, South Carolina, on February 24, 1811. He subsequently studied at the Lutheran seminary in Gettysburg, Pennsylvania, after which he was ordained in the Franken Synod of the Lutheran Church. Eventually moving to Philadelphia, Payne would join the AME church in 1842. From the time of his affiliation, Payne was a major advocate for an educated ministry within the AME Church. As a bishop, Payne was intent upon establishing a literate culture within the AME Church, so that requirements of education would have some substance to them. The renowned *AME Church Review*, a literary magazine, was established in 1884 under Payne's guidance. Payne also believed that the AME Church should have a seminary. He made more than one attempt at founding such an institution, but he would have the greatest success with an institution in southwestern Ohio, near Xenia, to which he would give the name "Wilberforce University," after the English parliamentarian William Wilberforce, who was instrumental in Britain's ending of the slave trade and of slavery itself within its dominions.

Morris Brown (1770–1847), the pastor of the congregation, had come north to meet with Allen. Two years later, a much-disputed conspiracy in Charleston was allegedly centered around Denmark Vesey, a lay member of Brown's flock. In the aftermath of that event, Vesey and more than 30 other black Charlestonians were executed, the Charleston AME Church was closed, and Morris Brown was exiled to Philadelphia, where Richard Allen welcomed him. The exiled Brown was to become the second bishop of the AME Church. The AME Church would not reopen in Charleston until 1865, but meanwhile the AME Church grew among African Americans in border cities such as Baltimore, Washington, D.C., Louisville, and St. Louis. John Mifflin Brown founded a congregation in New Orleans in 1843, and it remained open until 1858.

In 1841, a decade after Allen's death in 1831, another former Charlestonian, Daniel A. Payne (1811–1893), joined the AME Church, and he would prove to be a major influence in the church for most of the remainder of the nineteenth century. The thin, almost emaciated, puritanical Payne rose rapidly through the ranks of the denomination, becoming bishop in 1852.

In large part due to the efforts of Payne, the church would open Wilberforce University in 1856, with mostly white Methodist trustees; in 1863, the Methodist Episcopal Church wished to sell its interest in the property; Payne bought the property for the AME Church, and it was subsequently entirely under the control of the AME Church. Wilberforce University would have many subsequent challenges, including a disastrous fire in 1865. For a time, the state of Ohio provided substantial funding, but due to concerns of separation of church and state, Wilberforce University was divided in two in 1946, with the state-supported portion of the university adopting the name "Central State University."

The AME Church had an antislavery stand, at least from the time that Richard Allen, together with Absalom

Jones, had published in 1794 *An Address to Those Who Keep Slaves*. In effect, Allen and Jones, were building on the antislavery position of John Wesley, a stand that the latter had made public in his 1774 publication, *Thoughts upon Slavery*. Allen and Jones wrote to slaveholders, "if you love the God of love, clear your hands of slaves, burden not your children or country with them" (Campbell 1995, 24). The South Carolina exiles Brown and Payne preserved an antislavery stance within the AME Church, but as styles of antislavery proliferated in mid-nineteenth-century America, so such styles also proliferated within the AME Church; there was no single pattern. Of the 31 African Americans in one Pennsylvania county who were "agents" in the Underground Railroad, it appears that more were members of the AME Church than any other; i.e., of the 15 whose religious identity is known, 8 were AME.

Not all African Americans believed that the AME Church and its clergy were doing all that they might. The fiery 26-year-old Mary Ann Shadd decried the role played by AME clergy: "Their gross ignorance and insolent bearing, together with their sanctimonious garb [shows] the downright degradation of the free colored people of the North" (Kashatus 2002, 58). Indeed, when the subject of antislavery strategy reached the floor of the 1856 General Conference, a majority of the delegates voted against the ultraist position, apparently agreeing with the elderly Richard Robinson, who stated that it was unnecessary for African Americans to adopt an outright abolitionist position, because "every colored man is an abolitionist, and the slaveholders know it" (Payne 1891, 339). It was much to be preferred, believed

Robinson, for the AME Church to maintain a low profile. What both Shadd and Robinson pointed to, in very different ways, was the fact that AME clergy devoted far more of their efforts to community building in the antebellum era than to politics, although their community building may have undergirded antislavery politics in a more subtle manner than Shadd's comments would allow. Those African Methodists who sought refuge in Canada, seeking an extra level of protection from the pro-slavery laws of the United States, organized themselves in 1855 into the "British Methodist Episcopal Church" with the help of Payne and their American coreligionists. The BME Church would rejoin the AME Church in 1884.

One antebellum AME clergyman with a reputation for militancy was Thomas Henry, an Underground Railroad agent for two decades. In the late 1850s, he was pastor of the AME Church in Hagerstown, Maryland. Henry was a confidant of John Brown, and his name was found in Brown's papers. Before he could be arrested, Henry sought refuge in Philadelphia, and church leaders then assigned him to a circuit in upstate New York rather than send him back to Maryland.

When the Civil War broke out, AME clergy closely monitored the policies of the Lincoln administration. Bishop Payne, for example, successfully lobbied the president to sign the bill for the emancipation of slaves in the District of Columbia enacted in April 1862. When Lincoln signed the Emancipation Proclamation on January 1, 1863, William Hunter and Henry McNeal Turner were two AME clergymen who helped to recruit black regiments for the Union Army, subsequently serving the regiments they helped to raise as chaplains.

In the period from 1863 to 1868, there were numerous proposals made to reunify Methodism. Some proposals sought to bring together only black Methodists, while James Lynch and Daniel Payne, among others, looked favorably at a reunion of Methodism along racial lines. Many of these proposals would have involved changing the name of the AME Church and discarding the word "African," a nonstarter for many. None of these reunion proposals worked out, as the attachment to denominational prerogatives, including keeping all of the current AME bishops, remained strong.

The AME Church's post-emancipation advance into the South began with the arrival of James Lynch and J. D. S. Hall as missionaries to South Carolina's Sea Islands in May 1863. It would eventually reach to every southern state, although competition with other branches of black Methodism—especially the AME Zion Church and the CME Church—would greatly restrict AME prospects in such states as North Carolina and Alabama. Through successful revivals and transfers of membership from the Methodist Episcopal Church, South, the ranks of membership of the AME Church grew steadily. In 1858, the AME Church had only 20,000 members, and its southern members would have been almost entirely in border states. By 1896, it would have 452,725 members, and most of the increase occurred in the 11 former states of the Confederacy. By the 1990s, the AME Church would claim 3.5 million members worldwide.

In the area of education, AMEs in virtually every southern state established their own colleges, over the objections of Payne, who correctly believed that the denomination could not adequately support such a proliferation of colleges. Many of these institutions were eventually closed, but the denominational colleges and seminaries that survive include: Wilberforce University in Wilberforce, Ohio; Payne Theological Seminary, also in Wilberforce, Ohio; Allen University in Columbia, South Carolina, reorganized from an earlier educational venture in 1880; Morris Brown College, in Atlanta, Georgia, founded in 1881 (as of 2007, operating with reduced staff and student body and without accreditation); Paul Quinn College in Dallas, Texas, founded in 1872 (as of 2007, placed on probation by its accreditors); Turner Theological Seminary in Atlanta, Georgia, founded 1894 and, since 1958, a part of the Interdenominational Theological Center, a consortium of six seminaries; and Edward Waters College in Jacksonville, Florida, founded in 1883.

There were intensive discussions within the turn-of-the-century AME Church as to how to implement its educational mission, and these discussions often played out in denominational periodicals such as the *AME Church Review*. Many AME church leaders agreed with Bishop Payne about the need for a Christian education and with Booker T. Washington about the need for a practical (or, as often stated, an "industrial") education. However, Charles C. Cook, writing in the *Review* in 1904, was among those who discerned a false dichotomy between "industrial" and "classical" education: "No educational scheme can stand, whose high arch of family and social life does not rest upon twin pillars of industry and culture" (Angell and Pinn 2000, 90). Industry, he observed, bid to eclipse religion, book learning, and politics, because "behind industry, as it is at present regarded, lies wealth. The last has now become first" (Angell and Pinn 2000, 91), and the dollar sign has conquered. However, others, such as Will M. Jackson, writing in 1889, feared that African Americans were "educating the head at the expense of the hands" (Angell and Pinn 2000, 86) with the danger that honest toil might be treated disdainfully. This kind of controversy even raged about the AME ministry, with some denomination members stoutly insisting that educated ministers had such little regard for the old-time revival religion that they harmed the churches rather than building them up.

Ministers associated with the AME Church such as Daniel Coker and Scipio Beanes undertook missions outside North America in such locations as Liberia and Haiti as early as the 1820s, but these missions did not result in permanent churches being established. A much more concerted missionary effort began in the 1880s into the first two decades of the twentieth century, in Liberia, Sierra Leone, South Africa, Haiti, Bermuda, British Guiana, Cuba, and Mexico, among other locations. There were many reasons for such missions. African Americans who suffered from increasing segregation in the United States sought homes in countries where the color line was not drawn. Some also had a strong desire to assist those who had no knowledge of Christ to undergo moral reform. Some saw Christian missions undertaken by African Americans as a way to unify peoples of color and to build up churches without racial prejudice.

The AME Church experienced its greatest missionary success in South Africa, with the decision of Mangena Mokone to bring his Ethiopian Independent Church into affiliation with the AME Church in 1896, a merger facilitated by his niece, Charlotte Manye, who had experienced AME hospitality at Wilberforce University during a tour by the African Jubilee Choir of which she was a part. The flexibility of the leadership in applying church rules that had aided the AME mission to the southern United States also aided its spread in South Africa. Not very helpful, however, was the inconsistent leadership from the long succession of American ministers and bishops sent to guide the South African church and juggle admittedly conflicting demands from white officials and a wide range of colored and black constituents. Some, but not all, of the AME churches in South Africa proved to be hospitable to Black Nationalism. Some black South Africans sent their children to Wilberforce University and other American schools; one of the first sent across the ocean, Francis Herman Gow, became the first South African–born AME bishop. The AME Church has been slower in encouraging indigenization than some other American missionary churches; during the twentieth century, most of the episcopal leadership for the church would come from American bishops. By 2007, two of its African bishops, Wilfred J. Messiah and Paul J. M. Kawimbe, were African born. The Church hailed this as "a milestone in the reality that our church is global" (*Christian Recorder* online, July 13, 2007). The AME Church has expanded to having a presence in 22 African nations, most of which are in southern Africa.

Beliefs and Practices

The AME Church has been a pioneer in the "Black Theology" movement. Henry McNeal Turner, in the nineteenth century, was a pioneer in his oft-repeated admonitions to AME Church members to "respect black" and his controversial assertion in 1898 that "God is a Negro." Turner explained that "We have *as much right* biblically and otherwise to believe that God is a negro, as you buckra or white people have to believe that God is a fine looking, symmetrical, and orna-mented white man" (Angell 1992, 261), inasmuch as every race of people has a right to envision God in their own image. Other AME theologians explored the Biblical basis for Black Nationalism. George Wilson Brent, writing in the *Review* in 1896, explored Biblical refer-ences to Cush, Canaan, Egypt, and Ethio-pia, concluding that "Africa, our fatherland, the home of the Hamitic race, is the only country on earth whose past, present, and future so concerned our Lord, that of all notable events in the lives of Joseph, Moses, Jacob, Abraham, Solomon and Our Savior Jesus Christ, the fact of their being there became a turning point in their lives" (Angell and Pinn 2000, 148). In more recent times, James H. Cone, born (1938) and raised in the AME Church in Bearden, Arkan-sas, has pioneered the academic study of Black Theology with such works as *Black Theology and Black Power* (1969), *God of the Oppressed* (1975), and *For My People: Black Theology and the Black Church* (1986).

From Richard Allen's lifetime onwards, the AME Church has been faced with responding to women who have been called to preach and who claim the right to exercise their ministry. Allen himself gave informal permission to Jarena Lee to preach in 1818, but he did not ordain her. After Allen's death, Lee did not find AME leaders so hospi-table to her ministry. In 1835, for exam-ple, she recounted that she returned to Philadelphia and found the AME pulpits closed to her. In 1850, Bishop Payne

related that female preachers in the AME Church sought to erect a parallel structure for assigning women to congre-gations "after the manner of our Annual Conferences," but that their efforts "fell to pieces like a rope of sand" (Payne 1891, 237).

The influence of the Holiness Move-ment after the Civil War gave further impe-tus to the cause of women's preaching, most notably through the career of Amanda Berry Smith, an evangelist who preached in India, Africa, and England, as well as North America. After a well-received sermon delivered to the AME General Conference in 1872, Berry disclaimed any interest in churchly ordination, stating that she was "satisfied with the ordination that the Lord has given me" (Angell and Pinn 2000, 282). Other women who experienced the call did want that human recognition. One who succeeded, at least for a time, was Sarah Ann Hughes, an evangelist and pas-tor in North Carolina, who was ordained by Henry McNeal Turner in 1885. How-ever, her ordination was overturned two years later because of the opposition of many male ministers who claimed that the ordination of women was unbiblical. Doz-ens of women served as ministers in AME Churches during the next decades, includ-ing a few who accepted pastorates, but none of these women were ordained. By the mid-twentieth century, AME men's interpretations of Paul's epistles had shifted sufficiently that in 1948 when Rebecca M. Glover, assistant pastor of the Metropolitan AME Church in Washington, D.C., became only the second AME woman to be ordained, her ordination stood.

The first woman elected to the episco-pacy in the AME Church was Vashti McKenzie, a pastor from Baltimore, who was consecrated as a bishop in 2000. She now serves the Thirteenth

HENRY MCNEAL TURNER (1834–1915)

Standing increasingly in opposition to the elderly Bishop Payne during the Reconstruction era was one of Payne's former protégés, Henry McNeal Turner (1834–1915). Like Payne, Turner was from South Carolina, moving north to join the AME Church in 1858. Turner rose rapidly in AME ranks and, in 1865, took charge of AME missionary work in Georgia. He was a "race man" who accomplished an enormous amount in both the ecclesiastical and the political arenas, organizing AME congregations and the Republican Party in Georgia. Turner took an active role in Reconstruction politics, serving for one term as a representative in the Georgia State Legislature, and for a brief period as postmaster in Macon, Georgia. Turner's main involvement with African issues came in the last two years of Daniel Payne's life or after his death, including four missionary journeys to Africa and sponsorship through the International Missionary Society of two shiploads of African American emigrants to Africa after the demise of the American Colonization Society in the early 1890s, a Society of which Turner had been honorary vice president. Turner became a bishop at the General Conference of 1880, along with another southerner, Richard Cain (1826–1887) of South Carolina. Turner passed away in 1915.

Episcopal District, which comprises Tennessee and Kentucky. Two other women have subsequently been elected as bishops: Carolyn Tyler Guidry, who serves the Sixteenth Episcopal District, which comprises AME Churches in the Caribbean and in London; and Sarah Frances Davis, supervising the Eighteenth Episcopal District, which includes conferences in the smaller southern African nations of Lesotho, Swaziland, Botswana, and Mozambique.

Among the programs and stances taken by the AME Church and its bishops in 2007 were the following: an agreement that the AME Church should encourage HIV testing among its constituents; a pledge to support efforts to strengthen literacy among African American children; a resolution of opposition to "the unjust war in Iraq"; and the recommendation of a process to build up "an educational endowment fund for the church to undergird the financial health of our educational institutions" (http://www.ame-church.com/news-and-events/convoIX-highlights.php, 2007 Convo IX highlights).

Stephen W. Angell

SELECTED BIBLIOGRAPHY

African Methodist Episcopal Church. Official Web site. http://www.ame-church.com/index.php.

Angell, Stephen Ward. *Henry McNeal Turner and African-American Religion in the South* (Knoxville: University of Tennessee Press, 1992).

Angell, Stephen W., and Anthony B. Pinn. *Social Protest Thought in the African Methodist Episcopal Church* (Knoxville: University of Tennessee Press, 2000).

Campbell, James T. *Songs of Zion: The African Methodist Episcopal Church in the United States and South Africa* (New York: Oxford University Press, 1995).

Collier-Thomas, Bettye. *Daughters of Thunder: Black Women Preachers and Their Sermons, 1850–1979* (San Francisco: Jossey Bass Publishers, 1998).

Dodson, Jualynne. *Engendering Church: Women, Power, and the AME Church* (Lanham, MD: Rowman & Littlefield Publishers, 2002).

Kashatus, William C. *Just Over the Line: Chester County and the Underground Railroad* (West Chester, PA: Chester County Historical Society, 2002).

Libby, Jean, ed. *From Slavery to Salvation: The Autobiography of Rev. Thomas W. Henry of the A.M.E. Church* (Jackson: University of Mississippi Press, 1994).

Melton, J. Gordon. *A Will to Choose: The Origins of African American Methodism* (Lanham, MD: Rowman & Littlefield Publishers, 2007).

Payne, Daniel Alexander. *Recollections of Seventy Years* (New York: Arno Press, 1968 [first published, 1888]).

Payne, Daniel Alexander. *History of the African Methodist Episcopal Church* (New York: Arno Press, 1969 [first published, 1891]).

Pinn, Anthony B. *Making the Gospel Plain: The Writings of Bishop Reverdy C. Ransom* (Harrisburg, PA: Trinity Press International, 1999).

Walker, David. *Walker's Appeal, in Four Articles*. Electronic Edition (Chapel Hill: University of North Carolina, 2001 [first published, 1829]).

Wright, R. R., Jr. *The Bishops of the African Methodist Episcopal Church* (Nashville: A.M.E. Sunday School Union, 1963).

AFRICAN METHODIST EPISCOPAL ZION CHURCH

Historical Development

The African Methodist Episcopal Zion Church (AME Zion Church) recognizes its founding in 1796, the year in which a number of African Americans, the majority of whom were members of John Street Methodist Episcopal Church in New York, New York, petitioned for the privilege to hold meetings under their own leadership. This was the second secession effort of note by African American congregants within the Methodist Episcopal Church, the first being in 1787 by African American members of St. George's Methodist Episcopal Church in Philadelphia, under the leadership of Richard Allen. The denomination that grew out of the Philadelphia movement would take the name African Methodist Episcopal Church (AME Church). Unlike the Philadelphia community, however, there was not a single incident that served as a catalyst for a move toward separation. Instead, the African American congregants in New York simply seemed desirous of a place and a setting in which they might greater exercise their spiritual gifts and offer mutual support. This petition was granted by Bishop Francis Asbury. The leaders of this effort included Francis Jacobs, William Brown, Peter Williams, Abraham Thompson, June Scott, Samuel Pontier, Thomas Miller, William Miller, James Varick, and William Hamilton. Three of these individuals, Abraham Thompson, June Scott, and Thomas Miller, were already recognized preachers, and William Miller was an exhorter. Thus, some of this number already had limited opportunities to exercise their calling, albeit under the supervision of white Methodists and only as the opportunities presented themselves within the Church's association.

By 1799, the growth in participation of African Americans in the Methodist Episcopal Church in New York, led these members to propose the establishment of their own house of worship. In the interim period, their independent gatherings were taking place in space owned and

JAMES VARICK (1750–1827)

James Varick was born near Newburgh, New York in 1750. Raised for the most part in New York City, Varick appears to have been the recipient of some elementary education. At age sixteen, he would join the John Street Methodist Episcopal Church, the congregation at that time little more than a year old. He was eventually licensed to preach by this body. He would support himself and his family through the trade of shoemaking, opening his own business by 1783. Varick was one of the black members who participated in the development of separate meetings for black congregants, which eventually lead to the existence of the independent African Methodist Episcopal Zion Church. In 1806, Varick and two others were ordained as the first black deacons in New York. He would be instrumental in the spread of the AME Zion Church to New Haven, CT in 1818 and to Philadelphia, PA in 1820. Finally, following a two year struggle with the white church hierarchy, he was finally ordained as the first black superintendent (bishop) of the AME Zion Church in 1822. In 1817, he became one of the vice presidents of the New York African Bible Society. Before his death on July 22, 1827, he helped found the *Freedom's Journal.*

controlled by white Methodists. After initially failing to secure one site on Orange Street, between Cross and Chatham, they purchased a site situated at the corner of Church and Leonard Streets and fronting on Church Street. There they erected a building that they called the African Methodist Episcopal Zion Church, securing a charter in 1801.

The young congregation would confront various trials during its early formative years. For example, two of the earlier founders, Abraham Thompson and June Scott, attempted to start another society separate from the Zion Church, which they named the Union Society. Thompson would shortly return to the Zion Church while Scott remained with the Society until it soon folded, after which he joined another church.

In 1813, Thomas Simpkins was expelled from the Zion Church, where he had been a member and trustee. With the assistance of one of the early founders, William Miller, he was able to establish a new society, drawing several members of the Zion community. Around 1810, both Simpkins and Miller had begun to make overtures toward the Allenites in Philadelphia, much to the dismay of the Zion Church. The new congregation they founded was named Asbury Church, and though never officially associating with Bishop Allen's congregations, there were clear theological and liturgical influences derived from the Allen's African Methodist movement. Another point of contention between Zion and Asbury was the latter also receiving recognition from the Methodist Episcopal authorities.

Another person of note during the early days of the "Zionist" movement was William Lambert. One of those who left the Zion Church for the Asbury community, he continued to be thwarted in what he considered to be a calling to the ministry. He eventually left for Philadelphia, where he came under the influence of Bishop Richard Allen. Under Allen, he finally obtained a license to preach. Lambert subsequently returned to New York, were he was determined to found a congregation affiliated with Allen's Methodist movement. With the assistance of Rev. George White, he obtained property in the area of Mott Street. Significantly, these activities coincided with Bishop Allen's investigations into extending the jurisdiction of his denomination, an investigation that involved communication with several African American Methodists in the New York area.

Also at this time, Henry Harden, an African Methodist Episcopal elder from Baltimore, came to New York, joining Lambert and White in their efforts to form an association of African Methodists. Harden had been authorized by the denomination to head African Methodist Episcopal Church work in New York City. The Zionists' leadership promptly viewed this as an encroachment on their jurisdiction and appeared to take a stance of noncooperation with the "Allenites." Interestingly, the earlier separatists that constituted the Asbury Church aligned themselves with the Zionists in this dispute.

One should note, however, that while the leaders of these early African Methodist associations were often at odds with one another, this was not always the case. For example, Christopher Rush, who became one of the early bishops within the AME Zion Church, notes in his early history of the church that James Varick, the man who would become the denomination's first bishop, offered the opening prayer for a meeting during Bishop Allen's first visit to New York to assess the progress of Harden, Lambert, and White. Rush also notes that it was quite common for the laity of the various groups to attend one another's meetings.

Nevertheless, the dissension between the various groups persisted. Though similar in many ways, they possessed distinct and separate senses of identity associated with their particular histories. As mentioned earlier, the African Methodists under Allen had had a much more contentious relationship with the Methodist Episcopal Church than had the Zionists in New York. Consequently, the Philadelphia-based church tended to exhibit a stronger separatist politics than the New York–based community. This is not to say, however, that the Zionists did not value their autonomy. After all, their autonomy enabled them to more fully explore and express their gifts as Christians. It was in this context that the Zionists called for an official meeting on August 11, 1820, to discuss their future viability. Two questions were placed before the gathering: should they rejoin

Christopher Rush, second bishop of the African Methodist Episcopal Zion Church. (History of All the Religious Denominations in the United States. *Harrisburg: John Winebrunner, 1848)*

the white Methodist Episcopal Church or should they join with the Allenites? The prescient answer to both questions was no; i.e., neither option was acceptable. They would chart their own unique course.

The Zionists eventually followed in the footsteps of the Allenites and the Asbury Church in ordaining their own deacons and elders. Over the course of the next several years, they began a mission effort leading to the founding of congregations in Flushing, New York; New Haven, Connecticut; and even Philadelphia, Pennsylvania; assimilating a group of schismatics that had severed ties with Bishop Allen to found the Wesleyan Church.

Under the leadership of individuals such as James Varick, George Collins, Charles Anderson, and Christopher Rush, the Zionists drew up doctrines and disciplines, elected elders, and finally organized in 1821 as a national body, adopting the name "African Methodist Episcopal Church of America." In 1822, James Varick, then pastor of Zion Church, was elected their first superintendent (a designation that was later changed to bishop) and served until 1828. In 1848, Zion was officially added to the name of the denomination, to become the "African Methodist Episcopal Zion Church" to make clear the distinction from the African Methodist Episcopal Church.

Prior to the Civil War, the church experienced little growth. The growth that did occur during this period is generally attributed to the gifts and talents of Christopher Rush, who was Varick's successor as general superintendent. Rush, a native of North Carolina, had escaped from slavery when he was approximately 21 years of age. He traveled north,

eventually arriving in New York in 1798. The young man shortly affiliated with the Methodist Episcopal Church, eventually joining Zion Church soon after its founding. Before long, Rush discerned a call to the ministry. He was licensed to preach in 1815, and eventually was ordained seven years later in 1822. Over the next several decades, Rush would prove himself to be one of the most gifted leaders of the young denomination. He was a tireless advocate for the emancipation and formal citizen status for all African Americans. He was an important member of the Phoenix Society, founded in 1833 to foster the education of African American children and adults through classes, lectures, lending libraries, job centers, and mutual aid funds. He was also quite active in the American and Foreign Antislavery Society as well as the Convention of Colored People of the United States.

Indeed, the AME Zion Church as a whole was very much involved in the Abolitionist Movement. Many of its churches would serve as "stations" on the Underground Railroad, a vast informal network of routes, safe houses, and individuals that assisted fugitive slaves in reaching the relative safety of the North as well as Canada. This commitment to the antislavery struggle was likewise codified in the earliest documents of the denomination. For example, from its inception, the denomination's book of rules, regulations, and rituals known as the *Discipline* stated that no one who owned slaves could be a member of an AME Zion congregation. Further, among persons involved in the life of the AME Zion Church as well as the movement to abolish slavery in the United States, one will find the names of activists such as Sojourner Truth, Frederick Douglass (who was also an AME Zion lay minister), and Harriet Tubman, perhaps the most famous conductor on the Underground Railroad. With such a heritage, the denomination is frequently referred to as "The Freedom Church."

With the retirement of Rush as the General Superintendent of the Church in 1852, a power struggle ensued, resulting in a schism within the church that would eventually be resolved some eight years later, just before the start of the Civil War. Finally, in the period that followed, the postbellum Church experienced significant growth, expanded not only in the South but also in the West. This period would also mark the church's entry into serious mission outreach, leading to its having a noteworthy presence in the Caribbean and eventually Africa. For instance, Andrew Cartwright was the first Zionist missionary in Africa in 1878. In addition, Bishop John Bryan Small was also an early missionary to the continent, eventually heading the church's first Episcopal district there. To date, AME Zion mission churches and schools have been established in Liberia, Ghana, and Nigeria. The church also has a presence in Georgetown, Guyana, as well as several congregations in Canada, the latter due to the church's involvement in the Underground Railroad.

In 1996, the AME Zion Church celebrated its bicentennial, first with a gathering in Washington, D.C., in July of that year, and later in October, in the denomination's birthplace, New York, New York.

Beliefs and Practices

Social justice and democracy for all have been highly regarded within the denomination, to the point of being reflected in its ecclesiology. For example, initially favoring a more democratic structure than their white and black associates of the Methodist Episcopal and African Methodist Episcopal Churches, AME Zionists initially followed an organizational model more akin to the Methodist Protestant Churches, which meant that in lieu of bishops elected for life, they elected "superintendents" for their episcopal overseers with terms of four years. Interestingly, as part of their continuing rivalry, AMEs began to cast aspersions on the efficacy of the superintendents. The Zionists eventually adopted the title of bishop and extended tenure to life. The life tenure would be amended in later years with the institution of compulsory retirement for bishops at age 70.

In the contemporary context, AME Zion bishops collectively provide oversight of the entire Church, while exercising specific individual leadership responsibilities in a geographical area, called an episcopal district. These episcopal districts are composed of one or more annual conferences. Today, there are 12 episcopal districts covering the United States and abroad, ministering to the needs of over 1 million persons.

As the executive unit of the Church, the Board of Bishops exercises its authority by directing the Church's ministry and mission work on five continents. Indeed, it oversees and promotes the activity of the Church in the period between the General Conferences of the Church, which are held every four years. The Board of Bishops convenes twice a year, at such time and place where a majority attendance can be assured.

Another way in which the democratic and egalitarian principles characteristic of the denomination are shown is through the inclusion of laity on most of the high

JULIA A. J. FOOTE (1823–1900)

Julia A. J. Foote was born in 1823 in Schenectady, NY, the daughter of former slaves who had purchased their freedom. Her family moved to Albany, NY, and, it was there that Julia underwent a profound conversion experience and joined a local African Methodist church. After moving to Boston, MA, Julia would begin her affiliation with the African Methodist Episcopal Zion Church. She shortly became a presence in the community, exhorting persons within and without the congregation about the blessings of sanctification. Undeterred by criticism, Julia began to hold religious meetings in her home, open to all whom where interested. Just prior to 1845, Foote would meet with other likeminded women in Philadelphia, where they held a series of religious meetings. In 1851, she experienced throat difficulties and was forced to restrict her evangelistic efforts, settling in Cleveland, OH. She would not return to preaching until sometime in the early 1870's, joining a Holiness revival in the area. Foote eventually reaffiliated with A.M.E. Zion Church, receiving an appointment as a missionary. On May 20, 1894, she became the first woman in the AME Zion Church to be ordained a deacon. Before her death on November 22, 1900, she was ordained an elder in the Church.

councils of the Church. For instance, most of the administrative departments have their own governing board of lay and clergy members. Others are operated simply under the auspices of a supervising bishop. Members of these boards are selected from individuals nominated by annual conferences and other groups. In addition to board members, there are varieties of staff that coordinate and carry out the daily activities of each department. Through the work of these departments, the Church is able to maintain a common vision, mission, and ministry.

As noted in the previous section on the history of the Church, education has

JAMES WALKER HOOD (1831–1918)

James Walker Hood was born on May 30, 1831 in Kennett Township, Chester County, PA. He and his family moved to Wilmington, DE in 1841 where his father worked as a tenant farmer. In 1852, Hood moved to New York City. There he was licensed to preach in 1856, by the African Methodist Episcopal Zion Church. In 1957, he moved to New Haven, CT and joined the AME Zion Church in that city. In 1860, Hood was ordained a deacon and commissioned to do missionary work in Nova Scotia. Hood would return to the United States in 1863, serving on the staff of the church in Bridgeport, CT. In 1864, Hood was ordained an elder in the church, the same year that he moved to North Carolina, where he would spend the rest of his life. In 1872, Hood was elected a bishop in the AME Zion Church. In 1881, Hood was a delegate to the Ecumenical Conference in London. He later served as the president of the conference in 1891 when it convened in Washington, DC. In 1884, Hood published the first collection of sermons by an African American, entitled *The Negro in the Christian Pulpit*. Hood died on October 30, 1918.

traditionally been held in high regard. Thus, it should come as no surprise that one of the most influential administrative departments within the denomination is the Christian Education Department (CED). Founded in 1887, the CED provides supervision, guidance, direction, and programmatic support of the Christian training and development of the entire membership of the denomination. The Christian Education Department supports Christian development in homes, churches, camps, as well as church-related schools, colleges, and seminaries. This is accomplished through workshops, seminars, conferences, and conventions. The CED also establishes curriculum and other standards to support Christian education programs throughout the Church.

The department consists of two divisions: the Home and Church Division, and the School and College Division. The Home and Church Division includes Varick's Children, Youth Ministries, Young Adult Ministries, Adult Ministries, and Church School Literature. The School and College Division oversees the activities of the various institutions of higher education associated with the Church. These institutions include Livingstone College (Salisbury, North Carolina), Hood Theological Seminary (Salisbury, North Carolina), Clinton Junior College (Rock Hill, South Carolina), Lomax Hannon Junior College (Greenville, Alabama), A.M.E. Zion University (Monrovia, Liberia), and Hood Speaks Theological Seminary (Akwa Ibom State, Nigeria).

Another significant legacy of the Church has been the involvement of women in its growth and development. Indeed, the African Methodist Episcopal Zion Church was the first of the historically black churches to ordain women to full ministry. Beginning in 1891 at the second Ecumenical Conference, Bishop James Walker Hood defended the right of women to be elected delegates to the general conference of the denomination. At the 73rd Session of the New York Annual Conference held at the Catharine Street AME Zion Church in Poughkeepsie on May 20, 1894, Bishop Hood ordained Julia A. J. Foote as a deacon. On May 19, 1895 Mary J. Small, the wife of Bishop John Bryan Small, was ordained a deacon by Bishop Alexander Walters at the 67th Session of the Philadelphia and Baltimore Conference. In 1898, she became the first woman in Methodism to be ordained an elder by Bishop Charles Calvin Pettey at the Philadelphia and Baltimore Conference. Two years latter in 1900, upon transferring to the New Jersey conference of the Church, Foote was ordained an elder by Bishop Alexander Walters. Of the African American Methodist denominations, the AME Zion Church has continued to have the highest approval rate for women as pastors. Despite this early progressivism, however, they have yet to ordain a female bishop, an event that has taken place within the AME Church and the predominantly white United Methodist Church.

Another indication of the importance of women in the Church can be seen in the existence of the Women's Home and Overseas Missionary Society. Though not officially coordinated as a national organization until 1880, there were local and regional women's organizations in the African Methodist Episcopal Zion Church that antedate it. Among the early leaders of this body, one finds the names of Mary Jane Talbert Jones, Meriah G. Harris, and Annie Walker Blackwell. The purpose of the Women's Home and Overseas Missionary Society of the African Methodist

Episcopal Zion Church is to promote growth in the knowledge and understanding of God and the gospel as revealed through Jesus Christ; to teach the concepts of Christian missions and provide opportunities for participation in the work of mission and ministry; to live a life exemplifying and testifying to the power of Christ; and to support evangelism at home and abroad, through one's charitable gifts of money, time, and talents.

Finally, among the historically black churches, the AME Zionists are distinguished for their commitment to ecumenism, namely the promotion of unity and cooperation between various Christian groups or denominations. Their first serious ecumenical effort was during the Civil War in 1864 when the AME and AME Zion Churches almost reached an agreement that would bring the two denominations into one union. The efforts failed due to the failure of AME conferences to ratify the measure. In subsequent years, the AME Zion Church has engaged in discussions with the Christian Methodist Episcopal Church (formerly the Colored Methodist Episcopal Church—the third major historically black expression of Methodism in the United States) as well as with white Methodist communions. The AME Zion Church has also been involved with the National Council of Churches of Christ in the USA and the World Council of Churches.

Torin Alexander

SELECTED BIBLIOGRAPHY

Baldwin, Lewis V. *"Invisible" Strands in African Methodism: A History of the African Union Methodist Protestant and Union American Methodist Episcopal Churches, 1805–1980* (Metuchen, NJ: Scarecrow Press, 1983).

Bradley, David Henry, Sr. *A History of A.M.E. Zion Church*, 2 vols. (Nashville, TN: Parthenon Press, 1971).

Johnson, Dorothy Sharpe, and Lula Goolsby Williams. *Pioneering Women of the African Methodist Episcopal Zion Church* (Charlotte, NC: AME Zion Publishing House, 1996).

Martin, Sandy Dwayne. *For God and Race: The Religious and Political Leadership of AMEZ Bishop James Walker Hood* (Columbia: University of South Carolina Press, 1999).

McClain, William B. *Black People in the Methodist Church: Whither Thou Goest?* (Cambridge, MA: Shenkman Publishing Co., 1984).

Richardson, Harry V. *Dark Salvation: The Story of Methodism as It Developed Among Blacks in America* (Garden City, NY: Anchor Press, 1976).

Walls, William J. *The African Methodist Episcopal Zion Church: Reality of the Black Church* (Charlotte, NC: AME Zion Publishing House, 1974).

AFRICAN ORTHODOX CHURCH

Historical Development

The African Orthodox church is a Christian denomination in the Episcopal tradition, which was founded in 1919 in Chicago, Illinois, amidst the Pan-African Movement. Chicago at that time had become a place in the Midwest where thoughts and ideas of African unity flourished as many Africans in America attempted to understand themselves better. During this time the African Orthodox Church was competing with the growing movement of Black Muslim and Judaic groups that began to spring

GEORGE ALEXANDER MCGUIRE (1866–1934)

George Alexander McGuire was born March 26, 1866 in Sweets, Antigua. Records are not clear as to McGuire's parents, but it is known that he was a part of the Anglican church at an early age. He was formally trained at Moravian's Nisky Theological Seminary on the Island of Saint Thomas and became involved with the African Methodist Episcopal Church. Around the turn of the century, in 1894, McGuire made his way to the United States. In 1913 McGuire went back to Antigua for a few years feeling spiritually spent by his work in the United States. Five years later McGuire returned to the United States to continue his work in the Episcopal Church. In 1918 he became the Chaplain for Marcus Garvey's organization the UNIA. In 1921 McGuire was consecrated a bishop by Archbishop Vilatte and Bishop Nybladh. After his consecration he remained active in the UNIA until Garvey relocated to the Caribbean in 1924. The next year McGuire relocated to Florida and began expanding his Church internationally to South Africa, Venezula and his home island Antigua just to name a few. McGuire died in 1934.

up in the region as well as on the east coast of the United States. However, this tradition like the others was focused on the ideologies of Pan-Africanism and Black Nationalism as a cultural and political point of departure for all believers. Furthermore, like many of the religious groups, which sprang up during this time, the African Orthodox Church experienced periods of intense growth because of the migrating population of African Americans in the United States.

In particular, the African Orthodox Church is an Episcopalian congregation that felt it necessary to form its own church in order to meet the spiritual and communal needs of the Black population. This religious body was founded by George Alexander McGuire with other Black Episcopalians who wanted a home for worship that would speak to their needs. McGuire was consecrated bishop of the church on September 28, 1921, in Chicago, Illinois, by Episcopal Archbishop Joseph Rene Vilatte and

assisted by Bishop Carl A. Nybladh who had also been consecrated by Vilatte. At first the new denomination was called the Independent Episcopal Church to quite literally signify the church's independence from the White Episcopal tradition. However, this moniker was changed in 1924 to the African Orthodox Church to identify the church's ideological connection to Pan-African and Black Nationalist thought.

It is important to note that the Pan-African/Black Nationalist thought of McGuire did not just come about because it was the popular ideology of the times; the Archbishop himself was a member and the chaplain of the Universal Negro Improvement Association (UNIA), which was a nonreligious Pan-African organization founded by Marcus Mosiah Garvey in Harlem, New York. McGuire left this organization in 1924 only because Garvey decided to relocate the national headquarters of the organization from Harlem to the Caribbean. Unwilling to leave the congregation placed in his

DANIEL WILLIAM ALEXANDER (1882–1970)

Daniel William Alexander was born in South Africa, December 23, 1882. Early in his life Alexander was baptized in the Anglican Church of the Province of South Africa. Alexander became aware of the efforts of the African Orthodox Church through the UNIA's publication the *Negro World*. Not only was he exposed to the ideas and mission of the church through the periodical, more importantly he was exposed to the ideology of Pan-Africanism. These efforts on the part of Alexander attracted the attention of the South African government. The government had files on all Black or "Native" churches because they were not under direct European supervision and control. Alexander made his way to the United States in 1927 where he met with McGuire to be consecrated as a bishop of the African Orthodox Church in South Africa. After this, Alexander returned to South Africa to begin forming African Orthodox Churches. Furthermore, he made efforts to form congregations in Uganda, Kenya, and Rhodesia (now the Democratic Republic of Congo). In 1970 Alexander passed away.

care, he left the UNIA and began to concentrate on the growth and progression of his church.

Early in the history of the church much of the congregation was composed of Anglican Caribbean immigrants. This may be due to the connection between the African Orthodox Church and the UNIA, which was led by a Jamaican who also came from the Anglican Church. In 1925 the church began to spread to the southern United States, before they began having religious aspirations oversees. In 1927 Daniel William Alexander of the South African Anglican Church appealed to McGuire to be consecrated into the African Orthodox Church so that he may bring the teachings of the people of South Africa.

By the time of McGuire's death in 1934, his church had grown to over 30,000 members and had extensive international influence in the Caribbean and on the continent of Africa. The African Orthodox Church maintained organizational and ideological solidarity through the 1950s and 1960s. Further, the church has continued its efforts in reaching

Africans throughout the world. They continue to consecrate their own bishops and even lift certain individuals such as John Coltrane to the rank of sainthood, which demonstrates a continuously evolving and dynamic religious ideology, allowing members of congregations to grow spiritually as well as culturally.

Beliefs and Practices

The African Orthodox Church came to fruition during a very ideologically rich period in African American history. Like many religious and cultural groups of the time period the ideology of Marcus Garvey made up the material used as the foundation for theological structure. Particularly, Garvey's ideology of Pan-Africanism influenced the Church not only in their naming but more importantly in influencing their posture toward Africans from diverse regions of the globe. This is what inevitably led Alexander to McGuire in his attempt to address the spiritual and cultural needs of his people in South Africa. The organization teaches cultural pride and progress as well as endeavors to demonstrate the spiritual and cultural strength of African people.

The African Orthodox Church of South Africa took a similar posture because it was dealing with racial oppression. However, since this church was on the African continent, it had a different orientation with respect to the cultural practices of the people in the church. For instance, it was very important that the church be grounded in African philosophy, mythology, customs, and mores. However, despite this concern for culture, the African Orthodox Church was considered a reform church. Whereas some churches in South Africa were radical, meaning they held an anti-European militant posture toward the European colonizers and culture, a reform church, despite the connection to the African culture of the region, wanted to maintain European doctrinal and liturgical forms. This posture was a move away from McGuire's perspective in that he pushed a more radical approach to Christianity.

In practice, the African Orthodox Church in the United States as well as in South Africa and the Caribbean maintains a threefold ministry of deacons, priest, and bishops who emphasize apostolic succession of power. The church also observes the seven sacraments just as the Roman Catholic Church, and its worship style is liturgical and infuses elements of Eastern and Western rites of Orthodoxy. In this respect, the African Orthodox Church, while appealing to African culture mores and nuances, maintains its Episcopal identity through its beliefs and practices. However, it must be acknowledged that appeal to African culture makes all the difference for the congregation of the church. It is in this space that African people can worship in the fashion they desire while maintaining some semblance of cultural integrity.

Paul Easterling

SELECTED BIBLIOGRAPHY

Johnson, Morris R. *Archbishop Daniel William Alexander and the African Orthodox Church* (San Francisco: International Scholars Publications, 1999).

Terry-Thompson, Reverend A. C. *The History of the African Orthodox Church* (New York: Beacon Press, 1956).

JOHN COLTRANE (1926–1967)

Jazz saxophonist John William Coltrane received Sainthood from a San Francisco congregation of the African Orthodox Church. The sainthood of Coltrane was inspired by Archbishop Franzo King and his wife Mother Marina King who claimed to have felt the presence of God in Coltrane's art during a concert in 1965. The couple claimed to have received a "sounds" baptism when they heard Coltrane's song "The Love Supreme." For them Coltrane had the ability to wins souls for God through his music. Further, Coltrane felt that his gift was to be used for that central purpose. It was not enough to be understood as a jazz musician because his music could speak to hearts and minds. The name of the African Orthodox congregation that raised Coltrane to the position of saint is St. John Will-I-Am Coltrane Church of San Francisco, and it is still lead by Archbishop King.

AMERICAN MUSLIM MISSION

Historical Development

After his father's death from congestive heart failure on February 23, 1975 and his own elevation to the leadership of the Nation of Islam as Supreme Minister at the Savior's Day convention on February 26, 1975, Wallace Delaney Muhammad (Warith Deen Mohammad) began making plans to radically change the Nation of Islam and move it toward orthodox Sunni Islam. On March 7 he announced that members of the Nation would no longer refer to whites as "devils" because they have been treating blacks more fairly but they would not be allowed to join the Nation. But on June 18 at a meeting at McCormick Place in Chicago, he announced that "There will be no such category as a white Muslim or a black Muslim. All will be Muslims. All children of God" (*Nashville Tennessean*, 1975). This announcement sent shock waves through the audience and the national membership of the Nation because whites could now join their movement. Dorothy Dorsey became the first white person to join Wallace's new direction. We turn to a brief biographical sketch of Wallace Muhammad's background before analyzing the changes and schism in the Nation of Islam movement.

On October 30, 1933, Wallace Delaney Muhammad was born to Elijah and Clara Muhammad in a poor ghetto called Paradise Valley in Detroit, Michigan. He was the seventh child of eight children that Elijah originally had with Clara. Since Elijah Muhammad was deeply immersed in the activities of the new Nation of Islam, having joined in 1931,

he and Clara decided to name their new son after Master Wallace (Wali) Dodd Fard (Farrad) Muhammad, the founder of the new religious movement. The initials of "WDM," which appeared on the uniform lapels of male members, referred to Fard Muhammad but they were also the same as Wallace Delaney Muhammad's. This act of being named after Master Fard grew into a legend in the Nation with many stories developing around it. The legend was that Wallace Delaney Muhammad was "special" because he was named after Master Wallace Fard, Allah in person, and was also a son of the Messenger Elijah Muhammad. He was thus specially ordained for leadership from his birth. Immersed in the intense milieu of the Nation, Wallace Muhammad eventually believed in the legend that he was somehow special, and he has made reference to it in countless speeches. For example, he said:

> My father told me once, "son you're different." He didn't tell me this once, he told me this more than once and there are those who heard him say this to me. He said "Son you are different." He said "You are different because when you were formed, I was devoted to the teachings of Islam and I was new in it." Elijah also told Wallace: "When you were born son, what was in me went straight into you." (Mamiya and Lincoln 1992)

Wallace grew up in poverty on the South Side of Chicago after the Muhammad family fled there from Detroit to avoid the violent conflicts of succession after Master Fard disappeared in 1934. Since his father spent some time in the Washington, D.C. area, living alone, constantly moving, and using aliases to avoid being killed by his enemies (1935–1942) and later was incarcerated for failure to register for the military draft (1942–1946), Wallace was largely raised by his mother, Clara Muhammad, and became deeply devoted to her. That devotion was reciprocal because Clara also sought to protect Wallace from harm by Muslim "zealots," after Malcolm X's assassination. In a tribute to his mother's influence, Wallace changed the name of the University of Islam schools to the Clara Muhammad Schools in the masjids of the American Muslim Mission.

Wallace Muhammad in 1979. (Bettmann/ Corbis)

All of Wallace's education in elementary and secondary schools occurred at the University of Islam in Chicago. He developed a keen interest in science, psychology, and religion. He also attended Wilson Junior College, where he studied microbiology, and Loop Junior College, where he studied English, History, and the Social Sciences. However, he did not go further to complete a Bachelor's degree. Instead, like many black men his age, he began to develop his skills in the trades of carpentry, masonry, and plumbing, which became the main way he supported his family. Throughout his educational years and his work life, Wallace Muhammad was very active in the Nation of Islam. He moved through the ranks from the Fruit of Islam to assistant minister of Temple No. 2 in Chicago and for a while his father appointed him as the Minister of the Temple No. 12 in Philadelphia.

Wallace, like his younger brother Akbar, began to have doubts about the teachings and doctrines of the Nation of Islam. On his own, he began to read and study about orthodox Sunni Islam. His brother Akbar was fortunate to be chosen by Minister Malcolm X to receive a scholarship in 1963 to study at the University of Al-Azhar in Egypt along with another African American Muslim named Ahmad Khalid Tawfiq, whom Malcolm called the "little Samurai" because of his small stature and outstanding skills in the martial arts. Akbar eventually became a scholar and professor of Islamic Studies at SUNY Binghamton, and Tawfiq was the founder of the Mosque of Islamic Brotherhood in Harlem. As mentioned before, Wallace was incarcerated from October 1961 to January 1963 in a federal prison for failure to register for the military draft during the Vietnam era. Instead of being depressed Wallace reveled in the freedom from the responsibilities of running a Nation's temple so that he could spend all of this time studying about orthodox Islam, including learning some Arabic and reading the Qur'an daily.

When he returned from prison, he began to teach some of the things he had learned. Elijah Muhammad suspended Wallace in 1964 for the first of three times for teaching things contrary to the Nation and also for providing confirmation to Malcolm X about Elijah's paternity of other children with his secretaries. After Malcolm's assassination, Wallace quickly made amends with his father and apologized to the membership of the

Nation for his errant ways. He was afraid that the zealots who killed Malcolm would also be after him. However, in the ensuing years, he began to express his doubts publicly that Master Fard was Allah. He was suspended two more times, and returned each time to apologize. The fact that Wallace was once again back in the fold of the Nation in 1975 when his father died made it easier for Elijah's close advisers to choose him to become the next leader, the Supreme Minister of the Nation of Islam. Keeping the leadership of the Nation within the family contributed to the development of the concept of "the royal family," referring to blood ties to Elijah Muhammad.

Wallace has always been a humble person, never seeking the limelight. He also had a deep interest in spirituality. As Malcolm X once said of him, "I felt that Wallace was Mr. Muhammad's most strongly spiritual son, the son with the most objective outlook. Always, Wallace and I had shared an exceptional closeness and trust" (Malcolm X and Haley 1999, 303). He was not a great public speaker or charismatic personality the way Louis Farrakhan was. In fact, a *Playboy Magazine* article once said that Wallace had the charisma of "a post office clerk" (Gans and Lowe 1980). However, what the *Playboy* authors missed was the "spiritual charisma" that he possessed. This spiritual charisma enabled his followers to trust him and his teachings. In his appreciation for the teaching and leadership of Malcolm X, Wallace renamed Temple No. 7 in Harlem as the Malcolm Shabazz Masjid and he had Minister Louis Farrakhan lead the renaming ceremony in 1976.

In his personal life, Imam Muhammad has been married four times, has eight children from those marriages, and has ten grandchildren. He has shunned the ostentatious lifestyle that his father had. For example, he never moved into the "Palace," the large, luxurious quarters with an indoor courtyard area and marble floors that Elijah Muhammad had built for himself and two other similar houses for relatives in Chicago's Hyde Park district. Instead he sold the Palace buildings to Louis Farrakhan, who has resided there since. He also does not use the fancy limousines that Farrakhan prefers. Muhammad resides in a modest middle class house in a suburb of Chicago. He has never strayed far from his working class background. However, some practices from the Nation of Islam still affect him. Whenever he travels to give lectures or attend conferences, a security detail consisting of his chief aides, the local Imam, and Muslims from his movement quickly forms to provide transportation and protection for him. He also holds meetings with Imams and other followers before or after his speeches. Both his humbleness and his spiritual charisma have generated a loyal devotion and respect for his leadership. As some of his followers have written:

> African-Americans do not revere or worship the Imam as the whispers suggest: we follow the late Prophet of G-d. Our Imam points us to him and to the Quran with everything he does and says, he is so respectful of the common person that it would certainly be insulting and sinful not to return that respect. (Islamic History Group Project 2006, 123)

In order to move the Nation in the direction of Islamic universalism, Wallace Muhammad began by reinterpreting its basic racial doctrine in a symbolic manner. Following Malcolm X's lead, he put emphasis upon the attitudes, values, and behavior of a person, upon "mindedness," how a person thought. After his experience of the Hajj, Malcolm said:

> We were all the same (brothers)—because their belief in one God had removed the "white" from their minds, the "white" from their behavior, and the "white" from their attitude. (Malcolm X and Haley 1999, 347)

The new direction was formulated in the key phrase, "Man Means Mind." For Wallace, the devil is a "mind," an attitude. A person who is born white is not ipso facto evil or the Devil. Whiteness is a symbol of evil only when it is linked to the attitudes and values that characterize white supremacy and racism. Blackness, on the other hand, is a symbol for goodness and humaneness. Just as it is possible to have a black person with a white mind, i.e., one who acts and thinks white—the proverbial "oreo" or "Uncle Tom"—it is also possible to have a white person who thinks black—a "reverse oreo." This view opened the possibility of accepting white members. "Man Means Mind" also shifted the great significance that members of the Nation put on skin color since knowledge of self often meant emphasizing blackness and black nationalism. The new slogan meant to stress the character and thought of a person. It opened up levels of differentiation between people. Race and skin color were not the primary factors. In making the transition to Sunni Islam, editions of *Muhammad Speaks* showed a photo of Wallace Muhammad pointing to his head. Ministers of the Nation were instructed to preach and teach on the new theme of "Man Means Mind" (*Muhammad Speaks*, March and April 1975 editions; also Islamic History Group Project 2006, 148).

Besides opening the Nation to a path of Islamic universalism, one of his first tasks was to deal with the situation of Minister Louis Farrakhan, who had been chosen as National Representative by Elijah Muhammad to replace Malcolm X in 1965. As the second in command, Farrakhan had expected to be chosen as Elijah's successor. Popular and charismatic, Farrakhan had established a power base in Harlem as the minister of Temple No. 7. Wallace invited Farrakhan to join him in Chicago in order to monitor and control Farrakhan's actions. He also sent Minister Jeremiah Shabazz (Jeremiah X Pugh) from Philadelphia to become the interim minister of No. 7. Shabazz had a notorious reputation within the Nation as one of their tough strong-armed enforcers. Coming from the streets, Shabazz disdainfully referred to him as "pretty boy," instead of using Farrakhan's stage name, "The Charmer." Jeremiah Shabazz's presence at No. 7 was to make sure that Farrakhan left peacefully (Interview with Alfred Mohammed, June 15, 1994). Although he was still confused by the turn of events, Minister Farrakhan accepted Wallace Muhammad's invitation to move to Chicago.

The ultimate goal for Wallace's program of reconstruction and restructuring the Nation was to eradicate its black nationalist image completely. He has used allegory and symbolic reinterpretation of some basic doctrines and beliefs to reeducate his followers and has quietly dropped others. Ever since his prison years from 1960 to 1963 for refusing to register for the military draft, Wallace has had a great vision and desire for complete Islamic orthodoxy for

WARITH DEEN MOHAMMAD (1933–2008)

The son of the Honorable Elijah Muhammad, born Wallace, Warith Deen Mohammad (Wallace Delaney Muhammad) grew up holding various positions within the Nation of Islam. He served as a member of the Fruit of Islam (security force) and would also lead a mosque. However, his relationship to his father and the Nation was tense at times, and at one point he left the organization. It came as a surprise to many when he was appointed head of the organization after his father's death. Under his leadership the Nation of Islam was pushed in the direction of Sunni Islam and some of the more "un-orthodox" elements of its teachings and aesthetic were removed. Warith Deen Mohammad changed the name of the organization, eventually naming it the American Muslim Mission in 1978. He resigned leadership of the organization that same year, and in 1980 officially changed his name to Warith Deen Mohammad. Further pushing the organization toward the world community of Islam, Warith Deen Mohammad dismantled its national structure in 1985. His stature in the Islamic world has continued to grow over the years and has increased his profile in the United States. For example, he was the first Muslim to give the invocation at the U.S. Senate.

the Nation. He has said that his three years in prison were a fruitful time in his spiritual life because he could study the Qur'an, learn some Arabic, and not be bothered by the constant and daily burdens of running the Philadelphia Temple. Wallace has felt that some of his father's ideas had stifled the spiritual and moral growth of his people (Mamiya and Lincoln 1992). The task of reeducating and reconverting the members of the Nation of Islam to Sunni orthodoxy (or the "Second Resurrection" referred to by members of his movement) has been an enormous one, fraught with dangers given the past killings of members who defected such as Malcolm X. The difficulties of this change in direction cannot be underestimated.

Wallace taught about the unity of Allah and that Allah was not a man like Master Fard. He debunked the view that his father, Elijah Muhammad, was the Messenger of Allah. Both Fard and Elijah were men like other men. He pointed to Muhammad ibn Abdullah of Arabia as the final prophet of Allah. He directed his followers to study the Qur'an and the Sunna, as well as Islamic history. The meeting times of his movement also changed from Sunday afternoons, Wednesday evenings, and Friday evenings to the Friday noon Jum'ah prayer service and Sunday instructional classes on the Qur'an, Arabic, and Islamic history.

The changes were unsettling and caused a great deal of confusion and debate. Talmadge X Hayer (now Mujahid Halim), who was imprisoned for the assassination of Malcolm X, said the following about Wallace's attempts to change things:

He (Wallace) began to explain to us that his father was only a man like any other man. He said something to the effect that the Hon. Elijah Muhammad did father some children. And hey, man, this was heavy. I was a ball of clay that was rolled up—had to be put together again, man. Just broke down my whole concepts of things. It was like a birth coming about, a baby coming into the world—he's just got to come in man. (Goldman 1979, 427)

Khalil Islam (Thomas 15X Johnson), who was wrongly imprisoned for Malcolm's murder, said in his prison interview that he too had great difficulty coming to terms with the Elijah affair but that he finally accepted what Wallace said and chose to follow his leadership (Mamiya 1985).

In his major reorganization of the movement, Wallace Muhammad, who in the transition years (1975 to 1978) changed his titles from Supreme Minister to Chief Minister then to Chief Imam and finally to his current name Imam Warith Deen (Warith ud-Din—inheritor of the faith) Mohammad (adopting the British spelling instead of the Arabic in order to distance himself from his father), completely dismantled the Fruit of Islam (F.O.I.) and its female counterpart the MGT (Muslim Girls in Training). Trained in martial arts and sometimes in the use of firearms, the Fruit was created by Master Fard Muhammad to act as the "moral right arm" of the Nation of Islam. They provided security, searched everyone who entered a mosque or major meeting, acted as ushers, and sometimes acted as enforcers of the strict code of discipline. The Fruit of Islam had become an "elite organization" within an organization, or a paramilitary group. Raymond Sharrieff, Elijah Muhammad's brother-in-law, was the Supreme Captain of the F.O.I. Wallace claimed that this group had become a "political order," a "hooligan outfit, a hoodlum outfit." Men were "viciously beaten," he said in an interview with Peter Goldman, "simply for asserting their rights or for failing to sell their quota of newspapers." He was shocked to learn upon assuming leadership that more than ten believers were killed, "for no other reason than that they didn't want the F.O.I.

completely dominating their lives" (Goldman 1979, 433). If any group within the internal structure of the Nation would provide organized opposition to Wallace's ideas it was the Fruit; thus, along with its female counterpart, the MGT, it became the reason for dissolving them.

Besides the killings, Imam Mohammed also discovered that some of the Nation's ministers, especially those in Philadelphia, Newark, and Los Angeles, had used their temples as a cover to hide drug dealing and other criminal activity. Even Malcolm X had to suspend some members from Temple No. 7 for using drugs. Moreover, many of the Nation's business enterprises, restaurants, grocery stores, and bakeries, either were bankrupt or had accumulated too much debt. In response, the Imam ordered the closing of these enterprises.

Beliefs and Practices

In 1976 Wallace Muhammad changed the name of the Nation of Islam to the "World Community of Al-Islam in the West." His followers also gave him the title "Mujeddid" or reviver of Islam. Like many newcomers to the religion, he and his followers insisted on referring to "Al-Islam," including the Arabic article "al," instead of just Islam. For example, the largest mosque in Imam Mohammed's movement with some 3,000 members is called the Atlanta Masjid of Al-Islam. Besides changing the name of the Nation, he also introduced the name "Bilal" and made the term "Bilalian" the official replacement for other terms (Afro-American, Black, Negro, Colored, etc.) referring to all black people, believers and nonbelievers alike. Bilal Ibn Rabah, a tall, gaunt

Ethiopian, who had been brought to Arabia as a slave, became the first "muezzin" or caller to prayer in the Prophet Muhammad's earliest Muslim community in Medina. Bilal had been ransomed and given his freedom by one of the Prophet's companions, Abu Bakr. His strong melodic voice established the pattern of calling the faithful to prayer five times daily from the tops of minarets throughout Islamic history. The melodic chant in Arabic replaced earlier experiments in the fledgling Medina community that had used the wooden clapper of Christians or the ram's horn of Jews to call people to worship. The significance and prominence of an African in the first Muslim community has not been lost by Imam Mohammed. Bilal is not only an important black hero but he is also relevant to the quest for identity among Bilalian people in America.

Even the name of the Nation's newspaper changed its name from *Muhammad Speaks* to *Bilalian News* in 1976. The use of Bilal and Bilalian fits into a long historical tradition of "Ethiopianism" in black religion. As St. Clair Drake has argued in his perceptive monograph, *The Redemption of Africa and Black Religion*, the theme and myth of Ethiopianism has persisted from slavery to the present. Ethiopia has symbolically stood for all of Africa. The selection of Bilal, the Ethiopian slave, by Imam Mohammed's movement has struck deep chords of resonance in black religious and social history.

In 1977 all Bilalians were instructed to drop the remnants of their Christian names that had been used in the Nation of Islam and to take on Islamic names (Islamic History Group Project 2006, 154). Thus Wallace Delaney became "Warith ud-Din" or "Warith Deen."

Between 1978 and 1980, Warith Deen Mohammad's movement changed its name from the "World Community of Al-Islam in the West" to the "American Muslim Mission." The abrupt name change and internal organizational confusion led some key followers like Siraj Wahaj to leave the movement and to found his own independent masjid, Masjid Taqwa, in Brooklyn.

The first decade from 1975 to 1985 was spent making the changes from the Nation of Islam to Sunni orthodoxy and stabilizing the movement. Since so much of the movement revolved around Imam Warith Deen Mohammad, he formed a Council of Imams in 1978 to help him guide the movement and direct its activities. In 1980 the name of World Community of Al Islam in the West was officially changed to the American Muslim Mission. The movement's newspaper also changed its name several times from the *Bilalian News* to *World Muslim News* in 1982 to the *American Muslim Journal* and finally to the *Muslim Journal* in 1985. Two events stand out in this period: the first was the cooperative buying program (AMMCOP) and the second, the American Muslim Mission's drive to remove/destroy all images of God by the Committee to Remove All Images of the Divine (C.R.A.I.D.). The Council of Imams endorsed a cooperative buying program, i.e., buying in bulk as a path to economic development in black communities. For example, buying washing machines or refrigerators in bulk would lessen their costs to the buyers. C.R.A.I.D. activities were carried out by Muslim groups within their communities. Their attempts to convince black churches and clergy to remove pictures of Jesus depicting him as the son of God were not successful.

However, C.R.A.I.D.'s major point was to show the oneness of God in the monotheistic traditions of Islam, Judaism, and Christianity. The American Muslim Mission also acquired properties in Sedalia, North Carolina, to establish a teacher's college and high school and 4,600 acres in Terell County, Georgia, to establish Elijahville, a future Muslim city. However, both enterprises failed due to the lack of finances.

The mid-1980s were also a period of protracted and drawn out legal struggles between the American Muslim Mission and the probate court of Chicago that was acting on behalf of the children that Elijah Muhammad had with his secretaries. Their suit targeted the Muhammad Mosque's No. 2 Poor Fund, which the court contended was Elijah Muhammad's personal funds but the Mission argued that the funds belonged to the Muslim community, contributed by local mosques. Judge Henry Budzinski also sought to have 56 Muslim properties attached to Elijah Muhammad's estate. In 1987 Budzinski leveled a $12 million judgment against the Muslim community (Islamic History Project Group 2006, 167–171). As a result of these legal struggles and in an effort to prevent future suits, Imam Mohammed disbanded the American Muslim Mission in 1985, declaring that it was no longer an organized movement but that each imam and mosque were now on their own. He said to his followers: "You should put down the term [American Muslims] and never pick up any term again that lumps you all together in one community. You should be members of a Muslim community that's international" ("The Final Call," March 30, 1994; March 2000, 124). On December 7,

1986, he formally resigned as the Imam of Masjid Elijah Muhammad saying,

> My concern is that we don't allow our lives to be limited by organization . . . . I want reality to come to this masjid . . . . We don't need all of the facilities and attention that we are asking for . . . . My purpose is to free myself so that I will be able to propagate, teach, and demonstrate in my life the excellence of the Muslim life. (Marsh 2000, 172)

Although the American Muslim Mission was formally disbanded, the movement continued informally and acquired a 64 acre farm in Hattiesburg, Mississippi, which was called "New Medina." This farm has been used for youth conferences and Muslim retreats. New Medina still exists and is the longest lasting of the rural properties acquired by the movement. With funds and land donated by the former boxer Muhammad Ali, Masjid Al-Faatir opened in Chicago in 1987, led by Imam Mohammed's brother, Jabber (Herbert) Muhammad who had been Ali's boxing manager. In the late 1990s a conflict arose in Masjid Al-Faatir, and Jabber's son Omar with his support group of immigrant Muslims took over the leadership of the Masjid, ousting Jabber. In 1988 Imam Mohammed's movement was forced into bankruptcy by the probate court. Mohammed also decided to sell the building and land of the headquarters Temple No. 2, the former Greek Orthodox church building, which Elijah Muhammad purchased after he received a $3 million gift from Muammar Qaddafi, negotiated by heavyweight champ Muhammad Ali, in 1972. After his father's death, Imam Mohammed renamed the building Masjid Honorable

Elijah Muhammad. The Imam agreed to sell the property to Minister Louis Farrakhan's revived Nation of Islam. Farrakhan had obtained a $5 million interest-free loan from Libyan President Muammar Qaddafi for the purchase. He renamed the building Mosque Maryam in honor of the Mother of Jesus in 1988.

Another thrust of Imam Mohammed's program that began in the mid-1980s and lasted into the 1990s was his desire to establish an American-based Islamic school of law or "madh'hab." Throughout Islamic history there have been four Sunni orthodox schools of law established: Hanafi, Maliki, Shafi'I, and Hanbali. The schools are geographically distributed throughout the Muslim world and reflect different methodologies used by jurists in their interpretations of the sources of law. According to Imam Mohammed, every significant Islamic culture has produced a school of law. Thus, given its superpower status in the world, the Islamic community in the United States, immigrant and African American Muslims, should also produce an important school of law. He also emphasized the need to include immigrant Muslims in this endeavor. "If they [immigrant Muslims] share that interest in their life on this continent with us, I think we would have a much better school of thought developing with their participation. It can't be without their participation, it won't be good without their participation" (Mamiya and Lincoln 1992). Although Imam Mohammed has not completely given up his endeavor to establish an American school of Islamic law, he has not emphasized it beyond the mid-1990s.

By breaking the racial barriers in 1975 in allowing whites to join his movement, Imam Mohammed has also moved into interfaith dialogue with Christians and Jews. He and some of his Imams have participated in the Muslim/Christian conferences held at the predominantly African American Protestant Interdenominational Theological Center in Atlanta, for example. Imam Mohammed gave Islamic prayers at President Bill Clinton's two Inaugural Interfaith Prayer Services. He also addressed the Muslim-Jewish Conference on March 6, 1995, with leaders of Islam and Reform Judaism in Glencoe, Illinois. He met with Pope John Paul II twice in 1996 and 1999. However, his most serious foray in the interfaith area occurred in 1997, one year after he led a delegation to the Vatican and had a personal audience with Pope John Paul II. On May 18, 1997, a historic meeting was held at the Malcolm Shabazz Masjid in Harlem between Imam Mohammed and Chiara Lubich, President of the Focolare Movement, an outreach organization consisting of lay Catholics. Started by Ms. Lubich in Trent, Italy, in 1943, the movement took the name "Focolare," which means "hearth" or "family fireside." Its major goal is the "spirituality of unity," bringing together all forms of Christianity and other religions in interfaith dialogue. Since 1997 members of both movements have met either at the Malcolm Shabazz Masjid in Harlem or at the Mariapolis Luminosa center in Hyde Park, New York. The Focolare Movement presented Imam Mohammed with the "Luminosa Award" in 1997 for promoting Interfaith Dialogue, peace, and understanding in the United States. In April 2005, Imam Mohammed sent a delegation of Imams to Muslims-Christians in Dialogue, First Symposium sponsored by the Focolare Movement.

Imam Izek Pasha of the Malcolm Shabazz Masjid in Harlem has led the way for masjids in the Mosque Cares Ministry movement in pioneering economic development projects, including mixed income housing in the neighborhood of the masjid. Imam Pasha has been able to get city, state, and federal housing grants to develop a building with 246 mixed income apartments diagonally across from the masjid on Malcolm X Boulevard and 116th Street and 20 town houses on 117th Street. A tower of luxury apartments with space allotted for the Clara Muhammad School has been built next door to the masjid. Malcolm Shabazz also helps with the development of small businesses in the area, including an African marketplace for African immigrant entrepreneurs. Pasha has been consulting with other masjids in the Mosque Cares Ministry movement to develop housing in Atlanta and a shopping mall in suburban Chicago.

Since 1975, Imam Mohammed's movement has changed its name a number of times from the "World Community of Al-Islam in the West" (1976 to 1980) to the "American Muslim Mission" (1980 to 1986) to the "Muslim American Society" (in the 1990s) to "American Society of Muslims" (ASM; 1996 to 2003). The movement has also been disbanded several times, most recently in 2003. As the members of the Islamic History Project Group have written, "The American Society of Muslims was 'thunderstruck' at its Islamic Convention in September 2003 when Imam W. Deen Mohammed resigned as leader of the organization" Islamic History Project Group 2006, 200). He bluntly stated that he did not believe that he had the majority support of the Imams of the community and would not preside over a set of affairs that "did not genuinely heed his advice and counsel." In an interview with Nathaniel Omar, Imam Mohammed said:

(1) Many ASM imams have not given me (as their leader) their open and full support. They have a separate agenda. (2) Imams supporting me, if staying with the ASM, should want it to be better and I will be happy to see that. (3) They (Imams with separate agendas) will not support Muslim Journal because it brings my message to them. So the good leaders in the American Society of Muslims should really take up the slack and do for their members what these leaders won't do, who won't let people be free for G-d. (Islamic History Project Group 2006, 202)

At a conference in Newark on December 21, 2003, Imam Mustafa El-Amin received Imam Mohammed's blessings to attempt to hold the ASM together as an organization. However, since that time the majority of mosques and Imams have joined Imam Mohammed's Mosque Cares Ministry, which is an office in Chicago that has an administrative staff, a media productions staff, a committee on education, a business group, and other entities that support his personal ministry. Mosque Cares Ministry does not handle the daily organizational affairs of mosques or the convening of Imams.

Since 2000 Imam Mohammed and Minister Farrakhan have held joint Friday Jum'ah services over the Savior's Day weekend. Mohammed has declared that he accepts Farrakhan as a Muslim because Farrakhan has adopted the Friday Jum'ah prayer and the orthodox form of prostration prayer. Although both leaders do not see their movements unifying into one movement, Mohammed has indicated some interest in taking over the Nation of Islam due to the complications from prostate cancer treatment that have forced Farrakhan to take a medical leave in 2007. The question of who will succeed Imam Mohammed is highly uncertain since he has not designated any successors. Whether the Mosque Cares Ministry movement will disintegrate into independent masjids or continue in some form of a cohesive movement is not known. Imam Mohammed died of a heart attack on September 9, 2008.

Lawrence A. Mamiya

SELECTED BIBLIOGRAPHY

Curtis, Edward E., IV. *Islam in Black America: Identity, Liberation, and Difference in African-American Islamic Thought* (Albany: State University Press of New York, 2002).

Drake, St. Clair. *The Redemption of Africa and Black Religion* (Chicago: Third World Press, 1970).

Evanzz, Karl. *The Judas Factor: The Plot to Kill Malcolm X* (New York: Thunder's Mouth Press, 1992).

Evanzz, Karl. *The Messenger: The Rise and Fall of Elijah Muhammad* (New York: Pantheon Books, 1999).

"Final Call," March 30, 1994; March 2000, 124.

Gans, Bruce M., and Walter L. Lowe. "The Islam Connection." *Playboy Magazine*, May 1980.

Gardell, Mattias. *In the Name of Elijah Muhammad: Louis Farrakhan and the Nation of Islam* (Durham, NC: Duke University Press, 1996).

Goldman, Peter. *The Death and Life of Malcolm X* (Urbana: University of Illinois Press, 1979).

Islamic History Group Project. Hanif, C.B., associate editor. *A History of Muslim Africa Ameircans* (Calumet City, IL: WDM Publications, 2006).

Lincoln, C. Eric. *The Black Muslims in America* (Boston: Beacon Press, 1960).

Lincoln, C. Eric. "The American Muslim Mission in the Context of American Social History." *The Muslim Community in North America*, ed. Earle H. Waugh, Baha Abu-Laban, and Regula B. Qureshi (Edmonton, AB, Canada: University of Alberta Press, 1983).

Malcolm X and Alex Haley. *The Autobiography of Malcolm X* (New York: Grove Press, 1964; New York: Ballantine, 1999).

Mamiya, Lawrence. "From Black Muslim to Bilalian: The Evolution of a Movement." *Journal for the Scientific Study of Religion* 21, no. 2 (1982): 138–152. Reprinted in *Islam in North America: A Sourcebook*, ed. Michael A. Koszegi and J. Gordon Melton (New York and London: Garland Publishing Co., 1992), 165–182.

Mamiya, Lawrence. "Minister Louis Farrakhan and the Final Call: Schism in the Muslim Movement." *The Muslim Community in North America*, ed. Earle H. Waugh, Baha Abu-Laban, and Regula B. Qureshi (Edmonton, AB, Canada: University of Alberta Press, 1983).

Mamiya, Lawrence. Interview with Khalil Islam at the Green Haven maximum security prison, April 15, 1985. Islam was one of three men imprisoned for the assassination of Malcolm X.

Mamiya, Lawrence. Interview with Alfred Mohammed, member of Temple No. 7 under Malcolm X and Louis Farrakhan, who chose to follow Imam Warith Deen Mohammad. Congregational Studies Institute at the Hartford Seminary, June 15, 1994.

Mamiya, Lawrence. Interview with Imam Warith Deen Mohammad at an Islamic conference in Poughkeepsie, New York, May 15, 1998.

Mamiya, Lawrence, and Ihsan Bagby. Interview with Imam Talib Abdur Rashid at the Mosque of the Islamic Brotherood in Harlem, November 5, 1992.

Mamiya, Lawrence, and C. Eric Lincoln. Interview with Imam Warith Deen

Mohammad at Duke University, April 22, 1992.

Marsh, Clifton. *The Lost-Found Nation of Islam in America* (Lanham, MD: Scarecrow Press, Inc., 2000).

Mohammad, Imam Warith Deen. *Mohammed Speaks* (Calumet City, IL: WDM Publications, 1978).

Mohammad, Imam Warith Deen. *As the Light Shineth from the East* (Chicago, IL: WDM Publishing, 1980).

Mohammad, Imam Warith Deen. Black History Month Lecture at Vassar College, February 7, 1980.

"Rule Switch Allows Whites as Muslims," *Nashville Tennessean*, June 19, 1975.

Walker, Dennis. *Islam and the Search for African-American Nationhood: Elijah Muhammad, Louis Farrakhan and the Nation of Islam* (Atlanta: Clarity Press, 2005).

NEWSPAPERS

Muhammad Speaks.
Bilalian News.
Muslim Journal.

APOSTOLIC FAITH MISSION CHURCH OF GOD

Historical Development

Founded on July 10, 1906, in Mobile, Alabama, the Apostolic Faith Mission Church of God (AFM) was one of the earliest Pentecostal denominations established in the United States. Pentecostalism emerged as a distinct religious movement in America in the late nineteenth and the early twentieth centuries. Early adherents came primarily out of Holiness, Baptist, and Methodist churches. Known for their exuberant worship style and embrace of the practice of speaking in tongues or *glossolalia*, Pentecostals trace their heritage and their name to a passage in the Book of Acts that describes an event on the Day of Pentecost when a group of Christians "began to speak in other tongues as the Spirit enabled them" (Acts 2:4). Today the movement claims hundreds of millions of adherents around the world.

Frank W. Williams was one of many who carried the Pentecostal brand of Christianity to the South after having been introduced to the movement at the 1906 Azusa Street Revival in Los Angeles, California. Recognized by many as American Pentecostalism's birthplace, the revival is touted as one of the most influential events in American religious history as it attracted thousands of onlookers, critics, and new converts from all over the world. The Apostolic Faith Mission served as the revival's central headquarters. A former Holiness minister named William Seymour presided over the mission where spontaneous preaching, miraculous healings, and all night prayer services were typical. The revival lasted until 1913.

Seymour's small, unassuming, interracial congregation on Azusa Street influenced the preaching careers of several itinerant evangelists including that of Williams. The experience at Azusa inspired the newly converted to carry the Pentecostal message to all corners of the country and around the globe. Armed with fervor for proselytizing, missionaries planted churches and missions to entice the unsaved and win over other Christians to the Pentecostal way of life. Williams was part of an early wave of missionaries and preachers who enthusiastically took the message of the new Pentecost to the Deep South.

Continuing the legacy of itinerant preaching and church planting popular in Pentecostal circles, upon his return from Los Angeles Williams attempted to start a congregation in Mississippi but was unsuccessful. In a day when Pentecostal preachers needed little to no training to start their ministries, Williams tried again. He moved to Mobile, Alabama, and with few resources he conducted services under a tent until an entire Baptist church was converted to Pentecostalism. The church graciously offered their building as the first AFM sanctuary. In a brief report to the *Apostolic Faith Mission Newsletter* in 1907 the young pastor wrote of the challenges and successes of his new ministry:

> After a hard battle in this wicked place, the Lord gave me a tent in answer to prayer. We give God all the glory for victory. Five have been sanctified and three received Pentecost. One brother that has been crippled for years has been healed in his foot and can walk without a stick, and we are expecting a great work of the Lord here soon. (*The Apostolic Faith* 1907)

Williams named the congregation in Alabama *Apostolic Faith Mission Church* after Seymour's Mission in Los Angeles. But unlike Seymour, Williams professed the Oneness doctrine, a theological position that rejects the traditional Christian teachings about the Trinity. Williams insisted on Baptism in "Jesus' Name" (Acts 2:38) instead of immersion "in the name of the Father, Son and the Holy Ghost" (Matthew 28:19). This shift in understanding of the Godhead that gave rise to this baptismal formula became known as the "New Issue Controversy." It would divide the Pentecostal communities around the world and was the impetus for Williams's break

with Seymour. On October 9, 1915, he incorporated a new denomination and renamed his congregation the Apostolic Faith Mission Church of God. Less than a decade later he would sever his ties with the original Apostolic Faith Mission and its founder, William Seymour.

William's ministry was successful in influencing several up-and-coming Pentecostal evangelists. William Thomas Phillips (1893–1973) converted to Pentecostalism after hearing Bishop Williams preach a tent revival in Birmingham, Alabama. Williams ordained Phillips in 1913 and just three years later Phillips established the Apostolic Overcoming Holy Church of God (formerly Ethiopian Overcoming Church of God) in Mobile, Alabama. Bishop Williams passed away in December 1932.

Beliefs and Practices

Like other American Pentecostal denominations, the AFM Church of God adheres to social prohibitions. Members are forbidden to smoke, drink, or gamble. Church ordinances include foot washing and monthly communion. Members must be baptized in Jesus' name and receive the Baptism of the Holy Spirit to enjoy full membership. Unlike women in many Oneness and Trinitarian Pentecostal denominations who are not given space to preach, within the AFM women can be ordained.

Today a Board of Bishops called the Executive Board governs the church. Bishop Donice Brown Sr. became pastor of Ward's Temple in 1976 and presiding bishop of AFMCOG in 1993. Other members of the Board include: Bishop T. C. Tolbert Sr. (Anniston, AL), Bishop John Crum (Birmingham, AL), Bishop Samuel Darden (Hyde Park, MA),

Bishop James Truss (Lincoln, AL), Bishop T. C. Tolbert Jr. (Ohatchee, AL), Bishop Thomas Brooks (Decatur, GA), Bishop Johnny Cunningham (Century, FL), and Bishop Wayne Smiley (Mary Ester, FL).

Each district reports to a District Overseer. The National Departments of the church include the Sunday School under Superintendent Thomas Books (Decatur, GA), the Young People's Christian Association directed by President Johnny Kennedy (Birmingham, AL), the Mothers Band led by Mother Bessie Davis (Pensacola, FL), and the Missionary Department under the direction of Rosa Tolbert (Anniston, AL). Bishop Beter T. Nelson heads up the International Division of the church in Monrovia, Liberia. AFM Church of God quarterly publishes a newsletter called *The Three-Fold Vision.*

Apostolic Faith Mission's headquarters are housed at Ward's Temple in Cantonment, Florida. Ward's Temple bears the name of the immediate past presiding bishop, Houston Ward. The church maintains a Bible school, Florida Apostolic Bible Institute, where students can earn Associate's and Bachelor's degrees in biblical education. Most of the churches in the denomination are located in Alabama though the church maintains several congregations and schools in Florida, Ohio, Massachusetts, and West Africa, under the leadership of Bishop Mary Kolo.

In 2004 the church reported 10,340 members. The connectional church meets annually in the third week of June.

Anjulet Tucker

SELECTED BIBLIOGRAPHY

The Apostolic Faith 1, no. 6 (February–March 1907). www.wardstemple.org

Burgess, Stanley. *The New International Dictionary of Pentecostal and Charismatic Movements* (Grand Rapids, MI: Zondervan Press, 2003).

Dupree, Sherry Sherrod. *African-American Holiness Pentecostal Movement: An Annotated Bibliography* (New York and London: Garland Publishing, 1996).

Gordon, Melton. *Encyclopedia of American Religions*, 7th ed. (Detroit: Gale Research, 2003).

Yearbook of American and Canadian Churches (Nashville: Abingdon Press, 2007).

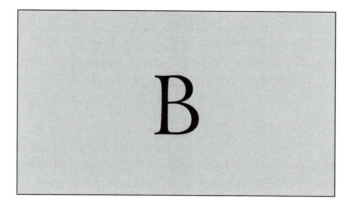

BAHÁ'Í FAITH

Historical Development

The Bahá'í Faith arose in Iran in the mid-nineteenth century and attracted African Americans to its membership starting in 1898. Its founder, Bahá'u'lláh (1817–1892), declared himself a divine messenger and composed thousands of works defining the teachings, organization, and practices of the religion, which have as their purpose the creation of unity among all humankind. His successors, 'Abdu'l-Baha (1844–1921) and Shoghi Effendi (1897–1957) continued to produce authoritative texts that clarified and amplified the Bahá'í teachings and developed institutions to express and channel them. The successive leaders and the nine-member governing council, the Universal House of Justice (1963–present), which succeeded them, guided a systematic growth plan that brought over 5 million people into the Bahá'í community, which is found in nearly every country of the world. The American Bahá'í community (164,000 members in 2009) is about 10 percent African American. Among the blacks attracted to its ranks have been Robert Abbott, Elsie Austin, Nina Gomer DuBois, Dizzy Gillespie, Louis Gregory, Robert Hayden, Alain Locke, and Harriet Gibbs Marshall.

The Bahá'í Faith arose in Iran from the Bábí Faith, which was established by 'Alí-Muhammad of Shiraz (1819–1850). In 1844 he took on the title of *the Báb* (the gate) and declared himself to be the fulfillment of Islamic prophecies. The Báb penned mystic commentaries on the Qur'án whose style and content signified a claim to divine revelation.

The claim to be the successor of Muhammad created immediate controversy. Followers of the Báb were arrested and expelled from cities, later beaten, and eventually executed. The Iranian army besieged two neighborhoods in which the majority of the inhabitants had converted to the new religion and killed most of the inhabitants. The Báb was

ALAIN LOCKE (1885–1954)

Locke, a Harvard trained philosopher and the first African American Rhodes Scholar, is perhaps best known for his intellectual work related to the changing culture of African Americans during the early twentieth century. One representation of this work is the book titled *The New Negro*. Locke also played a significant role in progressive activities toward the advancement of African Americans in the United States through community activism in addition to his scholarship. Locke became a follower of the Bahá'í faith as a young man and maintained the basic principles of the faith as a way to frame his social activism and intellectual life.

placed under house arrest, then consigned to two remote prisons in the mountains of northwestern Iran. He was tried, found guilty of blasphemy, and in 1850 executed in Tabriz. Estimates of the numbers of Bábís who were killed for their beliefs range as high as 20,000. Many of the Báb's extensive writings were lost; about 200 have survived. The Báb's teachings included new laws to replace Islamic shariah law and an emphasis on the coming of a successor, "He whom God would make manifest," who would appear soon and be a far greater messiah.

Among the early converts to the Bábí movement was Mírzá Husayn-'Alí, a nobleman born in northern Iran. As the Bábí leadership was killed, his role in the movement grew in importance. He took on the title of Bahá'u'lláh (the glory of God), which was endorsed by the Báb. Before his execution, the Báb recognized Bahá'u'lláh's teenage half-brother Yahyá (1831–1912) as a figurehead leader of the Bábí community, but gave him no explicit authority.

In August 1852 a group of Bábís attempted to assassinate Iran's king, resulting in a severe government-sponsored pogrom against the remaining Bábís. Bahá'u'lláh was arrested and imprisoned for four months. While there he received a revelation:

> During the days I lay in the prison of Tihrán [Tehran], though the galling weight of the chains and the stench-filled air allowed Me but little sleep, still in those infrequent moments of slumber I felt as if something flowed from the crown of My head over My breast, even as a mighty torrent that precipitateth itself upon the earth from the summit of a lofty mountain. Every limb of My body would, as a result, be set afire. At such moments My tongue recited what no man could bear to hear. (Bahá'u'lláh, *Epistle to the Son of the Wolf*, 22)

The event marked the beginning of Bahá'u'lláh's ministry, though he did not announce His status as "He whom God would make manifest," the successor to the Báb, for another decade.

When the Iranian government released Bahá'u'lláh from prison, they banished him. He departed for Baghdad. Over the next ten years Bahá'u'lláh penned several of his most important works: *The Hidden Words* (a collection of ethical and mystical aphorisms), *The Seven Valleys and Four Valleys* (two works about the mystic journey of the soul, in dialogue with Sufi concepts), and the *Book of Certitude* (a work delineating basic theological concepts and principles of personal spiritual development through commentary on passages from the Bible and Qur'án). His efforts to revitalize the Iranian Bábí community were so successful that the Ottoman government exiled him to Istanbul. On the eve of his departure, in April 1863, Bahá'u'lláh publicly declared to his close associates that he was the divine messenger the Báb had prophesied.

Bahá'u'lláh spent the next five years in Istanbul and Edirne in European Turkey. Utilizing diplomatic contacts made in the Ottoman capital, he sent epistles to the heads of state of Iran, Turkey, and major European powers, as well as to Pope Pius IX, announcing his claim to be God's messenger and Christ returned. He sent numerous *tablets* (a term for a writing of Bahá'u'lláh, usually a letter to an individual) to Iran's Bábís and sent teachers to explain his messianic claim. The vast majority of the Bábís converted to the Bahá'í Faith. Bahá'u'lláh's half-brother Yahyá, the figurehead leader of a now almost non-existent community, broke with him and attempted to have Bahá'u'lláh murdered. Because of the violence, the Ottoman authorities exiled Bahá'u'lláh and most of his followers to the prison city of Acre, in what is today northern Israel, in the summer of 1868. Yahyá and most of his handful of followers were sent to Cyprus.

In Acre, Bahá'u'lláh and his followers were confined in a prison under severe conditions for more than two years, then allowed to rent houses in the area. The flow of pilgrims resumed and they carried tablets to fellow Bahá'ís

in Iran. Bahá'u'lláh composed the *Kitáb-i-Aqdas*, or book of laws (a work that defines Bahá'í worship practices such as obligatory prayer and fasting, its laws of marriage and inheritance, and miscellaneous prohibitions, such as drinking alcohol); a series of tablets produced after the Aqdas that outlines basic social reform teachings; the *Epistle to the Son of the Wolf*, a major work of apologetics and a summary of many basic teachings; and *The Book of the Covenant*, Bahá'u'lláh's will.

The latter work specified that upon Bahá'u'lláh's passing, his eldest son, 'Abbás, was to become his successor. Other tablets praised 'Abbás as the exemplar of Bahá'u'lláh's teachings and the official interpreter of Bahá'u'lláh's revelation. Consequently, when Bahá'u'lláh passed in 1892, at age 75, 'Abbás, age 48, was quickly acknowledged by all as the rightful head of the Bahá'í Faith. He took the title of 'Abdu'l-Bahá, meaning servant of Bahá, to underline his subservience to his father's legacy.

Although the Turks renewed 'Abdu'l-Bahá's confinement within the city of Acre, he was able to receive visitors, letters, and cablegrams. The spread of the Bahá'í Faith to the United States and subsequently to Europe, Hawaii, Australia, and Japan resulted in a diverse group of pilgrims entering Acre—still a prison city—to meet 'Abdu'l-Bahá and receive his wisdom. Among the visitors was Robert Turner, the first African American Bahá'í.

In 1908 the Young Turk Revolution toppled the Ottoman sultan and released all political prisoners. 'Abdu'l-Bahá was now free to travel. In 1910 he visited Egypt; in 1911, Europe; in April 1912, North America. His nine-month sojourn extended as far south as Washington, as far north as Montreal, and as far west as Los Angeles. He spoke to thousands in churches, synagogues, theosophical lodges, university auditoriums, and the fourth annual conference of the NAACP. Hundreds of newspaper articles appeared. He made sure his public talks were held in places African Americans were welcome. In one case, he invited Louis Gregory, a prominent African American Bahá'í who was an attorney, to attend a private luncheon for prominent members of Washington society and sat Gregory at his right hand near the head of the table. He made special efforts to meet African American staff at hotels and servants in private homes. He even encouraged Gregory to marry an English woman; when they were wed in 1912 it was the first interracial marriage in the Bahá'í community.

'Abdu'l-Bahá left North America in December 1912 and visited Bahá'ís from London to Budapest before returning to Palestine months before the beginning of World War I. A contemplated trip to India was rendered impossible by the war and subsequent old age. He passed away in November 1921 at age 77.

In his will 'Abdu'l-Bahá named his eldest grandson, Shoghi Effendi Rabbani, to be his successor and Guardian of the Faith. As a result, aside from a few small efforts to split the Bahá'í community (none of which garnered more than a few hundred followers or lasted more than a generation), the Bahá'ís unitedly accepted Shoghi Effendi as their new head. 'Abdu'l-Bahá's will also specified the system whereby Bahá'ís would elect nine-member local spiritual assemblies (governing councils of local Bahá'í communities) and delegates who would elect nine-member national spiritual assemblies. The will stated that the members of all national spiritual assemblies would serve as the delegates to elect the Universal House of Justice, the supreme worldwide Bahá'í governing body. 'Abdu'l-Bahá's will asserted that while the Guardian had the power to interpret authoritative Bahá'í texts, the Universal House of Justice had the authority to legislate on matters about which the texts were silent.

Shoghi Effendi devoted much of his ministry to building local and national spiritual assemblies around the world. He utilized his Oxford education to translate major works of Bahá'u'lláh into masterful English of an elevated King Jamesian style that has become the

---

LOUIS G. GREGORY (1874–1951)

Gregory received his academic training from Fisk University and Howard University, and he began practicing law in Washington, DC after completing his training at Howard. While showing all the signs of a stellar law career, Gregory became a follower of the Bahá'í faith in 1909 and shortly after that he devoted the remainder of his life to lecturing across the country on the faith. During the years prior to his death, Gregory gained leadership positions in the Bahá'í community, including election to the national administrative organization. His work on behalf of the faith is recognized through the numerous centers and schools named in his honor.

model for subsequent translation of Bahá'í sacred texts. Among the 17,500 letters he wrote were a dozen epistles of book length in which he defined basic Bahá'í teachings and delineated the theoretical principles for the establishment of Bahá'í institutions. He wrote extensively about racial unity, calling it the "most vital and challenging issue" (*The Advent of Divine Justice*, xx) and repeatedly urged American Bahá'ís to be in the forefront of peaceful, legal efforts to break down racial barriers.

Shoghi Effendi's sudden death, without a will, in November 1957 plunged the Bahá'í world community into a crisis, because it deprived the community of its head and raised the specter of schism. But Shoghi Effendi had begun a ten-year plan for expansion of the Bahá'í Faith in 1953 that provided the Bahá'ís with clear goals until April 1963. He had also appointed a series of individuals as *Hands of the Cause of God* (a position created by Bahá'u'lláh). In 1951, immediately after Louis Gregory's death, he declared that African American the first of his race to be Hand of the Cause. In October 1957 he raised the number of living Hands of the Cause to 27, including Enoch Olinga, a Ugandan Bahá'í. He termed the Hands "the Chief Stewards of Baha'u'lláh's embryonic World Commonwealth, who have been invested by the unerring Pen of the Center of His Covenant with the dual function of guarding over the security, and of insuring the propagation, of His Father's Faith" (Shoghi Effendi, *Messages to the Bahá'í World*, 127). Consequently the Bahá'ís of the world turned to the Hands, who coordinated the Faith until the completion of Shoghi Effendi's ten-year teaching plan.

In April 1963 the Hands oversaw the election of the Universal House of Justice. One African American, Amos Gibson, was among the nine original members. Subsequently, the Universal House of Justice has been elected every five years by the members of all the national spiritual assemblies, who either send their ballots by mail or gather in Haifa, Israel, to cast their ballots in person. To date there has always been at least one African American among the nine members; there were two in 2000–2008. The Universal House of Justice has overseen continued expansion of the Bahá'í community and coordinated translation of more Bahá'í texts into English and other languages (including Bahá'u'lláh's most important work, the *Kitáb-i-Aqdas*). It has overseen a great increase in the public visibility of the Bahá'í Faith worldwide.

The Bahá'í Faith possesses authoritative written texts from the Báb, Bahá'u'lláh, 'Abdu'l-Bahá, Shoghi Effendi, and the Universal House of Justice. A significant feature of them is their sheer volume: 15,000 documents by Bahá'u'lláh, 27,000 by 'Abdu'l-Bahá, and more than 17,500 by Shoghi Effendi. No official estimate of the quantity of writings of the Universal House of Justice is known, but they employ a large secretariat to research and draft responses, producing thousands of letters per year.

Beliefs and Practices

Bahá'í teachings are often summarized as the unity of God, the unity of religion, and the unity of humankind. If one adds teachings about the creation of a Bahá'í community and about the personal

H. ELSIE AUSTIN (1908–2004)

Austin received her academic training at the University of Cincinnati College of Law, where she was the first African American woman to graduate from the Law School, and went on to have a highly distinguished career within the legal profession. This career included service as the first African American woman to serve as Assistant Attorney-General of Ohio. Austin also spent time in Africa, using her training in a variety of organizations as a Foreign Service Officer, and she also participated in numerous conferences sponsored by United Nations agencies. A long time follower of the faith, Austin served spiritual assemblies across the globe. In addition to her publications on the Bahá'í faith, Austin chaired the Bahá'í delegation to the International Women's conference held in Mexico City in 1975.

spiritual life, one has a useful division of Bahá'í teachings.

Unity of God. Bahá'u'lláh describes God as an unknowable essence—in other words, that ultimately God is beyond human ken and reckoning. Bahá'u'lláh's view, however, is not that humans can know nothing about God; on the contrary, even though the divine has an unknowable essence, it also has attributes such as mercy, justice, love, patience, self-subsistence, might, and knowledge that we can experience and know. By developing these qualities in their own souls, humans guide and foster their personal spiritual development and prepare themselves for the next life, in which spiritual growth occurs continuously and primarily through God's grace. Bahá'u'lláh says that all created things reflect divine attributes, a concept that is fundamental to Bahá'í environmental ethics.

Bahá'u'lláh notes, however, that the perfect reflector of divine attributes on this plane of existence is the Manifestation of God, a rare figure who receives divine revelation and guidance and manifests them in the language of his/her culture and through his/her own life and actions. In an epistemological sense the

manifestation *is* God, because in the mortal plane he/she is the only perfect source of knowledge of the divine. The Bahá'í authoritative texts identify Abraham, Moses, Krishna, Buddha, Jesus, Muhammad, Zoroaster, the Báb, and Bahá'u'llah as Manifestations and suggest that Adam, Noah, the founder of the Sabaean religion, Salih, and Hud were also Manifestations (the last three are figures mentioned in the Qur'án as well). The texts state that many Manifestations lived so long ago that their names have been lost and that humanity has always received divine guidance through Manifestations.

Unity of Religion. The Bahá'í recognition that the majority of the world's major religions were established by Manifestations is the basis of the Bahá'í concept of the unity of religion. All religions are ultimately based on divine revelation but, while they share certain basic ethical and metaphysical principles, they differ because revelation progressively unfolds from faith to faith and that it must be tailored to the social and cultural context in which it was expressed. The diversity of the world's religions—especially in ritual and practice—is attributed to differing cultural contexts and mistaken interpretations. Bahá'u'lláh states that God will continue to send Manifestations to humanity, but the next one will come only after the lapse of a thousand years (which is the time given the Bahá'í Faith to develop and mature).

Unity of Humanity. Bahá'u'lláh emphasizes that human beings are the "waves of one sea," "the leaves of one branch," and "the flowers of one garden," images that emphasize the overriding unity of all human beings. Shoghi Effendi notes that the oneness of humankind is the watchword and pivot of the Bahá'í teachings. Bahá'u'lláh and 'Abdu'l-Bahá strongly emphasized the implications of oneness: all persons are equal before God and therefore must have basic equality in human society; men and women are equal; races are equal and must be reconciled and united. Bahá'u'lláh stated that all people, including women, had the right to training so that they can pursue a trade or profession. He described Africans as black like the "pupil of the eye" through which "the light of the Spirit shines forth" (*'Abdu'l-Bahá in London*, 68).

Consequently, the Bahá'í principle of oneness has historically been particularly attractive to minorities, and the challenges of creating integrated local Bahá'í communities is an important theme in Bahá'í history. Women were first elected to Bahá'í local and national governing bodies as early as 1907 (in 2009 they constitute the majority of the membership of American local spiritual assemblies and four-ninths of the membership of the national spiritual assembly). Louis Gregory was the first African American elected to a local Bahá'í governing council (Washington, D.C., 1911) and to a national Bahá'í coordinating body (the American Bahá'í Temple Unity Executive Committee, 1912). The first African American woman elected to the National Spiritual Assembly of the Bahá'ís of the United States was Elsie Austin, in 1946. Two African Americans have served as Secretary-General of the American National Spiritual Assembly (Glenford Mitchell, 1968–1982, and Robert Henderson, 1984–2007). In 2009, three of the nine members were African American, one was American Indian, one was Iranian American, and four were of European American background. The chair was an American Indian woman, the treasurer an African American man.

In addition to its implications of unity, the oneness of humanity implies the need to establish a global governing system. Bahá'u'lláh called on all kings and rulers to end war, limit armaments, and meet in an international summit to establish common treaties and institutions. The Bahá'í texts call for an international language and script to supplement local languages, an international system of weights and measures, a world currency, an elected world legislature, an international collective security arrangement, and global measures to ensure universal education and health care, to create equitable access to resources, and to diminish the extreme imbalances of wealth and poverty. The texts include a critique of existing social norms and a vision for creating a just, unified world.

Building the Bahá'í Community. The Bahá'í community consists of all persons who have accepted Bahá'u'lláh and have requested membership in the body of his followers. It is conceived of as an evolving entity destined to reflect Bahá'u'lláh's teachings ever more perfectly and to embrace an ever-larger segment of humanity. The chief goal of the Bahá'í community is to achieve ever-greater unity. Bahá'u'lláh exhorts Bahá'ís to "be ye as the fingers of one hand, the members of one body" (*Kitáb-i-Aqdas*, para. 58), a utilitarian metaphor of working together that is reinforced by 'Abdu'l-Bahá's exhortation that "verily, God loveth those who are working in His path in groups, for they are a solid foundation" (*Bahá'í World Faith*, 401). More important is an ideal, spiritual unity expressed in the metaphor that the Bahá'ís should be "one soul in many bodies" ('Abdu'l-Bahá, quoted in Shoghi Effendi, *The Light of Divine Guidance*, vol. 2, p. 50).

Bahá'ís strive for spiritual unity through various means. Bahá'í gatherings begin with prayer. Discussion about any matter is conducted according to the principles of consultation, whereby individuals are encouraged to be frank but tactful in expressing themselves; where one should listen carefully and avoid offending or feeling offended by others; where ideas, once expressed, belong to the group and thus can be modified or rejected by all present, including the person first proposing the idea; where decisions ideally should be unanimous, but can be carried by a majority; and where the results of consultation must be trusted and not undermined by subsequent dissent, noncooperation, or backbiting. Consultation is simultaneously a set of principles of behavior, a collection of attitudes toward people and ideas, and a culture of discourse to model and perfect.

Reinforcing the goal of spiritual unity and the means of consultation are the principles of Bahá'í elections. The religion has no clergy; authority rests in nine-member elected bodies (local spiritual assemblies, regional councils, national spiritual assemblies, and the Universal House of Justice). Elections are based on the right of the individual to free and unfettered choice in voting. Voters are urged to consider "without the least trace of passion and prejudice, and irrespective of any material consideration, the names of only those who can best combine the necessary qualities of unquestioned loyalty, of selfless devotion, of a well-trained mind, of recognized ability and mature experience" (Shoghi Effendi, *Bahá'í Administration*, 88).

When Bahá'ís gather to vote, they begin by praying. All discussion of names of possible candidates, nominations, campaigning, straw votes, and other forms of influence are forbidden. If evidence of efforts to influence voters comes to light, the election is invalidated. If the election produces a tie, it is automatically broken in favor of the minority member. Such a system of elections, where voting is a sacred, spiritual act and campaigning is banned, fosters the conditions for consultation, greatly reduces opportunities for strife in the Bahá'í community, encourages involvement of minorities, and reinforces unity.

Complementing the elected bodies is a second arm of the Bahá'í administrative system, consisting of individuals who have no personal authority but who advise and encourage. Bahá'u'lláh appointed the first members of this arm, the Hands of the Cause of God, in the late nineteenth century. Shoghi Effendi appointed additional Hands and created a subsidiary institution under them, Auxiliary Board members, who were appointed by the Hands. He also said that Auxiliary Board members would appoint assistants. After the passing of

Shoghi Effendi, the Universal House of Justice determined that the Bahá'í scriptures did not authorize them to appoint Hands, so in 1968 they created a parallel institution, the Counselors, who would carry on their functions. In 2009 there were 81 Counselors worldwide; operating under them were 990 Auxiliary Board members; and under them were thousands of assistants. The Counselors meet with the Universal House of Justice annually; individual Counselors meet with national spiritual assemblies and regional councils several times per year; Auxiliary Board members and their assistants meet with local spiritual assemblies, and entire local Bahá'í communities frequently. The Bahá'í world is tied together in a series of face-to-face relationships and consultative gatherings.

Bahá'í communities do not regularly hold weekly worship services. Instead, community life centers on Feast, a gathering once every Bahá'í month (which lasts 19 days) wherein the Bahá'ís worship together, consult on local community activities, and socialize. The Feast provides the principal opportunity for local spiritual assemblies to share their ideas and plans and receive feedback from the local members. Nine Bahá'í holy days are observed throughout the year via events that are open to the public.

Bahá'ís also participate in a series of core activities: children's and youth classes (the equivalent of Sunday school, at the neighborhood level or more centralized), junior youth groups (which engage in service and other activities focused on moral empowerment), study circles (classes for youth and adults following the Ruhi curriculum, currently a series of seven books that teach community building skills), and devotionals (prayer meetings held in homes and public places). Bahá'ís are encouraged to conduct one or more core activities in their home for friends and neighbors. They also participate in firesides (gatherings, usually in people's homes, to introduce the Bahá'í Faith to others) and deepenings (meetings to study Bahá'í texts and principles together).

Many Bahá'í communities meet in the homes of the members, but rented and purchased Bahá'í Centers are becoming increasingly common. The United States has one Bahá'í House of Worship, located in Wilmette, Illinois, outside Chicago. It is a continental House of Worship (one of seven in the world) and does not serve a particular local Bahá'í community. It hosts daily worship programs, holy day observances, and a variety of classes, special gatherings, and interfaith activities.

The Spiritual Life. The Bahá'í scriptures state that the purpose of life is "to know and worship" God and to "carry forward an ever-advancing civilization," thus embracing both a vertical relationship with one's Creator and a horizontal relationship with one's fellow humans. Rather that stress instant achievement of personal salvation, like some Christian groups, or a moment of enlightenment, like some Buddhist groups, the Bahá'í scriptures stress ongoing personal transformation based on internalization of the Bahá'í revelation and its expression in service to others.

Bahá'u'lláh called on Bahá'ís to build their prayer life on the pillar of daily obligatory prayer; he gave three prayers among which Bahá'ís choose one to say daily. Bahá'ís also can choose among hundreds of prayers penned by

Bahá'u'lláh, the Báb, and 'Abdu'l-Bahá on a variety of subjects, such as forgiveness, assistance, healing, and grief; they may also pray spontaneously in their own words, but this is more typically done in private. Bahá'u'lláh ordained the repeating of the phrase *Alláh-u-Abhá* (God Is Most Glorious) 95 times each day as the basis for one's meditative and contemplative life. He established a period of fasting, which lasts from sunrise to sunset for 19 days from March 2 through March 20. In that period Bahá'ís abstain from eating, drinking, and tobacco. He granted exceptions to those under age 15, over age 70, the ill, travelers, women who are pregnant, menstruating, or nursing, and anyone performing heavy labor. He enjoined the practice of reciting the Word of God twice daily in order to connect the believer to the revelation.

The horizontal dimension of the devotional life has various aspects. Bahá'ís says Bahá'ís should be "anxiously concerned with the needs of the age ye live in, and center your deliberations on its exigencies and requirements" (*Gleanings from the Writings of Bahá'u'lláh*, selection CVI). Bahá'ís are thus encouraged, individually and collectively, to improve the world around them. Bahá'u'lláh requires all to "engage in some occupation" and exalts work performed in the spirit of service "to the rank of worship of the one true God" (*Kitáb-i-Aqdas*, para. 33), thus potentially spiritualizing the life of the individual, while simultaneously forbidding ordained priesthood and monasticism. He describes marriage as "a fortress for well-being and salvation" (*Bahá'í Prayers*, 105), thus sacralizing that institution and making it a vehicle for spiritual progress. Finally, the Bahá'í scriptures describe 'Abdu'l-Bahá as the personal exemplar Bahá'ís should emulate. His life of service to others serves as a model of behavior.

The dissemination of the Bahá'í Faith has been a systematic and active long-term goal of the Faith from the very beginning, which explains how it has achieved vast international spread (greater than Hinduism and Buddhism) even though it has far smaller numbers. A consistent effort to reach out to new ethnic groups is an important theme of its growth.

The Bábí community, starting in 1844, was largely confined to Iran and Iraq and their Shi'ite populations. Virtually all Bábís had become Bahá'ís by 1880. By the mid-1880s the Bahá'ís began to reach out to Iranian Jews and Zoroastrians, whose younger and more educated members soon became attracted to the religion's modernistic ideas and its claim to fulfill scriptural prophecies.

Commerce, flight from persecution, exile, and deliberate efforts to spread the Faith took the religion to India, Burma, Indonesia, the Ottoman realms, Sudan, and Central Asia during the years 1870–1892. Christians, Parsees, Sunni Muslims, and possibly Buddhists were attracted to the Faith. Iranian Bahá'ís fleeing persecution became one of the largest religious communities in Ashgabat (the modern capital of Turkmenistan) and constructed the first Bahá'í House of Worship in the world (1902–1908). In the 1920s, Stalin ordered the House of Worship confiscated. The vast majority of the city's 2,000 Bahá'ís were expelled to Iran, exiled to Siberia, or executed.

In 1888 two Lebanese Christians became Bahá'ís in Egypt and in 1892 immigrated to the United States. One of them, Ibrahim George Kheiralla

(1849–1929), brought the first Americans into the Faith in 1894. From a small group in Chicago, by 1900 the United States had four Bahá'í communities of 50 or more believers, plus scattered Bahá'ís in 23 states. At least two were African American: Robert Turner in San Francisco and Olive Jackson in New York City. By 1899 the Faith also spread to Ontario, Canada; Paris, France; and London, England. A convert in Europe took the Bahá'í Faith to Hawaii in 1901 and two Hawaiian Bahá'ís took it to Japan in 1914. In Shanghai, China, Occidental Bahá'ís met Persian Bahá'í merchants who had settled; at that point the Bahá'í religion had circled the globe from both directions. By 1921 American Bahá'ís had settled in Mexico, Brazil, Australia, New Zealand, and Korea. Four American Bahá'í women settled in Tehran, Iran, and helped the Bahá'ís build modern schools and clinics.

'Abdu'l-Bahá penned a series of 14 tablets to them in 1916 and 1917 entitled *The Tablets of the Divine Plan*, in which he enjoined them to spread the Bahá'í religion to every nation and island on the globe. He enumerated hundreds of places where there should be Bahá'í communities, all of which subsequently became goals. In the 1920s Shoghi Effendi gave the American Bahá'ís the chief responsibility for establishing Bahá'í elected institutions, and he patterned such bodies in Europe, Asia, and Australasia on the American model. He used the elected institutions as instruments for implementing the missionary vision in *The Tablets of the Divine Plan*.

Membership growth on the home front brought at least 21 African Americans into the Bahá'í community by 1920, located in nine localities. The number

exceeded 100 by 1934—about 5.5 percent of the community—located in 34 distinct localities. The most prominent were Louis Gregory, a Washington, D.C. attorney, who became an active traveling teacher for the Faith; Dr. Alain Locke, a Howard University philosopher; Robert Abbot, publisher of the *Chicago Defender*; Harriet Gibbs Marshall, founder of the National Negro Music Center in Washington; Nina Gomer Du Bois, first wife of W. E. B. Du Bois; and Elsie Austin, an attorney. Most of the prominent American Bahá'ís, in historical and cultural terms, were African American.

In 1937, when the North American Bahá'ís had established a strong national spiritual assembly, Shoghi Effendi gave them a Seven Year Plan (1937–1944). It was followed by a second Seven Year Plan (1946–1953). In 1953 Shoghi Effendi launched the Ten Year Crusade (1953–1963), which gave plans to 12 National Spiritual Assemblies. The number of countries, islands, and significant territories in which the Bahá'í Faith was established increased sevenfold compared to 1921 and the number of national spiritual assemblies rose to 56. The number of American Bahá'ís increased fourfold to 10,000.

The next decade—1963–1973—saw the fruits of the effort to spread the Bahá'í Faith widely but very thinly around the world. Latin American Bahá'ís settling in Bolivia reached out to the rural population, and tens of thousands became Bahá'ís. Similar efforts to reach entire villages brought thousands into the Bahá'í Faith in Kenya, Uganda, Swaziland, and several Pacific archipelagoes. Hundreds of thousands became Bahá'ís in India. In the United States, door-to-door teaching brought 10,000 to

15,000 rural African Americans into the Bahá'í Faith in South Carolina, North Carolina, and Georgia in the years 1969–1972. At the same time an unusual receptivity swept the college population, stimulated by the social unrest caused by the Vietnam War and the Civil Rights Movement, which many Bahá'ís participated in.

By 1974 the United States had 60,000 Bahá'ís. Subsequent conversion has been supplemented by immigration (some 12,000 Iranian Bahá'ís and perhaps 10,000 Southeast Asian Bahá'ís have settled in the United States since 1975), with the result that in 2009 the United States had 164,000 Bahá'ís and nearly 1,200 local spiritual assemblies. Notable is the presence of hundreds of native Bahá'ís on the Navajo and Lakota reservations, the involvement of several thousand Hispanic Bahá'ís (served by a quarterly Spanish-language Bahá'í magazine), and countless multiracial or multiethnic marriages within the American Bahá'í community. The National Spiritual Assembly of the Bahá'ís of the United States owns retreat and conference centers in five states; publishes a children's magazine, a bimonthly newspaper, and a quarterly scholarly periodical; operates a radio station in South Carolina to reach the large African American Bahá'í population there; runs two institutions for economic development and public health; and employs some 200 staff.

Expansion of the American Bahá'í community in the past 30 years has allowed resources to be channeled in new directions. The Bahá'í community has been able to sustain much greater commitment to the abolition of racism, the establishment of world peace, and the development of society. One result has been greater media attention. The larger community produced an expanded book market that stimulated writers and scholars, so that Bahá'í literature greatly expanded in scope and depth. Serious study of Bahá'í history, texts, teachings, and communities greatly expanded. Cultural expressions of the Faith became much more sophisticated. Robert Hayden,

---

DIZZY GILLESPIE (1917–1993)

Born John Birks Gillespie, "Dizzy" Gillespie is known as one of the most important and innovative musicians ever produced in the United States. Born into a musical family, with his father leading a band in South Carolina, Gillespie began playing the piano before he was five-years old. He began his career as a professional musician in 1935 working with prominent figure such as Roy Eldridge and Cab Calloway. Growing in stature as a musician, he played a major role in the development of bebop as a genre of jazz in the 1940s, as well as Afro-Cuban music. In 1968, Gillespie embraced the Bahá'í faith and served as an ambassador of the faith across the globe. Like so many other African Americans, Gillespie found the faith's appeal to the oneness of humanity and the concept of relationship between the divine and humanity inspiring and transformative. He creates the Faith with helping him to move away from destructive behavior. Gillespie's commitment to the Faith is recognized and celebrated through the weekly jazz programs held at the New York City Bahá'í Center in his honor.

a prominent poet who was African American, stimulated interest in poetry among American Bahá'ís. Many musicians joined the Faith, including Dizzy Gillespie, the prominent jazz trumpeter. In 1992 Bahá'í gospel music made its debut at a major international Bahá'í conference and immediately became popular.

Internationally, membership growth slowed throughout the 1980s and 1990s when no easy way was found to consolidate large numbers of converts. The advent of the core activities and the Ruhi curriculum, starting about 2000, offered a potential solution to the problem. The grouping of small local Bahá'í communities into units called clusters, and the provisioning of clusters with committees and officers dedicated to spreading the religion systematically, has brought about a resumption in membership growth.

Persecution has remained an important factor worldwide. The Iranian Bahá'í community was severely restricted after the Islamic Revolution of 1979, with many members facing harassment, denial of business licenses and pensions, vandalism, arson, physical violence, imprisonment, and execution. Bahá'í children are harassed in and occasionally expelled from the public schools. Bahá'ís are denied access to higher education, resulting in the creation of the Bahá'í Institute for Higher Education, a Web-based private university operating on computers in the West for educating Iran's Bahá'í youth. Defense of the Iranian Bahá'í community has become a stimulus for the development of external affairs and public information departments in many national Bahá'í communities.

In some countries, however, the situation improved. The Bahá'í Faith has become legalized in Indonesia, Vietnam, Cambodia, and Iraq. In Egypt, the Bahá'ís won a court case in 2009 that allowed them to obtain government identification cards, which are essential for obtaining driver's licenses, opening bank accounts, attending universities, and holding a job. The spread of the Internet and satellite radio have made it much easier to disseminate accurate information in the Arabic and Persian languages and refute false accusations and stereotypes. Web sites, listservs, and blogs have knit the worldwide Bahá'í community together in ways previously unimaginable.

The Bahá'í Faith's international governing body, the Universal House of Justice, is based in Haifa, Israel, close to the burial places of Bahá'u'lláh, the Báb, and 'Abdu'l-Bahá. Several official Internet sites are maintained at http://www.bahai.org/, http://www.bahai.us/, and http:/news.bahai.org/.

Robert H. Stockman

SELECTED BIBLIOGRAPHY

Note: For a full listing of Bahá'í sacred writings, see www.bahai.org/section5.html.

'Abdu'l-Bahá. *Some Questions Answered* (Wilmette, IL: Bahá'í Distribution Service, 1981).

'Abdu'l-Bahá. *'Abdu'l-Bahá in London* (Wilmette, IL: Bahá'í Publishing Trust, 1982 [reprint]), 68.

The Báb. *Selections from the Writings of the Báb* (Haifa: Bahá'í World Centre, 1978).

Bahá'u'lláh. *Gleanings from the Writings of Bahá'u'lláh*, trans. Shoghi Effendi, 2nd ed. (Wilmette, IL: Bahá'í Publishing Trust, 1976).

Bahá'u'lláh. *Writings of Bahá'u'lláh: A Compilation* (New Delhi: Bahá'í Publishing Trust, 1986).

Bahá'u'lláh. *Epistle to the Son of the Wolf*, 3rd ed. (Wilmette, IL: Bahá'i Publishing Trust, 1988), 22.

Bahá'u'llah. *Kitáb-i-Aqdas* ('Akká and Haifa, Israel: Bahá'í World Centre, 1992)

Bahá'u'llah and 'Abdu'l-Bahá. *Bahá'í World Faith: Selected Writings of Bahá'u'llah and 'Abdu'l-Bahá* (Wilmette, IL: Bahá'í Publishing Trust, 1976).

Bahá'u'llah, The Báb, and 'Abdu'l-Bahá. *Bahá'í Prayers*, 2nd ed. (Wilmette, IL: Bahá'í Publishing Trust, 1982).

Collins, William P. *Bibliography of English-language Works on the Babi and Bahá'í Faith, 1845–1985* (Wilmette, IL: Bahá'í Publishing Trust, 1991).

Hatcher, William S., and J. Douglas Martin. *The Bahá'í Faith: The Emerging Global Religion* (San Francisco: Harper and Row, 1984).

Shoghi Effendi. *Bahá'í Administration* (Wilmette, IL: Bahá'í Publishing Trust, 1968).

Shoghi Effendi. *The Light of Divine Guidance: Letters from the Guardian of the Bahá'í Faith to Individual Believers, Groups, and Bahá'í Communities in Germany and Austria* (Hofheim-Langenhain, Germany: Bahá'í-Verlag GmbH, 1985).

Shoghi Effendi. *The Advent of Divine Justice* (Wilmette, IL: Bahá'i Publishing Trust, 1990).

Shoghi Effendi, *Messages to the Bahá'í World* (Wilmette, IL: Bahá'i Publishing Trust, 1990), 127.

Smith, Peter. *An Introduction to the Bahá'í Faith* (Cambridge, U.K.: Cambridge University Press, 2008).

Universal House of Justice. *The Promise of World Peace* (Haifa, Israel: Bahá'í World Centre, 1985).

BATUQUE

Historical Development

"Batuque" (also used colloquially to refer to Afro-Brazilian religion in the Amazonian region) refers to Afro-Brazilian religious practices in the southern Brazilian state of Rio Grande do Sul, and, in some instances, beginning especially in the 1970s and 1980s, in Argentina and Uruguay. Batuque is practiced in groups that are each organized around a *mãe de santo* or a *pai de santo* ("mother of saint" and "father of saint," respectively) who presides over ritual, initiates new members, constitutes the ultimate authority in religious matters, and trains future *mães* and *pais de santo*. The word "batuque" also, and originally, refers to Afro-Brazilian traditions of dance, both secular and sacred, accompanied by drumming.

Relatively little is known of the early history of Batuque. (The following history is summarized mainly from Oro 2002 and Bastide 1978.) African religious traditions arrived in Rio Grande do Sul in the eighteenth century with the widespread introduction of slavery. By the early nineteenth century, persons of African ancestry, whether born in Africa or Brazil, accounted for about 40 percent of the population. While they comprised a number of different "nations," or ethnicities, their religious traditions had a great deal in common, most importantly the belief in a number of deities responsible for the forces of nature and key domains of culture, and the practice of ritual possession of adepts by those deities. While we do not know precisely when or where the first *terreiros*, or places of worship, were established, the historian Marco Antônio Líro de Mello (1994) asserts that Batuque was present at the beginning of the nineteenth century. By the latter decades of the century, the prevalence of Batuque is attested to by newspaper reports of police raids and arrests of practitioners.

Following abolition in 1888, Batuque continued to grow in popularity; by 1952, the last year such records were kept, 211 *terreiros* were officially registered with the police in the capital city of Porto Alegre.

In large part this growth was fueled by the increasing participation of non-Afro-Brazilians. (In fact, the percentage of persons identified as Black or of mixed ancestry in Rio Grande do Sul declined precipitously through the last century, now comprising approximately 13 percent.)

While Batuque is strongly rooted in centuries-old traditions, it is dynamically engaged in the present. Marginalized and suppressed for much of its history, Batuque has not only survived but flourished. During the 1960s, increasing numbers of Batuque centers incorporated doctrine and ritual practices associated with Umbanda (introduced in the 1930s), producing the so-called *"linha cruzada"* ("crossed line") that along with Umbanda now accounts for about 80 percent of Afro-Brazilian religion in Rio Grande do Sul. In recent decades Batuque has expanded beyond the borders of Brazil, attracting followers in Argentina and Uruguay. Batuque is a lively presence on the Internet, with blogs and homepages with links to discussions of the Orixás, the history of Batuque, and various aspects of ritual and belief. Recently, followers have used the Internet and other means of political mobilization to fight against discrimination from Evangelicals and legislation that would threaten their freedom to perform the ritual sacrifices required in their worship. It, along with Umbanda, is an important presence in local politics and culture. By 1996, the municipal government of Porto Alegre would sponsor an annual celebration of Afro-Brazilian religion, while leaders in the Afro-Brazilian religious community would receive commendations from the municipal and state governments.

Beliefs and Practices

Within Batuque, both historically and today, *terreiros* and practitioners identify with distinct "nations," based on ancestral homelands in Africa. (The following description of beliefs and practices is summarized from Bastide 1978, Herskovits 1966, and Oro 2002.) This is not to say that a person belongs to a given *terreiro* due to his or her actual ancestry, but rather that there are a number of different strains of religious practice and belief. The relative prominence of the various nations has varied over time. The Oyó, and Nagô nations, most dominant in the early years and well into the twentieth century, have practically disappeared, largely overshadowed by Ijexá. In any event, the various nations have far more similarities than differences.

When compared with Candomblé *terreiros* of Salvador, Bahia, Batuque *terreiros* display a somewhat simpler social structure. The leader, as elsewhere in Brazil, is the *mae de santo* ("mother of saint") or, if a man, the *pai de santo* ("father of saint"), also known as the *ialorixá* or *babalorixá*, respectively. He or she is the unquestioned authority in matters of ritual and belief, and bears the responsibility for training and initiating the *filhas de santo* and *filhos de santo* ("daughters of saint" and "sons of saint," respectively, as the adepts are known). The *mãe* or *pai de santo* is also responsible for developing the future leaders who will eventually carry on the tradition, a process involving years of training. Unlike in the traditional Candomblés of Bahia, where a special priest known as the *babalaô* performs divination, in Batuque this is done by the *mãe* or *pai de santo*. In Batuque there is also no special office of sacrificer, though animal sacrifice is essential to ritual. Animals are sacrificed by the leader, or by a *filho de santo*. There are, of course, drummers, but there are no *ogans*, the prestigious and well-connected patrons who hold honored places in Candomblé. This could reflect the fact that in Rio Grande do Sul, the Afro-Brazilian population during the twentieth century was much smaller proportionally than in Bahia, making the Batuques less attractive to elites who might seek the office as a way of cultivating politically advantageous relationships with the Afro-Brazilian community. The lengthy initiation process of Candomblé is considerably shortened in Batuque, often to merely a week, although to qualify for the office of *mão* or *pai de santo* requires at least seven years of apprenticeship, and thorough knowledge of all aspects of the tradition. Even the physical setting is simpler, generally lacking Candomblé's separate outdoor shrines for deities such as Ijexô. Most Batuque *terreiros* are located within the house of the *mãe* or *pai de santo*. The stones and metal implements that represent the Orixás are kept in a closet or small room, with a separate structure, outside the house, for Bara or Exu.

Central to Batuque are the African deities known as *Orixás*. In myth and practice, the Orixás embody the forces of nature and critical domains of culture. The Orixás worshipped in Batuque are the following: Bara (equivalent to Exu in Candomblé) is the messenger or intermediary between humans and the deities; the Ibejí are twins, child deities, representing both duality and the irrepressible energy and growth of children; Ogum is the Orixá of war, agriculture, blacksmithing, and transportation; Oiá (Iansã in Candomblé) is the tempest, a warrior goddess; Xangô, giver of law and justice, is manifest in thunder and lightening; Odé or Otim, the hunter, the Orixá of the forest, is equivalent to Oxossi in Candomblé; Xampanã (Omolu in Candomblé) is associated with disease and healing; Oxum, associated with fresh water and fertility, manifests in two forms—Oxum Pandá and Oxum Docô; Obá is the wife of Xangô; Ossain is the master of sacred and medicinal plants; Iemanjá is the sea goddess; Oxalá is the creator of humankind; and Orunmilá, one of the names of the Supreme Being according to some sources, second to Olorum, according to others, is the Orixá of divination. Besides their roles as forces of nature and principles of culture, the Orixás are believed to play a crucial role at the level of individual persons, in that every person is thought to be the child of a particular Orixá.

Ritual begins with an offering to Bara (Exu). This *despacho* "dispatches" Bara, the messenger who opens the way to the Orixás. Each Orixá is saluted in turn, by songs accompanied by drumming and dancing, the exact order varying according to the "nation." Three songs are performed for certain Orixás, four for others. The dancing culminates in the descent of the Orixás, who take possession of their "children," in effect bringing those in attendance into the presence of the deities. The ceremony ends with a ritual feast (Bastide 1978).

Lindsay Hale

SELECTED BIBLIOGRAPHY

Bastide, Roger. *The African Religions of Brazil: Toward a Sociology of the Inter-penetration of Cultures* (Baltimore and London: The Johns Hopkins University Press, 1978).

Herskovits, Melville. "The Southernmost Outposts of New World Africanisms." *The New World Negro*, ed. Frances S. Herskovits (Bloomington and London: Indiana University Press, 1966).

Krebs, Carlos Galvão. *Estudos de Batuque* (Porto Alegre, Brazil: Instituto Gaúcho de Tradição e Folclore, 1988).

Oro, Ari. "Religiões Afro-Brasileiras do Rio Grande do Sul: Passado e Presente." *Estudos Afro-Asiáticos* 24, no. 2. Available at http://www.scielo.br/scielo.php?script=sci _arttext&pid=S0101-546X2002000200006. *Axé Mercosul: As Religiões Afro-Brasileiras nos Países da Prata*.

THE BIG DRUM RITUAL

Historical Development

The ancient Big Drum Ritual continues observances initiated two centuries ago on the Caribbean island, Carriacou. Carriacou is populated by African descendants who host the family ritual, formerly called the Nation Dance. The Big Drum comprises songs, dances, and drumming performed within an outdoor ring formed by the community of Carriacouans.

The island, along with Petite Martinique, is administered by Grenada and is the largest of the Grenadines, lying 27 miles away from Grenada. "Carriacou is a simple, small island with about seven thousand people living on its arid soil, and, some say, with the majority of its population living in London and Brooklyn" (Hill 2003).

An open invitation to a Big Drum is extended to all and food, drink, music, and dance are presented to lively neighbors. This danced religion was originally sponsored primarily to call African Ancestors and petition their pardon. The ceremony is also intended for a return of thanks and the communal sharing of food, but also for pleasurable, unaffected entertainment. It inherits major themes from its extended past in its expression of one's relationship to another world and as a unified celebration of African memory.

With remnants of African religious thought infused within the Christian culture (Anglican, Catholic, and Spiritual Baptist), messages merge to form a double religious consciousness. Big Drum participants have been heard to say, "what better way to remember the Ancestors, but by having to feed them." They offer saltless food to Spirits who attend the Big Drum Ritual and extend to them a "free ring" to dance, which is reserved for them alone. Humans who enter the ring during the free ring may invite danger to themselves. During the opening phase of the ritual, the oldest male member of the family libates visiting Spirits by sprinkling *jack iron* (strong rum) on the earth. With the rum, he paints the paths of Spirit flight, east to west, and north to south. The fluid, imperceptible lines of rum (like the flour and meal *veve'* configurations of Haitian Vodun) intersect to create the form of a cross.

Beliefs and Practices

Anthropologist Donald Hill states: "Many people in Carriacou believe in

Musicians and dancers at a Big Drum, Carriacou. (Dean Conger/Corbis)

the importance of dreams as a way the dead contact the living'' (Hill 2009). A "dream message" or the vision of a departed family member elicits the planning of a Big Drum event.

The Big Drum Ritual was most likely initiated slightly after the era of France's colonial control of Carriacou (1650–1763) and at the British introduction of an enslaved Cromanti population. England took possession in 1763, but during the administration the French retrieved Carriacou for a short period of time (1779–1783) until its final restoration to England through the Treaty of Versailles.

Assembled from French and native languages, Patois survived the colonial exchange as a social language, but now it exists (with lost meanings) solely as an Ancestral ritual language. Despite the loss of language, the English-speaking

people of the island possess great love and respect for the historicity surrounding the French Patois lyrics of the songs.

Following is the text of a Cromanti song, "Ena-o," sung at a highly spiritual point in the ceremony, midnight. The original investigator of the Big Drum, Andrew Pearse (1956, 3), states that the figure in the song, which he spells as "Ina," is also known as "mama nu" which is the Patois term for "Our Mother." From this, Pearse argues that Ina is a Cromanti Ancestor/spirit (Pearse 1956, 3). "The Inna in the Hausa Bori religion is celebrated as the 'mother of us all,' and in a specifically Akan (Cromanti) context, Inna is a popular female kinship term which also means 'mother,' but spelled Ena'' (McDaniel 2002, 133). The words of the song are as follows, with the translation underneath:

Ena-o, Ena-o
Ena-o, Mama nu
Salamani-o

Ena-o, Ena-o
Ena-o, Our Mother
We greet thee

Each song of the Big Drum bears a name. In the oldest songs we discovered names of Goddesses, Gods, Ancestors, and Spirits forgotten by the population. Somehow, the holy names were kept and vocalized for two centuries: Sai Amba, Ena, and Oko (Cromanti Ancestresses or Goddesses), Anancy (the trickster deity), Cromanti Cudjo and Pa Beni (male Ancestors), and the Hausa spirit, Ahwusa. The deity found in Igbo songs, Ianman Igbo Le-le, a deity known to Haitian Vodun participants and the divinity discovered in a Manding song, Negesse Manding, whose name, similar to that of the Haitian Loa, Negesse Igbo, posits her as a Goddess.

Music is controlled by a female leader, the *chantwell*, who directs and trains the dancer/singer chorus. At performances, she introduces the call and response songs, selects songs and dancers from the 6- to 12-member troop and spurs on drummers with her *chac-chac* (maraca).

The female choristers/dancers wear multicolored dresses copied from the nineteenth-century French design. The trained skirt of the *douette* was split in front, and for Creole dances the performers would grasp the hem edges, opening the wide skirt to imitate wings. In former times the winged skirt exposed elaborate, luxurious, embroidered, white petticoats (MacDonald 1962, 48).

Without costume, a few men participate in the dance, but do not, as in former times, enroll in choral activity.

Drumming is exclusively performed by three dashiki-clad males. Two *boula* players perform a single significant rhythm and one *kata* (cutter, cut) player improvises a highly dramatic, improvised musical line. The *chac-chac* and iron (any hardware or bottle and spoon), which ring like an African bell gong, complete the instrumentation.

The adoration of the specialized African-type drumming is related to a covert history-keeping device. The musical line played by *boula* drums holds a vital rhythmic memory of the past that survives as the most intriguing element of the Big Drum. Coded drum rhythms accompany each dance style. The short, reiterative, musical phrases enunciate ethnic origins of the people from nine West African nations. This musical information in *boula* drumming has been documented, classified, and notated by their rhythmic coding (McDaniel 1998, 87). Cromanti, Igbo, Manding, Arada, Congo, Banda, Chamba, Temne, and Moko are the nine West African nations defined by discrete rhythms. These rhythms support songs and dances of the democratic congress of Carriacou's dance ring religion. And Carriacouans keep within themselves an ethnic/religious document, the Big Drum Ritual, and through it they "know their nation."

One speculates that the early stages of the ritual began with Cromanti dances in the late eighteenth century and later other nations attached their songs to complete the group called Nation Songs. Creole Songs were composed and borrowed during the late nineteenth century and, later, Frivolous Songs of the early twentieth century took root. Rather than dealing with spiritual matters of Ancestor veneration, calling, supplication, consolation,

Table 1   The Carriacou Big Drum Dances—Andrew Pearse

Nation	Creole	Frivolous
Cromanti	Old Bongo	Chattam
Igbo	Hallecord	Lora
Manding	Bele' Kawe'	Cariso
Arada	Gwa Bele'	Chirrup
Temne	Old Kalenda	Pike'
Congo	Juba	Chiffone'
Chamba	Man Bongo	
Banda	Trinidad Kalenda	

and homeland longing (appropriate to the Nation Songs), the succeeding Creole group exhorts social control, relationships, migration, and protest. The final accreted group, Frivolous Songs, projects humor, derision, satire, protest, and issues concerning migration.

Taken from Andrew Pearse (1956, 3), the Table I outlines the basic dances created during three eras (Nation, Creole, Frivolous) of Big Drum performance.

The first three dances performed at every ritual are the Cromanti, Igbo, and Manding solo offerings, which display a lowered stance, expressing penitent demeanor. This is dramatically expressed especially in the Manding dance, where dancers move and bend at low angles to the earth (unlike the upright posture of all other dances) with palms turned upward in a gesture of supplication. The Nation dances, the earliest dances, express a humble spirit of contrition.

We witness, from the nineteenth century, new Creole dances, many of which are borrowed types from Trinidad and neighboring islands. In the creation of an African dance repertoire, one questions the inclusion of dance styles with obvious European influence as seen in the dainty, mincing footwork of Creole dances. Couples dances (Bele Kawe', Juba) and the dance for two couples (Gwa Bele') are reminiscent of the English quadrille (Macdonald 1962, 574) with movements seemingly incongruous to drum accompaniment.

So, too, is the imitated colonial dress, the *douette*, an eighteenth century French fashion, a contradiction. With a frontal slit in skirt, opposite hems are held out by both hands (appearing much like the spreading of bird wings), exposing, in early styles, elaborate lacework of the white, flounced petticoat.

The inclusion of European style, whether coerced by slave owners, commanded by priests and missionaries (Daniel 2008, 7), or pursued by choice, is a curious innovation in African danced religion. Plantation dances served as entertainment for owners whose threatening advice assured compliance. The effects of such influence from the age of slavery can be seen in today's Big Drum, and even more clearly in the Quadrille and Lancers dancing of Carriacou, which are undiluted European dances performed with violin as the principal instrument.

Big Drum dance innovation in the early twentieth century (Frivolous Dances) promotes mirth, fun, and *winin'* (of the hips), The Frivolous group, as characterized by the Chirrup, Pike', and Chiffone', is danced near the end of the ritual and could be danced and enjoyed at any contemporary North American, swinging, urban club.

In this way, through the Big Drum, family history and lineage come alive as the ancient religion revives duty in the community with generous sharing that instills memory of the past.

Lorna A. McDaniel

SELECTED BIBLIOGRAPHY

Daniel, Yvonne. "A Critical Analysis of Caribbean *Contredanse*" (Unpublished, 2008), 7.

Herskovits, Melville J. "Drums and Drummers in Afro-Brazilian Cult Life." *Musical Quarterly* 30 (1944): 477–492.

Hill, Donald. " 'England I Want to Go': The Impact of Migration on a Caribbean Community" (PhD diss., Indiana University, 1973).

Hill, Donald. *The Impact of Migration on the Metropolitan and Folk Society of Carriacou, Grenada* (New York: American Museum of Natural History, 1977).

Hill, Donald. Personal communication, 2003, 2009.

Lomax, Alan. *Carriacou Callaloo*, produced by Anna Lomax Chairetakis and Jeffery A. Greenberg (Cambridge: Rounder Records Corporation, 1999).

Macdonald, Annette. "The Big Drum Dance of Carriacou: Its Structure and Possible Origins" (Master's thesis, University of California, 1962).

McDaniel, Lorna. *The Big Drum Ritual of Carriacou: Praisesongs in Rememory of Flight* (Gainesville: University Press of Florida, 1998).

McDaniel, Lorna. "Musical Thoughts on Unresolved Questions and Recent Findings in Big Drum Research." *Black Music Research Journal* 22, no. 1 (2002): 127–139.

Pearse, Andrew. "Aspects of Change in Caribbean Folk Culture." *Journal of the International Folk Music Council*, no. 7 (1955): 29–36.

Pearse, Andrew. "The Big Drum Dance of Carriacou." *Ethnic Folkways Library*, recording includes insert (FE411). 1956.

Pearse, Andrew. "Music in Caribbean Popular Culture." *Revista 1 Interamericana* 8, no. 4 (1978–1979): 629–639.

Smith, M. G. *Kinship and Community in Carriacou* (New Haven, CT: Yale University Press, 1962).

BLACK HEBREW ISRAELITE TRADITION

Historical Development

Since the mid-eighteenth century, African people in the United States have embraced the tradition of Judaism. At the beginning of the nineteenth century Denmark Vesey and Gabriel Prosser both identified with Israelites of the Old Testament in their respective rebellions. Identification with Israel at this time was identification through enslavement. African people read themselves into the Old Testament as a nation oppressed under the yoke of an evil empire. However, by the end of the century some began to claim to be the true descendants of the ancient Israel nation.

In 1886, the first Black Hebrew organization was founded by F. S. Cherry in Chattanooga, Tennessee, called the Church of the Living God. This organization incorporated both Judaic and Christian beliefs within their philosophy. They used the Jewish Bible and the Talmud as holy text as well as observed

Jewish practices and holidays. In 1915 the organization moved to Philadelphia, Pennsylvania, under the leadership of Cherry's son. Prophet William Saunders Crowdy also established a Black Hebrew movement called the Church of God and Saints of Christ in 1893 (see related entry on this organization). He started his tabernacles in Lawrence and Emporia, Kansas, and then moved to Philadelphia in 1899 where he established permanent residence.

Both of these organizations still function to this day in the United States; however, the Black Hebrew Tradition has taken different forms as it has evolved. Legend has it that in 1966 Ben Carter received a vision from the archangel Gabriel for the true Black Hebrew Israelites, African Americans in the United States, to reestablish their nation in Israel. He then began preaching and teaching his vision in the streets of Chicago and amassed a small but loyal following. Ben Carter changed his name to Ben Ammi ben Israel, and he and 350 of his followers moved to Liberia to live and work on their way to Israel. The time spent in Liberia was important because it was taught that this new nation had to learn how to be a nation before they entered the "promised land." Therefore, Liberia was to be a place where Ben Ammi and his followers learn to produce, build for themselves, and function as a nation of people.

Not everyone was up to the challenge of starting this new nation. Many people left and went back to the United States, and some died due to malaria, yellow fever, and other physical aliments. Still Ben Ammi was determined, and in 1969 he and 38 of his followers received permission to establish themselves within the nation of Israel. Although they were openly received at first as new immigrants, eventually the Israeli government saw them as a liability and began making their existence difficult within Israel. They were not entitled to health care or educational benefits as citizens, which forced them to establish their own institutions. There are now thousands of African Americans who have came into this organization and now live as a nation within Israel's borders. Also there are functional satellite synagogues within the United States.

Back in the United States, in the 1960s, Abba Bivens established the

---

BEN AMMI BEN ISRAEL (1939–)

Ben Ammi ben Israel was born Ben Carter in 1939. He grew up in Chicago and worked at an airline factory early in his life. While working at the factory, he was exposed to Black Hebrew thought and beliefs by a co-worker. Soon after, he joined a Black Israelites group in Chicago and, at the age of 22, he was ordained as Ben Ammi. In 1966, he claimed to have a vision from the archangel Gabriel to lead the true African Israelites back to the promised land. Later that year he and over 300 of his followers left for Liberia in preparation for their migration to the nation-state Israel. The Ben Ammi movement has grown into the thousands and has received international recognition for their mission and migration to Israel. He remains the leader of this nation and currently resides in Jerusalem.

HULEN MITCHELL JR. (1935–2007)

Hulen Mitchell Jr. was born in 1935, the first of 15 children, in Kingfisher, Oklahoma. His father was a Pentecostal preacher who focused his message on Old Testament teachings. Mitchell grew up during the Jim Crow era. As a young adult, he did some military service and went to Oklahoma University for a short period. During the 1950s and 1960s, he began to get active in civil rights organizations. Feeling unsatisfied with the progress of the movement, he started studying other Black Nationalist groups such as the Nation of Islam. During the 1970s, he began organizing followers based on his ideas of Black people being the chosen people of God. Mitchell changed his name to Yahweh ben Yahweh, which means "Lord Son of the Lord." As his organization grew during the 1980s, he was convicted on racketeering and conspiracy to commit murder charges in 1990 and was not released until 2001. While many members stayed loyal during ben Yahweh's incarceration, such issues eventually stunted the growth of the organization. Yahweh ben Yahweh died May 7, 2007, but his organization is still active in Florida.

Israeli School of Universal Practical Knowledge (ISUPK) in Harlem, New York. This organization grew and sought tax-exempt status as a religious organization, which led it to change its moniker from the Israeli School to the Israeli Church of Universal Practical Knowledge. Further, the organization had to change its name again to the Israelite Church of GOD in Jesus Christ to differentiate it from its Israeli organizations. Like other Israelite organizations with very Christian sounding titles, this organization adheres closely to Jewish laws and practices.

The Nation of Yahweh is a Black Hebrew movement, which began in Dade County in Miami, Florida. This movement began in the late 1970s by Hulen Mitchell Jr. who renamed himself Yahweh ben Yahweh. The primary focus of this group is to return the children of Israel (African people in the United States) to their homeland. Like most other Black Hebrew groups, they see European Jews as intruders on their original covenant.

In the later 1980s and early 1990s Yahweh ben Yahweh and several members of the movement were arrested and charged with racketeering and conspiracy to commit murder. Yahweh was convicted of these charges and was sentenced to 18 years in prison in 1990. He was released in 2001, and many of his followers remained loyal in keeping the organization intact. Despite these problems, this organization has grown and branched out across the United States; however, it is still centrally located in Florida.

Beliefs and Practices

Although there are many diverse movements that make up the tradition of Black Judaism within the United States, Black Hebrew Israelites share a lot of the same spiritual understandings and beliefs. Knowledge of self or racial pride is always a feature of the Black Judaic tradition. Theologically, Black Hebrews see themselves as holy and descendants of the ancient Judaic tradition. Most Black Jews claim they are the people of

Nation of Yahweh service. The Nation of Yahweh moved to Miami in 1979 and set up the Nation of Yahweh under the leadership of Yahweh Ben Yahweh. (Ed Kashi/Corbis)

the original covenant with God. They argued that they come from Ethiopian Jews of Northeast Africa and that European Jews are religious converts, not the original people of the covenant. Further, many Black Jews believe that European Jews are not only misrepresenting themselves as God's children but that the White race is evil and led by Satan, not the true living God. For them, White people are seen as thieves of the original covenant who have deceived the world and enslaved God's people.

With the belief in the right to the original covenant comes the necessity of Zionism. Without the promised land there is no covenant; there is no nation of Israel. This push for Zionism is relevant for all of the Black Israelite traditions, yet most organizations have not appealed to the current Israeli nation-state as have the African Hebrews.

As the Hebrew nation of the Old Testament, Black Hebrew Israelites observe many of the customs and cultural practices to solidify their connection to the divine. The Sabbath, for instance, is strictly observed and remains the holy day of the week. Beginning at sundown on Friday through sundown on Saturday, Black Hebrew Israelites are not to work. Circumcision is also a requirement of all Black Hebrew males eight days after birth. Women must adhere to the menstrual purity rites and customs. Jewish holidays such as Passover, Shavuout, Memorial Blowing of the Trumpets, Yom Kippur, and Succoth are also very important celebrations and are observed by the Black Hebrew movements. The observance of these rituals solidifies their connection to the divine as well as demonstrates their right to God's covenant. Further, many of the Black Hebrew communities observe certain rites that are specific to their particular history, such as the founding day of their movement or the birthdays of their founders.

For many of the Black Hebrew movements, strict adherence to a kosher diet is very important. The diet of the Hebrew nation is understood as being a divine mandate. African Hebrew movements, however, not only adhere to a kosher diet, they have gone further and made the vegan diet mandatory for all of God's people. Believers are not to eat any animal products, including eggs and dairy. The vegan diet is considered a divine diet focused on the divine health of every person within the nation. Such a diet is how a community maintains and sustains itself.

Paul Easterling

SELECTED BIBLIOGRAPHY

Chireau, Yvonne, and Nathaniel Deutsch, eds. *Black Zion: African American Religious Encounters with Judaism* (New York and Oxford: Oxford University Press, 2000).

Fauset, Arthur Huff. *Black Gods of the Metropolis: Negro Religious Cults in the Urban North* (Philadelphia: University of Pennsylvania Press, 1944).

Lounds, Morris, Jr. *Israel's Black Hebrew: Black Americans in Search of Identity* (Washington, DC: University Press of America Inc., 1981).

BUDDHISM

Historical Development

While the Buddhist Churches of America represents possibly the oldest institutional form of Buddhism in the United States, it is unwise to assume that this organization sets the tone and determines the texture of Buddhism within this context. Buddhism, the name given by Westerners to the tradition associated with Siddhartha Gautama's teachings, has grown to take numerous forms and presentations. Furthermore, it has grown to include Americans of various socioeconomic, racial, and ethnic backgrounds.

This diverse and complex Buddhist community is composed of immigrants who establish the tradition in their new home as well as American converts. According to some accounts, there may be as many as 4 million Buddhists in the United States, more than in any other Western country. And, of that number, almost 1 million are American converts. What may surprise some readers is that, as of the late 1990s, of these converts a noteworthy number perhaps somewhere around 30,000 are African American, and they are typically affiliated with Soka Gakkai International-USA.

A proper understanding of Soka Gakkai International-USA and its African American membership requires context, a general understanding of Buddhism's development. The story of Buddhism begins with Siddhartha Gautama, the historical Buddha, born during the sixth century BCE in what is now known as Nepal. Siddhartha Gautama was born into an important warrior class responsible for protecting the people, and as a result of its responsibilities this class held great social importance. Based on the stature and social ranking of his clan, he would have experienced a comfortable life, free from most discomforts.

At the age of 29, Siddhartha Gautama rejected this sheltered life and began a quest to understand and end human suffering. As part of this quest, he worked to control his body through extreme ascetic practices learned from various teachers encountered during his travels. These practices did not, however, serve to end suffering. It was not until seven years after he began this process that Siddhartha Gautama found the enlightenment he sought while meditating under a pipal tree. Engaged in deep meditation or *dhyana*, he worked through his various past lives, and from this rehearsing of his past he realized the manner in which karma influences the nature and contours of life. This awakening, the realization of suffering's causes and the way to eliminate it, resulted in his becoming enlightened—the Buddha.

Siddhartha Gautama not only recognized the nature of suffering and its causes, he also discovered the proper way to obtain liberation from suffering—nirvana—through the surrender of desires that produce suffering. This proper way is referred to as the "middle way." It moves between surrender to the senses and the attempt to control oneself through harsh, ascetic practices. In order to help others, the Buddha began teaching this new path, the *dharma* or doctrine, as well as *vinaya* or discipline. He first announced this new way during a sermon given outside Varanasi.

With time the Buddhist tradition grew throughout India, with written texts developing to form a canon of teachings and philosophy. Various schools emerged with the three dominant being Theravada (the most traditional and strictest form), Mahayana (the "Great Vehicle," so called because it considered Theravada too narrow for most), and Vajirayana, which involves an embrace of esoteric scriptures (*tantras*). These traditions differ in numerous ways, including: (1) disagreement on the nature of connection between *nirvana* (liberation) and *samaara* (this world); (2) the idea of the Bodhisattva (one who vows to assist others to become liberated from suffering) (Williams 2000, 83–84); and (3) the appeal to particular texts as vital on the path to liberation. Besides disagreements related to teachings, the complexity of this growing Buddhist tradition was also found in the formation of its ritual activities and the visual images associated with it. These differences would generate internal disagreements and spark various movements, but they did not stifle the religion's growth. Although Islam would supplant Buddhism in India, the tradition continued to grow over the centuries, reaching the United States prior to the twentieth century.

According to accounts by his followers, Nichiren, a Buddhist in Japan from the Mayahayana tradition, lamented what he considered the decline of *dharma*, and he attempted to correct this through emphasis on devotional practices geared toward laity who were not from the more socially elite groups. He emphasized chanting and the Lotus Sutra because he considered it the most complete Buddhist teachings. The supreme importance of the Lotus Sutra is expressed in the name change through which Zenshobo Rencho becomes Nichiren [Sun-Lotus] (Hurst, in Prebish and Tanaka 1998, 82). Missing from this approach was attention to the four noble truths and the eightfold path. Those involved in Nichiren Buddhism also participated in *kosenrufu*, or the push toward world peace.

Nichiren was not content to address the needs of Japan alone as they relate to practice and the study of Buddhism. In fact, he desired to take his understanding of Buddhism, which he considered the only true form of Buddhism, across the globe. While one can debate Nichiren's personal success as a missionary, it is quite evident that his movement eventually developed into various Nichiren Buddhism schools, including Soka Gakkai International, in various areas of the world.

Some trace the presence of Buddhism in the United States back to the mid-1800s through the rather superficial understanding promoted by transcendentalists such as Henry David Thoreau, who published in 1844 a translation of the Lotus Sutra (Prebish 1999, 3). With the arrival of immigrants, including some missionaries, as scholar Charles Prebish notes, Buddhism's presence only increased.

In addition to the early efforts of missionaries Shuei Sonoda and Kakuryo Nishimjimo, who came to the United States in 1899, D. T. Suzuki (a student of Buddhism from Japan) and Alan Watts (an Episcopal priest) aided the expansion of Buddhism's influence. The writings of Suzuki reached a diverse audience across several decades as Angel Kyodo Williams's, an African American Buddhist, experience suggests. She writes that her first acquaintance with Buddhism stems from an intense appreciation for the aesthetic of Japanese notions of home that led her in search of materials on Japanese culture. "What I found," she writes, "was a classic Zen book called, what else, *Zen and Japanese Culture*, by a scholar named D. T. Suzuki who happened to also study Zen . . . . His writing did a lot to bring Zen to the West and to America, but I didn't know that then. All I knew was that it wasn't Japanese culture that I was having a love affair with . . . .it was the culture and sensibility that came from Zen" (Williams 2000, 4).

One of the Buddhist organizations that began to flourish during the 1960s was Nichiren Shoshu of America. This organization, composed of priests and laity, was associated with the Nichiren Buddhist movement of Japan mentioned earlier. Nichiren Shoshu of America experienced tremendous growth, with estimates as high as 7,500 new members each month in 1969. And by 1976, Nichiren Shoshu Temple claimed some 200,000 members, with branches in cities such as Los Angeles, San Francisco, Philadelphia, Phoenix, Washington, D.C., and Seattle (Prebish 1999, 25). Internal conflict within this organization, however, eventually fueled a schism in 1991, resulting in the Nichiren Shoshu Temple led by priests and the laity-led Soka Gakkai International-USA.

Soka Gakkai was founded by Tsunesaburo Makiguchi, who became a teacher in Sapporo and eventually in Tokyo. In developing his ideas on Soka (or value creation), he drew on three fields of study—sociology, pragmatism, and geography. He was impressed by the manner in which these disciplines shed light on the nature of relationship and the reciprocal interaction between groups. Drawing on these disciplines and the teachings of Nichiren Buddhism, he set to work on the formation of an educational system bringing together individual improvement and social commitment—an effort to transform society through the practice of Buddhist teachings. By 1937, he had worked out the basic principles of value creation education and Buddhism, giving it institutional form as the Soka Kyoiku Gakkai (Value Creation Education Society). The society lasted only six years due to pressure from the Japanese government, with Makiguchi and other members of the Society's leadership being imprisoned on charges of treason because of their rejection of State-supported Shintoism. Makiguchi died in prison, but the movement he initiated continued under the leadership of Josei Toda, and with a new name—Soka Gakkai (Value Creation Society).

In 1951 Toda worked to have Soka Gakkai recognized as a religious organization, under the authority of the Nichiren priesthood. Prior to his death in 1958, he used an aggressive approach to proselytizing to increase the organization's size, and he gave Soka Gakkai a doctrinal base it lacked in its earlier years by appealing to the Lotus Sutra and the writings of Nichiren. Toda's goal for Soka Gakkai was to increase individual happiness within the context of a world marked by harmony.

Saisaku Ikeda became the next president of Soka Gakkai. Although aggressive proselytizing benefited Soka Gakkai, Ikeda diminished this aspect of spreading the organization's teachings while transforming the movement from a regional, Japan-based, religion (with political involvements through its *Komeito* or "Clean Government Party" founded in 1964) into an international movement. This process of internationalization in regard to the United States began in 1960 with Ikeda's first trip. This trip resulted in the formation of Soka Gakkai of America (Nichiren Shoshu of America). Initially, its membership was primarily Japanese immigrants, with meetings conducted in Japanese. The first meeting in English took place three years later.

Rather loosely organized, Soka Gakkai of America's leadership structure grew through the appointment of George Williams as the American General Chapter Chief in 1968. Invitations were extended to strangers to attend meetings during which they were introduced to the practice of chanting. They also heard testimonies from group members concerning the spiritual and material benefits of chanting. On a larger scale, the organization hosted "culture festivals" during which neighborhoods were introduced to the activities and teachings of Soka Gakkai.

By 1976, aggressive efforts to introduce Soka Gakkai to an American public were suspended because of the negative ramifications of the mass suicide/murder in Jonestown by followers of Jim Jones. In spite of this setback, the organization has paid attention to the racial and ethnic diversity of the United States and developed various initiatives (e.g., the Boston Research Center for the Twenty-first century in Cambridge, Massachusetts, and

---

HERBIE HANCOCK (1940–)

Herbie Hancock is an internationally known and respected musician, and he has been a Buddhist for almost 30 years. His musical skills were noticed early, and over the course of his career he has worked with figures such as Miles Davis, and he has also led his own jazz groups. Hancock has recorded numerous albums, and many of his compositions have become jazz standards. Among his many awards is an Oscar for his work on the film *Round Midnight*. As Hancock notes, Buddhism has played an important role in his personal life and the direction and shape of his professional development.

the Soka University of America in Southern California) to increase the diversity of its membership as well as to promote religious dialogue and understanding.

For some, the recognition that African American Buddhists exist is linked to the movie about singer Tina Turner's life in which she is shown chanting. Others might be aware of musician Herbie Hancock's link to Buddhism. However, these are only a few of the African Americans who claim Buddhism as their religion.

Soka Gakkai International-USA, a component of the larger Soka Gakkai International organization with members in over 100 countries, typically claims a membership of roughly 100,000 and maintains a headquarters in Santa Monica, California. Although actual membership is hard to calculate for this movement, what is significant is the fact that Soka Gakkai has a larger African American membership than any other Buddhist group in the United States. In fact, as Shelvia Dancy, notes in *The News & Observer*, African Americans constitute 20,000 of Soka Gakkai's total membership. Although most Buddhist communities are rhetorically committed to diversity, only Soka Gakkia has lived this out in ways that are reflected in the makeup of the membership (Chappell in Queen 2000, 184). For example, regarding district leadership (one of the basic units within Soka Gakkai), African Americans by 1990 "represented 26.74 percent of the district leaders: Atlanta—43 out of 67; Boston—24 out of 180; Chicago—75 out of 160; Los Angeles—101 out of 458; Miami—5 out of 64, New York—141 out of 465; Philadelphia—60 out of 1120; San Francisco—103 out of 599; Washington, DC—103 out of 336. Whites make up

38.67 percent, Japanese 18.66 percent and Hispanics, for example, 5.69 percent" (Chappell in Queen 2000, 190). While the executive committee for Soka Gakkai traditionally had been Japanese and male, this began to change when African Americans gained prominent positions: Sheilah Edwards became a vice-general director in 1997 and Ronnie Smith in 1998 (Chappell in Queen 2000, 203).

With such a long history of Christian church involvement, why have so many African Americans turned to Buddhism? This question is extremely pertinent when one considers that irrespective of conversation to the contrary, many American Buddhists have a difficult time actually applying notions of equality and "race-less" movement through the world that marks much of the Buddhist tradition. In an article titled "American Buddhism: What Does It Mean for People of Color?" frustration over this very issue is expressed in graphic terms:

> Separatism and mutuality are equally free to emerge in the splendor of freedom in America. For some Buddhists, this causes confusion. Some American Buddhists who believe in the mutuality of all beings conversely find themselves practicing racial, cultural, and economic segregation in their Dharma activities. Mere mention of this contradiction makes them very upset and can cause them to condemn, cold shoulder, reject, and even reject someone from their Dharma center. (http://www.Rainbowdharma.com/commentaries.html#Part1)

For Euro-American Buddhists, the article continues, this dilemma is at times dealt with in far from productive ways, through what the author refers to as a "loosely formed majority consensus" by which selection for inclusion involves:

> 1) people of color are allowed in as long as they do not bring up the heritage issue; 2) people of color who have no connection to the heritage issue, such as Tibetans, are welcome because their preoccupation is with Chinese heritage rather than American heritage; anyone, regardless of race or culture who speaks of these issues must subject him/herself to a verbal caution from a dominant culture senior student. (http://www.Rainbowdharma.com/commentaries.html#Part1)

Those who fail to adhere to the no-race-talk requirement after an initial reprimand are subject to dismissal for "non-Buddhist activity" (http://www.Rainbowdharma.com/commentaries.html#Part1). In another portion of the "American Buddhism: What Does It Mean For People of Color?" article, a rather troubling encounter based on American stereotypes was played out. The author notes that, "I had one newly arrived Asian Teacher tell me he was afraid of me when we first met. He said he had heard that, 'black people were violent', and challenged me to a battle of his Asian magic against my black magic" (http://www.Rainbowdharma.com/commentaries.html#Part1). The extent of such problems and the precise manner in which issues of race and ethnicity are handled is not exactly clear.

In spite of such problems, African Americans have found in Soka Gakkai a somewhat tolerant approach to multicultural religiosity, one that allows them to embrace both their African American heritage and the Buddhist teachings, fostering a synergy of sorts. In keeping with the more recent strategy of individual contact, word of mouth has been a primary way by which African Americans have come to embrace Buddhism through Soka Gakkai—seeing and responding to members of their family and friends who claimed major life changes through the tradition. Some scholars claim that Soka Gakkai is attractive to African Americans because its social sensibilities are in line with the dominant mind-set of progress that emerged out of the Civil Rights Movement. Coming into contact with Buddhism during the struggles for equality in the United States, some African Americans found in the teachings and practices of Buddhism a more productive way to understand and address racial discrimination. Rather than simply talking in terms of legislation or social transformation, the external world, Buddhism offered opportunity for introspection. It offered a way of promoting the healing of oneself through a better understanding of what actually allows for happiness and fulfillment, by pushing beyond material acquisition to spiritual healing and health. The concerns of social existence were, through Buddhism, put in perspective and placed within the context of larger issues of cosmic existence.

The leadership of Soka Gakkai supported the quest for civil rights, and this was meaningful to African Americans seeking both social improvement and spiritual health. While remaining important concerns, Buddhism, particularly as represented by Soka Gakkai's contact with African Americans, recognized as priority the nature of desire as the root cause of social discrimination. Yet, there was an expressed way in which people can address both social and spiritual difficulties, and this dual approach had great promise for African Americans who embraced Buddhism. The proper life path advocated by Buddhism served to enhance one's perception of life circumstances, and cut to the core of one's relationship to self, others, and world. The mutuality of all beings championed by Buddhism has had great appeal to some African Americans who find patterns of discrimination in the United States hard to understand and address.

African American members also at times speak of the "fit" between Buddhism and African American life in terms of Ikeda's appreciation for the plight of African Americans and those in the African Diaspora. Hence, joining Soka Gakkai did not result in cultural disconnect, a surrender of black pride, nor an eclipsing of a desire for social transformation. Soka Gakkai understands race as a social construct lacking deep or fundamental merit. There is recognition of the impact this social construct has had on life in the United States, while struggling to live in ways that move beyond race and ethnicity.

Beliefs and Practices

With time, the teachings of the Buddha were combined with various forms of devotion. While those who have achieved enlightenment provided texts or sutras that explain the Buddha's teachings, the elemental nature of Buddhism that guides most Buddhists is often described in terms of the "Four Noble Truths": (1) life is marked by suffering or *dukkha*, and this reality should not be lamented but rather acknowledged simply as a reality to be addressed and overcome; (2) *dukkha* is caused by desire or *tanha* through which people misunderstandingly seek happiness through temporal

realities, and this attempt to secure happiness through those things that cannot in actuality produce lasting happiness causes suffering; (3) *dukkha* or suffering ends when desires are surrendered; (4) *dukkha* ends through the eightfold path, the "middle way" described by the Buddha.

In addition to the four noble truths, there is the path that leads to the ending of suffering and nirvana through eight realizations: (1) right view—entails the understanding that our actions have felt consequences that shape our lives through the production of bad or good *karma* or action; (2) right resolve—involves a commitment to avoid all perceptions and actions that block movement toward complete liberation; (3) right speech—entails recognition that what we say has felt consequences in that it produces bad *karma* that harms us and others; (4) right action—avoid activities that harm ourselves and others; (5) right livelihood—undertake economic activities that are in keeping with the production of good *karma*; (6) right effort—consistent practice of right thinking; (7) right mindfulness—involves a recognition of the importance of the connection between the mind and the body highlighted in the process of meditation; (8) right concentration—proper focusing of the mind so as to achieve liberation.

Followers of the Buddha's teachings formed a community (*sangha*), based on various levels of engagements with the Buddha's principles of proper living. Monks (*bhikkhus*) and nuns (*bhikkunis*), who are most deeply devoted to the "middle way"—the path to liberation outlined by the Buddha—surrender all worldly attachments. While all followers of the "middle way" are expected to adhere to a particular life marked by a refusal to kill, steal, and so on, monks and nuns live an even more rigorous life involving many strict regulations concerning dress and so on. Those who maintained connections to family and the larger world express their devotion in part through efforts to care for monks and nuns. Monks, nuns, and laity play a role in the spread of the Buddha's teachings, sharing the "middle way" with converts. This movement into Buddhism involves "taking refuge": "I take refuge in the Buddha. I take refuge in the dharma. I take refuge in the sangha."

Soka Gakkai embraces Nichiren's teaching that there are three secret laws of Buddhism: (1) *gohonzon*—a small scroll (resembling the one written by Nichiren) containing the *diamoku* and embodying the dharma that is the primary object of devotion for Buddhists who follow the teachings of Nichiren; (2) *kaidan*—the sanctuary of Buddhism often associated with the temple, Taisekiji, founded by Nikko Shonin; (3) the true chant of the *daimoku*, at times said to be "hail to the wonderful dharma Lotus Sutra" or "homage to the Lotus Sutra." It is chanted quickly and for roughly 30 minutes. According to those in Soka Gakkai, the meaning of the chant—Myohorenge-kyo—is as follows:

> Myoho is the mystic law of the universe, the underlying principle of duality which is the basis of human life. Renge is the lotus flower, which can be understood as a metaphor for the simultaniety of cause and effect (karma) and the pure flower which blooms in a swamp. Kyo is the sound or vibration one creates in chanting which attunes the individual to the law of the universe. (Hurst in Prebish and Tanaka 1998, 84)

Various individual and communal concerns play into the general guidelines of Soka Gakkai International:

> 1—To work for the prosperity of society by being good citizens who respect the culture, customs, and laws of each country; 2—to promote humanistic culture and education based on the fundamental, humane principles of Buddhism; 3—to join our efforts for world peace, for instance, with those of the United Nations by supporting the spirit of its charter, thereby helping achieve our ultimate goal of the abolition of nuclear arms and universal renouncement of war. (Prebish 1999, 120)

Buddhists in America define themselves in various ways and participate in various traditions all linked in some way to the initial teachings of Siddhartha Gautama, the Buddha. Related to this, American Buddhists are involved in a diverse and complex community, one that at times is composed of an uneasy tension between various cultural backgrounds, socioeconomic positions, and political commitments.

The participation of African Americans in Buddhism adds to the rich religious landscape that marks their religious history. Buddhism has become one of the religious orientations allowing African Americans to make sense of the world and forge a firm and healthy sense of self within the context of a larger community of living beings. In short, it promotes a deep sense of happiness and points toward a path by which the various modalities of suffering or the cycle of suffering—and Buddhism allows African Americans to acknowledge the various ways in which injustice has meant suffering—can be understood and ultimately overcome.

Anthony B. Pinn

SELECTED BIBLIOGRAPHY

Prebish, Charles. *Luminous Passage: The Practice and Study of Buddhism in America* (Berkeley: University of California Press, 1999).

Prebish, Charles, and Kenneth Tanaka, eds. *The Faces of Buddhism in America* (Berkeley: University of California Press, 1998).

Queen, Christopher S., ed. *Engaged Buddhism in the West* (Boston: Wisdom Publications, 2000).

Seager, Richard. *Buddhism in America* (New York: Columbia University Press, 2002).

Williams, Angel Kyodo. *Being Black: Zen and the Art of Living with Fearlessness and Grace* (New York: Penguin Compass, 2000).

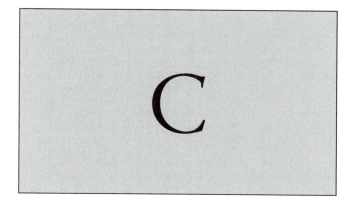

C

CANDOMBLÉ

Historical Development

Candomblé is an Afro-Brazilian religion that is known for the beauty and energy of its rituals, its fidelity to African traditions, and the devotion of its followers. Candomblé is centered around the African deities known in Brazil as *orixás*. (In the rest of Latin America, these are referred to as *orishas*; in this entry I will follow the Brazilian usage.) A recent study estimates there are approximately a million followers of Candomblé and other Afro-Brazilian religions, but the actual number may be substantially higher, in that many adherents consider themselves to be Catholic, while countless others attend ceremonies but do not actively participate in rituals. Candomblé churches, or *terreiros*, are found in most large cities throughout Brazil, but the religion is most strongly associated, both in history and in the popular imagination, with the city of Salvador, now the capital of the northeastern state of Bahia, and once the capital of Brazil. While Candomblé is rooted in African traditions, and developed through the agency of people of African descent both during and after slavery, people of all races and social classes participate in Candomblé. Further, in recent years it has become a potent symbol of Afro-Brazilian identity and resistance, as well as a symbol of Brazilian national identity.

In a sense, the history of Candomblé goes back to the beginnings of Brazil as a Portuguese colony. Almost from the start, African slaves played a crucial role in the economy, especially with the rapid demise of the native population. The Africans carried with them their own religious beliefs and practices, which were at odds with those of their Portuguese masters. As early as 1680, the Holy Office of the Inquisition in Brazil heard reports of animal sacrifices associated with funeral practices; a century later denunciations of decidedly non-Catholic rituals practiced by slaves

125

were recorded (Verger 1992, 26). From the beginning, both church and state attempted—at times with brutal violence, even into the twentieth century—to suppress African religion. The degree of suppression varied widely from time to time, and from place to place, but the threat was never entirely absent. The survival of African religion in those times testifies to the courage and devotion of its practitioners, but there are historical and sociological factors to be considered as well.

African religions survived in part because of the voracious appetite of the Brazilian economy for slave labor. There is always controversy regarding the numbers of slaves imported, but most estimates today are that somewhat over 3 million Africans were imported to Brazil, ending only in 1850. This meant that every year, tens of thousands of Africans arrived, their religion fresh in their minds and souls. Instead of dying out with the passing of time, traditions were continually renewed. Also, though we tend to think of plantations when we think of slavery, much of Brazilian slavery was urban. Africans and their descendants, slave and free (Brazilian owners not infrequently manumitted slaves—though often the slave actually had to purchase his or her freedom), were concentrated in large numbers in cities such as Rio de Janeiro and Salvador. This created an environment in which there were enough people available to carry out rituals, maintain religious specialists, and encourage the lively exchange of ideas and sentiment indispensable to religious vitality. Finally, and very importantly, Catholicism itself played an important role. Africans, slave or free, were allowed and even encouraged to participate in their own *irmandades*, "brotherhoods," ostensibly devoted to the worship of a saint or saints, but also concerned with mutual aid—providing for members' funerals or purchasing a member's freedom, for example. Beyond that, these brotherhoods provided a cover, and a framework, for the practice of African religion. As the brotherhoods often recruited members on the basis of their culture of origin (for example, Dahomey or Kêto), this fostered Afro-Brazilian religions remarkably faithful to African traditions. (See Bastide 1978 for a thorough discussion of these dynamics.)

In or about 1830 (more than half a century before abolition in Brazil), in Salvador, three free members of such a brotherhood—actually, a sisterhood, the Sisterhood of Our Lady of the Good Death of Barroquinha—founded the *Iyá Omi Ase Aira Intilé*, a *terreiro* that continues to this day, though not in the same location, and is now known as *Ilé Nasso* (after Iyanassô, one of the three founders) or, more commonly, as the *Casa Branca do Engenho Velho* (The White House of the Old Mill). Iyanassô, who may have been the first *mãe de santo* (literally "mother of saint," the colloquial term for a woman who leads a Candomblé *terreiro*) is said to have visited the land of Kêto, in Africa, along with Marcelina-Obatossí, who would be her successor. Upon Marcelina's death, there was a dispute over who should succeed her, resulting in a schism. The losing faction opened a new *terreiro, Gantois*, in 1849, led by Maria Júlia da Conceição Nazaré, whose great-granddaughter, Maria Escolástica da Conceição Nazaré (better known as Mãe Menininha), would lead *Gantois* from the 1920s until her death in 1986 and become among the

ANINHA (EUGÊNIA ANA DOS SANTOS) [1869–1938]

Aninha was born Eugênia Ana dos Santos on June 16, 1869. Her parents were Africans of the Grunci people, whose religious practices are related to those of Ketu (Nagô). Aninha was initiated at the relatively young age of 16 (in 1885) in the Casa Branca do Engenho Velho (Ilé Nasso). Aninha, who founded the Ilé Axé Apô Afonjá in 1910, was a guardian of the purity of Nagô traditions in Candomblé (portaldaco Huranegra). She spread her pure Nagô style of Candomblé to Rio de Janeiro, where she founded a terreiro that continues to function. Aninha not only powerfully influenced the Candomblé community from within, the profound impression she made on scholars, such as the ethnologists Edison Carneiro, Arthur Ramos, and the sociologist Donald Pierson through her appearance at the Second AfroBrazilian Conference in 1937 contributed immeasurably to the growing prestige of Candomblé among intellectuals, artists, writers and musicians that continues to this day. Aninha instituted the "Obás de Xangô" an honorary society of powerful individuals who would support the terreiro in its dealings with the outside community. Eugênia Ana dos Santos died on January 3, 1938.

most revered women in Brazilian history. In 1910, yet another *terreiro*, *Axé Apô Afonjá*, was founded by followers of Eugênia Ana dos Santos (better known as Mãe Aninha), who, like Maria Júlia da Conceição Nazaré, left *Engenho Velho* following a dispute. (The preceding history is summarized from Carneiro 1954, 56–57, and Verger 1992, 28–31.) All three of these houses—*Engenho Velho*, *Gantois*, and *Apô Afonjá*—not only continue to be active, but are internationally renowned. They also exercise tremendous influence on the thousands of Candomblé *terreiros* in Brazil, directly because so many of their initiates have gone on to become Candomblé leaders in Salvador and elsewhere, and indirectly through their position as prestigious models for the practice of Candomblé.

Candomblé continued to be the target of periodic repression by police and virulent criticism from Catholic authorities during the first decades of the twentieth century. This is no longer the case, for three major reasons. First, politicians found that by cultivating relationships with *terreiros*, they could gain access to a mostly poor, Afro-Brazilian populace, otherwise marginalized from political participation. Second, the attitude of the Catholic Church changed with the Second Vatican Council (1962–1965), which promoted much greater tolerance of other religious traditions, especially those associated with indigenous and formerly colonized people; indeed, the Church in many ways reached out to Candomblé. Third, profound cultural and ideological shifts, including the rise of the Black consciousness movement, the work of writers such as Jorge Amado and musicians such as Gilberto Gil and Gaetano Veloso, and the attention of Brazilian and international scholars and intellectuals, all contributed to a profoundly positive reevaluation of Candomblé as a symbol of Afro-Brazilian heritage and Brazilian national identity. In recent years, *terreiros* have become featured destinations for cultural tourism, promoted by state and private interests, and a number of *terreiros* have been declared sites of cultural and historical

MÃE MENININHA (MARIA ESCOLÁSTICA DA CONCEIÇÃO NAZARÉ)
[1894–1986]

From 1922 until her death in 1986, Mãe Menininha was the ialorixá of the Terreiro of Gantois, which her great-grandmother, Maria Júlia da Conceição Nazaré, had founded in 1848 or 1849 following a dispute over who should succeed Marcelina-Obatossí, ialorixá of the Casa Branca of Engenho Velho (Verger 1992, 29). Like Aninha, Mãe Menininha was an effective diplomat for Candomblé, gaining the respect of civil authorities, Catholic leaders, and influential scholars. Over the years, Mãe Menininha became the public face of Candomblé, the popular image of the mãe de santo. Many of the most important figures in Brazilian popular culture, such as the great novelist Jorge Amado, and musicians such as Tom Jobim, Dorival Caymmi, Vinicius de Morais, and Gaetano Veloso, and powerful politicians such as Antônio Carlos Magalhães were devoted followers and friends of Mãe Menininha. During her lifetime, Candomblé moved from being stigmatized and marginalized, to assuming its present position as a respected and even revered part of Brazilian national culture. At the same time, Mãe menininha and other Candomblé leaders spoke out against the "folklorization" of Candomblé and the exploitation of its symbols in tourism and Carnival performances.

significance by the state of Bahia (see Dantas 1988; Selka 2007; Prandi 1991 for discussions of the changing status of Candomblé). During the past 20 years, as well, Candomblé has enjoyed increasing popularity, not only in its traditional strongholds in the Northeast, but even in areas, such as São Paulo, where it had not been a major historical presence (Prandi 1991, 2004).

Beliefs and Practices

Slaves were brought to Brazil from different regions of Africa, so it is not surprising that there are various forms of Candomblé. These are referred to as "nations" and are named after the ancestral homeland. Major ones include Angola and Congo, from the Bantu regions; and Nagô, Ketu, Ijexá, and Gegê, from West Africa (Bastide 1978; Carneiro 1954, 1991). Differences between the West African traditions were largely superficial; the various deities are

called by different names due to the different languages; there are differences in songs, etc. Because of what the French sociologist Roger Bastide has called "Nagô prestige"—the ascendancy of the Yoruban traditions of Nagô and Ketu (Engenho Velho, Gantois, and Opo Afonjá are all in that line)—these West African traditions converged even more, so it is not misleading to describe Candomblé in general by referring to the specifics of Nagô ritual and belief, which I will do here. The Bantu traditions differ somewhat more, while in the *Candomblé de Caboclo* the African deities are represented by Amerindian spirits. Nonetheless, the similarities outweigh the differences. (The following discussion draws on Augras 1983; Bastide 1978; Carneiro 1954 and 1991; Lima 2003; Moura 1981, 1982, and 1987; Nina Rodrigues 1935; Verger 1992; Wafer 1991.)

Central to Candomblé is the veneration of the *orixás*, or African deities.

Practitioners of Candomblé sweep the steps of the Nosso Senhor de Bonfím in Salvador, Brazil. The ritual is part of the Festival of Iemanja and symbolizes the cleansing of the soul for a new spiritual year. (Stephanie Maze/Corbis)

(In Bantu traditions, these are referred to as *inkices*, and as *voduns* in Gegê, but the broad concept is the same.) There is a supreme *orixá*, Olorun (Zambi in Angola; Zambiapongo in Congo), creator of the world. Olorun is not represented, not invoked; Olorun is distant, beyond the present affairs of humankind. Below Olorun is Oxalá, his son, creator of mankind and de facto supreme diety. In addition to Oxalá, there is a pantheon of about a dozen *orixás* (compared with hundreds in West Africa).

Like the Greek, Roman, Hindu, and Norse deities, the *orixás* are imbedded in a rich mythology, in which they are portrayed in quasi-human form—they have personalities, they engage in adventures, rivalries, loves, and wars. They are associated with the forces of nature (and are often called just that) and are culture heroes, inventing and patronizing key aspects of human social life. Xangô, for example, brought law and justice to humankind; in nature, Xangô is manifest in thunder. His sometimes lover, Iansã, is lightening, wind, and tempests; culturally, she is a warrior goddess, the archetype of the tempestuous, indomitable woman. She is also the psychopomp, the conductor of the souls of the dead in the afterlife. Other *orixás* include Oxum (fresh flowing waters, fertility, beauty, and luxury), Ogum (war, agriculture, ironworking), Oxossi (the forests, the hunter), Omolu (sickness, but especially smallpox, traditionally, and now HIV-AIDS; healing), Nanã (still waters, swamps; mother of Omolu and Oxumaré, old age), Oxumaré (the rainbow, the serpent, always in motion; Oxumaré is both male and female, spending six months of the year as each), the child twins known as the Ibejí, Iemanjá (the sea; a maternal goddess), Irokô (his home is the sacred *gameleiro branca* tree; time), and Ossain (*orixá* of leaves, and the knowledge of their sacred and medicinal uses). And finally, there is Exu, a trickster, a being of enormous vitality, the messenger between humans and the *orixás*.

In Brazil, the *orixás* came to be associated with particular Catholic saints, a practice that has recently generated considerable controversy. While it can be argued that in some cases there is a metaphorical logic linking a saint and an *orixá*—for example, in Rio de Janeiro, Oxossi, the hunter and lord of the forest, is associated with Saint Sebastian, a martyr who is depicted tied to a tree and pierced with arrows, while Iansã is everywhere associated with Saint Barbara, whose father, legend has it, was struck by lightening as he attempted to cut her head off for refusing to renounce her faith—the associations vary from region to region and often seem to be completely arbitrary. It is frequently said that the association, or syncretism, arose during slave times, when Afro-Brazilians were forbidden from freely practicing their religion. According to the story, slaves would set up altars, with images of the Catholic saints on top, in plain view. Underneath, hidden, were placed the *assentamentos*, the sacred objects in which the *orixás* reside. Ostensibly praying to the saints, the slaves were really worshipping the *orixás*. The story, apocryphal or not, suggests what many followers today explicitly state: *orixás* and saints have nothing to do with each other, and their association is a product of history, not spiritual truth. In recent years, there has been a movement by some Candomblé leaders, most notably Mãe Stella (Maria Stella de Azevedo Santos) of Ilé Axé Apô Afonjá, to purge Candomblé of such syncretic practices (Prata 1983; Selka 2007, 76–79).

The relationship between the *orixás* and followers of Candomblé can be described as one of deep reciprocity, at both the communal and the personal levels. (The following discussion draws on Augras 1983; Bastide 1978; Carneiro 1954 and 1991; Lima 2003; Moura 1981, 1982, and 1987; Nina Rodrigues 1935; Verger 1992; Wafer 1991.) Every individual is said to be the

---

MÃE STELLA DE OXOSSI (MARIA STELLA DE AZEVEDO SANTOS) [1925–]

Mãe Stella is currently the Ialorixá of Ilé Axé Opô Afonjâ. She was initiated in 1939, and assumed the leadership of the terreiro in 1976, following the death of Mãe Ondina. Mãe Stella is probably best known for her campaign against syncretism in Candomblé; her argument is that Catholicism and Candomblé are separate religions, and that there is no basis to combine the two. She has spoken out against virulent attacks on Candomblé from Protestant Pentecostal ministers, which have grown more frequent in recent years. Mãe Stella came out against syncretism at the Second International Conference on the Traditions of the Orixás in 1983. At 82, Mãe Stella is modern and forward-looking. She articulates an environmentalist consciousness implicit in Candomblé.

"child" of a particular *orixá*. The *orixá* gives life, protection, and sustenance; in return, the person who takes up Candomblé has obligations to the *orixá*. These can include taking part in the annual celebration of the *orixá* (which occurs around the feast day of the Catholic saint associated with the *orixá*), making appropriate offerings of sacred foods and observing food taboos, and, most demanding of all, becoming initiated as a "daughter" (or "son") of the "saint" in Candomblé.

To be initiated is to take on a tremendous obligation. A *iaô*—a woman who has undergone initiation, also called by the Portuguese phrase, *filha de santo* ("daughter of saint")—serves the *orixás* in many ways, but perhaps the most important occurs during public rituals when the *orixás* are invited to descend and possess their daughters. That is to say, filhas de santo serve as the vehicles of the *orixás*, who dance and are otherwise manifested through their bodies. Initiation in itself involves considerable expense. The initiate must raise money for her *orixá* costume, as well as to purchase sacrificial animals and other items. Initiation practices vary and the process is not public, but the general outline is as follows. The *mãe de santo* (also referred to by the Nagô term, "*ialorixá*") verifies the identity of the prospective initiate's *orixás*. This is crucial; to serve the wrong *orixá* would be to not serve the initiate's real protector, with terrible consequences. The *orixá* determined, money raised, and costume sewn, the candidate is sequestered in the *terreiro*. Her (most initiates are women) regular clothing is taken away. In some *terreiros*, she is shaved completely; in others, just an area on the top of the head is shaved. She and her initiate colleagues

(collectively known as a *barco*, "boat") will spend the next many days (according to the Brazilian scholar of Afro-Brazilian culture, Edison Carneiro, the period is 17 days, but this varies) isolated from the outside world. She sleeps with the group on mats laid out on the floor, maintaining silence and rising at dawn to bathe in cold water outdoors. Her time is taken up learning the beliefs, rituals, practices, and obligations, and otherwise preparing herself to become an instrument of the *orixá*. When all is ready, the initiates emerge from their seclusion to a public celebration. They will be dressed in the costumes of their *orixás* (which cost the initiates considerable money); they will dance in the manner of the *orixás*, but most importantly, they will become the living vehicles through which the *orixás* become present to the community of believers.

The social organization of Candomblé is complex and hierarchical. (The following description is mainly based on Carneiro 1954, 103–123.) The unquestioned leader is the *mãe de santo* or the *pai de santo* ("father of saint"). To become a *mãe de santo*, at least seven years must have passed since her initiation as a *iaô*. Either she must have been chosen as the successor to the previous *mãe de santo* or, as in the case of Gantois and Apô Afonjá, she must start her own *terreiro*. While in Angola and Congo Candomblé men are more likely to be the leaders, in Nagô *terreiros* the leader will usually be a woman, a *mãe de santo*. Indeed, the anthropologist Ruth Landes, who did field research in Salvador in the 1940s, titled her monograph "The City of Women" and famously characterized Candomblé as a matriarchy. Moral, spiritual, and executive authority resides in these women. Perhaps the most important duty of the *mãe de santo* is to initiate and supervise the *filhas de santos*, because it is through them that the *orixás* are celebrated and it is from among the *filhas de santos* that future leaders emerge to carry on the tradition.

Assisting the *mãe de santo* is the *mãe pequena*, the "little mother." She takes considerable responsibility for the day-to-day administration of the *terreiro* and directly supervises the *filhas de santos* and sees to the myriad details of ritual. She will usually be the successor to the *mãe de santo*, but in most *terreiros* this must be confirmed through divination.

Of high prestige is the *axogun*, the sacrificer, sometimes called the *mão de faca*, "knife hand." His office is limited to carrying out the blood sacrifices to Exu and the Orixás. The sacrificial technique varies from species to species, and it is essential that it be done correctly.

Another office of high prestige, limited to males, is that of *ogã*. There are two kinds of ogã. There are the *ogãs de atabaque*, who play the sacred drums that call the Orixás, and the *ogãs honoríficos*, the honorary *ogãs*, men who have distinguished themselves through service to the *terreiro*. These can include wealthy patrons, politicians, and other public figures. *Ogãs honoríficos*, in general, can be seen as a crucial, protective connection between the *terreiro* and the outside world.

Lower on the hierarchy are the initiates, who treat both kinds of *ogãs* with considerable respect and deference. There are two ranks. The *ebomin* are those who have been initiated for at least seven years. Until then, the *filhas de santos* occupy the rank of *iaô*.

Assisting the *ebomin* and *iaôs* are the *ekedi*. Like the *iaôs* and *ebomin*, an *ekedi* is consecrated to her *orixá*, but the *orixá*

does not descend and possess her. She instead serves by seeing to initiates' costumes, arranging the altars, and attending to the details of ritual.

Candomblé *terreiros* periodically hold public rituals in celebration of the *orixás*. These are often referred to as *festas* (festivals), a word that well captures their energetic, communal, and celebratory dimensions. The *festa* is an event that renews and energizes the relationship of the *terreiro* with the *orixás*; it places the prestige and religious virtuosity of the *terreiro* on public display; and it constitutes a deeply moving and joyous encounter with the sacred (Bastide 1978; Carneiro 1954).

A *festa* involves weeks or even months of planning and preparation, as well as substantial expenditures of human energy and economic resources. *Festas* are often held on a Saturday night coinciding with the feast day of the Catholic saint traditionally associated with particular *orixás*—for example, the first or second Saturday of December falls close to the feast days for Santa Barbara (Iansã) and Our Lady of the Immaculate Conception (Oxum, in Rio de Janeiro and most Bahian *terreiros*). Fixing the date and details also involves divination. Various methods are employed to consult with *Ifá*, the *orixá* of destiny and divination, most well-known, perhaps, being the *dilogun* in which 16 cowry shells are cast repeatedly; the patterns in which they land are interpreted as a message from *Ifá*.

On the morning of the *festa*, in a ceremony closed to the public and all but the senior members of the terreiro, the *matança*, or sacrifice, is carried out. Different species of fowl and four-legged animals are specific to each of the various *orixás*. For example, Xangô might be honored with a sheep and roosters, while a goat and roosters would be appropriate for Ogum. The sacrifices are carried out by the *axogun*, generally by cutting the animals' throats. The blood is seen as a form of *axé*, the sacred energy on which life and spirit depend; shedding it gives energy to the ritual and to the *terreiro* and is a kind of reciprocity toward the *orixás*. The sacrifices are carried out with great respect, and death occurs quickly. The flesh of the animals is prepared in special dishes for the *orixás*, who partake of the spiritual essence of the food, which at the end of the *festa* may be served to the participants and guests.

Before the festa can go forward, an offering must be made to Exu, the intermediary between humankind and the *orixás*. A sacrifice will have been made to Exu in the morning, but later in the evening, before the public arrives, another offering is made, called the *padê*. A container of water and a clay bowl full of manioc flour and red palm oil is placed on the ground, above the spot where the sacred items said to be the "root" of the *terreiro* were planted. Hymns are sung asking that Exu provide protection and that he conduct the offerings and invitations to the Orixás. The offering is carried outside to the gate or to a crossroads.

The public ritual begins in the evening. The public, seated on benches, watches and listens as the *ogãs de atabaque* drum, and the *filhas de santo* dance in a circle. The three drums—*rum*, *rumpi*, and *lé*, from largest to smallest—are sacred and are themselves periodically honored and energized with the axé of sacrifice. To each *orixá* correspond a number of distinctive rhythms, or *toques*, which are used to summon them, and distinctive dances, suggestive

of the mythology and character of the *orixá*. There are also a number of hymns for each; in Nagô *terreiros*, these are more likely to be in Yoruba, while in Angola or Congo Candomblé, Portuguese is more common. These are sung in concert with the toques. Each *orixá* is in turn saluted with (usually) three toques. The exact order varies, but always begins with Exu and ends with *oxalá*. As the toques for an *orixá* are played, those *filhas de santo* that are its children are likely to go into trance and become possessed as they dance. They are led away by *ekedis*, who assist them in changing into the costumes of the *orixás*, after which they return to dance as the embodiments of the deities. There is enormous energy in the dancing, the music, the costumes, but it is all carefully controlled and channeled by the *mãe de santo*, the *mãe pequena*, and the sure hands of the drummers. After having summoned and celebrated each *orixá* in turn, the drummers play toques to send each away. When all have gone, the mãe de santo closes the ceremony. At some *terreiros*, this is followed by a meal, consisting of the "leftovers" of the dishes made for the *orixás*, served on big broad leaves, with ice cold beer, as the roosters began to crow in the hour before dawn.

Lindsay Hale

SELECTED BIBLIOGRAPHY

Augras, Monica. *O Duplo e a Metamorfose: A Identidade Mítica em Communidades Nagô* (Petrópolis, RJ, Brazil: Editora Vozes, Ltda., 1983).

Bastide, Roger. *The African Religions of Brazil: Toward a Sociology of the Interpenetration of Civilizations*, trans. Helen Sebba (Baltimore and London: The Johns Hopkins University Press, 1978).

Blog metropolitano, Iya Stella. http://blogmetropolitano.blogspot.com/2006/03/iya-stella.html.

Carneiro, Edison. *Candomblés da Bahia* (Rio de Janeiro: Editorial Andes, 1954).

Carneiro, Edison. *Religiões Negras e Negros Bantos* (Rio de Janeiro: Civilização Brasileira, 1991).

Dantas, Beatriz Góis. *Vovó Nagô e Papai Branco: Usos e Abusos da África no Brasil* (Rio de Janeiro: Edições Graal, Ltda., 1988).

Jornal da Bahia. "Candomblésays no to Syncretism," July 29, 1983. Available in English translation: http://74.125.47.132/search?q=cache:CPVQt4_VX_gJ:ifeaxejewelry.com/jornal%2520da%2520bahia%2520-%2520candomble%2520says%2520no%2520to%2520syncretism.pdf+%22m%C3%A3e+stella%22&cd=13&hl=en&ct=clnk&gl=us

Landes, Ruth. *The City of Women* (New York: The Macmillan Company, 1947).

Lima, Vivaldo da Costa. *A Família de Santo nos Candomblés Jejes-Nagôs da Bahia* (Salvador, Bahia, Brazil: Corrupio, 2003).

Lima, Vivaldo da Costa. "O candomblé da Bahia na década de 1930." *Estudos Avançados* 18, no. 52 (2004): 201–221. http://www.scielo.br/scielo.php?script=sci_arttext&pid=S0103-40142004000300014.

Matory, James Lorand. *Black Atlantic Religion: Tradition, Transnationalism, and Matriarchy in the Afrobrazilian Candomblé* (Princeton, NJ: Princeton University Press, 2005).

Moura, Carlos Eugênio Marcondes de, ed. *Escritos sobre as Religiões dos Orixás* (São Paulo: Agora, 1981).

Moura, Carlos Eugênio Marcondes de, ed. *Bandeira de Alaira: Outros Escritos sobre as Religiões dos Orixás* (São Paulo: Noble, 1982).

Moura, Carlos Eugênio Marcondes de, ed. *Candomblé, Desvendando Identidades: Novos Escritos sobre as Religiões dos Orixás* (São Paulo: EMW Editores, 1987).

Nina Rodrigues, Raimundo. *O Animiso Fetichista dos Negros Bahianos* (Rio de Janeiro: Civilização Brasileira, 1935).

Portadeculturnegra. (n.d.) http://portaldaculturanegra.wordpress.com/2008/11/26/mae-aninha-ialorixa-do-ile-axe-opo-afonja

Prandi, J. Reginaldo. *Os Candomblés de São Paulo: A Velha magia na metropole Nova* (São Paulo: Editora Huicitec; Editora da Universidade de São Paulo, 1991).

Prandi, J. Reginaldo. "O Brasil com Axé: Candomblé e Umbanda no Mercado Religiosa." *Estudos Avançados* 18, no. 52 (2004). http://209.85.165.104/search?q=cache:A4yEWL681d8J:www.scielo.br/pdf/ea/v18n52/a15v1852.pdf+umbanda+candombl%C3%A9+%22reginaldo+prandi%22&hl=en&ct=clnk&cd=7&gl=us.

Prata, Vander. "Iyalorixás assumen a crença como religião independente da Católica." Salvador, Bahia, Brazil: Jornal da Bahia, July 29, 1983.

Santos, Maria Stella de Azevedo. Interview by Max, Clécio. Salvador, Bahia, Brazil, May 2, 2007.

Selka, Stephen. *Religion and the Politics of Ethnic Identity in Bahia Brazil* (Gainesville: The University of Florida Press, 2007).

Uniafro. "Mãe Menininha de Gantois." http://www.uniafro.com.br/biografia_mae_menininha.htm.

Vensencher, Semira Adler. Mãe Stella de Oxossi. Fundação Getúlio Vargas. 2008. http://www.fundaj.gov.br/notitia/servlet/newstorm.ns.presentation.NavigationServlet?publicationCode=16&pageCode=309&textCode=11744&date=currentDate.

Verger, Pierre Fatumbi. *Orixás: Deuses Iorubás na África e no Novo Mundo* (Salvador, Bahia, Brazil: Corrupios Edições, 1992).

Wafer, Jim. *The Taste of Blood: Spirit Possession in Brazilian Candomblé* (Philadelphia: University of Pennsylvania Press, 1991).

CATIMBÓ

Historical Development

Catimbó is a religious and healing tradition of Amerindian origin found mainly in Northern Brazil. In addition to Amerindian traditions, Catimbó also draws on Catholicism and European traditions of witchcraft and magic. While many participants are Afro-Brazilian, Catimbó borrows relatively little from Afro-Brazilian religion and is quite distinct in terms of ritual, theology, and social organization. On the other hand, some symbols from Catimbó have found their way into Afro-Brazilian religion, especially Umbanda, where one finds frequent usage of the word *jurema*, a tree whose bark and roots are used in Catimbó to brew a psychotropic tea[1] that facilitates visions of the seven (in some versions, five) enchanted kingdoms.

The Catimbó religious specialist is often called *mestre* ("master" or "maestro"). The main function of the master is to serve as the vehicle whereby various spirits (also called *mestres*) from the enchanted realms appear to heal and in other ways help those who attend Catimbó rituals. (To avoid confusion, in this article the religious specialist will be referred to as "master" and the spiritual entities "*mestres*.") The master learns his craft through apprenticeship; proof of his qualifications comes not only through his performance but also from the presence of a small, soft cyst, often on the hand, that is said to be the seed of the *jurema* tree, granted him by a *mestre*. Although Catimbó draws on Catholic imagery, it is not a moralistic religion; *mestres* can be called on to do good or evil (Cascudo 1979, 1988).

Beliefs and Practices

Ritual is relatively simple and informal. In contrast to Afro-Brazilian religions, with their numerous initiates or mediums, the master works more or less alone. As described by Cascudo (1988), ceremonies take place in a simple room, the main feature of which is a table that serves as an altar. On it are arranged statues of Catholic saints, bottles of *cachaça*,[2] cigars, candles, a large metal key to "unlock the door" for the *mestres* to arrive, a maraca that the master uses to accompany his singing, a white ceramic bowl called the *princesa* ("princess"), used in the preparation of the *jurema*, and a pipe. The pipe, or *cachimbo* (the word from which Catimbó derives its name), and tobacco, play a central role in ritual. At the opening of the session, the master blows smoke from his pipe over the altar and around the room. Some masters achieve an altered state of consciousness by drawing deeply on the pipe and swallowing the smoke, and smoke is blown over injured or diseased bodies as a medicine; both practices are rooted in Amerindian tradition. As the ritual unfolds, the audience drinks cachaça and smokes, but refrains from talking. The master begins with a hymn declaring the session open, followed by another asking the permission of the *mestres* to work "with the power of Jesus Christ,"

---

[1]The psychotropic tea is not used in Umbanda, but "Jurema" is a frequent name for spirits of *caboclas*, that is, spirits of Amerindian women.
[2]*Cachaça*, distilled from sugarcane, is approximately 80 proof.

and then another invoking several Catholic saints, as candles are lit in their honor. The master "opens the [invisible] door" with the key and then receives a series of *mestres*, each announcing his or her presence through a song, often accompanied by the maraca from the altar. The songs are simple and usually short—several lines of verse—but vivid, evoking images of the forests, the ocean, animals, tropical birds, villages, and cities of the enchanted kingdoms, along with the characteristics of the *mestres*. The *mestres* represent a diverse panoply of spiritual beings. There are Indians, Afro-Brazilian slaves, cowboys, princesses, *caboclos*, and even *Orixás* from the Afro-Brazilian Candomblé (see "Candomblé," in this volume), and many other varieties of *mestres*. The various *mestres* specialize in curing particular illnesses and dealing with particular kinds of problems. As each appears, he or she tends to those thus afflicted, giving advice, blowing smoke, and prescribing any number of herbs, teas, and other remedies. This can go on for hours. The work of the *mestres* finally done, the session draws to an end. There may be drinking of the *jurema*, or not[3]; in any case, the master sings a hymn declaring the session closed, and, taking up his key once again, closes and locks the door to the enchanted realms (Cascudo 1988; Bastide 1978 gives a somewhat different description of ritual).

While Catimbó is not an Afro-Brazilian religion in the sense of having significant roots in African traditions, historically it has played an important role in the lives of many Afro-Brazilians in the northern regions of Brazil, and many of its masters and *mestres* share an Afro-Brazilian identity.

Lindsay Hale

SELECTED BIBLIOGRAPHY

Bastide, Roger. *The African Religions of Brazil: Toward a Sociology of the Interpenetration of Civilizations*, trans. Helen Sebba (Baltimore and London: The Johns Hopkins University Press, 1978).

Cascudo, Luis da Camara. *Dicionário do Folclore Brasileiro* (São Paulo: Edicões Melhoramentos, 1979).

Cascudo, Luis da Camara. "Notas sobre o catimbó." *Novos Estudos Afro-brasileiros*, ed. Gilberto Freyre et al. (Recife: Editora Massangana, 1988).

Gates, Louis Henry, and Kwame Anthony Appiah, eds. "Religions, African, in Brazil." *Africana: The Encyclopedia of the African and African American Experience* (New York: Basic Civitas Books, 1999), 1605–1606.

CHRISTIAN METHODIST EPISCOPAL CHURCH

Historical Development

Originally established as the Colored Methodist Episcopal Church, the Christian Methodist Episcopal Church (CME) is a historically African American denomination founded in Jackson, Tennessee, on December 16, 1870. Its polity and doctrines follow the pattern of other

---

[3]Bastide reports this from his observations in Paraíba; Camara Cascudo, reporting from Natal, does not.

organizations within the Methodist traditions. Initiated by black people during Reconstruction, the denomination came into being through the efforts of members of the Methodist Episcopal Church, South (MECS). The black leaders of this effort were former slaves, and many of the whites who joined with them were former slave owners. Other white participants had defended the rights of their church peers to own slaves. Today, churches in the denomination are spread throughout the United States, as well as in the Caribbean and Africa.

Historically, African Americans have practiced Methodism through four denominations: the United Methodist Church (UMC), the African Methodist Episcopal (AME) Church, the African Methodist Episcopal Zion (AMEZ) Church, and the Colored or Christian Methodist Episcopal (CME) Church. The first of these, the UMC, is the current iteration of the spiritual renewal movement within the Anglican Church transported to America from England in the eighteenth century. It is a predominantly white organization with congregations of various ethnic groups among its churches in the United States. The AME Church and the AMEZ Church were formed out of a predecessor denomination of the UMC, the Methodist Episcopal Church. These two Methodist bodies were formed from protests against second-class treatment, such as separate and unequal seating, in antebellum northern congregations in Philadelphia and New York. Black congregants left these fellowships and formed their own autonomous religious groups.

Finally, the formation of the CME Church came through a concerted, cooperative, social, and political effort between the MECS and the members of the nascent CME Church. The MECS had been established in 1844 from Methodist congregations located in the southern United States. These congregations had split from the American derivative of John Wesley's religious movement within the Church of England, which was known as Methodism. Methodism had been organized in America at the popularly named Christmas Conference of 1784. The MECS had become a denomination that formed in dispute with its northern sister churches over the matter of conference delegate privileges for slavery owners.

CME historians are intentional in noting the distinction that the Colored Methodists were "set up" by the MECS and not "set off." For them, this meant that the white Methodists were not attempting to get rid of them but rather were extending to them the opportunity for a limited autonomy, while still maintaining its relationship to the governing body or General Conference. This distinction also implied that the move toward independence had the full support of the MECS, including the property and financial and political resources to make the denomination a lasting reality. This was also important for the CMEs, who wanted to emphasize their relationship to white Methodists whose religious roots were linked to Methodist founder, John Wesley. Accordingly, they never seceded from the Methodist Episcopal Church, unlike their African Methodist rivals. The CME made many gestures to its white Methodist antecedent in its founding, one of which was to codify in its General Conference a prohibition against using churches and church property for political purposes.

Before the end of the Civil War, the MECS had as many as 207,000 black members, the majority of whom had been added to the membership rolls through mission outreach to the slaves. Slave owners often allowed—or even requested—missionaries to preach and teach the Christian message to their slaves with the expectation that the slaves would learn a message that would cause them to become more docile and more productive. In short, the belief was that Christian preaching would serve to make African Americans better slaves. By the end of the Civil War, congregations of the MECS reported that as few as 78,000 black members had retained their membership throughout the war and after the Emancipation Proclamation of 1863. Regular church membership for many congregants, black and white, became difficult, if not impossible, due to the general disruption of daily life during war time. Furthermore, through the missionary efforts of northern Methodists from black and white denominations, large numbers of black people affiliated themselves with other churches in response to the new sense of choice that emancipation from slavery offered them.

The 1866 MECS-wide national meeting, also known as the General Conference, was the first postwar opportunity for denominational leaders to discuss the matter of the "colored" people who remained members. As they had before the war, white leadership played a role in developing plans for the religious concerns of the black people among them. By the 1870 MECS General Conference, 26 black preachers from six geographic districts had been reportedly ordained and available for placement to the pastorates in black congregations and movement through the Methodist system of pastoral itinerant appointment. In December of that year, an organizing conference in the movement toward a black Methodist body settled on the name "Colored Methodist Episcopal Church in America."

The nomenclature "in America" was distinct from its parent group, the Methodist Episcopal Church, South. The new

---

WILLIAM H. MILES (1828–1892)

William H. Miles was born a slave in Kentucky in 1828. As an adult, he confessed his belief in Jesus Christ and was admitted to membership in the Methodist Episcopal Church, South. Later he was licensed as a local preacher and two years after that, in 1859, he was ordained by Bishop James Osgood Andrew. Miles moved to Ohio with his family, and he transferred—with the approval of the Methodist Episcopal Church South (MECS)—to the African Methodist Episcopal Zion Church (AMEZ). Miles returned to Kentucky and remained with the AMEZ Church after having been appointed to a pastorate. In 1868, Miles resigned his post and joined a colored conference that had been organized. Miles is credited with being the senior bishop of the church for 20 years. During his tenure, the new church grew to record 118,000 adult members. Miles's goal was to create a church as independent as possible from excessive control by former slave owners in the MECS as well as the northern Methodists who included the independent African Methodist churches. This desire for independence may be the reason for Miles's failed attempt to open the first CME (Colored Methodist Episcopal, later the Christian Methodist Episcopal) school without funding support from the MECS. Miles died in Louisville in 1892.

RICHARD H. VANDERHORST (1813–1872)

Richard H. Vanderhorst was elected bishop in 1870, along with William H. Miles. He was considered the more impressive of the two original bishops in terms of his physical presence and his oratorical abilities. Born in Georgetown, South Carolina, on December 15, 1813, his surname reflects the Vanderhorst clan who owned him and his family as slaves. Vanderhorst was industrious as a carpenter, and by the beginning of the Civil War, he had earned and saved enough money from his trade to purchase his own freedom. A former member of the AME Church, he had been introduced to the MECS by Betsy and Judith Wragg, two young women who owned him until his late teens. His Sunday duties included carrying the hymn books and Bibles of his young owners and taking his place on the slave bench at their side during the worship services. In addition, Samson Dunmore, a black carpenter who trained Vanderhorst, was a class leader and exhorter in the MECS. Vanderhorst, like Miles, was a key leader in the Organizing General Conference. Vanderhorst's legacy was curtailed due to the limited time he served as bishop. He died of pneumonia in July 1872.

organization later showed its interest in becoming a church body beyond the United States and dropped the "in America" in 1930, having moved into the western and northern United States. Furthermore, when the ex-slave organizers met in 1870 to transition to a separate Methodist organization, "colored" was the prevailing term used in America to refer to people of African descent. By 1954, CMEs were ready to discuss the elimination of the racial designation from their official name. In all likelihood, discussions of integration had become widespread in national black agendas. That year, the denomination adopted a resolution that embraced "inclusiveness in membership" and changed the name to "Christian" from "Colored.

At their official founding in 1870, the CME Church conferences were concentrated in the southern United States, primarily in Mississippi, Alabama, Georgia, Tennessee, and Kentucky, with unofficial and semiorganized delegations in East Texas, Arkansas, and South

Carolina. Likewise, the first two elected bishops were from two states with larger constituencies—William Henry Miles, born and formerly enslaved in Kentucky, and Richard H. Vanderhorst, an ex-slave of South Carolina and Georgia. Miles and Vanderhorst had been influential African Americans in the MECS, and, in addition, they may have been elected bishops because of their prior affiliation with the African Methodist churches. This was strategic, since confrontation between the CME churches and AME churches was inevitable. Therefore, the CME leadership believed that these men would be the most capable men to manage such issues. Finally, because these men represented large southern Kentucky and Georgia contingencies, the leadership believed them to be in a position to expand north into predominantly white areas and south into areas dominated by other black Methodists.

The CME development was swift and steady. In the first 20 years of its independence, for instance, the CME Church tripled its membership and added three

LUCIUS HENRY HOLSEY (1842–1920)

Lucius Henry Holsey was born in 1842 near Columbus, Georgia. His slave mother was the daughter of a "pure" African. His father, James Holsey, was also his owner. Lucius Holsey had an unusually close relationship with Bishop George Pierce of the MECS. Pierce performed the wedding ceremony between Holsey and one of Pierce's slaves, and he was the church official who granted Holsey a license to preach and subsequently ordained him and assigned him to his first pastorate. He was elected a bishop of the CME Church in 1873. Among his many activities, Holsey made an appeal to the General Conference of the MECS, in 1882, requesting funds for the education of colored youth and preachers. The MECS Conference responded by establishing an Education Commission, members of which had previously worked on issues of interests to African Americans. When Holsey, Bishops William Miles, Isaac Lane, and Joseph Beebe met with the Commission in August 1882, their work led to the founding of Paine Institute in Augusta, Georgia. Holsey is credited with having had a vision for a CME educational system for primary through college. He served as the Secretary of the College of Bishops for 40 years. Holsey died in 1920.

bishops—Joseph A. Beebe, Lucius H. Holsey, and Isaac Lane, for whom Lane College in Jackson, Mississippi, was named. As a church organized in the Reconstruction Era, the CME Church wanted to exercise their newfound freedom in a variety of ways. The establishment of a self-governed ecclesial body was important as was their setting an agenda for the uplift of the African American people. A vital strategy for such improvement of the lives of emancipated former slaves was development of educational opportunities—something that had been legally denied to most of them prior to Emancipation. To address the literacy needs of black communities and to train preachers, the CME Church made education a primary thrust of their denominational work. Nearly from its beginning, church leaders began raising funds to begin a school to educate its ministers and laity. The 1874 General Conference approved one to be opened in Louisville, Kentucky. It was to be a "Central University." Bishop William

Miles was the primary fundraiser. By 1876, the effort was defeated—no students had been enrolled. This attempt was a failure due to insufficient funding.

In 1882, Bishop Lucius Holsey, who envisioned an entire CME school system, from primary grades to college, made an appearance at the MECS General Conference. He felt strongly that whites had a moral obligation to their former slaves and that education was the key to fulfilling that obligation. The MECS named representatives to help the CMEs start a college. Shortly afterward, Holsey and the other CME bishops met with MECS representatives in Atlanta. They determined to open the first MECS-supported school in Augusta, Georgia. The subsequent school was named Paine Institute after Dr. Uriah Paine, who gave $25,000 to the effort.

From its inception, Paine was touted as the flagship college of the CME educational endeavors. It survived, in large part, due to ongoing MECS financial support. Another factor in Paine's ability to

ISAAC LANE (1834–1936)

Born near Jackson, Tennessee, on March 3 or 4, 1834, Isaac Lane was elected the fifth bishop of the CME Church. Lane was 20 years of age when he was converted to the Christian religion, and he was licensed to preach in the same year. Prior to this, he had been ordained a deacon by Bishop Robert Paine in 1866 and ordained an elder the following year. He has the distinction of being the first "Presiding Elder" of what was to become the CME Church, when in 1867 he was appointed to that position over the Jackson District of the Memphis Colored Conference. Lane was responsible for the first expansion of the church in the northern United States, and he was the moving force behind the founding and maintenance of Lane College, which continues to exist as a historically black college. When the school became a college, Bishop Lane chose a white minister, Thomas F. Saunders, to serve as its first president. In 1907, Lane's son, James Franklin Lane, who had completed his PhD, became president of the college. A World War II Merchant Marine Victory ship was named the USS *Lane* in honor of his commitment to education. Lane died in 1936.

flourish as a school was the 1968 reconciliation of several Methodist traditions into the United Methodist Church. Paine continued to receive financial support from that body. The cooperative nature of the work that helped to establish the institution became known as the "Paine College Ideal" or the "Paine Principle," a model for progress through interracial partnership. In 2007, the CME Church claimed a total of five surviving institutions: Paine College, Miles College, Texas College, Lane College and its seminary, and Phillips School of Theology of the Interdenominational Theological Center in Atlanta, Georgia.

In addition to the work across the United States, the denomination currently maintains missions and churches in Haiti, Jamaica, Nigeria, and Liberia.

CHARLES HENRY PHILLIPS (1858–1951)

Born in 1858 in Georgia, Charles Henry Phillips later took courses at Atlanta University before being turned away from the school. Phillips enrolled at Central Tennessee College in Nashville, earning a bachelor's degree. In 1882, he earned a medical degree from Meharry Medical College in Nashville. Phillips converted to Christianity in 1874, and he was ordained an elder in 1883. After some time as an educator, he was appointed to several pastorates, and he served congregations in Washington, D.C., Kentucky, and Georgia before becoming a presiding elder. Before becoming a bishop, Phillips served for eight years as editor of the denomination's official publication, *The Christian Index*, and he was a bishop of the church for 44 years from 1902 to 1946. Bishop Phillips wrote the first definitive history of the CME Church, published as *The History of the Colored Methodist Episcopal Church in America* in 1925. Because he was an educated man and scholar, Phillips School of Theology, the denomination's seminary in Atlanta, Georgia, is named in his honor.

Beliefs and Practices

Members of the Christian Methodist Episcopal Church ascribe to doctrines as set out by John Wesley in his sermons and treatises. These are interpreted in the *Articles of Religion*.

Members believe in a supreme God, who created the world including human beings. This God is spoken of in the masculine and "he" has three manifestations known as the Trinity: God the Father, God the Son, and God the Holy Spirit. These are three persons, but they are one being. Humans are believed to have been born defiant against God. Accordingly, God the Father rejects humans in this natural state. For this reason, the son is believed to have offered himself in sacrifice to the father as a substitutionary atonement for their salvation. He is said to have done so in order to "redeem" humans so that they can be in relationship with God and live forever in a life after death, in a world that God inhabits. So, according to members, each human who accepts that the son has acted sacrificially can be restored in relationship to God. In Wesleyan theology, this sacrifice becomes efficacious once one accepts it. It exists before such acceptance—humans do not need to seek it or perform particular deeds—only to evidence acceptance of it by confessing a belief in their own sinfulness and in the restoring act of Jesus, the Son. Finally, the Spirit of God is said to be ever-present, communicating between the father and the son as well as communicating the will of the father to human beings.

At the point that a person accepts the son, he or she has attained "salvation." In other words, one has established a reconciled relationship with God and will have an eternal afterlife. Furthermore, members believe this act of salvation means that humans are literally changed so that their nature will now be more like God's, that is, more apt to agree with the tenets of the Christian faith and to live a life of holiness. Children or infants of Methodist families, on the other hand, pose some special circumstances. Generally, a child born into a family that practices Methodism will normally be baptized, that is, ritually immersed in or sprinkled by water, during infancy. As the child matures, the child will be taught the matters of the faith then enter a class to specifically teach Methodism and the tenets of the Christian faith. At the end of the time of the class, the child—usually a teenager—will have an opportunity to acknowledge verbally his or her belief in Jesus Christ as the son of God.

The CME Church is a system of congregations linked together by a series of local, regional, and church-wide meetings on a quarterly, annual, and quadrennial schedule each known by the name of "Conference." A pastor and the local governing body are the officials of each local congregation. These representatives establish the regular times—generally at least one Sunday per month—for the worship ritual. This "worship service" is a gathering of all members of the congregation who choose to come. Members may also invite guests. The service includes prayers for the sick and grieving or otherwise troubled members of the congregation, as well as collection of any financial offerings that support the church and the General Conference. Services also include singing of songs to instruct or retell hearers the tenets of the faith, to encourage doubters and the discouraged, to highlight the faith of the community, and to adore, revere, and worship the Deity. The pastor or another speaker delivers a sermon or lesson with a similar theme often in a rhetorical fashion. Members of the audience who are not professed believers of the faith or who do not regularly worship with that congregation are usually invited to become confessors or to unite with the local body.

The ritual known as Communion or the Lord's Supper is a reenactment of the final meal that Jesus Christ shared with a group of his followers, known as "the Twelve" or "the disciples," before his death by crucifixion. The ritual includes broken pieces of "bread" or a bread substitute (such as crackers or wafers) and "wine" or a wine substitute, sometimes grape juice.

Members also maintain that a Christian can reach perfection, in the sense that one can attain a sinless lifestyle.

The CME Church also promulgates what they call a Social Creed, meant as a public statement of the relevance of their belief to human conditions of existence including the physical, intellectual, and social needs of human beings. The Social Creed asserts that all human beings are part of the human family and as such all represent the creation of God. The Creed addresses crime, war, military service, unemployment, human rights, poverty, gambling, sex, and health. The church locates this commitment to social concerns in the life of Jesus, in which, they maintain, can be seen a focus on the everyday needs of communities and individuals. Furthermore, members locate authority for such social practice in their own history, and they point to their own bishops, laity, and leaders as evidence of a CME heritage of social and racial justice. They believe that whatever is in the interest of human beings and their well-being should also be in the interest of the Church. Finally, they assert that the Social Creed is just as significant as a religious statement of concern, and any other official theological statements and creeds.

Stephen C. Finley and Terri Laws

SELECTED BIBLIOGRAPHY

Gilmore, Marshall. *The Larger Catechism: A Catechism for Members of the C.M.E. Church* (Nashville: The CME Publishing House, 1995).

Keller, Rosemary Skinner, and Rosemary Radford Ruether, eds. *Encyclopedia of Women and Religion in North America* (Bloomington: Indiana University Press, 2006).

Lakey, Othal Hawthorne. *The History of the CME Church*, rev. ed. (Memphis: The CME Publishing House, 1996).

Melton, Gordon J. *A Will to Choose: The Origins of African American Methodism* (Lanham, MD: Rowman and Littlefield Publishers, 2007).

Phillips, Charles H. *The History of the Colored Methodist Episcopal Church in America: Comprising Its Organization, Subsequent Development and Present Status*, 3rd ed. (Jackson, TN: Publishing House of the C.M.E. Church, 1925).

Publishing House of the Methodist Episcopal Church, South. *History of the Organization of the Methodist Episcopal Church, South with the Journal of its First General Conference* (Nashville: Publishing House Methodist Episcopal Church, South, 1925).

Richardson, Harry V. *Dark Salvation: The Story of Methodism as It Developed Among Blacks in America*. C. Eric Lincoln Series on Black Religion (Garden City, NY: Anchor Press/Doubleday, 1976).

Sommerville, Raymond R. *An Ex-Colored Church: Social Activism in the CME Church, 1870–1970* (Macon, GA: Mercer University Press, 2004).

Tribble, Jeffery L. *Transformative Pastoral Leadership in the Black Church*. Black Religion/Womanist Thought/Social Justice Series, eds. Dwight N. Hopkins and Linda Thomas (New York: Palgrave Macmillan, 2005).

Whelchel, Love Henry, Jr. *Hell without Fire: Conversion in Slave Religion* (Nashville: Abingdon Press, 2002).

CHURCH OF CHRIST HOLINESS USA

Historical Development

The Church of Christ Holiness USA (COCHUSA) represents an ecclesiastical body whose historical birth and maturation results from both rifts and alliances along theological and doctrinal lines. The presence of concurring schisms within Baptist and Methodist denominations and the development of new ecclesiastical alliances around "fresh" theological sensibilities created an ideal environment for the genesis of COCHUSA.

COCHUSA was not formally incorporated until 1907; however, its foundation extends back to the last decade of the nineteenth century. In 1894, Charles Price Jones, while serving as pastor of Tabernacle Baptist Church in Selma, Alabama, maintained that he experienced a personal encounter with the presence of God. Jones utilized these revelations of truth concerning the Trinity, especially with regard to the Holy Spirit, to formulate a holiness doctrine. Personal/social empowerment concerning both sin and physical illnesses through the process of sanctification was the primary tenet of this new truth revealed to Jones. After one year of pastoring in Alabama, Jones relocated to Jackson, Mississippi, where he began sharing these teachings with the congregation of Mt. Helm Baptist Church.

CHARLES PRICE JONES (1865–1949)

Charles Price Jones was born on December 9, 1865, in the northwestern portion of Georgia where the Weiss Lake and Oostanaula River converge. He moved to Arkansas in 1882 due to his mother's death. In Arkansas Jones converted to Christianity, which led to his ordination in 1887. In 1891 he graduated from Arkansas Baptist College. Although Jones served as a pastor in Arkansas, Alabama, and California, Mt. Helm Baptist Church in Jackson, Mississippi, would serve as the fertile ground in which Jones planted holiness doctrine. It is here that he taught Christ-centered theology, specifically stressing the importance of the Holy Spirit in the role of sanctification and personal/social empowerment. This notion led Jones beyond the walls of Mt. Helm to co-establish the Church of God and Christ and establish, after 1907, the Church of Christ Holiness USA in which he served as Senior Bishop until his death in 1949. Jones's theological perspectives concerning holiness can be attested to in the periodical entitled, *Truth*; within both of his primary works, *The Work of the Holy Spirit in the Churches* and *An Appeal to the Sons of Africa*; and lastly, in the over 1000 hymns he wrote and arranged.

The doctrine of holiness grew like a wildfire cutting across denominational and geographical boundaries. In response to this growth, Jones sent out a call to all ministers and laypersons who were interested in the promotion of holiness doctrine. The first holiness convocation occurred at Mt. Helm Baptist Church in 1897. Not only did this event serve as the first official attempt to nationally identify and organize various ecclesiastical bodies—many with established Baptist and Methodist denominational ties—but it also brought to the forefront of the movement other important figures like Charles Harrison Mason and J. E. Jeter who would participate in the spread of the holiness doctrine.

Since most of these pastors, specifically Jones and Mason, were clergy within the Baptist denomination, their promotion of holiness doctrine was deemed unacceptable. In 1899, various Baptist Associations, in Jones's case the Jackson Baptist Association, began the process of expelling clergy who taught the holiness doctrine within churches that were Baptist. Despite their expulsion from the Baptist denomination, Mason in 1899 and Jones in 1902 established nondenominational churches that solely promoted holiness doctrine. Christ Temple Church, built in 1903 under the leadership of Jones, served as the official meeting place for the annual holiness convocation that attracted churches from across the United States. This site also contained a printing shop that produced doctrinal material, hymnals, and the group's official periodical entitled, *The Truth.*

Between the years of 1903 and 1906, the various churches in attendance at the holiness convocation were organized into a single coalition known as the Church of God in Christ. Because of rapid growth within this alliance, the installation of a governing body soon followed with Jones serving as the presiding superintendent. Also, within this structural system Mason became the presiding officer over Tennessee, while Jeter was placed over churches located in Arkansas. Growth in membership, an increase in ministerial workshops, and constant educational training for laypersons concerning the holiness doctrine blossomed as a result of this coalition of holiness bodies.

Although this holiness alliance produced much fruit, it came to an end in 1907 when both Mason and Jeter attended the Azusa Street Revival in Los Angeles. After spending five weeks in Los Angeles, Mason returned to Tennessee armed with a holiness doctrine laced with Pentecostalism. It was his acceptance of glossolalia (i.e., ''speaking in tongues'') as the sole sign of receiving the Holy Spirit that caused the Church of God in Christ to split into two separate groups in August 1907. The first group, headed by Mason, adopted a Pentecostal orientation and retained the name Church of God in Christ, while the second group, which Jones led, maintained a non-Pentecostal orientation and adopted the name the Church of Christ Holiness USA.

Under the leadership of Jones, COCHUSA membership increased from 96 in 1907 to over 4,000 in 1936. An Episcopal framework was adopted in 1927 formally decreeing Jones as the Senior Bishop and creating seven dioceses, Northern, Southwestern, Eastern, South Central, Western/Pacific Northwest, Southeastern, and North Central. Each diocese has a presiding bishop, and these men along with the Senior Bishop make up the Board of Bishops. Women are not allowed to hold positions within this structure. It is important to note that some women were instrumental in starting the local churches, like Christ Temple Church of Christ Holiness USA founded over 80 years ago in Kansas City, Missouri.

Major Rudd Conic, after the death of Jones in 1949, served as the Senior Bishop of COCHUSA until 1992. With over 200 local churches and well over 11,000 adherents, the association flourished under the leadership of Bishop Conic. He stressed the importance of empowerment through land ownership, facility buildings, as well as personal financial stability. For example, he implemented the Master Plan Project in which the church purchased 340 acres of land. Bishop Conic's passion for the empowerment of COCHUSA served as a catalyst in the formation of the M. R. Conic Foundation. With land already purchased in Jackson, Mississippi, this nonprofit organization, initiated by the United Christian Women's Ministries of COCHUSA, plans to build a housing complex that would provide shelter,

fitness programs, educational resources, and technological training for senior citizens.

Presently, under the leadership of Bishop Emery Lindsay, COCHUSA continues to hold biennial national conventions and promote their system of core values, WHEAT—an acronym for Worship, Training, Evangelism, Administration, and Training. COCHUSA continues to stress the importance of education by financially supporting the Christ Missionary Industrial College in Jackson. The small printing shop built by C. P. Jones has now matured into the National Publishing House, which is located in Chicago and headed by church elder Dr. Dale Cudjoe. It is still responsible for publishing and disseminating projects, such as the *Truth* and *The Manual* periodicals. An organized system of governing, property ownership, maturation in doctrinal practices, and the extension of COCHUSA into Africa, serve as fruit to attest to this group's historical solidarity.

BISHOP MAJOR RUDD CONIC (1909–)

The union of Bishop J. L. O. and Louise Virginia Crawford Conic yielded the birth of Major Rudd Conic on December 22, 1909. Although Jackson, Mississippi, was his birthplace, Arkansas and Alabama served as instrumental locations in the childhood of M. R. Conic. He finished his secondary education at Dunbar High School in 1928; a year later he matriculated at C.M. and I. College. He received ordination in 1937 and became the pastor of Christ Temple Church in Jackson, Tennessee, three years later. In 1947 he served as both pastor of Christ Temple Church in Jackson, Mississippi (mother church of COCHUSA), and executive Secretary of the Trustee Board of C.M. and I. College. That same year a special National Convention was called during which M. R. Conic accepted the bishopric office overseeing the South Central Diocese. Following the death of Bishop Jones in 1949, he became the National President and Senior Bishop of COCHUSA, which lasted until 1992. Empowerment through the reduction of financial debt and initiation of massive building projects via land ownership stood as pillars within the 43-year tenure of Bishop M. R. Conic.

Beliefs and Practices

The 28 "Articles of Faith" housed in COCHUSA's manual illustrates the primary tenets of the group's belief system as well as its adherences to certain rituals. Although opening articles, especially as seen in 1–3, maintain belief in one God and the holy Trinity, Christ represents the focal point within their theological discourse. For instance, this body supports that only the birth, ministry, and death of Christ can lift man from a fallen state caused by the sin of Adam and grant restoration of this same body to its former, sinless state; therefore, Christ is the catalyst of atonement. Justification, the eighth article, is thought to be God's domain with absolution depending upon the individual's participation in repentance and reception of the incarnated Christ.

Repentance composes only a portion of the first of the three parts found in COCHUSA's "3-stage way of salvation." Conversion, including repentance and a confession of faith, represents the first stage. The second stage is characterized by eradication and is known as the "second blessing." It is within this stage that original sin transmitted through Adam undergoes eradication via the entrance of the Holy Spirit. Freedom from moral demise, transference from original sin to holiness, apprehensions of freedom through holiness, and empowerment to conquer sin are the fruits produced within this second stage of salvation. The power to conquer sin also gives one the ability to participate in divine healing, the final stage. Divine healing is believed to be a gift from God meant to be utilized by the ecclesiastical body. Each stage of salvation is supported by the Bible. Since the Bible itself for this group is viewed as the infallible words of God, the doctrinal belief system of COCHUSA maintains that the 66 books of the Bible contain all the knowledge needed to live as Christians.

The theological doctrine of this group also places emphasis of the role of the Holy Spirit in both the process of salvation and the daily existence of each individual. The Holy Spirit is an initiated gift of God and represents Christ in operation. Therefore, the two cannot be separated. The movement of the Holy Spirit within the lived experiences of individual members creates an environment of resistance to sin through holiness, producing a well-structured moral system. Accordingly, this doctrine upholds the ability of holiness to defeat both personal and collective oppression within society. Spiritual gifts, the twenty-seventh article of faith, are present only after the reception of the Holy Spirit. Although each gift, like "speaking in tongues," receives recognition within COCHUSA, it is doctrinally unacceptable to single out one specific gift to represent the reception of the Holy Spirit.

Baptism and the Lord's Supper represent the two major sacraments found within COCHUSA. Baptism is reserved for those who are considered to be of age. Infants are not baptized. Full immersion and the verbal proscription "In the name of Jesus" complete this sacrament. The Lord's Supper contains two Eucharistic elements: bread and unfermented wine. Foot washing is not an official mandate, but symbolizes an act of humility in which members of the local congregation submit and wash the feet of his/her neighbor. Each diocese decides whether to include foot washing as a local mandate. Also, 40 days of praying, usually during September and October, is not an official mandate, but can be seen on the national calendar of COCHUSA every year.

Margarita Simon Guillory

SELECTED BIBLIOGRAPHY

"The ARDA: Association of Religion Data Archives" (2006). Available from ARDA, http://thearda.com (accessed June 15, 2007).

Cobbins, Otho B., ed. *History of Church of Christ (Holiness) U.S.A. 1895–1965* (New York and Washington: Vantage Press, 1966).

"COCHUSA: Church of Christ (Holiness) USA." Available from faithHighway, http://www.cochusa.com (accessed July 2, 2007).

Goff, James R., and Grant Wacker, eds. *Portraits of a Generation: Early Pentecostal Leaders* (Fayetteville: The University of Arkansas Press, 2002).

MacRobert, Iain. *White Racism of Early Pentecostalism in the USA* (New York: St. Martin's Press, 1988).

Sidwell, Mark. *Free Indeed: Heroes of Black Christian History* (Greenville: Bob Jones University Press, 1995).

Simpson, George Eaton. "Black Pentecostalism in the United States." *Phylon* 35, no. 2 (1974): 203–211.

Sparks, Randy J. *Religion in Mississippi* (Jackson: University Press of Mississippi, 2001).

CHURCH OF GOD (CLEVELAND)

Historical Development

With a worldwide membership of over 4 million and affiliated churches located in 150 countries, the Church of God (Cleveland) is one of the largest Pentecostal denominations in the world behind the Church of God in Christ (COGIC) and the Assemblies of God. Like COGIC and the Assemblies of God, the roots of the Church of God (Cleveland) are found in the "holiness movement" of the nineteenth century, a movement begun among Methodists that called for spiritual renewal and church reform. And also like COGIC, the Church of God (Cleveland) became a Pentecostal denomination after its founder had an encounter with the Azusa Street Revival of 1906.

Having been established in 1886, the Church of God (Cleveland) is the oldest Pentecostal group with holiness roots. In that year, R. G. Spurling Sr. left the Baptist church, gravely dissatisfied with Baptist worship, culture, and polity and desiring a way of Christian life that more closely reflected the first-century church and New Testament teachings. He was also particularly keen to be free of denominational organization and official church creeds. With his son, R. G. Spurling Jr. and six other people, five of whom were women, Spurling Sr. gathered at the Barney Creek Meeting House on the Tennessee/North Carolina border to form what they called "Christian Union." As separatists, the group had no intention of forming a new church or denomination but nevertheless chose Spurling Jr. as its pastor. Spurling Sr. died not long after his son's ordination.

In 1896, the members of Christian Union participated in one of the most significant revivals in American history and became fully aligned with holiness teachings. The revival at Schearer Schoolhouse in Cherokee County, North Carolina, was significant for the way it anticipated many of the doctrines and worship practices that would characterize the Azusa Street Revival a full decade later. It started when three area evangelists, William Martin, Joe M. Tipton, and Milton McNabb, opened a series of meetings focusing their preaching on the doctrine of "sanctification" and holy living. The doctrine of sanctification held that a one-time, often dramatic, experience subsequent to conversion cleansed believers from all known sin and freed them from the willful desire to commit sin. Impressed by this message, the members of Christian Union moved to North Carolina and combined with the group to which the three evangelists belonged. The revival was enormously successful, garnering mass conversations and many demonstrations of the Spirit. The ministers placed an emphasis on "the Baptism of the Holy Spirit" and incidences of people "speaking in tongues" were noted.

The success of the revival, the growth in membership, and the spread of "fanaticism" challenged Christian Union's commitment to no governance, official creeds, or record keeping. Under the direction of William F. Bryant, whom Spurling chose to pastor in his absence, they began to move toward denominational formation after the revival, adopting some forms of organization to ward off interlopers and to bring some structure and governance. Clearly a church in the traditional sense by 1902, they dropped the name "Christian Union" for "The Holiness Church," the final step in becoming fully aligned with the holiness movement. Spurling was chosen as head pastor.

Further changes ensued when A. J. (Ambrose Jessup) Tomlinson joined the group in 1903. A former Quaker and amateur actor, Tomlinson had been born to a well-to-do family in Westfield, Indiana, and had attended Westfield Academy. After his conversion to holiness teaching, he made it to North Carolina and the newly formed "The Holiness Church" by way of an itinerant ministry that took him throughout the South and Midwest. Church of God legend has it that Tomlinson paid a visit to Spurling and Bryant at Bryant's home in June 1903. The morning after the meeting, Tomlinson is said to have ascended the mountain behind Bryant's home and in the "fields of wood" on the mountain received a vision about the church, which he was instructed by God to call "the Church of God of the Bible." Several months later Tomlinson joined the church and was ordained as its minister. He began immediately to put the church on the path to doctrinal coherency, denominational formation, and organizational structure. The church also began to grow and spread throughout other regions in the South. By 1906 it held its first General Assembly as a holiness congregation and moved to Tennessee.

Two of the most significant events in the denomination's history happened in 1907. The group agreed to drop the name "The Holiness Church" and adopted the name "Church of God," and Tomlinson began to preach the Pentecostal doctrine of Spirit Baptism. Like other Holiness-Pentecostal churches, the Church of God (Cleveland) is intricately connected to occurrences at the Azusa Street Revival in Los Angeles. The revival had been launched in 1906 through the efforts of an itinerant preacher, William J. Seymour. Seymour had been born in Centerville, Louisiana, in 1870 to parents who were members of the Missionary Baptist Church. After having traveled to the Midwest and converting to holiness teachings, he landed in Houston, Texas, where he was introduced to Charles Fox Parham, who had developed a notion of the Baptism of the Holy Spirit that necessitated "speaking in tongues" as "initial evidence." Tongue speaking, the ability to speak in a language not of one's origin or an "unknown" tongue, had been a feature of holiness teaching since the 1890s, but Parham formalized the practice into a central feature of the Christian experience. While in Texas, Seymour embraced this new teaching and upon invitation took the Pentecostal message to Los Angles, where he started a three-year revival in an old AME church and livery stable on Azusa Street. In addition to speaking in tongues, a range of ecstatic and demonstrative practices developed at Azusa, including prophecy and divine healing. The church Seymour founded, the Apostolic Faith Mission, is widely viewed as the birthplace of worldwide Pentecostalism.

In 1908, a year after he had begun preaching Pentecostalism, Tomlinson invited G. B. Cashwell to conduct a revival at the church. Cashwell had been to Azusa, received the baptism, and began traveling across the country spreading the message. Although Tomlinson had been preaching Spirit baptism for a year, he had not received the experience himself. During the revival, however, he had the experience and converted the church from a Holiness to a Pentecostal denomination. In 1909 he was elected "General Overseer" of the new Pentecostal church.

The years 1909 to 1920 were productive and prosperous ones for the Church of God (Cleveland). It was a time of great denominational growth throughout the country and across racial lines. Seven black congregations formed between 1909 and 1915. The first blacks to join the group were Edmond and Rebecca Barr, who evangelized parts of Florida as members of the church. From the start women have constituted the majority membership and have been allowed to preach and to pastor churches. The church began printing its own literature beginning with the *Church of God Evangel* in 1911. In 1918 Lee University, the first of many Church of God (Cleveland)–affiliated schools, was founded and named after the man who would become the denomination's second General Overseer, F. J. Lee. The Assembly Auditorium was erected in Cleveland, Tennessee, in 1920 and Cleveland became the denominational headquarters.

The prosperous years were immediately followed by crisis. Having gone through what some observers considered a great change in his personality, A. J. Tomlinson became autocratic and antidemocratic in his leadership style. Also, whether through carelessness or oversight, his handling of church finances incurred large debts. In 1922, an investigative committee found that over $14,000 was missing from the church's treasury and over $31,000 had been misappropriated. These and other findings led to a yearlong battle between Tomlinson and the other church leaders that resulted in his impeachment as General Overseer in 1923. The church split into two opposing factions of the Church of God, the name the Tomlinson group continued to use after his impeachment. When the original group asked him to stop using the name to avoid confusion, Tomlinson refused. So, in 1924 under the leadership of its new General Overseer, F. J. Lee, the group brought suit, and the Chancery Court of Bradley County, Tennessee, granted them the exclusive use of the name. Tomlinson's group continued to use "Church of God" in modified forms throughout the 1920s, prompting other suits. Not until 1953 when the supreme court of Tennessee finally settled the issue did Tomlinson change the name of his church to "The Church of God of Prophecy." Although they were given exclusive right to the name "Church of God," since the 1953 decision the church has identified itself as Church of God (Cleveland) to be distinguished from other churches that have some form of "Church of God" in their names, including the Church of God of Prophecy, the Church of God (Holiness), and COGIC.

Beliefs and Practices

The "Doctrinal Commitments" of the Church of God (Cleveland) show all the hallmarks of Pentecostal belief and practice. Typically, however, the church is also decidedly Weslyan/Armenian and fundamentalist. In keeping with tenets promoted by John Wesley, the Church of God (Cleveland) believes "sanctification" to be a dramatic experience subsequent to conversion or "justification" where the believer enters a state of Christian perfection and is removed from the desire to sin. Unlike other Pentecostal denominations, Church of God (Cleveland) uses the terminology "baptism of the Holy Spirit" to describe this experience. It is considered an "enduement" or special enabling with power to serve and to live a holy life. "Holiness," it is maintained, is the only way of life for all believers. In Armenian terms, salvation or "justification" is a free gift of grace—an act of God—available to all, not simply to the elect.

The Fundamentalist aspects of the Church of God (Cleveland) principally have to do with their beliefs about the Bible, the personhood of God, and eschatology. Church of God (Cleveland) holds that the Bible is completely without error. It is the divinely inspired Word of God and supreme rule of life. Additionally, they are Trinitarian, asserting that God exits in three persons, Father, Son, and Holy Spirit. Water baptism is performed in the Trinitarian form as apposed to "Oneness" Pentecostals who deny the Trinity and baptize in Jesus' name only. They expect the premillennial second coming of Christ to resurrect dead saints and to "rapture" living saints before a seven-year period of tribulation, followed by a thousand-year reign of Christ on earth. Church of God (Cleveland) theology has changed little over the years and is affirmed at its biannual conventions.

In addition to its Pentecostal theology, the Church of God (Cleveland) is known for its strictly conservative cultural aesthetic. The church has long adhered to a set of "practical commitments" that were designed to be Scriptural guidelines for practical Christian living (Crews, 63). The categories seemingly cover all aspects of life and potential behavior: spiritual example; moral purity; personal integrity; family responsibility; behavioral temperance; modest appearance; and social obligation. It is in the areas of moral purity and modesty that the church has made its distinctive mark. Over much of the twentieth century, the church has eschewed all "ungodly amusements," including watching TV, dancing, attending movies, and using tobacco. Men and women have been expected to dress modestly, and women are disallowed to wear makeup or sexually suggestive clothing.

Since the 1960s the Church of God (Cleveland) has attempted to relax some of its strident behavioral expectations as a way to deal with the modern world. For example, latter versions of the "practical commitments" regarding modest appearance simply urged members to demonstrate modesty by dressing in such a way as to enhance one's testimony and to de-emphasize personal pride and sexuality. Formerly, it had forcefully charged members to dress according to the principles of the Bible, a charge that had particular implications for women, who were to refrain from wearing, according to Deuteronomy 22: 5, "that which pertaineth unto a man" (Crews, 60). In 1964 the denomination passed a "Resolution on Human Rights" followed by a resolution on the "AIDS Crisis" in 1990 and a "Resolution Against Racism" in 1991. The "Resolution on Human Rights" was passed in recognition of racial tension within the denomination that emerged in 1958 when a decades-old ruling granting African American Church of God (Cleveland) members relative autonomy and the ability to chose their own Overseer was overturned. Since 1926 there had been black and white divisions of the denomination with separate supervision, governance, and national assembly, largely through the initiative of blacks. A. J. Tomlinson conceded to the split in order to stop the flow of African American members of the church into COGIC, which was predominately African American.

In recent years the denomination has attempted to heal its divisions. Self-governance was reinstated for African Americans and cooperation with the Church of God of Prophecy was initiated. With continued growth and extensive outreach, the Church of God (Cleveland) is poised to make a major contribution to Pentecostalism worldwide.

Wallace Best

SELECTED BIBLIOGRAPHY

Conn, Charles W. *Like a Mighty Army: A History of the Church of God, 1886–1976* (Cleveland, TN: Pathway Press, 1977).

Crews, Mickey. *The Church of God: A Social History* (Knoxville: University of Tennessee Press, 1990).

Duggar, Lillie. *A. J. Tomlinson: Former General Overseer of the Church of God* (Cleveland, TN: White Wing Publishing House, 1964).

Michel, David. *Telling the Story: Black Pentecostals in the Church of God* (Cleveland, TN: Pathway Press, 2000).

Robins, R. G. *A. J. Tomlinson: Plainfolk Modernist* (New York: Oxford University Press, 2004).

Simmons, E. L. *History of the Church of God* (Cleveland, TN: Church of God Publishing House, 1938).

CHURCH OF GOD AND SAINTS OF CHRIST

Historical Development

Shortly after Prophet F. S. Cherry began his work in Philadelphia (see "Church of the Living God" entry), William Saunders Crowdy's life changed. He began a path of religious awakening similar to Cherry's.

Born in 1847, in Charlotte Hall, Maryland, Crowdy spent the first 15 years of his life as a slave. Once an opportunity presented itself in 1863 to leave his position of servitude, he journeyed to the

---

WILLIAM SAUNDERS CROWDY (1847–1908)

Prophet William Saunders Crowdy was born on a Maryland plantation called Charlotte Hall in 1847. Crowdy prayed to be liberated from his captors and at the age of 17 was set free; he immediately joined the army. Working as a cook for 20 years until 1892, Crowdy claimed to have received a vision from God that he should lead his people to the true religion. In 1895, he received another vision, much more intense than the first, which pushed him to begin preaching in order to lead God's people. He began preaching in Guthrie, Oklahoma, then moved to Lawrence, Kansas, where he opened his first tabernacle. He migrated to New York, establishing tabernacles in small cities before he set up permanent residence in Philadelphia, Pennsylvania, in 1899. In 1903, the organization bought land in Suffolk County, Virginia, that he named Canaan Land. The movement also showed international aspirations by sending missionaries to South Africa in 1905. In 1906 he named himself Chief Joseph William Crowdy and declared the future leaders of his movement to be Bishop William H. Plummer and Elder Calvin S. Skinner. On August 4, 1908, Crowdy died.

---

north and became a cook for the Union Army. With the conclusion of the war, he held various jobs in Guthrie, Oklahoma, and Kansas City, Missouri. Accounts of his life indicate that it was while living in Guthrie for the second time that his religious life took a turn from a rather uneventful connection to the Baptist Church to contact with the divine that changed his behavior.

In 1893 he began having visions. The first occurred while he was farming: "He heard a loud sound that was similar to that produced by a large flock of birds. Amidst this noise he thought he heard a voice saying 'run for your life.' On hearing this he dropped his axe and cleared a trail into the forest . . . . There he fell into a deep slumber during which the vision came to him as a dream." This dream, the account continues, involved him being "in a large room and that tables were descending from above. The tables were covered with filthy vomit . . . . Each table was labeled with the name of a church . . . . At one point in the vision a small, clean white table came down with the name

Church of God and Saints of Christ on it" (Wynia 1994, 21). Crowdy understood the vision to mean a divine mission to start a tabernacle, as he called his congregations, rejecting the problems of the other denominations. His tabernacle would be true to the teachings of God, as provided in Scripture and through subsequent visions experienced by Crowdy.

In a manner meant to resemble the ministry of biblical prophets, Crowdy took to the streets and began sharing his vision for a new tabernacle with anyone who would listen. This ministry was based on the demands placed on him during that first vision. The organization's Web site describes the command to preach felt by Crowdy:

When afterwards I heard a voice speaking unto me; saying, as he had so said unto Ezekiel, "Son of Man, I send thee to the children of Israel, and to all nations of the earth that hath rebelled against me. They and their Fathers have transgressed against me, even unto this very day; for they are imprudent children and stiff-hearted. I do send thee unto them and thou shalt say unto them, thus saith the Lord God; not Elder Crowdy, or any other man or minister, but thus saith the Lord God who is Supreme above all, an in all; whether they will hear or whether they forbear, yet shall they know there has been a Prophet among them." The Lord let me know that I should look for trouble and tribulation, but be not afraid of them; neither be afraid of their words; though briars and thorns be with thee. And thou dost dwell among scorpions, be not afraid of their words or be dismayed at their looks and thou shalt speak my words unto them, whether they will hear or whether they will forbear. (http://www.churchofgod1896.org/founder.html)

From 1893 through 1895, he spread the teachings he received in the visions to his family and receptive members of the community. Feeling a need to spread these teachings beyond Guthrie, Crowdy made his way to Chicago and stayed there a short time teaching both African Americans and Whites.

Wanting to give his converts and the doctrine they embraced an institutional framework, he moved to Lawrence, Kansas, in 1896 and established his first organization. By 1898, he had more than 20 fellowships throughout Kansas. These somewhat loosely arranged fellowships took the form of a church in 1899 during the second general assembly organized by Crowdy. From this point until his death in 1908, the organization maintained a presence in various cities and established its headquarters in Belleville, Virginia, in 1917. The tabernacles varied in size, but it has been suggested that some, including one in New York City established in 1899 had roughly 1,000 members. Beyond efforts to reach potential converts in the United States, the church also established missionary outposts in the Caribbean and in South Africa.

To foster the smooth functioning of these various congregations, Crowdy arranged them into regional districts, each headed by one of his ministers. The elders, or ministers, who supervised these districts formed a group referred to as the Presbytery. These elders played an important role, but the organization clearly revolved around Crowdy who, in addition to being called the "Black Elijah" because of the prophecy and healing he offered his followers, was understood as the primary teacher. In order to manage the affairs of the organization, Crowdy was assisted by C. S. Skinner and W. H. Plummer, who served as counselor for and business manager of the organization, respectively. (Wynia 1994, 32–33).

While the total membership is uncertain, the Church of God and Saints of Christ Web site indicates a network of 32 tabernacles in cities in the United States such as Buffalo, New York; Detroit, Michigan; Newark, New Jersey; as well as in the Caribbean, South Africa, and England. In an effort to continue to advance its work, the Church of God and Saints of Christ argues that its "vision is presently focused on community development. The Church of God and Saints of Christ had embarked upon a multi-million dollar project, a multi-faceted building on 110 acres of land owned by the church in Galestown, Maryland. This project will include worship edifice, recreational and educational facilities" (http://www.churchofgod1896.org/mission&vision.htm).

Beliefs and Practices

Crowdy, who was understood to be one of God's prophets, taught his followers that African Americans were members of the lost tribes of Israel. Based on this, he pushed for strong adherence to various elements of Judaism. For example, Crowdy's churches followed the Jewish Sabbath by centering activities around Friday evening and Saturday. On Friday evening, the service began with the rabbi (teacher), assisted by the cantor, leading the congregation in silent meditation and prayer. Afterwards, the rabbi led the congregation in various readings, some of them from Scripture. Songs were sung throughout the service, and the service concluded with a sermon by the rabbi.

On Saturday, members of the various tabernacles gathered early, and after a time of fellowship during which songs were sung, people divided into Sabbath school classes. These classes provided information concerning the church's distinctive doctrine taught and significant scriptural stories. After Sabbath school, the main service began. As with the Friday service, singing was an important dimension of worship. However, the focus of the Saturday service was the presentation of the Torah and the rabbi, and this was followed by the sermon that outlined the origin and teachings of the organization. After the sermon, those present were given an opportunity to either join the tabernacle (if they were visitors) or renew their relationship with God if they were current members. Additional singing and a benediction brought the service to an end, but those gathered did not go to their homes until after a communal meal was eaten (Wynia 1994, 60–64).

Crowdy's organization recognized various rituals as central to church life, including Rosh Hashanah (Jewish New Year), Yom Kippur (the Day of Atonement), and Passover. Within this church, the Passover celebrations were distinguished by color. There was a purple Passover during which members of the church wore that particular color. There was also a black Passover, so called for the same reason. Members of the various local congregations were encouraged to travel to the headquarters for the denomination and there celebrate the Lord's safekeeping of the children of Israel when the angel of death killed the firstborn of the Egyptians (Exodus 11:4–6). Furthermore, the Passover allows for a recounting of the Exodus story in which the Jews were freed from bondage in Egypt. During the week of celebration, members of the organization attended services consisting of singing and sermons. Food consumed during this period centered around unleavened bread, and the week of activities culminated in a communal meal of bread and lamb.

While Crowdy's followers understood themselves to stand within the tradition of Judaism, their practices were not pure in that he sought to blend Judaism with Christianity. He gave a great deal of attention to Jesus Christ as the model of conduct. He does not refer to Jesus as the messiah, but the perception of Jesus seems to extend beyond traditional Jewish understandings of him:

> The scripture says when you are converted old things passed away. Now if you are converted, leave lying, whoremongering, idolatry, witchcraft, hoodooing, and all manner if isms, you want to leave that behind and take up the new things of Jesus Christ which by no means will suffer to do any of those things. I want members to stop evil speaking of one another, and don't care to undermine on another and let me know it, if you can't speak a good word for your neighbor, even if he is a sinner, hold your peace [*sic*]. (Wynia 1994, 52)

In addition to the life of Jesus Christ and an appreciation for other dimensions of the prophetic tradition as expressed in Judaism, Crowdy developed rituals unique to the church including Re-establishment Day that honors Crowdy and recounts the church's history.

These activities were practiced within the context of established doctrine, drawn loosely from the Bible, by which tabernacle members lived. Central amongst these innovations was the "Seven Keys":

1. The Church of God and the Saints of Christ.
2. Wine forbidden to be drunk in the Church of God forever.
3. Unleavened bread and water for Christ's body and blood.
4. Foot washing is a commandment.
5. The Disciples' prayer.
6. You must be breathed upon with a Holy Kiss.
7. The Ten Commandments. (http://www.cogsoc.org/our-doctrine/keys-commandments/)

The first key speaks to the significance of Crowdy's work by highlighting the truthfulness of the Church of God and the Saints of Christ. It, unlike traditional churches, and based on the revelations received by Crowdy, is in line with the will of God and is teaching the truth about God and God's relationship to African Americans. The Christian undertones of this religious organization are apparent in the centrality given to Jesus Christ. The third key speaks to this by describing the appropriate items to be used in celebration of what Christians refer to as communion—the ritual enactment of Jesus Christ's blood and body sacrificed on the cross. Most Christian churches celebrate communion using some type of bread to represent the body and wine (or grape juice) to represent the blood of Jesus Christ. However, as the second key stipulates, wine is not consumed by members of this community—not even as part of the communion ritual. Other important components of the organization's code include the ritual of foot washing through which members show their sense of humility and community by washing the feet of other members of the group. It is meant to represent the biblical tradition of cleaning the feet of guests as they entered the home. Jesus Christ does this for his disciples as a sign of humility in that the proclaimed "Son of God" lowers himself and provides this service. Also of symbolic importance is the "Holy Kiss" given to members as a sign of community and proper relationship. The final two elements of this code are the Disciples' prayer that plays a role in the worship experience of members of the church, and the Ten Commandments drawn from the Old Testament. Even after his death, the principles outlined by Crowdy hold sway over the Church of God and Saints of Christ.

Anthony B. Pinn

SELECTED BIBLIOGRAPHY

Brotz, Howard M. *The Black Jews of Harlem: Negro Nationalism and the Dilemmas of Negro Leadership* (New York: Schocken Books, 1970).

Chireau, Yvonne, and Nathaniel Deutsch, eds. *Black Zion: African American Religious Encounters with Judaism* (New York: Oxford University Press, 2000).

Fauset, Arthur Huff. *Black God of the Metropolis: Negro Religious Cults of the*

Urban North (Philadelphia: University of Pennsylvania Press, 2001).

Wynia, Elly M. *The Church of God and Saints of Christ: The Rise of Black Jews* (New York: Garland Publishing, Inc., 1994).

CHURCH OF GOD IN CHRIST

Historical Development

The Church of God in Christ (COGIC), the first African American Pentecostal denomination in the United States, experienced phenomenal growth during the twentieth century. From a mere ten congregations in 1907 it has become the largest Pentecostal denomination in the United States and claims over 6 million members worldwide. The origins of COGIC are inextricably linked to the two most significant movements in American Christendom, the "holiness movement" of the late nineteenth century and the Pentecostal movement of the early twentieth century. It is from these movements that COGIC has drawn its worship patterns, system of belief, social philosophies, cultural traditions, and organizational structure. Over the past century, the denomination has consistently maintained these aspects of its tradition, forged, as they were, in a time of great crisis and opportunity in American society.

The early development of COGIC took shape in light of the spiritual journeys of its two founders, Charles Harrison Mason and Charles Price Jones. Mason and Jones founded the denomination as a "holiness" body in 1897. Although they would part

company over a doctrinal dispute just ten years after establishing COGIC, both men played significant roles in setting the theological and cultural framework for the denomination. Charles Mason was born to former slaves Jerry and Eliza Mason on the Prior farm just north of Memphis, Tennessee, on September 8, 1866. The devout couple belonged to the Missionary Baptist Church and prayed fervently for their son's dedication to God. Those prayers were seemingly answered in 1880 when just shy of his fourteenth birthday Charles was healed of yellow fever. The family had left Memphis for Plumerville, Arkansas, in the wake of the yellow fever epidemic only to have Jerry Mason succumb to the disease in 1879 and Charles to fall ill within months. After his recovery, Charles's mother took him to the Mt. Olive Baptist Church in Plumerville, where he was baptized and dedicated to a life of Christian service.

Having been licensed and ordained to preach in 1891 and after a failed marriage to Alice Sexton, Charles Mason entered Arkansas Baptist College in Little Rock on November 1, 1893. The experience was not a good one, but it prompted the first stirrings of Mason's desire for personal and ecclesiastical holiness reform. Established by Elias C. Morris, Arkansas Baptist College had come under the influence of new "higher criticism" in biblical interpretation, largely through the influence of one of the school's professors, Charles Lewis Fisher. Exponents of higher criticism such as Fisher investigated the origins of the biblical text and the sociocultural context in which it was written as a means to decipher original meanings and author's intent. Developed in Europe

---

CHARLES HARRISON MASON (1866–1961)

The union of two former slaves, Jerry and Eliza Mason, resulted in the birth of Charles Harrison Mason on September 8, 1866, in a rural area that graces the outskirts of present-day Memphis. At the age of 12, his family moved to Plumerville, Arkansas. It is within this city's confines that Mason would receive baptism at Mt. Olive Missionary Baptist Church. In 1893, Mason matriculated into Arkansas Baptist College. In this same year, he received ordination under Baptist auspices in the small town of Preston, Arkansas. Although Mason entered into C. P. Jones's alma mater, he transferred and completed his educational and ministerial training at the Minister's Institute of Arkansas Baptist Church. Mason, also in 1893, experienced the "second blessing." This personal encounter with God transformed Mason into an espouser of holiness doctrine. His new theological perspective stressed the importance of the Holy Spirit in the process of sanctification, which yields both spiritual freedom and personal/social empowerment over sin. Mason's teaching of holiness doctrine led to the formation of the Church of God in Christ (COGIC) with C. P. Jones; however, in 1907 the alliance was severed, resulting in Mason's incorporation of COGIC. Until his death on November 17, 1961, he served as the Presiding Bishop over COGIC.

---

in the mid-eighteenth century, higher criticism was built on the work and assumptions of Enlightenment thinkers. While it was at times used to confirm traditional biblical teachings, higher criticism most often disputed them, and exponents employed a notion of the Bible as human and not Divine in origin as their hermeneutical starting point. Deeply suspicious of these new methods and philosophies, Mason left the college after only three months.

When Mason and Charles Price Jones met in 1895, the two men discovered that they had much in common, including having both attended Arkansas Baptist College. Jones was born near Rome, Georgia, to a slave mother on December 9, 1865. After his mother's death in 1882, Jones traveled throughout the South and the Midwest working menial jobs. Returning to Tennessee in 1884, he was converted, started teaching Sunday school, and began a preaching ministry. His desire to expand his ministry to Africa took him to Arkansas Baptist

College in 1888, and although he presumably experienced similar frustration with the college's liberal hermeneutical bent, he graduated in 1891. Even while completing his course of study, Jones was busy in Christian ministry, shepherding three congregations, Pople Creek, Mt. Zion, and St. Paul Baptist churches. It was after graduation and a move first to Alabama and then to Mississippi, however, that Jones expressed a need for a deeper Christian experience. Mason and Jones encountered one another at a meeting in Mississippi that had been organized by Jones and fellow pastors J. E. Jeter and W. S. Pleasant to study the Scriptures regarding the doctrine of "sanctification." Mason and Jones became convinced of the doctrine and the necessity of the experience for every believer. They saw it as key to a deeper Christian life.

Sanctification was the theological bedrock and the experiential core of the "holiness movement." The holiness movement began among Methodists who in the mid-nineteenth century began to call for spiritual renewal for the members of their denomination and all Christians. John Wesley, the founder of Methodism had taught that salvation was a two-part process. Conversion or "justification" should lead to "entire sanctification" or full salvation, which freed believers from conscious acts of sin and flaws of character. This one-time, dramatic experience enabled believers to enter into a "perfect" state despite dwelling in corruptible bodies. Christian perfection had to be sustained, however, by a daily commitment to holy living, which involved abstinence from all "worldly pleasures" and "desires of the flesh." By the 1840s, followers of Wesley sought to revive his notion of sanctification as the only way to reform individuals and the church as a whole. Their efforts were greatly assisted by a series of revivals that happened to coincide with them. Often called "the Second Great Awakening," the revivals of the 1830s and 1840s cascaded across many sections of the United States, prompting many conversions to Christianity as well as conversions to Wesley's notion of "entire sanctification." By the 1880s what had been a movement that spread out from Methodists to nearly all Protestant groups was formed into independent denominations. This road to denominationalization was precipitated by the withdrawal of several Methodist churches from the denomination in the 1840s and by the formation of the National Camp Meeting for the Promotion of Holiness in 1867. By the time this organization was reestablished as the National Holiness Association in 1893, there were hundreds of holiness churches teaching the doctrine of sanctification throughout the United States.

Mason and Jones began to preach the holiness doctrine of sanctification widely, becoming the major purveyors of the teaching among black Baptists throughout Tennessee, Mississippi, and Arkansas. By the mid-1890s both men were making direct challenges to Baptist authorities, calling for "holiness conventions" and the outright espousal of Christian perfection within the Baptist Church. Jones assumed the pastorate at the historic Mt. Helm Baptist Church in Jackson, Mississippi, in 1895 and immediately set out to place the church on the path to what he considered "deeper spiritual labors" (Clemmons 1996). His first sermon there was from Matthew 5:48, "Be ye therefore perfect, even as your Father which is in heaven is perfect." It caused a division among the congregation and incited even more troubles with the National Baptist Convention. A revival staged by Mason and Jones in 1896 drew them deeper into the holiness fold and further alienated them from black Baptist officials. Mason, who at the time was an itinerant preacher, found the doors of most Baptist churches in Jackson closed to him because of the enthusiastic response to the revival. But the response seemingly convinced both men to formalize their relationship with the holiness movement by establishing a holiness church. In 1897, Mason, Jones, W. S. Pleasant, and about 60 other charter members gathered to establish what they called the "Church of God," the first African American holiness congregation in the United States. The name was later changed to "Church of God in Christ" after a vision Mason experienced while walking down a street in Little Rock, Arkansas. He had wanted a way to distinguish his church from others in the holiness fold.

In an unprecedented move, Jones allowed the first conventional meeting of the nascent denomination to be held at Mt. Helm. He even attempted to change the denominational affiliation of the church to COGIC. That attempt failed but it was apparently the last straw for the National Baptist Convention. In 1899 Mason and Jones were expelled from the Convention for their actions. Mason had already been disfellowshipped from the Leavenworth Baptist Association. But by that time, however, the two men and a growing number of followers were fully ensconced in COGIC and its holiness teaching. The group organized themselves into an episcopal structure, electing Jones as General Overseer, Mason as Overseer of Tennessee, and J. A. Jeter as Overseer of Kansas.

In the same way that the history of COGIC is intricately bound up with the holiness movement, COGIC and Pentecostalism in America share a history. Indeed, the history of COGIC is a significant part of Pentecostal history. COGIC was transformed from a Holiness denomination into a Pentecostal one through events that Charles Price Jones set in motion. In 1906 Jones sent Mason, Jeter, and D. J. Young to Los Angeles, California, to investigate reports of a great revival taking place in a former African Methodist Episcopal (AME) church and old livery stable on Azusa Street under the leadership of an itinerant preacher, William J. Seymour. Mason and Jones had met Seymour in Mississippi the year before. In its early stages in 1906 (it would last for three years), the revival at Azusa was radically reshaping Christian worship and defying social convention at the height of Jim Crow segregation. Seymour had been a protégé of Charles Fox Parham, a holiness

teacher and former Methodist minister, who in 1901 developed Pentecostal doctrine, what he called the "third work of grace" or the "baptism of the Holy Spirit." Parham came to believe that there existed an experience beyond Wesley's notion of sanctification that completed a believer's salvific experience. When he posed this question to the students of his Bethel Bible College in Topeka, Kansas, they concluded that the experience was "speaking in tongues." Tongue speaking harkened back to a first-century episode found in the book of Acts, when on the day of Pentecost a gathering of Christians spoke in languages they had not learned. Followers of holiness teachings had long developed a notion of "spirit baptism" but understood it as a spiritual unction that allowed one to live a holy life—in effect, sanctification. Parham began to teach that the "baptism in the Holy Spirit" should always be accompanied by speaking in tongues and that tongues were the "initial evidence" that one had indeed been baptized in the Holy Spirit. Convinced that speaking in tongues had an evangelistic purpose, Parham at first espoused a notion of "Zenoglossy"—the ability to speak in a "known tongue" not of one's ethnic origin. This was, in fact, in keeping with the account in the book of Acts. However, early Pentecostalists soon embraced the notion of "glossolalia"—the ability to speak in an "unknown tongue" or a "heavenly language" as the sign of Spirit baptism.

Parham systematized the notion of Spirit baptism as a third experience that was as essential for salvation as conversion and sanctification. The new teaching began to take root among vast cross-sections of American Christians, but particularly among those from Methodist and Holiness denominations. Drawn to Parham and the Pentecostal experience, Seymour arrived at another school Parham had founded in Houston, Texas, in 1905, wanting to sit under Parham's tutelage. Seymour had been born to freed slaves in Centerville, Louisiana, in 1870. His parents were members of the Baptist church, but due in part to the religious diversity of the region Seymour's early religious influences included Baptists, Methodists, and Catholicism. As a young man he traveled to the Midwest, converted to Methodism, and joined the Church of God, Indiana, also called "The Evening Light Saints," a radically conservative wing of the holiness movement. While he was with this group, Seymour experienced sanctification and a call to preach. Following his call he moved on to Ohio where he caught smallpox and became blind in one eye, a characteristic by which he would be known for the rest of his life. It was in Ohio that Seymour heard of Parham's new teaching regarding the Baptism in the Holy Spirit. Traveling to Texas, he found Parham and enrolled in his school. Conceding to Jim Crow practices in American education at the time, however, Parham only allowed Seymour to sit outside the classroom. Despite this dehumanizing arrangement, his experience at the school and the new Pentecostal teaching had a profound effect on Seymour's life, and it was not long before he had his own Pentecostal experience.

Seymour's move from Texas to California—as well as the birth of the Azusa Street Revival—was initiated by the efforts of three women he came to know. During his time in Texas he attended a small African American holiness congregation that was shepherded by Lucy Farrow, a former slave and niece of Frederick Douglass. She had also been a household worker of Parham's. Neely Terry, a member of the congregation, persuaded Seymour that a man of his talents and spiritual vision was needed in her home state of California. She contacted Julia W. Hutchinson, her former pastor, who extended an invitation to Seymour requesting that he pastor a small holiness congregation she had formed. He set out for California with financial help from Parham and immediately began preaching the new doctrine. Although his initial efforts were rebuffed, primarily by those within the holiness movement who disavowed tongue speaking, and his meetings moved to various locations before settling at 312 Azusa Street, word of the meetings soon spread throughout Los Angeles and to many places throughout the world.

The Azusa Street Revival and the Apostolic Faith Mission, as it came to be called, quickly became a phenomenon and was one of the most significant events in American religious history. Scholars have long debated whether Parham or Seymour can rightfully be heralded as the founder of American Pentecostalism. Both men unquestionably played significant roles in the birth of the movement. Yet, while Parham is certainly to be credited for initiating the wave of interest in Holy Spirit baptism at the dawn of the twentieth century and for constructing the basis for Pentecostal theology, it was Seymour who development the liturgical and social practices that came to characterize Pentecostalism. Pentecostal worship at Azusa was lively, was exuberant, and allowed for the full expression of all the "spiritual gifts," including speaking in tongues, prophecy, and divine healing.

Early chroniclers of the revival also left written accounts of spontaneous testimony or preaching, "singing in the spirit," "writing in the spirit," and holy dancing. The regular church music, which was strongly influenced by African traditions, was sung without instrumental accompaniment or hymnbooks. The vivacious worship services generated constant complaints from the surrounding community and some pithy critique from the local press, who often called the attendees at Azusa "holy rollers," "holy jumpers," or "tangled tonguers." On April 6, 1906, the *Los Angles Daily Times* published a now-famous account of the revival with the headline, "Weird Babel of Tongues: New Sect of Fanatics Is Breaking Loose."

It was not only the worship practices at Azusa that caught the attention of the press and the general public. The interracial mixing and physical contact among blacks, whites, and an array of other ethnic minorities during the services defied social convention at the height of Jim Crow segregation. Unlike Charles Parham, who was rumored to be a racist and a Klan sympathizer, Seymour preached a gospel of social equality. Blacks and ethnic minorities were on equal footing with their white counterparts and shared equally in the power structure of the Azusa Street mission. Women were also equal to men and given broad sanction to preach, to lead worship, and to practice divine healing. Women such as Jennie Evans Moore, who later married Seymour, and Florence Crawford held prominent positions at the mission, and Clara Lum was chiefly responsible for editing the church's periodical, *Apostolic Faith.*

Charles Price Jones likely did not anticipate the crisis that would ensue within COGIC because of Mason's visit to Azusa. He merely wanted to investigate a revival that was greatly reshaping Christianity across the globe, as emissaries from around the world were coming to Azusa and taking the Pentecostal message back to their home countries. But his visit to Azusa had a profound impact on Mason's life and precipitated a break from Jones and the Holiness denomination similar to the break he had experienced from black Baptists a few years earlier. While at Azusa Mason became a disciple of William Seymour and was convinced of the necessity of Pentecostal Baptism for all believers. On March 19, 1907, he, Jeter, and Young all experienced Pentecostal Spirit Baptism under Seymour's guidance. Mason described his own baptism this way: "The Lord stood me up one day and I began to speak in tongues and interpret the same. He soon gave me all kinds of spiritual utterances" (Clemmons 1996, 62).

Upon his return to Memphis, Mason began to preach the Pentecostal message in COGIC churches. Jones, however, rejected the new teaching, principally because of the centrality of speaking in tongues to Pentecostal practice. He did not believe tongues to be the "initial evidence" of Spirit Baptism, and this became the central issue that generated tension between the two leaders and would eventually split the church. At the annual COGIC convocation in August 1907, the issue reached its crisis point. As General Overseer, Jones had urged Mason to reject the new teaching and to stop preaching its message. He requested that the elders of the denomination decide if speaking in tongues was, indeed, a scriptural practice. After three days of deliberation, they decided that it was not a scriptural practice and again requested Mason to reject Pentecostalism. He did not. Rather, Mason affirmed his belief in tongues, and the elders of COGIC withdrew the "right hand of fellowship" from him. It was the second time within a decade that Mason had been disfellowshipped from a denomination because of his embrace of a new spiritual practice.

When Mason parted ways with Jones, a reported half of the denomination left with him. These ministers and laity became the basis upon which COGIC was restructured as a Pentecostal denomination. In September 1907, Mason called a meeting in Memphis to discuss among his followers the formation of a new church. The church was agreed upon and Mason was elected "General Overseer" and "Chief Apostle." He was given complete authority over church doctrine, organizational structure, and discipline. The annual convocation was set for November 25 to December 14. A tradition with nineteenth-century revival, camp meeting, and holiness roots, the three-week-long annual convocation allowed time for COGIC members to fellowship and to transact church business. As the name "Church of God in Christ" had appeared

Members listen to a sermon in the Church of God in Christ, Washington, D.C., November 1942. (Corbis)

to Mason in a vision, the new church believed that it rightly belonged to them and not to the Jones faction. The court in Shelby County, Tennessee, agreed. In 1909, after a two-year battle between Mason and Jones, Mason was awarded the exclusive use of the name COGIC, and his church became the first major Pentecostal denomination generated from the Azusa Street Revival. Charles P. Jones and his followers restructured themselves in 1915 as the Church of Christ Holiness USA.

As a newly minted Pentecostal denomination, COGIC possessed legal authority to ordain ministers. So, in addition to rapid growth throughout many regions of the United States in the first decade of the twentieth century—particularly in the South—COGIC also gathered a significant number of white ministers into its fold. This apparent racial unity reflected the deepest values of Seymour and the Azusa Street Revival. White COGIC ministers soon bristled under Mason's leadership, however, and bowed to the pressures of societal racism. A delegation left in April 1914 to form the Assemblies of God in Hot Springs, Arkansas, citing a need for better organization and doctrinal stability. The move effectively ended the interracial experiment in American religion that began at Azusa, and Pentecostalism in America has been divided between black and white ever since.

From the start, Mason developed a distinct cultural aesthetic within COGIC. While black Methodists were known to emphasize the importance of education and many black Baptists concentrated efforts on social activism, COGIC churches strictly enforced the rules of personal piety. Modesty in dress was insisted upon in men and women, but

COGIC women in particular became identifiable by their austere clothing. COGIC members where forbidden to indulge in any of the pleasures of the body such as tobacco, alcohol, and, in some cases, caffeine. Premarital sex was taboo, as was divorce, remarriage, and most "worldly amusements." Throughout her long career, guitar great Sister Rosetta Tharpe found herself at odds with COGIC for her attempts to bridge the worlds of the sacred and secular in her music and the venues in which she played (Wald 2007). Members still address one another as "brother" and "sister" and collectively consider themselves "Saints."

As women have always constituted the majority membership in COGIC, women "Saints" have always been the most visible. Mason, however, did not follow Seymour's example of gender equality in his church. Rather, men have always constituted the 12-member general board of bishops (often considered "apostles"), and COGIC has never ordained a woman bishop, pastor, or preacher. COGIC pastor and gospel singer Andrae Crouch famously defied the denomination to ordain his twin sister, Sandra, in 1998, but she serves outside the COGIC fold. Undoubtedly recognizing the important roles women would play in COGIC, Mason established the "Women's Department" in 1911 and appointed Elizabeth "Lizzie" Woods Robinson as its first "General Overseer" and head "Mother" of the church. Robinson was born to slave parents in Phillips County, Arkansas, on April 5, 1860. A Baptist until she was Spirit filled and joined COGIC, Robinson was known to prize "motherhood" and oppose women preachers (Butler 2007). The Women's

Department in COGIC has wielded enormous influence in the denomination in what is effectively a "dual-sex," parallel power structure. In addition, despite the prohibition on women's ordination, throughout the church's history COGIC women have served informally as pastors, teachers, and ministers.

Beliefs and Practices

The cultural aesthetic within COGIC develops from its system of belief, which bears all the hallmarks of its Holiness and Pentecostal roots. The denomination's "Statement of Faith" affirms the Trinity, the infallibility of the Bible, the imminent Second Coming of Christ, and the necessity of Sanctification and the Baptism of the Holy Ghost. The principle beliefs of COGIC can be stated as follows: The Bible is the inspired, written Word of God, infallible and without error; there is One God, who exists in three persons, Father, Son, and Holy Ghost; repentance and regeneration are the only ways to be cleansed of sin, which is accomplished through the Blood of Jesus and water baptism; and Christ's work of redemption on the cross and the believer's prayer have power to heal body and mind. The sanctifying and indwelling power of the Holy Spirit allows the believer to live a holy life separate from the sins and corruptions of the world; the Baptism of the Holy Ghost is given to every believer who asks for it and is essential for salvation; and the Rapture of the church will occur at the Second Coming of Christ, when believers will be "caught up to meet Him in the air."

In accordance with Wesleyan notions, COGIC understands sanctification as a one-time, dramatic experience that leads to a life free from sin and the desire to commit sin. The COGIC official manual calls it "that gracious and continuous operation of the Holy Ghost, by which He delivers the justified sinner from the pollution of sin, renews his whole nature in the image of God and enables him to perform good works" (*Official Manual of the Church of God in Christ* 1973). In keeping with Pentecostalism, COGIC believes that the Baptism of the Holy Ghost is an experience subsequent to conversion and sanctification, and that speaking in tongues is the sign that one has been filled by the Spirit. In addition, the church observes three ordinances: The Lord's Supper (Holy Communion); Feet Washing (Ordinance of Humility); and water baptism (total immersion).

The death of Charles H. Mason in 1961 ended the early period of COGIC history and ushered the church into the modern era. Since the 1960s, the church has extended its reach into many places across the globe, including Africa, Haiti, Latin America, and Great Britain. It operates two schools, the C. H. Mason Bible College and Theological Seminary, and its leaders have become some of the most powerful men in Christendom. In the first decade of the twentieth century, G. E. Patterson, only the sixth Presiding Bishop since Mason, transformed COGIC into a global media empire, securing spots on radio and television and expanding the church's publishing enterprises. His death in 2007 marked COGIC's centennial year. Charles E. Blake of Los Angeles, California, succeeded him. Blake's church, the West Angeles COGIC, boasts a membership of 24,000. Since 1940, the "world headquarters" of COGIC has been Mason Temple in Memphis, Tennessee. Often called "the Holy Mecca of the Saints of God," it was the site of Martin Luther King Jr.'s "Mountain Top" speech delivered the night before he was killed on April 4, 1968.

With stalwart leadership, over 6 million members, vast media exposure, hundreds of auxiliaries, business enterprises, and charitable organizations, the church founded in 1907 seems poised to continue as a major force in American Christianity and global Pentecostalism. In recent years the church has reaffirmed its espousal of fundamentalist biblical doctrine and Christian conservatism, most notably in 2004 with a statement confirming its belief in marriage as exclusively between "a man and a woman." Although COGIC has experienced many changes throughout its history, primarily due to its tremendous growth, the leadership and laity seem committed to sustaining the ideals of a sanctified and Spirit-filled life as espoused by its original founder, Charles H. Mason.

Wallace Best

SELECTED BIBLIOGRAPHY

Bartleman, Frank. *Azusa Street* (New Kensington, PA: Whitaker House, 2000).

Borlase, Craig. *William Seymour: A Biography* (Lake Mary, FL: Charisma House, 2006).

Butler, Anthea D. *The Women of the Church of God in Christ: Making a Sanctified World* (Chapel Hill: University of North Carolina Press, 2007).

Clemmons, Ithiel C. *Bishop C. H. Mason and the Roots of the Church of God in Christ* (Lanham, MD: Pneuma Life Publishing House, 1996).

Gilkes, Cheryl Townsend. *If It Wasn't for the Women: Black Women's Experience and*

Womanist Culture in Church and Community (Maryknoll, NY: Orbis Books, 2000).

Official Manual of the Church of God in Christ (Memphis: COGIC, 1973).

Sanders, Cheryl J. *Saints in Exile: The Holiness Pentecostal Experience in African American Religion and Culture* (New York: Oxford University Press, 1999).

Synan, Vinson. *The Holiness-Pentecostal Tradition: Charismatic Movements in the Twentieth Century* (Grand Rapids, MI: Eerdmans Publishing Company, 1997).

Wacker, Grant. *Heaven Below: Early Pentecostals and American Culture* (Cambridge, MA: Harvard University Press, 2003).

Wald, Gayle. *Shout, Sister, Shout!: The Untold Story of Rock-and-Roll Trailblazer Sister Rose* (Boston: Beacon Press, 2007).

CHURCH OF THE LIVING GOD, PILLAR OF TRUTH FOR ALL NATIONS

Historical Development

African American history is peppered with conversation concerning the connections between African Americans and Jews. In large part this connection is described in terms of a common understanding of suffering based on the atrocities of the slave trade, the Holocaust, and continued racially and ethnically based discrimination. This general understanding of commonality based oppression is given more specific expression by African American Christians throughout history who speak in terms of a religious connection: Both groups have a profound connection to God based on what both perceive as a "special" relationship to God, a type of chosen status. That is to say, "the Jewish components of American Christianity were appealing to slaves and to post-abolition blacks. They identified with the stories of the embondaged children of Israel and had hopes of God's leading them out of their state of slavery in a similar manner" (Wynia 1994, 13). For the descendants of slaves in the United States, the story of bondage and freedom outlined in the Old Testament provided hope for a better time to come; and so, African Americans gravitated toward these stories and saw in their experience commonalities with the protagonists of the Old Testament stories—the Jews.

Most African Americans have expressed this sense of kinship within the context of the Christian faith by giving great attention to the biblical story of the Exodus, the Psalms, and Proverbs, and by appealing to the biblical prophets for ways to understand the demands of a proper relationship with God. Others have expressed this connection through involvement in predominantly white Jewish synagogues. As early as the Civil War, some Blacks participated in white Jewish synagogues in southern states (Singer in Chireau 2000, 57). Still others such as Arnold Ford, who was associated with Marcus Garvey's UNIA, have gone further to argue not only a general religious connection to Jews but also a claim on Judaism. In other words, "after 1900 a plethora of groups who characterized themselves as black Jews, black Hebrews, and black Israelites expanded the metaphorical kinship between black religion and Judaism" (Chireau 2000, 21). Many of these early, separate communities developed in New York City—Harlem—and in large part this was the case because Harlem, early in the twentieth century, was a heavily Jewish area. This made for ideal contact between African Americans, who worked in Harlem's neighborhoods, and Jews, who lived and worshipped in those areas.

Questions can be raised concerning the strength of their adherence to Judaism, in that for instance most of these African American groups walked a line between the Old Testament's laws and customs and the New Testament's celebration of Jesus Christ. Few of these congregations extended their appreciation for Judaism beyond the Bible to the oral law and commentaries (Talmudic Tradition) that inform traditional Jewry (Brotz 1970, 10).

The dating of these various communities is difficult, but it is often suggested that Prophet F. S. Cherry was one of the first to institute this appeal to Judaism when, in 1866, he organized the Church of the Living God, Pillar of Truth for All Nations. Originating in Chattanooga, Tennessee, Cherry moved his organization to Philadelphia sometime in the 1940s. Concerning the development of the Church of the Living God, Prophet Cherry told his followers that: "years ago, when he was far from his native land, the Lord approached him in a vision and touched him, thereby appointing him His

prophet. Thereafter he was led back to America and to Philadelphia, where he was directed to establish the Church of God" (Fauset 2001, 32). With this story of origin, it becomes clear that Prophet Cherry is the final authority in all matters within the church; but, like other charismatic leaders mentioned in this book, he has developed a hierarchy of assistants—including deacons, elders, secretaries, and preachers—who help him manage the church.

Prophet Cherry's work as leader of this organization continued until his death in 1965. After his death, Prophet Cherry's son, Benjamin Cherry, led the organization. Information concerning the church after Prophet Cherry's death is unavailable, but what is more certain is the manner in which Prophet's Cherry's ministry served to buttress the work of those who came after him.

Beliefs and Practices

Cherry proclaimed that divine visions instructed him to undertake the work of bringing African Americans to a proper understanding of themselves as the true Jews. Cherry's message was aggressive and nationalistic in that he argued God and biblical figures, such as Adam, Eve,

---

FRANK S. CHERRY (PROPHET CHERRY) (?–1965)

Documentation concerning the location of Prophet Cherry's birth and his years prior to his adult life is unavailable. However, it is known that as an adult he held various jobs as a daily laborer and as a sailor he traveled outside the United States. It was while abroad that Cherry says he was spoken to by God and instructed to work with African Americans in the United States. In the vision, God called him a prophet and told him to provide African Americans with proper information concerning their true religion—Judaism. In 1866 he organized the Church of the Living God, Pillar of Truth for All Nations. In the 1940s, the organization moved to Philadelphia. He led this congregation until his death.

and Jesus, were physically black. Furthermore, he argued whites, including white Jews, altered this information concerning the blackness of biblical figures to fit their purposes. African Americans are representative of the true people of God. His teachings are premised on his reading of the Hebrew Bible, which is the ultimate source of knowledge for his church.

Much of this doctrine is explored and explained within the context of worship. Prophet Cherry's services took place on Saturday—the Sabbath. Members of the church also gathered on Fridays and Wednesdays. But the most important was the Sabbath, Saturday, service. Those gathered started the service with songs, and after a few selections had been sung, Prophet Cherry took the pulpit and called the service to order. After the congregation sang another song and prayed, he read from the Bible and provided commentary on the meaning of the biblical passage.

Members of the congregation did not simply listen and absorb the Prophet's teachings. To the contrary, members of the congregation were invited to raise questions concerning the Prophet's teachings or to provide their insights concerning the biblical passages under study. After this portion of the service was completed, another song was sung, and this was followed by a sermon from the Prophet during which he expounded on the organization's teachings—including the status of his followers as the true people of God. He criticized Christian churches for embracing the incorrect teachings of white Christians and Jews, first by accepting the idea that Jesus is white. Also exposed to critique were white Jews, who, according to Prophet Cherry, are guilty of not understanding the true significance of Jesus Christ.

Clearly, Prophet Cherry combined elements of Judaism such as the Passover with Christian commitments such as the centrality of Jesus Christ.

After the sermon, another song was sung and the congregation was dismissed. These weekly teachings were supplemented on a daily basis by moral and ethical guidelines heavily dependent on the Ten Commandments. Requirements were strict, including no dancing, no heavy drinking of alcohol, avoidance of pork, and a prohibition on photographs of church members or pictures on the walls of their homes (Fauset 2001, 37–39).

Members argue that Judaism is a tradition associated with Africa and that African Americans are connected to the original Children of Israel discussed in the Old Testament. They are the descendants of the Children of Israel, whether they live in the United States or Israel. Such a position, however, requires rigorous discipline and attention to laws that included the Ten Commandments, but that also extended beyond these commandments.

An effort is made to separate its membership through attire and ritual. For example, members dressed in modest clothing that was often based on a combination of Jewish aesthetics and African American culture.

Members find in the aesthetics and rituals of the faith a language and pattern of behavior that helps make sense of the world.

Anthony B. Pinn

SELECTED BIBLIOGRAPHY

Brotz, Howard M. *The Black Jews of Harlem: Negro Nationalism and the Dilemmas of Negro Leadership* (New York: Schocken Books, 1970).

Chireau, Yvonne, and Nathaniel Deutsch,
    eds. *Black Zion: African American Religious Encounters with Judaism* (New
    York: Oxford University Press, 2000).
Fauset, Arthur Huff. *Black God of the
    Metropolis: Negro Religious Cults of the
    Urban North* (Philadelphia: University of
    Pennsylvania Press, 2001).
Wynia, Elly M. *The Church of God and Saints
    of Christ: The Rise of Black Jews* (New
    York: Garland Publishing, Inc., 1994).

COMMANDMENT KEEPERS OF HARLEM

Historical Development

The Commandment Keepers of Harlem is the most well-known congregation of Black Jews in New York and arguably the largest and most influential community of Black Jews in the United States. Established in 1919 by Rabbi Wentworth A. Matthew, this religious community evolved and developed significantly for nearly a century in response to both historical events, such as the Depression, World War II, the Italian invasion of Ethiopia, the emigration of the Hebrew Israelites to Israel in 1969, and the changing cultural movements that carried currency over the years: Garveyism, Ethiopianism, Civil Rights, and Black Power. Although many Black Jewish communities existed in New York and other large urban centers in the United States throughout this period, the Commandment Keepers was responsible for the form of Black Judaism that most closely resembled Jewish practices, rituals, and traditions associated with the recognized (and in the United States) mostly white Jewish community. They established the Ethiopian Hebrew Rabbinical College in 1925, and through this institution trained many rabbis and spiritual leaders who went on to found affiliate synagogues in other parts of New York, the United States, and the Caribbean. The Commandment Keepers' relationships with other communities evolved and changed in response to their treatment of and by those communities, yet their status as one of the foremost, respected, and influential Black Jewish groups is undeniable.

WENTWORTH ARTHUR MATTHEW (1892–1973)

Born in West Africa and raised in the Caribbean, Matthew moved to New York City in 1913. He was eventually attracted to the teachings of Marcus Garvey, and he joined the Universal Negro Improvement Association, where he met Arnold Josiah Ford. In spite of his earlier attention to Pentecostalism, Matthew found Ford's teachings concerning Judaism compelling. Although he initially worked with Ford, Matthew started his own community in 1919, and called it the Commandment Keepers, Holy Church of the Living God. Taking over Ford's congregation when Ford departed for Ethiopia, Matthew would incorporate his members and use the name Commandment Keepers Congregation of the Living God. While this church started as a blend of Christianity and Judaism, Matthew would eventually remove the Christian elements. He would lead the organization until his death in 1973. At that point, his grandson, David Dore, took charge.

It is impossible to discuss the development of the Commandment Keepers without putting them in the context of the larger Black Judaic movement in the United States. Since the nineteenth century, some Black groups in the United States had been identifying *with* and *as* Jews, Hebrews, and Israelites as evidenced in many of the slave spirituals' lyrics. The terms "Black Jew, Hebrew, and Israelite" have been used to describe a continuum of identities and practice. At one end are Black Jews who would be "accepted" by members of the recognized Jewish community as Jews either because they were born to an authenticated Jewish mother or because they had converted according to *halacha* (Jewish law). On the other end are Blacks who identify as either Hebrews or Israelites through race and/or nationality, but who may share very little if any ritual practice with the recognized Jewish community. Moreover, some of these groups may actively argue that *they* and *not* the recognized Jewish community are the "true Jews." In the middle are a variety of other groups who may use any of the terms: Jew, Hebrew, or Israelite, and who may perform rituals and practices that incorporate elements of recognized Judaism, Christianity, or both. In *Black Judaism: Story of an American Movement*, James Landing traces the development of Black Judaism as a social and religious movement and uses the term to account for all varieties along the continuum.

Although these groups differ as to how they define and trace their biblical ancestors (through Moses, King Solomon, Queen of Sheba) and whether or not they see themselves as one of the Lost Tribes, they all trace some kind of biblical lineage descended from the ancient Hebrews or Israelites depicted in the Pentateuch.

Moreover, these groups share a belief that their biblical descendants were Black and spent time in Africa, because they emphasize that Ancient Israel was part of the African continent, they believe that they are descendents of Ethiopians, or they believe their descendants lived in exile in Africa after the destruction of the Second Temple in Jerusalem. Some groups also trace Judaic heritage to descendants from Africa who practiced Jewish rituals such as circumcision or refraining from pork and were later brought to the United States or the Caribbean as slaves. Other groups claim Judaic heritage through ancestors who were the offspring of unions between Jewish slave owners and slaves living in the Caribbean.

Terminology is a sensitive issue and each group's choice of terms for self-identification is affected by a variety of cultural beliefs. Some groups eschew the use of the term "Jew" because it has come to be associated with whiteness in the U.S. context, and instead prefer the terms "Hebrew" and "Israelite" because they are associated with ancient, African roots, and have become a way to assert racial pride and affiliation with African customs, cultures, and traditions. For many Black Judaic groups, Hebrewism or Israelitism, and thus also identifying as Black Jews, is a way of reclaiming African heritage.

The various names associated with the Commandment Keepers reflect this preference for emphasizing their African heritage; their leader Rabbi Matthew stressed the connection with Ethiopian descent and connections with Africa. They and their affiliated organizations were known by the following titles over the years: Commandment Keepers: Congregation of the Living God, Pillar and Ground of the Truth, Inc. (1934), a secular arm called the Royal Order of Ethiopian Hebrew Sons and Daughters of Culture was formed in either 1926 or 1930 and was often described by observers as a Masonic organization, and the religious group later was known as the Commandment Keepers Ethiopian Hebrew Congregation (1962). The community also moved as congregational wealth and donations ebbed and flowed in consonance with the larger U.S. economy. Although their original worship place is unknown, in 1934 they were worshipping in Antillean Hall at 30 West 129th Street in Harlem, though in 1935 they had difficulty making ends meet and relocated the congregation to 87 West 128th Street on the corner of Lenox above a drugstore, where the congregation remained until 1962. In 1962, they moved to what would become their most recognized and historic building at 1 West 123rd Street in Harlem or 31 Mount Morris Park West on the northwest corner of West 123rd Street (photos available at http://www.nyc-architecture. com/HAR/HAR025.htm). The congregation's final home was a brownstone residence, originally designed by architect Frank H. Smith in the neo-Renaissance style for the John Dwight family of Arm and Hammer fame and converted into a synagogue in 1962 by the Commandment Keepers. Especially noted for its entrance, the building is listed as one of New York's historic landmarks. This building became the source of great controversy in the early twenty-first century, however, due to internal conflicts over the community's leadership that began after Rabbi Matthew's death in 1973.

Since Rabbi Matthew established the Ethiopian Hebrew Rabbinical College in 1925, many Black Jewish Rabbis and spiritual leaders were trained under his influence and beliefs. These spiritual leaders went on to found affiliate synagogues in other parts of New York, the United States, and the Caribbean. According to the official Web site of the Israelite Board of Rabbis, in 1970, the school's name was changed to the Israelite Rabbinical Academy by its chief Rabbi Levi Ben Levy. In 2001, the members of the Israelite Board of Rabbis voted at their International Convention to open the gates of this educational institute to train not only rabbis for the Israelite community, but also interested laypeople and members of the public, including women.

Rabbi Matthew, an immigrant from St. Kitts, was the Commandment Keeper's founder and respected leader for more than half a century. He was a charismatic leader strongly influenced by Garveyism and Ethiopianism, and the tenets of his congregation's beliefs reflect both. Although sources often differ about Rabbi Matthew's origins—some say Nigeria—Rabbi Matthew came to the United States in 1913 from St. Christopher (St. Kitts) in the Leeward Islands of the West Indies. According to Rabbi Sholomo Ben Levy, Matthew was born in 1892 and died in New York in 1973. Over the years, many observers came to worship with his community and often remarked upon his distinctive voice. He had close ties with Rabbi Arnold Josiah Ford, who was the founder and leader of the Beth B'nai Abraham Ethiopian Congregation and Hebrew School and who also directed the musical arm of Marcus Garvey's Universal Negro Improvement Association (UNIA). Although Rabbi Ford was quite influential in his own right, he eventually left the New York community to live in Ethiopia where he later died in 1935. Before his death, Rabbi Ford sent ordination papers written in English, Hebrew, and Amharic, from Ethiopia to Rabbi Matthew in 1929, thus intending to certify Matthew's legitimacy as a rabbi of the Black Jews. While Rabbi Matthew and those inside his community accepted Rabbi Ford's certification, unfortunately this recognition was never granted legitimacy by those outside the community. Rabbi Matthew reported the community's membership to number over 400 or 500 at its height in the 1920s and 1930s, though by 2004 official membership had dwindled to eight.

Under Rabbi Matthew's leadership, the community sought a range of interactions with the recognized Jewish community and attracted the attention of several scholars interested in Black Jews including Ruth Landes, Arthur Dobrin, Harold Brotz, Graenum Berger, and later James Landing, Roberta Gold, Marlaine Glicksman, and Rabbi Sholomo Ben Levy. On several occasions, Rabbi Matthew attempted to become an accepted member of the New York Board of Rabbis, first in 1931 and then again in 1952, and later he attempted to join the B'nai B'rith Lodge.

On all occasions his requests for membership and recognition from the mainstream Jewish community were denied. Although the rationale varied, in most cases the recognized Jewish community did not accept Rabbi Matthew's ordination by Rabbi Ford as legitimate according to Jewish legal standards, and consequently, Rabbi Matthew's congregation eventually had little to do with the recognized Jewish community.

Rabbi Matthew married and had two sons and one daughter, Florence; only his daughter and her son, Matthew's grandson, David, remained with the faith. Before his death in 1973, Rabbi Matthew ordained his grandson David Dore before he was 18 years old as a recognized rabbi of the Commandment Keepers congregation. Dore, then a student at Yeshiva High School, went on to study at Yeshiva University and become a practicing lawyer.

Unfortunately, after Matthew's death, an internal dispute erupted over who would become his legitimate successor and the congregation's recognized leader. In 1975, the synagogue board members elected Rabbi Willie "Chaim" White,

ARNOLD JOSIAH FORD (1890–1935)

Ford was born in Barbados and migrated to the United States in 1912. Having musical talent, he spent almost a decade in New York as the leader of the New Amsterdam Musical Association of New York. This work was in addition to his membership in Marcus Garvey's Universal Negro Improvement Association, a connection Ford developed in 1917. As a member of Garvey's organization he put his musical talents to use by creating much of the music utilized during its activities. Upon leaving Barbados, Ford dismissed much of the religious training he had received from his minister father. However, it is believed that in New York Ford encountered Judaism. In 1924, Ford organized Beth B'nai Abraham Congregation, and he began to teach African Americans that they were the true Hebrews. Six years after he founded this congregation, Ford left for Ethiopia because he was convinced the existence of the Falashas (Ethiopian Jews) proved his point concerning the African origin of the true Hebrews. He died in Ethiopia in 1935.

also ordained by Rabbi Matthew, to be the congregation's leader. Reportedly, Rabbi White and Rabbi Dore jointly led services until the 1980s, when Rabbi White began to exclude Rabbi Dore and others from services and participation. Rabbi White then led the services with Rabbi Bezzalel Ben Yehudah, though White was clearly the leader. Conflict continued throughout the 1990s and the beginning of the twenty-first century. In 2000 Rabbi Zechariah Ben Lewi was ordained, and a few years later, in 2004, he was appointed as the new leader. Although the Israelite Board of Rabbis suggested that the congregation resolve their internal disputes through a traditional, religious court known as a *bet din*, the congregants did not pursue this path and instead brought their grievances to the civil courts of New York. In April 2007, the synagogue board sold the historic building on Mt. Morris and 123rd Street for $1.6 million, and the loss of the building received widespread media coverage in the New York and Jewish presses. Rabbi Dore has legally contested the board's right to sell the building, and the issue remains unresolved.

While Rabbi Matthew's community does not continue to meet in its most recognized home, his teachings and beliefs live on in the successful sister congregations that grew out of his movement. Black Jews influenced by the Commandment Keepers continue to practice at Mt. Horeb Congregation in the Bronx; Beth Sholom in Bedstuyvesant, Brooklyn; B'nai Adat in Brooklyn; Beth Elohim in Queens; and B'nai Zaken in Chicago.

Beliefs and Practices

Although terminology varied over the years, members of the Commandment Keepers explicitly saw themselves as Black Jews, believed that they had direct lineage from the ancient Hebrews and Israelites depicted in the Pentateuch, and believed that ancient, biblical figures were Black. Specifically, Rabbi Matthew emphasized the story of Moses, who came from Egypt and therefore Africa, and also the story of King Solomon and Queen Sheba, who Matthew believed to have hailed from Ethiopia. Rabbi Matthew taught that all of these figures were Black, and though these "original Jews" were non-Europeans, he did not deny white Jews' legitimacy. Rather, he believed that white Jews had helped to preserve Judaism over the years. He also reasoned that since the original Jews were Blacks, those Blacks who returned to the faith did not need to undergo conversion procedures, because they were originally and ancestrally Jewish.

The community followed many traditional, orthodox Jewish practices. Seating was separated by gender, prayer services were conducted from a recognized Jewish *siddur* (prayerbook) in a combination of Hebrew and English, and male members wore head coverings known as *kippot* or yarmulkes as well as traditional prayer shawls called *tallitim*. Rabbi Matthew also introduced African and Caribbean customs by carrying an African cane to services. Additionally, many female members were reported to wear traditional African dress to worship. The group observed all major Jewish holidays, including Rosh Hashanah (the Jewish New Year), *tashlich* (the symbolic ceremony of casting one's sins into a river during Rosh Hashanah festivities), Yom Kippur (a day of atonement and fasting), *Sukkot*, Passover (*Pesach* in Hebrew), Hannukah, and traditional practices such as hanging mezzuzot on doorways, observing the laws of kashruth (abstaining from pork, shellfish, and not eating dairy and meat products at the same meal), and performing a Bar Mitzvah for male members at the age of 13. (A forthcoming hour-long, feature documentary film by Marlaine Glicksman about the community, *The Commandment Keepers*, includes original footage of many of the community's ritual practices and life-cycle events, including a Bar Mitzvah, a wedding, a Rabbi's retirement, as well as holiday celebrations for tashlich, Sukkot, Hannukah, and Passover, and original interviews with community members.) The community also held regular Sabbath services on Friday evening and Saturday, with congregants reading from a Torah Scroll during the Saturday service.

In 1942, Rabbi Matthew collected many of the group's beliefs and spiritual teachings into a document called the *Minute Book*, which also included his memoir. In the *Minute Book*, Rabbi Matthew included a summary of the community's early history and guide about their practices, a copy of the Rabbinical College's curriculum, "The Twelve Principles of the Doctrine of Israel" that he compiled, and the "Anthropology of the Ethiopian Hebrews and their Relationship to the Fairer Jews." A copy of the *Minute Book* is appended to scholar Howard Brotz's 1947 thesis about the Congregation, and its contents are also reproduced in Brotz's 1964 popular and oft-cited book *The Black Jews of Harlem: Negro Nationalism and the Dilemmas of Negro Leadership* and summarized in Landing's text *Black Judaism*.

Janice W. Fernheimer

SELECTED BIBLIOGRAPHY

Ben Levy, Sholomo. "Blackjews.org: A Project of the International Board of Israelite Rabbis." http://www.blackjews.org (accessed October 11, 2008).

Brotz, Howard. "The Black Jews of Harlem" (unpublished master's thesis, University of Chicago, Chicago, 1947).

Brotz, H. *The Black Jews of Harlem: Negro Nationalism and the Dilemmas of Negro Leadership* (New York: Free Press of Glencoe, 1964).

Dorman, Jacob S. "I Saw You Disappear with My Own Eyes: Hidden Transcripts of New York Black Israelite Bricolage." *Nova Religio: The Journal of Alternative and Emergent Religions* 11, no. 1: 61–83.

Glicksman, Marlaine. "The Commandment Keepers." http://thecommandmentkeepers.net/synopsis.htm (accessed October 11, 2008).

Landing, James E. *Black Judaism: Story of an American Movement* (Durham, NC: Carolina Academic Press, 2001).

"Matthew, Wentworth Arthur." In *African American National Biography* (New York: Oxford University Press, 2008).

"New York Architecture Images: Commandment Keepers Ethiopian Hebrew Congregation." http://www.nyc-architecture.com/HAR/HAR025.htm (accessed October 11, 2008).

West, Cornel, and Jack Salzman (eds.). "Judaism: Black Jews in America." In *Encyclopedia of African-American History and Culture*, Vol. III (New York: Macmillan Publications, 1996).

CONJURE

Historical Development

Conjure is the name for an African American magical system. Also known as tricking, goopher, mojo, and, since the late nineteenth century, hoodoo, it has long been a living link between black Americans and their African roots. Though most often found in the South, it has existed throughout the United States wherever a significant black population has settled.

Conjure began its history during the seventeenth century, with the rise of the British North American slave trade into the Atlantic Coast colonies. The African regions from which the unwilling laborers came were to influence its development enormously. In the Chesapeake, the African population was quite mixed, though by far the largest single ethnicity were the Igbo of the Bight of Biafra region of West Africa. Like most Africans and many Europeans of the day, the Igbo were firm believers in charms and spells. In Virginia, poisons were the most common weapon of the conjurer. Conceived of as spiritual instead of simply toxic substances, they were an integral part of Igbo beliefs as well. The Igbos' American descendants turned to poisons to punish enemies and even cruel masters. The term *mojo*, used either as a synonym for conjure or as a designation of a type of charm, may be another Africanism introduced by the Igbo.

Though Igbos were an early and persistent presence in the Chesapeake, the contributions of people of West Central African descent cannot be overlooked. Slaves of Kongo, Angolan, and related ethnicities were a numerical majority of South Carolina and Georgia's black population. One of their most obvious

The interior of Robinson Hall of Micanopy, Florida. This small-town example of a conjure shop carried the usual oils, candles, and herbal curios. Note the wall hangings, which represent from left to right Nelson Mandela, Martin Luther King Jr., and Malcolm X. (Jeffrey Elton Anderson)

contributions was the heavy use of grave-yard dirt, sometimes known as goopher dust, in their charms. *Goopher* appears to derive from the Kongo word *kufwa*, meaning "to die." This focus on the dead arose from West Central Africans' religious veneration for ancestral spirits, which was considerably stronger among the Kongo and related peoples than with most other Africans. Another West Central African import was the widespread use of roots in conjure charms, a practice in keeping with the beliefs of the slaves' homeland.

Though the preceding practices and terms are but a few of the African features of conjure, one thing that sets it apart from hoodoo, its Mississippi River Valley cousin, is the absence of many of the latter's overtly African features. Hoodoo, as the magical and ceremonial aspect of Voodoo, relied on a variety of African deities and specific spirits of the dead. Such practices were rare in the rest of the South, at least by the nineteenth century. Even African words, though present, were far less common in conjure than in hoodoo. By the nineteenth century, the most common names for the practice, including *conjure* itself, were English. *Goopher doctor* was an exception to the general rule. In place of the missing Africanisms were European-isms. Practitioners were sometimes known as *cunning men* and *women* and *high men* and *women*, English terms for magic workers. Likewise, Bibles had become powerful conjure tools well before the end of slavery, and prayers to the Christian God had supplanted the deities. Though English terms and concepts strongly influenced conjure, it had in no way ceased to be African. On the contrary, it had become African American.

Beliefs and Practices

Historically, conjure men and women were vital components of this magical system. These were supernatural specialists who worked for paying clients, selling charms and spells tailored to meet their clients' needs for love, luck, money, revenge, or virtually anything else they might request. During the antebellum era, some of the conjurers' most popular products were designed to help slaves avoid punishment or successfully run away.

The nature of conjurers' practice has changed significantly over time. Prior to the first half of the twentieth century, practitioners gathered most of their magical materials from nature. Their best-known curios were John the Conqueror roots, five finger grass, black cat bones, devil's shoe string, and Chewing John roots. Today, these items remain available, though few now collect them by hand. Instead, spiritual supply shops have largely supplanted the historical conjurers. These shops purchase their herbal and zoological products from supply houses. Alongside these traditional items now appear magical candles, oils, aerosol sprays, and other goods originating not in the wild but in a manufacturing company.

Whatever era they have inhabited, conjurers have been important people. Antebellum conjure men promised—and reportedly delivered—relief from the lash. After emancipation, African Americans needed money in addition to protection. Conjurers offered their magical assistance. Their versatility, coupled with a widespread belief in their powers, made many famous. Conjure men and women like Aunt Caroline Dye, Dr. Buzzard, and Dr. Jim Jordan are still talked about

---

"AUNT" CAROLINE DYE

By the time of her death in 1918, this well-known fortune-teller and conjurer had become a household name for hundreds of miles around her Newport, Arkansas, home. Her fame was such that she found her way into popular blues songs. Unlike many practitioners, Caroline Dye reportedly never used her powers to harm.

---

today. Some of them succeeded in doing more than building name recognition. Jim Jordan, for instance, used his conjure trade to build a large fortune, charging some customers thousands of dollars for his services. By the time he died in 1962, he had used his earnings to purchase several other businesses and to support a community of many dozens that grew up around his rural North Carolina shop. Scholars and popular authors, black and white alike, have often dismissed conjurers as mere superstitious charlatans. Clearly, they have been wrong.

Jeffrey Elton Anderson

SELECTED BIBLIOGRAPHY

Anderson, Jeffrey E. *Conjure in African American Society* (Baton Rouge: Louisiana State University Press, 2005).

Chambers, Douglas B. *Murder at Montpelier: Igbo Africans in Virginia* (Jackson: University Press of Mississippi, 2005).

Chireau, Yvonne. *Black Magic: Religion and the African American Conjuring Tradition* (Berkeley: University of California Press, 2003).

Georgia Writer's Project, Savannah Unit. *Drums and Shadows: Survival Studies among the Coastal Negroes.* With an Introduction by Charles Joyner and photographs by Muriel and Malcolm Bell, Jr. (Athens: University of Georgia Press, 1986).

Hyatt, Harry Middleton. *Hoodoo-Conjuration-Witchcraft-Rootwork.* 5 vols. Memoirs of the Alma Egan Hyatt Foundation (Hannibal: Western Publishing Company, 1970–1978).

Long, Carolyn Morrow. *Spiritual Merchants: Religion, Magic, and Commerce* (Knoxville: University of Tennessee Press, 2001).

McTeer, James Edwin. *Fifty Years as a Low Country Witch Doctor* (Beaufort, SC: Beaufort Book Company, 1976).

Yronwode, Catherine. *Hoodoo Herb and Root Magic: A Materia Magica of African-American Conjure and Traditional Formulary Giving the Spiritual Uses of Natural Herbs, Roots, Minerals, and Zoological Curios*

JAMES SPURGEON JORDAN

Dr. Jim Jordan of Como, North Carolina, was one of the most successful conjurers of the twentieth century. His practice earned him enough money to purchase a variety of other businesses, including a sandlot baseball team. Jordan's fame was such that a small community grew up around his country store, coming to be known as Jordansville. He died in 1962 at the age of 91.

"AUNT ZIPPY" TULL

Tull was a mid- to late nineteenth-century conjure woman who lived on the Delmarva Peninsula. She was so well regarded that stories were still being told about her during the 1930s, approximately two generations after her death.

(Forestville, CA: Lucky Mojo Curio Company, 2002).

CONVINCE (JAMAICA)

Historical Development

"Convince" is the name given to an ancestral cult of obeah men found in the parishes falling within the county of Surrey in Jamaica—St. Mary, St. Catherine, St. Andrew, St. Thomas, and Portland.[1] Donald Hogg (1964), the only scholar so far to have written about the cult, does not explain the name, but says that it is also known as "Bongo" in St. Mary where he conducted research. Warner-Lewis (2003, 17) gives "Bongo" a Central African derivation, thus validating popular perception of the cult's African provenance, and its similarity with Kumina. A more appropriate name for the cultists, therefore, is "science specialists" (Warner-Lewis 2003, 146), given the pejorative connotation of the word "obeah."

The cult has no organized structure, except the Bongo man and one or two "grooms," apprentices who will eventually become Bongo men themselves. Their main function is to attend to their charge when possessed. Each Bongo man is autonomous and organizes his

secret rituals and occasional public ceremonies as the needs demand, and to them he will invite other Bongo men.

Beliefs and Practices

Like Kumina, the possessing powers are the spirits of the once living, whether in Africa, under slavery, or more recently. They, therefore, have personalities and even names, such as Old Johnson, who "had been killed by a white planter and hated all white men"; Needles, "a sad, defensive spirit"; Kill-and-Cure, "an ill tempered, ugly old Maroon who delighted in frightening children"; and Fire Key Master, "a former boiler in a sugar factory who loved to dance on burning coals" (Hogg 1964, 271). Spirits become the familiars of the persons they choose to possess, thus initiating a relationship of mutual obligations. The Bongo man allows his body to be used to dance, smoke cigars, drink rum, insult people, simulate sex, curse profanities, climb trees and perform other dangerous feats, not without injury sometimes, and express anger and aggression. He is also expected to perform annual sacrificial feasts. For its part the spirit becomes his guardian and must comply with the Bongo man's requests when summoned. Multiple spirits may possess the same person, but not all at the same time.

---

[1]This account is based on the doctoral research of Donald Hogg (1964) and on this writer's visit to two ceremonies in the Bog Walk region of St. Catherine in 1997.

Hogg found three types of ceremonies: simple meetings, memorial services, and annual sacrifices. In the one he describes (1964, 267), the first stage incorporates the revival equivalent—hymns, choruses, and prayers—around such sacred icons as candles, flowers, and the Bible. The second stage begins with the entry of the Bongo man, at which point the spirits are summoned "by singing hymns in a slow, dirge-like tempo called 'long meter.'" It culminates in spirit possession, which comes with a sudden, headlong pitch to the ground. The groom struggles to secure a firm grip at the nape of the neck, a position he endeavors to maintain during this phase of the possession, as the now-stiffened body of the Bongo man is raised face-up from the ground and propelled backwards by the heels wherever he wants to go. The groom tries to steer him away from physical harm.

As the spirit gains control, the Bongo man grows calm and assumes the physical characteristics and personality of the spirit. Hogg (1964, 269) observed one "who had a paralyzed left arm, crossed eyes, and a limp." The Bongo man will remain in this state, smoking constantly, consuming rum liberally, using obscene language, and making lewd passes at young women, until satisfied the spirit departs, and the final stage is reached as people leave one by one.

Bongo spirits, which often require of their mounted hosts extraordinary feats of climbing trees or buildings, have a reputation of aggressiveness. According to Hogg, they seemed terrified of dogs. In one ceremony witnessed by this writer, the Bongo man seized hold of a dog that wandered too near the yard and hurled it squealing in terror 20 meters outside.

Spectators immediately retreated a safe distance from the circle.

Sacrificial ceremonies usually take three days, with the sacrifice of a goat performed on the second. The Bongo man blesses it with rum, before the groom beheads it with a single stroke. A portion of the meat is cooked without salt and set aside for the spirit, while the rest is consumed first by the Bongo man and groom, and then by the spectators. Dancing and possession will resume and continue into the third day, when the whole event is brought to a close "with a final Christian prayer and a solemn, ritual good-bye to the spirits" (Hogg 1964, 273).

Convince seems to have had an influence on the Rastafari movement, which appropriated and valorized the title "Bongo," as in Bongo Sam, or Bongo Jerry. In the 1960s and 1970s in Jamaica, "Bongo man" became a popular name for a dreadlocked Rastafarian. A noticeable feature of Rastafari nyabinghi celebrations is the sacred bonfire at the entrance of the sacred grounds that remains alive for the duration of the nyabinghi, which have been known to last as long as two weeks. Hogg makes no mention of a fire, but one was observed at each of the two ceremonies witnessed by this writer in St. Catherine. The ritual presence of fire serves as a source of spiritual power (Warner-Lewis 2003, 220–223). Rastafari abstention from salt may have derived from a more generalized tradition brought from Africa and strengthened in the post-Emancipation years by liberated Africans from the Kongo, but the movement's neutral attitude toward the use of expletives seems temptingly reminiscent of Bongo men's practice.

Alston Barrington Chevannes

SELECTED BIBLIOGRAPHY

Hogg, Donald William. "Jamaican Religions: A Study in Variations" (PhD thesis, Yale University, 1964).

Warner-Lewis, Maureen. *Central Africa in the Caribbean: Transcending Time, Transforming Cultures* (Barbados, Jamaica, Trinidad, and Tobago: University of the West Indies Press, 2003).

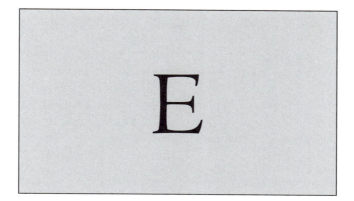

ESPIRITISMO

Historical Development

The early nineteenth century was a vibrant time for religious sentiment in both Europe and the United States. On both continents there was a renewed interest in the afterlife and methods for speaking with the dead. In the 1850s the young teacher and mathematician H. Leon Denizard Rivail began exploring the phenomenon of table turning. During the séances held in middle-class parlors, mediums attempted to contact the "other side." One evidence of such communication was when the table they were sitting around rose up and began to spin. Rivail began his investigation as a skeptic, but soon he was convinced of the veracity of these phenomena. He was especially convinced by the sophisticated responses to his questions given by the illiterate young female mediums. He began a systemic exploration of these ideas. Working under the pseudonym Allan Kardec, he wrote, under the direction of

some of the spirits, several books including *Le Livre des Esprits* (*The Book of the Spirits*), which served as the recognized textbook of Spiritism in France.

Kardec's form of communication with the dead was soon exported to the islands of the Caribbean and to South America where it became especially well established in Puerto Rico and Brazil. Originally a middle and upper-middle class phenomenon in France, in the Americas Espiritismo (Spiritism) quickly spread throughout these societies. Although the worldwide movement Kardec established did not survive his death, the forms of Espiritismo that developed in the Americas have continued to grow and develop. In the mid-twentieth century, Puerto Rican immigrants brought Espiritismo to the United States. Their Espiritismo *centros* (communities) attract not only other Puerto Ricans but also Spanish-speaking peoples from throughout the Americas as well as some non-Hispanic Black and White Americans. In addition, many non-Hispanics have been introduced to the beliefs and practices of Espiritismo by practitioners of other Caribbean religious traditions, including Santería. In New York City where members of vibrant Espiritismo and Santería communities often intermingle, a uniquely American form of Espiritismo, known as Santerismo, has developed (see entry "Santerismo").

Beliefs and Practices

Spiritist beliefs are based on eighteenth- and nineteenth-century Christian Catholicism, Hindu ideas that were circulating in Europe at the time, and the newly discovered ideas of electricity and fluid mechanics. The soul was understood to be an immaterial fluid that animates the human body. When a person dies, this fluid separates from the body and becomes a disembodied spirit that may roam the material and immaterial realms until it is reincarnated into a new human being in either this world or another. In the cosmology of Hinduism, one could be reborn as a person in any of the many castes or as an animal. One's rebirth depended on one actions in this life. If one is good and moral, one could expect to have an auspicious rebirth or perhaps even a release from the material world entirely; but if one is not good and moral, one might expect to be reborn into a lower level of existence, even as low as a dog or a pig or an insect. According to the laws of Karma as understood by spiritists, a spirit belongs to one of three categories and becomes more and more purified with each incarnation. Spiritists believe that among the disembodied spirits there are the impure spirits who roam the earth causing trouble and confusion and the pure spirits who work

with human beings sharing their wisdom and spiritual knowledge. Between these two types of spirits are the embodied spirits we call human beings. As embodied spirits humans are struggling to improve themselves so they may join the pure spirits upon their deaths. Important to Kardec's original followers were the scientific proofs it provided of continued existence. Although God stands behind the work of the spirits, He plays a minor role in the ritual activities of *espiritistas* (spiritists). Instead, it is the pure spirits that they look to for help and guidance.

Although Kerdac's principle concerns were theological and philosophical, in the Americas, Espiritismo provides spiritual, emotional, and physical healing. Professor Armand Andres Bermudez has identified four types of Spiritism practice. He calls these Scientific Spiritism (*Espirismo del Mesa*), Spiritualism of Charity (*Espiritismo de Caridad*), Spiritism of the Chain (*Espiritismo de Cordon*), and Mixed or Crossed Spiritism (*Espiritismo Cruzado*). The most common types of Espiritismo in the United States are Scientific Spiritism and the Mixed or Crossed Spiritism.

Table set for Misa Espiritual in Houston, Texas. (Mary Ann Clark)

In Scientific Spiritism, trained mediums led by the head medium gather at a table placed in the front of the meeting room. From there they communicate with the spirits associated with the community, providing practical and spiritual advice to the congregation that sit on the pews or chairs that fill the room. Only pure spirits are invoked, and if lower spirits manifest they are either driven away or provided with the light they need to continue their own spiritual evolution. Although some congregations use recorded music, in general, singing, dancing, drumming, and the like are considered inappropriate. Instead, prayers and simple chants are used to encourage the mediumistic trances.

Mixed Spiritism engages in a more free-flowing ritual known as *Misa Espiritual* (Spiritual Mass). Here the table is pushed to one end of the room and both the mediums and other participants sit in a semicircle. Singing, dancing, drumming, and even drinking along with prayers may be used. These sessions are known for mixing elements of traditional Espiritismo with Christian and African, particularly Yoruba and Bantu, practices. Prayers from Kardec's *Collection of Selected Prayers* in English or Spanish are common, but Protestant hymns, Black spirituals, and Catholic prayers may also be included. Although the experienced mediums provide most of the interactions with the spirits, all participants may exhibit forms of spirit communications. Whereas the Scientific Spiritism mediums generally work for the health and well-being of those nonmediums in attendance, in the Misa Espiritual all participants are encouraged to share in the spirit communications and all share in the benefits of these communications.

Mary Ann Clark

SELECTED BIBLIOGRAPHY

Bermundez, Armando Andres. "Notas para la historia del Espiritismo en Cuba." *Etnologia y folklore* 4 (1967): 5–22.

Gual, Candita C. *Collection of Selected Prayers: Devotion Manual A Spiritualist Prayer Guide* (New York: iUniverse, Inc., 2006).

Kardec, Allan. *Book on Mediums; Guide for Mediums and Invocators*, trans. E. A. Wood (New York: Samuel Weiser, 1970).

Kardec, Allan. *The Spirit's Book* (São Paulo, Brazil: Lake-Livraria Allan Kardec Editîra Ltda., 1972).

Kardec, Allan. *Collection of Selected Prayers* (Bronx, NY: De Pablo International Inc., 1989).

Kardec, Allan. *Coleccion de Oraciones Escogidas* (Bronx, NY: De Pablo International Inc., 1990).

Pérez y Mena, Andrés Isidoro. *Speaking with the Dead: Development of Afro-Latin Religion Among Puerto Ricans in the United States* (New York: AMS Press, Inc., 1991).

FIRE BAPTIZED HOLINESS CHURCH OF GOD OF THE AMERICAS

Historical Development

On August 1, 1898, William Edward Fuller Sr. mounted a mule and traveled more than 40 miles to attend the first nationally based organizing meeting of the Fire Baptized Holiness Association, an association that within three years (1895–1898) had grown from a locally based group located in a small rural area in Nebraska under the initiative of Benjamin Irwin to a nationally recognized force within the holiness movement. Fuller, the only black in attendance, embraced the theological principles of this newly formed association, and ten days later his zeal led to his appointment as overseer of all the "Negro Churches" within this group. Although racial tension disrupted interracial unity within the association, Fuller utilized this

opportunity to create the *Fire Baptized Holiness Church of God of the Americas*, an association that has grown from one church in South Carolina to over 1,000, extending into Canada, England, and the Caribbean.

In 1908, because of increasing discrimination within the organization and a growth in the viciousness of segregation, the interracial element that once promoted the growth of the Fire Baptized Holiness Church (Association) became terminus. Fuller, in this same year, along with 500 black members, agreed with the racialization of the group. Consequently, they left the group and formed a new ecclesiastical group called the *Colored Fire Baptized Holiness Church*. By the end of 1908, this new group, whose membership exceeded 900, under the leadership of Fuller, held its first Council Meeting in Greer, South Carolina, and formally appointed G. W. Gleen as its ruling elder and Fuller as General Overseer. The Sunday School Convention along with the formation of the Fuller Normal Industrial Institute in Atlanta,

---

WILLIAM EDWARD FULLER SR. (1875–1958)

On January 29, 1875, in Mountville, South Carolina, George and Martha Fuller became the proud parents of William Edward Fuller. Orphaned at the age of four, he was raised by his aunt Ida Fuller Vance. In 1892 Fuller joined New Hope Methodist Church and one year later received ministerial ordination. After attending the first meeting of the Fire Baptized Holiness Association in 1898, Fuller left Methodism, became the overseer of the black churches within the FBH Association, and by 1905 was appointed to the executive board of the group. In 1908, he departed this association to form the Colored Fire Baptized Church. Establishment of *The True Witness*, the first periodical of the association, the founding of Fuller Normal Industrial Institute, the adoption of a formal politico-religious framework, and a steady increase in membership numbers are key hallmarks of Fuller's leadership over the Fire Baptized Holiness Church of God of the Americas, which ended with his death in 1958.

Georgia, in 1910 and 1912, respectively, represented this group's early focus on education.

The Fire Baptized Holiness Church of God became the official name of the group in 1922. However, as a result of a General Council Meeting held at Mount Moriah Fire Baptized Holiness Church in Knoxville, Tennessee, in 1926, Fire Baptized Holiness Church of God of the Americas became the adopted name and still remains the official name of the organization. Between the 1930s and 1940s the association continued its expansion beyond South Carolina into the territories of Georgia, Tennessee, and North Carolina. A structural system of governance began in 1958, the same year in which Bishop Fuller died, with the instillation of C. C. Chiles, G. G. Gary, C. A. Mills, E. Z. Bowman, and W. E. Fuller Jr. into the bishopric.

Although men held the top-tiered positions within the Fire Baptized Holiness Church of God of the Americas, it is important to note the involvement of women within this ecclesiastical body. Women were not just members of the laity, they were also allowed to hold positions in the clergy. They were not only candidates of ministerial ordination, but they were also founding and acting pastors of local churches. For example, Mother Hazel L. Lindsay held a 34-year tenure at Antioch Fire Baptized Holiness Church in Cincinnati, Ohio. Women also served in positions of national capacity. For instance, Sister Caroline Williams Phelps and Mother L. E. Chiles were instrumental in the formation of the Sisters of Charity, the first service and mission organ of this association, in 1946. In the same year Sister Johnnie E. Fuller created the Young People's Institute.

Under the leadership of Bishop William Edward Fuller Jr., who received headship over the association in 1958 after the death of his father, organizational restructuring occurred in 1970 due to the growth in membership numbers. Remaining faithful to an Episcopal structure, there was an establishment of two additional dioceses in which Elder Abraham L. McCracken became bishop over the Second Episcopal Diocese and Elder Frank C. Canty began to oversee

MOTHER HAZEL L. LYNCH LINDSAY (1932–2003)

Hazel L. Lynch Lindsay was born on August 17, 1932. Mother Lindsay received her formal ministerial training from the Fuller Normal School of Religion. Armed with a Doctor of Divinity, she founded the Faith Chapel Fire Baptized Holiness Church of Gastonia in North Carolina where she remained pastor for ten years. Mother Lindsay would go on to serve as pastor of Mt. Sinai Fire Baptized Holiness Church located in South Carolina. She was not limited to only pastoral duties but diligently served as a regional supervisor in the Young People's Institute for eight years. In 1969, Mother Lindsay accepted a pastoral position at Antioch Fire Baptized Holiness Church in Cincinnati, Ohio. She became an advocate of community service, as seen in her reception of the Bishop N. T. Scott Service Award in 1992. The 34-year tenure of Mother Lindsay came to an end upon her death on May 30, 2003.

the Third Episcopal Diocese. Elders, pastors, evangelists, missionaries, deacons, and teachers are recognized as offices of ordination.

A continual increase in membership yielded not only organizational structuring, but it also led to the manifestation of organizations and additional schools focused on both missionary and educational pursuits. In 1974, the Junior Missionary Department was initiated in order to provide basic theological training for children and young adults in the church; however, this group became responsible for the expansion of the Fire Baptized Holiness Church of God of the Americas into international territories. For example, in 1977, the youth group built a local church in Jamaica, West Indies, and then in 1988 established the W. E. Fuller Jr. Headquarters and Mission Home in the same country. A continued commitment to youth can be attested to in the opening of the Fuller Normal Advanced Technology Charter School (FNATCS) in 2006. Nestled on

BISHOP WILLIAM EDWARD FULLER JR. (1921–2007)

William Edward Fuller Jr. was born in 1921 to Bishop William Edward Fuller Sr., founder of the association, and Mother Emma Fuller. Five months after the death of his father in 1958, Fuller, upon reception into the bishopric, became the new leader of the Fire Baptized Holiness Church of God of the Americas. With the addition of two dioceses to the association's governing body, the creation of the Junior Mission Arm, and the documenting of official church doctrine through two primary works, *Work of a Deacon: A Handbook* and *Introducing the Fire Baptized Holiness Church of God of the Americas*, both written by Bishop Patrick L. Frazier, the association continued to grow under the leadership of Bishop Fuller. He was also instrumental in expanding the Fuller Normal Industrial Institute's campus and the passing of Bill 731, a legislative bill passed in order to rename the highway that runs in front of the association's headquarters in Greenville, South Carolina, to the "Bishop William Edward Fuller, Sr., Highway."

75 acres of land in Greenville, South Carolina, FNATCS, with its small teacher-to-student ratio, well-established board of directors, and technically equipped building that can house 500 students, has made a commitment to equip those students labeled "at-risk" with literacy, technological proficiency, and a sense of community.

Beliefs and Practices

The "Basis of Union" contained within the "Discipline" symbolizes the written theological disposition of the Fire Baptized Holiness Church of God of the Americas. Redemption, justification, sanctification, and eschatology—a doctrine that deals with matters of finality like the afterlife—form the major theological categories utilized to organize this belief system. For this group the blood of Jesus serves as a catalyst in the propagation of redemption and absolution of past sins, yielding total restoration or regeneration. Although redemption from sin maintains a place in the "Basis of Union," it does not include an explicit statement about the origin of the sin, i.e., original sin.

Not only does Jesus' blood hold a significant place within this value system, but the faith of believers also maintains an important position in the aforementioned ideology. For example, justification results from faith in the redemptive power of Jesus' blood. Accordingly, faith serves as a precursor to grace, and this unmerited favor precedes the process of sanctification. Faith places believers into a posture of receptivity toward the "baptism of fire," in which glossolalia, i.e., "speaking in tongues," scripturally supported in Acts 8:14–17, emblematizes the initial sign of this reception. In summation, this group believes in the following

experiences: conversion, sanctification, and baptism of the Holy Spirit. Concerning eschatology, the group highlights the second coming of Christ with emphasis on his judgment yielding both rewards and punishments.

Spiritualism, Mormonism, Jehovah's Witnesses, and Roman Catholicism are rejected in the "Basis of Union." It is important to note these rejections are not a simple one line theological denial, but instead the "Basis of Union" meticulously presents each group in light of its documented history and theological dispositions in order to offer rejections. For example, the church denies Catholicism's acceptance of transubstantiation elements of communion actually becoming the blood and body of Jesus, and purgatory. Specific practices such as witchcraft and sorcery are also rejected. The church also rejects certain theological teachings like reincarnation.

Outside of the value system presented in the "Basis of Union," this body also maintains general rules generated to assist with the functionality of the group. Rejection of members joining secret societies and entering casinos or movie theatres signifies only 2 of the 15 ordinances. Considering that women are able to hold clergy positions within the group, it is important to note ordinance five in the system of general rules. Women are mandated to refrain from wearing pants and dresses with short sleeves. This dress code extends beyond an ecclesiastical setting; therefore, even if pants are required for work, women must wear a skirt/dress to work, change into pants, and then change back into the skirt/dress before leaving the employment location. Women are the only members who are subjected to an explicit dress code.

The Fire Baptized Holiness Church of God of the Americas professes two sacraments. The first is the Lord's Supper. Baptism, specifically "water baptism," is the second sacrament of this group. In order for members to progress toward perfected obedience and receive regeneration, baptism by full immersion must be completed. Cleansing the feet of saints (members) and marriage represent other rites within this ecclesiastical body.

Margarita Simon Guillory

SELECTED BIBLIOGRAPHY

Fire Baptized Holiness Church of God of the Americas. *Discipline of the Fire Baptized Holiness Church of God of the Americas* (Atlanta: Fuller Press, 1994). Available from the Fire Baptized Holiness Church at http://www.fbhchurch.org (accessed July 10, 2007).

Frazier, Patrick L. *Introducing the Fire Baptized Holiness Church of God of the Americas: A Study Manual* (Wilmington: Fire Baptized Holiness Church, 1990). http://www.fbhchurch.org (accessed July 10, 2007).

"Fuller Normal Advanced Technology Charter School" (2006). Available from FNTACS at http://fullernormalcharter school.org/home.aspx .

Hogan, Howard B. *Tongues and the Baptism of Holy Spirit: Their Place in the Fire Baptized Holiness Church of God in the Americas* (Chicago: Professional Paper, Chicago Theological Seminary, 1976).

Sanders, Cheryl J. *Saints in Exile: The Holiness Pentecostal Experience in African American Religion and Culture* (New York and Oxford: Oxford University Press, 1996).

G

GAGA

Historical Development

Gaga is a widespread African-based religious tradition in the Dominican Republic, formerly known as the Spanish colony of Santo Domingo, but it also exists on a much smaller scale in Eastern Cuba. The followers of this tradition consist primarily of poor Haitian immigrants who reside in rural areas. They and their ancestors fled from neighboring Haiti in several waves of migration to escape the endless economical hardship and violence in their home country. Unfortunately, many of these Haitians ended up living under equally impoverished if not worse conditions in the Dominican Republic, their hardship being compounded by the fact that large numbers of them do not have Dominican citizenship and suffer marginalization. In Eastern Cuba, the servants of the Gaga spirits usually do not have to carry this additional burden of political disenfranchisement.

Gaga or Rara—as it is called in Haiti— is an exuberant carnival-like spring festival associated with a certain cluster of Haitian Vodou spirits. Its highly popular ceremonies culminate during Holy Week with the Easter holidays. It is this celebration of Rara, hispanicized into the term "Gaga," that gave the name to this religious and cultural movement.

Beliefs and Practices

Gaga is a complex and intricate religion consisting of Haitian-derived beliefs and practices adapted and assimilated into their new Dominican diaspora environment. It is found mainly in rural areas and is widely practiced by Haitian contract laborers (i.e., recent noncitizen migrants), but Gaga has also attracted followers among *Dominicanos* of Haitian descent and has even spread into the wider Dominican population of any ethnic descent. Hence, Gaga is a highly adaptive social and political movement that serves primarily the needs of these Haitian immigrants. The religion offers its followers an elaborate system of magical beliefs and practices that enable them to cope with the problems and uncertainties of everyday life. Moreover, it provides them with a welcome escape from persistent patterns of political oppression, degradation, and abuse. Gaga processions and street parades allow them to transform their often harsh reality into a festive and entertaining mystical journey.

While the followers of Gaga serve a multitude of Haitian spirits, they have a particular affinity with the Rara spirits. The origin of these spirits has been associated with the Arada region of the former Kingdom of Dahomey in West Africa, but has also synthesized other West and especially Central African traditions from the former Kingdom of the Kongo. In addition, like many African diaspora religions in the Caribbean, Gaga reflects the influence of both French and Spanish Catholicism. Like in Haitian Vodou, the sacred cosmology of the religion of Gaga, includes an almighty supreme being, the spiritual presence of the ancestors, and most significantly a pantheon of intermediary spirits grouped into distinct families. It is the intermediary spirit entities that are the focus of most religious activity. They have their own characteristic attributes, food offerings, color preferences, rhythms, songs, dances, places of power in the natural world, and location in the cosmos that are individually allocated to them. Depending on the context, these spirits can be seen as either malevolent or beneficial. Dominican followers of Gaga maintain that proper ritual behavior and appropriate offerings appease all spirits, Rada, and Petwo, and ensure balance, happiness, good luck, and success in life. The spiritual forces are understood as just acting as they are (according to

whatever their nature is, regardless of whether wild and ferocious or tame and sweet), and it is how the human *serviteurs* relate to these spirits that determines ultimately the nature of their behavior and their relationship with the individuals who serve them. Bad luck and unfortunate events are thus explained by enraged and unhappy spirit entities that have been offended or neglected in some form or another. Nevertheless, when properly addressed and satisfied through offerings or animal sacrifices, all spirits can turn around and become supportive spiritual allies.

Overall, Gaga rituals are similar to those rituals performed in Haitian Vodou. However, given the circumstances over time, some differences between Dominican and Haitian ritual traditions have evolved. These differences become most evident in the Dominican emphasis on Amerindian spirits and shamanic practices (Alegria-Pons 1993) as well as differing patterns of influence between Vodou practitioners in Haiti and the Roman Catholic Church (Deive 1988). Most of these differences can be traced to historical dissimilarities. Following the Haitian Revolution, the Roman Catholic Church withdrew all priests from Haiti for a period of about 50 years. This complete absence of Catholic clergy allowed Haitian Vodou to develop independently from the Church. By contrast, African diaspora religions in the Dominican Republic remained continuously under the watchful surveillance of the Catholic Church.

The most important public ceremony of Dominican (and Cuban) Gaga is the annual rite that marks the celebration of the end of the sugarcane harvest and the beginning of spring. The rituals begin with the washing of hands and feet on Holy

Thursday, followed by a blessing of clothing. On the next day, Good Friday, pilgrimages to other villages take place. The week-long festivities are marked by keeping a perpetual flame, and include also spectacular performances of secular and religious music as well as mock battles between villages. According to Alegria-Pons (1993, 61), these harvest rites are simultaneously rituals of reconciliation and rituals of rebellion and hence serve a variety of spiritual, social, and political functions.

The priesthood of the Gaga religion includes powerful *reinas de Gaga* (Gaga queens) and priests who assume complex roles of leadership during the annual rites of Holy Week. They also assist their community all year round as spiritual advisors in every aspect of life. Similar to Haitian *manbos* and *oungans* they function—always for a small fee—as the physicians, legal advisors, psychologists, and personal counselors for the marginalized and impoverished people they serve. These religious leaders often have an enormous influence on their constituency because of their profound magical and esoteric knowledge, their vast ritual and healing expertise, and their magnetic and charismatic personalities. For instance, baseball superstar Sammy Sosa, a native Dominican, is alleged to have sought the spiritual assistance of a Gaga priest who enabled him to reach fame and fortune in the United States.

Ina J. Fandrich

SELECTED BIBLIOGRAPHY

Alegria-Pons, Jose Francisco. *Gaga y Vudu en la Republica Dominicana* (San Juan, Puerto Rico: Editorial Chango-Prieto, 1993).

Deive, Carlos Esteban. *Vodu y Magie en Santo Domingo* (Santo Domingo: Museo del Hombre Dominicana, 1988).

Interviews with Marily Gallardo De La Rosa, performing artist, community activist, and *Reina de Gaga* (Gaga Queen) from the Dominican Republic. (July 2007) [translation provided by Mara Rivera].

Levinson, David, and Stephen Glazier. "Gaga (Rara cult) in the Dominican Republic." *Encyclopedia of African and African-American Religions*, ed. Stephen Glazier (New York: Routledge, 2001), 127–128.

McAlister, Elizabeth. *Rara! Vodou, Power, and Performance in Haiti and Its Diaspora* (Berkeley: University of California Press, 2002).

Rosenberg, June. *El Gaga: Religion y Sociedad de un Culto Dominicana* (Santo Domingo: Editoria de la UASD, 1979).

GARÍFUNA RELIGION

Historical Development

The ethnic group known as the Garífuna, or Black Caribs, live today in Central America, the Caribbean, and various cities in the United States, Canada, and England (a total population of about 100,000–150,000) and can be distinguished by their unique cultural patterns: language, religion, crafts, music, dance, and lifestyle.

The history of the Garífuna (cassava-eating people) begins on the island of St. Vincent in the eastern Caribbean, which was originally inhabited by a mixture of Carib and Arawak tribes (linguistically Maipuran and Arawakan, or Island Carib) from mainland South America prior to the period of Spanish colonization that began in 1492. Soon after their initial contact with Europeans, the Island Caribs began to absorb individual Europeans (from Spain, France, and England) and West Africans (mainly from shipwrecked Spanish slave ships) by means of capture or rescue. By 1700, a new ethnic group emerged on St. Vincent that was racially and culturally distinct from that of the Island Caribs: the Garífuna.

In terms of their language and cultural patterns, the Garífuna are an Afro-Amerindian people (called Zambos by the Spanish) who have blended various traits of their ancestors to create a unique social system with a strong emphasis on music, dance, and storytelling and with its own unique brand of religion, which consists of a mixture of Indian, African, and Catholic beliefs. Another distinction is that the Garífuna are matrifocal, which means that the women are the center of the household and that people trace their bloodlines through their mother's family.

In November 1997, the Garífuna celebrated the 200th anniversary of their arrival on the shores of Central America, after being forcibly removed by the British from the island of St. Vincent in 1797. After conquering many of the Spanish-held islands in the Caribbean, the British decided to take control of the French-held island of St. Vincent during the 1770s. By 1783, the British had dominated the French inhabitants and their slaves and attempted to subjugate about 7,000–8,000 Garífunas. However, many Garífunas were killed in battles with the British or died from European diseases during this period. During 1795–1797, the British hunted down, killed, or captured the remaining Garífuna population, destroyed their homes, and deported on eight or nine ships about 2,250 survivors to the island of Roatan in the Bay Islands, off the coast of Honduras. However, the Garífuna leaders considered

Roatan to be unsuitable for such a large population and requested help from the Spanish authorities at Trujillo, on the mainland of Honduras. By the end of September 1797, about 1,700 Garífuna had been resettled near Trujillo by the Spanish, who hoped that the Garífuna would provide them with needed manpower for the development of farming communities on the north coast of Honduras.

By 1900, the Garífuna had established their own settlements along the Caribbean coast of Central America, predominantly in Honduras, Guatemala, and Belize (known at that time as British Honduras), but also at Sandy Bay in Nicaragua. The principal settlements were at Stann Creek and Punta Gorda in Belize; at Livingston, near Puerto Barrios, in Guatemala; and at scores of locations along the northern coast of Honduras, near the major cities of Puerto Cortés, Tela, La Ceiba, and Trujillo. In 1974, it was estimated that the Garífuna population in Honduras was about 60,900, with about 10,600 in Belize, 5,500 in Guatemala, and 800 in Nicaragua. With few exceptions, most of these settlements were located within 200 yards of the sea, near river mouths, freshwater lagoons, and protected bays. Also during the 1970s, thousands of Garífuna were reported to have migrated to U.S. cities (New York, Boston, New Orleans, and Los Angeles), where the men typically served in the U.S. merchant fleet. More recently, Garífuna families have been reported in port cities of Canada and Great Britain.

Beliefs and Practices

Soon after their arrival in Central America in 1797, the Garífuna were considered by the Spanish and British settlers to be ''devil-worshippers, polygamists and speakers of a secret language,'' which strengthened the Garífunas' resolve to live apart in their own settlements, maintain their independence, and preserve their culture. Garífuna songs and dances display a wide range of subject matter; for example, there are work songs, social dances, and ancestral ceremonies centered on traditions. One of the most popular dances is called ''La Punta,'' which is performed at wakes, holidays, parties, and other social events. Some of these traditional dances and ceremonies have to do with the Garífunas' respect for the dead: the Amuyadahani (bathing the spirit of the dead), the Chuga (feeding the dead), and the Dugu (feasting of the dead).

The Garífuna perform these religious rites and ceremonies because, like many Amerindian and African societies, they believe that the spirits of their dead ancestors, which are both good and evil and have a direct impact on the lives of people in the living world, must be respected, worshipped, and appeased. This religious tradition bears some resemblance to Spiritism (see ''Spiritualism'').

Although some Garífunas adopted Catholicism on the island of St. Vincent during the French occupation or after arriving on the Spanish-controlled mainland of Central America, this was rather a ''political decision'' than an authentic conversion to Christianity. After migrating to the south coast of Belize and establishing permanent settlements, some Garífunas accepted the presence of Anglican, Methodist, and Baptist missionaries in their villages and eventually the establishment of English-speaking Protestant churches and schools, beginning in the early 1800s. Later, the Seventh-day Adventists and the Church of the Nazarene developed churches and schools in Garífuna villages in Belize. In Honduras, there are a few Baptist churches among the Garífuna, near Tela.

However, the core of Garífuna culture consists of their traditional Afro-Amerindian rites and rituals, which are practiced in every Garífuna settlement, and the *buwiye* (shaman [male or female]) is the direct psychological link between the ancestors and the souls of the living. An important part of their religious ceremonies involves the use of songs, drinking, and dance, accompanied by drums and other musical instruments, a combination that sometimes induces a trance-like state of consciousness (called ''spirit-possession'') during which time a person is believed to enter the spirit world and communicate with the ancestors, according to practitioners (see ''Spirit Possession''). These ceremonies, which are similar in some respects to Vodou, Santería, and obeah (see entries on these three traditions) practices in Haiti, Cuba and Puerto Rico, and Jamaica, respectively, are used to mourn the dead, heal the sick, protect family members from harm, do harm to one's enemies, discern the future, assure good fishing and harvests, find a mate, help the dead achieve peace and happiness in the next world, appease alienated spirits, and so on. Rum is often administered ritually to begin a ceremony or induce a trance; it is thrown out of the doors and windows to attract the spirits; it is sprinkled upon the dancers, drummers, and the possessed to cool and sooth; it is used to cure those seeking relief from physical and psychological ills; and it is used to anoint the sacred table at the end of the ceremony. Food, flowers, and candles are normally used in these ceremonies as well, but there is no mention of animal sacrifices being used as in Vodou,

Santería, and obeah rituals. Although many Garífuna today speak Creole English and/or Spanish, most continue to use their traditional language, which is a unique blend of Arawak, Carib, French, Yuroba, Bantu, and Swahili.

Clifton L. Holland

SELECTED BIBLIOGRAPHY

Davidson, William V. "Black Carib (Garífuna) Habitats in Central America." *Frontier Adaptations in Lower Central America*, ed. Mary W. Helms and Franklin O. Loveland (Philadelphia: Institute for the Study of Human Issues, 1976).

"The Garífuna of Belize and St. Vincent." http://www.centrelink.org/Belize.html (accessed October 15, 2001).

Gonzalez, Nancie L. *Sojourners of the Caribbean: Ethnogenesis and Ethnohistory of the Garífuna* (Urbana: University of Illinois Press, 1988).

Olmos, Margarite Fernández, and Lizabeth Paravisini-Gebert, eds. *Sacred Possessions: Vodou, Santería, Obeah and the Caribbean* (New Brunswick, NJ: Rutgers University Press, 1997).

H

HOODOO

Historical Development

Hoodoo is an African American magical tradition that developed in the Mississippi River Valley. Practitioners, who could equally be male or female, have been known by a variety of names, including but not limited to *hoodoo doctors* and *two heads*. Their art consists of making magical charms and casting spells for paying clients and has historically also included the performance of ceremonies, including ritual initiations for new hoodoo doctors.

Hoodoo is closely related to Voodoo. Most researchers of the nineteenth and early twentieth centuries, including Zora Neale Hurston, treated them as synonyms. Recently, however, scholars and a growing number of popular authors have drawn a sharp distinction between them, describing Voodoo as a religion and hoodoo as supernaturalism. Historical evidence indicates that hoodoo is best understood as the ritual and magical aspects of Voodoo. According to one Voodoo practitioner interviewed by the Federal Writers' Project in the late 1930s, "*Voodoo* means the worker, *hoodoo* the things they do." This distinction is in keeping with West African practice, which defines "Vodu" as a religion and "hudu" as working with the spirits of that religion.

Scholars frequently use *hoodoo* as a synonym for a related magical system known as *conjure*. Though this terminology reflects modern usage among practitioners and believers, it obscures some of the historical differences in the two magical systems, which arose because of the distinctive religions of the Mississippi Valley's African slaves and their French masters. Hoodoo has roots stretching back to peoples of the Senegambian region of West Africa, as reflected in its name for charms, *gris-gris*, a Mande term of the same meaning. Contributions from the Bight of Benin and West Central Africa had also entered the practice by the late eighteenth century. Conjure, in contrast, has incorporated few elements from Senegambia or the Bight of Benin. Instead, it originated primarily among peoples from the Bight of Biafra and West Central Africa. In addition, hoodoo has long included such Roman Catholic paraphernalia as altars, candles, and saint images. These items were virtually unknown outside of the Mississippi River Valley until the twentieth century, largely because of the paucity of Catholics in the Anglo South.

Beliefs and Practices

Prior to the twentieth century, hoodoo doctors' chief duties were the manufacture of charms and casting of spells for paying clients. They obtained most of their supernatural materials from nature, and these consisted of a wide range of botanical and zoological items as well as some minerals. Though charms took many forms, a particularly popular type were bags containing bundles of magical objects. The uses of these magical items varied enormously. During the era of slavery, protective powders and root charms were common. Items promising to bring luck, money, and love to their owners were likewise prominent.

Modern practitioners obtain most of their materials from spiritual supply shops, which are also known as candle shops and sometimes hoodoo stores. Today, spiritual supply shops are common across the nation, but the somewhat scant evidence for their origins indicates that they arose out of pharmacies in the Mississippi Valley. George Washington Cable, who demonstrated substantial knowledge of hoodoo in his 1891 novel, *The Grandissimes*, hints at this possibility. At one point in the book, an African American attempts to purchase hoodoo supplies from a New Orleans pharmacy. The implication was that pharmacies were appropriate places to purchase such items, at least in the lower Mississippi Valley. Though Cable wrote near the end of the century, his tale is set in the years just after 1800. If the author was accurate in his depictions, then the spiritual supply industry of New Orleans was almost certainly the oldest in the nation.

In addition to making charms and casting spells, hoodoo doctors were ritual leaders. Some of the best-documented ceremonies were initiations. Many practitioners considered these necessary to become adepts. There were several types of initiations, likely reflecting a progressive hierarchy of spiritual power.

JAMES ALEXANDER

Little is known about the particulars of his life, including information related to his birth, childhood, and training. What is known tends to be rather sketchy. A late nineteenth-century hoodoo practitioner, generally known as Dr. Jim Alexander, he was best known for his curing ceremonies. One eyewitness described the ritual as including dancing, distribution of fruit covered in burning brandy, and head washings with the same brandy. This particular ceremony, which was probably similar to the others of his repertoire, ended with a collection. A later hoodoo practitioner, Oscar Felix, performed ceremonies that were in many ways reminiscent of Alexander's.

Though initiations were small affairs, including only the aspiring practitioners and one to a few hoodoo doctors, large-scale ceremonies also existed. Some of the most popular supposedly cured attendees of illness. Nineteenth- and early twentieth-century authors reported many others as well. When one bears in mind that Voodoo and hoodoo were not distinct systems prior to the mid-twentieth century, any Voodoo ceremony could be equally defined as a hoodoo ritual.

The rise of spiritual supply shops has significantly affected the practice of hoodoo. Most continue to stock a selection of traditional herbal and zoological curios. Their primary business, however, consists of selling manufactured items of recent vintage. These include a wide selection of candles, oils, incenses, bath salts, aerosol sprays, and other items.

Those who in earlier days would have become clients of supernatural specialists today patronize spiritual supply shops. In place of hoodoo doctors are salespeople who determine consumers' problems and recommend items to aid them in their magical endeavors. Much of the knowledge and repertoire of the historical hoodoo practitioner is now embodied in the advice of shop clerks and an array of do-it-yourself books, spell kits, and other magical items. The decline of the hoodoo doctor also

F. and F. Botanica and Candle Shop in New Orleans. It is the largest hoodoo shop in the city and caters to traditional hoodoo practitioners, members of Spiritual churches, and adherents of a variety of Afro-Caribbean faiths. (Jeffrey Elton Anderson)

saw the disappearance of the ritual aspect of their roles. Though it is tempting to disparage the transformation of the practitioner-client relationships of the past into the business-consumer transactions of the present, it must be remembered that hoodoo's ability to evolve has kept it a vital part of black life from Africa to twenty-first-century America.

Jeffrey Elton Anderson

SELECTED BIBLIOGRAPHY

Anderson, Jeffrey E. *Conjure in African American Society* (Baton Rouge: Louisiana State University Press, 2005).

Cable, George Washington. *The Grandissimes: A Story of Creole Life* (New York: Charles Scribner's Sons, 1891).

Hyatt, Harry Middleton. *Hoodoo-Conjuration-Witchcraft-Rootwork*. 5 vols. Memoirs of the Alma Egan Hyatt Foundation (Hannibal, MO: Western Publishing Company, 1970–1978).

Jacobs, Claude F., and Andrew J. Kaslow. *The Spiritual Churches of New Orleans: Origins, Beliefs, and Rituals of an African-American Religion* (Knoxville: University of Tennessee Press, 1991).

Long, Carolyn Morrow. *Spiritual Merchants: Religion, Magic, and Commerce* (Knoxville: University of Tennessee Press, 2001).

Long, Carolyn Morrow. *A New Orleans Voudou Priestess: The Legend and Reality of Marie Laveau* (Gainesville: University Press of Florida, 2006).

Rosenthal, Judy. *Possession, Ecstasy, and Law in Ewe Voodoo* (Charlottesville and London: University Press of Virginia, 1998).

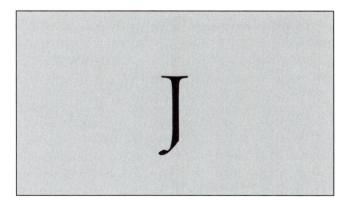

JEHOVAH'S WITNESSES

Historical Development

Almost from its very inception, African Americans have been involved with or become subjects of attention and controversy within the Jehovah's Witness movement. Many famous African Americans have been associated with the religious group, including the late Michael Jackson and the Jackson family, actors Lark Voorhies and Terrence Howard, tennis sensations Venus and Serena Williams, musical artists such as Prince, Jill Scott, Ja Rule, Wilton Felder, Wayne Henderson Sr., and Larry Graham, and notables like Evelyn Mandela and former Witness Gloria Naylor, a literary scholar whose novel *The Women of Brewster Place* was made into a highly lauded television movie.

Founded in Allegheny, Pennsylvania, by Charles Taze Russell in 1872 (at the age of 20) and incorporated in Pennsylvania in 1884 as the Zion's Watch Tower Tract Society, the group has been called by various names. Part of the challenge with respect to what to call itself was the movement's desire simply to be known as "Christian," but given the numbers of groups that call themselves Christian and the fact that Jehovah's Witnesses perceive themselves as a distinctive and separate body of people who are exclusively God's ("Jehovah's") chosen religious assembly, not having a name with which to identify the group became an obvious problem.

Prior to adopting the name Jehovah's Witnesses, the group was called many different names, including Russellites, Dawnites, Dawn Bible Students, Watch Tower Bible people, and Rutherfordites, after Joseph Franklin "Judge" Rutherford. It was Rutherford, in fact, who proposed that the group accept "Jehovah's Witnesses" as its official designation. The resolution, made at its Washington, D.C., international convention in 1931, passed at the annual meeting in Columbus, Ohio.

As God's visible, earthly organization, the argument went, it has existed for thousands of years from the time of Adam and Eve, but especially since Abel, God's first faithful Witness. Because of this, Rutherford suggested that the organization had actually been on earth for more than 5,000 years (Stroup 1945, 3). And, thus, the name "Jehovah's Witnesses" was considered appropriate.

With respect to African American members in the history of the group, like many religious traditions, the development of the Watch Tower organization is neither neat nor clear-cut. While the group taught that racial distinctions were not significant, some black Jehovah's Witnesses had negative experiences due to intentionally segregated Kingdom Halls (Jehovah's Witness "churches") and little or no opportunity for leadership, albeit the organization, according to some scholars, is more than 50 percent people of color and as much as one-third African American. (This was even more challenging for black women, given that the organization did not allow women to hold leadership positions based on a strict understanding of gender roles. Men were the leaders in the group and in the home.) Because of Jim Crow and anti-integration laws down South, for example, black and white Jehovah's Witnesses had to meet separately. While distasteful, the Society did not fight these laws with vigor. Russell perhaps did not agitate for change regarding such discrimination because his perspective was that the preaching of the good news was more worthy of the Society's attention than racial justice issues. Also, from the late 1920s to the early- to mid-1930s there was a "Colored Branch" within the headquarters of the Watch Tower Society in Brooklyn, New York. (By 1934 this branch was merged into one branch to serve the U.S. territory.)

African Americans were members of the group from the early years of its history. Thomas E. Banks joined the "Bible Students" in 1901, as Jehovah's Witnesses were then known. He is thought to be the first African American Witness official when, in the early 1920s, the President of Watch Tower Society, Joseph F. Rutherford, asked him to represent the Society to the "colored" Brethren

WILLIAM K. "BILL" JACKSON

Bill Jackson is argued by scholar Firpo Carr to have been the first leader of African descent on the Governing Body (not to be confused with the Watch Tower Society, a *legal* apparatus), the Bible-based legislative entity of Jehovah's Witnesses. The issue is controversial, since Jackson was believed by his colleagues to be white, and his birth certificate (first made public by Carr himself) ostensibly indicates this. According to Carr, strong evidence suggests that he lived his life "passing," a term in African American vernacular that implies that a black person who is lighter in color and lives as "white" in order to avoid the challenges of being black and conversely to share in the privileges of being white in America. Jackson served on the Governing Body from 1971 until his death in 1981. Headquartered in Brooklyn, New York, the members of this group of leaders are considered elders, and they make all the major decisions, both legal and theological, of the group.

throughout various parts of the United States, as well as in Panama, Costa Rica, and Jamaica. Banks eventually worked part-time out of Witness headquarters in New York until 1938 when he was permanently assigned to Jamaica.

Though details are scant, in the late 1930s and early 1940s, it is thought that James Otis Boone emerged as the next prominent African American traveling overseer of Jehovah's Witnesses. He was in his early twenties at the time. Furthermore, the first African Americans to attend the newly opened prestigious school for missionaries called Gilead were George Richardson and Charles Fitzpatrick. In the early 1950s William J. Douglas of New York City was one of the youngest traveling overseers at age 21. African American participation and visibility would increase over the decades, with many gaining key leadership positions.

Beliefs and Practices

Among the more public practices is the refusal to allow members to undergo blood transfusions and organ transplants, which, for this community amounts to a form of cannibalism. Moreover, members of the group do not celebrate birthdays,

since the practice would amount to aggrandizement, and no Witness is considered better than another. Furthermore, the community considers saluting or pledging allegiance to the American flag to be a form of idolatry. Finally, typical American holidays such as Easter and Christmas are considered pagan celebrations and not Christian ones.

Jehovah's Witnesses assert that their beliefs are based exclusively on the Bible, the unerring Word of God (2 Timothy 3:16, 17). While they have their own version of the Bible, *The New World Translation of the Scriptures*, members are not forbidden to read other versions. The following is a synopsis of their major beliefs drawn from information made available by the Jehovah's Witnesses (see http://www.watchtower.org/e/jt/article_03.htm): "God's name is Jehovah." Jesus Christ, God's Son, "was the first to be created and is inferior to God," understood in male terms. "Christ died on a stake, not a cross, and his human life was paid as a ransom" to redeem humanity. Having been raised to "immortal spirit" life in heaven, "Jesus' one sacrifice is sufficient." His "presence is in spirit" rather than in body, and the earth will be a paradise of peace under his righteous Kingdom rule. "Earth will never be destroyed nor depopulated." Instead,

SAMUEL HERD

Presently, Samuel Herd is a member of the Governing Body. And, as a member of this Body, Samuel Herd is the highest-ranking African American within the Jehovah's Witness Governing Body. Prior to this, he was the first African American "circuit servant." In this capacity he was a traveling overseer with authority of a number of congregations and was assigned to the Watts section of Los Angeles after the "Watts Riots" of 1965. Having served in that capacity in the Southern United States among African American congregations, he was eventually given greater responsibilities as a District Overseer, serving numerous circuits in the process.

J. RICHARD BROWN

J. Richard Brown is the official spokesman for the entire worldwide organization of Jehovah's Witnesses. He heads the Office of Public Information located at Witness headquarters in Brooklyn, New York. Fluent in French, Brown has served as both circuit and district overseer for both French- and English-speaking congregations, circuits, and districts. When summoned to headquarters ("Bethel") in 1980, Brown initially was assigned to the Service Department, which is responsible for coordinating the Witness preaching work. However, realizing that his talents were underutilized, he was reassigned to the Writing Department, generally thought of as being more prestigious than the Service Department. He then became a member of the Public Affairs Office, now the Office of Public Information.

"God will destroy the present system of things in the battle at Har-Magedon" (Armageddon).

The incorrigibly wicked will be "eternally destroyed." "People who God approves will receive eternal life." "We are now in the time of the end. Human death is due to Adam's sin. The human soul ceases to exist at death. Hell is humankind's common grave, where the majority of people will end up. The hope for the dead is resurrection, but only a little flock of 144,000, all born again, will go to heaven and rule with Christ." (Available at http://www.watchtower.org /e/jt/article_03.htm.) A version of this doctrine as well as Jehovah's Witness practices of predicting the end of the age and many other tenets of Watch Tower religion influenced Nation of Islam leader Elijah Muhammad, who reportedly listened to early radio broadcasts of Judge Rutherford.

Jehovah's Witnesses are always politically neutral and ideally do not exalt one race above another. All their religious gatherings are integrated. They ritualistically meet together in local congregations of approximately 100 on a weekly basis at the local Kingdom Hall, their place of worship. Several times a year a number of congregations forming a circuit meet at Circuit Assemblies and Special Assembly Days. A number of circuits form a district and meet at annual district conventions. There are also national and international gatherings.

African American traveling circuit and district elders sometimes oversee predominantly white congregations, circuits, and districts. Both African American Witnesses and their white American counterparts believe the earth will soon be restored to a plush, African-like paradise where people of all races will live together in peace and harmony. While emphasizing racial harmony, Jehovah's Witnesses rarely, if ever, acknowledge racist ideology that was part of its early history. Borrowing from Mormons (the Church of Jesus Christ of Latter-day Saints), for example, the Watch Tower (c. 1902), including its founder Pastor Russell, taught that African Americans' skin would eventually turn white in order for them to gain salvation. They claimed to have documented evidence that this process of skin whitening had occurred for Rev. William H. Draper (an African Methodist Episcopal minister rather than a Witness), who turned white in response to his earnest desire and prayer to be so (Carr 1993, 92–95).

Following the death of Charles Taze Russell, the "cult of personality" (or "creature worship" according to the Bible Students) manifested itself when certain ones attached themselves reverentially to him. Because of this, the organization strongly discouraged unnecessarily "drawing attention to oneself." Those in responsible positions frowned on or cast a suspicious eye on anyone who began to gain prominence. For this reason, there were no real "official" African American "leaders" among Jehovah's Witnesses. However, there were *de facto* ones.

Stephen C. Finley and Firpo Carr

SELECTED BIBLIOGRAPHY

Carr, Firpo W. *A History of Jehovah's Witnesses: From a Black American Perspective* (Lakewood, CA: Scholar Technological Institute of Research, Inc., 1993).

Carr, Firpo W. *Jehovah's Witnesses: The African American Enigma—A Contemporary Study*, Vol. 1 (Lakewood, CA: Scholar Technological Institute of Research, Inc., 2001).

Maesen, William A. "Watchtower Influences on Black Muslim Eschatology: An Exploratory Study." *Journal for the Scientific Study of Religion* 9.4 (Winter 1970): 321–325.

Pike, Royston. *Jehovah's Witnesses: Who They Are, What They Teach, What They Do* (New York: Philosophical Library, 1954).

Stroup, Herbert Hewitt. *The Jehovah's Witnesses* (New York: Columbia University Press, 1945).

Watch Tower Society. *Jehovah's Witnesses—Who Are They? What Do They Believe?* (Brooklyn, New York: Watchtower Bible and Tract Society, 2000).

"What Jehovah's Witnesses Believe." http://www.watchtower.org/e/jt/article_03.htm.

K

KUMINA

Historical Development

Kumina is a Jamaican ritual in which communities remember their past members. The word *kumina* derives from the Kongo verb *kamama*, meaning "to feel an obligation to carry out an act or keep a promise." The promise or act takes the form of a ceremony during which participants dance clockwise in a ring, singing songs in the Kongo language or in Jamaican Creole to drum accompaniment. The ceremony climaxes with the slaying of a goat as a sacrificial offering to those for whom the occasion has been held. The goat is then prepared for cooking, and goat mutton and rice are served to participants and onlookers in attendance. The meal is cooked without salt, out of reverence for the spirits of the departed whose spirit essence is incompatible with salt.

It is these spirits, the *kuyu*, for whom the ceremony is held. The ceremony allows the kuyu to return and possess the bodies of living community members who "go inna [into] *mayal*," that is, spiritual possession, by acquiring rigid facial features, trembling, threatening to fall to the ground, or climbing along rafters until they are ministered to by other celebrants who remove all constricting items of clothes from them and generally support them physically in their convulsions.

Kumina seems to have been introduced by West Central African indentured laborers initially captured as slaves and brought to Jamaica after the British had outlawed the slave trade in 1807. Their religious traditions emerged particularly in the southeastern parishes of Jamaica, some Kongo in the northwestern Trelawny parish having established the *tambu* song-and-dance ancestral rite there. The parishes of St. Thomas and Portland are considered the seats of Kumina, but rural-urban migration in the early twentieth century accounts for its presence now also in the adjacent parishes of St. Andrew (Kingston) and St. Catherine.

Apart from maracas and a metal scraper along a grater, the instrumental accompaniment to the short repetitive choruses of Kumina are two skin-headed wooden drums, the *bandu* or *kibandu*, and the playin' kyas [cask]. The drums are laid along the ground and the drummers are seated on them, each facing the other. The drums are played with the palms and cupped fingers, and tonal variation is achieved by tightening and loosening the drum-skin with one heel on the drum-face. The bandu beats a pulsating 2/2 rhythm, the same rhythm of the inching step made by the dancers as they bend forward their torsos, horizontally waggle their rears and their shoulders while either dropping their hands loosely at their sides or keeping their elbows pointed outwards. The cask supplies accentuating counter-rhythms and rolls.

Beliefs and Practices

No deity is worshipped within Kumina, but adherents recognize the Supreme God or Creator whose element is thunder. As happens among western Kongo ethnic groups, this Creator's name is *Zaambi*, *Zaambi Ampungo* (God Almighty), *Kinzaambi* (God as abstraction). The latter word is often anglicized as "King Zaambi." Kumina adapts use of a number of fossilized Kongo phrases intercalated with Jamaican Creole as instructions to the spirits, among themselves, and in explanations.

Ancestors may appear in dreams and make requests of their dreamers for commemoration. The dreamer would then arrange a Kumina ceremony, and the English term used for such an event is "a duty." *Kamama* is used as an exclamation during the ceremony, but seems not otherwise used. Kumina ceremonies are also put on to celebrate birthdays, to mark the anniversary of a death, or to accompany the "tombing" of graves, that is, the cementing over of a grave a year or two after burial. Kumina feasting also takes place to mark the New Year and the anniversary of the declaration of emancipation of slaves in British colonies on August 1, 1838. Ceremonies may also be a means of enlisting ancestral help in the face of physical and mental illness, and for favor in pending legal matters.

Kumina ceremonies are held in temporary sheds decorated with streamers in colors appropriate to the mood of the event. For mourning, black and white ribbons are wound around the poles supporting the roof. Red signifies that "judgment" (a decision for justice; vengeance) is the main purpose for the ceremony. The shed is called a "bood" (booth). Offerings of alcohol are sprayed toward the four corners of the enclosure from the mouth of the "king" or "queen" who leads the ceremony and dances in the ring. The participants wear normal Western dress, but some may wear head wraps. The head tie of the "king" or "queen" may be more elaborate than the wear of other members and may consist of one or two thick swathes of cloth. Food offerings to the spirits are laid on the ground in front of the drums and at the booth corners. In cross-fertilization with Revival (Afro-Christian) practice, the paraphernalia of some Kumina ceremonies include a rectangular table on which are placed sodas, fruits, cakes, and loaves of bread, interlaced with lit candles. As with other African-derived religious occasions in the Caribbean, Kumina ceremonies are held during the night.

Maureen Warner-Lewis

SELECTED BIBLIOGRAPHY

Bilby, Kenneth, and Fu-Kiau kia Bunseki. *Kumina: A Kongo-Based Tradition in the New World* (Brussels: Centre d'étude et de documentation africaines, 1983).

Carter, Hazel. "Annotated Kumina Lexicon." *African-Caribbean Institute of Jamaica Research Review* 3 (1996): 84–129.

Lewin, Olive. *Rock It Come Over: The Folk Music of Jamaica* (Kingston: University of the West Indies Press, 2000).

Ryman, Cheryl. "Kumina: Stability and Change." *African-Caribbean Institute of Jamaica Research Review* 1 (1984): 81–128.

Warner-Lewis, Maureen. *Central Africa in the Caribbean: Transcending Time, Transforming Cultures* (Kingston: University of the West Indies Press, 2003), 146–48.

Warner-Lewis, Maureen. "The *Nkuyu*: Spirit Messengers of the Kumina." *Caribbean Women: An Anthology of Non-Fiction Writing, 1890–1980*, ed. Veronica Gregg (Notre Dame, IN: University of Notre Dame Press, 2005), 415–446.

M

MACUMBA

Historical Development

"Macumba" is used to refer to the highly syncretic blends of Afro-Brazilian, Catholic, and Spiritualist traditions prevalent in Rio de Janeiro in the late nineteenth and early twentieth centuries. Recent scholars and practitioners of Afro-Brazilian religion tend to avoid the term, mainly because of its history: for many decades, "Macumba" was the word used by those who attacked Afro-Brazilian religion and attempted to equate it with ignorance, evil, and charlatanism. The fact that in its generic sense the word lumps all Afro-Brazilian religions within one category is equally problematic; there are real differences between the various forms of Candomblé and Umbanda. Nonetheless, it is important to discuss Macumba, in the specific sense of the word, that is, as it refers to the syncretic blend of traditions in Rio de Janeiro in the decades around the turn of the century, not only for our understanding of Afro-Brazilian religion during that epoch, but because it is from Macumba that the highly popular Umbanda religion would develop. (I make use of Barreto 1976; Bastide 1978; Brown 1994; Hale 2004, 2009; Ortiz 1978; Ramos 1939.)

According to the French sociologist and renowned scholar of Afro-Brazilian religion, Roger Bastide, Macumba was the product of "disintegration" at several levels. Sociologically, turn of the century Rio de Janeiro, with its rapid growth and industrialization, represented a chaotic environment for the urban poor, themselves a mosaic of recent migrants from the postslavery rural economy; longer-term Afro-Brazilian residents, either recently freed or freedmen and their descendants; and an influx of immigrants from Portugal, of course, but also from other Mediterranean countries. Culturally, a diverse array of traditional patterns of belief and behavior were brought into proximity within the context of a new and difficult urban reality. While Bastide is no doubt correct in

211

emphasizing the disintegrative forces, Macumba can also be seen as an attempt at a new, integrative synthesis.

Beliefs and Practices

Afro-Brazilian religion was the main source for Macumba, but even here *Macumbeiros*, as practitioners were often called, drew from a range of sources. Mainly because of the demographics of the slave trade, the Bantu traditions of Angola and Congo predominated in Rio, but there was also a strong West African (often referred to as "Nagô") influence, evidenced by the existence of Nagô *terreiros*, or religious centers. Indeed, in Macumba the Bantu deities or *inkices* generally took on the names of the West African *orishas* (in Brazilian Portuguese, these are referred to as *orixás*, a convention followed in this article), reflecting this strong influence. To this mixture of African traditions were added Catholic influences. *Orixás* or *inkices* were syncretically associated with Catholic saints (e.g., the *orixá* Iansã, equivalent to the Angolan inkice Matamba, is represented as Santa Barbara). The Roman Catholic devil, Satan, enters Macumba, where he is associated with the orixá Exu/inkice Bombongira—bringing with him a whole complex of symbols and concepts foreign to the African traditions. *Macumbeiros* also reached out to a new source of beliefs and symbols in *Espiritismo* (see "Espiritismo" entry), or Spiritism. Inspired by the writings of a former French schoolteacher who went by the name of "Allan Kardec" (actually, Hyppolite Leon Denizard Rivail, 1804–1869), Spiritism spoke to key issues such as the nature of spiritual beings, reincarnation, and ethics;

perhaps most importantly, Spiritist practice included communication with "disembodied" (i.e., deceased) spirits through séances in which the spirits would speak through mediums. By the turn of the century, Spiritism was quite popular in Brazil, and especially in Rio, among the more privileged classes. Macumba incorporated elements of Spiritist metaphysics, while communication with the spirits, through spirit possession, was a major focus of ritual.

Detailed accounts of Macumba are lacking, largely due to a bias against Macumba by anthropologists and sociologists working in the first half of the twentieth century. Researchers were much more interested in Candomblé, which was seen as an "authentic" representation of African religion in the New World. Nonetheless, there is enough to sketch the broad outlines of ritual, belief, and organization, and these largely overlap the better known facts about Candomblé and Umbanda.

Macumba groups were hierarchically organized. The group leader, known as the *Embanda* or *Umbanda*, was equivalent to the *mãe de santo* or *pai de santo* (literally, "mother of saint" and "father of saint," respectively) of Candomblé and Umbanda. He or she directed the ritual, and initiated the *mediuns* (Bastide 1978, 296; Ramos 1939, 89–93). (These are "mediums," a term borrowed from Kardec's Spiritism, equivalent to *iaôs* or *filhas de santo* in Candomblé. Initiation of mediuns seems to have taken the general form of initiation in Candomblé.) The mediums in turn were ranked. Bastide tells us that the "top category" was known as *sambas*, the highest ranked samba apparently functioning as would "the *mãe pequena* of the Candomblé"—

that is, presumably, as the direct supervisor of the mediuns. In addition to the mediums, there were drummers whose rhythms invoked the various spirits; and *cambones*, who assisted with ritual (Bastide 1978, 296; Ramos 1939, 89–93).

While the *orixás* of Candomblé—identified with various Catholic saints—were invoked during ritual, the main focus was on the spirits of Indians, known as *caboclos*, and those of old Africans or Afro-Brazilian slaves. Arthur Ramos identifies this practice with the "worship of ancestors and family gods among the Bantu peoples" whose descendants made up the majority of Afro-Brazilians in Rio. (The *caboclo* and Afro-Brazilian spirits would come to be the main focus of Umbanda ritual as well.) Ramos tells us that ritual begins by invoking the

"patron saint" (in his example, the Afro-Brazilian spirit Father Joaquim), followed by drumming to call the other spirits. As in contemporary Umbanda, much of the ritual was devoted to consultations between these spirits (embodied in the mediums) and persons who would come seeking their help for various problems such as illness, romantic entanglements, etc. As in contemporary Umbanda, the sessions closed with a Catholic hymn and/or prayer.

While "Macumba" became a pejorative term in popular discourse, and despite the bias against Macumba by scholars more interested in "pure" Afro-Brazilian religions, such as the Nagô Candomblés associated with Bahia, a more objective reading suggests both the religious value and historical importance of Macumba. Like Candomblé, it kept alive the

Macumba practitioners prepare food for the orixas *before a ceremony begins honoring a novice being inducted into the temple, Rio de Janeiro. (Stephanie Maze/Corbis)*

veneration of the orixás and transmitted tradition through the rigors of initiation. The combining of African, Catholic, Spiritist, and Indigenous traditions, derided by "purists" can be read not as "disintegration" but as an active, imaginative search of new religious synthesis and meaning. And finally, it was from Macumba that the popular religion of Umbanda (which shares many of its characteristics), would emerge.

While individual embandas no doubt exercised strong leadership within their groups, no leaders of major national or regional importance emerged in Macumba, in contrast to the situation in Candomblé.

Lindsay Hale

SELECTED BIBLIOGRAPHY

Barreto, Paulo. *As Religiões no Rio* (Rio de Janeiro: Novo Aguilar, 1976).

Bastide, Roger. *The African Religions of Brazil: Toward a Sociology of the Interpenetration of Civilizations*, trans. Helen Sebba (Baltimore and London: The Johns Hopkins University Press, 1978).

Brown, Diana. *Umbanda: Religion and Politics in Urban Brazil* (New York: Columbia University Press, 1994).

Hale, Lindsay. "The House of Father John, the House of Saint Benedict: Umbanda Aesthetics and a Politics of the Senses." *Race, Nation, and Religion in the Americas*, ed. Henry Goldschmidt and Elizabeth McAlister (Oxford, U.K.: Oxford University Press, 2004).

Hale, Lindsay. *Hearing the Mermaid's Song: The Umbanda Religion in Rio de Janeiro* (Albuquerque: University of New Mexico, 2009).

Ortiz, Renato. *A Morte Branca do Feiticeiro Negro* (Petropolis, Rio de Janeiro: Editora Vozes, 1978).

Ramos, Arthur. *The Negro in Brazil* (Washington, D.C.: The Associated Publishers, 1939).

MAROONS

"Maroon" is the name applied to escaped slaves in the wider Caribbean region, and "marronage" is the term given to the practice of running away from plantations. "Maroon" is an anglicized form of the Spanish term "cimarrón," which was itself based on a Taíno (Arawak) word. Originally, "cimarrón" was the name given to cattle that had turned feral and escaped to the hill country of Hispaniola (modern Haiti and the Dominican Republic). It was soon applied also to the Taíno Amerindians who had similarly fled the depredations of their new Spanish masters. It quickly took on the meanings of "fierce" and "wild," and by the 1540s was mainly being applied to African-Caribbean slaves who had run away from their owners. Slaves escaped their bondage also in mainland South America (from the Guianas to Brazil, Colombia, and Peru) as well as in Mexico and parts of the United States. In these countries, Maroons were variously known as palenques, mocambos, or ladeiras. Today, the descendants of the first Maroons still live in Jamaica, Suriname, French Guiana, and Belize.

Maroons settled in their own communities either on the fringes of the plantations from which they had escaped or in isolated areas that protected them from raids. These communities forged their own cultural traditions in opposition to the European society that had enslaved them. In some places, such as Haiti, marronage was responsible for preserving enclaves of African religious beliefs such as Vodoun, as well as facilitating the mixing of new hybrid spiritualities where individuals belonging to different African tribes came together.

The first Jamaican Maroons may well have been the surviving remnants of the island's Taíno population escaping from Spanish servitude. Nevertheless, marronage in Jamaica is most commonly associated with some 1,500 slaves of African descent who took the opportunity of freedom offered by their former Spanish masters when the British took the island in 1655. As the Spanish departed for Cuba, the newly freed slaves took to the hills and soon began engaging in guerrilla attacks on the British.

Organizing themselves into small bands, the Maroons began raiding the plantations of their former masters, stealing and killing cattle, carrying off slaves, and sowing fear and resentment among the white settlers. In 1690 in the area of Clarendon, one such group belonging to the African Coromantee tribe fled their plantation and joined their comrades in the isolated heart of Jamaica. Further localized slave uprisings occurred in 1694 and 1702, and after a crackdown by the planters and militia, more slaves escaped to swell the numbers of the Maroons.

Jamaican planters increasingly resented the fact that Maroon communities remained unpunished and acted as a magnet and refuge for runaway slaves. When the British authorities responded to the threat, the small groups of Maroons operating in the western-central part of Jamaica came together and appointed an overall chief called Cudjoe (also spelled Kojo) to lead them, along with his brothers Accompong and Johnny. Cudjoe was a brave and resourceful warrior of whom it was said that he never lost a battle

against the British. His success and fame soon attracted other scattered groups of Maroons—many with their own languages and ethnic traditions. These events led to the so-called First Maroon War that lasted from 1720 until 1739. The British suffered militarily against the cleverly camouflaged Maroon fighters and their guerrilla tactics and could never achieve a decisive victory.

After Cudjoe's ambush and massacre of British soldiers at Peace Cave in 1738, the British signed a peace treaty, ending hostilities and granting these western or Leeward Maroons their freedom, land, and limited self-governance. Cudjoe was appointed chief commander of Trelawney Town. In return, the Maroons had to agree to help defend Jamaica against foreign invasion and return any future runaway slaves to their owners. In 1739, a similar treaty was signed with Chief Quao of the eastern or Windward Maroons and with this the First Maroon War came to an end. Today in Jamaica, the two main Maroon communities of the Leewards and Windwards still survive and flourish. The Windward Maroons occupy the villages of Moore Town and Charles Town in the Blue Mountains of eastern Jamaica. Moore Town is said to have been founded by the renowned female Maroon warrior, Nanny, who is now a Jamaican national hero. Granny Nanny, as she was known, was a skilled and cunning guerrilla fighter whose exploits and character have been embroidered over the centuries to such an extent that history and legend are hopelessly intertwined.

Nanny is said to have practiced obeah and to have had such supernatural power that she could spirit away slaves from plantations. She is also alleged to have caught the white man's bullets in mid-flight and returned them at speed to their owners. Nanny played an important role during the First Maroon War and is believed to have opposed the peace treaty signed by Cudjoe. She was finally killed in 1734 when the British Captain Stoddart, accompanied by Amerindians brought from Central America's Mosquito Coast and tracker dogs, attacked and destroyed the village of Nanny Town. Archaeological investigations at the site have revealed not only Maroon objects but items belonging to Taíno Amerindians as well, thus raising new questions about the relations between the two groups. Nowadays, every October, celebrations take place in Moore Town that honor the redoubtable Granny Nanny.

In the western part of the island, the Leeward Maroons live in and around the settlement of Accompong in the remote area known as the Cockpit Country. Accompong New Town today is relatively new, having been moved from the ancestral location of Cudjoe's time that is now sacred ground. Every January, celebrations in honor of Cudjoe are held in Accompong and the festivities attract thousands of visitors to watch the singing of the so-called Treaty Songs, the dancing of ancestral Maroon War dances, and the telling of folk tales.

Daily life in Jamaican Maroon communities was simple and hard but free. People lived in small houses with thatched roofs and earth floors. Maroons practiced a basic form of agriculture with the women cultivating such staples as maize and yams. These foods were supplemented by the men, who concentrated on hunting wild boar and, in the early days, anything they could plunder from the white man's plantations. They also bred cattle and raised pigs and chickens. After the peace treaty of 1739, Maroons would also ransom escaped slaves they had captured. As Maroon communities were often made up of different African societies, their languages also varied. European accounts of everyday Maroon life noted the mix of African languages together with the use of broken Spanish and English. The Maroons appear to have devised a unique way of communicating that did not depend on dialect or language. This was the cow's horn, or abeng, with which each Maroon could be summoned by his own individual call. It is said that in the Cockpit Country the blast of the abeng could be heard up to 15 kilometers away and it is still used in festivals and funerals.

Aside from Jamaica, Hispaniola, and elsewhere in the Island Caribbean, Maroon communities also existed in mainland areas of North and particularly South America. One of the most unusual of these groups is the so-called Seminole Maroons. This group originated with slaves who escaped their masters in South Carolina and Georgia and made their way to Spanish Florida during the eighteenth century. Here, they associated themselves with the local Seminole Amerindians but kept their own distinctive cultural traditions. In 1842, after the Seminole War, they were forcibly removed, along with their Amerindian allies, to Oklahoma, and subsequently many ended up in Mexico, Texas, and the Bahamas.

In those parts of South America that fringe the Caribbean, Maroon societies also survive today. In Suriname and French Guiana, six communities have a combined population of around 60,000. Apart from being politically distinct, these groups also differ in their basic ways of life, such as language, dress, marriage customs, and diet. These differences are most marked between the groups of Saramaka, Matawi, and Kwinti who live in central Suriname and those of the Ndyuka, Aluku, and Paramaka who occupy an area that spans eastern Suriname and western French Guiana. The Saramaka's ancestors began escaping from Dutch plantations in Suriname during the seventeenth century, fought their previous owners for almost 100 years, and then signed a peace treaty in 1762. The Aluku crossed from Suriname to French Guiana between 1776 and 1777 and eventually signed a treaty jointly with the French and Dutch in 1860. As with other Caribbean Maroons, their society is strongly matrilineal. Religious practices vary and can focus on spirit possession, the interpretation of visionary dreams, and the consultation of objects known as oracle bundles.

The religious life of these Maroon communities is full of elaborate participatory ritual and includes special languages such as Púmbu and Papá, drumming rhythms, and invocations to ancestors. Snake gods (vodu) and warrior gods (komanti) are often at the heart of religious beliefs and prayers. Misfortune, childbirth, and illness are all considered the consequences of antisocial behavior that can be alleviated by talking to spirits. The most elaborate ritual expressions focus on funeral ceremonies that can last for several months and involve hundreds of people. Dancing, singing, and the carrying of the coffin as part of divinatory rites are all practiced during such events. Although some inroads have been made by Christianity among the Maroons of Suriname, in general the ever-changing nature of their religious and ritual life makes their beliefs the most rooted of all in their African origins.

The artistic and material life of mainland South American Maroons—

especially those in Suriname—is particularly rich and creative, especially in relation to rituals associated with birth, reaching adulthood, and death. As anthropologists Richard and Sally Price have observed, Maroon art is not a static leftover from seventeenth-century Africa but a creative and innovative adaptation and development of an African heritage to the new social and environmental conditions of the Americas.

For example, where the first Maroons possessed basic clothing and rustic wood carvings, the twentieth century saw an explosion of stunning and seemingly African wooden sculptures, multicolored textiles, and calabashes elaborately carved inside and out by men and women with newly created tools. Stringed musical instruments made from wood and stingray tails, elaborately carved-wood attaché cases, and artfully designed and decorated folding stools are all new forms ingeniously made and for sale to tourists and museums. Throughout the twentieth century, it is African ideas about aesthetics, color, and the place of art in everyday life that has survived and not a simple fossilized adherence to African objects and forms.

While many consider contemporary Maroon societies and their material culture to be totally African and displaced to the Americas as a consequence of slavery, the situation is more complex. Maroon people themselves, their beliefs, practices, values, and the cultural world of objects they make undoubtedly originate in the varied tribes of Africa. Yet, as with African-Caribbean peoples more generally, they are remarkably open and inventive, and elements of their religious beliefs and material culture are dynamic, creating new hybrid forms that are neither purely African nor American but truly African American. Some Maroons, like the Aluku of French Guiana, have funerary customs influenced by the local Amerindians, and, more widely, the creole languages they speak are a mix of primarily European words with African and Amerindian additions.

The place of the Maroons in the contemporary cultural and political life of the Caribbean and adjacent areas of South America is ambiguous. The colonial realities that created marronage are long gone and the once isolated Maroon communities are increasingly accessible. The attitude of modern postcolonial governments (for whom eighteenth- and nineteenth-century peace treaties are an embarrassing and anachronistic legacy of colonial rule) and the pressures of tourism and the global economy are all impinging on Maroon culture and identity, whether in Jamaica or Suriname. The younger generation, as the carriers of Maroon culture into the future, is increasingly attracted to the westernized towns and cities of their own countries and beyond, and consequently their connections to their ancestral homelands and traditions are weakened. In response, groups of Maroon elders and representatives are actively promoting links to pan-Amerindian networks of indigenous peoples, documenting their own cultural patrimony and promoting educational programs in efforts to secure the survival of their remarkable heritage.

Nicholas J. Saunders

SELECTED BIBLIOGRAPHY

Agorsah, E. K. "Archaeology and the Maroon Heritage in Jamaica." *Jamaica Journal* 24, no. 2 (1992): 2–9.

Agorsah, E. K. "Archaeology and Resistance History in the Caribbean." *The African Archaeology Review* 11 (1993): 175–196.

Agorsah, E. K., ed. *Maroon Heritage: Archaeological, Ethnographic and Historical Perspectives.* Kingston: Canoe Press, 1994.

Barker, D., and S. Balfour. "Afro-Caribbean Agriculture: A Jamaican Maroon Community in Transition." *The Geographical Journal* 154, no. 2 (1988): 98–208.

Bilby, K. "Jamaica's Maroons at the Crossroads: Losing Touch with Tradition." *Caribbean Review* 9, no. 4 (1980): 18–21, 49.

Campbell, M. C. *The Maroons of Jamaica 1655–1796.* Trenton, NJ: Africa World Press Inc., 1990.

de Groot, S. W. "A Comparison between the History of Maroon Communities in Surinam and Jamaica." *Slavery and Abolition* 6, no. 3 (1985): 173–184.

Heuman, G., ed. *Out of the House of Bondage: Runaways, Resistance, and Maroonage in Africa and the New World.* London: Frank Cass, 1982.

Kopytoff, B. K. "The Development of Jamaican Maroon Ethnicity." *Caribbean Quarterly* 22, no. 2–3 (1976): 33–50.

Weik, T. "The Archaeology of Maroon Societies in the Americas: Resistance, Cultural Continuity, and Transformation in the African Disapora." *Historical Archaeology* 31, no. 2 (1997): 81–92.

METROPOLITAN SPIRITUAL CHURCHES OF CHRIST, INC.

Historical Development

Chicago, Detroit, and New Orleans have been historically identified as instrumental locations in the birth and maturation of Spiritual associations and independent churches. Nevertheless, this historical excavation of the "Spiritualist Movement" must include Kansas City, the birthplace of the Metropolitan Spiritual Churches of Christ, Incorporated. The one seed, Metropolitan Spiritual Church of Christ (mother church), planted by Bishop William F. Taylor and Elder Leviticus L. Boswell has grown both domestically, as one of the largest Spiritual associations in the United States, and internationally with local churches in Jamaica, Liberia, and Ghana.

With 22 members, including Cora Murray whose residence served as the initial sanctuary, the "mother church" of the Metropolitan Spiritual Churches of Christ, Incorporated (MSCC) was born under the leadership of Bishop William F. Taylor and Elder Leviticus L. Boswell in Kansas City, Missouri. The group, in 1926, due to the spike in membership, acquired a new location for services, which had a 1,500 seating capacity, and held its First Congress Meeting in Kansas City. Also, in this same year, women were formally seen as candidates for ordination within the MSCC's clergy.

One such figure is Mattye B. Thornton who served as assistant pastor to the Reverend Clarence H. Cobbs, founder of First Church of Deliverance. By 1939, Taylor was ordained as overseeing bishop and the MSCC represented an association on the rise with 13 local churches, including First Church of Deliverance in Chicago and other churches in Tulsa and Los Angeles; female pastors headed 39 percent of these churches.

A significant shift occurred in 1942 when the MSCC merged with the Divine Spiritual Churches of the Southwest ("Southwest Association") to create the United Metropolitan Spiritual Churches of Christ. However, Bishop Taylor's appointment of Cobbs as president of the association following his death initiated a schism in 1945, dividing the association into two segments: The United Metropolitan Spiritual Churches of Christ under the leadership of Bishop Thomas B. Watson and the Metropolitan Spiritual Churches of Christ, Incorporated led by Cobbs. Since the geographical

---

BISHOP WILLIAM F. TAYLOR (1886–1942)

On May 14, 1886, in Jacksonville, Texas, James and Mattie Taylor became the proud parents of William F. Taylor. It is in the lone star state that he became an evangelist in the Colored Methodist Episcopal Church. Taylor would leave Texas to explore opportunities in Chicago, initially becoming a member of St. Paul Baptist Church, but soon joined the Metropolitan Community Church. By the age of 39, not only had he changed his location to Kansas City, but also, with the partnership of Leviticus Boswell, he co-established the "mother church" of the MSCC. Since Taylor operated under the belief of egalitarian methods, ordination into the association's clergy became available one year later in 1926. Taylor, in 1934, accepted the bishopric overseeing the MSCC, which had grown to 11 churches. From 1934 to 1942, under the leadership of Bishop Taylor, the MSCC ecclesiastical network grew to include 29 local churches that span across the United States. In 1942, Taylor moved to Los Angeles and in this same year he died in the home of the Reverend Mother Pearl C. Woods.

ELDER LEVITICUS L. BOSWELL (1891–?)

On the last day of 1891, December 31, Leviticus L. Boswell was born to the union of Major and Roseline Boswell in Selma, Alabama. Boswell's childhood and early adulthood were spent between Selma and Birmingham, Alabama. Leaving behind a houseman job in Birmingham, he moved to Chicago. While in Chicago he became a member of the Metropolitan Community Church, where he both met William F. Taylor and became assistant director of the choir due partly to his classical musical training from teachers like Julia Mae Kennedy during his formative years in Alabama. Boswell stepped down from his position as elder within the Church of God in Christ to co-establish the MSCC with William F. Taylor in 1925. Although Boswell was ordained overseeing elder of MSCC, he was best known for his musical abilities and accomplishments within the association. For example, while serving as musical director of the "mother church" of MSCC, the choir became nationally recognized. His voice penetrated the airwaves of Kansas City with the MSCC's weekly program yielding testimonies of healing due to the music ministry. After the death of Taylor, Boswell was appointed overseer of the "mother church." Ten years after this appointment, Elder Boswell also made his transition and was buried in Highland Memorial Gardens, the same resting place as his friend and co-laborer William F. Taylor.

location of the president determines the headquarters location, the MSCC moved from Kansas City to Chicago where Cobbs presided over First Church of Deliverance.

Through continued utilization of radio ministry and Cobbs's unique appeal to the poor and working class, MSCC's composition, by 1968, included 125 local churches. Cobbs became the first international president of the association with the induction of the Reverend James Vos's congregation located in Jamaica. The international initiative surpassed the boundaries of Jamaica and stretched into both Liberia and Ghana by 1975. The Reverend Lucretia L. Smith served as interim international president for only

REVEREND CLARENCE H. COBBS (1907–1979)

Although little is known about the Reverend Clarence H. Cobbs's early life, his legacy in the MSCC is not a secret. Cobbs began his ecclesiastical quest in 1929 with the founding of First Church of Deliverance in Chicago, Illinois. In this same year not only would he appoint Mattye B. Thornton as assistant pastor but his church also became a part of the MSCC. Cobbs, known as "preacher" by the masses, possessed a universal appeal, impressing the older generation with his spiritual knowledge while attracting the support of the working class and poor with his message of hope and prosperity. In 1942, Cobbs became the president of the MSCC. By 1968, the MSCC flourished to include 130 churches. At the time of his death in 1979, the MSCC's membership had expanded beyond domestic boundaries due to Cobbs initiating visits to Jamaica, Liberia, and Ghana, making him the first to serve as "International President" of the association.

one year following the death of Cobbs in 1979. The movement of the national headquarters to Baltimore due to the appointment of Dr. Logan Kearse as the second international president led to further secession within the MSCC. For example, from the period of 1980 to 1984 groups such as the United Evangelical Churches of Christ resulted from this schism. As a result of the cleavage of the internal lattice of the association, Indianapolis, a more neutral locality, became the new headquarters location.

Structural organization and modernization were the primary tenets of the Reverend Arthur L. Posey, third president of the MSCC. The College of Bishops, Board of Directors, National Officers, and Officers in Aeterna became the solidified structure of the church with the ordination of the Reverend Posey as Archbishop. Although one-half of the National Board is composed of women, there are no women serving in the bishopric. Current National Offices include the Healer's Board, Prophets Board, Home/Foreign Missions, and Mother's Board. With the expansion of its radio ministry, development of both a national and an international headquarters and the continuation of outreach programs such as "Operation Reach Out," a program committed to the evangelization of youth, the MSCC has matured into a major heavyweight among Spiritual associations in the United States.

Beliefs and Practices

The *Catechism of the Metropolitan Spiritual Church of Christ* contains the guiding principles of the MSCC. Serving as an official doctrinal organ of the association, this textual work displays these principles in the form of the "Declaration of Truths" and "Declaration of Principles."

The foundation of the MSCC's belief system involves the promotion of a triune doctrine in which God, in the form of Spirit, is Creator; Jesus symbolizes the womb of creation and maintains sole lordship; and the Holy Spirit emblematizes and embodies the Spirit of God and Christ. Thus, the Trinity—a representation of the Father, Son, and Holy Spirit—is the foundational element of this group's belief system. The catechism also reveals the presence of four primary cornerstones—healing, prophesy, preaching, and teaching—operating in the belief system of the MSCC known as the "four square gospel." Healing and prophesy, which are two primary tenants found embedded in the beliefs of most Spiritual churches, along with preaching and teaching compose this quadrilateral belief system.

The vibrant colors of this "four square gospel" becomes a visible reality on the canvas of rituals. For instance, in "bless services" a medium or pastor/medium serves as a vessel in which the Spirit manifests itself in the form of either spoken prophecies or healings. It is important to note that séances, a vital element found in the association's earlier history, have been slowly displaced with "bless or deliverance services." The MSCC does not negate the occurrence of spiritual communication, as seen in its "Declaration of Truths" and the continuation of private consultation by mediums, but in an attempt to set up definitive differences between itself and such religions as Voodooism and Spiritualism séances have been discontinued.

Margarita Simon Guillory

SELECTED BIBLIOGRAPHY

Baer, Hans A. "The Metropolitan Spiritual Churches of Christ: The Socio-Religious Evolution of the Largest Black Spiritual Associations." *Review of Religious Research* 30, no. 2 (December 1988): 144–150.

Baer, Hans A. "The Limited Empowerment of Women in Black Spiritual Churches: An Alternative Vehicle to Religious Leadership." *Religion and Gender Relationships* 54, no. 1 (Spring 1993): 65–82.

Baer, Hans A. *The Black Spiritual Movement: A Religious Response to Racism* (Knoxville: The University of Tennessee Press, 2001).

Baer, Hans A., and Merrill Singer. *African American Religion: Varieties of Protest and Accommodation* (Knoxville: The University of Tennessee Press, 2002).

Houston, Otto T. "History of the Metropolitan Spiritual Churches of Christ Inc. 1925–1942" (2003). Available from Metropolitan Spiritual Churches of Christ, Inc. athttp://www.metrospiritualchurch.com (accessed July 30, 2007).

MOORISH SCIENCE TEMPLE OF AMERICA, INC.

Historical Development

Initially known as the Canaanite Temple, the Moorish Science Temple was founded by Timothy Drew (aka Noble Drew Ali) in 1913 in Newark, New Jersey. It claims to have been the first organized Muslim community in the United States. Within the first ten years of the organization's history it had roughly 30,000 members scattered throughout many cities of the Midwest and Northeast, such as Detroit, Pittsburgh, Chicago, Milwaukee, Philadelphia, Lansing, Cleveland, Richmond, and Baltimore. The organization was renamed the Moorish Holy Temple of Science when Ali established the organization's headquarters in Chicago in 1923. This move was caused by a split in the organization that took place in 1921. The other group remained in Newark and renamed itself the "Holy Moabite Temple of Science." However, folklore related to Noble Drew Ali suggests he did not arrive in Chicago until 1925. Legend has it that he showed up on the streets of Chicago bearing a "flaming red fez" proclaiming the word of Allah. Regardless of the particular date of his arrival, it is clear that he moved the organization from Newark to Chicago and this allowed the organization to grow. Finally, one year before his death in 1928, Ali again renamed the organization the Moorish Science Temple of America (MSTA).

There is mystery surrounding Noble Drew Ali's death. Some say he died a natural death; however, it is reported that he may have been murdered by a member of a rival religious group. (The problem with this theory is that Ali was not in Chicago at the time of the murder.) Nevertheless, almost immediately after his passing two of his associates—John Givens-El and Wallace D. Fard—proclaimed themselves his reincarnation. John Givens El, who was the chauffeur for Ali, is said to have fainted shortly after the death of Ali and upon awakening he bore the sign of the star and crescent in his eyes, which was a sign for some that he was the reincarnation of Ali.

While it is not clear if Wallace D. Fard was a paying member of the MSTA, it is clear that certain ministers went from door to door in Detroit selling herbs and charms and proclaiming the Moorish doctrine. It is argued by some that W. D. Fard was one of these ministers. Some followers understand Fard as a crook and a false prophet who purposely took advantage of the people to destroy Ali's legacy and damage the movement. Others argue Fard was merely attempting to fill a spiritual void left after the passing of Ali and the deportation of Marcus Garvey. As a peddler in Detroit Wallace D. Fard, who would take the name Master Fard Muhammad, gained access to many homes through his business and thereby was able to spread the message of the Asiatic Black Nation in America, which would eventually lead to the development of an organization called the Lost-Found Nation of Islam (see "Nation of Islam" entry).

It is estimated that upwards of 8,000 were recruited between the time Fard proclaimed himself to be the reincarnation of Ali and the time of his disappearance, roughly 1930–1933. One of the people he recruited was an out-of-work auto mechanic named Elijah Poole who would later be renamed Elijah Karriem and then Elijah Muhammad.

After the passing of Ali and after Fard's proclamation of divinity, the Moorish Science Temple reorganized under the leadership of C. Kirkman Bey as president and John Givens-El as the reincarnation of the prophet. Kirkman Bey remained president for roughly 30 years, and during that time the organization maintained and grew despite attacks and harassment from the state and local law enforcement agencies. During the 1960s and 1970s investigation of the temple began to wane as the FBI started to investigate other Muslim organizations. During the 1980s and 1990s Moorish Americans (a label given to organization members by Ali) began pushing for more outreach in the community as well as within the prison system. Moorish publications circulated during the last part of the twentieth century, allowing the organization

---

TIMOTHY DREW (NOBLE DREW ALI—1886–1929)

Noble Drew Ali was born Timothy Drew on a Cherokee Reservation in North Carolina in 1886. Legend states that Ali, from 1902 until about 1910, traveled back and forth between the United States, Morocco, Egypt, and Saudi Arabia as a merchant seaman receiving education and training from prophets, sages, and sheikhs of Islam. It was at this time that he claims to have been endowed with the title "Noble Drew Ali" and given a charter to teach Islam in the United States. In 1910, Ali returned to the states for good to join the Prince Hall Freemasons, and he also worked as an "expressman" on a train. The year before he founded his organization in Newark, New Jersey, it is reported that Ali contacted Woodrow Wilson in order to ask him for permission to teach Islam to his people in the United States, and that his people would be given a new identity as Moorish Americans. Upon his death several members of the organization claimed to be the reincarnation of Ali that sustained the organization and allowed it to develop into a diverse Muslim movement in the United States.

to reach a large base of constituents. In 2006 the University of the Moorish Science Temple of America was founded, offering more in-depth studies into Islam.

Beliefs and Practices

Moorish beliefs and rituals are centered on five ethical values of righteousness and moral living: Truth, Love, Peace, Freedom, and Justice. Although Moorish Americans recognize the evil of the U.S. government through its treatment of Black people, the organization teaches all Moors (members of the Moorish Science Temple of America) to respect the United States because they are citizens of the country.

The Moorish Flag includes key symbolism that also addresses the moral posture of the organization. The flag is set against a red background with a circle split into four quadrants, which represent Love, Truth, Peace, and Freedom. Within the circle the letters "L.T.P.F." line the top with a curved Arabian sword called a Scimitar Shamshir, and the word "Justice" written across the blade. Underneath there is a five-point star, which is representative of the five points of moral living.

For Ali "Moslem" is not simply a designation given to those followers of Mohammed, but for all those who believe in Love, Truth, Peace, Freedom, and Justice. So in that spirit the MSTA is not to be understood as simply a Muslim or Christian organization nor a fraternal order; however, all of those elements combined speak to the organization's structure and understandings.

Ali taught that Islam was a very simple faith, which centers on obligations and duties to Allah. The supreme duty of living is to be at peace and to find harmony with one's surroundings. The object of the person's life is goodness and peace. Ali taught that humans are born with unlimited potential for growth and progress, and without "original sin."

While Islam is a very important element of the MSTA, at times Christianity seems to be the more prominent religious element, as represented by the sources for its holy book the *Circle Seven Koran*: the Quran, the Bible, *The Aquarian Gospels of Jesus Christ*, and a Masonic text entitled *Unto Thee I Grant*. In the *Circle Seven Koran* Ali narrates Jesus' travels to India, Europe, and Africa. According to Ali, before there was a word for religion, Jesus broke bread and shared ideas with the early founding priests of what are now considered major world religions of Hinduism and Buddhism.

Moorish education requires memorization of the sacred catechism written by Ali. This catechism consists of 102 question and answer lessons that outline the basic beliefs of the organization. For instance, the Moorish catechism asks members, "Who is Allah?" which requires the answer "Allah is father of the universe." The subsequent organizations branching off from the Moorish Science Temple (the Nation of Islam and the Nation of Gods and Earths) also have similar methods of educating their members with catechisms of 154 and 120, respectively. Furthermore, naming is also very important for the respective organizations. In particular, Moorish Americans all add a suffix to their surname, Bey or El, to indicate their ancestry as Moors. Ali is also a suffix that is used at times but not as consistently as Bey or El. Moorish Americans retain their identity as Americans through the retention of their birth names and designating themselves as Moors by adding a suffix, thus cementing their identity as Moors born in America. Likewise the dress of the Moors demonstrates a keen understanding of national identity. Robes and Fezzes are worn by most men much like the dress of Arabic Shriners, and women also always keep their bodies and heads covered when in public.

Prince Hall from Barbados organized what would become the first African Lodges of Freemasonry in the United States. Black Freemasonry provides the esoteric underpinning of the MSTA. The Moorish Science Temple has a twofold relationship with the Freemasons. On one hand, Masonry is a part of Moorish culture in that its signs and symbols are used as part of the overall structure of the organization. Ali, in the *Holy Koran*, uses Masonic symbolism to illustrate his understanding of humanity and human freedom. As in masonry he used the tools of building: the square, compass, the axe, hammer, etc., to draw out his understanding of Truth, Peace, Love, Freedom, and Justice. Although the Moorish Science Temple is not a Masonic organization, it makes use of Masonic symbolism and folklore, which begs the question: was Noble Drew Ali a mason? There is no evidence to concretely suggest that he was a mason. However, Ali does claim to be the keeper of sacred knowledge about Jesus Christ and other ancient sages.

For Ali, Islam was not to be understood as it is by modern definitions, that is, an adherence to the 5 Pillars of Islam and/or qualified by "Sunni," "Sufi," or "Shi'ite." There is a clear distinction between al-Islam and what the MSTA understands as Islam or Islamism. For example, the MSTA is not bound by the ritual of five prayers, nor are members of the MST required to visit Mecca at least once. Once again, ancient lineage is critical for Ali's understanding of Islam. The Moors teach that al-Islam is the translation of the wisdom of the Egyptian (Kemetic) Mystery System into the Arabic language by the Prophet Mohammad. For the Moors, al-Islam is a piece of the true understanding of Allah in Arabic form. What Ali taught, he called Islamism. Islamism was to be understood as much older than al-Islam, the "Old Time Religion" that descends from the ancient mystery systems of Kemet (Egypt). The mysteries of Kemet represent humanity's earliest recorded understanding of God or the Divine, and as such it is the foundation for all the world's religions.

Despite the fact that Ali held Marcus Garvey's UNIA movement in high esteem, he actually disagreed with Garvey's ideas on emigration to Africa. However, Garvey's ideology and organization were credited with being the divine "front runner" to the Moorish Science Temple of America. Instead of advocating a physical return to Africa, Ali argued for a spiritual return that was based more on theological mythology than on cultural continuity.

For Ali, the Moors are an Asiatic Nation descended from the ancient peoples of the Bible. Further, the Hindus, Japanese, Chinese, and the indigenous North, Central, and South Americans are all descended from the lineage of Hagar and can be identified in the Bible as Moabites, Canaanites, Hittites, Cushites, and Hamites. These peoples are considered Moslem or Moorish by Ali because of their perceived lineage or connection to the ancient peoples of Quranic and Biblical Scripture.

Paul Easterling

SELECTED BIBLIOGRAPHY

Clegg, Claude Andrew. *An Original Man: The Life and Times of Elijah Muhammad* (New York: St. Martin's Press, 1997).

Dannin, Robert. *Black Pilgrimage to Islam* (New York: Oxford University Press, 2002).

Evanzz, Karl. *The Messenger: The Rise and Fall of Elijah Muhammad* (New York: Vintage Books, 1999).

Gomez, Michael. *Black Crescent: The Experience and Legacy of African Muslims in the Americas* (New York: Cambridge University Press, 2005).

Marsh, Clifton E. *From Black Muslims to Muslims: The Resurrection, Transformation and Change of the Lost-Found Nation of Islam in America 1930–1995*, 2nd ed. (Lanham, MD: Scarecrow Press, 1996).

Moses, Wilson Jeremiah, ed. *Classical Black Nationalism: From the American Revolution to Marcus Garvey* (New York and London: New York University Press, 1996).

Turner, Richard B. *Islam in the African American Experience* (Bloomington and Indianapolis: Indiana University Press, 1997).

Walker, Dennis. *Islam and the Search for African-American Nationhood: Elijah Muhammad, Louis Farrakhan and the Nation of Islam* (Atlanta, GA: Clarity Press, Inc., 2005).

MORAVIAN CHURCH

Historical Development

The Moravian Church continues the attempts at reformation of the Roman Catholic Church that were made by Jan Hus (c. 1373–1415). Because of his oratorical skills as the preacher at the Bethlehem Chapel in Prague, Hus gained a popular following. His calls for reform came just as the papacy was divided between two claimants to Peter's chair, and Prague was divided between its German-speaking and Bohemian-speaking populations.

After his excommunication in 1410, Hus became a popular hero among the populace. He attacked corruption in the Church and its granting of indulgences as a means of raising money, and he upheld the authority of the Bible as a standard by which the Church and its leadership could be judged. In 1414 Hus was invited to present his views at the Council of Constance, called by the Roman Catholic Church to deal with issues of reform. Though he was granted safe passage, when he arrived the protection was withdrawn, and he was condemned and executed.

Hus was condemned in part for his belief that the Eucharist, the sacrament recalling the sacrificial death of Jesus, should be served to the people in both kinds, that is, bread and wine, rather than just as bread, the common practice at the time. After Hus's death, the serving of the Eucharist in both kinds became characteristic of his followers, known as Hussites, and the Roman Catholics were unable to suppress the revolt immediately. A temporary compromise was worked out in 1436. Amid the spectrum of opinion in Bohemia and neighboring Moravia arose a new mediating group, the Unitas Fratrum.

During the sixteenth century, the Reformed Church (with teachings based on John Calvin's [1509–1564] theology) emerged in Bohemia and Moravia and held sway until the beginning of the seventeenth century. Then after the Thirty

Years' War, Protestant leaders in Prague encountered Catholic leadership in the Holy Roman Empire bent on Counter-Reformation. In 1620 a Catholic army defeated the Bohemian forces and began to impose Catholicism anew throughout the land. In 1652 the expulsion of all Protestants from Catholic-controlled lands was implemented. Many members of the Unitas Fratrum went underground, and others fled their land. They settled first in Poland, and then, after 1722, they found refuge on the Prussian estate of Count Nikolaus Ludwig von Zinzendorf (1700–1760), where they founded the village of Herrnhut. Here they developed an order to rule both their spiritual and secular lives. The acceptance of this new order in 1727 by the Czech brethren marks the beginning of the reorganized Moravian Church.

Within the church, new ministerial leadership soon developed. Zinzendorf wanted the church to remain as an ordered community within the Lutheran Church, while many of the community's leaders looked for the development of a revived separate Moravian church. In 1835 the ancient episcopal lineage was passed to the community by Daniel Ernst Jablonski (1660–1741), a German Calvinist who had been consecrated by the Polish Moravians. Zinzendorf was consecrated in 1837. In 1845 the Moravian Church was more formally organized as a new episcopal body. It was recognized by the Church of England and the British Parliament in 1749.

The Moravian Church would develop two important emphases. First, the church developed in Germany just as a scholastic approach to Protestantism was becoming dominant, and in reaction the Moravians absorbed the lively spirituality of the Pietist movement, which had spread through Germany in the seventeenth century from the University of Halle. Thus, Moravians would become known for their heartfelt religion, which would have a significant effect upon a youthful John Wesley (1703–1791), the founder of Methodism.

Second, beginning with Zinzendorf's encounter with natives of the Danish West Indies and Greenland in 1731, the movement became enthusiastic proponents of a missionary enterprise. The Moravians sent the first missionaries to the West Indies in 1732 and to Greenland the next year. Through the rest of the century, the work would spread to England and the American colonies. Within the first generation, missions would follow to Labrador, South America, and Egypt. Stemming from this effort, the Methodists and then the Baptists would begin their own mission programs, and from this new venture would come the world-changing missionary enterprise of the nineteenth century, which would carry Protestantism around the globe.

During the mid-1700s, Zinzendorf assumed both temporal and spiritual powers as the leader of the Moravian Church. After his passing in 1760, the church organized its General Synod as the highest legislative body and appointed an executive board to administer the affairs of the synod. The executive board would in time evolve into the Unity Elders' Conference. Doctrinally, the church saw itself in general agreement with the Augsburg Confession (Lutheran), though there was no attempt to enforce assent to every sentence of this lengthy statement. A brief statement of essential beliefs was accepted in 1775. In practice, the church made or confirmed many of its practical decisions, especially concerning the deployment of personnel, by the casting of lots.

Through the early decades of the nineteenth century, the Moravian Church continued to expand globally. Partly because of the slowness of response from Europe, the church faced an increasing number of requests for grants of self-government from mission centers abroad. In 1857 the church established four provincial synods—one in Continental Europe, one in England, and two in the United States, one in the north and one in the south. These provinces were given limited autonomy.

In 1879 the mission in Jamaica organized a governing board with a protoprovincial organization, indicating that in the future, missions would grow to become discrete provinces. The twentieth-century problems of continuing financial support for the ever-growing world membership, the transformation of Europe in the wake of two world wars, and the changing perspective on missions within ecumenical Christianity led the Moravians in 1957 to extend the process of dividing the church's membership geographically into autonomous provinces. Meanwhile, in Europe, the work was divided into two independent provinces, setting off the work in what was then the German Democratic Republic of Germany, including the headquarters church at Halle. The European work was again combined after the reunification of Germany in 1990.

The Continental Province continues to have responsibility for Moravian life in Europe apart from the British Isles. The Moravian Church in the United States maintains an Internet site with links to Moravians around the world. The church has been active ecumenically and is a member of the European Council of Churches and the World Council of Churches.

Moravian Church in America

The Moravian movement was brought to North America in 1735, when a group under the leadership of Bishop August Gottlieb Spangenberg (1704–1792) moved to the new colony of Georgia. Because of the group's pacifism and refusal to serve in the militia, they left Georgia for Pennsylvania, where they initially settled on land owned by Methodist evangelist George Whitefield (1717–1770). They purchased 500 acres for the original settlement of what became Bethlehem, Pennsylvania, in 1741, and shortly thereafter obtained another 5,000 acres for the settlement they called Nazareth. Later, other settlements were created in neighboring New Jersey and Maryland, all positioned to carry out the primary goal of the movement from Germany, the evangelization of the Native Americans.

Spangenberg then led a group to North Carolina, where a large tract of land became the sight of three settlements—Bethabara, Bethania, and, most importantly, Salem (now known as Winston-Salem). Over the next century, Bethlehem, Pennsylvania, and Winston-Salem, North Carolina, emerged as the centers for the spread of the movement throughout North America and the headquarters of what would later become the two provinces (Northern and Southern) of the American Church. The Moravian Church in America became autonomous following the international Unity Synod of Moravian leaders in 1848. The church found its best response in communities of German immigrants, especially in the Midwest. Then at the end of the nineteenth century, the movement spread into Canada.

During its earlier years, the church adopted a communal organization that had been proposed by Spangenburg. The pooling of economic resources, which lasted for about two decades, allowed the church and its members to prosper quickly and led to a close communal life that persisted for several generations after the communal living experiment ended.

The Moravians retain the essentials of Protestant Christianity, but they have adopted a motto to govern their approach to theology: "In essentials unity; in nonessentials liberty; in all things love." They accept the Bible as the source of Christian doctrine. Central to the Moravian life is what is termed "heart religion," a personal relationship with Jesus being more important than doctrinal purity. They continue to hold simple communal meals called love feasts and developed an early emphasis on music.

The Moravian Church in America has two headquarters: one for the Northern Province and one for the Southern Province. The Northern Province is divided into an Eastern District, Western District, and Canadian District. Of the church's 50,000 members, approximately half live in the states of Pennsylvania and North Carolina. The church regularly participates in the meeting of the Unity (the international Moravian movement), which is held every seven years. The Moravian Church supports the Moravian College and Theological Seminary in Bethlehem, Pennsylvania. It is a member of the World Council of Churches.

Moravian Church, Eastern West Indies Province

Interest in the plight of Africans in the West Indies launched the entire Moravian missionary enterprise. In 1731 in Copenhagen, Moravian leader August Gottlieb Spangenburg (1704–1792) encountered an African man named Anthony, who told him of the deplorable conditions faced by Africans in the West Indies. Spangenburg's decision to respond to these conditions led Leonhard Dober (1706–1760) to offer his services as a missionary to the Dutch West Indies, thus becoming the first Protestant missionary of the modern era. Dober began his work on Saint Thomas. It was soon extended to Saint Croix (the site of a bloody slave revolt in 1833) and Saint John, the Virgin Islands then being in Danish hands. In 1734 a team of 18 missionaries arrived on Saint Thomas, and Dober turned the work over to them and returned to Germany with his first convert, an orphan boy named Carmel Oly whose freedom Dober had purchased.

The work grew in spite of opposition from most of the plantation owners and the high toll of lives among the Moravians unable to cope with the climate. When Count Nikolaus Ludwig von Zinzendorf (1700–1760), the Moravian bishop, visited the islands in 1739, he found the missionaries in prison as a result of a conflict with the local Dutch Reformed Church minister. On a more positive note, he also found some 800 African converts.

In 1772 the islands were hit by a major hurricane that destroyed much property; indeed, bad weather would periodically produce temporary setbacks throughout the history of the mission. However, as the work was established in the Danish East Indies, it built up enough momentum to carry the mission to the neighboring islands of Barbados (1765), Antigua (1771), Saint Kitts (1777), and Tobago (1790). The effort on Tobago, then a French possession, was halted almost as soon as it began by the unrest at news of the French Revolution. The revolution also stimulated efforts that grew in

England for the abolition of slavery. With the abolition of slavery on Haiti in 1793, hope for freedom spread throughout the Caribbean. Through the nineteenth century, one by one, the islands would become free states.

In 1830 the centennial of the mission was marked when the Danish king recognized the Moravians and granted them equal status with the state church (Lutheran). The next step in the mission's growth would be its maturation into an autonomous church, a process that began in 1879 when the West Indies work was organized as a province, accepted the challenge to become self-supporting, and established a semiautonomous governing board. The Europeans continued to provide some financial support, but they set a schedule to gradually decrease it. In 1886 the theological seminary was established at Nisky on Saint Thomas.

In 1899 the Moravians moved to restructure their international fellowship as a federation. This restructuring brought a new level of independence to the island church. In 1922 the Moravian British Province assumed responsibility for the work in the West Indies. In 1931 the International Missions Board was abolished. Finally, in 1967, the work in the Eastern West Indies was set apart as a fully autonomous province.

The Moravian Church, Eastern West Indies Province is at one with the beliefs and practices of Moravians worldwide. It now includes work in the U.S. Virgin Islands, Saint Kitts, Barbados, Antigua,

Nisky Moravian Mission house on St. Thomas, British Virgin Islands. The mission was established in about 1755 by missionaries who came to minister mainly to the slave population. (Library of Congress)

and Trinidad and Tobago. It is a member of the World Council of Churches.

Moravian Church in Jamaica

The impetus for Moravian work in the West Indies came in the eighteenth century directly out of the church's international center in Germany. The West Indian effort had spread through the easternmost islands but had not opened a station on Jamaica. Then in 1754, two plantation owners, John Foster Barham and William Foster, who resided in England and also happened to be Moravians, asked for missionaries to minister to the Africans residing on their lands in Jamaica. Zacharias George Caries and two companions pioneered the work, and with the initial support of Foster and Barham they soon gained the support of other plantation owners.

The work got off to a slow start; there were frequent changes of personnel, disease took its toll, and on occasion the converts returned to the religions they had brought from Africa. Then in 1834, slavery was ended in all British colonies. The church had taken special efforts to prepare its members for the new era. Some 26 schools had been opened. Membership shot upward in the years immediately after emancipation. In 1847 a conference structure replaced the rule of the mission's superintendent.

Representatives from Jamaica attended the 1863 conference on Saint Thomas (Virgin Islands), where the process of transformation in the Caribbean toward more indigenous leadership and eventual self-support was discussed. The Jamaicans agreed to move toward self-support if the European church would continue to supply financial support for building and the travel of missionaries.

As a first step, in 1876 a seminary was opened at Fairfield. In 1879 the work was reorganized as a separate province with semiautonomous status. The first bishop, Peter Larsen, was consecrated in 1901.

Most of the congregations were located in the western and especially the southwestern parts of the island. The church developed under the most trying of conditions, including epidemics, hurricanes, and a devastating earthquake in Kingston in 1907. The bad times drew together the various denominations represented on the island, and in the 1920s union negotiations began between the Moravians and the Methodists, Presbyterians, Disciples of Christ, and Congregationalists. Though they did not bring union, these discussions did bring closer relations and a new commonly supported seminary.

Soon the work had grown enough to enable Jamaican Moravians to give more systematic attention to their responsibility for the church's world mission. In 1925 the Moravian Missionary Society held its initial gathering and focused concern for the missions in West Africa and Egypt.

The independent province of the Moravian Church in Jamaica was set apart in 1967. It is at one with the beliefs and practices of Moravians worldwide. It is a member of the World Council of Churches.

Beliefs and Practices

The Moravian Church holds much in common with other Protestant denominations. The various providences that compose the Unitas Fratrum ("Unity of Brethren") or worldwide Moravian Church abide by creeds such as the

Apostles' Creed. The Moravian Church holds to a conception of the Trinity—defined as "God the Father, the Son, and the Holy Spirit." It is held that the Christ Event—the birth, ministry, death, and resurrection of Jesus Christ—serves to provide salvation for all humans who will accept Christ. As part of this Christian process, the Moravian Church believes in infant baptism. The truth of this Christ Event, according to the Church, is located in the Bible—Old and New Testaments. Furthermore, we are assisted in understanding the Bible, the Word of God, through the Holy Spirit. The Moravian Church also argues that the Church is unified through Christ and should not accept divisions based on race, gender, and so on. Rather, a unity of origin and purpose should mark the Christian church and the various denominations that compose it.

Holding to these beliefs, the Moravian Church understands service to humanity as the primary purpose of Christian fellowship. And this in part involves missionary activity, which would come to include the Americas.

J. Gordon Melton

SELECTED BIBLIOGRAPHY

Fogleman, Aaron Spencer. *Jesus Is Female: Moravians and the Challenge of Radical Religion in Early America* (Philadelphia: University of Pennsylvania Press, 2007).

Gillespie, Michele, and Robert Beachy, eds. *Pious Pursuits: German Moravians in the Atlantic World* (New York: Berghahn Books, 2007).

Hamilton, J. Taylor, and Kenneth G. Hamilton. *History of the Moravian Church: The Renewed Unitas Fratrum, 1722–1957* (Bethlehem, PA, and Winston-Salem, NC: Interprovincial Board of Christian Education, Moravian Church in America, 1967).

Maynard, G. O. *A History of the Moravian Church: Eastern West Indies Province* (Port of Spain, Trinidad: Yuille's Printerie, 1968).

MORMON CHURCH

Historical Development

African Americans in the Mormon Church have had a long and tumultuous history, and, simultaneously, African Americans have been central figures in the history of the church. Among prominent African Americans in the Mormon Church's history are R&B singer Gladys Knight, well known Black Panther Eldridge Cleaver, former Utah Jazz basketball player Thurl Bailey, and professional football players Burgess Owens and Jamal Willis (who played for the Oakland Raiders and the San Francisco 49ers, respectively). Efforts to proselytize African Americans have been limited by the history, theology, and politics of the church, in particular the at times blatant white supremacy in its mythology and historic practices. Conservative estimates suggest, however, that the African American membership in the church is less than 200,000, and the majority of them live in Sub-Saharan Africa, Brazil, throughout South America, and the Caribbean, with a smaller number of them residing in North America.

Also known as the Church of Jesus Christ of Latter-day Saints (LDS), the church had its genesis in 1830 when founder, 24- or 26-year-old (his age is disputed), Joseph Smith reported having a revelation that claimed to restore true and authentic Christianity to its primitive state—as it was practiced and lived by the biblical apostles. According to Smith, this revelation was given to him directly by God the Father and God the Son, who counseled him not to unite with any of the established Christian denominations, for they had fallen away and erred regarding true Christianity. Several reported revelations followed the initial disclosure that led to the founding of the church. For example, Smith maintained that he encountered an angel known as Moroni, the son of Mormon, who directed him to the location of a set of inscribed gold plates that Mormon had written. As the story goes, Moroni revealed the translation of the plates to Smith, and after a four-year period of probation in which he was "tried and tested," this translation became the Book of Mormon, the sacred text of the Mormon Church that serves as a companion text to the Bible.

The Smith family had migrated to New York State, where the church was founded west of the Catskills and the Adirondacks, in particular, in the city of Palmyra. At the time influenced by the Second Great Awakening, Western New York was the scene of fervent and intense religious activity. The area of Western New York in which Mormonism arose was increasingly middle class and cosmopolitan, albeit it was agrarian and rural. It was precisely in this middle-class and religiously enthusiastic context, wherein children were educated and people were seen as sophisticated and prosperous, that the church began. Another important dimension of life in the region, which would become a contributing factor in Mormon ritual, was the strong presence of Masonic lodges. In fact, it was in this area of the country that Captain William Morgan was allegedly killed in 1826 to prevent him from revealing Masonic secrets.

(His book, *Exposition of Freemasonry*, was published in 1827.) Apparently, Captain Morgan's widow later became one of Smith's numerous wives as Mormonism flourished.

The Mormon movement proselytized primarily in New York in its early years and expanded into Kirtland, Ohio, where they converted people in well-settled communities. From there, the church headed westward and settled outside Independence, Missouri (in what is now a part of Kansas City). Smith would continue to travel to Kirtland and to Mentor, Ohio, where he worked on a "translation" of the Bible. It was in Mentor in 1832 that he was tarred and feathered by a mob led by a former Mormon who had turned against him. Smith returned to Missouri. The church in Missouri grew tremendously in the subsequent years, but it was in Kirtland that Smith established what records suggest was the first Mormon Temple and the headquarters of the church. Missouri, on the other hand, posed some challenges that would lead to significant developments or clarifications of Mormon doctrine regarding African Americans.

The most important theological development that emerged, in part, in response to the Mormon presence in Missouri is called the Missouri Thesis. Mormons faced great threats from the residents of Missouri, who believed that their land and property might be in jeopardy from the Mormons who were seen as interlopers. Though the conflicts eventually led to the expulsion of Mormons from the state (c. 1838), Smith initially promoted an ideology, in support of African American slavery, that was meant to ingratiate them to their new neighbors. According to proponents of the Missouri

---

ELIJAH ABEL

Born in Maryland in 1810, Elijah Abel was the first known person of African descent to be a member of the LDS church and to be ordained to the Melchizedek Priesthood. From Maryland, he migrated to Kirtland, Ohio, a Mormon stronghold. There, he embraced Mormon teaching, and he was subsequently baptized in 1832—only two years after Smith's initiated the movement. Abel assumed an active role in church, and he was ordained an elder in the Melchizedek Priesthood in 1836. He advanced in authority within the priesthood, moving up to the Third Quorum of the Seventy leadership and serving at least three missions. Abel's mission fields included New York, Ohio, and Canada. Abel moved from Kirtland to Nauvoo, Illinois, in 1836, where he became a mortician in the church, an official LDS "calling." One interesting note is that people who were ordained to the priesthood by the LDS church were issued a license by the state of Ohio. Brigham Young, who assumed leadership after Smith, tried to take the priesthood away from him, and it was the Ohio-issued license that prevented Young from being successful. Young's successor, John Taylor, also refused to recognize Abel's history and credentials. Abel died in the Utah Territory.

Thesis, Mormon racism against African Americans and their exclusion from holding the Mormon priesthood begins here.

The first scholar to articulate this Thesis was Fawn McKay Brodie, author of *No Man Knows My History: The Life of Joseph Smith* (1945). Brodie argues that Mormons who immigrated to the slave-holding state of Missouri in the 1830s were anxious to deflect criticism and misunderstanding about their religion, so they adopted a position that denied the priesthood to African Americans, linking this practice with extant discriminatory ideology against African Americans in their Book of Abraham (i.e., Pearl of Great Price), albeit some still suggest that Smith was an advocate of African American rights and freedom. Unsuccessfully navigating the slave culture of Missouri, the Mormons' excursions would lead them to Illinois and eventually to Utah in 1847 under Brigham Young's leadership, where their headquarters remains in Salt Lake City to this day.

Smith was killed on June 27, 1844 (some suggest for revealing Masonic secrets and reproducing them in and as the Mormon temple ceremony), when a group overran the Carthage, Illinois, jail where he was being held on charges of ordering the destruction of the *Nauvoo Expositor*, a newspaper that had published an edition that was extremely critical of Smith, Mormonism, and polygamy (several founders of the paper were former Mormons who claimed that Smith tried to take their wives). The mob that had broken into the jail ran up the stairs, first killing Smith's brother Hyrum, then shooting Smith, who was heard to give the Masonic signal of distress as he tried to elude his pursuers. Brigham Young, who had joined the movement in 1832, succeeded him as president of the group, although Hyrum, who was killed with Smith, would have been the most likely successor. Young's most inflammatory contribution to Mormon doctrine that affected African Americans was his forceful iteration and codification that

WALKER LEWIS

Born Quack Walker Lewis in Lowell, Massachusetts, on August 7, 1798, he was the second known African American to hold the Mormon priesthood during the time of Joseph Smith. He was an abolitionist, and he came from a prominent family of abolitionists. Lewis was a founding member of the Massachusetts General Colored Association in 1826, one of the first all-black abolitionist groups. A middle-class Freemason leader and barber, Lewis appears to have joined the LDS church in 1842. He was ordained to the priesthood in 1843 by Smith's younger brother, William Smith. Lewis's son, Enoch Lovejoy Lewis, was also a Mormon, who married a white Mormon woman by the name of Mary Matilda Webster in 1846. Sources suggest that this event may have inflamed forces that sought to restrict African Americans from the priesthood, given that the priesthood is the entrance to the afterlife in which men will be able to practice polygamy. Moreover, it may follow that such cases, and this one in particular, led the first governor of the Utah Territory to make interracial marriage illegal, after being pressured by Young to do so in 1852.

they were subhuman, inferior in intelligence, and unfit for the priesthood, and that "Negroid" features were the result of a curse in the preexistent realm. Young based many of his interdictions and pronouncements on the idea that black people were the "seed of Cain," a people said to be cursed in the Hebrew Scriptures/Old Testament. Notwithstanding, some scholars argue that it was not Smith, but Young, who codified racism and exclusion within the LDS church.

One of the most significant developments for African Americans in LDS history occurred on June 8, 1978, when President Spencer Kimball announced that he had received a revelation that the priesthood would be open to "all worthy

JANE ELIZABETH MANNING JAMES

Born Jane Elizabeth Manning in southwestern Connecticut between 1813 and 1822, Jane joined the LDS Church in 1842, after hearing the proclamation of LDS missionary Charles Wesley Wandell. Jane and her family, also members of the Mormon Church, relocated to Nauvoo, Illinois, which was the LDS headquarters at the time. On their journey by boat to Nauvoo, the family ran out of money in Buffalo, New York, and walked the subsequent 800 miles. The family arrived in Nauvoo in November 1843 and was directed to the home Joseph Smith and his wife Emma, where shortly thereafter, Jane lived and worked. While in Nauvoo, Jane met and married Isaac James, a free black man and LDS convert from New Jersey. The couple divorced in 1869 or 1870, and Isaac apparently left the church for 20 years, returning briefly before his death in 1890. Two of Jane's children would die within three years of Isaac. By 1884, Jane had begun contacting LDS leaders in order to challenge the barriers in the Church for African Americans and for women. She died in 1908 at the age of 95.

male members of the Church . . . without regard for race or color" (Bringhurst and Smith 2004, 1). This was viewed as a significant event, though the announcement of the revelation included neither an explanation for racism in Mormonism's history nor an apology for such ideals and behavior. The Genesis Group, a collective of African American Mormons, had been founded unofficially on June 8, 1971. The group considered it prophetic that their organization began, as an instrument to address African American LDS cultural and social issues, exactly seven years to the date of the purported revelation. In 2008, the group led the celebration of the thirtieth anniversary of the change in LDS policy in a Salt Lake City ceremony, in which the central event was a video commemorating the occurrence.

African Americans, including those in the Genesis Group, continue to challenge the Church on its race relations and its apparent reluctance to evangelize in black communities in America. Yet, African American Mormons insist that they are black in healthy and positive ways, and that the LDS church does not

inhibit them from developing such an identity. In fact, some of them deny that the Church was ever racist, suggesting that it was misunderstanding and anti-Mormon propaganda that resulted in the notion that the religion was ever white supremacist in its values, beliefs, and rituals.

Beliefs and Practices

Mormon beliefs and rituals are far too many and detailed to present here, but a few are imperative to mention because of their importance. To that end, at the core of Mormon belief is the idea that the LDS Church is the reinstitution of true Christianity, since, according to Joseph Smith's report, the Christian denominations (e.g., Baptists, Methodists) had all "apostatized" or fallen away from the faith as it was originally intended by God. As such, the LDS church is the "true" Christian Church. Closely tied to this notion is the idea that God called the prophet Joseph Smith to develop authentic Christianity. As the Mormon narrative goes, God and Jesus warned Smith to avoid the denominations, which had been

---

RUFFIN BRIDGEFORTH

One of the most important modern black Mormons, Ruffin Bridgeforth was one of the founding members and the first president of the Genesis Group, an officially sanctioned African American LDS auxiliary that serves as a cultural, social, and outreach unit for its members. Originally from Louisiana, Bridgeforth arrived in Salt Lake City in 1946 with his wife, a Latina Mormon. In 1953, Bridgeforth joined the LDS church and remained a Mormon until his death in 1997. He also served as president of the Genesis Group from 1971 until 1997. Furthermore, Bridgeforth was the first African American to be ordained a high priest in the LDS church. Bridgeforth was such a prominent member of the church that he was eulogized by LDS President Gordon B. Hinckley. Darius Gray, a colleague, friend, and important African American Mormon, succeeded Bridgeforth as president of the Genesis Group.

corrupted. The key to the original religion of God, then, is contained in what was to be called the Book of Mormon—books that were reportedly translated from ancient gold plates to which Smith was directed in a divine visitation by the angel Moroni. The Book of Mormon is understood as the companion Scripture to the Christian Bible. It gives further details of the visitations of God and Jesus to North America as well as the story of the original inhabitants of North America. Therefore, the book participates in locating America and race as the center of divine activity.

Mormons have complex and intricate beliefs and rituals, some of which are directly and indirectly related to African Americans and race relations in America. Substantial beliefs and rituals revolve around their mythology of preexistence. In short, Mormons believe that human spirits preexist in a spiritual world that is prior to bodily existence. As the mythology goes Jehovah, the preincarnate Jesus, and Lucifer (later Satan) were spirit brothers in this world, whose father was the God Elohim, who had millions of children with his celestial wives. Jehovah and Lucifer were chosen to present plans for salvation for God's children who would advance to mortal life. Lucifer presented his plan first. It was rejected. Lucifer then rebelled against his brother, and war broke out in heaven. One-third of the spirit brothers sided with and fought on the side of Lucifer. Likewise, one-third sided with Jehovah. The one-third who did not take sides in the fight, who were not "valiant," was cursed as a result. The mark of the curse was "blackness"—the sign of inferiority. According to Mormon records, the lineage of this curse runs through Cain, a biblical character who Mormon sources suggests was the father of the Negroid races. The result of the curse, of which black skin was the marker, entailed African Americans not being allowed to progress to godhood and procreate eternally.

Through a great deal of effort, African Americans have pushed the Church to expand its thinking in ways that produced greater opportunity for involvement by African American members.

Stephen C. Finley

SELECTED BIBLIOGRAPHY

Bringhurst, Newell G. *Saints, Slaves, and Blacks: The Changing Place of Black People Within Mormonism* (Westport, CT: Greenwood Press, 1981).

Bringhurst, Newell G., and Darron T. Smith, eds. *Black and Mormon* (Urbana and Chicago: University of Illinois Press, 2004).

Brodie, Fawn McKay. *No Man Knows My History: The Life of Joseph Smith* (New York: Alfred A. Knopf, 1945).

Mauss, Armand L. *All Abraham's Children: Changing Conceptions of Race and Lineage* (Urbana and Chicago: University of Illinois Press, 2003).

Morgan, William, Capt. *Morgan's Freemasonry Exposed and Explained* (Pomeroy, WA: Health Research Books, 1993).

O'Dea, Thomas F. *The Mormons* (Chicago: The University of Chicago Press, 1957).

Stark, Rodney. *The Rise of Mormonism* (New York: Columbia University Press, 2005).

NATION OF ISLAM

Historical Development

The Nation of Islam is an American religious movement, consisting largely of African American members. Its history has been divided into several phases: Master Wali Fard Muhammad led the Nation of Islam from 1930 to 1934; the Honorable Elijah Muhammad was the leader from 1934 to 1975; and the Honorable Louis Farrakhan has led from 1977 to the present. The Nation was a "proto-Islamic" movement, using some of the symbols, rituals, and beliefs of Islam mixed with a core ideology of black nationalism.

On July 4, 1930, an amiable but faintly mysterious peddler suddenly appeared in a black ghetto of Detroit called Paradise Valley. At first he came to sell raincoats, silks, and other sundries to the poor residents of the area, but later he also began teaching them about their "true religion"—not Christianity, but the religion of the "Asiatic black man."

In spreading his message in people's living rooms and kitchens, he used both the Bible and the Qur'an. Soon the popularity of these meetings outgrew individual homes and a hall was rented and christened "Temple of Islam," which was later given the numeric designation "1" to signify its foundational character in a growing movement. This mysterious stranger who referred to himself as Mr. Farrad Muhammad, or sometimes as Mr. Wali Fard or W. D. Fard or Wallace D. Fard or Mr. Ford, was considered to be a prophet by some of his followers. He later came to be recognized as the "Great Mahdi," or "Savior," who had come to bring a special message to the suffering blacks in the teeming ghettos of America.

Master Fard taught his followers about the deceptive character and temporary domination of "blue-eyed devils," or white overlords. He also stressed the importance of attaining "knowledge of self" and "doing for self" as a prerequisite for achieving black liberation. He told the story of Yakub, a black mad

239

scientist who rebelled against Allah by creating the white race, a weak hybrid people who were permitted temporary dominance of the world for a period of 6,000 years. Whites had achieved their power and position through devious means and "tricknology." They had perpetuated "devilish acts" against black people through slavery, brutality, and lynching, and even by using alcohol and narcotics. He instructed his followers that they were not Americans and therefore owed no allegiance to the American flag and to refuse being drafted into the American military. He wrote two manuals for the movement, *The Secret Ritual of the Nation of Islam*, which is transmitted orally to members, and *Teaching for the Lost-Found Nation of Islam in a Mathematical Way*, which is written in symbolic language and requires special interpretation.

Within three years, Fard had founded an effective organization with a Temple of Islam that had its own worship style and rituals and a "University of Islam" with a special curriculum made up largely of Fard's teaching. The "university" was essentially a combined elementary and secondary school, but for his followers, it was the first step toward cultural and psychological freedom. He also established the Muslim Girls' Training (MGT) Class to teach young women the principles of home economics and their proper role in the Nation of Islam. Finally, in 1933 he created the Fruit of Islam (FOI), a paramilitary organization of male Muslims who served as honor guards, ushers, and enforcers of internal discipline within the temples, as well as security agents for the Minister of Islam and other leaders. Members of the Fruit and the MGT

learned how to frisk and search everyone entering a temple.

One of the earliest officers of the movement who became Master Fard's most trusted lieutenant was Elijah Poole who had to drop his slave name Poole and was first given the Muslim name Elijah Karriem and then Elijah Muhammad. Born on October 7, 1897, Poole was the son of a rural Baptist minister and sharecropper and his wife, Willie and Marie Poole, from Sandersville, Georgia. The family moved to Cordele, Georgia, where as a teenager Elijah witnessed the public lynching of his good friend Albert Hamilton. The lynching of Hamilton deeply affected Elijah so that he ordered a picture of a black man lynched from a tree be placed in the front of every Nation of Islam Temple when he became the head of the movement. The lynching also made him open to the racial doctrines of Master Fard's teaching, which he encountered later in Detroit, especially the view that the "white man is the devil" who dominates the world through devious tricks or "tricknology."

Elijah married Clara Evans in the town of Cordele in 1919. Faced with continued racial discrimination and job loss in Georgia, the couple took their two young children and other family members to join the black migration to Detroit in 1923. The Pooles eventually settled in one of the poorest black ghettos in Detroit, aptly named "Paradise Valley." After a dinner meeting with Master Fard at his home, Elijah Poole converted to the Nation of Islam in 1931. Despite his third-grade education, Elijah's shrewd native intelligence and devotion to Fard enabled him to rise rapidly through the ranks, and he was eventually chosen by Fard in 1933 to be the Chief Minister of

HONORABLE ELIJAH MUHAMMAD (1897–1975)

Born in Georgia, and given the name Elijah Poole, the Honorable Elijah Muhammad followed the Great Migration north and settled in Detroit with his family. During this time, a gentleman who would come to be called Master Fard Muhammad moved through the African American communities of Detroit spreading word concerning the glorious past of African Americans and their great future if they return to the original religion. Poole eventually met Master Fard Muhammad and became a member of his following. Poole became a key figure with a new name—Elijah Muhammad. Upon the disappearance of Fard Muhammad in 1934, Elijah Muhammad gained control of the organization. With time the organization grew and entered the popular imagination of the nation through charismatic figures such as convert Malcolm X. Among the Honorable Elijah Muhammad's more controversial teachings was the notion that African Americans were the original people of the earth, created for good, and whites were a demonic race created by Mr. Yakub, a mad scientist. (Under the leadership of Farrakhan this teaching was softened.) In 1975, the Honorable Elijah Muhammad passed away, leaving his teachings in texts such as *Message to the Black Man*.

Islam, to preside over the organization. In a short period of time, Fard's Temple of Islam had attracted more than 8,000 members.

After Master Fard mysteriously disappeared in 1934, rivalries and factions within the Nation of Islam broke into open hostilities in the struggle for the power to

Elijah Muhammad, spiritual leader of the Nation of Islam in the United States, established a religious organization that gave poor urban African Americans a sense of racial pride and economic and political self-sufficiency. (Library of Congress)

command the organization. Part of the controversy involved Elijah Muhammad's bold proclamation that Master Fard was Allah and that he himself was Allah's prophet or messenger. As a result of the factional rivalries and death threats, Muhammad fled Detroit, moving constantly back and forth by himself between Washington, D.C., and Chicago, while his wife Clara Muhammad and their children stayed in the family's residence in the South Side of Chicago. Besides trying to build his movement by preaching and recruiting in the late 1930s and early 1940s, another reason for Elijah's constant evasive tactics was to elude the FBI agents who were searching for him for failing to register for the military draft. Eventually, Elijah was arrested on May 8, 1942 ,for nonregistration and sentenced to serve three years at the Federal Correctional Institute in Milan, Michigan. While Elijah was in prison, his wife, Clara, ran the affairs of the Nation of Islam. He was released from Milan on August 24, 1946.

In the same year that Elijah Muhammad was released from prison, Malcolm Little, a small time petty thief, pimp, alcohol and drug addict, and street hustler was entering the prison system in Massachusetts. He was born in Omaha, Nebraska, on May 19, 1925, to the Reverend Earl Little and his wife, Louise. The loss of both parents led to an unstable childhood and teenage years. Tired of shuttling between foster parents, Malcolm moved to Boston to live with an older half sister named Ella. As an unemployed street hustler and leader of an interracial gang of thieves in Harlem and Roxbury, he was known as "Big Red" and "Detroit Red" for the reddish tinge in his hair.

Sentenced to 8 to 10 years in prison for armed robbery and larceny, Malcolm was first introduced to the Nation of Islam in 1948 at the Norfolk Prison Colony by his favorite younger brother Reginald who had joined the Nation earlier in Detroit along with other siblings (Wilfred, Philbert, Wesley, and Hilda).

Malcolm described the powerful, jarring impact that the revelation of religious truth had upon him when Reginald told him during his visit, "The white man is the Devil" (Malcolm X and Haley 1999, 162). This doctrine along with the myth of Yakub and other creedal beliefs of the Nation have functioned as a theodicy for Malcolm and for thousands of black men in a similar predicament, as an explanation and rationalization for all of the pain and suffering inflicted upon black people in America. It all began to make sense: the chaos of the world behind prison bars became a cosmos, an ordered reality. "The white man is the Devil" explained his father's death at the hands of whites and the extreme poverty suffered by his mother and nine children. It gave him a reason for his mother's being taken away to an insane asylum by white social workers, it rationalized his dropping out of school in the eighth grade when a white teacher told him "niggers can't be lawyers"

MALCOLM X (1925–1965)

Born Malcolm Little, in Nebraska, Malcolm X was early influenced by his father's Baptist preaching and the allegiance of his father to Marcus Garvey. Family tragedy, including the murder of his father and his mother's nervous breakdown, resulted in the disruption of life for Malcolm X. Disillusionment with his life options resulted in rebellion, particular in Boston where he moved to live with his eldest sister. Malcolm's criminal activities resulted eventually in his arrest and a ten-year sentence in state prison. It was in prison that Malcolm X became aware of the Nation of Islam. He joined in 1952. Malcolm became the organization's first national spokesperson in 1963. Friction within the organization concerning Malcolm's growing popularity would eventually become the pretext for his silencing. Malcolm X left the Nation in 1964. That same year he would found the Muslim Mosque, Inc., and would travel abroad to go on pilgrimage to Mecca. In Mecca he took a new name: El-Hajj Malik El-Shabazz. Upon his return to the United States, he founded the Organization of Afro-American Unity and began to address issues related to human rights abuses within the United States. He was assassinated on February 21, 1965.

(Malcolm X and Haley 1999, 38), and it made sense of all the years of hustling and pimping on the streets of Roxbury and Harlem as Detroit Red.

Elijah Muhammad began the practice of each new member of the Nation dropping their slave surname and substituting an "X," which became an outward symbol for inward changes. The "X" carried a number of meanings for members. It meant "undetermined" or an unknown quantity as in mathematics, as well as ex-slave, ex-Christian, ex-smoker, ex-drinker, or ex-mainstream American. After a period of time and demonstrating one's faithfulness, a Muslim name chosen by Muhammad is given to a member. For example, Malcolm X became "Malik Shabazz" and Louis X was named Louis "Abdul Haleem Farrakhan."

The years between Malcolm X's release from prison and his assassination, 1952–1965, mark the period of the greatest growth and influence of the Nation of Islam under Elijah Muhammad's leadership. Minister Malcolm X was a man of enormous physical and intellectual energy. He added 27 more Muslim temples across the country to the seven already in existence in 1952. He established the Nation's newspaper, *Muhammad Speaks*, by printing the first issues in the basement of his home until it was taken over by Elijah Muhammad. Malcolm also made it mandatory for every male Muslim to sell a set number of newspapers. This gave members of the Nation an opportunity to recruit new members, while also raising funds for the organization's work. Failure to do so often led to physical punishment. In his outreach to the black community, Malcolm preached on street corners of Boston and Harlem and often participated in "fishing" for lost souls in the bars and cafes and even in front of Christian churches as their Sunday services let out (Malcolm X and Haley 1999, 222–223). In recognition of

LOUIS FARRAKHAN (1933–)

Farrakhan entered the Nation of Islam under the tutelage of Malcolm X. His energy and abilities resulted in his moving through the ranks rather quickly, ultimately becoming the head of the most important mosque in the organization. He also became the organization's national spokesperson. After the death of the Honorable Elijah Muhammad, Warith Deen Muhammed became head of the Nation of Islam, and the changes he imposed eventually resulted in Farrakhan's breaking with the organization in 1978 and developing the Nation of Islam under the original teachings of the Honorable Elijah Muhammad. Under Farrakhan's leadership, the Nation has evolved to include a membership extending beyond African Americans. Also, members of the organization are encouraged to participate in the political process, something the Honorable Elijah Muhammad rejected. Farrakhan has become a controversial figure, whose statements concerning Jews and whose relationship with Islamic leaders rejected by the United States have resulted in heavy critique. However, his appeal is represented in events such as the Million Man March sponsored during the late twentieth century. This event, held in Washington, D.C., brought together a reported million black men for the purpose of atonement for their lack of leadership within their families and communities.

his energetic preaching and organizing, Elijah Muhammad made him the minister of Boston Temple No. 11 in 1953, and in 1954 he rewarded Malcolm with the post of minister of Temple No. 7 in Harlem, the Nation's largest temple outside of Chicago. Despite his constant travels and busy speaking schedule, in 1958 Malcolm briefly courted and married Betty Sanders, a nursing student from Detroit. Within seven years of marriage, Malcolm and Betty had six daughters.

Beliefs and Practices

The Honorable Elijah Muhammad recognized his organizational talents and his enormous charismatic appeal and forensic abilities by naming Malcolm his national representative of the Nation of Islam, second in rank to the Messenger himself. Inspired by his work, the Nation of Islam achieved a membership estimated to have ranged from 20,000 to 500,000. But like other movements of this kind, the numbers involved were quite fluid and the influence of the Nation of Islam refracted through the charisma of Malcolm X greatly exceeded its actual membership.

As a leading media personality, Malcolm became one of the most important critics of the Civil Rights Movement. He challenged the strategy of "integration" and the nonviolent Christian ethic upon which it depended. More than anyone else, Malcolm predicted that even if King's movement succeeded, the black subculture and its vital contributions to the American experience would be submerged in a sea of whiteness, leaving blacks with no history and no identity. Malcolm X believed more important than integration was the integrity of black

selfhood and its independence. Malcolm's challenge to the "so-called Negro" (Malcolm X, "Africa and Self Hate," in Breitman 1969, 184–185) and his emphasis upon the recovery of black self-identity and independence shaped the "Black Power" and Black Consciousness movement that emerged in the late 1960s and early 1970s in American society.

Malcolm's alternative to King's nonviolent stance was clearly enunciated in the time-honored right to self-defense he found in the prevailing Hebraic, Islamic, and American social and political credos. While Malcolm and the Black Muslims never advocated a violent revolution or overthrow of the American government, members were instructed to defend themselves, their families, and their homes "by any means possible" (Breitman 1970, 119). He made an enormous contribution to Americans by helping them to come face to face with the consequences of racial paranoia. He articulated the pent-up anger, the frustration, the bitterness, and the rage felt by the dispossessed black masses, the "grass roots." Perhaps more clearly than other leaders of his time, he foresaw the violent consequences of the repressed anger and bitterness that exploded in large-scale urban rebellions in Harlem, Watts, Newark, and Detroit after his death.

While he often paid tribute to his teacher and mentor, the Honorable Elijah Muhammad, Minister Malcolm X felt personally constrained from his own desire to participate actively in the politics and struggles of the Civil Rights Movement. After President John F. Kennedy's assassination, Malcolm was suspended for 90 days for making a controversial statement in the press that the assassination was comparable to "chickens coming home to roost," implying that a violent nation produced this kind of violence directed toward its leaders (Malcolm X and Haley 1999, 307). For Malcolm, the suspension was a pretext to cover up a deeper moral problem and conflict within the Nation of Islam, namely, Elijah Muhammad's consorting with and fathering 13 other children with seven of his secretaries. He received confirmation of these alleged affairs from one of Elijah's sons, Wallace Muhammad. He said that he was close to Wallace and trusted him. Malcolm also told Minister Louis X (Farrakhan) of Boston and Captain Joseph who headed the FOI in his Temple No. 7 in Harlem. Both Louis X and Captain Joseph informed the authorities in Chicago that Malcolm was spreading false rumors about Elijah Muhammad.

After resigning from the Nation in March 1964, Malcolm supported the paternity lawsuits of two of the secretaries against Elijah Muhammad. His support ended any chances of reconciliation with the Messenger. Malcolm also made the Hajj (Pilgrimage) to Mecca where he underwent another conversion to Sunni Islam, changing his name to El-Hajj Malik El-Shabazz. After returning to the United States, Malcolm created two organizations, the Muslim Mosque, Inc. and the Organization of Afro-American Unity, covering both his religious and secular followers. He was assassinated on Sunday, February 21, 1965, at the Audubon Ballroom in Harlem.

Minister Louis Farrakhan of Boston took over Malcolm's position as the minister of Temple No. 7 and was also appointed by Elijah Muhammad as the national representative, second in command to the Messenger himself. Farrakhan played a major role in stirring up dissent against Malcolm, who was once his mentor. As a charismatic speaker, he was one of the few leaders of the Nation who could match Malcolm's forensic abilities. Farrakhan also had to rebuild the membership base of Temple No. 7 since a number of members left after Malcolm's death.

On February 23, 1975, the Honorable Elijah Muhammad died of congestive heart failure at the age of 78. Close advisers and family members decided to keep the leadership of the Nation of Islam within the Muhammad family and announced at the Savior's Day rally that Elijah's fifth son, Wallace Delaney Muhammad, would become the new leader of the organization. This decision for hereditary leadership elevated the Elijah Muhammad family to the status of being considered "the Royal Family" among the members of the Nation of Islam. Within a few months of taking office, Supreme Minister Wallace Muhammad began making sweeping changes in the organization, getting rid of all of the black nationalist teachings of Master Fard and Elijah Muhammad and moving the Nation closer to orthodox Sunni Islam. (See the "American Muslim Mission" entry for the changes Wallace made and the direction of his movement.)

The death of the Honorable Elijah Muhammad and the quick succession of Wallace Delaney Muhammad replacing his father as the supreme leader of the Nation of Islam in February 1975 left Minister Louis Farrakhan in a state of shock and confusion. As result of his confusion, he did not challenge Wallace Muhammad's ascent to leadership, although as the national representative and second in command, there had been a widespread expectation that Farrakhan would become the next leader. When

Farrakhan was asked to relocate to Chicago by Supreme Leader Wallace Muhammad, he quickly complied. In 1960 Elijah Muhammad wanted all "Temples of Islam" to be called "Mosques," but the changeover did not completely occur until after his death in 1975. Rather than being given a prominent place in the leadership of the Nation and an important mosque to lead in Chicago, Farrakhan was shunted to the side and appointed to a small rundown mosque. Instead of responding immediately to this insult and his marginalization in the movement, Farrakhan kept silent and watched the directions of Wallace's leadership. When Wallace began criticizing his father, the Nation's teachings, and organizations like the FOI, Farrakhan withdrew from the World Community of Al-Islam in the West in 1976 and began a series of travels abroad. During his travels in African countries and throughout the Middle East, Farrakhan learned about the continued oppression of black people and began to see the need for the special message of Elijah Muhammad and Master Fard to awaken their consciousness.

Beginning with a meeting in a Los Angeles hotel with Bernard Cushmeer (Jabril Muhammad) in September 1977 and later with other devoted followers in meetings in Florida and Las Vegas, Farrakhan began laying the groundwork for a rebirth of the Nation of Islam based on the work and message of the Honorable Elijah Muhammad, which he announced on November 8, 1977.

Louis Abdul Haleem Farrakhan was born Louis Eugene Walcott on May 17, 1933, in the Bronx, New York. His mother, Sarah Mae Manning who came from St. Kitts-Nevis, moved to Boston to raise her two sons, Alvan and Louis, as a single mother. Deeply religious, Gene, as he was called, faithfully attended the St. Cyprian Episcopal Church in his Roxbury neighborhood and became an altar boy. At the age of six he began violin lessons under Preston Williams and later a Russian Jewish teacher. With the rigorous discipline provided by his mother and his church, Gene did fairly well academically and graduated with honors from the prestigious Boston English High School, where he also participated on the track team and played the violin in the school orchestra. In 1953, after two years at the Winston-Salem Teachers College in North Carolina, he dropped out to pursue his favorite avocation of music and made it his first career. Gene also married his pregnant high school sweetheart, Betsy Ross, who later took the Muslim name Khadijah Muhammad. They had nine children together. An accomplished violinist, pianist, and vocalist, Walcott performed professionally on the Boston nightclub circuit as a singer of calypso and country songs where he made $500 a week. He was called "the Charmer." His stage presence and experience before large audiences also helped him in his career as the leader of the Nation of Islam. In 1955, at the age of 22, Louis Walcott was recruited by Malcolm X for the Nation of Islam. However, it was not until he had met Elijah Muhammad, the supreme leader of the Nation of Islam, on a visit to the Chicago headquarters that Louis X converted and dedicated his life to building the Nation. After proving himself for ten years, Elijah Muhammad gave Louis his Muslim name, "Abdul Haleem Farrakhan," in May 1965. As a rising star within the Nation, Farrakhan also wrote the only song, the popular "A White Man's Heaven Is a Black Man's Hell," and the only dramatic play, *Orgena* ("A Negro" spelled backward), endorsed by Mr. Muhammad.

After a nine-month apprenticeship with Malcolm X at Temple No. 7 in Harlem, Minister Louis X was appointed as the head minister of the Boston Temple No. 11, which Malcolm founded. Later, after Malcolm X had split with the Nation, Farrakhan was awarded Malcolm's Temple No. 7, the most important pastorate in the Nation after the Chicago headquarters. He was also appointed national representative after Malcolm left the Nation in 1964 and began to introduce Elijah Muhammad at Savior Day rallies, a task that had once belonged to Malcolm. Like his predecessor, Farrakhan is a dynamic and charismatic leader and a powerful speaker with an ability to appeal to masses of black people.

After deciding to begin the rebirth of the Nation of Islam based on the teachings of Elijah Muhammad in the fall of 1977, Farrakhan made the effort to purchase the licenses from the American Muslim Mission to Elijah Muhammad's books such as *Message to the Black Man*, *How to Eat to Live*, *Our Savior Has Arrived*, as well as other Nation publications such as *Flag of Islam* and *Muslim Prayer Book*. In May 1979 in the basement of his home, Farrakhan began working on *The Final Call News*, taking its name from the first publication that Elijah Muhammad published in the 1930s, *The Final Call to Islam*. The purpose of Farrakhan's newspaper was "dedicated to the resurrection of the Black Man and Woman of America and the world." The first Savior's Day event was celebrated in February 1981.

On September 12, 1982, Farrakhan mortgaged his home to purchase the Final Call Administration Building at 734 W. 79th Street in Chicago's South Side. During this rebuilding period, the Final Call Building was used as the Nation's headquarters as well as the site for Farrakhan's speeches and meetings until Mosque Maryam was purchased.

After successfully securing the release of Robert Downing, an African American pilot, from the Syrian government in 1963, Minister Farrakhan and the Reverend Jesse Jackson began to work together during Jackson's presidential campaign in 1984. Both men participated in the debacle caused by Jackson's "Hymietown" remarks to a black reporter, and they were considered anti-Semitic by Jewish groups. Throughout the years, Farrakhan's critical statements about Jews, especially the Israelis' treatment of the Palestinians, the exclusion of blacks from Hollywood, and the role of some Jews in the African slave trade, have fanned the flames of the conflict. Jewish groups have tried to prevent Farrakhan from speaking in public venues in major cities. The B'nai B'rith Anti-Defamation League has singled Farrakhan out as America's leading anti-Semite. Farrakhan has refused to bow to these criticisms and has stood firm against apologizing because he has seen how Jesse Jackson was treated after his numerous and profuse apologies before Jewish groups, who still considered him to be anti-Semitic.

In 1985 Farrakhan released his economic vision called People Organized and Working for Economic Rebirth (P.O.W.E.R.), calling for a mass movement for the economic rebirth of black people. In the same year, he appointed five women ministers, breaking the tradition of having only males as ministers.

The first woman appointed was his lawyer, Ava Muhammad (Atkinson), whom he heard as a panelist on a Nation's radio broadcast for a charity event in January 1985. After appointing Ava, Farrakhan appointed four other women as ministers, including one of his daughters, Donna Farrakhan. All of the women ministers led study groups instead of a mosque, although Ava acted as the minister of Mosque Maryam for six weeks when Farrakhan and a contingent of Nation leaders attended the Hajj (Pilgrimage) that year. Farrakhan has said that he was just building on one of Elijah Muhammad's intentions of increasing the role of women in the Nation. In 1998 he went further and appointed Minister Ava Muhammad as the Southern Regional Minister of the Nation of Islam and the minister of Mosque 15 in Atlanta. His appointment of a woman as a minister of a mosque makes his treatment of women more progressive than the tradition of Sunni groups, which refuse to have women as imams.

Besides launching the "Clean and Fresh" products in 1986 as part of the Nation's economic project, the biggest event of the 1980s was the Nation's purchase of Mosque Elijah Muhammad from Imam Warith Deen Mohammed's movement in 1988. With a $5 million interest-free loan from Colonel Muammar Qaddafi of Libya, which was later turned into a grant, Farrakhan was able to purchase the property of the former Greek Orthodox Church for $2.175 million. He renamed the headquarters Mosque Maryam and had Muhammad's University of Islam attached to it. With Qaddafi's loan, he was also able to purchase from Imam Mohammed the three stylish Middle Eastern designed houses that Elijah Muhammad had built for himself and his family. The house that Farrakhan lives in is referred to as "the Palace" among members.

During 1990 to 1995 the following issues dominated Nation of Islam (NOI) activities: the 1992 release of Spike Lee's famous movie, *X*, refocused the public's attention on Malcolm X's life and relations to the Nation, which included a reconciliation between Malcolm's widow, Betty Shabazz, and her daughters with Minister Farrakhan; continued international outreach and economic development; and a national speaking tour preceding the NOI's preparation for the Million Man March.

AVA MUHAMMAD (1951–)

Ava Muhammad is a trained attorney, who worked as a criminal attorney before health issues raised for her religious questions that she answered through the Christian Church and eventually through the Nation of Islam in 1981. As a member of the Nation she has risen through the ranks, at one point serving as Farrakhan's personal attorney. During the course of her membership in the organization, she has served as the first woman to lead a mosque and has also been a regional minister (1998). More recently, she served as Minister Farrakhan's national spokesperson. Much of the theological materials available in the Nation of Islam, including commentary on its doctrinal beliefs, has been produced by Ava Muhammad.

Farrakhan has occasionally addressed the topic of Malcolm X's assassination. For example, for the first time he claimed at a closed meeting in May 1984 at the Final Call Building that as far as he knew, no direct orders were given by anyone in the Nation's hierarchy to kill Malcolm, and that he (Farrakhan) probably contributed toward creating an emotional climate that led to Malcolm's death. However, the release of Spike Lee's *X* in November 1992 exacerbated the debate. Farrakhan immediately ordered a 90-day period of silence for members of the Nation of Islam in discussing the film on Malcolm publicly. He broke the silence by making this topic the central part of his Savior's Day talk, "The Honorable Elijah Muhammad and Malcolm X: 25 Years Later." Farrakhan defended the domestic life of Elijah Muhammad against slander and introduced four of the seven women, now called "wives" instead of secretaries, to the audience.

The tensions between Betty Shabazz and Minister Farrakhan also reached a peak during this period. In the past, Shabazz had always blamed Farrakhan and the Nation of Islam for Malcolm's death. However, on January 12, 1995, FBI agents contacted Farrakhan to let him know that they had arrested Quibilah Shabazz, one of the daughters of Malcolm and Betty, in a murder-for-hire plot against Minister Farrakhan. In a press conference, Farrakhan blamed the intelligence agencies for hatching this plot, similar to what they did in the 1960s Counterintelligence Program to disrupt black leaders and groups such as Dr. King, the Nation of Islam, and the Black Panther Party. Shabazz said, "I was totally surprised at the extent of his humanity of understanding that my daughter had nothing to do with this."

In fact, Michael Fitzpatrick, a former member of the Jewish Defense League who had been convicted for a 1978 bombing of a Russian bookstore in New York City, was both the informer and conspirator, who tried to entrap Quibilah in this plot. On May 6, 1995, at a "Free Quibilah" fundraiser at the Apollo Theatre, Minister Farrakhan and Betty Shabazz met and reconciled.

In October 1990, the Nation of Islam Ghana Mission information center was opened in Accra. International Minister Akbar Muhammad headed the Mission. In ensuing years, Akbar has established both a home and a Nation of Islam mosque in Accra. Under Farrakhan, the Nation has built upon its international outreach so that study groups and mosques were established in London and Paris and throughout the Caribbean. A study group was also established in South Africa.

On November 26, 1994, the Nation of Islam repurchased 1,500 acres of land in Dawson, Georgia, in order to reestablish the farming operation that Elijah Muhammad had started earlier. Part of Elijah's plans were to establish an internal economy from farm to grocery store within the Nation. On February 21, 1995, the $5 million Salaam Restaurant and Bakery complex was opened.

From 1991 to 1995, Minister Farrakhan had a national speaking tour of American cities and drew very large crowds. Part of the tour focused on the theme of "Stop the Killing," working on bringing about gang peace among the Bloods, Crips, and other gangs. On October 18, 1992, he spoke on "A Torchlight for America," which was later published as a book, at the Georgia Dome to an audience of 55,000, which was larger than the number of fans attending the World Series game between the Braves and the Twins.

Besides the larger audiences, he also had smaller meetings that were advertised as being "for men only," because that was the target audience for the Million Man March on October 16, 1995, in Washington, D.C. Although he had separate meetings for women, he made clear that this march would focus on the needs and concerns of black men for apology, repentance, atonement, and reconciliation with black women, families, and the community.

Apparently, his call touched a deep responsive chord in black communities and more than a million people showed up, largely men but also including some women and children. The Million Man March was four times larger than the 250,000 people who attended the March on Washington in 1963, which featured Dr. Martin Luther King Jr.'s "I Have a Dream" speech. Many black men stood up with tears streaming down their faces and took the pledge litany that Farrakhan led them in, apologizing for their failure to protect black women, for abandoning their responsibilities to black children and families; repenting and atoning for these failures; and seeking forgiveness and beginning the hard road toward reconciliation. Some of the results of the March included: more than 1 million blacks were registered to vote, and many church groups have had Million Man March committees that lasted more than a decade, trying to fulfill the pledge and work actively in their communities.

In 1996 Farrakhan began a World Friendship Tour of African nations and Muslim countries, visiting Nigeria, Zaire, Sudan, Egypt, Libya, Syria, and Iraq among other countries. Because of the success achieved by the Million Man March, he was often treated as a head of state.

In 1997 Minister Farrakhan learned that he had prostate cancer. In 1998 he opted for treatment with radiated seed implantation, which caused further health problems for him in ensuing years. In 1999 he claimed that he had a "near death" experience from the severe infection caused by the implantation. This experience led him to move the Nation closer to Sunni Islam. He changed the month of fasting during Ramadan from December, which Elijah Muhammad used as a challenge to the Christmas celebration, to the lunar calendar tradition of the Sunnis. For a while Nation members were fasting for two months, once in December and the other during the lunar cycle for Ramadan. Farrakhan also ordered that all members of the Nation learn how to do the orthodox "prostration prayer" and all mosques were required to institute the Friday Jum'ah prayer service.

On October 15, 2005, the tenth anniversary of the Million Man March, the Nation of Islam held the Millions More Movement in Washington, D.C. This event, which also attracted about 1 million black people, was more inclusive and politically focused. Besides women and families and representatives from disempowered racial minority groups, the coalition also included representatives from African American gay/lesbian groups. In his 75 minute speech, Minister Farrakhan criticized the Bush administration's mishandling of the Hurricane Katrina disaster in Louisiana and the disastrous war in Iraq. The Millions More Movement also issued a pamphlet listing its public policy initiatives and political direction.

After undergoing a 14-hour operation, dealing with severe infection of his lower intestines, in December 2006, Minister Farrakhan took a leave of absence in 2007. Since then, the daily operations of the Nation of Islam are in the hands of a selected leadership council.

Lawrence A. Mamiya

SELECTED BIBLIOGRAPHY

Ansari, Z. I. "Aspects of Black Muslim Theology," *Studia Islamica* 53 (1981).

Ansari, Z. I. "The Religious Doctrines of the Black Muslims of America, 1930–1980," *Journal of Islamic Social Sciences* 9 (1987).

Benyon, Erdmann D. "The Voodoo Cult among Negro Migrants in Detroit." *American Journal of Sociology* 43 (July 1937–May 1938).

Breitman, George, ed. *Malcolm X: The Man and His Ideas* (New York: Pathfinder, 1965).

Breitman, George, ed. *Malcolm X Speaks* (New York: Grove/Atlantic, Inc., 1969).

Breitman, George, ed. *By Any Means Necessary* (New York: Pathfinder, 1970).

Breitman, George, Herman Porter, Baxter Smith, and others. *The Assassination of Malcolm X* (New York: Pathfinder, 1991).

Breitman, George, Robert Vernon, and Jack Barnes. *The Last Year of Malcolm X* (New York: Pathfinder, 1997).

Clegg, Claude Andrew, III. *An Original Man: The Life and Times of Elijah Muhammad* (New York: St. Martin's Press, 1997).

Curtis, Edward E., III. *Islam in Black America: Identity, Liberation and Difference in African-American Islamic Thought* (New York: State University of New York Press, 1992).

Curtis, Edward E., III. *Black Muslim Religion in the Nation of Islam, 1960–1975* (Chapel Hill: University of North Carolina Press, 2006).

Essien-Udom, Essien U. *Black Nationalism: A Search for an Identity in America* (Chicago: University of Chicago Press, 1962).

Evanzz, Karl. *The Judas Factor: The Plot to Kill Malcolm X* (New York: Thunder's Mouth Press, 1992).

Evanzz, Karl. *The Messenger: The Rise and Fall of Elijah Muhammad* (New York: Pantheon Press, 1999).

Farrakhan, Louis. *Seven Speeches by Minister Louis Farrakhan* (Harlem, NY: Ministry Class, Muhammad's Temple No. 7, 1974.

Farrakhan, Louis. *A Torchlight for America* (Chicago: FCN Publishing, 1993).

Gardell, Mattias. *In the Name of Elijah Muhammad: Louis Farrakhan and the Nation of Islam* (Durham, NC: Duke University Press, 1996).

Goldman, Peter. *The Death and Life of Malcolm X* (Champaign: University of Illinois Press, 1979).

Gomez, Michael. *Black Crescent: The Experience and Legacy of African Muslims in the Americas* (Cambridge, U.K.: Cambridge University Press, 2005).

Lee, Martha F. *The Nation of Islam: An American Millenarian Movement* (Lewiston, NY: Edwin Mellen Press, 1988).

Lincoln, C. Eric. *The Black Muslims in America* (Boston: Beacon Press, 1994 edition of the 1961 publication).

Lincoln, C. Eric. "The American Muslim Mission in the Context of American Social History." *The Muslim Community in North America*, ed. Earle H. Waugh, Baha Abu-Laban, and Regula B. Qureshi (Edmonton, AB, Canada: University of Alberta Press, 1983).

Lincoln, C. Eric, and Lawrence Mamiya. Interview with Minister Louis Farrakhan at his home in Hyde Park, Chicago, October 2, 1992.

Lincoln, C. Eric, and Lawrence Mamiya. Interview with Minister Ava Muhammad at Mosque Maryam, Southside Chicago, August 21, 1993.

Lomax, Louis. *When the Word Is Given* (New York: Signet Books, 1963).

Malcolm X and Alex Haley. *The Autobiography of Malcolm X* (New York: Random House, 1999 edition of the 1965 publication).

Mamiya, Lawrence H. "From Black Muslim to Bilalian: The Evolution of A Movement." *Journal for the Scientific Study of Religion* 21, no. 2 (1982): 138–152. Reprinted in *Islam in North America: A Sourcebook*, ed. Michael A. Koszegi and J. Gordon Melton (New York and London: Garland Publishing Co., 1992), 165–182.

Mamiya, Lawrence H. "Minister Louis Farrakhan and the Final Call: Schism in the Muslim Movement." *The Muslim Community in North America*, ed. Earle H. Waugh, Baha Abu-Laban, and Regula B. Qureshi (Edmonton, AB, Canada: University of Alberta Press, 1983).

Mamiya, Lawrence H. "Minister Louis Farrakhan and the Nation of Islam." *Contemporary Black Leaders*, ed. David DeLeon (Washington, D.C.: Howard University Press, 1994).

Mamiya, Lawrence H. Interview with Minister Louis Farrakhan at the Marriott Hotel in Washington, DC, June 7, 2006.

Muhammad, Elijah. *Message to the Blackman* (Chicago: Muhammad's Temple No. 2, 1965).

Muhammad, Elijah. *How to Eat to Live* (Chicago: Muhammad's Temple No. 2, 1967).

Muhammad, Elijah. *The Fall of America* (Chicago: Muhammad's Temple No. 2, 1973).

Muhammad, Elijah. *Our Saviour Has Arrived* (Chicago: Muhammad's Temple No. 2, 1974).

Muhammad, Elijah, with Abass Rassoul, ed. *The Theology of Time* (U.B. and U.S. Communications Systems, 1992).

Toure, Muhammad. *Chronology of the Nation of Islam History: Highlights of the Honorable Minister Louis Farrakhan and the Nation of Islam from 1977–1996*. Edition One. (Toure Muhammad and Steal Away Creations, November 1996).

Turner, Richard. *Islam in the African American Experience* (Bloomington: Indiana University Press, 1997).

NATIONAL BAPTIST CONVENTION OF AMERICA, INC.

Historical Development

The National Baptist Convention of America, originally called the National Baptist Convention, Unincorporated, was formed in 1915. This organization, developed because of disagreement over the Convention's publishing house, was the principle product of the second major split (the first was the Lott Carey split in 1897) within the National Baptist Convention, Inc.

Prior to 1915, the National Convention Publishing Board had been led by Richard H. Boyd, along the lines of a Booker T. Washington self-help approach to advancement and productivity. Having conceived the nature and function of the publishing board in 1896, Boyd held firmly to the idea that African Americans had to help themselves by way of self-produced economic opportunity and growth. The overall importance of the National Baptist Publishing Board to the National Baptist Convention as well as to the broader African American community during that time cannot be overstated. In 1905, with plans to solidify its publishing arm underway, the Convention sought to separate the management for Home Mission Board and the Publishing Board, with little support from the auxiliary boards. By 1906, the National Baptist Publishing Board had become the premier African American publisher in the United States. As a major provider of church-related materials they supplied books, pamphlets, booklets, and Sunday school materials. What is more, they utilized the most modern equipment among black publishers of the day. In fact, given their advanced business practices and largely good standing with the broader black community under Boyd's leadership, the National Baptist Publishing Board became in large part an umbrella organization for other black businesses in Nashville, its headquarters, such as the production of furniture. The growing success and diverse activities of the Publishing Board fueled growing tensions from within the National Baptist Convention regarding its aim and direction under Boyd's leadership.

Seeds of discord were evident by 1914, as rebellion against the separate management requirement of 1905 continued and caused the Convention to consider a new direction regarding this matter. Boyd's independent business style ultimately led to consternation among those within the National Baptist Convention leadership. Boyd's belief in cooperation with white Baptists, such as James M. Frost of the Sunday School Board of the Southern Baptist Convention, concerned several members of the convention. Boyd's simple premise for this cooperation was that such a partnership had to be based on equality rather than dependence. Even with the concerns from convention leadership at play, Boyd argued that the publishing board's affiliation with the national convention did not mean that the latter had full authority over the actions of the publishing board's activities. Connected to the resentment was the significant issue, and point of dispute for the NBC leaders and pastors, of the receipt of reports from the Publishing Board. Ultimately a debate ensued concerning the ownership of the Publishing Board. During this time the convention's publishing board became the largest black-owned publishing enterprise in the United States.

The central players within this dispute and 1915 court case were R. H. Boyd and E. C. Morris, the president of the National Baptist Convention (NBC). Morris was concerned with the depth and breadth of Boyd's influence over the Publishing Board. Accordingly, Morris and his supporters demanded Boyd produce all financial records demonstrating that funds were being used appropriately. This demand prompted leaders within the convention to form two factions, one pro-Morris and one pro-Boyd. The result was a complete split, supporters of Boyd and his position

---

RICHARD HENRY BOYD (1843–1922)

Richard H. Boyd was born a slave and attempted various occupations before finding his place in ministry. In 1897 Boyd founded the Publishing Board, which was then associated with the National Baptist Convention, USA, Inc. In addition to the Publishing Board, he was instrumental in the development of other businesses, such as a doll-making company and a bank. Through Boyd's efforts, the Publishing Board saw many successes, including the publishing of its own materials. Boyd's full control over the Publishing Board was a concern for the leaders of the convention and ultimately led to the formation of the National Baptist Convention of America, where Boyd moved the Publishing Board.

regarding the possibilities that would come from an independent publishing board not controlled by the convention formed the National Baptist Convention of America (NBCA) at the Salem Baptist Church in Chicago. It was initially known as the unincorporated convention.

By 1917, a constitution of the new convention was adopted. Those who remained with the Morris faction retained the original name. In response to the question of incorporation, those leaders remaining a part of the original convention endeavored to incorporate and thus became the National Baptist Convention, USA, Inc. (see entry "National Baptist Convention, USA, Inc."). The unincorporated National Baptist Convention of America would remain so (in name) for some time. Early efforts to solidify the new convention can be seen in their drawing an agreement in 1924 between themselves and Lott Carey regarding missions. Ultimately, in 1928 the new Convention incorporated its Foreign Missions Board, Baptist Young People's Union, and Sunday School Publishing Board. In 1987 the National Baptist Convention of America was incorporated in Shreveport, Louisiana, becoming the National Baptist Convention of America, Inc. The National Baptist Convention of America, Inc. does not have a centralized national headquarters, but the publishing house is in Nashville. In 1988 the National Baptist Convention of America, Inc. voted to operate its own National Congress.

The organizational structure of the unincorporated convention was similar to that of the National Baptist Convention, USA, Inc. The current organizational structure is composed of 16 national officers. The major offices are that of the president, three vice presidents, and a series of associate vice presidents, functioning as state leaders and moderators of general associations on the state level. There are seven program boards overseeing missions, publications, evangelism, youth issues, and charitable concerns. Additional auxiliary units such as the Woman's Missionary and Junior Woman's auxiliaries and the Nurse's Corps along with commissions on Christian education and social justice added to the variety of service and ministry efforts of the NBCA. The Lott Carey Baptist Foreign Mission Convention eventually became the foreign mission wing of the National Baptist Convention of America, Inc. It supports missions in the Caribbean, the Virgin Islands, Panama, Haiti, and Ghana in West Africa.

To uplift African American communities, the National Baptist Convention of America, Inc., in conjunction with the National Baptist Convention, USA, Inc., made commitments to the economic welfare of African Americans by means of the formation of the Minority Enterprise Financial Acquisition Corp. Through this initiative both organizations sought to secure financial assistance for the building of low-income housing. By way of these and other efforts, the NBCA seeks to remain involved in the social concerns of black Americans. Of the three major African American Baptist conventions—the National Baptist Convention, USA, Inc. and the Progressive National Baptist Convention, Inc. (formed in 1961)—the NBCA boasts the second largest membership. Part of their growth is attributed to its long-standing commitment to education and diverse ministries.

Beliefs and Practices

As is the case for most of the black denominations, the National Baptist

Convention of America holds to a creed that is Bible-based, drawing its major theological points from the Bible— understood as the word of God, written by humans through divine inspiration and guidance. It holds to a typical Trinitarian view whereby it is understand that God exists in three related and dependent realities—God, Jesus Christ, and the Holy Spirit. God "the Father" is the creator of all things and giver of life. Jesus Christ is understood and accepted as the Son of God and is in essence equal with God the Father. They believe that while on earth Jesus lived a sinless life. According to God the Father's plan for humanity, Jesus offered himself as the perfect and once-and-for-all atonement for the sins of all people through his sacrificial death on the cross. Thereafter, Jesus arose from the dead after three days, possessing all power and authority over sin and death. Jesus ascended to heaven and will ultimately return again to earth to reign as Lord of all humankind. The Holy Spirit is also equal in essence with the other members of the Trinity, yet with a distinct role in relation to believers. The Holy Spirit is present in the world to make believers aware of their need for Jesus Christ and make clearer the precepts of God in the Holy Scriptures. The Holy Spirit also provides the Christian with power for living, understanding of spiritual truth, and guidance in doing what is right. The Christian, in turn, is daily and willingly controlled by the Holy Spirit.

Humans, by way of their special creation have a unique relationship to God in that they bear in their being the image of God. Hence, humans are the paramount and supreme object of God's creations. Although humanity has the potential for good, humans are flawed with proclivity toward disobedience to God, or sin. Humanity was created to exist forever, but only those who accept Jesus Christ as personal savior will livet with God in Heaven. Because God gives humanity eternal life through Jesus Christ, and a proper relationship with God is maintained by the grace and power of God, not through any self-effort of the Christian, those who reject Christ will experience Hell.

Derek S. Hicks

SELECTED BIBLIOGRAPHY

Lincoln, C. Eric, and Lawrence H. Mamiya. *The Black Church in the African American Experience* (Durham, NC: Duke University Press, 1990).

Lovett, Bobby L. *A Black Man's Dream: The First One Hundred Years, Richard Boyd and the National Baptist Publishing Board* (Jackson, NC: Mega Corporation, 1993).

Pinn, Anthony B. *The Black Church in the Post-Civil Rights Era* (Maryknoll, NY: Orbis Books, 2002).

Pinn, Anne H., and Anthony B. Pinn. *Fortress Introduction to Black Church History* (Minneapolis: Fortress Press, 2002).

NATIONAL BAPTIST CONVENTION, USA, INC.

Historical Development

The National Baptist Convention, USA, Inc. was established in 1895 and is the second largest Baptist organization in the United States, second only to the Southern Baptist Convention. This organization came into existence after the merger of the Foreign Mission

Baptist Convention (organized in 1880), the American National Baptist Convention (organized in 1886), and the Baptist National Education Convention (organized in 1893). Estimates are that over 41,000 churches with over 8 million members comprise the National Baptist Convention, USA, Inc.

During the antebellum period, several Protestant denominations sought to evangelize and convert slaves to Christianity. Within such an endeavor, Baptists made concerted efforts to convert slaves, though mostly as second-class church members, to their faith and churches. Often slaves were compelled, if not mandated, to sit in slave galleries—often in the balcony—or other designated areas during worship. In some plantation churches the slaves would be offered a separate "sermon" through which their servitude was justified and the superiority of whites was championed. Black plantation preachers were sometimes used alongside white evangelical counterparts as exhorters, but their conversation and preaching was monitored in an attempt to make certain they did not counter efforts to use religion to justify and reenforce the slave system.

Increasingly, slaves sought independent religious experience within the Baptist tradition to exercise faith and religiosity. Outside the Deep South, black Baptist churches began to emerge in Virginia as early as 1774; Massachusetts around 1805; Pennsylvania in 1809; New Jersey in 1812; Manhattan in 1809; and Brooklyn in 1847. Within these developing churches slaves could more freely express themselves. However, this situation was not without its problems in that white slave owners and religious leaders expressed concern over autonomous meetings of slaves, fearing

that such meetings had the potential of inciting insurrections.

Among the several notable early black Baptist leaders were David George (1742–1810) and George Liele (1750–1820). Liele was ordained as a minister to the slaves and was instrumental in the conversion of George. Liele also began mission work in Jamaica, becoming one of the first African Americans in the mission field. Both men were principle figures in the founding of the Silver Bluff Baptist Church in South Carolina between 1773 and 1775, often viewed today as the first African American Baptist church in the United States. African American Baptist churches were also established in the North. Notable among these early congregations are Joy Street Baptist Church (Boston, 1804), the Abyssinian Baptist Church (New York City, 1808), and the African Baptist Church (Philadelphia, 1809). While these churches were autonomous, without obligations beyond the needs and concerns of the particular congregation, they recognized the benefits of collaboration. This connection across a geographical area took the form of associations by which congregations were able to pool resources, etc., to address commonly held concerns and issues such as abolition and mission work (both domestic and foreign). With time more local groupings of churches would give way to collective extending beyond narrow geography to include state conventions and national conventions.

Many black Baptists during the 1800s worked with white Baptist organizations through what was known as the African Baptist Missionary Society. This subordinate organization initially existed under the patronage of the American Baptist Union. The primary efforts of this

Society were to send missionaries to Africa. The earliest of the all-black Baptist associations were organized in the Midwest: Providence Association (Ohio, 1834); Union Association (Ohio, 1836); Wood River Association (Illinois, 1839); and the Amherstburg Association (Canada and Michigan, 1841). As early as 1840, black Baptists endeavored to develop a cooperative movement beyond state lines. For example, Baptists in New York and the Middle Atlantic states formed the American Baptist Missionary Convention. In 1864 the black Baptists in the Western and Southern territories founded the Northwestern Baptist Convention and the Southern Baptist Convention. In 1866, these two conventions held a meeting with the American Baptist Convention and formed the Consolidated American Baptist Convention. Perhaps the most significant accomplishment of the Consolidated American Baptist Convention was the support it offered black Baptists in the South to form their own state conventions. Post-emancipation black Baptists in the South, some with the support of the Consolidated Convention, were able to form state conventions in Alabama, North Carolina, Virginia, Arkansas, and Kentucky. Yet, despite the groundbreaking efforts and early success of the consolidated convention, regionalism and fragmentation emerging through conflict over resources and convention agendas continued among black Baptists. In 1873 black Baptists in the Western regions formed the General Association of the Western States and Territories, and in 1874 the individual Eastern groups organized the New England Baptist Missionary Convention. Continued regionalism and other factors brought about the eventual decline and

demise of the Consolidated American Baptist Missionary Convention.

The National Baptist Convention, not officially founded until 1895, was made up of representative delegates from three separate African American organizations: the Baptist Foreign Mission Convention (1880), the American National Baptist Convention (1886), and the National Baptist Educational Convention (1893). The formation of the Foreign Mission Convention was partly a result of the demise of the Consolidated Convention. Its death adversely affected efforts in the mission field, especially for African missions. This loss of production prompted Rev. William W. Colley, a missionary to Africa under the Foreign Mission Board of the Southern Baptist Convention, to issue a decree for black Baptists to meet in Montgomery, Alabama. In the initial meeting, convened by Rev. Colley, approximately 150 Baptist pastors and delegates from 11 states met in Montgomery, Alabama, on November 24, 1880, and formed the Baptist Foreign Mission Convention. Originally headquartered in Richmond, Rev. Colley served as the corresponding secretary. The purpose of this meeting was to organize a national convention to do extensive foreign missionary work. Accordingly, the major thrusts of this convention were to discuss the trajectory of planned mission work in Africa and domestic social issues such as the use of tobacco and alcohol. While this convention had connections with white Baptists, this relationship was far from ideal and at points problematic. However, some African American Baptist leaders still held out hope that working across racial lines would be fruitful. Most others simply sought independent black autonomy in conventional affairs. Both sides were represented at the 1880 convention. The result was rather large-scale infighting as well as the eventual formation of the American National Baptist Convention in 1886.

With Rev. William J. Simmons leading the formation and serving as its president, the American National Baptist Convention convened on August 25, 1886, the second of these important early groups. The paramount objective at this meeting was to unify the church regarding pressing racial issues. This meeting was made up of 600 delegates from churches in 17 states convened in St. Louis. Claiming over 1 million constituents from some 9,000 churches and 4,500 ministers, this convention represented their significant efforts to create a black Baptist denomination. Such an endeavor was pursued in spite of Northern white Baptist resistance.

The third convention, held in 1893 and led by Rev. W. Bishop Johnson of Washington, D.C., sought as its primary goal to address the issue of educating and training black clergy and missionaries. Ultimately, they desired to develop an educational framework of comprehensive formal education and training of black clergy who would normally be denied such opportunities because of racism. Moreover, they felt it necessary for trained black clergy to be capable of leading Baptists in the achievement of an agenda that primarily included the important component of uplifting the black race. Johnson was also a leading figure in the formation of the National Baptist Convention. At the 1894 annual meeting of these various organizational bodies in Montgomery, a motion was cast proposing the merger of the three separate groups into one convention. Thereafter a joint committee was appointed to report on the viability of

such a plan the following year. The year 1894 also saw the establishment and initial publication of the *National Baptist Magazine*.

With the desire to have the convention remain viable, this movement officially came into being on September 24, 1895, at the Friendship Baptist Church in Atlanta, when the merger was finalized and these three conventions came together to form the National Baptist Convention of the United States of America. As part of the merger, it was noted that the three former conventions would serve as subsidiary boards of the convention: Foreign Missions (in the form of the National Baptist Foreign Mission Board), Home Missions, and Education. The Reverend E. C. Morris was elected president and presided for 27 years.

His tenure was important for laying the foundation of the Convention. Beyond the significance of the general growth of the organization, his presidency brought with it significant accomplishments: one example was the formation of the National Baptist Publishing House in Nashville, Tennessee. One of the motivating factors for the formation of the National Baptist Convention was the desire of blacks to publish literature written by their own ministers. The American Baptist Publication Society had refused to publish writings by black ministers due to vigorous resistance from its Southern clients. Richard Boyd was called upon to give leadership to the National Baptist Publishing House. One of its principle roles was to supply National Baptist churches with all of their church and Sunday School supplies. Within a reasonably short amount of time this publishing house was the world's largest black publisher of any print material. With regard to its early

SUTTON ELBERT GRIGGS (1872–1933)

Best known as a Baptist minister and social activist, Griggs was born in Texas and attended Richmond Theological Seminary in Virginia. He entered the pastorate in 1893, serving in both Virginia and Tennessee. He is known for his novel *Imperium in Imperio*, which was published in 1899. This work advanced an idea of a utopian African American state within the United States and was considered one of the first protest novels written by an African American. Other protest novels, *The Hindered Hand* and *The Klansman* in 1905 and later *One Great Question: A Study of Southern Conditions at Close Range*, followed this work. Through his social concerns he became involved with W. E. B. DuBois and the Niagara Movement.

formation, many consider Morris's 27 years of leadership the most important period for the Convention.

Despite the positive accomplishments during his tenure as head of the Convention, Morris's presidency saw two major splits. In 1897, the Lott Carey Baptist Home and Foreign Mission Convention was formed by a group of National Baptist pastors who left the existing convention. The initial president of this newly constructed convention was C. S. Brown. This abrupt separation was centered on two issues: the location of the foreign mission board and collaborative efforts with white Baptists. That year Convention members demanded complete separation from Northern Baptist Societies. With respect to the former, the prominent issue centered on loyalties to the old Foreign

Mission Convention, which had been based in Richmond (as had the African Baptist Missionary Society). A plan was underway to relocate the Foreign Mission Board's headquarters from Richmond to Louisville. Added to this, resentment grew toward the publishing board's activities within the new convention, which, as a result, adversely affected the relations of the Richmond group with other local white Baptist organizations.

Those interested in cooperation with whites argued that this proposed move, in conjunction with separatist publication efforts, would be a destructive and counterproductive maneuver away from white Baptists. This move would thus significantly affect their joint mission and educational efforts. In addition, it was believed that such a move would

ELIAS CAMP MORRIS (1855–1922)

From Georgia and born into slavery, Morris was ordained into the Christian ministry at 19 years of age. He was pastor of Centennial Baptist Church in Arkansas for his entire ministerial career. Early in his career as pastor he was elected secretary of the state convention and rapidly moved through the ranks. He was later elected president of the state convention and helped found Arkansas Baptist College. His notoriety outside of the state of Arkansas led to him being elected president of the National Baptist Convention after it merged with the American National Baptist convention and two other organizations.

hamper the National Baptist Convention's efforts to generate the necessary income to achieve its lofty missionary goals. Further, they saw cooperation with white Baptists a sign of necessary gratitude for early white support. The Lott Carey withdrawal contingent was made up of better educated members and delegates from North Carolina, Virginia, and Washington, D.C. Accordingly, issues of class and differing ideology, which had long plagued the movement toward denominational independence, resurfaced. Among this period's continued accomplishments during this time, in 1899 the National Baptist Young Peoples Union organized.

In 1905 the Lott Carey Convention and the National Baptist Convention made new efforts to form a partnership. Formed in accordance with an understanding based upon a previously submitted proposal, the two conventions opened up dialogue regarding concessions. The pressing concern, advanced by C. S. Brown, was the readjustment of the foreign mission endeavors so that they reflected cooperation between both sides. Moreover, he requested that each side refrain from unwarranted attacks between officers' permission regarding the use of materials from either publishing house for Sunday School classes. While resulting cooperation was gained by these attempts, efforts to officially unite the two ultimately failed. Thereafter these two entities remained separately functioning bodies, though several of their members and officers would have dual membership. This set of circumstances was followed by two additional prominent schisms—in 1915 and 1961—within the National Baptist Convention.

The seeds for the next split were planted in 1897 with the internal debates over the publishing board. Before the second schism the National Baptist Convention had roughly 3 million members and some 20,000 affiliated churches. However, even after these splits, the National Baptist Convention, USA, Inc. remained the major black Baptist convention. Disagreements over the ownership and operation of the Publishing Board, also incorporated in 1897, prompted the second major split that came in 1915. Of all of the agencies of the convention, the Publishing Board, under the leadership of R. H. Boyd, was the most successful. Among the Publishing Board's various projects, in 1908 they began building church furniture. The following year the Publishing Board would develop the National Baptist Teacher-Training Service. Leaders and pastors of the convention became suspicious of the Publishing Board's actions when they did not receive anticipated reports on the Board's activities and financial gains. The ensuing debate regarding the ownership of the Publishing Board pushed Boyd's supporters, most of whom agreed with his view that the Board was independent of the convention, to form the National Baptist Convention of America (see entry "National Baptist Convention of America"). This group would become known as the unincorporated convention.

Fueled by a question and resulting debate over incorporation, those leaders remaining in the original convention moved to incorporate it. The constitution was amended in 1916 and the original convention was later incorporated, naming itself the National Baptist Convention, USA, Inc. Also as a result of this split, other boards within the original convention became subordinate to the convention. The Reverend E. C. Morris, who had been initially elected president when the National Baptist Convention was created in 1895, was allowed to continue in that role with the incorporated body until 1922. In addition, following the events of 1915, the convention created a new board—the Sunday School Publishing Board of the National Baptist Convention. However, it was the Foreign Mission Board that replaced publishing as the central and galvanizing concern of the convention's operations.

At this juncture the original convention devoted itself even more to domestic concerns. From Reconstruction through World War I, the National Baptist Convention had already advocated self-sufficiency among African Americans. Ministers from among the convention's fold encouraged high levels of education, temperance, and other forms of social respectability. Their goal was to make thoroughgoing efforts at securing for themselves a greater role in the life of the nation. Accordingly, they ventured to show other institutions, such as banks and major businesses, that the Black Church should be considered a viable starting point and source of support for their ventures. Convention president Morris argued that the church was the very centerpiece of the African American community; which, as a result, would instill blacks with the necessary moral fiber and social adeptness to function as productive members of society. He reasoned then that African American Christians, by way of positive example, would inspire white Americans to act with more tolerance and fairness, reducing levels and social maltreatment. What is more, the National Baptist Convention in the first decades of the new century initiated campaigns against racial violence and segregation in public buildings,

establishments, and schools. The basis for such campaigns was the notion of self-help, based on the ideology and programs of Booker T. Washington.

E. C. Morris was succeeded by W. G. Parks who served only one year as president before L. K. Williams gained office in 1924. L. K. Williams served until 1940. Several notable accomplishments were made during his 16 years, including the establishment of a Laymen's Department. He was chiefly concerned with the issue of a publishing board. Williams offered the role of General Secretary of the Board to L. G. Jordan. Upon laying plans for a new building in Nashville, which opened in 1925, paying honor to the Convention's influential and arguably its most important early leader, this new building was named the Morris Building. In 1939 Dr. Williams gave a speech at the World's Fair in New York.

Following Williams as president was David V. Jemison who served from 1940 to 1953. Under his leadership the Convention was able to pay off the mortgage on the Morris Memorial Building. In addition, they were able to purchase a building that would eventually become the National Baptist Bath House in Hot Springs, Arkansas. This establishment would offer African Americans vacation opportunities long denied them in the highly segregated South.

Joseph H. Jackson of Chicago became President of the Convention in 1953. Jackson's presidential tenure spanned the longest of any Convention head, from 1953 to 1982. At the beginning of Jackson's presidency the National Baptist Convention had nine boards and commissions. During his tenure the Convention moved from nine boards and commissions, whose responsibilities included internal operations, foreign operations, and domestic concerns, to 22 such divisions. Each board included a representative from each state in conjunction with eight at-large members. Such a board was free to develop its agenda and all necessary regulations to accomplish the goals set out on the agenda. In addition, he purchased the National Baptist Freedom Farm and set up an unrestricted scholarship at Roosevelt University.

It was during the time of Jackson's leadership that a third major conventional split occurred. In 1956 a symposium titled "National Baptists Facing Integration: Shall Gradualism Be Applied?" was held to discuss the best approach to social transformation. The issues of social transformation and civil rights represented one side of two

significant issues fueling conventional disputes, the other was the question of tenure. Ultimately, this split would ensue due to the lack of support of the Civil Rights Movement. As a result, advocate for black civil rights Dr. Gardner C. Taylor of New York made an unsuccessfully bid to challenge Jackson's presidency. After his unsuccessful election, a group of convention members, who were led by Dr. L. Venchael Booth, formed another new convention at the Zion Baptist Church, Cincinnati, Ohio. Formed in 1961, this new group called itself the Progressive National Baptist Convention (see entry "Progressive National Baptist Convention, Inc.").

In 1983 the leadership baton was passed to the pastor of Mount Zion First Baptist

Nannie Helen Burroughs holds the banner of the Women's Convention of the National Baptist Convention, 1900. (Library of Congress)

Church in Baton Rouge, Louisiana, the Reverend T. J. Jemison. Jemison served as president for 12 years. His notable development was the building of the Baptist World Center. This project was projected to cost over $12 million, and eventually functioned as the headquarters of the Convention.

The Jemison presidency ended in 1994 and Henry Lyons of Florida was elected the new president. Lyons's time as president was a productive one. Under his leadership the Convention experienced a reduction in the debt on the Baptist World Center and dissolved the debt on the Sunday School Publishing Board. In addition, several commissions were added to the convention. Lyons was compelled to resign from the presidency due to legal issues. Specifically, Lyons was forced to step down due to financial mismanagement of convention funds, which resulted in a jail sentence for his actions. Serving out the remainder of Lyons's tenure was Dr. S. C. Cureton, the vice president-at-large.

William J. Shaw, pastor of the White Rock Baptist Church of Philadelphia, Pennsylvania, became the Convention's president in 1999 and currently serves in that role. A new motto and theme was introduced that marks the nature of his presidency. This theme is termed VISA: *V*ision, *I*ntegrity, *S*tructure, and *A*ccountability. Shaw works to reestablish integrity and credibility in the Convention, and to make the Convention a leader for black people in the nation. In recent years, the Convention has made a major commitment to the economic welfare of African Americans through the formation of the Minority Enterprise Financial Acquisition Corp., which aids with financial assistance for the building of low-income housing.

Baptist as well as Methodist denominations shared a common struggle with the acknowledgment of women and the importance of their contributions to religious life. Spawned by gender conflicts existent within the National Baptist Convention, USA, Inc., the Woman's Convention, defined as an auxiliary, encouraged and sought sisterhood among the many female supporters of the Convention and the Baptist tradition in general. Since its inception the Convention sought to give voice to the issues of both black men and women. Yet, it did not encourage expression from men and women as social equals. Accordingly, the Convention's structure was decidedly masculine, which was most noticeable in its institutional structure. Whereas

---

NANNIE HELEN BURROUGHS (1878–1961)

Born in Virginia but raised in Washington, D.C., Burroughs moved to Kentucky in 1900 and worked as a secretary for the Foreign Mission Board of National Baptist Convention. Within this role, she taught several courses on domestic issues, notably concerning women. Ultimately she would help develop the Woman's Industrial Club, an organization that helped to feed African Americans in Louisville. In addition to this work, Burroughs helped in founding the Woman's Convention in 1900, appearing as its initial corresponding secretary, and playing an important role in its development. She was also an active and highly sought after lecturer.

Methodist churches eventually made noticeable strides toward recognition of women, Baptist denominations did not. While since the 1970s female ministerial leadership has increased, general tolerance and acceptance for women and their contributions remain lacking. Yet, without the work of black women within the Convention in the areas of fund-raising, missionary work, women's conventions and clubs, and many other duties necessary for keeping the church together and thriving, the Convention would have had a far more difficult time meeting the needs of the African American community.

The Women's Convention of the National Baptist Convention was formed in 1900 principally through the efforts Nannie Helen Burroughs as well as a host of others. Existing under the umbrella of the National Baptist Convention, its membership essentially belonged to them. Accordingly, its annual meetings were held in conjunction with the Convention's. This organization was committed to issues both within and outside of the walls of the church. Many of these women gave speeches and lectures across the country, outlining high moral and ethical standards necessary for the uplifting of the black race. They also considered women as holders of the keys to social transformation, with the United States as its massive mission field.

Beliefs and Practices

The National Baptist Convention, USA, Inc. ascribes to Articles of Faith, which are to be adopted by any Baptist church seeking affiliation at the time of organization. The core of these articles begins with the Bible. In this regard the Convention holds that the Bible was written by humans who were divinely inspired, and it is perfect and without error. Further, it, the Bible, sets the standard by which all human conduct, creeds, and opinions are measured. Drawing upon Scripture the Convention's doctrine of God holds that there is but one living and true God, who is an infinite, intelligent Spirit, and is the creator and Supreme Ruler of heaven and earth. Following the theological doctrine of the trinity, the Convention holds that in the unity of the Godhead there are three equal persons—the Father, the Son, and the Holy Ghost.

The Convention also believes in the fall of humankind precipitated by Adam and Eve's original sin and the resulting need for salvation through the Son of God, Jesus Christ, the second entity within the trinity. They believe, then, that Jesus came to earth, died on the cross, conquered sin and death, sits at the right hand of God the Father, and functions currently as mediator on behalf of all who believe. It follows that, upon placing faith in Christ, the believer is justified—that is, declared righteous by God—through their faith. Consequently, salvation is understood to be a free gift of God granted by way of faith and trust in Jesus Christ as personal Lord and Savior. Through faith, the believer is regenerated, or "born again." The Convention holds that Jesus Christ will return again and will judge unbelievers and reward those who have been faithful to his teachings.

The Holy Spirit functions as guide and as an aid in the perfecting of one's faith. With regard to living one's faith within the world, the process of one becoming perfected in Christ is the process of sanctification. Through this process believers partake in God's holiness, which is a progressive work. This work is begun at regeneration and continues throughout the Christian pilgrimage. Sanctification is facilitated through self-examination and reflection, prayer, and the work of the Holy Spirit.

The church of Christ is a congregation of baptized believers who are bonded by a common faith in God through Christ. The church functions as a community that encourages faith and common experience. Baptism, through immersion in water, is a sign of this common belief to the world. Baptism thus functions as an emblem of faith. As a privilege of shared faith, the church is granted the opportunity to remember and reflect upon the death, burial, and resurrection of the Savior, Jesus Christ, through the ritual of the Lord's Supper (communion). Through the Lord's Supper the members of the church, by the sacred use of bread and wine, are to commemorate together the dying love of Christ, preceded by solemn self-examination.

Derek S. Hicks

SELECTED BIBLIOGRAPHY

Higginbotham, Evelyn Brooks. *Righteous Discontent: The Women's Movement in the Black Baptist Church 1880–1920* (Cambridge, MA: Harvard University Press, 1993).

Leonard, Bill J. *Baptists in America* (New York: Columbia University Press, 2005).

Lincoln, C. Eric, and Lawrence H. Mamiya. *The Black Church in the African American Experience* (Durham, NC: Duke University Press, 1990).

Pinn, Anne H., and Anthony B. Pinn. *Fortress Introduction to Black Church History* (Minneapolis: Fortress Press, 2002).

Pinn, Anthony B. *The Black Church in the Post-Civil Rights Era* (Maryknoll, NY: Orbis Books, 2002).

NEW AGE MOVEMENT

Historical Development

The very term *New Age* is problematic, and defining it poses a number of challenges, from the chronology of the movement to its defining features. Is the New Age only an American phenomenon dating from the mid-twentieth century, or do its roots stretch back further, connecting it to other American and global traditions? Is the New Age limited to crystals, channeling, and UFOs, or does it include other alternative religious, spiritual, and medical practices? Is the term itself pejorative or a positive identifier? Part of the complexity is that, within the New Age itself (however defined), one finds individuals and groups that claim each of these positions, and more. This makes the New Age broader and more amorphous than what is normally understood as a religious movement or tradition: it has no founder, no set canon, no binding creed, and no core beliefs that can be identified as universally shared. Rather, it is an eclectic movement consisting of a loose collection of practices and practitioners, some of whom will adamantly insist they are part of a larger movement, while others will vehemently deny this, and some will ignore the issue entirely.

Importantly for this encyclopedia, the New Age is also a virtually exclusively Caucasian phenomenon: there are very few African American figures in its accepted histories, and while the number of African American practitioners (as well as that of other non-Caucasian groups) is growing, they still represent a significant minority in the movement as a whole. While the dominant explanation for this is a traditional, class-based analysis (that the New Age is a movement by the privileged for the privileged, requiring significant resources—both financial and in terms of leisure time—for participation), we believe the reality to be more complex than that—indeed, studies show that, while certainly not a "bottom-up" movement, the New Age is far more diverse in terms of its class composition than prior thought would indicate. In spite of the radically pluralistic and heterogeneous backdrop described above, it is possible both to discern common themes and practices that identify the New Age and to historically locate the movement. There is an emerging consensus that the New Age is the most recent manifestation of a distinct lineage of alternative Western religiosity, arriving in the New World with the first European settlements, and ultimately connecting with much older European esoteric and Hermetic movements.

In exploring this lineage, one might follow the American religious historian Catherine Albanese, for whom the New Age is merely the most recent manifestation of an enduring form of religious expression that she terms the "metaphysical," which Albanese argues represents a recurring and pervasive feature of the American religious landscape, appearing in elite and vernacular cultures alike. From its precolonial roots in European Hermetic and magical traditions, she traces metaphysical religion through early colonial America and the Revolutionary War era, from the nineteenth century to the Civil War and the following years, and finally to its twentieth-century reconfiguration as the New Age. This places the current New Age in a tradition that includes, among other movements, Freemasonry, Mormonism, the Shakers, Unitarianism, Mesmerism, Spiritualism, the Theosophical Society, New Thought, and Christian Science. With this wider lens in place, it becomes easier to observe the influence and impact of African Americans in the development of the New Age, beginning with the Africans brought to America through the slave trade of the seventeenth and eighteenth centuries. The interactions between the incredible diversity of African cultures and the emerging culture of White America have been treated from many perspectives. Some authors point to themes that will emerge as key to the New Age, specifically the relationship between humanity and the natural world, the presence and possibility of communion with spiritual guides and helpers, and the construction of a world where the sacred is infused into matter. Using these as a base, Albanese argues for the beginnings of a "revelation epistemology," where knowledge is passed through unseen methods (dreams, visions, etc.) for the spiritual health of an individual or community. Albanese continues her explorations of the interaction between African American religious expression and the American metaphysical up to the present day, highlighting the close connections between African American religious communities and the Spiritualist movement (where African Americans participated both as mediums and as spirits) and the activities of individual African Americans within metaphysical movements ranging from the Black Shaker Spiritualist Rebecca Cox Jackson (1795–1871) to the influence

Paschal Beverly Randolph (1825–1875) had on the Theosophical movement.

Shifting to more recent phenomenon, two leading scholars of the New Age, Wouter Hanegraaff and Steven Sutcliff, have identified two distinct streams within the New Age, one referring to a specific historical movement (the *Strict Sense New Age*) and the other to a larger, more varied movement (the *General Sense New Age*). The Strict Sense New Age refers to an Apocalyptic/Millennial movement that emerged in the 1940s and 1950s when a number of Anglo-American groups announced they were receiving messages from intelligent beings from other planets who were coming to bring a New Age to the peoples of the Earth. These groups believed there would be an apocalyptic catastrophe followed by a new era of spiritual evolution, peace, and prosperity with only those sharing such "New age" values surviving. Predominantly populated by White, middle-aged, and elderly adherents and characterized by a culture of austerity and traditional morality that emphasized community, service, and altruism, these groups also reflected a strong British influence. Of particular importance was Alice Bailey (1880–1949), an English Christian Theosophist who channeled "The Great Invocation." In the early 1960s some of these groups began to form utopian communities dedicated to awaiting the coming of the imminent New Age, the most famous and significant of which was the Findhorn Community in Scotland.

In response to the absence of an actual apocalypse, the Strict Sense New Age underwent a radical shift, internalizing the apocalyptic narrative and relocating the dramatic coming changes from the external world to the landscape of the psyche and spirit. Eileen Caddy, one of the founders of the Findhorn Community, declared in 1968 that rather than the New Age being brought about by intelligent beings in the near future, it would be activated through human psychological and spiritual growth in the present moment. Following this (that is, from the 1970s onwards) an understanding of the New Age as an exterior apocalypse in the physical world was superseded by an understanding of the New Age as a global transformation where an old, rationalistic, negative mind-set would be destroyed, paving the way for a radically new state of human consciousness—famously characterized as the "Age of Aquarius," a designation that was to gain widespread use in American popular culture. There was clear resonance with the emergent counterculture, which quickly adopted the expression "new age" into its ongoing discourse. The same year Findhorn was founded, Dick Price and Michael Murphy started Esalen in Big Sur, California, which would become a central location for the development of this more loosely defined "New Age."

Building on sociologist Colin Campbell's identification of the General Sense New Age as a "cultic milieu," Hanegraaff sees the New Age emerging when this cultic milieu becomes aware of itself as an invisible community of like-minded individuals aimed at widespread transformation. (Note that Campbell is not equating the New Age with the common associations of "cults"; rather, he is referring to a cultural underground consisting of unorthodox science, heterodox religion, alternative medicine, magic, and the occult.) Hence, it is not a singular unified movement but a broad, leaderless network sharing often overlapping visions of transformation and containing a bewildering array of diverse practices and beliefs. The General Sense New Age has a dominant American influence, from the metaphysical lineage traced above (particularly New Thought and Spiritualism) up to the more recent human potential and transpersonal psychology movements; additionally, the encounter with and subsequent assimilation and appropriation of Asian religions has been hugely significant. The General Sense New Age is often seen as being geographically centered in (although certainly not limited to) California, where the counterculture has perhaps taken root the deepest. Demographically, adherents tend to represent the upper-middle class, are mostly Caucasian, and tend to value emotional expressiveness, body awareness, and the belief that the transformation of the world can only come about as a result of individual transformation. Classic texts from across the decades include Ram Dass's *Be Here Now* (1971), David Spangler's *Revelation: The Birth of a New Age* (1976), Marilyn Ferguson's *The Aquarian Conspiracy: Personal and Social Transformation in the 1980's* (1979), Shirley MacLaine's *Out on a Limb* (1986), and James Redfield's, *The Celestine Prophecy* (1995).

Since its inception, the General Sense New Age has been the subject of much critique, most commonly targeting its focus on the individual (which is seen as a form of narcissism), its perceived apoliticism, its commercialism, its demographics, and its appropriation of various religious traditions (often seen as a form of religious and/or cultural colonialism). However, recent scholarship has defended the New Age from these claims; Albanese, for example, argues that

American religiosity—both mainstream and metaphysical—has *always* included a strong dose of syncretism. From a different perspective, British scholar Christopher Partridge argues that New Agers are deeply concerned with the search for and maintenance of community: where critics find individualism, self-indulgence, and appropriation; Partridge unearths the search for community, individual responsibility, and creative "bricolage."

While the New Age has drawn heavily on Native American and Asian religious resources, there has been an overall lack of interest in a similar assimilation of African or African American material. Additionally—and clearly related—there is a paucity of scholarly inquiry into the relevance of the New Age for African American religiosity. As an example, in British scholar Darren Kemp's recent extensive and interdisciplinary study of primary sources in both popular and academic literature on the New Age, there are *no* mentions of any links to African American culture. Additionally, even within those African American practices that can be seen as sympathetic to the concerns of the General Sense New Age, there is often a reluctance to identify with the New Age, largely due to its historically negative portrayal in the mainstream media. Still, the absence of explicit involvement between African American traditions and the New Age (which does have some notable exceptions, especially in discussions of Vodou and other "magical" traditions, and in research on specific individuals, such as John Patrick Deveney's biographical work on Paschal Beverly Randolph) may very well be the result of a lack of attention and insight, not because of a dearth of raw material.

Finally, because of its associations with commercialism and predominantly negative media attention, as well as to a growing desire among current New Agers to differentiate themselves from the previous generation, the term "New Age" itself has fallen out of favor. This is reflected in both the academic and commercial worlds: "alternative spirituality" is growing to be a preferred term in scholarship, and it is more common in bookstores to see sections marked as "Spirituality," "Holistic," or "Mind-Body-Sprit" than "New Age." At the same time, practices and themes associated with New Age are gaining both in their mainstream acceptance, and in their integration into existing social and religious structures (see, for example, the growing attention to "holistic" practices in mainstream medicine or the increasing use of Eastern meditation in various forms of Christian practice). From this perspective, there is certainly no evidence that the practices and concerns of the General Sense New Age are diminishing; indeed, if anything, the movements and practices that fall under the rubric of the New Age are growing and seem sure to influence the international religious landscape of the next century.

Beliefs and Practices

In examining the General Sense New Age, a number of shared characteristics emerge, among them the themes of a spirituality concentrated on the transformation of the self, a close integration with various psychological models, strong tendencies toward monism and/or pantheism, and a stress on an integrated, holistic view of the world and humanity's place in it. A common thread is the blurring of the boundaries between psychological and spiritual development and the replacement of religious salvation with personal growth and self-actualization. This leads to a sacralization of the Self, where it is seen not as the conventional individual ego, but rather as a type of inner divinity or deity, a Higher Self that is the source of all value and meaning. The goal of these "Self Spirituality" movements is to remove our identification with the egoic self and connect with higher and more sacred levels of this inner divinity. Similarly, a core mythology of the New Age is the journey of the Self through many incarnations toward increasing levels of spiritual knowledge. The physical world, then, is embraced as it serves as the physical manifestation of the opportunity for spiritual growth: the world is a school, and a single lifetime an opportunity for increasing one's spiritual knowledge and depth. Unlike its role in the Asian religions from which the concept is often appropriated, reincarnation is seen as positive, enabling additional learning and the chance of proceeding to the next level of spiritual maturity. Emerging from this, evolution and the related concepts of growth, change, and development are all metaphors central to the General Sense New Age, where they are seen as creative processes leading humanity toward greater and greater heights of potential and accomplishment.

In terms of ontology, the New Age tends to promote a basic Neoplatonic model of a hierarchical cosmos with a myriad number of spiritual beings existing on ascending planes of existence, each corresponding to progressively higher levels of spiritual development and culminating in an

270 I New Age Movement

impersonal monistic Absolute. (Across the New Age, there is quite a bit of flexibility in terms of how this Absolute is referenced and described: in general, New Agers are very accommodating in terms of language, allowing terms like "God," "Spirit," "Higher Power," etc., to coexist quite peacefully.) Pantheism, the concept that the Absolute is identical with the natural universe and Panentheism (the belief that the Absolute contains—but is not reducible to—the natural world) are also popular models. The most important point to note is that the New Age rejects dualistic and materialist ontologies in favor of unified, holistic, and interdependent visions. New Age practices encompass an incredibly wide range of activities, from aromatherapy to astral projection to channeling to various forms of "energy work" (Reiki healing practices, various Asian medical practices such as acupuncture, etc.); however, Hanegraaff has helpfully identified four major trends that may help identify at least the larger groupings: Channeling, Healing and Personal Growth, New Age Science, and New Age Neopaganism. Briefly, *Channeling* refers to various methods of communicating with other entities, usually either the spirits of the dead or beings from other dimensions and/or planets. Channeling is usually aimed either at personal communications for the development of the self or at the transmission of the knowledge crucial for the coming shift in consciousness. Three of the earliest and perhaps most well-known examples of New Age channeling are Jane Roberts's interactions with an extraterrestrial entity named "Seth," which began in 1963 and is collected in numerous books; J. Z. Knight's ongoing relationship with "Ramtha"; and Helen Schucman's

experiences in the mid-1960s that led to the dissemination of the highly popular *A Short Course in Miracles.*

Healing and Personal Growth may encompass the widest swathe of the General Sense New Age, including everything from energy work to forms of alternative medicine such as homeopathy and hypnotherapy to psychotherapeutic therapies such as psychosynthesis and transpersonal psychology. As such, a wide diversity of perspectives exist, but in general these practices are positioned as *against* modern Western medicine, which is seen as overly impersonal and invasive, and *for* a healing of the person as a holistic entity where psychological states and reactions are seen as being intimately tied to the physical manifestations of illness and disease. Additionally, there is a stress on healing as opposed to curing; on illness being seen as the result of an imbalance or a disharmony between mind, body, and spirit; on the potential meanings and lessons entwined with illnesses; and on the need for individuals to take responsibility for their own health.

The General Sense New Age has always paid close attention to emerging scientific knowledge, primarily in the areas of theoretical physics, evolutionary biology, and the mathematics of complexity, leading to *New Age Science,* which focuses on the creation of a bridge between the religious behavior of the New Age and science. The most common areas of focus are theoretical physics (see Fritjof Capra's *The Tao of Physics* [1975] as an early and influential example) and an emerging field of "holistic ecology" largely based on the ramifications of James Lovelock and Lynn Margulis's "Gaia Hypothesis" (see Lovelock's *Gaia: A New Look at Life on Earth* [1979]). While there are great debates as to the legitimacy of these claims—for some, New Age Science is simply a gross misunderstanding of *both* the scientific and religious content—the overall direction is clearly in sympathy with the General Sense New Age goals of holism and of the creation of a new, revolutionary paradigm for humanity.

Finally, some words need to be said about *Neopaganism* and its relationship to the General Sense New Age. In doing so, we are explicitly not referring either to the many historical movements that are also termed neopagan or to the various modern, revivalist movements centered around notions of racial purity that are sometimes grouped into that category; additionally, it must be noted that many members of the neopagan communities we *are* describing remain quite resistant to the term "New Age," and position themselves very explicitly as outside of the New Age umbrella. Defining neopaganism can be as tricky as defining the New Age itself; again we are reduced to identifying common threads that are *not* canonical or shared among all varieties of practice. These include a commitment to a deep relationship between humanity and the natural world, a belief in the divinity of the self, the practice and ritual use of magic, and an insistence on direct, unmediated experience of the divine through ritual and individual practice. Neopaganism is often associated with feminism and female-centered spirituality, although this is certainly not a ubiquitous feature. For more detailed explorations, see, among others, Starhawk's *The Spiral Dance: A Rebirth of the Ancient Religion of the Great Goddess* (1979), Janet and Stewart Farrar's *The Witches' Way: Principles, Rituals and Beliefs of Modern Witchcraft*

(1984), and Tanya Luhrmann's *Persuasions of the Witch's Craft* (1988). As a final note, remember that, in each of these four areas, you will find practitioners that embrace their inclusion under the New Age rubric as well as those that are, for a variety of reasons, vehemently opposed to it: these are intended solely as useful categories for exploration and analysis, as they may be applied across large groupings of heterogeneous beliefs and practices.

Some common characteristics that in many ways mirror the themes outlined above can be identified across the New Age. First, the General Sense New Age tends to be highly *individualistic and experiential*, where each person is seen as the highest authority for him/herself and as the final arbiter of truth: personal experience is valued more than tradition or dogma. Second, New Age practice tends, at least on the surface, to embrace a *democratic* position that rejects, or, at a minimum, is highly suspicious of, various forms of authority; and most New Age practice claims to be open to all individuals, regardless of their social identity. Third, New Age practice tends toward the *relativistic*, where different approaches are seen as not being exclusionary and where different claims about reality are seen as "different," and not "better or worse." This relativism legitimates the incredible diversity and *syncretic/eclectic* nature of the New Age, whereby elements from widely disparate traditions may be combined into new and innovative forms of spiritual activity. This has lead to the New Age being referred to as "supermarket spirituality," a normally pejorative term where religious consumers are seen as picking and choosing from a wide range of religious commodities. Finally, this eclecticism exists hand in hand with *perennialism*, where all spiritual activity is seen as leading to or as a manifestation of a common sacred Absolute. This allows the different practices—meditation, ecstatic dance, psychotherapies, shamanic ritual, etc.—to support each other in an interconnected network: metaphors of different paths leading to the same goal abound, as does a belief in unifying oneness existing behind the diversity of spiritual practice.

As discussed above, the role of and the contributions to the New Age by African Americans remain an under-researched and undertheorized area. Recent reformulations of the New Age, especially those that, as we have here, tie it to earlier, widespread movements in American religion, should lead scholars to the assumption that African Americans have played as vital, and as complex, a role in its development as they have in other forms of American religiosity. For example, into the mid-1990s, it was taken for granted that African Americans were unimportant in the American magical traditions that many see as the direct precursors of the New Age. However, we are now aware of the absolutely formative contributions of Paschal Beverly Randolph (1825–1875), a key figure in the evolution of Western sexual magic and in Western esoteric theory in general. While John Patrick Deveney's biography of Randolph (as well as Hugh Urban's later work on his impact and role in America) was revelatory, the role that Randolph's race—of which he was quite aware and quite conflicted—played in his religious behavior remains underinvestigated. It is our belief that in the next decades, scholarship will greatly expand our understanding of the role of African Americans in the formation and continued existence of the New Age, both by reinterpreting various African American practices through the lens of the new conceptions of the New Age (for example, Father Divine, the Nation of Islam, the United Nuwaubian Nation of Moors, or the similarities between the New Age and the Pentecostal movements of the African American church) and by the recovery of previously ignored or unknown historical figures.

Daniel M. Levine and Ann Gleig

SELECTED BIBLIOGRAPHY

Albanese, Catherine. *A Republic of Mind and Spirit: A Cultural History of American Metaphysical Religion* (New Haven, CT: Yale University Press, 2007).

Barrett, Leonard E. *Soul-Force: African Heritage in Afro-American Religion* (Garden City, NY: Doubleday, 1974).

Campbell, Colin. "The Cult, the Cultic Milieu and Secularization." *A Sociological Yearbook of Religion in Britain* 5 (1972): 119–136.

Deveney, John Patrick. *Paschal Beverly Randolph: A Nineteenth-Century Black American Spiritualist, Rosicrucian, and Sex Magician* (Albany: State University of New York Press, 1997).

Hanegraaff, Wouter. *New Age Religion and Western Culture: Esotericism in the Mirror of Secular Thought* (Albany: State University of New York, 1998).

Hanegraaff, Wouter. "New Age." *Encyclopedia of Religion, 2nd Edition*, ed. Lindsay Jones (New York: MacMillan Reference Books, 2005).

Heelas, Paul. *The New Age Movement and the Sacralization of the Self* (Oxford: Blackwell Publishers, 1996).

Hess, David. *Science in the New Age: The Paranormal, Its Defenders and Debunkers, and American Culture* (Madison: University of Wisconsin Press, 1993).

Karenga, Maulana. "Black Religion: The African Model." *Down by the Riverside: Readings in African American Religion*, ed. Larry G. Murphy (New York: New York University Press, 2000).

Kemp, Darren. *New Age: A Guide* (Edinburgh: Edinburgh University Press, 2004).

Kripal, Jeffrey J. *Esalen: America and the Religion of No Religion* (Chicago: University of Chicago Press, 2007).

Lewis, James, and J. Gordon Melton, eds. *Perspectives on the New Age* (Albany: State University of New York Press, 1992).

Partridge, Christopher. *The Re-enchantment of the West: Alternative Spiritualities, Sacralization, Popular Culture and the Occulture, Vols 2 & 2* (London: T &T Clark/Continuum, 2006).

Pike, Sarah M. *New Age and Neopagan Religions in America* (New York: Columbia University Press, 2004).

Sobel, Mechal. *Trabelin' On: The Slave Journey to an Afro-Baptist Faith* (Princeton, NJ: Princeton University Press, 1988).

Sutcliffe, Steven J. *Children of the New Age* (London & New York: Routledge, 2003).

Thornton, John. *African and Africans in the Making of the Atlantic World, 1400–1680* (Cambridge: Cambridge University Press, 1992).

NEW THOUGHT RELIGIONS AND THE AFRICAN AMERICAN EXPERIENCE

Historical Development

While the term "New Thought religion" is still largely unknown to most people, the teachings and principles permeate American and, more specifically, African American religious culture. Many people are acquainted with these religious principles through the more popular "prosperity," "Name it and Claim it," or neo-Pentecostal Word of Faith ministries that pour out from such well-known televangelists as T. D. Jakes, Creflo Dollar, Eddie Long, and Fred K. C. Price. While these ministries do not align themselves with New Thought religions as such, their teachings exhibit a similarity with these principles and thus warrant examination within this context. Thus, I include them in this discussion. New Thought religious teachings are strongly influencing the current context of American Protestant Christianity. Yet, very few people seem to know what it is.

New Thought is a general term used to describe a particular set of abstract or metaphysical religions that share a common history as well as beliefs, doctrines, and practices. While there are many different religions that have been categorized as New Thought, the term is best understood as an umbrella that encompasses numerous individual religions that share a set of core beliefs. Much in the way that the term "Protestant" is used in a general sense to refer to Christian denominations that, while sharing a common core, also differ in some ways and yet are still considered Christian, New Thought religions can be understood as similar, yet distinct from one another.

Among the ties that New Thought religions share is their connection to a common founder. Most, if not all, American New Thought religions still trace their historical, philosophical, and theological foundations back to the person of Phineas Parkhurst Quimby. Quimby began this movement in the nineteenth-century New England context of religious liberalism and experimentation. The late 1800s gave birth to liberal forms of Christianity, spiritualism, spiritual healing, and transcendentalism. Quimby lived from 1802–1866 and was informed by much of these liberal religious views, particularly spiritual healing, which he reinterpreted into a brand of mental healing or Mind Science, through which he taught that human beings have the power to heal one another in body and circumstance using the same spiritual gifts that Jesus had demonstrated in his lifetime. Quimby became extremely successful as a healer, ultimately becoming known as Dr. Quimby, though he was never formally trained as a physician. He continued to attribute his healing abilities to the right use of God's gifts that he believed to have been given to all of humanity. He taught that Jesus was not unique. Instead, he was a way-shower who embodied the consciousness and wisdom of God, and who was meant to be emulated as one who simply understood the proper way to channel God's pure energy to correct situations of illness or persistent personal problems. Quimby's technique of spiritual healing was to correct the thought pattern of the suffering person away from illness or problems toward the perfection of God. In effect, he healed by teaching people to release their negative thoughts and replace them with positive thoughts of health and wholeness. Quimby taught his method and his message to a small group of followers who continued in his stead after his death.

These followers began to heal and teach others, eventually developing into a new religious movement. The movement grew as new teachers, leaders, and believers rose to prominence preaching this Mind Science. As a system that taught the power of the mind to correct circumstances such as illness and suffering, Mind Science is the phenomenon that paved the way for what soon developed into New Thought religions. By 1895, Quimby's legacy was being formulated by his followers Warren Felt Evans, Julius Dresser, and his wife, Annetta Seabury Dresser, into a comprehensive religious system with its own cosmology, philosophy, and theology, specifically emphasizing the founder's original (though unorthodox) Christian interpretations. A new religious movement was born in America.

PHINEAS PARKHURST QUIMBY (1802–1866)

Phineas P. Quimby was born in Lebanon, New Hampshire, in 1802, and lived most of his life between Belfast and Portland, Maine. He is considered to be a pioneer in the area of mental healing. He had a simple education but became known as Dr. Quimby for his abilities to intuitively and spiritually heal the sick. He based his abilities on following the example of Jesus. Quimby maintained a practice in Maine, and began a movement that over time became known as New Thought religions, and he would be known as its founder. Quimby trained many others who would succeed him and carry on his teachings following his death in 1866. Although he did not leave any formal writings, some of his followers retrieved and published his personal papers. These writings are available today in *The Quimby Manuscripts* and *The Complete Writings*.

This trajectory from Quimby is most apparent in the three major New Thought denominations, Unity School of Christianity, Divine Science, and Religious Science/Science of Mind. While each of these denominations has its own immediate founder(s), each one of these also acknowledges a debt of tradition and historical origin to Quimby. Moreover, New Thought also consists of independent churches, groups, and individuals too numerous to name, who also affirm the same or similar beliefs and practices that began in the United States with Quimby, but who do not choose to affiliate with any one of the major denominations. These nondenominational New Thought believers prefer to maintain independent standing, conducting their religious practices outside the purview of any doctrinal or ecclesiastical authority.

While nineteenth century New England had its particular religious developments, the evangelical fervor of the Second Great Awakening (1800–1830s) reached southern states and African Americans with great enthusiasm. Enslaved African Americans living on plantations were being exposed to Christianity through ecstatic worship gatherings. Dynamic preachers at all night revival meetings and Baptist and Methodist missionaries zealously reached out to the enslaved people, baptizing them in large numbers and providing (segregated) worship spaces for them. Thus, African Americans were not learning about New Thought religion. For most, Christianity had replaced any form of traditional African religions or Islam that they may have brought over with them. African Americans began to forge a very intimate relationship with Christianity through the figure of Jesus Christ, whom they perceived as both co-sufferer and liberator.

The nineteenth century was also the time in which great African American Methodist and Baptist denominations were established. The energetic efforts of the missionaries had borne fruit, and most African Americans became staunch Christians.

Until emancipation in 1865, and the following great migrations north and west, only a small number of African Americans had been introduced to new and different forms of religion. African Americans who had migrated to the north in search of better opportunities found themselves once again discriminated against and segregated, this time into urban ghettos. This urban setting provided a fertile atmosphere for the introduction of New Thought principles such as self-help and positive thinking to African Americans looking for a way to improve their circumstances.

A handful of northern African American ministers had begun teaching and preaching in ways that borrowed heavily from New Thought religious teachings in their efforts to uplift their people. Some of these ministers were Father Divine, Father Hurley, Daddy Grace, and Rev. Ike. Although they each encountered criticism and suspicion from the larger society, particularly traditional

Rev. Ike delivers a sermon in 1977. (AP Photo)

Christians, for their unorthodox teachings and flamboyant lifestyles they can be considered to be the forerunners of African American New Thought minister/teachers. They saw that African-Americans were discouraged, impoverished, and disenfranchised from social opportunities and offered their own religious solutions. During this period from the 1920s to the 1960s, African Americans were beginning to integrate New Thought teachings into their Christian practices. They recognized some similarities between those teachings and the long-standing spiritual healing traditions of Spiritualist, Holiness, and Pentecostal Christianity. For example, they already believed in the power of the Holy Spirit to heal and transform, they already believed in a liberating God to whom one might appeal through ritual and prayer for favor, wealth, and well-being. So, when they were introduced to the New Thought ideas of the healing and transformative power of the indwelling spirit, and the rituals of affirmation and visualization to improve their life circumstances, they were hearing a familiar message. Sociologists such as Hans Baer and Merrill Singer have used the term "thaumaturgical" to categorize these types of religions, meaning that followers of these religions believe in the power of ritualistic behavior to change their life circumstances. For example, a believer's act of anointing the body with oil or lighting candles during prayer for the purpose of experiencing physical healing would be considered thaumaturgical. It is a religious ritual performed to attain a desired outcome. The ongoing development of New Thought religions was beginning to incorporate and appeal to African Americans who sought a different religious approach to their issues and needs.

Beliefs and Practices

There are similarities between New Thought teachings and more traditional forms of Christianity such as Spiritualist, Holiness, and Pentecostalism. These followers believe that God responds to these rituals by granting or allowing the believer's request. Some of these rituals might be particular forms of prayer, burning candles or incense, the use of consecrated water or oils, prayer cloths or beads, fasting, or anything else determined by the group to be sacred and effective. Likewise, in New Thought religions a foundational tenet of faith is that the universe is responsive and always affirms the dominant thought patterns of the believer. Thus, there is an emphasis upon positive thought and affirmative prayer as critical components of faith and practice. These are not carried out in a separate ritual apart from the rest of one's day or routine. New Thought believers are taught that affirmative thought and prayer must be one's natural and consistent form of being because the universe is always receiving one's thoughts and acting upon them to bring them into being for the individual. Despite the diversity among New Thought denominations such as Unity School of Christianity, Divine Science, Religious Science, and the multitude of independent groups, this point of faith is shared among all as a basic belief.

This belief may be better understood when placed in perspective with other core beliefs of New Thought, particularly the nature of reality as they define it. These religions affirm a metaphysical idealism, which for New Thought believers, means that the nature of the universe is based upon thoughts or ideas, and that all visible objects that we can observe are created by an invisible first cause (God), who creates through the medium of thought. By extension, it is also taught that the universe is responsive to human thoughts as well. Thus, every human being naturally has the power to create and change his or her circumstances by virtue of being created in the image and likeness of God. Human beings are created by God, and thus are endowed with the same creative capacity by properly using the power of the mind. Another core belief shared among New Thought religions is the idea of a monistic or unified deity. God is understood to be singular in existence, in contrast to Christian trinity, for example. This God manifests itself as the body of the universe, creating a pantheistic universe in which everything is created by God, out of God's own being, and therefore is God. Furthermore, God operates impersonally according to divine law or principle, and for this reason, many New Thought followers alternatively use God, universe, law, or principle to mean God, the original, creative force. Consequently, New Thought followers believe that God has established these impersonal principles or universal laws to respond to the creative thought patterns of each individual mind. A common statement among these believers is, "God is no respecter of persons, and will do for any what God will do for one."

New Thought believers practice these foundational beliefs in a variety of ways. One of the denominations, Religious Science, commonly uses the acronym, A-T-M, affirmation, treatment and meditation, to describe some of these practices. Religious Science, or Science of Mind as it is also called, was founded in 1927 by Ernest Holmes and is recognized as one of the more systematized New Thought religions, perhaps along with Unity School of Christianity. Both have presented a cosmology, philosophy, theology, and ecclesiology.

Religious Science seeks to teach a reliable system for creating positive life experiences. Its approach is to raise the consciousness of its adherents to a level of personal empowerment and responsibility grounded in the idea that human beings are created in the image and likeness of God even to the extent that individuals have the same creative power in microcosm that God has in macrocosm. In fact, Religious Science teaches that human beings are always creating their own experiences whether they are conscious of it or not. It is the conscious use of the Universal Principle that allows people to consistently (i.e., scientifically) create desired experiences. If individuals are only unconsciously using this Universal principle, then at best they live in a world of seemingly random events, coincidences, and luck, or at worst, a world of unhappiness, disease, lack, and limitation.

Affirmation, treatment, and meditation are the tools by which individuals change their thinking and improve their life circumstances. These methods are ways of rooting out old, dysfunctional thought patterns and replacing them with new more positive ones, so that they become the dominant way of thinking and lead to better life experiences. Participants are asked to claim their desires or state their claims of well-being even in the face of contrary feelings. Such feelings should be examined and recognized as not being consistent with one's desires and thus reprogrammed via affirmations. These are the beliefs that have previously manifested in one's life but have remained hidden from conscious thought, thereby causing seemingly random or negative experiences. The use of affirmations helps believers to recognize these hidden beliefs and to create more desirable experiences.

Treatment or Spiritual Mind Treatment is acknowledged by followers as the most powerful technique that Religious Science teaches, and is also known as affirmative prayer. It is a method of prayer that differs in that it is not done in a petitioner mode or from a mental position of lack asking God to bestow something upon the one praying or perform a miracle on his or her behalf. This would portray God as arbitrary, granting mercy and special favor to a select few. To the contrary, Religious Science teaches that God operates impartially through the impersonal nature of the Law or Principle; therefore one must approach prayer from this perspective. They understand affirmative prayer not as supplication or petition, but recognition and acceptance that God is all there is; and that all the abundance of the universe is already available to be accepted and embodied. Treatments consist of five steps: recognition, unification, declaration, thanksgiving, and release. The first two steps are regarded by many Religious Scientists as the two most important as they are akin to meditation in which one acknowledges the Oneness of God and one's own unity with God. This allows for one's consciousness to attain the highest possible level of meditative state.

The third step is the declarative stage of stating the object or condition of one's desire. This statement is really an affirmation. It is the point of claiming and accepting the desired outcome with faith and conviction that it is already accomplished. In the last two stages the practitioner gives thanks in the knowledge that the prayer is complete and then releases the prayer without any further worry or concern over the situation. It is then given over to God in the form of Universal Law with the expectation that the prayer will manifest accordingly.

Spiritual Mind Treatment can be done for oneself, for another whether present or not, or by a Practitioner (lay leader) of the Church. It is taught as a powerful tool for consciously creating one's own reality, moving people away from the idea that they are victims of circumstance or powerless to achieve their goals. It reflects Ernest Holmes's systemization of earlier Spiritual Mind healers all the way back to Quimby. Holmes studied their methods and their results and concluded that anyone could put these techniques into practice for themselves. His Science of Mind represents his attempt at putting this process in the hands of the average person in a practical and reliable fashion.

Finally, meditation is taught and encouraged as a means of listening to God. Affirmation and Treatment are initiated by the individual, as a means of either talking to oneself or to God, but meditation is the act of getting still and quiet to listen to the guidance that comes from within. It is a tool by which believers may acknowledge the unity principle that then informs all other thoughts and activities. From a position of understanding oneself as spiritually at-one with God, all obstacles and problems are acknowledged as illusory, not the real truth in light of God's perfection and wholeness. Meditation reminds the believer that he or she shares this perfection and wholeness, acting as a kind of mental housecleaning to allow the desired circumstances to manifest into one's life.

Religious Science stands as one of the contemporary bastions of New Thought religions. Its founder took the philosophical and religious teachings of many who had come before him, and coalesced them into a systematic formula for well-being. It was important to Ernest Holmes that his teaching was not exclusive and that anyone could apply the principles within the context of their own religious beliefs, and still make good use of Religious Science.

While it seems evident that ministers such as T. D. Jakes, Creflo Dollar, LeRoy Thompson, and Fred Price are teaching a brand of religiously based self-empowerment and wealth building, it is also clear that they remain rooted in conservative, evangelical Christianity. Their messages preach that God wants every saved Christian to be wealthy, and their programs for accomplishing this are rich in New Thought principle. These ministers teach positive confession, visualization, praying "prosperity" Scriptures from the Bible, and "naming and claiming" any object or situation that is desired, believing in faith that it will occur. In New Thought, these practices are called affirmation, treatment, and meditation.

What is interesting to note is that New Thought teachings that began with Phineas Quimby in the nineteenth century, geographically isolated away from most African Americans of the time, have periodically throughout the twentieth century emerged within the contours of Christianity, finding a niche with some otherwise traditional Christians. Neo-Pentecostal megachurches are some of the largest and fastest-growing churches in America today, with individual congregations soaring to 20,000–30,000 members according to the respective church reports.

We are seeing resurgence in the acceptance of teachings that at least have a strong affinity with New Thought religions. More to the point, contemporary neo-Pentecostal ministries are intentionally and strategically borrowing from New Thought principles as they build their religious empires. Ministers such as Jakes and Dollar keep these teachings grounded in familiar Christianity and do not adopt all New Thought teachings, but they are indeed using such principles as the power of the mind to create circumstances, as they lead their congregations to "name it and claim it."

Of course, this selective borrowing from another religious tradition is problematic on a number of levels; namely, it does not fully or accurately present the original religion, nor is it entirely forthcoming to its members regarding the nature of these Word of Faith teachings. In light of the criticism that is being leveled against these Christian churches for teaching a controversial, unorthodox, and possibly heretical doctrine, New Thought religions could well experience a backlash due to this negative publicity. People who might have otherwise been curious or open to New Thought as a religious or philosophical system may be scared away from it through its misrepresentation in Word of Faith ministries. This is an important point in the development of American Protestant Christianity, and African Americans are a focal point as these developments are largely taking place within their churches and from their long-trusted ministers.

Frederick J. Eikerenkoetter II, better known as Rev. Ike, began his "success and prosperity" preaching to the public in 1972. His ministry was large and nationally televised. Rev. Ike describes his message as self-image psychology, through which positive self-awareness can help an individual change the conditions of his or her life. His teachings

REV. JOHNNIE COLEMON

Rev. Johnnie Colemon was born in Columbus, Mississippi, to parents who were active in their church, and they encouraged her to participate as well. Demonstrating achievement and leadership at an early age, Rev. Colemon graduated as valedictorian of her high school class. She received her B.A. at Wiley College and became a teacher in the Chicago Public Schools. In 1952 she followed her mother's advice to enroll in the Unity School of Christianity. In that same year Colemon was diagnosed with an incurable disease. Using the principles that she had learned through Unity, she was cured, and she went on to become an ordained minister in that tradition. In the 1970s Rev. Colemon left the Unity organization and founded Christ Universal Temple in Chicago, Illinois, and in 1974 founded the Universal Foundation for Better Living, a new Unity-based New Thought denomination. Rev. Colemon is the author of *Open Your Mind and Be Healed*, which relays her remarkable personal healing story. Rev. Colemon retired from her post as senior minister of Christ Universal Temple in 2007, but she retains her title, the First Lady of New Thought.

emphasize visualization, affirmation, and meditation as tools for spiritual and material well-being. Today, Rev. Ike maintains a ministry in New York City, with services held in the Palace Cathedral. Although the height of his popularity has waned since his heyday in the 1970s, Rev. Ike stands as a major forerunner of African American New Thought teachers and ministers.

Rev. Dr. Johnnie Colemon was a contemporary of Rev. Ike. Dr. Colemon's presence, teachings, and impact are legendary. She is considered by many to be the "First Lady of New Thought." She is the founder of Christ Universal Temple in Chicago, Illinois, a Unity-based New Thought church that she formally founded in 1956. Additionally, in 1974 Dr. Colemon founded an entire New Thought denomination, the Universal Foundation for Better Living (UFBL). This denomination defines New Thought as a set of spiritual tools that empowers people to realize their potential by becoming consciously aware of spirit within them. These tools

help people to change their circumstances by changing their thoughts, feelings, and beliefs.

Dr. Colemon was introduced to New Thought through the Unity School of Christianity denomination in 1952. Her testimony states that she was cured from a physical ailment by applying the teachings of Unity and was therefore convinced of its validity and ability to help others. She remained with Unity until she began to experience instances of racism, limiting her advancement within the organization. She ultimately decided to leave Unity and start her own church, beginning in her home with only a handful of members. This small group developed into Christ Universal Temple with a membership of approximately 20,000 and occupies a 32 acre multiplex. Church reports state that they are the largest New Thought church on earth.

Because of Dr. Colemon's early affiliation with the Unity denomination, she developed and continues the UFBL ministry under the banner of "Practical Christianity," which maintains an understanding of Jesus as way-shower and example, not savior, but still utilizing the principles that Jesus taught as their primary guide for life. They also use the Bible as a principle text, although interpreted allegorically. The UFBL defines New Thought as a set of spiritual tools that empowers people to realize their potential by becoming consciously aware of spirit within them. These tools help people to change their circumstances by changing their thoughts, feelings, and beliefs.

The UFBL is largely an African American denomination, and it consists of 30+ churches and study groups located throughout the United States, Canada, and many Caribbean Islands. Rev. Mary Tumpkin serves as president of the denomination, and as of mid-2007, she will also act as Interim Senior Minister of Christ Universal Temple as Dr. Colemon steps down to retire. Rev. Mary is a high profile, well-known New Thought minister in her own right, maintaining a UFBL church in Miami, Florida, the Universal Truth Center, which she founded in 1982. She has been an important leader under Dr. Colemon for more than 25 years.

Rev. Dr. Michael Beckwith, of the Agape International Truth Center in Culver City, California, founded Agape in 1986 as a spiritual center based in Eastern and Western religious traditions. Rev. Michael was ordained as a Religious Science minister in 1985, and started Agape as a Religious Science/Science of Mind church. In 2006, the community declared its independence from the denomination, becoming a transdenominational spiritual community teaching New Thought–Ancient Wisdom. These teachings do not differ significantly from Religious Science; they are based in the understanding that Ultimate Reality or God is the source of all life, and that human beings are made in its image and likeness, making humans co-creators of their lives. The community teaches the practical application of universal principles, cosmic laws, meditation, prayer, and visioning for the enhancement of all life.

As senior pastor of Agape, Rev. Michael is internationally known as a

---

REV. DR. MICHAEL BECKWITH, D.D. (1956–)

Michael Beckwith was born in 1956 into a Methodist and Congregationalist family. He later graduated from Morehouse College and, like many people, set out to discover his own spiritual path. After living a life as a self-proclaimed militant who always challenged authority, Beckwith came to the study of Eastern and Western spiritualities in the 1970s. Following his ordination into the church of Religious Science in 1985, Rev. Michael began to teach spiritual principles from his home, and in 1986 he founded the Agape International Spiritual Center in Culver City, California. Today, Rev. Michael ministers to a congregation of 9,000+ members and speaks to audiences around the world on New Thought spirituality. In addition, he has been recognized with numerous humanitarian awards and honors for his work on issues of world peace and justice. He has met with the Dalai Lama of Tibet, Arun Ghandi, grandson of Mahatma Ghandi, and many other world luminaries. Rev. Michael is married to Rickie Byars-Beckwith, musician and director of Agape's music ministry, and they share a blended family of 4 children and 6 grandchildren.

dynamic visionary, who is setting a new course in New Thought spirituality. Agape is an enormously popular church community in the Los Angeles area, with a reported membership of 9,000 members. The already large membership has experienced explosive growth since Rev. Michael's appearance on *The Oprah Winfrey Show* and *Larry King Live* in support of the docu-film, *The Secret*, in which he also appeared. Rev. Michael has achieved celebrity status in a town of celebrities, and he maintains an extensive schedule of ministry, international speaking engagements, and co-leadership of the Association for Global New Thought, a separate organization seeking to apply spiritually motivated activism to justice issues around the world. Rev. Michael is helping to popularize New Thought spirituality into mainstream American life through his own status and the tremendous outreach of the Agape community.

Darnise Martin

SELECTED BIBLIOGRAPHY

Ahlstrom, Sydney E. *A Religious History of the American People*, vols. 1 and 2 (Garden City, NY: Doubleday & Company, 1975).

Braden, Charles S. *Spirits in Rebellion: The Rise and Development of New Thought* (Dallas: SMU Press, 1963).

Fauset, Arthur. *Black Gods of the Metropolis* (Philadelphia: University of Pennsylvania Press, 1944).

Holmes, Ernest. *The Science of Mind* (New York: Tarcher/Putnam Publishing, 1998 [1926]).

Lincoln, C. Eric, and Lawrence Mamiya. *The Black Church in the African-American Experience* (Durham, NC: Duke University Press, 1990).

Martin, Darnise. *Beyond Christianity: African-Americans in a New Thought Church* (New York: University of New York Press, 2004).

Synan, Vinson. *The Holiness-Pentecostal Movement in the United States* (Grand Rapids, MI: Eerdmans, 1971).

O

OBEAH

Historical Development

Like other African-Caribbean spiritual practices, such as Santería, Vodoun, and Shango, Obeah is an animistic religion that sees the natural world as alive with spirits of ancestors and supernatural forces. In this worldview, as late as the nineteenth century in Jamaica, descendants of African slaves believed that silk-cotton trees gathered together after sunset, and even today that tree is commonly called the God Tree, associated with *duppies,* or ghosts. Sometimes referred to as Afro-Caribbean shamanism, Obeah is far less well known and researched than its more high-profile relatives. Obeah is shrouded in secrecy, and even the meaning of its name is unclear; some consider that it originated from *Obeye*—the name given to a supernatural force that resides in African sorcerers—while others see the West African Akan word *Obayifo* (witch) as the likely source. Those who practice it are known

as Obeahmen, and can be considered a mix of shaman, sorcerer, and Vodoun witch doctor. Obeah is often divided into two types known as "science" and "bush magic"; adherents of the former use commercial charms and conjuring books while the latter prefer the more traditional talismans of dog teeth, bones, feathers, and minerals.

Today, Obeah is increasingly a catch-all term for many different types of spiritual activity, often appearing to blend with other African-Caribbean religions and influenced also by other faiths such as Islam, Hinduism, and Christianity. In Trinidad and Tobago, for example, Obeah is mixed with Orisha in several different forms. Originally, Obeah was practiced solely by enslaved West Africans brought to the Caribbean to work on plantations. Its origins can be traced particularly to the peoples of Dahomey and the Ashanti, arriving in the Caribbean during the seventeenth century. The colonial British rulers of the time used the term "Obeah" indiscriminately to describe any type of magical or mystical activities by

African slaves. Such was the reputation of Obeahmen for evildoing that they were often blamed for misfortune, unrest, and disaster on plantations by the European planters and African slaves alike.

Beliefs and Practices

Although usually credited with malign influence, in fact the Obeahmen who arrived on the first slave ships had the same supernatural qualities possessed by indigenous Amerindian shamans. They were ritual specialists who guarded their society's spiritual and ethical traditions; they were supernatural warriors who could kill at a distance, steal souls, raise the dead, and cure and send illness. While Taíno and Carib shamans were also accomplished herbalists, the African Obeahmen seem to have specialized in using plants to conduct apparently miraculous cures and to send magical death through poisoning.

Apart from their role as living links between the traditions of Africa and the new African-Caribbean society that was coming into being, Obeahmen also played an important political role during the slavery period. Their ostensibly religious meetings could be used to disguise opportunities for planning insurrection. Obeahmen were often believed to be at the heart of slave rebellions and of less violent forms of resistance. Often charismatic individuals, Obeahmen were believed to be able to protect their followers from the white man's weapons by rubbing special powders or substances on their bodies. In one case, recorded by Edward Long in his 1774 *History of Jamaica*, one Obeahman was believed to be able to catch the white man's bullets in his hand and hurl them back at those

who had fired them. Whatever the credibility of such stories, they served to embolden the slaves and make the plantation owners anxious.

Obeahmen made their followers swear bloody oaths of secrecy on pain of death to carry out any instructions that they might be given. These rites of obedience and the other rituals associated with Obeah involved a host of objects and materials deemed to be powerful weapons in the right hands. Plant poisons, powdered glass, gun powder, bird beaks, and animal teeth were all considered ingredients in Obeah sorcery. Eventually, rigorous searches of slave quarters every two weeks were carried out by the white planters, and in Jamaica increasingly harsh penalties were imposed for their possession. The link between Obeah witchcraft and slave unrest was finally recognized in 1816 when a law was enacted that sentenced the guilty to deportation. If anyone died through being poisoned, the occupant of the house where Obeah poisons were found was judged to have committed murder and could be hanged or burned. Obeahmen also sold their services, sometimes being commissioned to poison one person on behalf of another. More often, perhaps, they were employed for more mundane purposes—to cure illness, divine the future, or unmask an adulterer or thief. They were paid in food or money but also might defer payment by requesting a future favor. An astute Obeahman could build up a network of people who owed such favors and so achieve great personal power and influence. The ability of Obeahmen to be in one place while someone died in another location was presented as a sign of his ability to kill at a distance, whereas in fact he had simply called in a favor owed to him by someone else.

Obeahmen flourished in the harsh and often cruel conditions of slavery in the Caribbean. The injustices that white plantation owners and overseers visited on the slaves were such that acts of rebellion, large and small, were also desperate forms of resistance against oppression. In the hothouse conditions of plantation life, where slaves outnumbered their white owners, it is not surprising that Obeahmen were feared equally by their African-Caribbean compatriots and European masters. These situations magnified and emphasized the malign aspects of Obeah sorcerers at the expense of their equally important role as healers, ritual experts, and keepers of cultural traditions.

Steve Weaver

SELECTED BIBLIOGRAPHY

Bell, H. H. *Obeah, Witchcraft, and the West Indies* (Westport, CT: Negro Universities Press, 1970 [1889]).

Hedrick, B. C., and J. E. Stephens. *It's a Natural Fact: Obeah in the Bahamas.* Museum of Anthropology Miscellaneous Series No. 39 (Greeley, CO: University of Northern Colorado Museum of Anthropology, 1977).

Kalafou, Azoth. *Obeah: Afro-Caribbean Shamanism* (n.p./n.d.).

Long, E. *History of Jamaica* (London: T. Londwes, 1774).

Morrish, I. *Obeah, Christ, and Rastaman: Jamaica and Its Religions* (Cambridge, MA: James Clarke Press, 1982).

Schuler, M. "Myalism and the African Religious Tradition in Jamaica." *Africa and the Caribbean: The Legacies of a Link*, ed. M. E. Graham and F. W. Knight (Baltimore: Johns Hopkins University Press, 1979).

Sereno, R. "Obeah: Magic and Social Structure in the Lesser Antilles." *Psychiatry* 11, no. 1 (1948): 15–31.

Williams, J. J. *Voodoos and Obeahs: Phases of West India Witchcraft* (New York: Dial Press, 1932).

THE ORISHA RELIGION IN TRINIDAD

Historical Development

The *Orisha* religion in Trinidad is one of many African-derived religions in the New World whose origins can be traced back to the interaction between European colonials and African slaves. It is this European/African religious dynamic in Trinidad, dating back approximately 200 years, that eventually gave rise to the most salient characteristic of the *Orisha* religion (and many other African-derived religions as well): a syncretism (the blending of traits from diverse cultures, resulting in the creation of a new trait) involving African religious beliefs and practices (in the case of *Orisha*, primarily Yoruba) and Christian beliefs and practices (primarily Catholic but in some cases Protestant as well). The term "*Orisha* religion" was coined by Houk (1995) to replace the term "*Shango* cult" that had been favored by earlier ethnographers; "*orisha*" is the Yoruba term for "god" and can be used in the singular or plural sense.

"*Orisha* religion" or simply "*Orisha*" is an "umbrella" term that serves more as a category rubric rather than a specific identifier of a homogeneous religious practice; the term, thus, functions in a manner somewhat similar to "Hinduism," a term that also refers in a very general, categorical way to a variety of religious beliefs and practices that one finds in the

Indian subcontinent. In Trinidad, those who are adherents of *Orisha* may also practice the Spiritual Baptist religion (a syncretic African/Protestant faith with an emphasis on the latter), a uniquely Trinidadian form of Kabbalah, or, in a small number of cases, Catholicism. Many *Orisha* worshippers also incorporate Hindu icons into their worship practices although they cannot be said to "embrace" or practice Hinduism; the Hindu influence on *Orisha* is attributed to the pervasive presence of Hindu Indians on the island. Of course, the foundation of *Orisha* is strongly African, which can be seen in the many prayers and songs in the Yoruba language as well as the worship of many Yoruba gods, most of whom are referred to by their Yoruba names.

We can trace the beginning of *Orisha* in Trinidad back to around 1838 or so,

when thousands of indigenous Yoruba peoples arrived in Trinidad; most were freed slaves who immigrated to the island. (Complete emancipation of African slaves occurred in 1838.) The religious landscape of the island was predominately Catholic at the time due to the colonial and missionary activities of first the Spanish and later the French. Hence, the earliest syncretism in *Orisha* involved the amalgam of Yoruba and Catholic beliefs and practices. There are a few theories regarding precisely why this African/Catholic syncretism, so salient in the New World, occurred. In regard to *Orisha*, however, it appears to be the result of "reasoned analogy"; i.e., the two religious systems, in the eyes of the transplanted Africans in Trinidad, seemed to possess similar pantheons. *Orisha* worshippers today will often refer to Catholicism with its cult of saints as

An Orisha *service, Trinidad. (Roberta Parkin/Impact/HIP/The Image Works)*

the "white man's version" of African orisha worship. Many *Orisha* adherents in Trinidad still refer to the *Orisha* by their Catholic names, for example, St. Michael as opposed to *Ogun* and St. John as opposed to *Shango*.

The next major development in the *Orisha* religion probably occurred sometime in the 1920s and 1930s when the Spiritual Baptist religion began to influence *Orisha*. While it is true that the Spiritual Baptist religion is primarily a Protestant faith and, given the general nature of Protestantism, would not easily syncretize or mix with a polytheistic or henotheistic African religious system (or a Catholic religious system for that matter), the Spiritual Baptists themselves are primarily drawn from the same ethnic group and socioeconomic class as are *Orisha* worshippers. For reasons noted above, what we find here is not really a true syncretism or blending but rather the wholesale borrowing of traits. So, for example, it is quite common for *Orisha* worshippers to practice "mourning," a Spiritual Baptist sensory deprivation ritual in which "pilgrims" undergo a series of "spiritual travels" to Africa, China, the United States, and often other Caribbean islands as well. During this ritual, which can be repeated annually, *Orisha* worshippers are often given "spirit work" to do or instructions for building an *Orisha* shrine on their property. The more experienced *Orisha* worshippers claim that Spiritual Baptist practices prepare the individual for entry into the more "mature," "sophisticated," and "spiritually powerful" *Orisha* religion.

The next major development in the history of *Orisha* occurred sometime around the 1950s or so when *Orisha* worshippers began to incorporate Hindu icons and, on occasion, "prayers" into the *Orisha* belief system. Both the opportunity and the motivation for this practice are well understood. In regard to opportunity, it should be noted that approximately 40 percent of the Trinidadian population is Indian and well more than half of those practice Hinduism, so this ancient old world religion is popular and quite visible all over the island. Also, the Hindu pantheon was viewed by many *Orisha* worshippers as yet another variation on the polytheistic theme found in African *Orisha* worship and Catholicism; a few Hindu gods and goddesses have been syncretized with particular *Orisha*. Finally, in regard to motivation, it seems clear that *Orisha*, a "primitive" and coarse religion in the eyes of most Trinidadians including many African Trinidadians, would gain for itself some degree of legitimacy by associating itself with Hinduism, one of the classic "great" or "world" religions.

Finally, the last addition to this eclectic mix of beliefs and practices occurred when some *Orisha* worshippers began practicing the Kabbalah in the 1970s. In Trinidad, this practice involves the invocation of a variety of Kabbalistic spirits known as "entities" and entreating them to do "spirit work" of some kind. Because this practice is generally viewed as being spiritually negative, it is generally kept separate from *Orisha* worship proper; so while a *mongba* (male Orisha shrine head) or *iya* (female *Orisha* shrine head) may engage in the practice of the Kabbalah, he or she will have a separate physical structure devoted to this activity and special times during the year that will be devoted only to this practice.

Beliefs and Practices

These various religiocultural traditions, then, African Yoruba, Catholic, Spiritual Baptist, Hindu, and Kabbalistic, all combine in a rather complex way to give us what today is known as the *Orisha* religion in Trinidad. While Orisha may appear to be a "hodgepodge" of this and that thrown together in a haphazard fashion, nothing could be further from the truth. Each component plays a specific role and the syncretism, borrowing, and incorporation of various traits has been guided by reasoned choices and rational decisions. Furthermore, while it may appear that *Orisha* is overly eclectic, a religion without its "own" corpus of beliefs and practices, it should be noted that this religion (the New World variant, that is) is only about 150 years old and is, thus, in its infancy, and all religions at a comparable stage, including the "great" or "world" religions, were similarly syncretic and eclectic.

Given the existence of so many religious traditions and groups on the island (in addition to those noted above, there are independent Baptists, Seventh Day Adventists, Anglicans, Muslims, and a variety of Pentecostal/Fundamentalist faiths), individuals from a variety of different religious backgrounds are drawn to *Orisha*. Edmond David, for example, was christened and confirmed as a young man in the Anglican Church and became interested in *Orisha* when he finished high school. He had actually been a drummer in an African folk music group and, at some point, began to play the drums at *Orisha* ceremonies. One of the appeals of *Orisha* for Edmond was the link or connection with his African ancestors that the religion emphasized and celebrated. Edmond was eventually initiated in the religion and is today one of the most important *mongba*, directing *ebo* (ceremonial "feasts") activities as the primary drummer and singer.

Because of the popularity of the Spiritual Baptist religion in Trinidad (there are roughly five times as many Spiritual Baptist churches than *Orisha* shrines), many worshippers come from that tradition to *Orisha*. One prominent "Leader" (a title that signifies that this individual is a male leader in the Spiritual Baptist church), Aldwin Scott, even maintained his Spiritual Baptist honorific even after he became involved with *Orisha*. Leader Scott eventually became one of the most "religiously fluent" elders in the religion as he "pastored" his own Spiritual Baptist church, held an annual *ebo* at his own *Orisha* shrine, assisted in Kabbalah ceremonies, and even conducted Hindu prayer ceremonies before his annual feast. Leader Scott's ability to "manipulate" these various traditions made him one of the most prestigious *Orisha* elders on the island.

There are approximately 150 *Orisha* shrines in Trinidad, most of which will sponsor an annual *ebo*. The first night of the *ebo* begins around 10 PM on a Tuesday and concludes around dawn Wednesday morning. The feast continues in this manner for three more nights, concluding on a Saturday morning. The typical feast night begins with Spiritual Baptist prayers and songs. At the conclusion of this activity, there is a short break during which time the *palais* (a rectangular, covered structure, with benches along the four sides and surrounded by a fence or wall that is about waist-high) is swept out and readied for the African part of the night's activities. The three drummers will begin beating drums and directing songs for the "trickster god"

Eshu (recognized throughout the New World as *Exu*, *Eleggua*, *Legba*, and *Elegba*) who will be respectfully "asked" through offerings of his "food" (ashes and water) not to disrupt the ceremonies. Once this is done, songs for a variety of other gods and goddesses are sung with the intention of drawing the spirits down to earth to possess one of the worshippers. Spirit possession of this sort is considered a positive and uplifting religious experience that serves both to energize the activities and to validate the *Orisha* religious system in the eyes of its adherents. Sometime around dawn, various animals (generally, chickens, "morocoys" [land turtles], and goats) are sacrificed to particular gods or goddesses (depending on the night), the blood of the carcass is drained into the earth at the outdoor shrine for the various *Orisha*, and the animal is cooked with some of the food being offered to the *Orisha* and the rest being consumed by worshippers.

While it is true that a viable community of *Orisha* worshippers does exist, given the eclectic and variegated nature of the religion, disputes and disagreements among worshippers, including even the elders and *mongba* and *iya*, regarding various aspects of the religious system, are quite common. This is, however, precisely what one would expect for a religion in the incipient stages of development. Nevertheless, as the *Orisha* religion, from its beginning an "open" religious system that was constantly adjusting to the contingencies of its multicultural legacy and its worshippers' needs, grew ever more complex, the already tenuous web of commonality that held the religious community together became increasingly frayed. It is precisely at this point, conceptually, that the organic structure of the religion becomes apparent.

On the one hand, there are "centrifugal forces" that are acting to expand the religious system; this would include primarily the historical tendency to "fill out" a religion that was originally an incomplete version of its African counterpart, the prestige conferred on *Orisha* leaders who were adept at manipulating all of the various religious traditions that make up the system, and the "mourning" ritual that allowed for the incorporation of individual or subjective experiences into the religious system. On the other hand, there are "centripetal forces" at work that are tempering the historical tendency toward expansion including the formation of the *Opa Orisha (Shango)*, an organization that oversees liturgy and practice in an effort to standardize the religion, and "Africanization," an attempt on the part of generally younger worshippers to pare down the religion to its original African roots. It should be noted here that these two "centripetal" mechanisms, formation of the *Opa Orisha (Shango)* and "Africanization," only appeared in the past 20 to 30 years or so. In other words, it seems clear that the tendency toward expansion of the *Orisha* religious system had, in some sense, be it psychological, conceptual, or institutional, become too eclectic, too complex, and too confusing.

So, if one views the *Orisha* religion from the broadest perspective possible, it is clear that two essential needs are being met. All individuals need some sense of permanence in their religion, some indication that their faith is, in fact, not misplaced or superfluous; what is being referred to here is a religion in the Durkheimian sense, i.e., religion as a social institution, enduring and immutable, that both symbolizes and validates the social system as a whole. On the opposite end of the spectrum, so to speak, are more individual, existential concerns that can only be addressed by a flexible, protean religious system.

This religion will, no doubt, continue to change and adjust to both the culturally diverse Trinidadian society and the needs of its adherents. Although, one cannot predict the future course of the *Orisha* religion with any degree of certainty, it does appear as though a stabilization point of sorts has been reached and there will be very little "expansion" of the system in the future, if any at all.

James Houk

SELECTED BIBLIOGRAPHY

Elder, J. D. *African Survivals in Trinidad and Tobago* (London: Karia Press, 2001).

Houk, James. *Spirits, Blood, and Drums: The Orisha Religion in Trinidad* (Philadelphia: Temple University Press, 1995).

Lum, Kenneth Anthony. *Praising His Name in the Dance: Spirit Possession in the Spiritual Baptist Faith and Orisha Work in Trinidad, West Indies*. Studies in Latin America and the Caribbean (London: Routledge, 2000).

Simpson, George E. *Religious Cults of the Caribbean: Trinidad, Jamaica, and Haiti*, 3rd ed. Caribbean Monograph Series, no. 15 (Rio Piedras: University of Puerto Rico, Institute of Caribbean Studies, 1980).

Warner-Lewis, Maureen. *Guinea's Other Suns: The African Dynamic in Trinidad Culture* (Dover, MA: Majority Press, 1991).

OYOTUNJI AFRICAN VILLAGE

Historical Development

Oyotunji African Village is an intentional community in Beaufort, South Carolina. Founded in 1970, and by the late 1970s boasting a residential population of 191 residents, today the village's community base spans thousands of practitioners both within it and in affiliated communities throughout the United States. Oyotunji represents the home of black people in America whose ancestors were enslaved and transported to the Americas as captives. As a result, and over a period of 300 years, the United States became the home to millions of black Americans sold into slavery. The development of religious revivalist movements, as part of a counterculture, is not new. It reflects various practitioner's attempts to respond to historical conditions that led to black disenfranchisement. It is a community of African American converts to Yoruba religious practices that is part of a larger network of Yoruba American revivalist practitioners throughout the Americas and Africa.

As African religions moved with the spread of African captives into transatlantic slavery, there developed a repressive sphere of plantation slavery that led to the transformation of *orisa* ritual practices in the Americas. These vast numbers of practitioners who trace their lineage to predecessors in West and Central Africa were transported as captives to the Caribbean and North and South America and in that process participated in the transformation of ritual and religious practices that have endured over centuries. These changes have led to the reconfiguration of *orisa* ritual practices, including the reconfiguration of ways that the *orisa* were represented. In Brazil, the spaces of interpretive production led to the development of a variation that became Candomblé; in Cuba, it became Santería; in Trinidad and Tobago, it became Shango (see entry "The Orisha Religion in Trinidad"); and in the United States, among black American cultural nationalists interested in Africanizing *orisa* practices, it became *orisa* voodoo or a return to the Yoruba *orisa*. These variations are reflective of the encounter between the West and Sub-Saharan Africa in the making of the modern world; and increasing numbers of these *orisa* adherents are contributing to the growth of multiple networks of *orisa* knowledge outside of the African continent.

The late twentieth- and twenty-first-century proliferation of groups of *orisa* practitioners outside of West Africa is expansive, ranging in the millions of adherents of *orisa* voodoo, Santería, and Candomblé religious practices. And today, practitioners in the Caribbean and South America are increasingly in conversation with practitioners from the global North. Now, more than ever, vast numbers of Americans in the United States are reclaiming or converting to Yoruba religious practices and playing central roles in reshaping how *orisa* traditions are to be practiced. The widening constituencies of changing Yoruba *orisa* practitioners, though not mutually exclusive, can be classified in four significant groups. (1) The first are the *orisa* practitioners, principally in Nigeria and Benin as well as various surrounding West African countries; they tend not to be educated in the West, have limited financial resources, and claim *orisa* worship as their religious faith. (2) The second are Orisa/Santería/Lukumi practitioners in the Americas who constitute the largest group of religious worshippers and in varying degrees tend to accept the hybridization of *òrìsà* practices. Practitioners in this group span regions

throughout Cuba, Haiti, Trinidad, Puerto Rico, Brazil, and the United States. (3) The third are *orisa* worshippers and Yoruba or *orisa* revivalists who are part of a relatively new (post-1960s) *orisa* economy of practitioners who are interested in the return to a more orthodox traditional practice; this return sometimes includes the purging of whiteness, but, more fundamentally, it is manifest through the reconfiguration of changes to the religion that were important because of the criminalization of the religion during conditions of enslavement. (4) The fourth, *orisa* modernists, are a relatively new (post-1980s) group of initiates, led by predominantly white American and European practitioners, who are part of a growing movement interested in the transcendence of racial membership through the emphasis of ancestral lineage.

These four groups constitute multiple networks of *orisa* practitioners that have produced *orisa* institutional practices throughout the Americas and reflect, to a greater or lesser extent, the African origins of *orisa* practices. However, Oyotunji practices are reflected in the third category and through beliefs that blackness is the modality through which African ancestral lineages are lived; their mission is a cultural and religious reclamative one.

During the formation of Oyotunji Village, knowledge of *orisa* practices took shape through the prism of Santería practitioners from Cuba. "Santería," a word derived from the Spanish *santo*, or saint, means the worship of saints—as in Catholic saints (see entry "Santería"). On Cuban plantations Yoruba *orisas*, once outlawed, led to the production of two stages in the development of *orisa* transformation. The first stage, the establishment of the *regla de ocha*, occurred during the first generation of African slaves in Cuba in which the Spanish colonial government encouraged enslaved Africans to create mutual aid societies. (It is believed that the *regla de ocha* was encouraged in order to avoid slave uprisings.) The second critical moment took place during the second and third generations of enslaved Africans who adapted *orisa* practices based on their social circumstances. These circumstances led to the production of new hybrid representations of *orisa* icons in which various Catholic iconic symbols came to stand in for *orisa* religious objects and cosmologies. It was these Santería conceptions and practices and their related histories of regimentation and exclusion, post-1960, that became part of the widespread development of *orisa* practices in the Americas—Oyotunji practices included.

By the mid-1970s, the membership of the growing Yoruba movement comprised hundreds of U.S. voodoo practitioners spread throughout the United States and Canada to establish networks of Yoruba *orisa* practices. This form of Yoruba religious practice took shape alongside the proliferation of Afrocentricity and was self-consciously driven by the growing tide of black nationalism in the 1960s. The founders of Oyotunji, many of whom apprenticed with Cuban Santería practitioners up until the height of the *black power movement* of the 1960s, developed an African-centered religious and cultural movement to counteract the history of the loss of African religious practices. It was in this context that black Americans involved in this movement reconceptualized the form of Santería ritual practices that they were taught in order to disentangle it

from its history of Spanish and Christian regulation.

Oyotunji Village contemporary membership and affiliation cannot be understood in relation to its physical location alone. Late twentieth-century and early twenty-first-century processes have presented new developments such as distance learning and "mobile" computer databases for divinatory interpretation across scales of use, and Oyotunji members of satellite communities are able to use these technologies to gain access to Oyotunji knowledge practices and to maintain connections and alliances. Thus, Oyotunji societies operate through a network of linkage and obligations and society membership. Society members pay yearly fees to their local and transnational member associations, they participate in voting and decision making well outside of their regions, and they refer clients to each other throughout the society network. The growth of a national and international membership that is mobile and intersects with other *orisa* sects has led to a need to develop institutional infrastructures to coordinate interrelated satellite communities globally.

Lying outside of the geographic boundaries of African nation states, Oyotunji African Village is a small community built to accommodate up to 25 housing compounds with a potential capacity of over 500 people. With the mission to bridge ties to an African homeland as a postslavery revivalist and reclamative project, the Village began with the following founding families: Adefunmi, Adesuji, and Olafemi. The families of Ajamu, Adeyemi, Awolowo, Olaleye, and Ajanaku set the terms for what would become a vast cultural mission.

Over the years the number of residents at the Village has fluctuated, ranging from eight to ten families. Despite this small contingent of residents, Oyotunji's network is part of a wider configuration of hundreds of thousands of *orisa* practitioners and today the network of Oyotunji practitioners has produced spaces for the growth of *orisa* voodoo practices throughout the Americas and beyond. Oyotunji is a place for making and maintaining an Africa denied by the historical practices of American slavery and continually thwarted by contemporary processes of U.S. American daily life. Viewed as strange and odd by some, Oyotunji practitioners use notions of ancestral continuities to recast Africa in America.

Oyotunji is organized around three main sectors: political and educational governance, religious ritual and organizations, and a small-scale market economy. The community's claims to African ancestry are signified through its grand political organization. In keeping with the nobility of Empire, Oyotunji is politically structured according to hierarchies of grandeur and social status. Embracing these symbols—signs of Yoruba institutional power—the formation of Oyotunji governance marked the development of a new kind of black nationalist governance in the 1970s that required an ideological framework from which to determine what is counted as Yoruba.

Oyotunji is hierarchically divided into various levels, ranging from a political leader—the Oba—to the chiefs, the priests, and the nonpriest practitioners for Oyotunji is a democratic dictatorship. Through a structure of hierarchy and nobility, the Oba represents the symbolic head of the Oyotunji kingdom. The first leader, His Royal Highness Oba Adefunmi, ruled the community for 35 years and on February 11, 2005, he died and was succeeded by his son and heir, H.R.H. Obalola A. Adefunmi II.

His Royal Highness Oba Efuntola Oseijeman Adelabu Adefunmi I (born Walter Eugene King) (October 5, 1928–February 11, 2005) was the first known twentieth-century African American to

---

OBA EFUNTOLA OSEIJEMAN ADELABU ADEFUNMI I (1928–2005)

Oba Efuntola Oseijeman Adelabu Alladahunu Adefunmi I (name at birth Walter Eugene King) was born on October 5, 1928, in Black Bottom, Detroit, Michigan, and died on February 11, 2005. In 1959 he traveled with his friend and godbrother, Obalumi (Chris) Oliyana to Matanzas, Cuba, and became the first known African American to be initiated into the Yoruba priesthood of the *orisa*. Reborn Efuntola, he returned to New York and founded the Order of Damballah Hwedo, the Sango Temple, the Yoruba Temple, and incorporated the African Theological Archministry.

After a decade of organizing, he relocated to South Carolina in 1970 and founded Oyotunji African Village in Sheldon, South Carolina. In 1972 Efuntola traveled to Nigeria and was initiated into the Ifa priesthood and became a *babalawo* (father of secrets). During the same period, the people of Oyotunji named Adefunmi their formal leader and gave him the title "Oba" (King). Nine years later, Oba Efuntola Adefunmi traveled to Ile Ife, Nigeria, for the first World Orisa Congress and was given the title of "Bale" (Town King) by the Ooni of Ife, the spiritual leader of all Yoruba worldwide.

A man representing an egungun *(sacred ancestor) at Oyotunji African Village, South Carolina. (Bob Krist/Corbis)*

be initiated into the Santería *orisa* priesthood. Adefunmi's initiation paved the way for other African Americans to engage in *orisa* practices. Having grown up as Walter Eugene King, however, Oba Adefunmi I underwent significant transformations from a dancer for the Katherine Dunham Dance Company to a cultural activist to a central leader of the Oyotunji movement. In 1959, just before the Cuban Revolution, the then Walter King traveled to the Matanzas region of Cuba to be initiated into the *orisa* priesthood of Obatala. As a result of that initiation, he returned to the United States reborn as Efuntola Oseijeman Adefunmi and founded the Order of the Damballah Hwedo. He later transformed it into the Shango Temple and later incorporated it as the African Theological

Archministry (ATA). The ATA would eventually become the Yoruba Temple, marked by increasing concern for black nationalism.

By 1969, Oba Oseijeman developed a new lineage of *Orisa* worship that placed what was seen as the *orisa* homeland— Nigeria—at its core. With this lineage Oyotunji Village was founded in Beaufort County, South Carolina, and by 1972, Oba Adefunmi was initiated into the *Ifa* Priesthood in Nigeria. This placed him in the highest rank of *orisa* religious practitioners—the rank of *Babalawo*— a by its inhabitants. And there they lived, polygamous, Afrocentric, and ten families strong.

At the apex of Oyotunji's zones of governance is the palace, a signifier of ancient ancestral leadership. The Öba (king), sophisticated and learned, is currently under the reign of Oba Adefunmi II— the son of Oba Oseijeman I. He claims a constituency of thousands of African Americans in the United States, hundreds of whom have lived and trained in Oyotunji African Village.

On December 21, 1976, Prince Obablola II was born the fourteenth child of 22 children to His Royal Highness Oba Efuntola Adefunmi I, and the third child of five born to Iya Esu Ogo Oyewole. Prince Obalola was raised in Oyotunji African Village. At a young age, Obalola under the teachings of H.R.H. Adefunmi I, was schooled in the cultural lessons of Yoruba leadership and cultural practices. Raised in the traditional lifestyle of Oyotunji African village, Obalola learned at the feet of his father. Upon graduating from the Yoruba Royal Academy, Obalola was an initiate of several sacred Egbes (African societies), as well as the worship of Ifa. And since 2005, Obalola, now Oba

OBA A. ADEFUNMI II (1976–)

Prince Obalola was born on December 21, 1976, as the fourteenth child of 22 children to His Royal Highness Oba Efuntola Adefunmi I, and the third child of five born to Iya Esu Ogo Oyewole. The Prince Obalola was raised in the Kingdomj of Oyotunji African Village. By the time of his graduation from the Yoruba Royal Academy, Prince Obalola was an initiate of several sacred Egbes (African societies), to name a few: Egbe Egungun, Egbe Obatala, Egbe Onilu, Egbe Akinkonju, and he was a sophisticated drummer. As a young man, Prince Obalola followed his first love of drumming into many performances internationally and nationally. In 2001, Obalola moved to Key West, Florida, as an artist in residency at the Lofton B. Sands African Bohemian Museum. H.R.H. Oba Adejuyigbe E. Adefunmi II has a wife and two sons and sees his goal as one by which he fulfills his father's vision for the expansion of the Kingdom of Oyotunji, and passes on to the next generations the customs, traditions, cultural lifestyle, and skills of African peoples.

Adejuyigbe E. Adefunmi II, has been the reigning leader and lives in Oyotunji with his wife and two sons.

The political governing body of Oyotunji is the Ogboni. This body consists of the land owners and titled persons of Oyotunji. The Ogboni is a two-chambered council. The house of chiefs and the house of other landowners. The Ogboni makes laws, rules, and ordinances for the village. This body also hears complaints between its members as well as adjudicates trials within the community. As of 2007, the following are the members of the Oyotunji Ogboni Society:

1. Oluwa Olaitan (Apena—Head of the rules committee)
2. Iya Oba Adaramola (Iya Sanla—Chief Priest of Obatala Temple)
3. Oluwa Akintobi (Olotu—Chief Sacrificial Priest)

OLOFUNDEYI OLAITAN (1950–)

Born January 25, 1950, in Buffalo, New York, Olofundeyi Olaitan became aware of Yoruba cultural practices in the 1970s after a friend gave him a book entitled, *The Religion of the Yoruba*. This book answered questions about what religion and culture African people had before they were enslaved. He began a search for his African ancestry. A former radio announcer, Olaitan became associated with the Founder of the African Cultural Center in Buffalo and they with seven others (Iya Lode of Buffalo, Iya Oyelana and her child [Olokunwumi], Iya Osadele and her two children [Olojuokun, Ifategunse], and Iya Makinde) founded the Yoruba Foundation Inc. Olaitan became aware of Oyotunji after seeing an article in *Ebony* magazine in January 1978. Since arriving at Oyotunji, August 6, 1978, Olaitan has received several Chiefly and Priestly titles. Under his leadership as head of the Ancestor Society, Egbe Egungun has been presented Egungun (Ancestor Masquerade) throughout the United States, in England, in Belize in the Caribbean Islands, and West Africa.

CHIEF ADENIBI IFAMUYIWA S. AJAMU (1940–)

Chief Adenibi Ifamuyiwa S. Ajamu was born on October 31, 1940, in Chicago Illinois. Throughout the early and middle 1960s Chief Ajamu was the "Staff Coordinator" of the "Southern Christian Leadership Conference" on the west side of Chicago in the Lawndale area. By the late 1960s he was introduced to black nationalism and followed this concept until 1968 when he met the late Queen Mother Moore who introduced him to the notion of African Nationalism. Through this association he was led to the late Chief Medahochi Kofi Zanu, and it was through this association that he was introduced to the first Oba of Oyotunji, His Royal Highness Oseijeman Adefunmi. In 1970, Chief Ajamu joined Oba Adefunmi in Beaufort County, South Carolina, to establish the Oyotunji African Village. He was initiated in 1972 to the Yoruba deity Obatala. Leaving South Carolina, he traveled to Los Angeles, California, where he established a Yoruba shrine and community. In 1989 Chief Ajamu was initiated into the mysteries of Ifa in Oyo Town, Nigeria, on the compound of Ona Ilemole.

4. Oluwa Osadele (Chief Priest of Sango Temple)

5. Oluwa Ajamu (Chief Priest of Ifa Temple)

6. Oluwa Adeyemi (Otun Alagba of Igbale Egungun)

7. Baba Akinwon (Landowner)

When the first reigning King, Efuntola Adefunmi I started the Ogboni Society, it was in the 1960s in New York City. This Society was formed to spread the cultural/political message of African Cultural Restoration. At that time the society included Chief Akinbaloye, Chief Ogunseye, Chief Oyeilumi, Chief Awolowo, Queen Mother Moore, Iya Keke, Baba Gbumi, and others. In 2005, H.R.H. Adefunmi II, at his installation as Oba, selected a new cadre of mostly nonresident Chiefs of Oyotunji:

1. Oluwa Abisegun (Balogun—Oba's Road Opener)

2. Ijoye Adegbolola (Head of Egbe Egungun, NY)

3. Ijoye Oludoye (Igberohinjade—Oba's Secretary)

4. Ijoye Akinsegun (Iyalode—Head of Women, SC)

5. Ijoye Okunwale (Iyalode—Head of Women, NC)

6. Ijoye Akinsegun (Iya Magbaje—The Healer)

7. Ijoye Igunmuyiwa (Baba Alaje—Owner of Wealth)

8. Ijoye Gbolagesin (Agbede—Senior Teacher)

9. Ijoye Zannu (Igbabowo—Owner of Wealth)

Beliefs and Practices

Although it was their contact with Santería practitioners that enabled the survival of Yoruba traditions in the New World, in an attempt to reclaim Yoruba practices as a *phenotypically black African* phenomenon, the founders of Oyotunji formed a black separatist movement in which they rejected Santería and instead strengthened their ties with Nigerian Yorùbá *traditionalists* and cultural workers.

The development of *orisa* voodoo Yorùbá revivalism led to symbolically

CHIEF ADELAGBARA ADEYEMI (1945–)

Chief Adelagbara Adeyemi was born 1945 in Chicago, Illinois, and attended high school in the Gary public school system. He graduated in 1963. From 1964 to 1969, Chief Adeyemi majored in music therapy with a minor in psychology at Indiana University and Lincoln University, Jefferson City, Missouri. He moved to Beaufort County, South Carolina, in 1970 to take part in the establishment and building of Oyotunji African Village. Chief Adeyemi became one of the liaisons and diplomatic links to the community surrounding Sheldon, South Carolina, and Atlanta, Georgia, and in 1971 Chief Adeyemi directed the all "African Peoples Pre-school Program" in Sheldon, South Carolina. On October 17, 1978, he was initiated into the priesthood and cult of Obatala. In 1981 he earned his certificate of completion and passed the diviners test from Igbimolosha Priest College in Oyotunji. In 1983 he was appointed as the Alagba of the Egungun Society. In 1986 he departed from Oyotunji, but returned in 2000 to assist with a new phase of the Village's development.

"blackening" Santería and drawing ties to the West African Empires and kingdoms that preceded the colonization of Nigeria by the British Empire. The Oyotunji rejection of particular signs of *whiteness* in favor of the realignment of *blackness* with Africanness shaped a new Yoruba movement in the United States that shifted the criteria for African authenticity by privileging *blackness* and contesting the increasing racial marginalization of African Americans in the United States.

On a basic level of signification, Oyotunji practitioners argued for the need to culturally Africanize Santería as fundamentally Yoruba and visibly "African." Therefore, spurred by ideological clashes over the "whitening" of Yoruba ritual practices in Cuba, Yoruba revivalists in the United States—i.e., black American nationalists—renamed their version of Yoruba-Santería, orisa-Voodoo, substituting Spanish-language words and pronunciations with African

AYABA OLUBUNMI ADESOJI

Olubunmi Adesoji was born Eula L. Mayzck in South Carolina and started fighting for civil rights at the age of 12. At the age of 14 she was arrested and kicked out of the state of South Carolina. She relocated to Harlem, New York City, with her biological mother, and started attending Julia Richmond High School where she saw her classmate James Powell slain. As a result of this horrific experience, she was then hurled into the full fight for civil rights. She became interested in the cultural traditions of Yoruba peoples after the world fair and upon being introduced to the late King of Oyotunji. So enchanted was she upon meeting him that she joined the Yoruba cultural revolution and accepted her new name: Olubunmi Adesoji. In 1966 Adesoji was initiated into the Orisha miotho house. During that same year Olubunmi and Oseijeman married and had their first child named Fabayo Adefunmi.

words. Using representations that incorporated the mythic visual imagery of the old empire from which Yoruba people are known to have descended, the founders of Oyotunji created landscapes that resembled Nigerian Yoruba religious and political institutions thought to be more "authentically" African. They substituted their Anglophone names with Yoruba names, producing performative cartographies of Yoruba membership. These reformulations of Africanness shaped the terms of contestations, which developed in the United States, between early black nationalists and new Cuban immigrants to the United States.

The name, "Oyotunji," meaning "Oyo Returns," refers to the old ancestral city state of the Oyo Empire in West Africa that toppled and lost power in the nineteenth century as the transatlantic slave trade was on the decline and the British colonial Empire gained strength. Today, Yoruba traditionalism in the Americas is connected to the history of fifteenth- to nineteenth-century trans-Atlantic enslavement of Africans to the Americas and black American attempts to reclaim African traditions as their own. As a result of the belief that they have a right to control the African territory that they believe was their homeland—prior to European colonization—residents of Oyotunji Village have reclassified their community as an African Kingdom. This process has involved claiming diasporic connections to the ancestral history of the Great Ôyõ Empire of the Yoruba people.

The priesthood, following West African traditional practices, is trained in the practice of divination and the ritual slaughter of livestock and the practice of healing techniques. During the first years after the founding of Oyotunji African Village several priests were initiated into the priesthood. The first ones included:

1. Orisamola Awolowo—Priest of Obatala
2. Monilade Ogundupe—Priestess of Yemoja
3. Sangodele Omowale—Priest of Sango

Persons seeking the service of priests can visit an Oyotunji priest and receive advice, often referred to by Benjamin Soars as "fee for service." The governing and licensing body of the priesthood in Oyotunji is the Igbim Olosa. This body qualifies and licenses priests to practice and arbitrate disagreements between and among priests and also adjudicates complaints brought by clients against priests.

Priests are grouped into orders. These orders, each maintaining a house of worship, is situated on a lot that is roughly 50 feet by 100 feet. These houses of worship may be referred to as temples or shrines. No special requirements are necessary for a person or organization to participate in or receive benefit from the activities except belief in or curiosity about the religious and cultural programs of the African Theological Archministry Inc. (ATA). These activities accomplish a degree of healing for the believer and/or entertainment for the spectator and as such provide opportunities for economic viability.

Oyotunji residents earn a living through their religious services, tourism, market sales, commerce, lecture tours, and research, as well as other miscellaneous means; but the largest economic attractions are its religious festivals. Annual religious ceremonies, called festivals, are celebrated by each order of priests and bring in considerable amounts of monthly revenue. There is a senior priest who acts as the master of ceremonies and who leads prayers, singing, dancing and directs placement of offerings on altars to the patron saint or divinity of the order hosting the festival. No collection is made at annual festivals, but contributions in the form of animals and money are often offered to the Shrines as sacrifices. The major portion of all monetary contributions and donations are used to finance repairs or expansion and operation expenses of the several houses of worship.

These festivals provide priests and spectators a spiritual exuberance related to the holistic healing process. This tradition of annual festivals originated in West Africa, but in Oyotunji they are conducted on a monthly basis. They are held in the outdoor courtyard or lot provided for each house of worship. The dances of worship are costumed presentations. Music is provided by drums and accompanied by gongs and various shakers and rattles.

Oyotunji has its own formal educational system as well as a priestly training institution. The ATA was founded in 1959 in New York City as a center for dissemination of knowledge and information about religious traditions of the Yoruba people of Southwest Nigeria, Southern Dahomey, Togoland, and regions adjacent to the city of Accra in Ghana. The ATA's activities operated for the first ten years in New York City and centered on ordination of an Oyotunji priesthood, presentation for ceremonies, chants, preaching, divination, and dances dedicated to the deities of the Yoruba people. In 1970, the ATA relocated in South Carolina on a small tract of land and dubbed its location as Oyotunji African Village. It became a settlement for black Americans interested in the study of such cultural traditions. In 1980, the directors of the Oyotunji African Village applied

for and were granted a religious charter in the name of the ATA. The activities of the village have remained in the subsequent years a project of the ATA.

The ATA offers a series of religious services and cultural activities for visitors, tourists, colleges, high schools, grade schools, and researchers and also sponsors an annual convention and revival for national, as well as international, bodies of priests, congregants, or laypeople. These activities include demonstrations of Yoruba religious customs and practices, ritual dances, lectures, books, pamphlets, and arts and crafts. Also offered are workshops in holistic healing and open discussions of Yoruba social organization. The ATA provides weekly religious services of worship for the residents of the Yoruba African Village and for the general public who may regularly attend. The priests provide spiritual counseling to all who seek it. It provides, on occasion, shelter, clothing and food for arrivals to Oyotunji Village who do not have a place to go.

As part of an African American revitalization movement, Oyotunji practitioners recreated their identities through the adoption of Yoruba kingships and family codes seen by practitioners as being "traditionally" Yoruba. Contemporary dominant representations of African cultural traditions or indigenous African cosmologies as uncivilized and unworthy of serious attention (read "heathen/pagan") have also influenced significantly the discourses of African nobility that have become central to Yoruba practices. Therefore, the revival of African American interests in Yoruba-based religious cosmologies centers on the redemption from racial oppression and the revival of African-based cultural practices—known by them as those practices that predate European colonization.

When the builders engaged in the creation of the spatial layout, they started with small compounds that encircled the Ààfin. They changed the spelling of Spanish/Lucumi ritual words, as well as the pronunciation of ritual objects, and created a landscape that referenced the symbolic prestige of precolonial African village life in which they replaced the symbols of Santería saints with disembodied *orisa* shrines. They organized these reconfigurations to indexically reference key regions in West Africa, from which nine of the most popular Yoruba American *orisa* were known to emerge, and the Ààfin, the center for noble governance, and employed Yoruba names and terminology.

Today, the village is divided into five main districts: the Ààfin, Igbóòsà, Ìká gbó (Ìkabó), Ànàgó, and Ìgbàlê (sacred forested district). Each of these districts is governed by a series of town chiefs or a political or civic society (Egbë). Each of the districts houses living quarters, public buildings, and private and public temples and/or shrines for venerations by the practitioner. The Ààfin, the seat of leadership, seen as the central most important district, was configured as a large compound that houses the oba (king), his four wives and children's houses, as well as the ancestral shrines. One such shrine represents the embodiments of the oba's ancestors, as well as of the venerated unknown ancestors, Dombalahwedo. Other shrines housed in the Ààfin include the *orisa* sango (a symbol of kingship), the oba's *orisa* of Ifá (the deity of destiny), onile (owner of the earth), and obatala (creator of the human form). The Ààfin also houses the school complex, the museum, and guesthouses for new residents, indentured workers, and unmarried women (ayaba) who are betrothed or otherwise accountable to the oba.

The Ànàgó district, named to honor the Nago of Dahomean people, is adjacent to the eastern border of the Ààfin. At the front gate of the Ààfin is what is referred to as the shrine of Esu/Elegba. Extending westward, beginning with the Igbóòsà district, is the area popularly referred to as temple row. This district houses the temples of the Öya, Olókun, and Yemöja Òrìýàs. The Ìká gbó district begins with the Osun temple and includes the shrine to ogun and Ososi, as well as public and private buildings. The *orisa* Ôbalúaye is located in the forest adjacent to the Ìká gbó district. The final district, the place of ancestral veneration for the community, is known as the Ìgbàlê grove, the home of the sacred egungun (ancestors). These configurations of community were developed to produce a sense of connection to Africa that was represented not only as ancestrally legitimate but also as originary.

Cyclical and seasonal rituals of the ancestral *orisa* traditions are central to Oyotunji daily life. This extreme adherence to "tradition" is part of the means by which Oyotunji practitioners and related adherents are attempting to find their way back to Africa, back to a "homeland." In 1990, with the introduction of the African Cultural Restoration Plan, the elders of the Oyotunji Village outlined a program that seeks to develop and expand the consciousness of African Americans.

AFRICAN CULTURAL RESTORATION PLAN

- ANCESTOR WORSHIP: ERECT AN ANCESTOR SHRINE
- CULTURAL IMAGE: TAKE AN AFRICAN NAME, WEAR AFRICAN ATTIRE, BE A POSITIVE

ROLE MODEL, MAKE AFRICA THE CENTER OF YOUR WORLD VIEW

- SEXUAL CODE: AFRICAN IDEALS, VALUES AND MORALS MUST BE STUDIED, LEARNED AND EXPLAINED TO MALES AND FEMALES
- EDUCATION PROGRAM: WE ALL MUST BE REEDUCATED ABOUT AFRICA 24/7/365
- ECONOMIC PROGRAM: START YOUR OWN BUSINESS, FORM BUSINESS ASSOCIATIONS
- LEGAL CODE: LEARN AFRICAN TRADITIONAL AND CUSTOMARY LAW
- MARITAL CODE: LEARN TRADITIONAL AFRICAN MARRIAGE TYPES
- SOCIAL CODE: JOIN OR START AN AFRICAN GENDER SOCIETY, GO THROUGH A RITES OF PASSAGE PROGRAM
- RECREATION PROGRAM: THE ADULTS MUST INSTRUCT THE YOUTH AS TO THE CONCEPTS OF TEAMWORK, FAIR PLAY AND GOOD CHARACTER
- ARTS PROGRAM: CREATE AFRICAN ART, RESPECT, DISPLAY AND BUY AFRICAN ARTS AND CRAFTS

The Cultural Restoration program is a ten-year plan with a goal of invigorating, regenerating, and empowering those of African descent to a return of their royalty and majesty. All of the major aspects of African Cultural lifestyle are researched and presented for accurate incorporation in the day-to-day activities of African Americans.

Two of the most widespread and transnationally far-reaching societies founded by Oyotunji residents are the Egbe Akinkonju men's and Egbe Moremi women's societies. The Egbe Akinkonju is a society of males of African descent. Its mission is described as organizing and developing males to grow to be dedicated men committed to the work of *orisa* revitalization and black empowerment. The society uses the iconic symbol of the deity Ogun—warrior, pioneer, and advocate for justice. The Society of Men at Oyotunji Village incorporates the egbe of men in their various functions: The militia, the dopkwe (work group), Egbe Akinkonju, and the Onilu (musicians/drummers) are some of the manifestations of the Society of Men. The militia is the paramilitary department of the men's society, which oversees the community watch system, the raising and lowering of the community flags, as well as village security during festivals, and its parade unit is called upon to greet and is in procession on formal state occasions. The dopkwe oversees construction and public works in the African community. Under the auspices of the dopkwes training program, young men are taught the various facets of the building trades necessary to build and maintain a community. Public works include not only the building and maintenance of public as well as private facilities but landscaping, road maintenance, recycling, plumbing, and electrical systems. The Onilu (musicians/drummers) are the society of drummers and represent another important component of any spiritual-religious, civic-social function.

Since the late 1980s, the national appeal of this society has been its male initiation rites programs known as the Egbe Akinkonju. Boys join at young ages and over time accomplish various tasks toward their "manhood rites" tests. At puberty they undergo a series of rites, and after passing them they are admitted for life to the Egbe Akinkonju. Interested practitioners in various U.S. cities can establish affiliations with Oyotunji through membership in the Egbe Akinkonju's men's society. As members, they must pay dues, viewed as important to group cohesion and to the support of group activity and productivity.

In both London and Birmingham, England, there are also Oyotunji-allied practitioners who have undergone Egbe Akinkonju rituals and maintain affiliation through the payment of dues, yearly rites, and occasional attendance at meetings. Male members of Oyotunji also join other male societies based in England, Benin, Nigeria, and Brazil, among other places. Their ritual initiations in men's societies in these various sites further concretize their claimed spiritual affinities with African societies.

Similarly, the Egbe Moremi women's society boasts widespread membership in a range of institutional networks within and outside the United States. Its mission is to educate and train girls and women to understand and transmit traditional African values. The Egbe Moremi society celebrates womanhood each June through the figure of the patron orisa Yemoja Moremi. This annual Yemoja festival includes the celebration of affiliated members of Egbe Moremi. To become members, girls must undergo a yearlong female rite of passage; grown women follow an adapted version of the training rituals and ceremonies. With the successful completion of such rites, girls and women are admitted to the society and considered members for life and even in death.

Kamari Maxine Clarke

SELECTED BIBLIOGRAPHY

Clarke, Kamari M. "Governmentality, Modernity, and the Historical Politics of Oyo-Hegemony in Yoruba Transnational Revivalism." *Anthropologica: The Journal of the Canadian Anthropology Society* 44–42 (December 2002): 271–93.

Clarke, Kamari M. *Mapping Yoruba Networks: Power and Agency in the Making of Transnational Communities* (Durham, NC: Duke University Press, 2004).

Clarke, Kamari M. "Transnational Yorùbá Revivalism and the Diasporic Politics of Heritage." *American Ethnologist* 34, no. 4 (November 2007).

Gregory, Steven. *Santería in New York City: A Study in Cultural Resistance* (New York: Garland, 1999).

Hurt, Carl M. *Oyotunji Village: The Yoruba Movement in America* (Washington, DC: University Press of America, 1979).

Johnson, Samuel. *The History of the Yorubas: From the Earliest Times to the Beginning of the British Protectorate* (London: Routledge and Kegan Paul, 1921).

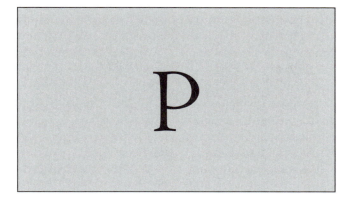

PALO MONTE

Historical Development

Regla de Palo Monte Mayombe, more commonly known as Palo Monte or Palo Mayombe, or simply Palo, is the general term given to the Afro-Cuban religions that are based on the traditions of the people who lived in the Kongo River region of west central Africa. (This area and the people that inhabited it during the precolonial and colonial periods are designated as "Kongo" with a "K" to distinguish them from the area and people of the contemporary countries of Congo and the Democratic Republic of the Congo, both of which contain many non-Kongo people.) The Kongo River area had been a highly developed, centralized kingdom for over a century and a half when Portuguese sailors first landed in 1483. The first Catholic priests arrived in the Kingdom of Kongo in 1491 and begin baptizing the king and his principle nobles. In a short time the Kongoese aristocracy accepted Christianity

as their state religion and began to develop a version of Catholicism that integrated Christian beliefs with their own indigenous beliefs and practices. Although the Kingdom of Kongo was a major source of slaves for the Portuguese and other European traders from as early as 1502, it was the settlement of Brazil in 1630 with its concurrent demand for slaves that accelerated the importation of peoples from this area. By 1670 as many as 3,000 people a year were being sold out of the Kongo river basin. In all, it is estimated that between 40 and 45 percent of the 11 million Africans imported to the Americas were from this part of Africa. Because of their early exposure to Catholicism in their homelands, many of the Kongoese people who arrived in the Americas also came practicing their own unique form of Christianity.

Kongolese people were imported to Cuba from the early sixteenth century until as late as the last quarter of the nineteenth century. Although originally predominant in the eastern end of Cuba, by the time of the Haitian Revolution between 1791 and 1804 the Kongolese had spread throughout the island and were a major ethnic group working as stevedores in the ports of Havana and Santiago as well as workers on the sugar and tobacco plantations and the sugar mills throughout the island. During the colonial period, Afro-Cubans both in Havana and in the smaller towns were encouraged to organize religious and self-help organizations known as *cabildos*. Since the cabildos were organized along ethnic lines, members were able to reestablish their religious ceremonies and other cultural traditions. Records of Kongo-based religion in Cuba go back as early as 1796 when it is reported that a certain Malchor ruled one of most famous cabildos in Havana, *Cabildo de Congos Reales*. Each year, members of this cabildo engaged in street performances and masquerades as part of the Epiphany celebrations as well as during Carnival and Holy Week.

In 1799 the colonial authorities ordered that the cabildos be moved outside the city walls because of their music, ceremonies, and public displays. Later during the wars for independence and in the early Republican eras, when the cabildos became highly regulated and even prohibited, the religious centers moved to home temples, an organization structure that continues today both on the island and in the United States. When great numbers of Yoruba people were brought to Cuba in the mid-nineteenth century, there was originally much conflict between the two groups but by the Cuban Revolution in the mid-twentieth century many people had become practitioners of both Palo Monte and the Yoruba-based religion of Santería, and many contemporary practices in the Palo

tradition show the influence of this interaction with Santería (see entry "Santería"). By the twentieth century subgroups under the umbrella of Palo Monte Mayombe include la Regla Conga, la Regla Biyumba, la Regla Musunde, la Regla Quirimbaya, la Regla Vrillumba, and la Regla Kimbisa del Santo Cristo del Buen Vieje.

With the flight of Cubans following the Cuba Revolution and Castro's rise to power and the second exodus in 1980 when the marielitos took advantage of Castro's temporary opening of the Port of Mariel to émigrés, the African-based religions of Cuba have spread beyond the island. Anywhere Cubans landed also became the center of religions such as Palo Monte, including Miami, New York, and Panama. Today there are strong Palo communities along both the East and West coasts of the United States as well as Chicago, Houston, and many smaller communities. Because this tradition is even more secretive than its sister tradition of Lukumi (Santería), it is difficult to give any estimate of the total number of practitioners

Beliefs and Practices

Because of the similarities between Kongolese beliefs and those of the Catholic priests, it was easy to incorporate Catholic ideas into the existing Kongolese cosmology. Kongolese cosmology included a supreme God, Nzambi (known as Sambia among Palo Monte practitioners), who was approached through the mediation of land and sky spirits, most of whom were understood to be ancestors who had once lived on the earth. Principal spirits in Palo Monte include Lucero Mundo, who is associated with Anima Solo Purgatory (the lonely soul in Purgatory) and the Orisha Eleggua; Sarabanda, who is associated with St. Peter, St. Michael the Archangel, and the Orisha Ogun; Insancio, popularly known as Siete Rayos (Seven Lightning Flashes), who is associated with St. Barbara and the Orisha Shango; Baluanda popularly known as Madre de Agua (Mother of Water), who is also known as Siete Sayas (Seven Skirts) and is associated with the Virgin of Regla and the Orisha Yemaya; Chola also known as Mama Chola or Chola Awengue, who is associated with the Virgin of Charity of El Cobre and the Orisha Oshun. In addition, there are many other spirits and the ancestors of individual family lineages. All of these are believed to be highly advanced and powerful ancestors who have died and continue to work for the welfare of their children and devotees. There are no "gods" within Palo Monte; rather all of the spirits were once human beings who, having died, have gained additional power and abilities. The oldest of these ancestors, Sarabanda, Siete Rayos, Baluanda, Chola, and even Nzambi are all powerful spirits, who after centuries of worship have become godlike in their power and abilities. However, they are still continuous with their human devotees in that they are not a different order of beings, but merely extremely old and powerful ancestors. These ancestors, although separated from their living families, maintain a link to them so that they might counsel them and provide healing and support. During rituals they are invited back into the circle of the family, offered food and other gifts, and consulted by their living descendants. Whatever organized pantheon of these spirits that had existed in Kongolese mythology has been lost in the Americas, and Paleros depend on the correspondences between these spirits and the Orisha of Santería to form the mythological relationships between these spirits.

This cosmology was represented by a circle surrounding an equal-armed cross. The horizontal bar of the cross separates the world of the living (above) from that of the spirits (below). The four moments of the sun (sunrise, noon, sunset, and midnight), as well as the journey of human life (birth, adulthood, old age, and the afterlife) are represented by the points where the end of the cross intersects the circle (right, top, left, bottom). This and other cosmograms, also know as *firmas*, are used to inscribe the ground of ritual space, and the inside of the sacred *nganga* described below. Most *firmas* are the signature of a specific spirit or religious congregation and as such resemble the *vèvès* of Haitian Vodou. Some *firmas* are as simple as the cross bisecting a circle; others are quite a complex group of circles, lines, curves, arrows, crosses, skulls, suns, and moon that represent the spiritual force in amazing detail and serve as altars for the spirits to interact with their devotees. *Firmas* drawn on the ground accompanied by the appropriate singing during rituals serve as centering spaces and the connections between the world of the spirits and that of human beings. For those who can read the symbolism, the *firmas* contain the stories and characteristics of the spiritual entity portrayed. Initiation into this tradition is commonly referred to as having been "scratched" or "cut": as the ritual includes having small *firmas* incised onto the body of the initiate.

The most important icon of Palo Monte is the *nganga* or *prenda* (Spanish for jewel, treasure, or pawn), a metal caldron that contain sticks (*palo*) from the woods (*monte*) as well as Spanish coins,

Nganga *at Calixto Garcia Museum, Holguin, Cuba. (Mary Ann Clark)*

a piece of sugar cane filled with sea water, sand and mercury, dirt, human and animal bones, herbs and spices such as chili, pepper, garlic, ginger, onion, cinnamon, and other items. *Nganga* containing human skulls are considered especially powerful as the skull contains the seat of intelligence. The *nganga* becomes a microcosm embodying these objects and the qualities they represent. Each item lends its own characteristic to the whole. With it the priest has harnessed all the energies of the plants and animals of the wilderness for his own use. Once sacralized the *nganga* becomes home to the spirit or spirits who work for the priest (called a *palero/a* or *mayombero/a*) who owns the *nganga*. Often this spirit is called the *nganga-perro* or "nganga dog" as it works under the control of the palero and guards the microcosm contained in the *nganga*. If the *nganga* is dedicated

to only good works, it is baptized with holy water from a church and is said to be *christana* (Christian) while one used for less savory ends is considered unbaptized or *judía*. A *christiana nganga* may also be called a *nkisi* while a *judía nganga* may be called a *ndoki* reflecting their positive and negative attributes, respectively. Some people consider the *nganga judía* more purely African than the *nganga christana* as they think it represents a refusal to incorporate Christianity into Kongolese practices. Each *ngnang*, said to contain the cosmos in microcosm, bears the name of the spirit of a deceased person (*muerto*) ensconced inside. Names such as *Paso Larog* (Long Steps), *Viento Malo* (Bad Wind), *Remolino* (Whirlwind), and *Rompe Monte* (Forest Breaker) are common.

During the initiation ceremony referred to as *rayamiento* or "being scratched," a pact is made between the priest and the spirit of the *nganga*. This pact enables the priest to direct the spirit to perform healing and other "magical" activities on his behalf. Although the work of the palero/a is often described as *brujería* (witchcraft), most of the rituals are designed to protect the palero, to help overcome obstacles, and to bring spiritual, mental, physical, or emotional healing to the palero, his family, or client. Although the relationship between the priest and the spirit is often described as one between a master and his slave, the spirits of Palo are believed to be powerful and dangerous beings. They must be treated appropriately according to the agreements made by the priest and his client to avoid having the spirits turn against and destroy them. Traditionally only senior priests, commonly known as *tata* (father) or *yaya* (mother) maintained a *nganga*, and it was common for a *nganga* to be passed down through the family line. Such old *ngangas* were said to be very powerful, having been used by generations of priests. The junior member of the religious group would petition the spirits through the senior priests. Today, however, it is much more common for even new initiates to be given their own *nganga* born from the *nganga* of their initiating priest. Many people are initiated into both Palo Monte and Santería. Santeros generally say that a person should be initiated into Palo Monte before their initiation into Santería as "the dead come before the Orisha" but, although it is considered spiritually dangerous to do so, there are some santeros that have been initiated into Palo after their initiation as priests of Santería.

As in many African-based religions, drumming, dancing, possession trance, divination, and animal sacrifice are integral to this tradition. A drum ensemble accompanied by wrist maracas and a plowshare or other piece of iron generally provides music for dance rituals. These rituals generally result in one or more of the devotees being possessed by the spirit of the *nganga*. Once it has possessed a devotee, the spirit can communicate with the assembled congregation, blessing individuals and working toward their physical, emotional, and spiritual betterment. As with other African-based traditions, the singing tends to be in a call and response form. Divination is performed using piles of gunpowder, a mirror embedded in a cow horn known as *mpaka*, or pieces of coconut shell.

Before the rise of modern medicine and readily available pharmaceuticals, herbalists were the primary healers in all communities. Paleros were known as especially knowledgeable and powerful healers whose knowledge of local herbs supplemented their spiritual healing work. Many paleros continue to work as herbalists and healers, integrating a wide range of healing arts into their religious practice.

It is commonly the case that both scholars and the general public compare Regla de Ocha (Santería) and Regla de Palo. Santería is often described as more refined, effete, and developed than Palo, which is described as cruder, "darker," and less sophisticated but also as more powerful, pragmatic, shrewd, and unhampered by strong ethical considerations. Although both men and women are initiated into Palo Monte, many people consider it more masculine and instrumental in its approach and style. Because paleros work with spirits of the dead rather than gods, their rituals are sometimes described as "witchcraft" or "evil." The dead, being at base human beings, are thought to be subject to the failings and foibles of the living. Often people will say that the Kongo spirits are less ethical than the Orisha of Santería and thus can more easily be enticed to perform unsavory or unscrupulous actions by their priests, and many think Palo rituals are more expeditious and effective because the spirits invoked are less hampered by ethical considerations. At the same time, Palo practitioners are quick to point out situations where a palero misused the power of the *prenda* and was subsequently punished by its spirit.

The use of the term "witchcraft" to describe the religious work of Palo is fraught with difficulties as African, European, and American concepts are interwoven in the various connotations of the term, and most of these connotations include the idea of power used for evil or immoral ends. Although much of this religious work involves healing of spiritual, emotional, and physical imbalances, it tends to be oriented toward individuals whose concerns may not be completely ethical. The Palo Monte *prenda* also looks scary to the uninitiated with its sticks and chains gathered together into a three-legged pot similar to the witch's caldron of popular imagination.

Palo Monte is sometimes identified as the "dark" side of Santería in spite of the fact that these are two separate traditions. Because none of the Afro-Cuban religions are exclusive, it is quite common for practitioners to be initiated in both systems (and others such as Espiritismo as well). However, the two traditions are independent, each coming from a different geographic and historical context and both containing both "light" and "dark," positive and negative, elements. Those practitioners who are initiates of both traditions are very strict about keeping the rituals of the two traditions apart so that they are

never performed in the same ritual space and time.

Mary Ann Clark

SELECTED BIBLIOGRAPHY

Cabrera, Lydia. *El Monte (Igbo, Finda, Ewe Orisha, Vititi Finda): Notas Sobre Las Religiones, La Magia, Las Supersticiones Y El Folklore De Los Negros Criollos Y Del Pueblo De Cuba* (Miami: Ediciones Universal, 1975).

Matibag, Eugenio. *Afro-Cuban Religious Experience: Cultural Reflections in Narrative* (Gainesville: University Press of Florida, 1996).

Olmos, Margarite Fernandez, and Lizabeth Paravisini-Gebert. "Creole Religions of the Caribbean: An Introduction from Vodou and Santería to Obeah and Espiritismo." *Religion, Race and Ethnicity*, ed. Peter J. Paris (New York and London: New York University Press, 2003).

Palmié, Stephan. *Wizards and Scientists: Explorations in Afro-Cuban Modernity and Tradition* (Durham, NC, and London: Duke University Press, 2002).

Thompson, Robert Ferris. *Flash of the Spirit: African and Afro-American Art and Philosophy* (New York: Random House, 1984).

PEACE MISSION MOVEMENT

Historical Development

The early twentieth century in the United States marked a period of great change. The aftermath of the Civil War and Reconstruction included entrenched patterns of discrimination referred to as "Jim Crow" that through social code and law made African Americans inferior. These sociopolitical problems combined with World War, economic challenge to make the early twentieth century a challenging time. And many African Americans responded by moving to new locations in search of better economic opportunities and a decrease in racial oppression. This movement—called the "Great Migration"—that took African Americans west and north to cities like Chicago began shortly after the Civil War and continued into the mid-twentieth century. This was a period of important and somewhat rapid cultural and social change in the United States, and the cultural production of African Americans often chronicled these shifts. African Americans moving north, for example, spread the influence of the blues—detailing their lives in music. Literature also gave voice to the struggle for a "good life" within the context of oppressive circumstances.

Changing life in the United States was not simply a secular matter. The early twentieth century was also a time of the growth of a diverse range of religious communities and beliefs. Some African Americans continued to embrace African American churches because, for them, these churches met a full range of their needs. But this did not mean that only the long-standing and dominant denominations were the target of devotion. No, the late nineteenth and early twentieth centuries also marked the emergence of new Christian denominations such as the Church of God in Christ. In addition, some African Americans found churches of limited assistance to them; both theologically and sociopolitically they found church supported the status quo and did little to help African Americans face the new challenges in front of them. It is in part this discontent that gave energy

to the development and growth of alternate religious orientations such as the Nation of Islam, the Universal House of Prayer for All Peoples, and Father Divine's Peace Mission.

Scholars of religion began giving attention to the development and activities of Father Divine's Peace Mission by the 1940s, with one notable example being Arthur Huff Fauset's *Black Gods of the Metropolis* (1944) in which he chronicles several key religious developments in African American urban communities. How could Father Divine not generate this sort of interest when one considers his financial means during a time of great socioeconomic want and need? For example, as many scholars note, during the Great Depression, Father Divine fed and housed many people, when the United States government seemed of little assistance. This religious organization marks one of the more intriguing religious developments of the early twentieth century.

It is believed that "Father Divine" or Father Major Jealous Divine was born George Baker, in Georgia. The actually date of his birth is unknown, but generally placed in the late 1870s or early 1880s. There is general consensus that Father Divine traveled as a preacher, but ministered without the benefit of formal education. Some scholars argue that at the turn of the century he worked for religious leader "Father Jehovia" (Watts 1995). Father Divine was influenced by the energy and thought of the growing Pentecostal movement and New Thought movement, and he used this combination of theologies and rituals to form a rather unique and "unorthodox" religious organization.

Eventually making his way to New York in roughly 1919, Father Divine

---

FATHER MAJOR JEALOUS DIVINE [FATHER DIVINE] (?–1965)

It is possible that Father Divine was born in either Georgia or Maryland, with the name George Baker. Little is known of his early life, although it is assumed he may have been a Baptist preacher, but one without the benefit of formal training. Having come under the influence of New Thought, Holiness teachings among other philosophies and theologies, Father Divine preached in various locations before moving to Long Island. It was in Long Island that he began holding the banquets that would define his movement. During these events his followers received his teachings, expressed their appreciation, and developed a sense of religious community outside the confines of strict hierarchy and organizational structure. His movement, known as the Peace Mission Movement, grew slowly until public speculation concerning his powers increased interest in him on the part of white Americans and African Americans. He would eventually move his organization to Harlem, but within a short period of time he would establish his primary location in Philadelphia, where he worked until 1960. At that point he stopped speaking and died in 1965.

---

began holding small meetings during which he preached his message. For the first decade of his New York ministry, there was slow growth among African Americans. In fact, it was not until white Americans took notice of his teachings and began to participate in his activities that numbers (and resources for the movement) grew in a noticeable manner. Figures with public visibility began to join the organization by the third decade of the twentieth century, and Father Divine continued to impress not only through his teachings but also through alleged healings (Fauset 1944; Watts 1995). The energy of his message, combined with what appeared to be supernatural power, helped a growing number of people make sense of a troubled world. His appeal would continue to grow, and an event in 1932 solidified his standing as a spiritual leader with great cosmic authority. I recount the story as told by numerous scholars and members of the Peace Mission: Father Divine and several of his followers were arrested on Long Island for disturbing the peace. In May 1932 he was found guilty and

sentenced. However, and this is key, a short number of days after the verdict, the judge in the case died. Father Divine claimed to have used his spiritual power to bring about the death of the unjust judge. As one might expect, his public exposure and appeal only grew because of this event (Fauset 1944; Dallam 2007; Watts 1995).

This boost to his popularity and visibility was matched by efforts to establish a more institutionalized approach to his work, and to more clearly and systematically present to the public his teachings as they related to the equality and value of all people. To achieve the former, Father Divine moved his organization to Harlem (New York City), the recognized "center" of African American cultural life. The plan was to grow the scope and reach of the organization through public exposure and the securing of property for housing Father Divine's ministry. This growth required the type of organized presentation of his teachings made possible through their media outlets such as the *New Day* (1937). As a consequence of these activities,

Father Divine's organization grew and by the early 1940s a name change spoke to this new status. The organization became the Peace Mission Movement (Watts 1995).

Father Divine's exposure was great, and national media outlets routinely covered him; but his activities were not without challengers. Most notably, as scholar Marie Dallam makes clear, Sweet Daddy Grace would be responsible for a major shift in Father Divine's popularity and a relocation of his movement to Philadelphia. Sweet Daddy Grace and Father Divine were chief rivals, in part because of overlap in their New Thought–Pentecostal influenced teachings, but also their powerful presence and personas often brought them into comparison. Both leaders claimed special status, Sweet Daddy Grace as a powerful and anointed spokesperson for God and Father Divine as God (Dallam 2007, 112). The degree of similarity between these two religious leaders is less the point here. What is more important is the friction between them and the nature of their interaction. Harlem, where both would settle, was a substantial geographic and cultural location, but not so big that these two major figures, with different theological perspectives and strong claims to special status, would be able to coexist without any conflict. The desire of both to punctuate their authority eventually brought them into conflict.

Problems for Father Divine would mount, and would create vulnerabilities others would seek to exploit. Regarding this, the late 1930s marked a change in the "fortune" of the Peace Movement, as controversy challenged its public reputation. For instance, at least one key member of the organization—"Faithful

Father Divine holds a parade in Harlem to celebrate the acquisition of a new communal dwelling that he calls Heaven, July 31, 1938. (Bettmann/Corbis)

Mary"—left the Mission and began to critique the teachings and practices of Father Divine (Dallam 2007, 123–124). Such fracturing of the Peace Mission and the rhetoric surrounding it suggested the high moral standards endorsed by its members were not always practiced. Conflict developed between members based on shifting loyalties to Father Divine versus those who had a growing level of suspicion toward Father Divine. In addition, the illness of Father Divine's wife, Peninniah, caused stress in that she had been a major source of support for him (Dallam 2007, 123–124). These problems and challenges were not simply addressed within the context of the Peace Mission but also within the larger Harlem community, and within both scholarly and popular publications.

Disagreeing with much of Father Divine's teachings and practices, Sweet Daddy Grace took his move to Harlem as an opportunity to distinguish what he considered the truth and power of his teachings from the teachings and practices of Father Divine. Targeting the headquarters of the Peace Mission—"Number One Heaven"—Sweet Daddy Grace sought to secure the building during a time of financial stress for the Peace Mission Movement. Through securing this property, Sweet Daddy Grace would be able to critique Father Divine's claim to be God and establish his authority (Dallam 2007, 125–126). The manner in which Father Divine taught his members to avoid debt such as mortgages made this property vulnerable in that it was rented and available for purchase from the bank (see appendix "Explaining the Peace Mission"). Sweet Daddy Grace bought the property, evicted Father Divine, and proclaimed that he had "kicked God" (i.e., Father Divine) "out of Heaven" (i.e., the Peace Mission Headquarters).

Father Divine eventually moved the Peace Mission headquarters to Philadelphia (some three years after the eviction), claiming that in fact the Harlem location was not adequate for the needs of his organization. While the loss of his Harlem location meant a challenge to his organization and teachings, Father Divine remained active but modified his practices. For example, he began to secure personal property that was something he avoided prior to 1938. Furthermore, some scholars speculate that the loss of his Harlem property also demonstrated to him the vulnerability of an organization that was not properly and firmly structured. So, Father Divine worked to develop all the elements of a solid and sustainable organization—incorporation, a governing board, and so on. Change in business perspective allowed the Peace Mission to regain material health and both national and international growth. Father Divine continued his teachings and practices, until

1960 when he stopped speaking. At that time his second wife, Edna Rose Ritchings ("Mother Divine"), had to expand her work within the organization. After his death in 1965, Edna Rose Ritchings maintained the activities of the Peace Mission.

Beliefs and Practices

Expressed through publications and provided often through weekly banquets during which Father Divine taught his followers, the beliefs of the Peace Mission Movement entail a blending of New Thought, Holiness, and Pentecostalism among other minor influences. As scholars have noted, those who lived in the "compound" were called "Angels" and took large responsibility for the financial needs of the movement, while those who commuted in for the weekly banquets but lived elsewhere were called Father Divine's "Children" (Dallam 2007, 113). The organization lacked the type of hierarchy and structure associated with traditional churches, preferring instead a more community-centered model. Followers of Father Divine believed that he, as God in the world, had been given to them to teach them and guide them toward healthy and prosperous existence on earth. Father Divine's teachings, according to scholars of religion, revolved around the belief that the universe is defined by its beauty and positive value and that each individual is a representation of this value and beauty (Dallam 2007, 113; Burnham 1979; Watts 1995). Hence, their activities in the world should speak to this goodness and should represent commitment to harmony between the physical and the spiritual. In a way that would be later mirrored in the prosperity gospel, Father Divine taught that material wealth reflected spiritual health. Therefore, physical discomfort or hardship corresponded to poor spiritual health (Dallam 2007, 113–114; Watts 1995). This theological perspective, however, did not justify greed and the harming of others for personal wealth accumulation. Father Divine taught that spiritual and social equality and harmony were fundamental aims. Meaningful life in this world took precedence over any talk of heaven or hell.

As existing scholarship on the Peace Mission suggests, Father Divine's perspective on financial responsibility urged proper management of resources, and denounced the borrowing of money and credit. Instead, members were to work hard, monitor their resources, and stay within their means. Moral conduct, according to Father Divine, demanded sharing of resources; therefore, community assistance represented the proper mode of healthy material and spiritual life (see appendix "Explaining the Peace Mission"). And while material health was important, Father Divine did not personally own property and business; everything, instead, belonged to the Peace Mission.

While this attention to prosperous living on earth did not justify greed, it also did not allow for questionable practices in securing material happiness. To the contrary, members of the Peace Mission believed in the need for strict rules for life, and failure to abide by these rules could result in dismissal from the community. They were to live a healthy and socially modest life by avoiding things such as alcohol, wagers, immodest clothing, and questionable conversation (Dallam 2007, 114; Watts 1995).

In terms of ritual practices, the banquets mentioned at the start of this section entailed the most sustained and regularized gathering for the membership. It was during these weekly sessions that Father Divine spread his wisdom and those committed to him celebrated the strength of their community and the power of his teachings. Members testified to the progress they had made regarding proper living (Dallam 2007, 114). These ritual gatherings and the teachings they reinforced fostered strong bonds with Father Divine that often resulted in separation from birth families and friends outside the movement. This in part stemmed from the nature of life within the Peace Mission, but also from a desire to keep at a distance nonmembers who might try to harm the Movement and soil the reputation of Father Divine through their disbelief.

Anthony B. Pinn

SELECTED BIBLIOGRAPHY

Burnham, Kenneth E. *God Comes to America: Father Divine and the Peace Mission Movement* (Boston: Lambeth Press, 1979).

Dallam, Marie W. *Daddy Grace: A Celebrity Preacher and His House of Prayer* (New York: New York University Press, 2007).

Fauset, Arthur Huff. *Black Gods of the Metropolis: Negro Religious Cults of the Urban North* (Philadelphia: University of Pennsylvania Press, 1944).

Watts, Jill. *God, Harlem U.S.A.: The Father Divine Story* (Berkeley: University of California Press, 1995).

Weisbrot, Robert. *Father Divine and the Struggle for Racial Equality* (Urbana: University of Illinois Press, 1983).

PEOPLES TEMPLE

Historical Development

The Peoples Temple movement began in the 1950s as an independent Pentecostal congregation of white and black working-class families in Indianapolis, Indiana. Seventy members of this congregation followed their leader to northern California in the mid-1960s. Here they were joined by a number of young, middle-class, professional whites who in turn helped recruit hundreds of urban African Americans. In the mid-1970s, the movement built a utopian community in the country of Guyana that was named for its founder and leader, Jim Jones. The movement ended in 1978 after more than 900 members died in Jonestown in a mass homicide and suicide.

In part because of its tragic and apocalyptic ending, this movement has frequently been labeled a "cult" by both scholars and members of the communications media. (Scholars today prefer the language of "new religious movement" or "alternative religion.") Some argue it was initially a Christian sect that then became a new religious movement. Mary Maaga suggests that the movement can best be described as including various types of religious organization, according to different time periods and different membership groups. Thus, the members from the first stage of the movement can be regarded as sect-like, younger white members from the second stage on were more cult-like, and African American members who joined in later years were neither.

With regard to the African American members, Mary Sawyer makes a case that those who retained a Christian orientation constituted a "church" within the larger movement. Anthony Pinn argues that African American members could well have represented a range of religious orientations, including humanism. Certainly the movement's emphasis on community-building and social justice was resonant with the values of black religious traditions that have their roots in the cosmology of African traditions.

Peoples Temple was a complex movement that offered hope to thousands of individuals. The overwhelming majority of people who affiliated with the movement had a vision of peace and equity and a commitment to match the vision. In many respects, it was a mini-version of the civil rights movement. It was also a movement full of contradiction. While the leader of the movement, at least in its earliest years, was undoubtedly sincere in his quest of these goals, his manner of pursuing them ultimately degenerated into a nightmare of control, hypocrisy, paranoia, and abuse. In the end, he was a contradiction of everything he had claimed to hold dear.

Focusing solely on the leader or leaders of a movement tells us little about who joined, and why, and what meaning the experience had for them. At the same time, the leadership of the movement cannot be discounted. Most especially, the fact that Jim Jones, as well as some 60 percent of the movement's governing group, was white cannot be discounted.

Within the movement's Planning Commission was an inner circle of staff members who were especially close to Jones. Most of them were white, most were women, and most were well-educated professionals. The majority of the members were poorly educated and unskilled. While the movement membership was diverse, including Native Americans, Latinos, and Jews, it was not integrated at the leadership level.

The paradox is that the primary goals of the movement were racial integration and class equality. Personally, Jones and his wife, Marceline (Marcie) Baldwin Jones, lived this commitment by adopting a number of children who, together with their biological son, formed a multiracial family.

James Warren Jones was born during the Great Depression in a rural county of southern Indiana on May 13, 1931. An only child, Jones and his parents soon left their farm, moving into the small town of Lynn, Indiana. Jones's father was a disabled World War I veteran of Quaker and Baptist heritage who purportedly was also a member of the Ku Klux Klan and virulently anticommunist. His mother carried much of the financial responsibility for the family, working odd jobs and volunteering as a labor organizer. She did not share the bigoted views of her husband and his family, a point that she impressed upon her son. In terms of religious views, Jones's mother believed strongly in the presence of spirits in the world, but rejected the idea of a monotheistic, all-powerful God. This perspective was also not lost on young Jim.

Beliefs and Practices

Jones defied his father by embracing socialist tenets of equality and becoming an ardent proponent of racial integration. Although he never embraced the Christian understanding of God, he was impressed by the teachings of Jesus. His engagement in organized religion appears to have been largely a matter of convenience and utilitarianism. He was attracted to Pentecostalism, finding its emphasis on the "gifts of the spirit" especially appealing. Jones apprehended the ways in which claims of spiritual gifts, especially those of discernment, healing, and prophesying, could be used to gain power over people. The apocalyptic worldview of Pentecostalism also was important, connecting, as it did, with Jones's conviction that nuclear annihilation was imminent. In later years, Jones invoked the Pentecostal expectation of a second coming of Christ, declaring himself to be the divine embodiment of Christ. However, Jones rejected the otherworldly salvation claims of traditional Christianity, instead emphasizing social salvation in this world. He rejected the Bible as Holy Scripture, though he pointed to the early communities of Jesus' followers that are described in the Book of Acts as the ideal model of human relationships. He knew the contents of the Bible well and became skilled at using biblical language, as well as Marxist language, to assert the imperative of equality. He rejected institutional religion, though he was not averse to using these forms of organization to attract and mobilize followers.

Jones's first attempts at weaving together these disparate strands occurred in 1952 when he served as a student pastor at a Methodist Church located in an all-white, economically impoverished section of Indianapolis. His championing of racial integration resulted in a number of black Pentecostals joining the church, which in turn led to his dismissal. Within the year, however, while attending a black Pentecostal church convention, he was proclaimed a prophet and called to the ministry.

In 1954, Jones started his own church. The church initially was called

Community Unity, then Wings of Deliverance Church, and finally Peoples Temple Full Gospel Church. In 1955, his congregation elected to affiliate with the Christian Church (Disciples of Christ) denomination. Four years later, Jones was ordained a Disciples of Christ minister.

His choice of denomination is interesting, but in hindsight not surprising. Disciples of Christ differs from other mainstream Protestant denominations in significant ways. The church does not believe in the concept of "original sin," for example, and declines to use the phrase "Holy Trinity." It has no creed and emphasizes freedom of thought and individual interpretation. These positions of the church were compatible with many of Jones's personal biases. In addition, at the time Jones was ordained, church authority rested in the local congregation; not until some years later did the denomination develop a significant national structure to provide oversight of individual churches.

At the time the Jonestown tragedy occurred, Jones was still credentialed as a Disciples minister and Peoples Temple was still in good standing as a Disciples of Christ congregation. In a statement issued shortly after the tragedy, however, Dr. Kenneth L. Teegarden, general minister and president of the denomination, made it known that a review of Jones's ministerial standing had been underway. He also noted that, "When James W. Jones affiliated with the Disciples and during his ministry in Indianapolis there was no forewarning of what was to come. His early ministry was considered something of a model for inner city work, with strong interracial aspects and community service to the poor."

More so than the tenets of the Christian Church, Jones was influenced by the teachings of the black messianic leader, Father Divine. Divine was the founder of the movement known as *Peace Mission Movement* (see entry "Peace Mission Movement"). Concurrently, Jones was preparing for ordination in a mainstream Christian denomination while he was visiting Father Divine in Philadelphia where he studied the programs and organizational structure of the Peace Mission Movement. The Peace Mission Movement was itself a communal movement devoted to racial equality and alleviation of poverty. Its goals were pursued through two strategies: urban outreach and social service in the city, and the building of interracial, cooperative communities in rural areas of upstate New York. Urban social service and migration to escape the racism and classism of American society became the twin foci of Jones's own movement. The sharing of personal economic resources, communal living, and the operation of various service entities (e.g., nursing homes and drug counseling) became the means for financing these endeavors.

When Jones was named executive director of the Indianapolis Human Rights Commission, he launched an aggressive program to desegregate Indianapolis. While he achieved some success, he also generated fierce hostility and opposition. As early as 1961, he explored the possibility of building a settlement in a South American country that, following independence, became known as Guyana. However, in 1962 Jones and his wife, Marci, along with their children, relocated to Brazil, where he inquired about obtaining land on which to build a settlement. Failing in this endeavor, they returned to Indianapolis in 1964. Upon being met with the same hostility they had experienced previously, Jones and members of his congregation began looking to California as a more favorable climate for their social ministry and as a location safer from nuclear destruction.

By 1965, Jim Jones and his followers had migrated to Mendocino County in the Redwood Valley of Northern California. Initially, membership growth was slow. A few families continued to relocate from Indianapolis, and some recruits were drawn from among black residents recently arriving from the Bay Area. But the primary growth consisted of young professional whites—teachers, social workers, and lawyers—who were drawn to the movement by its program of social transformation and socialist lifestyle. Among these new members were several individuals who assumed important positions in the leadership circle of the movement. Sharon Amos, Teri Buford, Carolyn Moore Layton, Michael Prokes, and Timothy Stoen joined older members such as Rick Cordell and Archie L. James as confidantes and disciples of Jones.

In 1968, Peoples Temple began reaching out to African Americans in San Francisco. Two years later, a church building was purchased in San Francisco that in short order became the primary headquarters of the Peoples Temple movement. A church also was established in Los Angeles and, for several years, Jones and hundreds of members caravanned by bus to other California cities, as well as to major cities around the country, where evangelistic-style rallies were staged to draw new recruits.

At its peak, Peoples Temple had a membership of some 3,000. The largest proportion of its members consisted of disaffected black youth, single mothers with children, and elderly black women. The ranks of Peoples Temple included some who had little political consciousness, but were simply seeking a better life. Black youth found help with legal problems, addiction issues, and educational and employment deficiencies. Single mothers were assisted in obtaining social services. Elderly people, especially women, responded to the promise of lifelong care and security. But the majority of members also were impassioned about the movement's overt political values and activities.

While the well-educated whites who had joined earlier were products of the countercultural challenges to authority of the 1960s, African Americans were more influenced by the liberation struggles of the day. For whites, the student protest and anti–Viet Nam war movement were pivotal; for blacks, the context was defined by the Civil Rights Movement, the assassinations of Malcolm X and Martin Luther King Jr., and the flourishing of black power groups such as the Black Panther Party and the Nation of Islam.

Activist members campaigned for ballot initiatives, worked for tenants' rights, and protested on behalf of journalistic freedom. They supported gay rights, protested the California Supreme Court decision in the anti-affirmative action *Bakke* case, and joined the movement to abolish apartheid in South Africa. They were connected to well-known social change activists, including Dennis Banks, one of the leaders of the American Indian Movement; Dick Gregory; Daniel Ellsberg, of Pentagon Papers fame; and defense attorney William Kunstler. Locally, Peoples Temple took control of the San Francisco chapter of the National Association for the Advancement of Colored People.

Jones himself had the ability to develop relations with key government representatives that gave him entrée to power circles denied to most social change activists. He was appointed to the influential San Francisco Housing Authority, which gave him an official platform from which to speak on behalf of citizens who were being displaced by urban renewal programs. On a moment's notice, Jones could mobilize hundreds of people for a campaign or protest rally. The power he wielded at election time in getting out the vote was legendary. For a few brief years, he and his aides were a public force to be reckoned with.

The Temple became known for its charitable giving, some of which had transparent political motives. But it also held clinics for testing sickle cell anemia and hypertension, and for administering flu shots. Hundreds of people were provided daily meals; others were offered shelter in the complex of homes for the elderly, foster children, and mentally challenged individuals that the movement owned and/or operated.

This extraordinary demonstration of commitment to social service and social justice, along with its public presentation as a Christian Church, garnered the movement support from such entities as the San Francisco Council of Churches. Peoples Temple also successfully cultivated relations with representatives of the local Muslim and Jewish communities. No entity was more supportive of the movement than the local black newspaper, *The Sun Reporter*, which consistently ran stories and articles favorable to the Temple's activities.

Black ministers in San Francisco initially embraced Jim Jones as a gospel-preaching "brother," disregarding his racial heritage in the face of his public ministry to "the least of these." They fairly quickly became hostile, however, as members of their churches left for Peoples Temple. Many individuals and families who changed affiliation came from local black churches that had a reputation for their otherworldly focus. Members who were frustrated with the conservative theology and passivity of their home congregations saw in Peoples Temple a religious organization that lived out the principles of equality and justice that were the bedrock of their Christian faith. Of the few progressive ministers in the Bay Area at this time, some were skeptical of Jones, but others saw him as functioning in accord with the prophetic biblical tradition.

As the character of Jones's power changed and as his behavior during the movement's San Francisco years became erratic, he grew increasingly defensive and punitive. Members who were perceived to be obstructing his program were punished both psychologically and physically. An elaborate system of spying and reporting on one another was instituted. False rumors were started, causing friend to turn upon friend, all in the interest of maintaining control.

In 1973, Peoples Temple negotiated the purchase of land in the country of Guyana for the purpose of building a utopian community. This new settlement was envisioned as the Promised Land, a place in which people—young and old, black and white—could live lives of peace and harmony, free from the racism of American society. The country of Guyana, which had first been considered by Jones a decade earlier, was appealing for several reasons: it was a Cooperative

Socialist Republic, its leadership was Afro-Guyanese, and it was strongly anticapitalist.

The project of clearing the land in the midst of jungle terrain began in 1974 and quickly became a primary focus of the movement. As houses, a school, and a health clinic were erected, visitors to the site returned to California with glowing reports and photos that excited the members and friends of the movement alike.

Things began to unravel in San Francisco as rumors surfaced in the larger community that all was not well within the movement. Allegations ranged from misuse of public funds (none of which were ever substantiated) to abuse of individual members. The most damaging critique of the Temple took the form of an article published in August 1977 by *New West* magazine, but articles by the *San Francisco Chronicle* and *San Francisco Examiner* newspapers added to a growing public suspicion.

As the attacks on the movement mounted, Jim Jones and hundreds of Peoples Temple members relocated to Jonestown, Guyana. According to the accounts of nonmembers who visited the settlement, it was an extraordinary accomplishment. Hundreds of people were fed, clothed, and sheltered. Children were educated. All were provided high quality medical care. Many residents rejoiced in the sense of freedom and self-worth that came from living in an atmosphere where all were treated equally. Meanwhile, however, Jones himself descended into a world of illness, paranoia, and drug addiction.

Most of the allegations made against the movement came from disaffected former members. Most of the critics were white, and many of them had been out

of the movement for a number of years. Some of them became part of a group calling itself "Concerned Relatives." In general, the practices used to maintain social control that former members had come to find intolerable were not unusual in the history of utopian communities. But outside the context of the communities themselves, such practices engendered even more alarm. The concern that defectors felt for friends and relatives still in the movement was undoubtedly genuine.

At the same time, the full range of motives of persons alienated from a movement that had at one time been meaningful to them is rarely transparent. Some, for example, had given large sums of money to the movement and later came to regret having done so. Consequently, parties to whom they took their concerns were invariably ambivalent about how to respond. One person who did respond, Congressman Leo Ryan, unwittingly triggered the chain of events in Jonestown that led to the movement's demise.

In November 1978, Congressman Ryan led a delegation to Guyana to investigate the concerns of members' relatives. The delegation, which included several staff members as well as journalists and photographers, visited Jonestown and spoke to Jones as well as numerous members. Upon returning to the airfield with several defectors, Ryan and others were attacked by a small contingent of Jonestown members. Ryan and four others were killed; a number of people were injured.

When word of these shootings was received in Jonestown, Jones, fearing military retribution that would destroy the entire community, led the residents in a ritual of what he termed revolutionary suicide. The ritual had been rehearsed a number of times previously. This time, however, it was the real thing. On November 18, 1978, 909 people died in Jonestown; four more died in Georgetown, Guyana.

A few individuals escaped through the jungle and eventually returned to the United States. Other members, including three of Jim and Marci's sons, were away at the time of the violence. About a hundred members remained in California, the majority of them in San Francisco. But the movement was effectively eliminated.

Speculation about CIA or other government involvement in the demise of the community ensued. In fact, from the time significant numbers of people migrated to the settlement, Jonestown was under surveillance by various government agencies—Guyanese, United States, and international. No evidence has surfaced to date that any of these agencies were directly responsible for what transpired. But the surveillance and continuous allegations against the movement were experienced by the leadership as harassment, and the people collectively developed a siege mentality that made them vulnerable to engaging in extreme behaviors.

It is plausible that, by the end, the capacity of adult members to choose their fate was compromised by the effects of the extreme duress they had endured. Clearly, for some time before the end, Jones himself, having succumbed to drug addictions and mental aberrations, was incapable of exercising rational judgment.

Among the survivors were countless friends and family members of those who died, who were not themselves formally affiliated with Peoples Temple.

Their healing and recovery from this traumatic experience was severely impeded by the inflammatory media coverage of the deaths, and by the shroud of silence woven by the insensitive and unsympathetic sentiments of most Americans. For many years—in some instances, decades—survivors did not even acknowledge having had a connection to the movement.

Annual memorial services held at the Oakland cemetery where some 400 unclaimed bodies are buried, and the establishment of the Jonestown Web site and a regularly published newsletter (called *the jonestown report*) by Rebecca Moore and Fielding McGehee, have been primary avenues for voicing thoughts and feelings, as well as for reporting research and insights about the movement.

Peoples Temple representation of itself as a black church was critical. This representation began with Jones's own self-presentation. Jones was so invested in the principle of racial equality that he appropriated a personal identity of blackness and spoke the inclusive language of "we blacks." Ultimately, he even claimed to have African ancestry. While in Redwood Valley, he encouraged both black and white members to adopt the African dress and Afro hairstyles of the black consciousness movement.

Jones also appropriated the theological vocabulary, autocratic leadership style, and messianic themes characteristic of many black ministers. The services conducted at Peoples Temple had the ambience of black worship services, with strong emphasis on gospel music, testimonies, and healing. Many black members who participated in this culturally familiar milieu undoubtedly did so with sincerity and integrity, but Jones did not. Black members were part of the larger of the two orientations that comprised the Redwood Valley organization. The smaller of the two orientations was secular and Jones made an effort to appeal to their Marxist inclinations. The larger orientation entailed a highly religious perspective that Jones nurtured through attention to the gospel message of community involvement and justice.

The economic and political objectives and the religious rhetoric came together in Jones's program of "apostolic socialism." A central component of this program involved drawing black religious members away from an escapist, otherworldly version of Christianity to a set of social principles that mandated activism in order to create more just conditions in the world. Jones often expressed frustration that the people he was seeking to free from the "opiate of religion" insisted on remaining tied to old forms and understandings of their faith.

At the same time, Jones gave his political program religious status through his claims of having special powers of perception and healing. Testimonies abound of Jones's extraordinary charisma. Still today, some survivors remain persuaded that Jones had unusual, if not supernatural, power; some among these have spoken of his powers for good that over time were transformed into powers for evil.

In the very last years of the movement, references by the movement's leadership to conventional Christianity were made only during the Temple's public worship services when "outsiders" might be present, some of whom it was presumed would be Christians. Insincere as it may have been on the part of the leadership, Christian language was spoken and heard by religious members who attended these services. Even when scriptural language was forbidden in private Temple meetings, those terms that had been so prevalent in the years of the Civil Rights Movement—such words as freedom, equality, integration, and community—continued to be primary.

When Jones or members of the leadership team exchanged visits with black churches, they spoke in the language of Christianity. Christian language was also used by Temple staff whenever they interacted with prominent individuals in the black community, the ecumenical religious community, and government offices. To the very end, the letterhead of the movement's stationery read, "Peoples Temple of the Disciples of Christ, Jim Jones, Pastor." On the sideboard was printed the text of Matthew 25: 35–40: "For I was hungry and you fed me; I was thirsty and you gave me drink; I was a stranger and you took me in; naked, and you clothed me . . . . Inasmuch as you have done it unto one of the least of these . . . you have done it unto me."

It is noteworthy that, following the dissolution of Peoples Temple in California, a number of survivors returned to conventional Protestant churches. What the religious journey of all the black members who joined Peoples Temple was or would have been will never be known. Evidence argues that at least some of them kept the faith of Christian orthodoxy—the faith that Jesus was Lord and Savior, the faith that God had sent a servant to lead the people out of bondage in biblical times and would do so again, the faith that all people were the children of God and ought to be accorded equal respect and opportunity.

It was the resonance of Jim Jones's words with these core tenets of Christianity that brought many of them to the movement in the first place; it may in part have been these tenets—along with the historic African values of community and kinship so deeply embedded in the souls and psyches of the people—that kept them there. At least some among them retained a capacity for questioning what was presented to them and made conscious choices to remain with the community that had become their family and the church that was real for them in spite of Jones's apostasy. That is to say, the people retained agency; they were not merely puppets of a deranged leader.

For all of their leader's deceit, the people of Peoples Temple recognized that Jim Jones spoke a truth. That truth was that America's "self-evident" principles were not evident in practice. In despair that it would ever be otherwise, they sought to build a community in another land. Persuaded that the very existence of their community was threatened, and believing they could never return to a racist American society, the majority of adult members concurred with the decision to die—together, as a community. It goes without saying that the infants, children, and youth, who numbered nearly 300, had no power to choose.

While the killing of the children was incomprehensible to most outsiders, there is historical precedent. Their deaths, which Marceline Jones reportedly protested until the end, are reminiscent of the stories of captured Africans killing their children to spare them the worse fate of slavery. Reprehensible as the acts may have been, they provide a measure of how horrific the members of the movement understood racism in American society to be: Being denied one's humanity on account of color was regarded as the worse fate.

Mary Sawyer

SELECTED BIBLIOGRAPHY

Hall, John R. *Gone from the Promised Land: Jonestown in American Cultural History* (New Brunswick, NJ: Transaction Publishers, 1989).

Maaga, Mary McCormick. *Hearing the Voices of Jonestown* (Syracuse, NY: Syracuse University Press, 1998).

Moore, Rebecca. *A Sympathetic History of Jonestown* (Lewiston, NY: The Edwin Mellen Press, 1985).

Moore, Rebecca, Anthony B. Pinn, and Mary R. Sawyer, eds. *Peoples Temple and Black Religion in America* (Bloomington, IN: Indiana University Press, 2004).

POCOMANIA

Historical Development

Pocomania is an African-based religious tradition indigenous to the island of Jamaica in the Caribbean. Pocomania adherents are generally drawn from the poor and depressed sector of Jamaican society. The name "Pocomania" is generally attributed to the Spanish word *pocomania*, meaning "small madness."

This Jamaican indigenous religious tradition is also spelled as "Pukumina." Some scholars question the Spanish derivation of the name. They argue that the spelling "Pukumina" signifies the religion's derivation from the West African Twi words *po*, meaning "small," and *kumina*, referring to the dance of ancestral possession. According to this argument, "Pukumina" means "small kumina" or the "small dance of ancestral possession" (Thelwell 1988, 397). Nevertheless, Pocomania or Pukumina refers to the same African-based religious tradition indigenous to Jamaica. We shall here use the term "Pocomania," since it appears to be the more popular term used to refer to the religion. However, it must be pointed out that the term "Pukumina," referring to the "small ancestral dance," brings out the images of dance and music that are associated with the religion, as well as emphasizing through reference to ancestors the African base of the religion.

Millions of Africans were brought to the New World, including Jamaica, to work as slaves on the sugar plantations or estates that developed as the base of the modern industrial and economic system. Most of the slaves, who came from West Africa, carried their ancestral or traditional African religious and cultural system with them across the Atlantic, and used it to develop new religious and cultural systems in response to the hardships and brutality of slavery and plantation life. Pocomania belongs to what is called Revivalism in Jamaican religions. Consequently, the terms "Revivalism," "Pocomania," "Kumina," and "Zionism" are frequently used to refer to various indigenous Jamaican religious traditions that bear similar features. For example, it is possible for Pocomania to be referred to as "Revival" by members and nonmembers. Nonetheless, we shall here distinguish Pocomania from other forms of Revivalism.

The umbrella term "Revivalism" hides what distinguishes Pocomania from other Revival cults in Jamaica (Hogg 1964). The difference between Pocomania and other Revival traditions in Jamaica revolves around the kind of spirits Pocomania band leaders and adherents collaborate with. It is easy to understand the perception that Pocomania leaders use obeah (see entry "Obeah") or witchcraft, since they work with the "ground spirits." Pocomania is predominantly African in its rituals and beliefs.

Pocomania emerged in Jamaica during the 1860s. It was influenced by Myalism, the Great Revival of the 1860s. Myalism is an amalgamation of religious observances in Jamaica, contained, in varying proportions, African and Christian religious elements, concepts, and practices. Myalism, first documented in the late eighteenth century, was the crucible out of which present-day Revival, Zion, and Pocomania religions evolved (Warner-Lewis 2003, 190–198). Myalism first gained attention during the 1760 Taki Rebellion. The Taki or Tacky Rebellion occurred when Tacky, a Coromanti slave, led a small band of slaves and captured Fort Haldane at Port Maria, Jamaica. The rebels set fire to Heywood Hall Plantation and destroyed some buildings at Esther Estate. There was no general uprising, though a number of slaves joined the rebels. The uprising was eventually put down, but in the same month there was another slave uprising in the Parish of St. Thomas-in-the-East, as well as uprisings on several plantations in the Parish of Westmoreland. The Coromantin slaves were at the center of these rebellions in the 1760s. The role of Myalism in these rebellions means that it had been in gestation for some time prior to the rebellion. In other words, Myalism was a form of religious resistance to the oppression experienced in plantation life. Myalism enabled a rebellion to be organized on pan-African, instead of strictly ethnic, lines for the first time in the history of the Africans in Jamaica (Warner-Lewis 2003, 190–198). Dreams of freedom, the growth of the Native Baptist Church, and Myalism increased in Jamaica around the time of the American War of independence.

Following the commencement of the American War of Independence in 1776, a number of American planters, loyal to the British crown, migrated to Jamaica with their slaves. In the group were a Baptist preacher named George Liele, Moses Baker, and George Lewis. Some planters with abolitionist sentiments permitted Lisle and Baker to proselytize the slaves. Lisle's work focused in Kingston where he established the first Baptist church in Jamaica. He used the class-leader system in which the most talented converts were appointed leaders over classes of new converts. As soon as these converts were baptized, they passed on the gospel to others. The Baptist church grew in this process. However, it was Myalism that was really growing (Chevannes 1994, 20–21). The class-leader system allowed greater autonomy and freedom for Myalism to refashion the symbols and teachings of Christianity in its own image. This new development made it possible to identify and distinguish some of Myalism's teachings and practices, with Christianity as the basis of comparison. Myalism modified Christianity's central doctrine of Jesus Christ as the Mediator between God the Father and humankind; the Holy Spirit is the sole Mediator between God and humankind in Pocomania. Myalism's emphasis on the experience of the Spirit was strategic. Ritually, the centrality of spirit possession in Myalism defines it as a space of experience in which a horizon of expectation is constructed. In other words, it is the liberation of eschatology, in keeping with the conviction of those formerly enslaved, that their masters were withholding, the freedom that the British monarch had granted them. In contact

with the Great Revival of the 1860s, Myalism underwent further development.

The Great Revival that swept the world in the 1860s impacted the development of Revivalism, Myalism, and African religions in Jamaica. Under the general name of Revival Zion, the intensity of the Great Revival transformed Myalism into two streams, Zion and Pocomania. Zion, the first to become public, like the Native Baptists, retained close resemblance to Christianity. It made greater use of the Bible and other Christian symbols. Above all, it refused to show any respect for the belligerent and dangerous spirits that it acknowledged existed but kept under control through the power of ritual symbolisms. Pocomania emerged after Zion in the early months of 1861. This is why Pocomania is referred throughout the Revival world as "Sixty-One" and Zion as "Sixty." Pocomania modified the African and ancestral heritage, adapted them to the Jamaican context, and provided healing from the trauma of displacement from ancestral homelands and the brutality of slavery and plantation society.

Writers and scholars like Edward Seaga, Rex Nettleford, Barry Chevannes, and Noel Erskine would appreciate the argument that through Pocomania African-descended peoples in Jamaica expressed self-agency to reclaim their subjectivity (Chevannes 1994; Erskine 1998; Nettleford 2001; Seaga 1969). They recognize Pocomania's significance in the construction of Afro-Jamaican humanity, Jamaican culture, and the evolution of post-emancipation Jamaican sovereignty. Seaga, an early Pocomania researcher and former Jamaican prime minister, knows the political significance of Pocomania, with respect to the mobilization of the Jamaican masses for political transformation. Nettleford would argue that people express their inherent need to name God or the Divine in their own image. Chevannes, in the context of indigenous Jamaican religions, would call for a radical rethinking of Pocomania in relationship to peasant religious traditions and their role in the revolutionary process of creating Jamaican nationhood. Though Erskine subsumes Pocomania within the phenomenon of Revivalism, he defines it as a form of Black religion designed to help Black people in the Caribbean become more fully human. These perspectives point to the historical struggle of Jamaican and Caribbean peoples of African descent for sovereignty, full emancipation, self-determination, and the right to represent themselves authentically.

Beliefs and Practices

The major Pocomania beliefs and rituals must be interpreted within the framework of a myth or drama of cultural regeneration. Belief in spirits is central in the Pocomania worldview. A pivotal belief in Pocomania is the coexistence of the ancestral spiritual and temporary world. Pocomania, by virtue of its very name, indicates the centrality of the spirits in the tradition. One knows one's identity in Pocomania through relationship to the spirits that include, amongst others, the ancestors. That all spirits are powerful in Pocomania is closer to traditional African religions. Since all spirits can possess, they deserve respect (Chevannes 1994, 20–21; Simpson 1956). The "spirits" include Old Testament prophets, New Testament saints, other Biblical figures, and the ancestral dead. The spirits must be venerated since the spirits of the dead may affect the fate of the living in important ways. There are three

categories of spirits in Pocomania: (1) the Heavenly spirits, (2) "Earthbound" spirits, and (3) "Ground" spirits (Seaga 1969, 10). The Heavenly spirits are made up of the Triune God, archangels, angels, and saints. The Earthbound spirits include the "Fallen Angels" or satanic powers. The Ground spirits are the human dead who are not mentioned in the Bible. Pocomania's orientation to ground spirits distinguishes it from Revival Zion, Kumina (see entry "Kumina"), and Covince, other members of the Revival family in Jamaica. Whereas Pocomania followers collaborate with Ground spirits and Fallen Angels, other Revival groups do not, since they consider these beings evil. Pocomania followers maintain that the "Ground spirits" are more useful than those used by Zion. These spirits are closer at hand and more accessible. According to Edward Seaga, "they are more attentive and quicker in action than the other powers who are too busy to give personal attention and too cautious in action" (Seaga 1969, 10–11).

Pocomania groups are organized into "bands" under the leadership of a Shepherd. In the case of Pocomania, the leader or Shepherd is always a male. Since the spirits are essential to healing, the Pocomania leader is a type of shaman. He must know how to negotiate with the spirits, with the visible and invisible worlds, to exorcize devotees of the evil and traumas they experience, individually and collectively. To a large extent the life of a Pocomania band depends on the leadership skill of the Shepherd or leader. The Shepherd or leader is critical to the maintenance of the Pocomania "band" as a support group or structure for those who find themselves at the margins of Jamaican society.

As in other religious traditions, ritual or sacred spaces are marked off in Revivalism, and in the Pocomania tradition, from ordinary space. Hence there are Revival or Pocomania churches, healing centers, and balm yards that are decorated with poles and flags of different colors to attract passing spirits. Sometimes, the pole is planted in the "Seal" or mission ground. The seal is considered to be sacred and is the center or axis mundi for most of the important ritual activity. The belief is that the spirits of all the dead who work for the revival "bands" inhabit these spots. Features of a Revival yard would include an altar covered with a white cloth on which a number of items such as flowers, fruits, Bibles, hymnals, and candles are placed. Revival yards also contain a water pool or a large earthenware jug with water that is used in various rituals. In Pocomania, the water is understood to be "home" of all the functionaries who perform with water such as the River Maid and the Diver.

Major rituals in Pocomania include prayer meetings, street meetings, and rituals for specific purposes such as feast tables or duties, altars, and baths (Seaga 1969, 9–10). Prayer meetings are held for different purposes. They usually take the form of Bible reading, hymn singing, and discussion. Street meetings are held to gain new members, preach biblical doctrine, make the Pocomania "band" or group known, and even to utter prophetic warnings to the society as a whole. Street meetings or public processions in rural or urban spaces in Jamaica combat invisibility, create community, and make a space for Pocomania in Jamaica's culture and religious landscape.

The "Tables" or "Duties" are ritual features in Pocomania. Each is a ritual held for a specific purpose. In some cases a number of purposes could be linked within the observance of a particular "Table." Though they vary in detail, they generally follow similar procedures (Hogg 1964, 309). According to Seaga, tables are held for "thanksgiving for a particular event, prosperity, deliverance, memorial, death and judgment, mourning, consecration, pole-planting, ordination, dedication, and baptisms" (Seaga 1969, 9). They could also be held for marriage, birth, or success of a child or family member, for personal or family success, for safe travel, and for healing. The list is endless. It depends on the circumstances and the felt need. Participation in the table expresses hospitality and commensality. The most common table is the thanksgiving table since it reciprocates or shows appreciation to the spirits for benefits received. Shepherds, band members, and sometimes well-wishers hold them after recovery from serious illnesses or success in major economic ventures. Observance of tables also helps to build community amongst the members of a Pocomania "band," as well as with other bands, well-wishers, and other members of the wider community. The observance of tables helps to structure a sense of collective identity, both with the living and the dead. In Pocomania, the feasting table is usually held on Sunday nights. It is covered with fruits, drinks, bread, candles, and vegetables. Following the reading of the Bible and the greeting and welcoming of visitors and those who have responded to the invitation to attend the ceremony, the table is "broken" at midnight. The food is then distributed amongst those present as a form of communal meal. The entire ritual ceremony connected with the table fuses Bible reading, preaching, singing, dancing, and movement to invoke the spirits to enter and participate in the ceremony. In this sense the table can be understood as a kind of "birth-night" or spiritual regeneration of the group present. In keeping with Pocomania's African orientation, the invocation and participation of the spirits at the table is a way of honoring the ancestors, a major feature of African traditional religion.

An essential part of Pocomania meetings is the tramping and the cymbals. This occurs after the singing and the Bible reading part of the program. Members gathered move around in a circle, counterclockwise, each using forward stepping motions with a forward bend of the body. Songs or hymns used in the Revival tradition, including Pocomania, usually vary in beat and rhythm, and include the familiar African American lining or call-and-response feature. The songs, hymns, and choruses are often adaptations of spirituals and Christian hymns, particularly those from the Protestant nonconformist tradition. This mode of singing is Africanized with the accompaniment of the beating of drums such as the kettledrum or the bass drum. Tambourines are also used, along with other instruments. On the whole, the mode of singing and worship is lively, as is expected of the Revival tradition.

One of the major functions of the Pocomania leader or Shepherd is to distribute "portions" or alternative identities to members of a "band." The Pocomania Shepherd is critical in the process of individual and collective cultural regeneration. The "portions" or roles assigned to members give them meaning and purpose that are alternative to those Jamaican society has imposed on them. In Pocomania, they have an alternative portrait of themselves, one in which they are regenerated or "born again." The Shepherd must give gifts, portions, to the different members of his band to construct individual and collective identity, to incorporate them into the mythological journey or pilgrimage beyond the Middle Passage. It is a form of religious resistance. These portions include Armor Bearer, Bands Mother, Explorers, Ambush women, and Water Maiden (Hogg 1964). The Pocomania imagination is similar to that of the carnival bands and celebrations throughout the Caribbean and the New World. Pocomania band members take on roles contrary to those assigned by the social status quo.

The Pocomania leader creates this sense of alternative reality through the portions he assigns to members. This distribution of charisma, for which each adherent is responsible, is framed in emancipatory terms. It sets the imperative to create a post-emancipatory identity. Myth, rituals, and portions integrate in Pocomania as they symbolize a journey or pilgrimage into the Land of Promise. Portions such as the "Water Maids" or "River Maids" symbolize, in Pocomania, someone who will swim through, and lead others across, waters from slavery into freedom. In terms of Jamaican history it signifies return across the Middle Passage and a reversal of slavery through return to Africa.

The Pocomania Shepherd must periodically issue new portions to his followers. Failure to grant new portions will destroy the vitality of the tradition. The Sundial orients Pocomania members to a new sense of time and eschatology. The in-breaking of freedom, newness, and the experience of a new day, resonate the J'Ouvert celebrations that open carnival celebrations in the Caribbean. Though freedom is conceived in different ways in Pocomania, the Nine Night ceremony that marks the final passing of the dead from the terrestrial into the spiritual nuances freedom in Pocomania. As a liminal or threshold space in Pocomania, death symbolizes freedom that includes repatriation to Africa or Guinee.

As a myth of return, Pocomania highlights the concept of return to Africa, physically or metaphorically, in Afrodiasporic religion and culture. Comparatively, the carnival aspect is one of several that links Pocomania myth and ritual to the African-diasporic tradition in the New World. Carnivals are forms of resistance to the dominant construction of reality. In carnival individuals organize themselves into bands around a particular leader and theme, with kings and queens. To "play mas" is to break out from their prescribed roles in the dominant status quo. Pocomania bands, like those of carnival, are organized in private. At the appropriate time, they take to the streets. In the public showcase or spectacle, the boundaries between the sacred and the secular are erased; the street space becomes the scene of primal power. Pocomania resembles other indigenous Afro-diasporic religious traditions in Jamaica, the Caribbean, and the Americas.

The Pocomania leader, usually a male, is a kind of shaman. However, there are female leaders. Pocomania Shepherds operate in network fashion, some leaders gravitating to and oscillating between Revivalism in general and Pocomania in particular. The most outstanding Revivalist leader in Jamaica's history was Alexander Bedward (1869–1935) who gained prominence as a healer and prophet at the turn of the twentieth century. Strictly speaking, Bedward was not really a Pocomania leader. Among Pocomania leaders, Donald Hogg identified Father Leslie, who at the turn of the twentieth century, had tremendous prestige and influence among other Pocomania leaders in St. Mary's Parish, possibly a major center for the development of modern Pocomania (Hogg 1964, 281). Francis Walker, who succeeded Father Leslie, joined the group in 1900 at the age of 18. Within a short time, Walker became a Shepherd, married Leslie's daughter, and took over Leslie's Obeah practice and leadership of his band when the latter died in 1912. Walker gained regional prestige and influence, was subsequently appointed Father, the highest rank in Pocomania, by the Shepherds who led other bands in St. Mary (Hogg 1964). Walker's relationship with Pocomania, as well as his religious career, was somewhat checkered as he moved between Pocomania, different Revival traditions, and Christianity. Criticism of Pocomania, fear of being considered non-Christian, and loss of influence were some of the reasons Walker shifted adherence between Pocomania, Presbyterianism, and Zion Revivalism. Shepherd Trashy, another Pocomania leader referred to by Hogg, operated in the parish of St. Catherine's within the ambit of Walker's group (Hogg 1964). Walker's band was apparently a kind of centrifugal force around which other Pocomania bands, mainly in rural Jamaica, revolved. Within Pocomania, women's status is to a large extent defined by its traditional, patriarchal, hierarchical leadership structure. Nevertheless, there are female leaders, called Mothers. Hogg identifies one such female leader, Chichi from Spanish

Town, who suffered loss of prestige in a challenge with Shepherd Luther from Clarendon (Hogg 1964, 383).

From the perspective of peasant religions, therefore, Pocomania served to keep Afro-Jamaicans close to their African roots. Pocomania is a classic illustration of the interface between myth, fable, religion, and the imagination in Afro-Jamaican religion. (Harris in Bundy 1999, 152–166). It is an important interpretive tradition within the set of Afro-Jamaican and Afro-diasporic religious traditions. It opens horizons of interpretation and consciousness that can be defined as gateways through which devotees experience insight into the human condition as they know it, experience individual and collective healing, and resolve identity and other conflicts.

Focus on the Afrocentric core of Pocomania is critical to understand its role in the preservation and maintenance of African-diasporic humanity. It is also important to explore Pocomania's relationship to other Afro-diasporic religions and the role that religion played in the survival of African-descended peoples in the New World. The Pocomania leader is a virtual shaman who plays a critical role in leading his followers through the gateway of consciousness into alternative realities. Since reality shifts, Pocomania will also because it is a valid mirror of the fluid Afro-diasporic experience in Jamaica.

Concerning Pocomania's future, George E. Simpson did not foresee an "early disappearance" of syncretistic revivalist cults in Jamaica. "Pure and reinterpreted Africanisms are deeply embedded, integral parts of the Pocomania-Revivalism-Obeah complex and they will last as long as revivalism lasts" (Simpson 1956, 401). For Seaga, it remained "to be seen whether the forces of social and economic change will either modify or obliterate the revival practices of a significant sector of the Jamaican population" (Seaga 1969, 9). To Simpson, who defined "Jamaican revivalism [as] an adjustive-escapist type of activity," the future of Revivalism, including Pocomania, depended on two factors: first, changes "in the economic, educational, and social conditions of the lower-class population" in Jamaica, and second, on the increase or decrease in appeal of "functional alternatives as the established religious denominations, the Pentecostal sects, and the Ras Tafari movement" (Simpson 1956, 401). Jamaica's history, especially since the independence era that began in the 1960s, validates the wisdom of these insights. An anatomy of Pocomania shows the integral relationship between religion and politics in Jamaica, an axiom well known to Jamaican politicians.

The religiosity of Jamaican society is well known. Though the Revival tradition, including Pocomania, might not be numerically strong in the Caribbean island nation, there is no reason to doubt that it is an important aspect of the Jamaican religious and cultural landscape. Revivalism and Pocomania contribute to Jamaica's religious distinctiveness. Revival churches can be found all over Jamaica, particularly in the deep rural areas and in the inner-city sections of the corporate Kingston–St. Andrews area. Watt Town in the Parish of St. Ann's, the same parish out of which came Marcus Garvey and Bob Marley, is one of the most popular revival meeting places or pilgrimage sites. In addition to being a site to which Revivalists flock on a quarterly basis each year, Watt Town has become a kind of museum for the Revival tradition. At this location the various aspects of the tradition, Bible readings, the singing of hymns and choruses, trumping, dancing, spiritual possessions, healing, and prophecy, are there to be seen. Pocomania is therefore very much alive in Jamaica. Amongst other things, in Jamaica, which is almost 90 percent Black, it helps to keep Jamaicans rooted to their African ancestry and heritage. Pocomania's influence transcends more than the narrow boundaries of religion, as it is usually understood. Its impact of Jamaican music, dance, art, and other forms of expressive culture is significant since Pocomania is a classic manifestation of the persistence of the African influence in Jamaican religion. Much of the vitality of Jamaican life and culture stems from the persistence and preservation of African religion and culture. It is therefore easy to imagine that this pattern will continue since Jamaica has been a major African Diasporic center for the preservation of African traditional religion and culture, as well as the site for the emergence of important African Diasporic religion and philosophy.

Leslie R. James

SELECTED BIBLIOGRAPHY

Bundy, Andrew, ed. *Wilson Harris: The Unfinished Genesis of the Imagination* (London, New York: Routledge, 1999).

Chevannes, Barry. *Rastafari: Roots and Ideology* (New York: Syracuse University Press, 1994).

Erskine, Noel L. *Decolonizing Theology: A Caribbean Perspective* (Trenton, NJ, Asmara, Eritrea: Africa World Press, 1998).

Hogg, Donald W. "Jamaican Religions: A Study in Variations" (Graduate School of Yale University Dissertation in Anthropology, 1964).

Nettleford, Rex M. *Mirror, Mirror: Identity, Race and Protest in Jamaica* (Kingston C.S.O., Jamaica: LMH Publishing Limited, 2001).

Seaga, Edward. *Revival Cults in Jamaica: Notes Towards a Sociology of Religion.* Reprinted from *Jamaica Journal*, Vol. 3:2 (Kingston, Jamaica: Institute of Jamaica, June 1969)

Simpson, George Eaton. *Jamaican Revivalist Cults.* Institute of Social and Economic Research Social and Economic Studies, Vol. 5:4 (Jamaica: University College of the West Indies, December 1956).

Thelwell, Michael. *The Harder They Come: A Novel* (New York: Grove Press, 1988).

Warner-Lewis, Maureen. *Central Africa in the Caribbean: Transcending Time, Transforming Cultures* (Kingston, Jamaica: University of the West Indies Press, 2003).

PROGRESSIVE NATIONAL BAPTIST CONVENTION, INC.

Historical Development

Founded at Zion Baptist Church in Cincinnati, Ohio, on November 14–15, 1961, by 33 delegates from 14 states, Progressive National Baptist Convention, Inc. (PNBC) has its immediate roots in the turbulent environment of the Civil Rights Movement and in the National Baptist Convention, USA, Inc. (NBC USA). The Reverend Dr. Martin Luther King Jr. was a pivotal figure in each of the intertwined streams of thought and political activities. Dr. King's concerns and the concerns of numerous others centered on two critical issues—first, the issue of term limits within the NBC USA (see entry "National Baptist Convention, USA, Inc."), and second, the NBC USA's engagement and active (or in this case lack of) participation in the Civil Rights Movement.

MARTIN LUTHER KING JR. (1929–1968)

Born into a Baptist family in Atlanta, Georgia, on January 15, 1929, Martin L. King Jr. received his education at Morehouse College and Crozer Theological Seminary, and he received his PhD from Boston University. He was central to helping to create the environment that led to the founding of the PNBC. King, while having been involved in church ministry, is best known as the central figure of the Civil Rights Movement. His work on behalf of civil rights would result in new legislation and new opportunities for African Americans and other oppressed groups. King's activities would result in his receiving numerous honors, including the Nobel Peace Prize, the Presidential Medal of Freedom, and the Congressional Gold Medal. His birthday is a national holiday.

The men who had held the presidency of the NBC USA generally stayed in that position until they died. At the time Joseph H. Jackson wrote and published his account of the history of the NBC USA, Inc. in 1980, for example, Jackson was one of only four men who had served as president of the organization established in 1895. Likewise, two of the three previous presidents had died in office, and this was the case despite the fact that the Convention's bylaws called for annual elections. In 1952, the body amended this "governing" document to limit the annual reelection of the same president to no more than four consecutive terms and the requirement that if the maximum terms had been served, the same person would be eligible to run again only after vacating office for one year. This amendment had been proposed by a special study committee. Indeed, annual elections were supposed to apply to all leadership positions in the NBC USA. Ironically, Jackson had been the presiding officer of the 1952 convention session at the time of this constitutional revision, and he, in fact, announced the revised policy to limit the tenure of the presidency.

Some members of the Convention had become increasingly concerned that the leadership of the NBC USA was autocratic, given that one could be elected president of the Convention and remain in leadership of the organization indefinitely. This meant that the president could wield enormous power over the group and could position himself to maintain power and to limit what other leaders were able to accomplish within the Convention. In other words, some members of the NBC USA contended that President Joseph H. Jackson was dictatorial in his leadership style, that he did not rule by committee or consensus, but rather issued solitary edicts. They were also concerned that Jackson, in their opinion, was manipulative and not forthcoming about the business of the Convention and that financial management of the organization needed more oversight. That is, his word was law and was not subject to sufficient checks and balances by the members and churches of the Convention. One of the ways to undermine such authoritarian leadership, they believed, was to try to enforce term limits on the presidency, so that, by rule, the president would be able to stay in power for only a limited and defined extent of time. This issue of term limits, of course, was a contentious one because it was a direct affront and threat to President Jackson and the continuation of his leadership.

Regardless of the policy of term limits that had been ostensibly enacted in 1952, Jackson was elected to his fifth consecutive term as president of NBC USA at the annual meeting of 1957. Later that year, ten ministers filed an initial law suit, charging that Jackson's reelection had violated the organization's constitution. Among those filing the suit were T. M. Chambers, W. H. Borders, L. K. Jackson, and Marshall Shepard. These men's names would later appear during the birth and formation of the PNBC. The U.S. District Court ruled on the suit just prior to the 1958 Convention meeting, suggesting that Jackson was "the titular head of the largest Negro church organization in the world." Details are scant about how the court arrived at such a decision despite the fact that the group's bylaws apparently required term limits.

Notwithstanding, it was clear that the lawsuit cemented the rupture between factions in the Convention. Undocumented historical accounts note, for instance, that some NBC USA members believed that those who had filed suit should apologize to the Convention before being fully restored. What this "restoration" entailed is not altogether clear. Likewise, if these were indeed the stipulations, no public apologies ever appear to have been issued, and strong disagreements remained among some of the members over the issue of the number of terms one could hold office. Tension about the issue of tenure grew among members of the NBC USA at subsequent annual Convention meetings

between 1959 and 1961. One plan was to unseat the then Convention president by vote—something that had never successfully occurred since its founding in 1895.

In November 1959, a group of Convention ministers began meeting secretly to devise plans to nominate and support an alternative candidate for the presidency of the NBC USA, the oldest and largest national, black Baptist convention. By June 1960, the number of these conferees had grown to nearly 300. At their June meeting, this alternative leadership movement called upon Gardner C. Taylor, a member of the Board of Education of New York City, internationally noted preacher, and pastor of the Concord Baptist Church of Christ in Brooklyn, to allow his name to be placed in nomination at the September 1960 NBC USA Convention meeting in

Gardner C. Taylor, pastor of the Concord Baptist Church and a member of the New York City School Board, in August 1961. (Bettmann/Corbis)

GARDNER C. TAYLOR (1918–)

Taylor was born in Louisiana and entered church ministry early. He received his education at Oberlin School of Theology. Taylor pastored several churches before moving to Concord Baptist Church, the pastorate that would bring him national attention. Some writers have credited Taylor as the founder of the Progressive National Baptist Church. However, the history as documented on the Convention's Web site does not mention this. Correspondence related to the development of the denomination indicates that Taylor's participation was highly sought in the new effort and clearly his name remains most prominent among the members of the ten pastors expelled from National Baptist Convention, USA Inc. Taylor, also known as the "Dean of black preaching," is recognized as one of the greatest African American preachers of all time.

Philadelphia. Taylor was widely known for his ability as a gifted preacher and leader and for his ability to build meaningful relationships across religious traditions.

The details of the 1960 meeting are disputed by various writers. Apparently, it was Martin Luther King Jr. who had nominated Taylor, but it is clear from all accounts that the dissenters mounted a massive disruption at the Convention. To that end, Jackson referred to their activities as a "sit-in" and compared their tactics to those used in the Civil Rights Movement. The men who would later be known as the "Taylor Team" failed in their attempt to unseat Jackson and to elect Taylor president.

Sources often ignore the influence of Dr. King in the issues that led to the founding of the PNBC, not only in his nomination of Taylor but in the Civil Rights activities that led to some of the contention between King, the Taylor Team, and President Jackson. Dr. King desired to use the resources of the NBC USA in the struggle for African American civil rights, and he attempted to appeal to Jackson to make the Convention a more meaningful part of the movement. King thought the Convention should either enter the Civil Rights Movement or meet its demise as irrelevant to the social conditions faced by the majority of black people in America.

The second critical issue was that Dr. King and several prominent members of the Convention had become concerned that the president of the NBC USA and his position on social progress for African Americans was too conservative and laid an excessive amount of the responsibility for the improvement of race relations and quality of life on African American communities. In a philosophy that was reminiscent of Booker T. Washington's appeal in his address to the Atlanta Exposition of 1895, President Jackson called on black people to focus on self-help and intraracial uplift rather than large public demonstrations and boycotts that were becoming the preferred method to effectuate social and political change. Jackson believed that such activity was un-American and inappropriate. Given the cumulative effects of Jackson's philosophy and the tumultuous relationship between Jackson and those who wanted the organization to be more engaged with the Civil Rights Movement, the end of the 1961 meeting of the NBC

USA signaled the end of Dr. King's relationship with denomination. King and the others would hold a "March-In" during the 1961 Kansas City Convention.

The "March-In," as it was called, was the name given to the civil disobedience method meant to disrupt the Convention. Some suggest "confusion" began when Taylor supporters rushed the main platform, where the Convention leadership was seated, to fill seats that had been designated for denominational officers—positions to which they believed they had been legitimately elected at Philadelphia. In the end, the Convention Board of Directors removed Martin Luther King from his office as vice president responsible for the Congress of Christian Education.

The Reverend Martin Luther King Sr., the father of Dr. King, and other officers and Board members associated with the Taylor Team were also reprimanded for their actions. A special meeting was called just two days after the "March In" (September 9, 1961). Apparently laying the blame for the crisis within the Convention on Dr. King, Jackson indicated that King Jr. was removed because he had caused disruption to the Convention by using civil disobedience tactics against NBC USA in 1959, 1960, and 1961. According to Jackson, King had used a "type of militant campaign against his own denomination and his own race" (Jackson 1980, 486).

These events led directly to the founding of the PNBC. Given the vision for relevance and social equity that the PNBC founders wanted to create in its formation, it is also ironic that one of the main critiques leveled at the PNBC is that it is considered by some to be among the most elite of national black Baptist conventions. Even with fewer affiliated churches, the average PNBC congregational size—approximately 1,000 members—was initially significantly higher and more middle class than that of its predecessor, the NBC USA. Writers have attempted to explain this disparity by pointing out that the difference in size and social class exists because the PNBC churches tended to be in urban areas rather than in rural locations whose churches tended to be smaller. One PNBC president, Bennett W. Smith (1995–1998), noted this difference and focused some of the Church's outreach to rural congregations as part of his vision for a more inclusive Convention. Indicative of this concern for class difference, early key leadership of the Convention was often more highly educated than the majority of African American Baptist ministers.

Famous members of the Progressive National Baptist Convention, Incorporated (PNBC) have included Martin Luther King Jr., Gardner C. Taylor, Benjamin Mays, Ralph Abernathy, Jesse Louis Jackson, former NAACP President Benjamin Hooks, former U.S. Representative and President of the United Negro College Fund William Gray III, and U.S. Representative and founding member of the Congressional Black Caucus Walter E. Fauntroy.

Beliefs and Practices

Consistent with other Protestant denominations, the PNBC believes in the notion of the Trinity—the belief that the Father, Son, and Holy Spirit equally and together are the One God. Furthermore, as a Baptist denomination, PNBC churches teach the "brotherhood" of humankind by which human beings are related, and that followers of Jesus Christ will live eternally in heaven.

BENJAMIN MAYS (1894–1984)

Though he never served as an officer of the PNBC, Benjamin Mays was active in Baptist denominations and was an outspoken supporter of an educated clergy. Mays had been appointed to the team of observers who would oversee the ill-fated 1960 NBC USA, Inc. election that would contribute to the departure of many ministers who would later serve the PNBC. Benjamin Elijah Mays is most noted for serving as the president of Morehouse College in Atlanta, Georgia. Under his leadership, this private institution became the premier black men's college in the United States. Among its most celebrated students and scholars were Martin Luther King Jr. and Howard Thurman. Mays was highly influential in the life of Dr. King, but before his tenure as Morehouse president, Mays was a scholar and administrator at the Howard Divinity School. In the late 1930s he co-authored the sociological study, *The Negro's Church* with Billy Nichols, and he wrote the influential book, *The Negro's God*. A theological education fellowship was named for him in order to promote an educated black clergy.

The denomination maintains two sacraments or ordinances, that is, ritual practices they believe are sacred: water baptism and communion. Persons who attend PNBC member churches become eligible for baptism upon confession of their belief in Jesus Christ as God, who came to live on earth in human form. Jesus' mission on earth was to demonstrate to humans how to live with one another as well as to allow himself to be killed in order to restore the relationship between God and humankind broken when humans disobeyed God while living in the Garden of Eden. The conversion experience in which the person confesses that he or she adheres to this belief often occurs in early adolescence or teenage years, although it is not unusual for the experience of conversion to be publicly confessed in adulthood or childhood. Baptism of the confessor is generally done by immersion into a pool or body of water such as a river or pond and is performed by an ordained minister—a person who has been authorized by officials of the denomination. This ritual imitates the baptism of Jesus that was conducted by John the Baptist in the Jordan River and symbolizes the death, burial, and resurrection of Jesus from the dead.

The other sacrament practiced by PNBC churches is communion. In this ritual, worshippers reenact a meal shared by Jesus and his disciples on the night he would be arrested by Roman soldiers. According to each of the gospels of the New Testament, Jesus broke a loaf of bread, served it along with wine to his 12 disciples, and instructed them to do the same in the future in remembrance of him. Accordingly, for PNBC churches, the bread represents Christ's body. The wine represents his blood that flowed from his body when he was killed. PNBC churches believe that Jesus' death was necessary to redeem human beings from sin, or transgression and "spiritual" separation from God.

The PNBC has a strong belief in the priesthood of all believers, meaning that they support the notion that lay members, not just clergy, have a divine ministry to fulfill. To that end, the laity should rely on their faith as a foundation to guide them to the service that they are to provide other believers, members of their congregation, and society. The PNBC motto incorporates these theological positions in its thrust for "fellowship, service, progress, and peace." In its formative years, leaders in this new National Baptist convention worked to avoid the types of disrespectful exclusion that many of them believed they had experienced as a result of challenging the leaders of their parent convention, the NBC USA, Inc. Inclusive fellowship was a practice meant to foster respect, deference, and spirit of collegiality and discourse in accordance with their belief that God has taken all believers into the same family, God's family. Throughout the history of the PNBC, its presidents have emphasized various portions of this motto, but the commitment to racial progress for African Americans and ecumenism has always remained prominent.

Progressive National Baptists pride themselves on their heritage of ministry that is intertwined with social progress. Data on the PNBC's social teachings indicate that "progress" relates to a realized view of the future—that is, a constant and forward historical movement of "God's revelation" that makes imperative Christian service to humanity. This notion served as the foundational basis for the birth of the PNBC, that it would be "progressive" and active in its social outlook and practices.

Annual Convention agendas provide evidence of other PNBC social teachings. Ongoing agenda items include support of higher education and historically black colleges and universities, especially Shaw University in Raleigh, North Carolina; Virginia Union University in Richmond, Virginia; Howard University Divinity School in Washington, D.C.; and Spelman College, Morehouse College, and the Interdenominational Theological Center, in Atlanta, Georgia.

One of the areas in which the PNBC views itself as distinct from the NBC USA is with respect to women, who, unlike in their parent group, were invited to participate in the PNBC from its inception as seen in the initial press release calling for the formation meeting that included "men and women." One woman, Mrs. Thelma Walton of Antioch Baptist Church in Cincinnati, is listed among the registered attendees at the November 1961 organizational gathering. The bylaws of the organization note that men and women are eligible to hold the office of president; however, no woman has served in that role to date. Women have provided leadership, however, in the Women's Department and the Board of Christian Education and Publishing. Furthermore, being highly supportive of education, one of the first acts of service of gender inclusion was to garner support for the Nannie Helen Burroughs School in Washington, D.C. The school had been founded by its namesake, a long-time Baptist activist and corresponding secretary of the NBC USA Women's Department during the early and mid-twentieth century. Its original purpose was to train women and girls for advancement rather than the domestic and servile employment of that era. It is now a private Christian elementary school.

Albert Avant interviewed female leaders in the PNBC through the year 2000. Few women have noted gender inequality as an issue, and none made gender

LAVAUGHN VENCHAEL BOOTH (1919–2002)

Lavaughn Venchael Booth was born into poverty in rural Mississippi in 1919. He became acquainted with church at an early age. By the age of 17, Booth had decided to enter the ministry. He left his family to attend Alcorn A&M College. While there, he was on the debate team and was an itinerate preacher in the local area. In Atlanta, Booth attended the Wheat Street Baptist Church and worked under the tutelage of William Holmes Borders. Booth struggled financially, but completed one academic year at Gammon. He transferred to Howard University School of Religion in Washington, D.C. While in Washington, Booth accepted his first pastorate only to leave shortly thereafter to attend the University of Chicago Divinity School on scholarship. In addition to his theological education, L. V. Booth was trained in practical ministry while serving Chicago's Olivet Baptist Church. By 1944, Booth had accepted a pastorate in nearby Gary, Indiana. He was active in the community and in the Baptist denomination. Eventually, he was called to the Zion Baptist Church in Cincinnati, Ohio, where he was the pastor for over 30 years. He left Zion Baptist Church in 1984 and accepted the pastorate of Olivet Baptist Church. In 1990, he played a role in the founding of the Marva Collins Preparatory School, which began in the basement of Olivet Baptist Church.

issues a key part of their leadership agenda. Despite this fact, the convention has taken no official stance on the ordination of women as ministers. L. V. Booth appointed a committee to make a theological inquiry into the issue of women's roles in ministerial leadership. (The issue was precipitated by the fact that former Women's Auxiliary president Uvee Mdodana-Arbouin had begun preaching.) The committee determined only that congregations ordain ministers and preachers, and that this issue was deferred to local congregations. (The PNBC relies on a standard understanding of Baptist congregational polity, meaning that each local church determines its own perspective on governance matters and voluntarily associates with other churches and conventions.) Author William D. Booth interpreted this stance as an essential agreement that women could be called by God to preach. But Avant interprets the move less

generously, pointing to an L. V. Booth statement that indicates that the position on the ordination of women was much more politically motivated. The Convention may have failed to take a definite position on the issue because of its potentially inflammatory and divisive nature, which could divide the new and therefore vulnerable organization. Some leaders in the denomination have been more intentional in noting that sexism must be structurally rooted out of PNBC operations and strategies. The 1990s chair of the Goals Commission, Gary Simpson, successor to Gardner C. Taylor as pastor of Brooklyn's Concord Baptist Church, is one PNBC leader who has been documented as much more vocal on the issue. Los Angeles pastor and late 1990s PNBC president Bennett W. Smith proactively appointed two women to his executive cabinet, namely, Rev. Ella Mitchell and Mrs. Brenda Little.

Stephen C. Finley and Terri Laws

SELECTED BIBLIOGRAPHY

Avant, Albert A., Jr. *The Social Teachings of the Progressive National Convention, Inc., Since 1961* (New York & London: Routledge, 2004).

Booth, William D. *The Progressive Story: New Baptist Roots* (St. Paul, MN: Braun Press, 1981).

Booth, William D. *A Call to Greatness: The Story of the Founding of the Progressive National Convention* (Lawrenceville, VA: Brunswick Publishing Corporation, 2001).

Fitts, Leroy. *A History of Black Baptists* (Nashville, TN: Broadman Press, 1985).

Jackson, Joseph H. *A Story of Christian Activism: The History of the National Baptist Convention, USA, Inc.* (Nashville: Townsend Press, 1980).

Lincoln, C. Eric, and Lawrence Mamiya. *The Black Church in the African American Experience* (Durham, NC: Duke University Press, 1990).

Paris, Peter J. *Black Religious Leaders: Conflict in Unity* (Louisville, KY: Westminster/John Knox Press, 1991).

Pinn, Anne H., and Anthony B. Pinn. *Fortress Introduction to Black Church History* (Minneapolis: Fortress Press, 2002).

Washington, James Melvin. *Frustrated Fellowship: The Black Baptist Quest for Social Power* (Macon, GA: Mercer University Press, 1986).

R

RADA

Historical Development

The term "Rada" refers to the people and spirits of the Arada region of the former Kingdom of Dahomey in West Africa. In 1860, free Rada persons under the leadership of Abojevi Zahwenu (Robert Antoine), known as Papa Nanee, began to reproduce their Dahomean-based cultural traditions in Trinidad. Papa Nanee came to Trinidad around 1855 as a trained diviner and skilled herbalist in the traditions of Dahomey. In 1860 he was able to purchase a parcel of land in Belmont on the outskirts of Port of Spain and began to create a residential compound on Belmont Valley Road that eventually formed the center of Rada religious life on the island.

Like many African-based religions, Rada was rejected and even persecuted by the dominant society. One of the consequences of colonialism throughout the Caribbean was the overvaluation of all things European and the depreciation of African and Native cultures. African traditions are often pejoratively referred to as *obeah* (see entry "Obeah"), a variant of the Ashanti term *obayifo* and the Twa term *obeye*, both of which refer to spiritual energy. *Obeah* practitioners used this energy to manipulate spiritual powers on behalf of themselves or others for physical, emotional, or social healing and protection. Caribbean colonial powers often used the term *obeah* to associate any African-based tradition with witchcraft, sorcery, and other types of harmful magic in the same way that "voodoo" is often used in American culture to denigrate an idea or practice. In both cases the term entered the culture as an easy way to discount an idea or practice by characterizing it as ignorant, primitive, or barbaric.

In 1868 Trinidad passed a series of laws outlawing what the authorities saw as *obeah*. Rada practitioners were caught in this legal net; and although his sentence was eventually commuted, Papa Nanee was sentenced to jail time

339

ABOJEVI ZAHWENU (1800–1899)

Abojevi Zahwenu, who adopted the French name Robert Antoine, was born in Whyda in the West African Kingdom of Dahomey about the year 1800. As a young man he served in the Dahomean army under the monarch Ghezo. He immigrated to Trinidad after both the abolition of slavery in 1833 and the apprenticeship system that followed. It is thought that he arrived in about 1855 as a 55-year-old man. He was not a member of the Dahomean priestly caste but was an experienced bokono or diviner. He was held in great respect by his neighbors and became known as Papa Nanee. In 1868 he was able to buy a parcel of land and establish a compound where he could live with his family and establish the shrines necessary to perform ceremonies for the earth, sky, and thunder deities. He died in 1899 and was buried in the private cemetery within his compound.

---

and lashes. More laws were passed in 1921 prohibiting essential elements of African religious practice including public dance processions, singing and dancing in public or private yards, and drumming. It was not until the Black Power movement in the 1970s that these traditions were perceived as important contributions to the culture of the island. Unlike many other African-based traditions of the Caribbean, Rada has not expanded outside its homeland of Trinidad. Always small, the number of initiated Rada practitioners continues to be limited to members of Papa Nanee's extended family and close neighbors. Today Rada practice is being replaced by the more popular Yoruba-based traditions.

Beliefs and Practices

Although little is known of the rituals performed by Papa Nanee and his companions, we do know that his compound included a *vodunkwe* or "house of the gods" and numerous shrines. Rituals were performed according to a yearly cycle and new *vodunsi* or priests were regularly initiated. The compound survived Papa Nanee's death in 1899 and continues to exist into the twenty-first century, although it has been overshadowed by other Trinidadian African-based traditions. It appears that most potential Rada members have been absorbed into the more popular Orisha religion.

The focus of Rada rituals is the deities known as *vodu*. The principal *vodu* include Dada Segbo, the creator deity; Dangbwe, a serpent deity; Elegba, the owner of the crossroads; Age, the patron of the hunt; Sakpata, an earth deity associated with smallpox; Ogu, the deity of iron; and Legba, the divine messenger. In addition, practitioners engage in a type of ancestor veneration. Significant rituals, known as *vodunu*, include food offerings and the sacrifice of common barnyard animals, divination, and the embodiment of the deities through the medium of trance possession. Often these celebrations are referred to as sacrifices because of the offerings made to the spirits to ask for blessings for one's household, the health and well-being of children, and thanksgiving for past blessings. Although these rituals continue to be performed throughout the year, according to the Rada ritual calendar, their frequency has decreased significantly since the death of Papa Nanee.

Mary Ann Clark

SELECTED BIBLIOGRAPHY

Eastman, Rudolph, and Maureen Warner-Lewis. "Forms of African Spirituality in Trinidad and Tobago." *African Spirituality: Forms, Meanings and Expressions*, ed. Jacob K. Olupona (New York: The Crossroad Publishing Company, 2000), 403–15.

Warner-Lewis, Maureen. *Trinidad Yoruba: From Mother Tongue to Memory* (Tuscaloosa: The University of Alabama Press, 1996).

RASTAFARI

Historical Development

Rastafari is an Afro-Jamaican religion that holds together Jamaican folk Christianity with pro-Africa perspectives inspired by Marcus Mosiah Garvey. Garvey articulated a vision of life for Afro-Jamaicans and people of African descent highlighting racial pride, race consciousness, and educational uplift. He challenged social inequality in Jamaica and insisted that as Jamaicans viewed reality through African lens racial pride and self-esteem would ensue. While Garvey insisted that Afro-Jamaicans view God and the world through the spectacles of Ethiopia, he never explicitly stated that God is black. Garvey said:

If the white man has the idea of a white God, let him worship his God as he desires. If the yellow man's God is of his race let him worship his God as he sees fit. We, as Negroes have found a new ideal. Whilst our God has no color, yet it is human to see everything through one's own spectacles, and since the white people have seen their God through white spectacles, we have only now started out (late though it be) to see our God through our own spectacles. The God of Isaac and the God of Jacob let Him exist for the race that believes in the God of Isaac and the God of Jacob. We Negroes believe in the

---

MARCUS MOSIAH GARVEY (1887–1940)

Marcus Mosiah Garvey, the founder of the Back to Africa Movement, was the foremost prophet of black liberation in the early twentieth century. He taught that black Jamaicans, like the children of Israel, were captives in the white man's land, and it was God's will that they experience exodus. "Africa for Africans" was the essence of his cry for self-awareness and liberation. Born in Jamaica August 17, 1887, he belonged to both the nineteenth and twentieth centuries. His central contribution to Jamaica and the rest of the African Diaspora was not only to keep Africa central in the consciousness of black people but to press black people in the Diaspora to clarify where they stand in relation to Africa. It is no secret that the unseen hand that guided Rastafari from its initial impulse was that of the Jamaican visionary Marcus Garvey. His emphasis on Africa as an organizing principle and his insistence that black people view God through the lens of Ethiopia was decisive in shaping Rastafari thought and practice. Wherever Garvey went he bemoaned the plight of black people. Garvey felt that he could help change occur by creating the Universal Negro Improvement Association with chapters in strategic locations.

God of Ethiopia .... We shall worship him through the spectacles of Ethiopia. (Garvey 1974, 44)

In spite of such pronouncement, Garvey was not radical enough for the Rastas. Garvey was not willing to identify God with a black man in Ethiopia. The Rastas understood that there was a theological and spiritual basis for the poor self-esteem and the loss of racial pride that afflicted Afro-Jamaicans. They understood that there was a correlation between construing God as white or colorless and having poor self-esteem. The main problem as the Rastas understood it was not that Afro-Jamaicans saw God as colorless, as Garvey implied, but that they saw God as white. The implication was that they interpreted themselves in the light of a white ideal. The Rastas turned this around by seeing God as a black man, the emperor of Ethiopia, Haile Selassie I. This reversed the anthropological implication and gave them permission to revalue and view themselves in the light of the divine image of blackness (Owens 1995, 57–63).

If Garvey's insistence that Afro-Jamaicans look to Ethiopia was one of the triggers that led Rastas to construct a new social reality in Jamaica, the other was the coronation of Ras Tafari as emperor of Ethiopia in November 1930. Ras Tafari who assumed the name Haile Selassie I ("Might of the Trinity") claimed that he was a descendant of the biblical King David through the union of King Solomon and the Queen of Sheba. Haile Selassie's titles include King of Kings, Lord of Lords, and Conquering Lion of the Tribe of Judah. These titles anchored the new emperor in the

Judeo-Christian tradition and allowed the Rastas to look to Ethiopia and the new emperor for deliverance from the harsh conditions and grinding poverty that confronted them in Jamaica. The Rastas felt that what was being signified in Garvey's prophecy and the coronation of an African emperor was nothing less than the death pangs of colonial rule in Jamaica and the signal for black people to repatriate to Africa.

A new theology emerged on Jamaican soil as four followers of Marcus Garvey—Leonard Howell, Robert Hinds, Archibald Dunkley, and Joseph Hibbert—preached that the new emperor was the incarnation of Jah (Rastafari's name for God). According to these founding fathers, the new emperor was the messiah who had come to liberate Africans and people of African descent everywhere. In the early years, the tenets of the new teaching were clear: Haile Selassie I was the black Christ and black people everywhere shared in his divinity. Furthermore, redemption came only through repatriation to the homeland of Ethiopia—the "New Zion." In light of this final point, the central question highlighted during this early period of the tradition's formation was short and to the point: Where do you stand in relation to Africa?

Howell held his first public meetings on the subject of "Ras Tafari, King of Abyssinia" in Kingston, Jamaica, during January 1933; but, failing to attract the community of followers he had hoped for, he shifted the center of his activities to St. Thomas where he made his earliest converts. And it was there, after a meeting held in Trinityville on April 18, 1933, that he attracted the attention of authorities when he urged the audience to sing the national anthem, but pointed out that before they sang, they should

ROBERT HINDS

Robert Hinds, a Garveyite, was the most successful of the early Rastas. At one time his "King of Kings Mission" numbered over 800 adherents. Hinds was also closely related to the early revivalist Alexander Bedward and worked closely with Leonard Howell. Hinds was able to merge Revivalist and Rastafari principles. At the King of Kings Mission there were fasts, feasts, and baptisms—these practices remembered Revivalism. Women also outnumbered men, which was also a carryover of the Revivalist faith. Rastafari as practiced by Hinds indicates that in the early years the place of women in the movement was not an issue. In both Howell's and Hind's communities, women were key players. One area in which Hind's mission differed from the Revivalist community was that he established a court for hearing grievances internal to the mission. Related to the court were seven security guards who were charged with the safety of the meetings who also served as members of the court. Hind's version of Rastafari thrived because on the one hand it provided continuity with Revivalism and on the other hand it signaled a forging with new practices and beliefs.

remember that they are not singing for King George V, but for Ras Tafari, our new king (Edmonds 2003, 36–40).

It is important to note elements in the social context that provided fertile ground for the new teaching. There was a widening gap between rich and poor. Key resources were owned by foreigners, and a handful of white people were in charge of the society. The masses of black people were at the bottom of the society. The country was in the grip of high unemployment and poor housing, and there were many malnourished children. The people revolted against these atrocities in 1938. The revolt began with the field workers—those who worked on the sugar estates—but very soon they were joined by workers in factories, sanitation workers, and dock workers.

JOSEPH N. HIBBERT (1894–1985)

Hibbert was born in 1894 and died in 1985. Raised a Baptist, at the age of 17 Hibbert migrated to Costa Rica, where he lived for 20 years. There he became a member of the Ancient Order of Ethiopia, a Masonic Lodge. Upon his return to Jamaica, Hibbert began preaching a message that drew from his association with the Ancient Order of the Ethiopian Masonic Lodge and Ethiopian Orthodoxy, and that related to Haile Selassie, whom he proclaimed was more than a political leader. Hibbert proclaimed Selassie divine. He became a significant figure in the Rastafarian Movement in Jamaica. Hibbert's fascination with the secrets of the Bible, which were hidden by the clergy from the wider society, and his embodying a sense of dread as a "scientist" steeped in the "occultism" for which the Ethiopian Coptic League was known certainly set him apart. From this perspective, Hibbert tapped into a culture of magic and redemption made possible by practitioners of African medicine and culture. One reason for the decline of Hibbert's approach to Rastafari is that Hibbert did not pass on his secrets to new initiates.

Eventually, the colonial powers with the help of former Prime Ministers Alexander Bustamante and Norman Manley were able to quell the revolt.

Rastas did not participate in the uprising. They did not join the masses in blocking roads, wielding machetes, and disrupting the infrastructure. They regarded Jamaica as Babylon and did not believe that Babylon could be transformed. (For Rastas "Babylon" points to oppressive social and political conditions of Jamaica.) Instead, they focused on talk about repatriation to Ethiopia, where Haile Selassie I would provide redemptive space for the healing of black people. The theological and philosophical basis for this position is that Jamaica, which is enmeshed in the "Babylonian system" must be destroyed as it is not capable of transformation. Based on such reasoning, it is not surprising that toward the end of the 1930s Howell and his group retreated to Sligoville and founded Pinnacle, a commune in the hills in St. Catherine, where they received a respite from the harassment of police brutality. Howell called his newfound community the "Ethiopian Salvation community" (Barrett 1997, 68–102).

The second phase of the movement begins with the issuance of the University Report. The government of Jamaica asked three academics from the University of the West Indies to undertake a study of the movement. The study, which in many respects was sympathetic to Rastafari, sought to help Jamaicans rethink policies and perceptions of Rastafari. The report pointed out that there were vast cleavages in Jamaican society, many of which were caused by the colonial education system. The system trained the middle class, who had matriculated through the secondary school system, to view Jamaica through European eyes. This placed the middle class on a collision course with Rastafari, who viewed life through Afrocentric lenses. The University Report helped middle class Jamaica see that the Rastas were not as unpatriotic as they had originally thought. Their desire to repatriate to Ethiopia was presented as not un-Jamaican but rather was likened to migration of middle-class Jamaicans in search of their destinies. The issuing of the report two weeks after it was commissioned began the process of middle-class Jamaicans attempting to accommodate Rastafari as a way of life. The report helped the wider society understand that the desire to physically move to Ethiopia was fueled in part by the lack of an infrastructure in Rasta communities. The University Report accomplished two objectives. First, it signaled a rapprochement between Rastas and the wider society, with the university serving as broker. Second, it gave the Rastas a stake in Jamaica as the report called on the government to provide employment, housing and other necessities to rehabilitate Rastas into Jamaican society (Edmonds 2002, 84–88).

It is reasonable to believe Rastas were never passive, sitting on the margins of Jamaican society waiting for change. They continued to threaten the colonial system—Babylon—and critique the educational and church establishments that they considered oppressive. However, it was not until after the University Report that they began to consider the Africanization of Jamaica. Although Ethiopia was their spiritual home, they lived in Jamaica and now had a vested interest in their homeland. They began in practice to parallel the approach of some Christian churches that regard heaven as their home but must come to grips with the reality that they live on earth. While they had not given up on Ethiopia, in the meantime they lived in Babylon. Rastafari began to move from being only a millenarian community to one that would work for social change.

The third stage in the development of the movement is marked by the advent of reggae lyrics and the creation of the "Twelve Tribes" of which Bob Marley was a member. With the national embrace of reggae, Rastas became bearers of the cultural heritage of Jamaica. Reggae music remembered Africa and used African history as a tool for the liberation of oppressed Jamaica. Learning from Rastas, reggae artists used their experience of suffering and victimization as the prism through which to criticize Jamaica as Babylon and to work for social change in Jamaica. No one understood better the heartbeat of the Jamaican people than Bob Marley, who had spent many years as a youth in one of the harshest ghettoes of western Kingston, Trench Town. Marley became a member of the Twelve Tribes along with several women, Rita Marley, Judy Mowatt, and Minnie Phillips among others. Through Twelve Tribes many women found a home in Rastafari (Marley 2004, 116–124).

Beliefs and Practices

The twin concepts of the divinity of Haile Selassie and the redemption of black people—the sons and daughters of God—have distinguished Rastafari from other Afro-Caribbean movements that seek to promote an awareness of black consciousness. It must be kept in mind that the discourse concerning the divinity of Haile Selassie I and the claims

concerning biblical warrants that justify their positions are made in the sociopolitical context in which the vast majority of Rastas are at the base of the social and economic ladder. The unwillingness to accept spirit possession within the movement and the sense that Rastafari was driven by a strong sense of the divinity of Haile Selassie came to full flowering in the life and ministry of Archibald Dunkley. He was clear that Rastafari was to be differentiated from the practices of the Revivalists. Spirit possession was a central element in Revivalist teaching and practice but not in Dunkley's version of Rastafari. While it is clear that Rastafari borrowed Revivalist practices such as chanting, drumming, and dancing, it is also clear that Dunkley did not deem dancing in the spirit as a central tenet of Rastafari. Rastafari, like Revivalists, believed in the Bible. For Rastafari, the category of blackness—both in relation to their messiah and in relation to themselves—functions as an interpretive key; for the Revivalists, the key was the power and presence of the spirit.

Rastas' practice of "I-and-I consciousness," or an awareness of the link between God and the divinity of black people, which is the result of a new awakening of the self, results in a high anthropology that contradicts the "anthropological poverty" that was the lot of Rastas before the awareness of this new consciousness. For Rastas the mark of anthropological poverty in Babylon is the need to look to authorities outside the self, the tendency to deprecate self and to marginalize self as was typical in colonial and neocolonial Jamaica. The mark of anthropological poverty is to associate blackness and Africanness with bondage, psychological dependency, and the spirit of victimization. The practice of I-and-I consciousness breaks this cycle of poverty as through the process of Jah indwelling the self a new collective self emerges—a new self in terms of collaboration and cooperation. This is the basis for a unifying context for Rasta ideology, theology, and organization. A Rasta never loses his or her Africanness, and this is what makes it possible to survive life in Babylon. It is this Africanness that provides the interpretive and unifying key in which doctrine, lifestyle, and organizational ethos are mediated.

Rastas seek in their living to preserve a rhythm between themselves and nature. Nature is closely related to the power of Jah (God) and as such demands respect from everyone. Rastas proceed at a very local level to advocate that streams are not polluted and that pesticides and chemical waste are not buried in Mother Earth. But there is also a sense in which nature expresses the will of Jah. Nature is not merely neutral; it is the vehicle of Jah's judgment. There are times when, as Rastas press for justice, they call on nature to embody the word. Often as judgment is pronounced on Babylon or the agents of Babylon, they will call on nature to assist: "may lightning and thunder strike the downpressors" ("downpressor" is the Rasta term for

Rastafari men play drums, Jamaica. (Bojan Brecelj/Corbis)

oppressor). Closely related with Rastas' organic view of human beings' relationship with Mother Earth is their understanding of natural living. Natural living does not mean to live naturally but to live in an awareness of the organic relationship between human beings and Mother Earth. The way of wholeness is to live in harmony with the principles of creation. Everything is given in Mother Earth for sustenance, healing, and wholesome living. Emerging from this notion that the earth is sacred and that it provides everything for human beings' wholeness and healing is the concept of "Ital living." "Ital" means related to the earth— one with nature, of the earth. "Livity" is to live according to the strict principles of Rastafari. This is one way in which Rastas differentiate their lives from those lived in Babylon. One can easily identify the ways of Babylon. For example, the people who embrace the Babylonian way of life use tobacco, alcohol, synthetic materials, and chemically treated foods. Rastas warn against the use of manufactured foods, especially canned foods, as they contend that these foods are made by the Babylonian authorities to destroy the minds of Black people. Most Rastas try to adhere to a vegetarian lifestyle—rarely eating meat and prohibiting the consumption of pork, shellfish, and scaleless fish.

Closely related to the notion of ital living is herbal healing and the role of ganja (marijuana). Rastas believe that Jah chooses to reveal God-self to human beings through herbs. Herbs, they contend, are intended for the healing of the nations, and if a people will seek to understand Jah it is through the use of herbs. And chief among these is ganja. Rastas who are versed in the Bible cite Genesis 1:29 to provide biblical warrants for their use of the "holy herb": "And God said, Behold, I have given you every herb bearing seed, which is upon the face of the earth, and every tree, in which is the fruit of a tree yielding seed; to you it shall be for meat." Another text that underscores their use of ganja is Revelation 22:2: "the leaves of the tree were for the healing of the nation." Using Scripture for their own ends, Rastas suggest that even God enjoys smoking by citing Psalm 18:18: "There went up a smoke out of his nostrils, and fire out of his mouth devoured: coals were kindled by it." Because Rastas live in a fractious society that is divided by inequalities of class, economics, and privilege, they contend that in this society the smoking of ganja is for the healing of the nation. For Rastas, smoking ganja is the medium of contemplation, inspiration, and insight. Through this sacrament they are able to plumb the depths of wisdom and discover the revelation of God that is given to reason. Smoking the herb intensifies the reasoning process and opens up new worlds of illumination, visions, and enlightenment. In the 1950s and 1960s there were clashes between Rastas and the police, and in each instance the public claimed that the confrontation was caused by Rastas smoking ganja. This perception changed in the 1970s and 1980s as the public came to better understand Rastas. It was discovered that Rastas were peace-loving people and that much of the conflict with the police was caused by others in the society posing as Rastas. The difference in perception came as many Rastas began to make it into middle-class Jamaica and as ganja use in Jamaican society began to be demystified.

The smoking of the herb is a deeply religious ritual. Rastas concoct a pipe specifically for the smoking of ganja that is called the chalice. Before the smoking begins, the pipe is blessed and prayer is offered to Jah. Through the smoking of ganja Rastas attain I-and-I consciousness, which is regarded as a fusing of the experience of the individual and Jah. Rastas insist that ganja smoking assists them in praying, contemplating, reasoning, and exposing the trickery of Babylon. There is the potential for conflict between Rastas and the government that has made the smoking of this herb illegal. Rastas attest to the sacramental value of the herb and its potential for awakening mind and spirit; the government prosecutes for possession of it

What has been described thus far is within the context of a patriarchal worldview. However, Obiagele Lake questions how a community such as Rastafari that purports liberation for African peoples could advocate male dominance, hence the subjugation of women (Lake 1998). Lake contends that the immediate answer is that the subordination of women in Rastafari parallels that of women in the larger Jamaican and Caribbean context. Furthermore, Obiagele claims that Rastafari is at its very core a patriarchal movement that looks to the Bible, especially to the Old Testament, for its structure and philosophy. The Bible is often used in Rastafari to validate the subordination of women, and because this way of life in which women accede to male privilege is also practiced by many Christian churches and has a foothold in Jamaican culture, many people—including Caribbean scholars—are reluctant to criticize.

Maureen Rowe, herself a Rasta woman, agrees with Obiagele Lake that Rastafari is essentially a patriarchal religion (Rowe 1998). She is able to nuance her assessment with a historical profile of women's relationship to the movement and their impact on the movement. Because Rastafari emerged from a long line of African religious experiences, Rowe argues that to understand the role of women in Rastafari one needs to pay attention to how African patriarchy functions in the Caribbean, over and against European patriarchy. European patriarchy is based on wealth. In this setting, male authority has a direct connection to wealth. In the European construct of male authority, the male is the chief breadwinner; if the female works, she does so in order to support the male. In instances where the male does not work or makes less than the female, the male is emasculated. Maleness and authority are related to wealth. However, in African patriarchy maleness is the source of authority. The African male is expected to wield power in the family by virtue of being male.

It is clear from both perspectives that women are not the equal of men in Rastafari. The male in Rastafari is the representative of His Imperial Highness Haile Selassie I. The woman's role approximates that of the Empress, in relation to Emperor Haile Selassie I. Both scholars assert that Rastas need to become aware of the importance of releasing women from the shackles of second-class citizenship and subjugation within Rastafari. The hope for a breakthrough in terms of the place of women in Rastafari cannot be modeled in terms of the relationship between His Imperial Highness and his Empress but in terms of the relationship with Jah who indwells Rastas and allows them to view the world, including their relationship with women from a different place. This new place from which they view the world is not Babylon. It is "Zion," or "Ethiopia," the place in Rasta theology where the ways and practices of Babylon have no currency. This new vantage point means that they cannot relate to others, be they men or women, along the traditional lines of Babylon. The practice of I-and-I consciousness places each Rasta, whether male or female, in a direct relationship with Jah.

There is a liberating individualism that is pervasive of Rastafari thought and practice. Each Rasta is encouraged to forge a personal relationship between self and His Imperial Highness, Haile Selassie I. There is no set format dictating or governing how one may pray or worship Jah (God). Prayer and worship even if done communally is at its core a personal relationship between the individual Rasta and Jah. There are some Rastas from the Bobo community in Jamaica who prefer to worship on Friday evenings and on Saturdays. Drums are the preferred musical instruments.

There are important celebrations that are important for Rastas such as the celebration of Haile Selassie's birth date and in more recent years that of Bob Marley's in Ethiopia. These occasions are referred to as "Nyabinghi," the coming together of Rastas from many places for celebration. These meetings are comparable to a synod or convention, and often last for a week.

There are no formal requirements for membership in Rastafari faith. Anyone may become a Rasta. Entry to Rastafari is usually signaled by a new awareness of one's relationship to Jah (God). This relationship between the individual and Jah allows each Rasta to claim divinity, and it is this new sense of self, I-and-I consciousness, that constitutes authority.

While the Bible (usually the King James Version) is an important text for Rastas, it is not the main source of authority. Each Rasta, because of his or her relationship to Jah, constitutes the primary source of authority.

Noel Leo Erskine

SELECTED BIBLIOGRAPHY

Barrett, Leonard. *The Rastafarians* (Boston: The Beacon Press, 1997).

Chevannes, Barry. *Rastafari: Roots and Ideology* (Syracuse, NY: Syracuse University Press, 1995).

Edmonds, Ennis Barrington. *Rastafari: From Outcasts to Culture Bearers* (New York: Oxford University Press, 2002).

Erskine, Noel Leo. *From Garvey to Marley: Rastafari Theology* (Gainesville, FL: University Press of Florida, 2007).

Garvey, Amy Jacques, ed. *Philosophy and Opinions of Marcus Garvey*, vol. 1 (New York: Atheneum, 1974).

Lake, Obiagele. *Rastafari Women: Subordination in the Midst of Liberation Theology* (Durham, NC: Carolina Academic Press, 1998).

Lewis, Rubert. *Marcus Garvey* (Trenton, NJ: Africa World Press, 1998).

Makeda, Barbara, and Blake Hannah. *Rastafari: The New Creation* (Kingston, Jamaica: Headstart Publishers, Ltd., 1980).

Marley, Rita. *My Life with Bob Marley: No Woman No Cry* (New York: Hyperion Books, 2004).

Owens, Joseph. *Dread: The Rastafarians of Jamaica* (Kingston, Jamaica: United Co-operative Printers Ltd., 1995).

Rowe, Maureen. "Gender and Family Relations in Rastafari: A Personal Perspective." *Chanting Down Babylon*, ed. Nathaniel Samuel Murrell, William David Spencer, and Adrian Anthony McFarlane (Philadelphia: Temple University Press, 1998).